CONSUMER BEHAVIOUR IN INDIAN PERSPECTIVE

(TEXT AND CASES)

SUJA R. NAIR
B.A. (Hons.), M.B.A.
Consultant
Educe Micro Research
Bengaluru

ISO 9001:2015 CERTIFIED

First Edition : 2001
Reprint : 2002, 2003, 2004, 2005
Reprint : 2006, 2007, 2008, 2009
Second Revised Edition : 2010
Reprint : 2011, 2012, 2014, 2015
Reprint : 2017, 2019, 2020
Reprint : 2023
Reprint : 2025

Published by : Mrs. Meena Pandey for **Himalaya Publishing House Pvt. Ltd.,**
"Ramdoot", Dr. Bhalerao Marg, Girgaon, Mumbai - 400 004.
Phone: 022-23860170, 23863863; **Fax:** 022-23877178
E-mail: himpub@bharatmail.co.in; **Website:** www.himpub.com

Branch Offices :

New Delhi : "Pooja Apartments", 4-B, Murari Lal Street, Ansari Road, Darya Ganj, New Delhi - 110 002. Phone: 011-23270392, 23278631; Fax: 011-23256286

Nagpur : Kundanlal Chandak Industrial Estate, Ghat Road, Nagpur - 440 018. Mobile: 09325409992, 09325908881

Bengaluru : Plot No. 91-33, 2nd Main Road, Seshadripuram, Behind Nataraja Theatre, Bengaluru - 560 020. Phone: 080-41138821; Mobile: 09379847017, 09379847005

Hyderabad : No. 3-4-184, Lingampally, Besides Raghavendra Swamy Matham, Kachiguda, Hyderabad - 500 027. Phone: 040-27560041, 27550139

Chennai : No. 34/44, Motilal Street, T. Nagar, Chennai - 600 017. Mobile: 09380460419

Pune : "Laksha" Apartment, First Floor, No. 527, Mehunpura, Shaniwarpeth (Near Prabhat Theatre), Pune - 411 030. Phone: 020-24496323, 24496333; Mobile: 09370579333

Cuttack : Plot No 5F-755/4, Sector-9, CDA Market Nagar, Cuttack - 753 014, Odisha. Mobile: 09338746007

Kolkata : 3, S.M. Bose Road, Near Gate No. 5, Agarpara Railway Station, North 24 Parganas, West Bengal - 700109. Mobile: 09674536325

DTP by : Page Designers, Bengaluru

Printed at : Geetanjali Press Pvt. Ltd., Nagpur. On behalf of HPH.

PREFACE

A decade has elapsed since the onset of the millennium and there have been many changes occurring across global economics which has had its repercussions on the Indian economy. Since the time of the liberalization of our economy, Indian markets have been greatly influenced by the global economy and global markets. The recession in the developed economies such as the U.S. and Europe has had its impact on the Indian markets. Inspite of being a king or queen in the buyers market, customer's were adopting a cautious approach while purchasing things. This was in total contrast to their buying behaviour during the boom period, when they had displayed a splurge while purchasing goods or services. Nevertheless, the Indian markets were not greatly affected due to the global slowdown because of the efforts put in by the organisations at constant innovations (and change) and the ability to adopt to evolving market conditions.

Now with the revival of economies across the world, marketers are once again busy making attempts to woo the consumers through tailormade products and brand offerings. The Indian market is well known for its diversity and marketers here are engaged in marketing a host of products and product variants in order to cater to the large consumer tastes differences that can be categorized regionally, religiously etc.

Consumers today are tech savvy and have started using the internet for purchasing products and services. So, a separate chapter on Online Consumer Behaviour has been included in this text book.

This second edition is a modest effort on the part of the author to give in hands of the students a text book, which will look into the various facets of consumer behaviour. The language used throughout the text is simple and can be easily understood by the reader. The subject matter in the text is ably supported by real Indian market examples, wherever possible. The source material for this book has been obtained from various secondary sources such as books and periodicals etc.

Each chapter in the book commences with a **Real Indian Case** and the concluding session is also devoted to another relevant case study. Further, each chapter also has a **Summary** covering the topics discussed and **Chapter Questions for Discussion** have been provided for. For all those interested in further reading, a separate list titled **Suggested Readings** has been given towards the end of each chapter.

Organisation of the text

This text book has been organised into six units:

- Unit I deals with Chapters 1 (An Introduction to consumer behaviour) and 2 (Consumer Modelling). This part gives an introduction and overview to the study of consumer behaviour.

- Unit II, speaks on the various individual determinants of consumer behaviour through Chapters 3 to 7 these include Consumer Perception, Consumer Learning, Personality and Lifestyle Influences, Attitude Behaviour and Motivation.
- Unit III deals with social processes affecting consumer behaviour such as Demographics, Social Class and Culture (Chapter 8) and Reference Group Influences (Chapter 9)
- Unit IV covers topics relevant to consumer decision making, after sales and related issues. This includes Chapter 10 (Consumer Decision Making), 11 (Diffusion of Innovations and Opinion Leadership), 12 (Consumer Satisfaction) and 13 (Relationship Marketing).
- Unit V includes Chapters 14 (Consumerism) and 15 (Market Segmentation). These two chapters convey about ethics and the application of consumer behaviour.
- The concludutory unit VI refers to the Organisational Buying Behaviour (Chapter 16) and Online Consumer Behaviour (Chapter 17)

ACKNOWLEGEMENTS

I would like to acknowledge all those who have either directly or indirectly helped and inspired me in writing the second edition of this book.

I am specially thankful to Mr. Anuj Pandey, Mr. Niraj Pandey and Mr. Vijay Pandey, my publishers, for their valuable suggestions and whole heated commitment in bringing out this book. My heartfelt thanks to Ms. Nimisha, Mr. Adiga and the entire team of Himalaya Publishing House for their continuous co-operation and support in the development and publication of the work. I would like to thank Mr. Madhu for the computer support and Ms. Shyamal for the lively illustrations presented in the book. Finally, and most importantly, I would like to convey my heartfelt gratitude to my spouse Ravi and children Sulekha and Swati for their critical appreciation and continuous support.

SUJA R. NAIR
BANGALORE

BRIEF CONTENTS

CONTENTS

UNIT I : INTRODUCTION & OVER-VIEW TO THE STUDY OF CONSUMER BEHAVIOUR

UNIT II : INDIVIDUAL DETERMINANTS OF CONSUMER BEHAVIOUR

15. MARKET SEGMENTATION 537 - 582

UNIT VI : ORGANISATIONAL AND ONLINE BEHAVIOUR

16. ORGANISATIONAL BUYING BEHAVIOUR 583 - 604

17. ONLINE CONSUMER BEHAVIOUR 605 -632

CHAPTER 

AN INTRODUCTION TO CONSUMER BEHAVIOUR

- Case : **'Raj Travels'** - Going Places
- Meaning, definition and relevance of consumer behaviour study
- The development of consumer behaviour as a separate field of study
- Growth of consumer research
- Managerial versus a holistic perspective on consumer behaviour
- Consumer behaviour and marketing management
- Few models of Consumer Decision Making
- Trends in consumer behaviour
- Summary
- Chapter questions for discussion
- Suggested readings
- The case study of **'Marico Industries'**

CASE

"RAJ TRAVELS" - GOING PLACES

Today, **Shree Raj Travels and Tours Ltd.,** is one of the biggest names in the travel business in India, having crossed many milestones. However, for Mr. Lalit Sheth, Chairman and Managing Director (and the man behind the wheel at Raj Travels) the climb to the top hasn't been easy.

Raj Travels had a fairly humble beginning when it was established in 1976. During those early days, Lalit Sheth started by conducting small excursion tours for people from his hometown in Burra Bazar in Kolkata. At that time, *Lala Tours, Rajaram Travels* and *Universal Travels* were considered to be the domestic superstars. In order to understand how these tour operators worked, Sheth approached one of the travel agent's posing as a customer. It was then that he heard horrifying tales of their operations:

In the absence of long distance trains, in those times customers were forced to travel on many different passenger trains, making the journey a long and tiresome one. Further, in order to get the meals ready, the cooks would convert toilets into kitchen.

Once the customers arrived at their destination, three or four people would have to share a room causing inconvenience to families who were traveling. It was such experiences, which prompted Sheth to think of creating a customer centric, well-differentiated tour and travel brand.

Sheth had a vision **'to provide the Indian traveler with superior quality package tour facilities'**. The objective was to make family holiday tours more comfortable, more exciting and most memorable. Sheth wanted to change the entire scenario that existed in the Indian markets by offering an array of new services. He started by introducing pre-departure get-together's - a concept which is very popular today. Says Sheth "I called the first group of 23 people to Sheraton as I thought it would be a good idea for them to get to know each other. Then I went to the market and bought around 100 books for a small library for travelers to read during the tours. Along with the books, I also bought some games and a television set to make the tours more interesting." All the changes were accepted by customers with open hands.

Raj Travels believes in giving their customers a product and not a price. For, the customers are provided exactly what they require like having cooks in hotels all over the world, who will offer them a varied spread, at all-inclusive prices and no hidden costs. Yet customers have no complaints considering the quality and transparency in Raj Travels dealings.

Slowly Raj Travels began to grow and also became the first outbound tour operator in the country. It was the first outbound tour operator to introduce Indian Meals on its Globe Tour packages to Australia and New Zealand. Way back in 1986, when Raj Travels launched Caravan Kitchens and started serving "Indian Cuisine – Hot Meals" in Europe, the customer response was so dynamic that it changed the face of 'Indian Tours' forever. The biggest players in the industry were compelled to follow suit and it was a do or die situation for many. Raj Travels continues to enjoy the number 1 position in the outbound tours industry with 54 operational offices spread across India. (BBC World Wide, in 2003, had rated Raj Travels as India's premier outbound tour operators).

Raj Travels has also ventured into road travel with the Raj National Express (RNE). Claims Akash, Sheth's son, who heads Raj National Express, that the occupancy rate of RNE is 97% during peak season and around 84% during the off season period. The fleet currently comprises of 41 coaches and plans are afoot to take the number to 100 by the end of this year and 300 by the end of next. RNE aims to have a fleet of 1000 coaches in five years time.

Raj National Express is also planning to go global with offers coming in from Thailand, South Africa and Mauritius. The company is also looking at extensions related to the travel business. It is planning to build India's tallest Hotel at Ahmedabad and creating an online travel portal for customers to make reservation in real time.

Thus, Raj Travels which started as a single table operation, has today grown to become a Rs. 180/- crore tour and travel brand. All this was possible only because it understood and pioneered in offering most admired "Customer services to its customers".

As the above case on Raj Travels indicates, even business establishments all over the world have acknowledged the importance of understanding consumer behaviour as the main key to their success. But understanding of consumer behaviour is a challenge for the marketers. It requires them to probe and investigate a wide range of responses including *affective responses* (feelings and emotions are experiences), *cognitive responses* (beliefs, opinions, attitudes and intentions related to products and services) and the *behavioural responses* (action involved while obtaining, using and disposing goods or services.) Moreover, in the long run it is only those organizations that have been close to their customers and understood their needs and wants that have been able to compete effectively at the market place.

Although the marketing concept has been in vogue since the past many decades, today, when the market is flooded with so many me-too products, it is all the more necessary that marketers understand the uniqueness and diversity of consumer behaviour and make product or service offerings accordingly. The success of organizations will be reflected when consumers accept such offerings and continue to patronise it for a long period of time.

Today we are living in e-technology age. The revolution in this e-technology age facilitates marketers to go for more customisation of products, services and media usage. This is possible because marketers take the help of technology to collect and analyse all the complex information available on consumer's characteristic features and buying pattern. Similarly, e-technology has also helped consumers to obtain more information on various product and service offerings and at times even converting them to online buyers. This clearly indicates that marketers as well as all those interested in the success of the organization need to understand the - what, why, when, where, how frequently and so on questions related to the study of consumer behaviour.

In this chapter we start by trying to understand the meaning, definition and relevance of consumer behaviour study. Then, development of consumer behaviour as a separate field of study, growth of consumer research and managerial versus a holistic perspective on consumer behaviour have been discussed. We have then had an overview of few models having relevance to consumer behaviour. Finally there is a brief discussion on the trends in consumer behaviour.

MEANING, DEFINITION AND RELEVANCE OF CONSUMER BEHAVIOUR STUDY

Marketers have noticed that there have been key changes occurring in consumer attitudes, especially in the recent past. Not too long ago, debt was viewed as a detested thing by Indian families. But now, Indian consumers have developed a huge change in the attitudes towards debt. Today, it is considered to be perfectly legitimate and an easy way to create assets and aspire for a better lifestyle. This change in consumer attitudes has led to the emergence of a number of very easy credit options. There has also been a shift in the mind set towards rising aspirations and changing attitudes to lifestyle, recreation and entertainment expenditures. As a result, today a basic product such as a soap or detergent is competing with a credit card, cell phone or digital camera – all of which are bought with the same money.

There has been a shift in the mind set of consumers towards rising aspirations and changing attitudes to lifestyle, recreation and entertainment expenditures.

Added to this is the fact that the market is flooded with an explosion of choices of products with seemingly very little differences between one and the other, which are often not even perceptible to consumers. The result of such imperceptible differences is that, the consumer is confused on which product and brand to select from the wide range of choices. Thus, the urge to motivate the consumer to develop a positive buying behaviour towards their brand, has resulted in a vicious spiral of consumer down-trading, price based competition, value destruction, erosion in profit margins at times even leading to the death of the brands.

Successful marketers have realised that the formula for success will be based on how effectively they have identified their customers' expectations from products and brands and provide the same with a very high value satisfaction level. These marketers are engaged in gauging the behaviour of consumers (or customers), identify the sources, timing and direction of the changes in their behaviour, the emerging new competencies and perspectives …….. all of which will enable them to respond to the changes in the most effective manner.

Definition of Consumer Behaviour

Consumer behaviour can be said to be *the study of how individuals make decisions on how to spend their available resources (time, money, effort) on various consumption-related items.* This simple definition of consumer behaviour tells marketers to revolve every activity around the ultimate consumer and gauge their behaviour by specifically focusing on:

Who buys products or services?

How do they buy products or services?

Where do they buy them?

How often do they buy them?

When do they buy them? and

How often do they use them?

The behaviour displayed by consumers while searching for, purchasing, using, evaluating and disposing of products and services that they expect to satisfy their needs is referred to as consumer behaviour.

These questions will help in understanding better what factors influence the decision making process of the consumers. The decision making process identifies the number of people who are involved in this process and ascribes a role to them – like the user, decider, influencer and buyer.

It is believed that consumers or customers make purchase decisions on the basis of receipt of a small number of selectively chosen pieces of information. Thus it will be very important to understand what and how much information is required by the customer to help him evaluate the goods and services offerings.

Thus, the term *consumer behaviour* is defined as *the behaviour displayed by consumers in searching for, purchasing, using, evaluating and disposing of products and services that they expect will satisfy their needs.*

For example, FMCG products such as, a soap or a shampoo or say coffee are usually bought by the consumer either for her own use or for her immediate family. She uses these products (as brands) in the privacy of her bathroom, kitchen or home. Further, she needs these brands more often, because of their very nature, and also shares a very personal, often intimate moments especially where the use of them either gives her personal joy as she cares for herself or experiences the joy of caring for those she loves.

The ad on Nescafe 3-in-1 give in to the formula which gives the pay off that "with a hot cuppa, everything feels perfect no matter what"

For instance the advertisement on *Nescafe 3-in-1* is based on a brilliant consumer and category truth. Coffee is said to be a mood uplifting magic brew which restores our equilibrium, sets our world right, puts us back in step with life around us. And its power is most noticed in its absence. In the ad we get to see people (young IT/ITES/BPO professionals) with real life depictions (shared digs, housekeeping helplessness in the absence of family support) all suitable for the product which indicates a convenience cuppa for the bachelor pad. In fact, the ad even has a vanished PYT neighbour reappearing and flashing a smile at the protagonist.

Products such as *Nescafe* or *Barista* can be said to be brands, which have a truly intimate relationship with the consumer. Such brands appeal to the inner self of the individual and inspire them to live their life with joy.

Relevance of Consumer Behaviour Study

Consumer behaviour study will enable marketers to develop powerful insights based on a deep understanding of what consumers seek and then ensuring that these are easily available and at affordable prices too. Through the consumer behaviour study, the marketer seeks to understand the functional, psychological and emotional gratification which consumers seek to desire from the product. Take *for example,* how *Hindustan Lever Limited,* had to change the brand positioning of *LUX* with the change in consumers' mind set towards the emotional and functional attributes being associated with the brand.

For more than 50 years *LUX* has been marketed as the 'soap of the stars', endorsed by film stars and has always stood for glamour and luxury. However, over the past few years studies showed that the consumer in LUX's target segment was looking for luxurious products that make her feel beautiful and special. A deep understanding of this desired 'feeling of specialness' led to creating a new position for Lux. It led to strengthening the position of Lux from 'The soap of the stars' to a soap that 'brings out the star in you! This shift recognizes that each woman is special, that there is something magnetic and star like in every women and that the consumer is not willing to buy into a brand whose only reason for existence is that it is endorsed by stars. This shift in consumer's mindset indicates that the consumer was clearly looking beyond the functional aspects with an inclination more towards the emotional and psychological facets that can be associated with the new 'LUX' brand of soap. The outcome of this shift led to creating the brand LUX, which connects more deeply with the consumer and placing it more uniquely and distinctively in the consumer's mind in comparison to other products with similar functional attributes.

The study of consumer behaviour is very relevant for marketers because information and knowledge of buyer motives and habits will enable them to draft suitable marketing programmes accordingly.

The study of consumer behaviour is very relevant, especially for marketers because knowledge of the buyer(s), his or her buying motives and buying habits will help them in drafting the marketing programmes. Specifically put, organizations try to study and analyse consumer behaviour in order to :

- **Adopt a customer culture**, which incorporates customer satisfaction as an integral part of the company mission.
- **Follow the marketing concept** where the organization plays a consultative role, helping consumers to select (or identify) products and services, which would best meet their needs.
- **Solicit support from the society** by focusing on serving its members through giving consumers the freedom of choice and catering to their needs and wants.

Inspite of their best efforts, analyzing the consumers' buying behaviour is not only a puzzle but also a challenge for the marketer. For, the consumer has always displayed a complex buying behaviour. They have different needs and wants, often at various stages of emergence and actualization, displaying various degrees of prioritisation (some are latent, some manifest, while some others are highly dominant). Every buyer may relish her own unique way of realising these needs and wants especially since she is exposed to a very wide world of information. Even after she takes a buying decision, her actual buying behaviour will be influenced by many individual and environmental factors. All this clearly shows that the marketer has got a tough task to study and analyse the complex consumer behaviour and draw marketing plans accordingly.

THE DEVELOPMENT OF CONSUMER BEHAVIOUR AS A SEPARATE FIELD OF STUDY

Consumer behaviour as a separate field of study has only gained attention from the 1960s. In the absence of a history or a separate research of its own then, this new discipline drew/or borrowed concepts from other scientific disciplines such as :

- Psychology (the study of individuals)
- Sociology (the study of groups)
- Socio-psychology (the study of how persons are influenced by groups)
- Cultural anthropology (the influence of the culture and society on the individual)
- Economics (relationship between demand and supply in the flow of marketing activity).

Initially, the study of consumer research was emphasizing a managerial perspective. In that, if the marketing manager could obtain consumption related behaviour *i.e.,* if they are able to predict consumer behaviour, then they could influence it. This type of consumer behaviour approach came to be known *positivism*.

The managerial perspective of approaching consumer behaviour study going by the premise that if they are able to predict consumer behaviour, they can influence it, is called *positivism*. Where as, the approach of studying consumer behaviour with a view of understanding consumption behaviour and interpreting such behaviour is called *interpretivism*.

But there are a group of academicians, who are interested in the study of consumer behaviour, so as to understand it better. This approach is of interest to the academicians because they are more interested in knowing consumption behaviour going by the influence of the various disciplines on the consumer behaviour. This approach of studying the consumer behaviour with a view of understanding consumption behaviour and the interpretations of such behaviour is known as '*interpretivism or post-modernism*'. These interprevists have included many subjective aspects of consumer behaviour such as the effect of moods, emotions, type of situations etc. These interprevists have also treated each purchase experience as unique because of the many variables which influence the behaviour at that particular moment of time. On account of its focus on the consumption experience, the interpretive approach is also referred to as *experientalism.* (*Consumer Behavior,* L.G. Schiffman, L.L. Kanuk, 1997.)

While conducting consumer researches, it was realised that in spite of easy acceptance of fashion and fads, consumers also had a preference for *differentiated products* matching their special needs, personalities and lifestyles. Thus, came into existence the importance of *market segmentation*. Thus, the field of consumer behaviour will be helpful for adopting the process of market segmentation. This is a process of dividing the total potential market into smaller, homogeneous segments, based on similar needs of the target market and producing a product that will meet those needs at a profit (Refer to the separate chapter on Market segmentation in this book for more information).

Similarly, the study of consumer behaviour will also help in the process of *product positioning*. This refers to a marketing strategy adopted so as to position the product with a specific image in the minds of the people. This is usually done with the aid of various promotional techniques, that can be adjusted to vary the perceived product image to match the specific

Bharat Petroleum makes use of research to give consumers information on the performance of 'Speed'

Consumer behaviour studies help in the development of new products, growth of non profit marketing, working out market segmentation strategies and international marketing.

needs of the target market. Other fields which can make use of consumer behaviour studies is the *development of new products*, *growth of non profit marketing* and *international marketing*. Today with most of the firms going global, there is an increasing importance being given to consumer behaviour across borders to have more information about cross cultural consumer needs and preferences and consumption habits. This information can help marketers devise the necessary promotional strategies to be adopted to meet the needs of target foreign consumers (For more details refer to the Chapter on Social stratification).

GROWTH OF CONSUMER RESEARCH

Consumer research, as mentioned earlier has developed as an extension to the field of marketing research with more emphasis on the consumer behavioural aspects. The initial thrust on studying consumer behaviour, by marketers was done for two reasons:

- To determine as to why consumers made the purchase decisions.
- To understand how consumers would react to promotional messages.

It was presumed that if they (the marketers) could have access to all the information about the consumer decision making process, it will help them in formulating various marketing strategies and in developing appropriate promotional messages, which could induce consumer's to take a positive purchase decision. Prior to this, it was believed that Economics was Marketing's "Mother discipline". Thus going by the economic presumption that consumers are rational human beings (or decision makers), it was assumed that they would evaluate the goods and services available and make the choice based on maximum utility value at less price.

Then came the *modernist era*. The positivists (researchers who endorsed the assumptions of modernism) conducted research studies by adopting the methods of experimenting, through observations and survey techniques. Since the data collected by this method was quantitative in nature, various statistical methods had to be used for analysis purposes.

Product positioning can influence consumer behaviour.

Another important research technique called the *Motivational research* came to be widely used by marketers and advertising agencies in the late 1950s. This research methodology was developed by Earnest Dichter, a Psycho – analyst, with the help of various Sigmund Freud's psycho analytic techniques. Motivational research method involves using projective techniques and indepths interviews. The effectiveness of motivational research depends on having a highly trained personnel who are required to collect data and analyse research findings. Since such research studies involve probing into their (consumers) basic motivations, usually the sample sizes are small and hence the findings cannot be extended to larger populations. Moreover, such research findings are subjective and qualitative involving a lot of analyst interpretations.

While working out strategic marketing programmes, marketers prefer to make *use of a combination of qualitative and quantitative research techniques*. Qualitative research findings enable marketers to gain insights into some of the psychological aspects of consumer behaviour which will help in the generation of new product ideas. While quantitative research help in analysing the likely behaviour to be adopted by the consumer based on various promotional inputs.

Marketers prefer to use a combination of qualitative and quantitative research techniques. Interpretivists are engaged in qualitative researches and use methodologies such as ethnography, semiotics and in-depth interviews to get an insightful understanding of consumer behaviour.

There is another group of researchers (academicians) interested in the act of consumption rather than in the act of buying adopted by the consumers. These researchers are more interested in the consumer experiences. This approach when used for consumer research can also be known as *experientialism* and those researchers engaged in such research activities are known as *experientialists* or *interpretivists*.

Interpretivists are engaged in qualitative research. That is, they are interested in getting an insightful understanding of the consumer behaviour. The research methodologies used by them are ethnography, semiotics and in-depth interviews. (*Consumer Behavior,* L.G. Schiffman, L.L. Kanuk, 8th Edn., 2005.)

- *Ethnography* – is related to cultural anthropology, where in the researchers put themselves in the society under study so as to absorb all the implications of the cultural practices.
- *Semiotics* – The study of symbols and their interpretations or meanings.
- *In-depth Interviews* – It is a method where the questions are asked to obtain a gainful insight into the understanding of consumer behaviour.

The interpretive research findings will be dependent on the capability of the researcher and the active role played by him or her during the interview purpose. This is because such research findings are often unique to the particular researcher consumer interaction.

The positivists and interpretive research studies can both be helpful to take marketing related decisions. Both these research paradigms – positivism and interpretivism can be said to be complementary to each other. To have a gainful and correct profile of the consumer behaviour, it will be necessary to consider the predictions of consumer behaviour made possible by positivists research and the probing and insightful understanding of consumer behaviour, which can be obtained through interpretivist research findings. So marketers use a combination of both positivists and interpretivists research findings, while designing more effective and meaningful marketing strategies and programmes.

TABLE 1.1

COMPARISONS BETWEEN POSITIVISM AND INTERPRETIVISM

Positivism	Interpretivism
• Consumer research carried out, from a managerial point of view to take strategic marketing decisions is called positivism.	• Consumer research carried out for the purpose of probing deep into the consumer's mind to understand the motivations, feelings, emotions etc., affecting their consumer behaviour is called interpretivism.
• Positivist research is quantitative and empirical in nature.	• Interpretivism involves qualitative research which cannot be projected to larger population.
• Positivist research tries to identify cause-and-effect relationship in buying situations.	• Interpretivism research is primarily concerned with understanding the act of consuming and can be used to provide insights for working out various positioning strategies.
• Positivists typically use probability studies, which can be generalised to larger populations.	• Interpretivists usually view consumption experiences as unique situations occurring at that specific time and hence cannot be generalised to larger populations.

Importance of Consumer Research

Consumer Research helps in providing marketers with vital information which in turn will help to form a good marketing information system.

As mentioned earlier in the text, the success of an organisation will greatly depend on the constant efforts made by it to identify consumers' unmet needs and match them with suitable product or service offerings. This is where marketing research (especially consumer behaviour research) will play a big role in providing it.

Marketing research is the collection and analysis of data from a sample of individuals or organizations related to their characteristics, behaviour, attitudes, opinions or possessions. It includes all forms of research such as consumer and industrial survey, psychological investigations, observations and panel studies. (Market Research Society, 1995)

Consumer research is very much an integral part of the marketing research and helps the marketer by:

- Providing information on how the consumers are behaving at the market place.
- Using it as a means of identifying future consumer needs or marketing opportunities.

Thus consumer research will provide marketers with vital information, which can help to form a good marketing information system.

Box 1.1, gives excerpts of an interview Tim Balbirnie, (CEO-Asia Pacific for Synovate, a global marketing research company in customised research) gave to the Economic Times, on the relevance of customer research in the fast changing Asia Pacific Market.

As shown in figure 1.1, the consumer research process involves various stages, right from the development of the research objectives till the report or presentation of data.

➲ MANAGERIAL VERSUS A HOLISTIC PERSPECTIVE ON CONSUMER BEHAVIOUR

Broadly stated, there can be a managerial view as well as a holistic view on the study of consumer behaviour. The managerial view is that consumer behaviour study is an applied social science. That is, consumer behaviour study is used as an adjunct to and as a basic for developing marketing strategies. Whereas, the holistic view considers consumer behaviour to be pure rather than as an applied social science. This implies that consumer behaviour study involves a legitimate focus of inquiry in and of itself without necessarily being applied to marketing.

Managerial Perspective

Under the managerial perspective, individual customerised information is obtained on their needs (desired product benefits), thought processes and characteristics, which is aggregated and targeted to specific consumer segments.

As per the managerial perspective, the consumer behaviour tends to be more 'micro' and 'cognitive' in native. *Micro* because, here the emphasis is on the individual consumer: his or her attitudes, perceptions and lifestyle and demographic characteristics. The *cognitive* aspect emphasises on the thinking process of the individual consumers and the thought process which influences their decision making process. Moreover, even the environmental factors (such as the social, reference groups, family and cultural) are studied in terms of how they can influence the individual consumer.

Marketing managers justify such a focus by saying that this view is correct since the ultimate goal of the marketing strategy would be to satisfy the needs of individual consumers in a socially responsible manner. Under this approach, individual customerised information is obtained on their needs (desired product benefits), thought processes and characteristics, which is aggregated to specific consumer segments, who are later on targeted with specific product or service offerings.

BOX 1.1

CHANGE IN CONSUMER TRENDS

What kind of consumer trends are you witnessing in the Asia-Pacific region? Is the Indian market different from other Asian ones?

There is a boom in consumerism. An average Asian Consumer is a 'value' seeker and is willing to pay more for value. Here value means 'premium products' and not necessarily, 'value for money'. This trend also emerged from Synovate PAM (Pan Asia Cross Media) study. Consumers are also buying products that are aspirational; enhance the quality of life. The Indian market is similar to other Asian markets – an average consumer is acquisitive, a value-seeker and is embracing big-ticket items like iPods, MP3s, mobile phones, digital cameras, plasma TVs, among others.

Our research shows that affluent Asians are enjoying a greater sense of security that has come from the improved economic environment. This is translating to greater spending and a willingness to acquire new products that will improve their lifestyle.

Which sectors will be the ones to look out for in the next few years in India? How does the Indian market fare compared to China's?

In the next few years, the sectors poised for boom would be retail, service and lifestyle products. Wellness and personal grooming is another area to watch out for. The Indian consumer is evolved and discerning. In the Indian marketplace, there is a fair bit of competitive activity – every brand has to fight for its place in the sun in India. In China as liberalization started much early, the market is huge. Players focus on how to manage growth as opposed to increasing market shares.

With the retail boom and entry of luxury brands in India how well do you think will they do? Foreign food brands have had to adapt to the Indian taste.

Compared to the last few years, Indians have witnessed an increase in disposable incomes. An average Indian shopper is a lot more exposed to international brands and is well travelled. While the affluent account for a small percentage of the population, the absolute numbers are huge and growing. The Indian market is now ready for luxury products. The critical part is to provide the same shopping experience that Indians get exposed to when they travel abroad. After all, international travel and shopping is accessible to a number of Indians now – the Indian retail experience has to match what exists abroad or surpass it.

Can you think of any successful branding exercise in this region / India?

I think, mobile phones, retailing – have defined the norms and set new benchmarks to delight the customer. Completely out-of-the-box branding wins.

How has market research evolved in the past few years? What's is the client's perspective on the same?

Market research has extended from 'supplier' status to partnership. The research needs are more and more formalised as a part of the overall marketing activity. Research usage is also becoming more planned and changing from data gathering to strategy.

(*Source : Economic Times*, Bangalore, 25 February 2006)

However, the managerial perspective has certain limitations:

- This approach overemphasises on the rationality aspect of consumers. For all practical purposes, the consumer may not always adopt a systematic manner to process information. This will especially hold true when they purchase products for their symbolic value or on impulse or on an addictive basis. During such instances, purely a cognitive view will not help to reveal the underlying motive of the consumer's decision-making process.
- Purely a micro view may tend to overlook the dynamics of external (environmental) factors independent of the individual. For instance, consider the example of an individual (say the father) who is making purchases for his daughter's wedding. This individual's purchase decisions would be in the context of ritual behaviour and thus be culturally derived and can provide a lot of insight to most marketers. And yet, such a perspective might be overlooked if the focus is only on individual consumer.

FIGURE 1.1

CONSUMER RESEARCH PROCESS

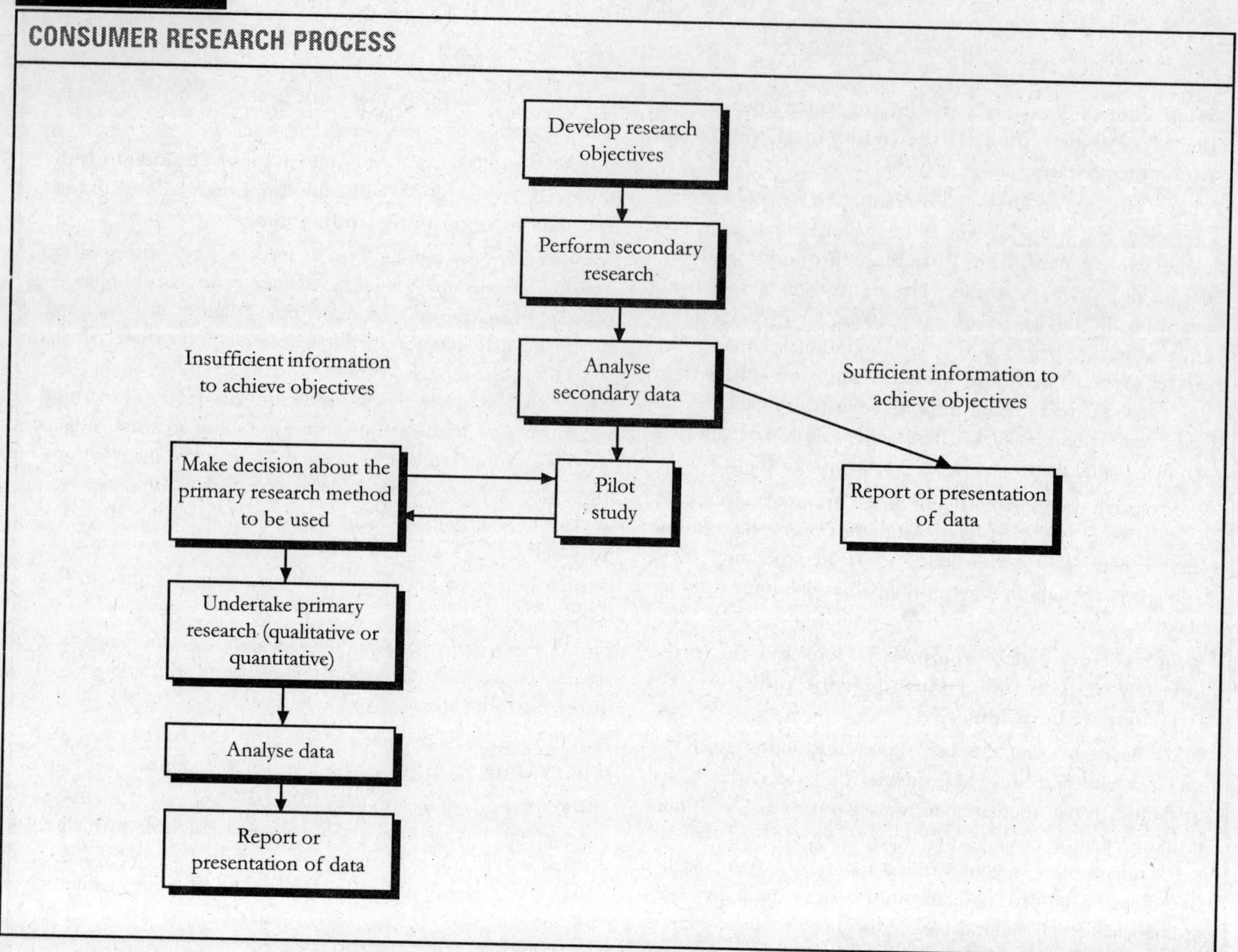

- The managerial perspective tends to focus more on the purchase experience. But the long term strategy of the successful organisations have revealed that more than anything, it is the post purchase satisfaction which has helped it to remain in the market for a long time. For instance, Toyota Kirloskar Motors (TKML) began their joint venture in India by offering the *Qualis* (a Multi-utility vehicle) in the least populated segment of a crowded automobile market. But very soon it became the best selling product in its segment. This was partly due to its features of ruggedness and driving ease and more because the company paid attention to suitable pricing, quality and best-in-class suppliers resulting in post purchase satisfaction.

A Holistic Perspective

A holistic perspective tends to focus more on the nature of consumption experience rather than the purchasing process.

A holistic perspective is more *macro* in its orientation. It tends to focus more on the nature of consumption experience rather than the purchasing process. The purchase behaviour is viewed (or studied) in the context of shopping rather than merely as taking a purchase decision. This means that the purchase behaviour is of little inherent interest outside its impact on the consumption experience. Unlike the managerial perspective, which is more interested in predicting what the consumer might do in the future, the holistic perspective focuses more on understanding the environmental context of the consumer's actions.

TABLE 1.2

LIMITATIONS OF THE MANAGERIAL VERSUS HOLISTIC PERSPECTIVES

Managerial Perspective on Consumer Behaviour	Holistic Perspective on Consumer Behaviour
• This perspective over-emphasises on the 'rationality' of the individual consumer, which may not be practically correct.	• It will be difficult for organisation's to act and work out marketing strategies merely based on culturally derived meaning of consumer's actions.
• This perspective takes a micro view, with a tendency to overlook the dynamics of the external environment, which can influence the consumer behaviour.	• This perspective does not put much emphasis on understanding the consumer's purchase decisions.
• This perspective gives more emphasis to the purchase experience, where as the long term strategy must ideally concentrate more on the long term customer satisfaction.	• This perspective does not 'involve' a systematic processing of consumer's cognitive process, which is necessary for developing marketing strategies.

The holistic perspective also suffers from certain drawbacks:

- Findings from the culturally derived meaning of consumer's actions and consumption experiences may not always help in working out marketing strategies in the business context.
- This perspective does not place sufficient emphasis on purchase decisions. But unless marketers understand how consumers reach at purchase decisions, how can they work on strategies to influence them?
- Although, many consumer decisions are not made through a process of systematic processing, it will help marketers if they try to develop an understanding of such cognitive processes. For, this will be necessary when marketers attempt at meeting consumers needs and wants.

World over, successful organisations have been those whose marketers have made attempts to know their customers and reach out and satisfy them more efficiently.

A Balanced View

World over successful organisations have been those, whose marketers have made attempts to know their customers and reach out and satisfy them more efficiently. Moreover, marketers and organisations who really understand their customers have been able to develop better products and services, promote these more effectively and also devise marketing plans and strategies that foster sustainable competitive advantages over their competitors.

So it will be apt to take a balanced view on the study of consumer behaviour. *i.e.,* along with the managerial perspective in studying consumer behaviour it will be necessary for organisations to also take a broader, holistic and macro view while trying to understand the purchasing and consumption experiences of consumers.

Consumer's Perspective on Consumer Behaviour

In the above discussion we have referred to the consumer behaviour study from the marketing manager's and organisation's point of view. However, the study of consumer behaviour can take a different perspective when seen through the consumer's eye.

Lifestyle can influence consumer's buying decisions.

- Consumers are interested in evaluating information provided by marketing organisations in order to make better product choices.
- Consumers are interested in taking buying decisions across a broad range of brand alternatives in order to select that product and brand which match their lifestyle.
- For consumers, more choices (or competition) among products is viewed as an opportunity to make a choice and gain from additional alternatives and at times, at lesser prices or discounts too.
- The study of consumer behaviour has not only made them better consumers but also given rise to the consumer awareness movement. The latter has helped in the protection of the consumer rights as well as ensured that organizations do not make false claims about their product or service offerings and take the consumers for a ride.

Consumer's perspective on consumer behaviour will help them to become more knowledgeable and better consumers.

Where there's energy, there's HP

Propelling airplanes, mechanizing agriculture, energizing industries, igniting stoves, lighting lanterns ...
HP is synonymous with energy in India.

For the last 25 years and more, Hindustan Petroleum has been meeting India's energy needs in many ways. It's been powering the nation ahead with an inexhaustible supply of petrol, diesel, LPG, lubricants, kerosene and other petroleum products. In the new millennium HP is all set to unveil an exciting new phase in its growth. Diversifying into oil exploration and production, power generation, renewable energy ventures and much more. Confident of creating a future full of energy. Confident of enriching the lives of millions.

Future full of energy

DIESEL • LPG • KEROSENE • AVIATION FUEL • NAPHTHA • FURNACE OIL • BITUMEN • LOW SULPHUR HEAVY STOCK • LUBES & GREASES • SOLVENTS • INDUSTRIAL SPECIALTIES

HP attempts to convey about its ability to satisfy consumer's various energy needs

CONSUMER BEHAVIOUR AND MARKETING MANAGEMENT

Only an understanding of the relevant markets can help marketers to analyse marketing opportunities and then devise suitable marketing programmes accordingly. Market itself means – buyers, that is, it is necessary to understand the buyers around whom all the marketing plans are formulated and implemented. In order to meet competition at the market place, the marketing managers are using various methods to add value to the final product which will reach the hands of the consumers. This means in the everchanging marketing environment, there is a growing concern or awareness among marketers to go for a careful study of the buying behaviour, which will provide the basis for all marketing activities.

In the ever changing marketing environment, there is a growing concern among marketers to opt for a careful study of consumers buying behaviour, which will provide the impetus for all marketing activities.

Samsung's DigitAll attempts to appeal to the young tech savvy consumer's of today

Broadly, buyers can be classified into two major categories:

- Consumers (in the household sector, who buy goods or services for personal consumption).
- Industrial buyers (who purchase goods and services for carrying out activities in the various industrial units)

Philip Kotler has suggested the 'Feed' to probe and find answers to four basic questions to understand buyer behaviour. These are :

- What (products or services) do the consumers buy?
- Why do they buy the products or services?
- What is the buyer behaviour process adopted by them?
- Who buys the various products and services?

The Domestic Consumers

It is widely acclaimed that India has one of largest consumer markets in the world. But the consumers in India show wide variations in the size and potential of the various consumer market segments. Such variations can be seen in terms of the geographical differences, urban – rural consumers (their style of living, consumption pattern etc.), age and family life cycle, income level, education levels, linguistic and religion diversity, food habits, festivals etc. These differences can be visible in the pattern of spending adopted by the domestic consumers. Added to this, with the availability of products 'anywhere' and 'everywhere', customers have also become more demanding and choosy.

India has one of the largest consumer markets in the world. However, the consumers buying pattern can be identified on the basis of their differences in geographical location, urban-rural divide, style of living, age and family life cycle, income level, education, linguistic and religion diversity etc.

The revolution in communication technology, are forcing marketers to look beyond time tested concepts such as brand loyalty and mass marketing. Marketers are tying to determine the underlying *needs and motives* of consumers as well as the various factors which influence the formation of these needs and the satisfaction of these. Simultaneously, marketers are also trying to understand the '*learning*' process adopted by consumers and buyers. The learning process can also be linked to other cognitive structures such as (values) *attitudes* and *beliefs*. Buying behaviour is also influenced by other psychological concepts such as perception, motivation, and personality. Knowing the impact of these concepts on buying behaviour will help marketers in the generation of new products ideas and adopt customization for – the core product, with some additional features and services offerings all done with the intention to add to customer delight.

FIGURE 1.2

MARKETERS TRYING TO CREATE THE CUSTOMER VALUE CHAIN

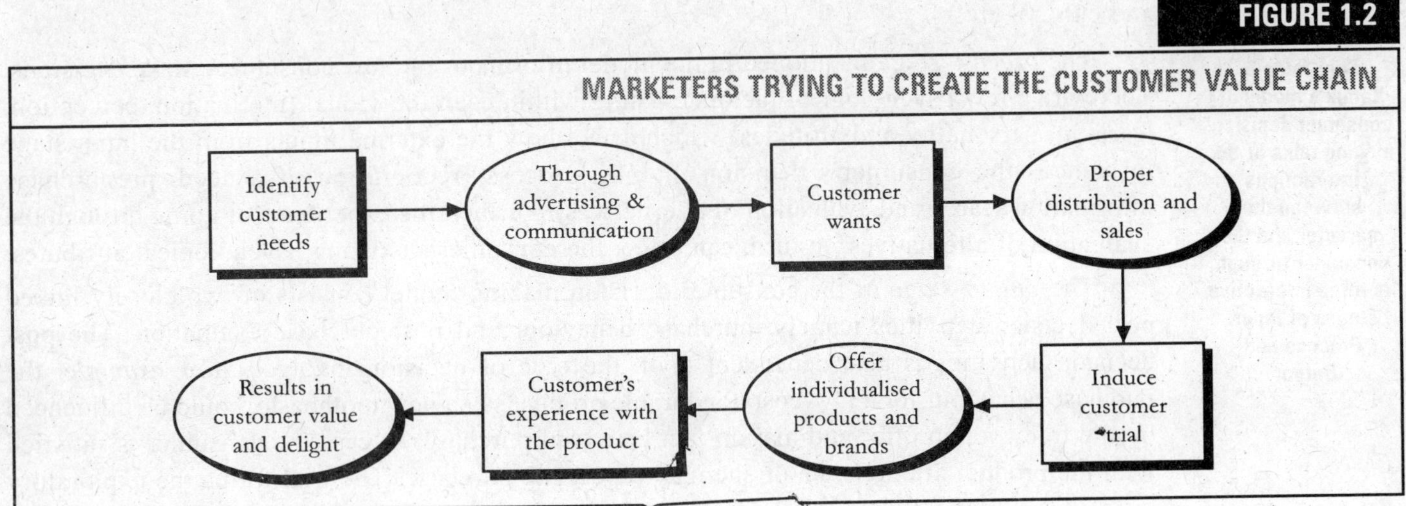

Firms have realized that it's sole dependence on the traditional demographic factors or past purchase behaviour or consumption pattern cannot be indicative of the present day consumer buying behaviour. That is why as shown in the Figure 1.2 above, most of the marketers in order to adopt to the new marketing paradigm shift in consumer tastes and preferences are going for a fundamental shift in their market research techniques, product development, advertising and promotional strategies. All such attempts such as advertising, proper distribution and inducing trial through individualised product offerings can help to create a customer value chain. Added to this, in this age of information explosion where internet marketing is a reality, it is all the more necessary that they (marketers) go for the creation of appropriate data base which can help them to make 'tailor made' products to suit individual tastes, preferences and buying behaviour.

The *industrial or organisational* markets consists of buyers who buy goods and services needed in the process of furthering their industrial and institutional activities. The behavioural differences between the domestic consumers and industrial buyers can be done on the basis of the ultimate objective sought by them. While the domestic consumers seek need satisfaction and value added by the purchase of the product, the industrial buyers seek profit or measurement of improved operational efficiency. The latter's behaviour, thus, will be influenced by the objectives of the organisation they serve.

➲ FEW MODELS OF CONSUMER DECISION MAKING

Typically, all marketing strategies are evolved on the basis of all those factors which influence consumer behaviour. We will discuss three such models here which will examine the consumer decision making process.

[A] Schiffman & Kanuk's Model of Consumer Decision Making

This model speaks of the interactions between the marketer and consumer. This process can be seen in the form of three distinct though interactive (or interlocking) stages.

The *input stage* in the consumer decision making model consists of external environmental influences, or two major sources of information. These sources are the firm's marketing mix elements (including the product or service, its price, its promotion and location of availability) as well as the external sociological influences on the consumer (family, peer and friends, neighbours, other informal and non commercial sources, social class, group influence, religion and cultural etc.).

Schiffman & Kanuk's model of consumer decision making talks of the interactions between the marketer and the consumer through its three interactive stages of Input, Process and Output.

The *process stage* mentioned in the model informs us on how consumers make decisions. There are a few psychological factors existing within each individual (motivation, perception, learning, personality and attitudes) which affect how the external inputs from the input stage influences the consumer's decision making process (recognition of a need, prepurchase information search and evaluation of alternatives). Further, the experience of going through the evaluation of alternatives, in turn, can affect the consumer's existing psychological attributes.

The *output stage* of the consumer decision making model consists of two closely linked post decision activities namely, purchase behaviour and post purchase evaluation. The post decision activities is also dependent upon the type of decision involved. *For example,* the purchase behaviour for a low-cost nondurable product say a new toothpaste, could be influenced by the free coupon offer and may in fact be a trial purchase. In case the consumer is satisfied with the product after use, he or she may repeat the purchase. The trial forms the exploratory

FIGURE 1.3

L.G. SCHIFFMAN AND L.L KANUK'S MODEL OF CONSUMER DECISION-MAKING

Input

External Influences

Firm's Marketing Efforts
- Product
- Price
- Place
- Promotions

Socio cultural environment
- Family
- Informal sources
- Other non-commercial sources
- Social Class
- Subculture and culture

Process

Consumer decision-making

- Need Recognition
- Prepurchase Search
- Evaluation of Alternatives

Psychological Field
- Motivation
- Perception
- Learning
- Personality
- Attitudes

Experience

Output

Post decision behaviour

Purchase
- Trial
- Repeat purchase

Post purchase Evaluation

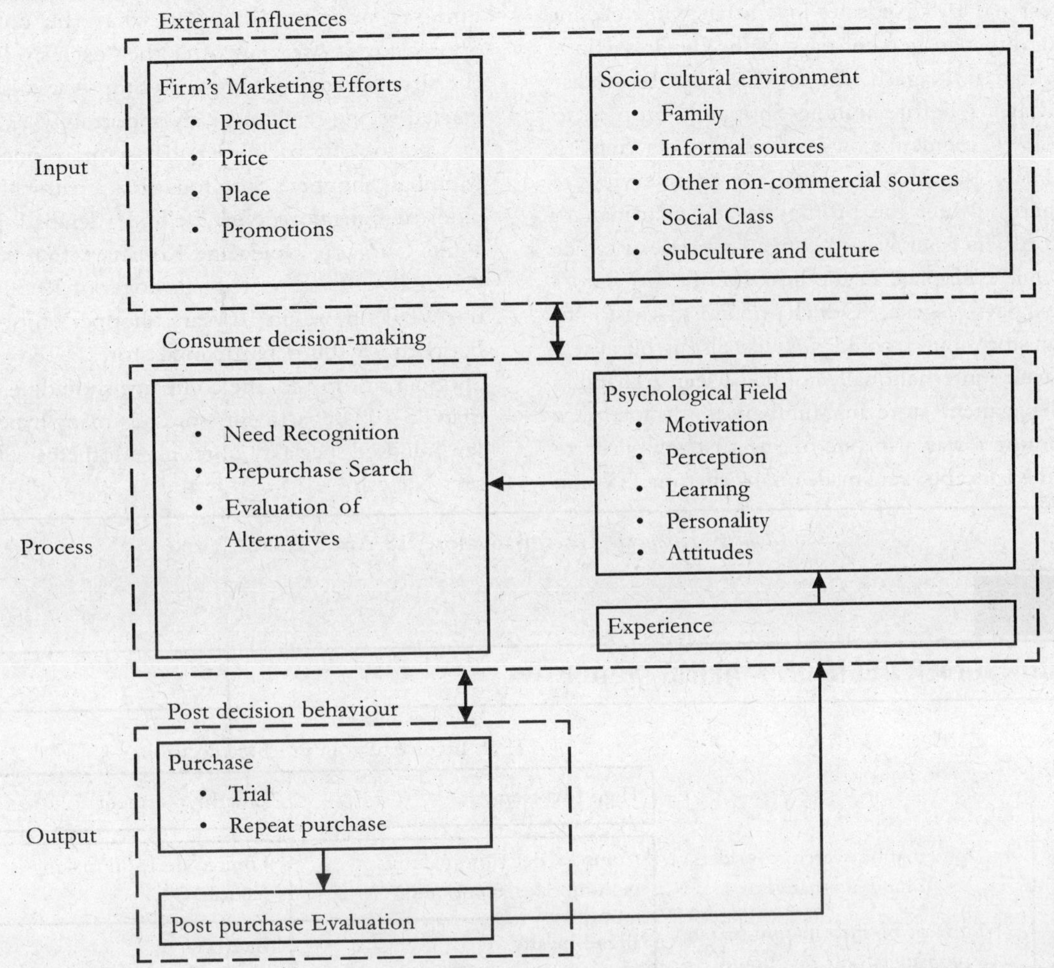

(*Source : Consumer Behavior;* Leon. C. Schiffman, Leslie Lazar Kanuk, Prentice Hall of India Private Limited, New Delhi, pp. 565, 1997)

phase of the purchase behaviour, when the consumer evaluates the product through direct usage. A repeat purchase will indicate product adoption by the consumer.

For a relatively durable product such as 'ipod' (because such products have a rapid rate of obsolescence), the purchase is more likely to signify adoption.

The above Schiffman and Kanuk's model of consumer decision making is only briefly touched upon here.

Given in Box 1.2 is an overview on how B.S. Nagesh of Shopper's Stop helped the departmental store grow by understanding what consumer's appreciated.

(B) Assaell's Consumer Decision Making Model

Assaell's model on consumer decision making as seen in figure 1.4 indicates that the consumer's involvement in the decision making will vary depending upon the type of purchase involved. For instance, in case of high involvement purchases (or complex decisions) the decision making process will involve information search and evaluating brand alternatives. Whereas, in case of low involvement purchases the consumer make seek little or no information and considers only one brand.

BOX 1.2

FOR THE LOVE OF RETAIL

Forty five year old B S Nagesh's love affair with retailing started during his management days at the Benares Hindu University, Varanasi. Nagesh who worked with Blowplast, Orson and Carona before joining Shopper's Stop at its inception in 1991, claims his biggest learning was "retail is detail". In 1991, Nagesh was called for an interview to Mumbai, where he met the promoters and chairman of Shopper's Stop. The brief was to convert a property which was an erstwhile multiplex, in the heart of the city, into a retail complex. Says Nagesh, "Our chairman had a vision of a department store, but I could nor visualise it because I had never traveled internationally not had I seen Akbarallys (a famous department store in Mumbai) as my interview with the promoters was also one of my first few visits to Mumbai. So the concepts were made on my chairman's vision and my understanding of what the consumer would appreciate. It was only after the "exclusively male store" – the first version of Shopper's Stop – was launched that we started seeing retailing as an opportunity". Of course, there was no looking back after that. From a one-store set-up in Mumbai, Shopper's Stop today has a national presence in the cities of Bangalore, New Delhi, Hyderabad, Jaipur, Chennai, Pune, Gurgaon, Noida and Kolkata with retail space of over 9,50,000 sq.ft and posted a turnover of Rs 505 crore in 2004-05. What's more, in 10 years Shopper's Stop hopes to have between 75-100 departmental stores. "Ten years from now Shopper's Stop Ltd, the company, should be operating more than 75-100 department stores, as many hypermarkets and a few hundred speciality stores like Mothercare, Crossword etc," says Nagesh.

(*Source : Economic Times*, Bangalore, 18 April, 2006)

FIGURE 1.4

ASSAELL'S CONSUMER DECISION MAKING MODEL

Decision making →		High Involvement in purchase decision →	
		High Involvement	Low Involvement
	(Information search, considers brand alternatives)	Complex decision making (automobiles, computers)	Limited decision making (cereals)
	(Little or no information search, considers only one brand)	Brand loyalty (Personal care products, cigarettes)	Inertia (canned food, paper napkins)

(*Source :* Understanding Customers 1996-97, Rosemary Phipps and Craig Simmons 1996)

The Assaell's consumer decision making process goes beyond the traditional facets of marketing. It says there are various individual and environmental factors which can influence buyers purchase decisions.

Figure 1.5 given below shows the various individual and environmental factors, which can influence consumers purchase decisions. The consumer decision making process goes beyond the traditional facets such as product features and design, benefits sought from the product (or brand), suitable pricing and ideal location. It is the post purchase satisfaction or dissatisfaction behaviour, which will count. For, a positive or post purchase satisfaction will induce adoption and loyalty. Whereas post purchase dissatisfaction could result in discontinuing usage of the product. Ultimately the post purchase behaviour of consumers will have repercussions on the communication (or word of mouth) they have with the prospective customers.

Figure 1.5 shows that right from stimuli till consumers' response there are many individual (perception, attitudes, needs and motives, demographics etc.) and environmental factors (culture, social class etc.) influencing the consumer's purchase decisions.

For industrial buying process, the buying situations involved are straight re-buy, modified re-buy and new task. Here also, even though the types of buying situation may vary, the categorisation in terms of low involvement and high involvement purchases made by individuals is similar.

The marketer generally looks into the decision making unit of both personal as well as industrial purchases. There after, depending upon the 'role' of the person, most likely to influence the purchase decision, all promotional efforts are directed towards that individual.

FIGURE 1.5

THE INDIVIDUAL AND ENVIRONMENTAL FACTORS INFLUENCING PURCHASE DECISIONS

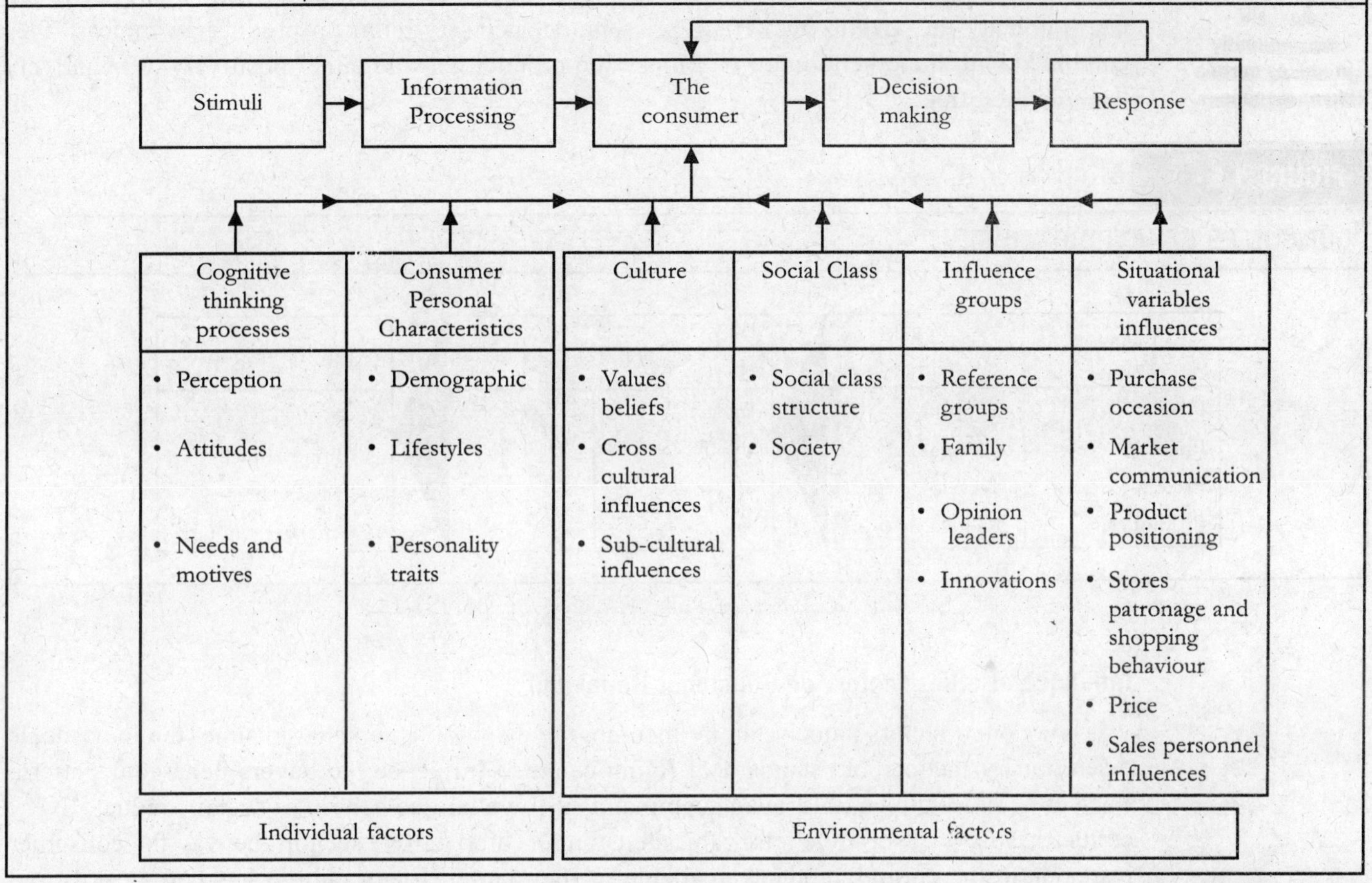

Stimuli → Information Processing → The consumer → Decision making → Response

Cognitive thinking processes	Consumer Personal Characteristics	Culture	Social Class	Influence groups	Situational variables influences
• Perception • Attitudes • Needs and motives	• Demographic • Lifestyles • Personality traits	• Values beliefs • Cross cultural influences • Sub-cultural influences	• Social class structure • Society	• Reference groups • Family • Opinion leaders • Innovations	• Purchase occasion • Market communication • Product positioning • Stores patronage and shopping behaviour • Price • Sales personnel influences
Individual factors		Environmental factors			

(*Source :* Henry Assael, *Consumer Behavior and Marketing Action*, Thomson Learning, Singapore 2001, pp. 69-83)

BOX 1.3

SURVEY CHARTS THEIR BRAND BEHAVIOUR

Survey Charts Their Brand Behaviour

INDIAN children are increasingly tech savvy, have their favourite brands, aspire to own fancy gadgets, and be like Shah Rukh Khan - the best, says a survey conducted by kids' channel Cartoon Network.

The study, New generations 2005, covered 14 cities and over 8,900 respondents. The survey showed that 39% of the children are computer users and within this, one out six surf the internet regularly, said Krishna Desai, senior manager research, Turner International India, said at a press meet here on Thursday. Up to 58% of the children access the Web from their schools. Gadgets like mobile phones with camera, Apple ipods and X-box figured high on the list of desired gadgets. Brands like Nokia, Sony, LG and Reliance topped on the "cool brands" list. Video games and remote controlled toys are gaining over soft toys, toy cars and other conventional toys. Children have a great influence on their parents when it comes to shopping and brand choices.

(*Source* : *Economic Times*, Bangalore, 7 April 2006)

Box 1.3 throws light on how children are involved in the decision making process.

[C] SIMPLE STIMULUS – RESPONSE MODEL

As per the *stimulus-response* model, there are marketing and other stimuli which enter the *consumer's black box'* and subsequently produces certain buyer responses.

As per the stimulus-response model, there are marketing and other stimuli which enter the *'Consumer's black-box'* and subsequently produces certain buyer responses. The marketing environment comprise of various marketing mix elements which act as cues in influencing consumer response. The buyer is exposed to a variety of information which informs and educates him or her on the product's existence, price to match the product features, availability at the various outlets, ably supported by the promotional tools such as advertisement, contests, sweep take publicity etc., while marketing environment helps to build up product awareness. This combined with the other stimuli will make the product respond either positively or negatively towards the offer.

FIGURE 1.6

CONSUMER BEHAVIOUR MODEL

Marketing stimuli	Other stimuli	Buyers black box		Buyers' response
		Buyers' Characteristics	Buyers' decision	
Product Price Place Promotion	Economic Cultural Technological Political			1. Product 2. Brand choice 3. Dealer choice 4. Purchase timing

(*Source : Principles of Marketing*, Philip Kotler, 1985, pp. 121-122)

Influence of other Factors on Consumer Behaviour

Economic factors namely family income, the disposable personal income, the individuals discretionary income and standard of living can also influence the buyers behaviour pattern. Each culture, religion and language commands its own unique pattern of social conduct. Every culture has its own set of beliefs, values, customs, which will be seen in the way the consumer responds to the various products available in the market. Every culture has certain do's and dont's which will significantly control the individual's lifestyle and buying behaviour. If the technology adopted in the making of the product is something unique or latest, the consumers must be made aware of this. Here the marketer will have to analyse the buying motive of the consumer. *'Buying motives can be defined as "all the impulses, desires and considerations of the buyer" which induces him to purchase a given product'*. People are very much concerned about their image and status in the society. Status is indicated by the possession of products made from the latest technology. So if a new product that constitutes a status symbol is within their reach, their aspiration to possess it, will influence the decision making process. Similarly, the political environment will play a role in the availability of the category of products in the market. The Government has adopted new policies and reforms in the form of industrial licensing policies and trade policies, which has had a direct impact on the economic institutions like the banking sector and capital market in particular. This is turn will affect the savings of the consumers, a large chunk of which will flow into the capital markets and this will have a direct effect on the consumption of the buyer.

Thus, all the above factors will play upon the buyers black box and make him respond to the product either positively or negatively. The buyer is a complex entity. He has always been a puzzle for the marketers. It has been observed that the buyer does not follow rigid rules while making buying decisions and though he is exposed to a lot of information about the product, he filters it out and perceives and retains information only what he would normally like to perceive and retain.

The buyers purchase decision is very often influenced by the social environment - consisting of his family, his society, neighbours, his friends, his job and his colleagues. Such influences will be seen in his response to the product brand, store patronage and purchase timing. Yet the buyer cannot be said to be a passive person, who will allow himself to be manipulated by the marketing man. So the marketing manager has to work out the marketing strategies and plans to influence the buyer behaviour.

TRENDS IN CONSUMER BEHAVIOUR 

Understanding of trends in consumer behaviour will give organisations certain strategic advantages. If the organisation is the pioneer in foreseeing the coming trends in consumer's needs and wants, it can be the first to introduce the product in the market and gain the initial advantage. *Sabeer Bhatia* was the first to anticipate the impact of free e-mail (*hotmail*). Similarly *Citibank* had been an early entrant to be successful in the acceptance of the credit card concept by Indian customers.

Secondly, on sighting a trend, it becomes possible for the industry to create a market by channeling a latent need. For this, the cellular phone industry can be quoted as an example. The cellular (or mobile) phone has gained wide acceptance among consumers because of the benefits of wireless technology. The cellular phone industry comprising of names such as *Reliance, BSNL, Airtel, Hutch* etc. have been able to attract customers by offering wide network coverage, attractive service contract and all at suitable prices.

And lastly, anticipating trends in customer needs and wants and responding to them will not only earn positive public opinion (for the organisation and industry) but also communicate a social responsible image of them. Examples can be quoted of organisations which endorse advertisements issued in public interest such as, banning of smoking at airports, aeroplanes and restaurants, and usage of organically grown vegetables/fruits, recycled paper products etc.

For understanding the trends in determinants of consumer behaviour, we have broadly viewed them under three categories:

- Customer demographic trends
- Technological trends
- Trends in public policy.

The trends in determinants of consumer behaviour can be broadly viewed under three categories:

a. Customer demographic trends

b. Technological trends and

c. Trends in public policy.

(a) Customer Demographic Trends

Changes occurring in customer demographics will help marketers to anticipate the needs and wants of their customer. A few visible changing trends affecting the demographic profile of customers at the market place are :

- The trend of aging population is visible due to *declining birthrate and rising life expectancy.* The aging of the population creates new needs and wants. A few of their concerns are related to health, financial security, personal safety and recreation facilities. Related to these concerns will be changes occurring in their purchase behaviour. Senior citizens will seek food items offering nutritional and dietary value, easy availability of products and services (suitable location of the store), attractive health insurance schemes and willingness to spend discretionary income for travel, eating out and other recreational activities.

Thus marketers will have to work out suitable product and services offerings to suit the changing consumer behaviour of senior citizens.

- Another changing trend is the increase in the double income households with more and more *women opting to work outside the home.* The increase in the number of working women has particularly affected the 'time resource' and a shift in the lifestyle of such households. With 'time' being a scarce resource at their disposal, working women are postponing their purchase time to weekends or holidays. They also prefer to purchase products from shops which are conveniently located along with the facility of ample parking space. To serve this category of customers, marketers must understand their changing needs and offer suitable products made available, at certain strategic locations.
- *Emergence of single individual households.* With both the sexes being (equally) qualified, there is another visible trend. Being more career conscious, educated youth have developed a tendency to postpone marriage, preferring to living alone, in order to enjoy their economic independence. Such households enjoy their personal lifestyles and freedom. Being away from their family, such households at times purchase goods which convey a feeling of belonging, takeup social causes etc. in order to escape loneliness. This category of customers may invest in cellular phones (or telephones), and other electronic goods.

  For the marketer, this trend indicates that they need to offer more customised products and services (say, instant food preparations etc.) which are appealing and available at convenient locations. [For instance; stores (or services like beauty parlours, restaurants etc.) where the sales personnel are similar to them in demographics and lifestyles].

The change in consumer demographic trends such as: shift in the definition of middle class customers, ethnic diversity especially in metros, and the geographic shifting of population are compelling marketers to customise product and service offerings to suit the particular market.

- *Shift in the definition of 'middle class' customers.* Due to the boom in the economy, the middle class has been growing. Our economy is constantly being fuelled with demand for goods and services from the rapidly expanding middle class. These middle class customers have high aspiration levels, with more disposable income and purchasing power in their hands.

  Alongwith these growing middle class aspirations and purchasing power, the neo rich (the affluent class and wealthy) are seeking ways to abandon old symbols of affluence and patronise new symbolic conspicious products.

  The implications for the marketer will be to offer customised product and service offerings to cater to the different needs of both the aspiring middle class and neo rich customers. To, encourage increased buying among consumers, marketers have brought out appliances, automobiles and even consumables with attractive financial schemes — like the *SOTC Holiday Packages,* Time share options, Low EMIs for purchasing cars (*Santro Xing, Honda City, Baleno etc.)* and so on.
- *Ethnic diversity especially in* metres and minimetros cities. To avail of better economic integration, people are seen to be migrating to metro cities and minimetros to enjoy better standards of living. This has resulted in more cultural and ethnic diversity

especially due to increasing globalisation of the economy and the availability of job opportunities.

The implications of this for the marketers will be the need to segment the market carefully so as to effectively serve the distinct ethnic groups or diverse segments. This could be the reason behind wide acceptance for departmental stores, *(Lifestyle, Shopper's Stop* etc.) supermarkets (*Nilgiris, Foodworld, Fabmall etc.),* shopping malls and so on among the diverse customer market segments. Simultaneously, marketers are also required to deal with various marketing communication tools (internet, labelling of products in more than one language etc.) so as to tackle the cultural diversity.

- *Geographic shifting* or *redistribution of population.* India has been a witness to shifting of people from the rural to urban areas. However, the influx of more and more people to the urban areas has made the city expand beyond its geographical boundaries. This has resulted in the breaking down of infrastructure such as roads, transport system and other public utilities. To partly solve this problem many organisations are relocating themselves to new locations to avail of the economic incentives and better infrastructure facilities. For instance, the *ITPL park* (Bangalore), Techno Park (Trivandrum). With the necessary support provided by the state governments, relocation of industries will be an attractive option.

  In rural India also there has been an increase in the purchase of goods. Although as seen in Box 1.4 there still exists differences in the consumption of consumer goods between rural India and urban Indian consumers.

  Each region will have a greater mix of people from various places. Even procurement and consumption pattern of customers are likely to be divergent. Accordingly, the marketers will have to modify their marketing plans based on the regional tastes and preferences of the divergent group of customers.

(b) Technological Trends

Technology also plays a role in shaping future customer values. Customers are now at the receiving end of information explosion, especially due to the technological advances. The benefits of technological advances are many :

Technological revolution has resulted in display of consumer behaviour which is more liberal, demanding, information seeking and individualistic.

- Customers have more *control over market place information.*
- The market has opened up to the new generation of smart *products* with voice-recognition capabilities, designed to the selected preferences of their owner or users.
- Today's customer has got the purchasing power and ability to have access *to products anytime, anywhere.*
- With technology, it is also possible to have products and services customised and delivered to consumers.

With technological advances, it will be easy to picturise future customers as being very knowledgeable and drivers of all marketing activity. Technological revolution will result in consumer behaviour which is more liberal, demanding, information seeking and individualistic.

(c) Trends in Ethical Concern, Economic Pragmatism and Regional Economic Integration

There is more *ethical consciousness* with organisations adopting certain explicit code of ethics for decision-making throughout the organisation. The widely accepted societal marketing concept calls for marketers to offer products and services which fulfill the needs of the target market with a long term perspective of improving the society as a whole. This trend of ethical

BOX 1.4

CONSUMPTION TRENDS AMONG RURAL AND URBAN CONSUMERS

HIGHER per capita income has brought about significant changes in consumption patterns in both rural and urban India. However, differences still exist between the overall composition of consumption, with consumers in urban India spending a greater proportion of their income on high-end luxury-related goods than rural India.

For instance, urban households spend about 41% of their monthly per-capita consumption expenditure on food and about 37.1% on expensive/high-end goods and services, while rural households spend close to 55% of their monthly per-capita consumption expenditure on food. The growing number of super markets and malls in urban India, has only helped in fueling urban expenditure on higher-end luxury-related products.

Rising incomes in urban India, and the changing relative prices of cereals and non-cereal foods have led to a diet diversification away from cereals and towards high-value agricultural products in urban India.

For instance, cereal consumption used to be as high as 14% to 15% of monthly per-capita consumption expenditure in the 90's but it has now come down to around the 10% mark.

Like-wise, the overall share in foods consumption has declined sharply in urban India, and expenditure on energy expenses, high-end goods and services and durable goods are rising. All these goods, barring energy expenses, can be classified as high-end products.

Increases in energy costs seen in urban India is a reflection of higher oil prices, and higher power prices. In the 90s, as much as 54% of monthly per-capita consumption expenditure was spent on food. This figure now stands at 41%. Similarly in the 90s, close to 26% of monthly per-capita expenditure in urban India was spent on high-end goods and services, which currently stands at 37%.

Even though per capita income levels haven't grown at a rapid pace in rural India, there are indications of improving quality of goods purchased. For instance, the share of non-food articles consumed has been spiraling upwards, while the total quantum of food articles consumed has been on the downtrend. In 1987-88 as much as 63.8% of the overall rural monthly consumption expenditure was spent on food-related products. That figure currently stands at about 53.9%.

SPENDING SPREE **TABLE 1.3**

Composition of Monthly Per Capita Consumption Expenditure in Rural And Urban Areas

	Urban	Rural
Food	41.6	53.9
Pan & Tobbacco	1.6	2.5
Energy Costs	9	9.6
Clothing	6	7.1
Footwear	1.1	1
High-End Goods & Services	37.1	22.5
Durable Goods	3.6	3.4

Source : NSSO (%)

Suorce: Shivom Chakravarti & Anupam K Gupta, Intelligence Group, *Economic Times*, Bangalore, 18 April '06

Today's consumer is also more ethically concerned, shows economic pragmatism and is all for regional economic integration.

ethics for decision-making throughout the organisation. The widely accepted societal marketing concept calls for marketers to offer products and services which fulfill the needs of the target market with a long term perspective of improving the society as a whole. This trend of ethical concern will continue to be a focus area, with consumer behaviour becoming an integral part of strategic market planning. Even in future the marketers will continue to focus and address moral issues and ethical behaviour at the market place.

Economic Pragmatism on the part of government is seen in the way the market economy has been opened up giving way to greater participation of the private sector, deregularisation and internationalisation of products and services. The long term benefits which will affect the consumer behaviour will be seen through increased productivity, better allocation of resources and higher standards of living with increased purchasing power. Customers will stand to gain because in order to compete, the organisations will become customer oriented, offer better products and services at lower prices with more standardisation due to internationalisation and global competition.

More and more national governments are seen accepting regional economic integration. For instance, the Association of South East Asian Nations (ASEAN), which includes countries such as Malaysia, Indonesia, Singapore, Brunei, Thailand, Philippines and Japan (which is moving towards integrating its economy). Eventually, Australia, China and India could also join the alliance. Such alliances could be more than trading partners, integrate production facilities and currencies, with even the tariff barriers being pulled down. Such regional economic integration could occur even across cultural and climatic boundaries. The impact of this on consumer behaviour will be seen in the form of :

- Consumers will be able to enjoy goods throughout the year due to the blending of climatic boundaries with economic blocs.
- With liberalisation of international trade, consumers can enjoy purchasing goods and services from anywhere across the world.
- With globalisation of the consumer, inspite of there being national, geophysical, climatic and cultural boundaries, when it comes to consumption of goods and services, it will be a global village.

SUMMARY

Today when the market is flooded with many me-too products, it is highly imperative that marketers make products to suit the uniqueness and diversity of consumer's tastes and preferences. Consumer behaviour can be said to be the study of how individuals make decisions on how to spend their available resources (time, money, effort) on various consumption related items.

The field of consumer behaviour study gained prominence only from the 1960's and has borrowed concepts from related scientific disciplines such as Psychology, Sociology, Socio-psychology, Cultural Anthropology and Economics. While undertaking consumer research, marketers use a combination of qualitative and quantitative research techniques, whereas, academicians are interested in the act of consumption *i.e.,* post positivism or experimentalism. As per the managerial perspective, the consumer behaviour tends to be more micro or cognitive in nature. Whereas, the holistic perspective tends to focus more on the nature of the consumption experience rather than the purchasing process.

Few models of consumer decision making namely, Schiffman & Kank's model of Consumer Decision Making, Assaell's Consumer Decision Making and a Simple Stimulus-Response Model were discussed. The chapter concludes with a brief discussion on the trends in consumer behaviour through a look at the customer demographic trends, technological trends and trends in public policy.

CHAPTER QUESTIONS FOR DISCUSSION

1. Assume a NRI friend of yours is planning set up a chain of fast food restaurants in cities like Ahmedabad, Pune, Jaipur, and Indore. Knowing the Indian consumers, which cultural, social, personal and psychological variables you think will work for or against the success of the proposed business? Why?
2. "The Uncola", "yeh dil maange more" and "Jashan Mana Le" are the taglines of 7-up, Pepsi and Coca-Cola respectively. Which consumer behaviour trends, you think might have been considered while the taglines were worked out for the ads?
3. According to you which of the two: holistic perspective or the managerial perspective, on the study of consumer behaviour is more apt today? Explain?
4. Describe the meaning of the term Consumer Behaviour? Why is the study of consumer behaviour very relevant in today's context, Explain?

➲ SUGGESTED READINGS

1. www.rajtravels.com
2. Riya-Kartha, 'Going Places', Brand Equity, *The Economic Times*, Bangalore, 14 June, 2006.
3. M.S. Banga (Chairman, Hindustan Lever); Brand Power, *Business Today*, January 16, 2005, pp. 56-62.
4. Dr. V.S. Ramaswamy, S. Namakumari, *Marketing Management Planning, Implementation & Control,* 3rd edition, Maxmillan India Ltd, 2005, pp. 219-261.
5. Frank R. Kardes, *Consumer Behavior and Managerial Decision Making*, 2nd Edition, Prentice Hall of India Pvt. Ltd, New Delhi, 2002, pp. 5-21.
6. Rosemary. Phipps; and Craig. Simmons; *Understanding Customers,* 1996-97, Butter Worth Heinemann Oxford, 1996.
7. Philip Kotler, *Principles of Marketing*, 2nd Edition, Prentice Hall of India Pvt. Ltd, New Delhi, 1985, pp. 121-141.
8. Liz Hill & Terry O' Sullivon, *Foundation of Marketing*, 3rd Edition, Pearson Education Limited, England, 2004, pp. 2-3.
9. Leon G. Schiffman, Leslie Lazar Kanuk, *Consumer Behavior,* 6th Edition, Prentice Hall of India Pvt. Ltd. New Delhi, 2005, pp. 5-10.
10. Henry Assael, *Consumer Behavior - A Strategic Approach,* (2005 Indian Adaptation Edition), Biztantra (Dream tech press) New Delhi, 2005, pp 2-21.

CASE

MARICO INDUSTRIES

INTRODUCTION

Marico Industries is a leading Indian FMCG Group dealing in consumer products and services and has successfully created brands in the largely commoditised business of hair oils and edible oils. Company sources reveal that Marico's producs and services in hair care, skin care and healthy foods generated a turnover of about 19.1 billion during 2007-2008.

Marico's branded products are present in Bangladesh, other SAARC countries, the Middle East, Egypt and South Africa. The overseas sales franchise of Mario's consumer products is totally in branded products and is also one of the largest amongst Indian companies.

THE BEGINNING AND THE SUBSEQUENT GROWTH

Marico's business lies in manufacturing and retailing personal consumer products as well as providing services in the skincare and beauty care area. The beginning of the company can be traced to 1948, when the Mumbai based Mariwala family which was already involved in the trading business set up the Bombay Oil Industries Ltd. (BOIL). The manufacturing unit at BOIL was utilized for coconut oil extraction plants, for vegetable oil refinery purpose and as a chemical plant. Over a period of time, BOIL expanded and diversified into branded consumer products subsequently. The promoter family went on to incorporate a company, initially called Marico Foods Limited, then Marico Industries Limited and later on became Marico Limited, in 1988 and BOIL consumer products division was transferred to the company.

In 1990, Marico entered into an agreement with BOIL to use its brands **'Parachute'** and **'Saffola'**. It also purchased a unit at Jalgaon for using it as a manufacturing base and then made several acquisitions in order to add to its product portfolio. The prominent acquisitions include:

- In 1999, Procter & Gamble's anti lice brand **'Mediker'**.
- In 2000, acquiring the facilities of Kanmoor Foods, Saswad, Maharastra for manufacture of jams, sauces and other fruit and vegetable products.
- In 2001, acquired the **Parachute** and **Saffola** brand from BOIL.
- In 2003, Marico acquired **Sundari LLC** from the USA, a manufacturer of luxury ayurvedic products.
- In 2004, Marico commenced offering scientific, unisex dermatological procedures as well as skin care products under the banner of **Kaya Skin Clinics**.
- In 2006, Marico, after acquiring the herbal bath soap brand **'Manjal'** from Kerela-based Oriental Extractions, made a direct entry into the soap market in India.

PRODUCTS AND BRANDS

Over the years, Marico has established itself and come to be known as a consumer focussed FMCG Company through its 12 well accepted brands. It has three business segments:

- **Consumer products** (includes the consumer products business of Marico Limited, Marico Bangladesh Limited and MBL Industries Limited).
- **Skin Care** (services and products retailed through Kaya Skin Clinics)
- **Global Ayurvedics** (Sundari)

Marico's Products and Brands

Hair care	• Parachute • Oil of Malabar
Hair Oils	
	• Parachute Lite, Parachute Jasmine, Parachute Rose, Parachute Advanced Parachute Sampoorna • Hair & Care • Shanti Amla
Hair care	• Silk-n-Shine conditioner, Parachute after shower hair cream
Anti-lice treatment	• Mediker
Processed foods	• Sil (jams, sauces, baked beans, Chinese vinegar, sweet corn soup, mayonnais) • Saffola salt
Edible oil	• Saffola and its extensions – Saffola Kardi, Saffola Tasty Blend, Saffola Gold • Sweekar
Fabric care	• Revive instant starch
Skin care services	• Kaya Clinic, Sundari

(*Source :* Company website, *IMaCS analysis*)

The product lines in the **consumer products segment** include coconut oil, fabric care, processed foods and its distribution alliance with Indo Nissin Foods. The various brands and their extensions in this segment not only have a significant market share in the particular product categories but even enjoy leadership positions. In fact, Marico's flagship brand **'Parachute'** has been maintaining a market share of over 50 per cent in India, in the coconut oil category.

In the **skin care services segment**, Marico's **Kaya Skin Clinics** offer US FDA approved dermatological procedures such as anti-ageing services, face rejuvenation, pimple remover etc., as well as beauty products like skin lightening complex, under-eye gel, moisturizing sunscreen and night crème. The Kaya clinics target high-income customers in the age group of 16-60 years across metros and mini metros in India.

The Global Ayurvedic segment is sold under the Sundari skin line with 28 products including cleansers, moisturizers and essential oils with formulations using plants and floral extracts sourced from India. This Sundari range of beauty products is used to target the spa market.

Marico Core Competence

Marico has adopted a methodical approach towards building its business after making a strong presence in its core business and identifying new growth drivers in the Kaya Skin Clinics and Sundari Ayurvedic business.

Marico's core competence lies in its ability to innovatively brand and packaging commodity items. Two of Marico's well known brands are *'Parachute'* and *'Saffola'*, with the former maintaining a market share of nearly 50 per cent. This was done with regular packaging innovations, increasing user base with low-cost blister packs targeted at lower income classes and many other focused micro marketing initiatives. In the past, coconut oil was sold loose in India as a commodity. Marico claims to be the first company to have branded and sold this commodity under the brand name 'Parachute'. The company has introduced brand extensions in the value-added coconut oil segment, which has found consumer acceptance and grown to command 34 per cent share in the segment in India.

Another core competence has been in its ability to create new niche categories for growth. It has indentified categories that do not have any product offering to serve the customers needs. *For example,* noticing the age-old habit of starching fabric in hot water, provided an opportunity to create a new category of instant cold water starch and led to the launch of its brand **'Revive'**. Similarly, with **Mediker**, Marico created another new category of anti-lice treatment. Both these brands 'Revive' and 'Mediker' have gone on to become dominant players in their respective categories and face limited competition.

Marico's efforts have been recognized through various awards received by it. To quote a few of the awards:

- Marico's "Saffola World Heart Day", campaign has won a Bronze at the first-ever Asia Pacific Effie Awards, Singapore, 2008.
- Marico Uncommon sense case study has been showcased in the Annual World Effie Coffee Table Book, 2008.
- Kaya – Best retailer in the Beauty and Fitness category, India Retail Forum, September 2007.
- One of India's 10 best marketers (*Business Today*, Sept. 2006).
- Brand Leadership Award at the India Brand Summit 2006 (September 2006).

Marico has leveraged its core sources of competitive advantage *viz.,* Brand building, Cost Management, Innovation and Technology to set up a fast growing franchise of new products and services.

FUTURE FOCUS

During the past two years, Marico has been on a high growth path (in FY 07, it grew by 36% followed by 22% in FY 08). The company generated a turnover of about Rs. 19.1 billion during 2007-2008. In future also the company sources indicate that their focus will remain on delivering healthy growth. The company's flagship brand 'Parachute' which has grown over 10% in volume during the past two years and is expected to sustain a growth rate of 6% to 8% in the category. Its second flagship, 'Saffola' which has been showing high growth rates in the recent past, the company believes that this premium niche segment of refined edible oil should grow by around 15% since the company's hair oils portfolio grew at 16% in FY-8, it expects this segment (comprising of Hairs care, Parachute Jasmine, Nihar perfumed oil, Shanty Amla and Parachute Advanced) to contribute to a significant part of the top line in the next few years.

During the past few years, the company has been launching new products in the pre and post wash hair care, which it plans to continue doing so and participate in category-creation and growth. Moreover, Saffola brand's role has been extended beyond edible oils towards functional foods. The company is working towards investing in promoting acceptance of functional foods as a part of changing lifestyles of the consumers. They also plan to explore the launching of new health food products in various formats.

In Kaya, the company plans to expand its skin services by adding about 15 clinics each year. This means apart from investing in manpower, the marketers have also to work towards advertising for customers acquisition and brand building. Further, to supplement its organic growth, Marico is open to exploring opportunities which matches its focus on the beauty and wellness segments.

(*Source :* www.marico india.com, www.maricoindustries.com, Rajiv Banerjee, Marico's strategy. On the Prowl', Brand equity. *Economic Times,* Bangalore 22-03-06)

QUESTIONS FOR DISCUSSION

1. Do you feel Marico is right in extending its Saffola brand's positioning more towards acceptance of functional foods' to match the changing lifestyles of today's consumers? Why?
2. Even though Parachute and Saffola hold very strong positions in the market, discuss what steps, according to you need to be taken by Marico to counter the entry of other large players/ FMCGS/MNCs in the future?

CHAPTER 2

CONSUMER MODELLING

- Case : **Falafel's** (Veg Hummus House)
- Models of Consumer Behaviour.
- The Howard-Sheth Model of Buying Behaviour.
- The Nicosia Model.
- The Engel - Kollat - Blackwell Model.
- Engel, Blackwell and Miniard (EBM) Model.
- Webster and Wind Model of Organisational Buying Behaviour.
- The Sheth Model of Industrial Buying.
- Summary
- Chapter Questions for Discussion
- Suggested Readings
- Case : **Booming Batter Business**

CASE

FALAFEL'S (VEG HUMMUS HOUSE)

Falafel's is one of the second rung of international fast food (originally from Israel) chains to have set up outlets in India to serve Indian customers and build up a strong customer base before the big chains such as Burger King, Star Bucks among others come to woo the customers here. An incident at Falafel's, made the management realize that it is good to follow the 'Economic Model" *i.e.,* localizing the offerings suitable for the diverse Indian taste buds at affordable prices.

Falafel's, the West Asian Cuisine Chain, had just opened its first Indian Outlet in South Mumbai, when Eli Zedaka, the Director of JB. N. JEG Foods, that owns Falafel's in India, was approached by a customer asking if they served "Jain" cuisine. For Zedaka who had lived in Israel for more than three decades, the "Jain" request though globally a first, many more similar requests came trickling in. This was because the outlet had opened in a locality predominantly inhabited by the jain community in Mumbai. The Jain community consume a strict vegetarian food without ever garlic, onion and potatoes. Very soon after receiving the 'jain' request, Zedaka got in touch with chef Guy Itzhaki, his partner who handles Falafel's operations globally, to localize the Falafel Hummus. The result was the birth of 'Jain Falafel' the company's first localized offering-minus the onion and garlic, but with the original taste of Hummus intact.

A research survey carried out by consulting major AT Kearney revealed that the Indian quick service restaurant (QSR) market is expected to grow at a compounded annual rate of 10%, to touch Rs 30,000 crore by 2011. This conclusion was made on the basis of the increase in frequency of eating out, by consumers today. This is unlike a decade ago, when the eating out frequency was only 3-4 days in a month, especially in the metro cities.

However, with the aim of attracting volumes, the strategy followed by Falafel was to make offerings at a low entry level price *i.e.,* the economic model. It was seen that a majority of the Indian consumers were not willing to spend much in the quick service formats, with an average per head spend in a QSR ranging between Rs 75 and Rs 100 across cusine formats. So in order to attract consumers who would evaluate all the alternatives in terms of the price and value received and derive satisfaction Falafel's had offerings in the price ranges between Rs.45 to Rs.125.

It was also learnt that apart from affordability and taste, availability (location) also played key factors in the success of a QSR. Implying that the right catchment area is imperative for higher footfalls and better visibility. Thus, accordingly *Falafel's* prefers to be located on the main roads, which are easily accessible to customers.

Falafel's is only one name amongst the several fast food chains offerings that Indian customers are slowly learning to relish and enjoy.

The above case on *'Falafel's* can to a certain extent be compared to the Economic and Learning Models of consumer behaviour. Although in the above case the comparison has been made only to these two models, as one goes through the chapter, one will be exposed to many more models. But first we will start by defining a model.

A model is very often referred to as an abstract representation of a process or relationship. We (human beings) hold various models in our minds which allow us to make sense of the world and also help to predict the likely course of events. Simply stated models help us in the following ways:

- They help in the development of theories.
- They help to understand complex relationships.
- They provide the framework for discussions and research work.

In this chapter effort has been made to examine the various models having relevance to the consumer decision making process. The primary concern is to use the models to understand consumer behaviour. Consumer behaviourists as well as marketers are interested in understanding how and why certain decisions are made. The discussions in the chapter are related to some of the important models of consumer behaviour, with an attempt made to give a comprehensive view of all those aspects of the buying situations which are deemed as significant by their creators. In particular, the models discussed in this chapter are:

- The Economic Model
- Learning Model
- Psychoanalytic Model
- The Sociological Model
- The Howard Sheth Model of buying behaviour
- The Nicosia Model
- The Engel-Kollat-Blackwell model
- Engel, Blackwell and Miniard (EBM) Model
- Webstar and Wind Model of organisational buying behaviour
- The Sheth Model of Industrial buying.

MODELS OF CONSUMER BEHAVIOUR

TRADITIONAL MODELS

The early or traditional models were developed by economists with a view to understand economic systems. Economics helps to understand how scarce resources are allocated among unlimited wants and needs. The first four Models give a general view in terms of the Economic model, Learning model, Psychoanalytic model and the Sociological model.

Economic Model

The economic model assumes that with limited purchasing power and a set of needs and tastes, a consumer will allocate his/her expenditure over different products at given prices so as to maximize utility.

Under economics, it is assumed that man is a rational human being, who will evaluate all the alternatives in terms of cost and value received and select that product/service which gives him/her maximum satisfaction (utility). Consumers are assumed to follow the principle of maximum utility based on the law of diminishing marginal utility. It is assumed that with limited purchasing power, and a set of needs and tastes, a consumer will allocate his/her expenditure over different products at given prices so as to maximise utility.

I. Economic Model

II. Learning Model

Various models affecting consumer behaviour.

The law of equimarginal utility enables him to secure maximum utility from limited purchasing power.

Economic model of consumer behaviour is unidimensional. This means that buying decisions of a person are governed by the concept of utility. Being a rational man he will make his purchase decisions with the intention of maximising the utility/benefits.

Economic model is based on certain predictions of buying behaviour.

1. *Price effect* - Lesser the price of the product, more will be the quantity purchased.
2. *Substitution effect* - Lesser the price of the substitute product, lesser will be the quantity of the original product bought.
3. *Income effect* - More the purchasing power, more will be the quantity purchased.

The assumption about the rational behaviour of human beings has been challenged by the behavioural scientists. They are of the opinion that while the predictions are useful, the model only explains how a consumer ought to behave, it does not throw light on how does the consumer actually behave.

Behavioural scientists feel the economic model is incomplete. They feel that Economics is assuming the market to be homogeneous where all the buyers will think and act alike and also focuses only on one aspect of the product *i.e.,* income. It has been argued upon that man is a complex entity and hence the need to adopt a multidisciplinary approach to understand consumer behaviour. Whereas, the model has ignored all vital aspects such as perception, motivation, learning, attitude, personality and socio-cultural factors. Added to this, man is today living in a technologically advanced age with constant exposure to the various marketing variables such as superior technologically advanced quality products (and services), efficient network distribution centers, highly interactive media exposure etc. Under such circumstances man cannot be assumed to be a rational person who only treats 'price' as the deciding factor in his consumption related decisions.

Behaviour scientists have opined that a broader perspective need to be adopted while analysing the buyer behaviour. So apart from economics, even the role played by needs, motives, personality, self concept and the socio-cultural factors have to be considered for understanding the buyers responses to various stimuli, which in turn could influence their buying behaviour.

Learning Model

The learning model will help marketers to promote association of products with strong drives and cues, which would lead to positive re-enforcement from the consumers.

Unlike the economists, classical psychologists have been interested in the formation and satisfaction of needs and tastes. They argued that living beings were influenced by both innate needs such as the primary needs of hunger, thirst, sex, shelter and learned needs like fear and guilt. A drive (internal stimulus) which when directed towards a drive reducing object becomes a motive. The various products or services will act as stimuli to satisfy drives. For instance, a hungry person will be driven towards food, which after consumption will reduce the drive and also provide satisfaction. According to learning theorists, this response of satisfaction (feeling) reinforces the relationship between drive and the drive reducing stimulus object as well as the related cues. Further, when consumers learn to associate connection between stimulus and response, it becomes a habit. There are certain cognitive theorists, who have advocated that human beings not only learn to link stimulus with response (S-R) but also about the formation of other cognitive processes such as, attitudes, values, beliefs, motivation etc.

In marketing context, 'learning' will help marketers to understand how consumers learn to respond in new marketing situations, or how they have learned and responded in the past in

III. Psychoanalytical Model

IV. Sociological Model

Various models affecting consumer behaviour.

similar situations. Very often it is observed that consumer's experience with one product from an organisation is likely to be generalised to the other products of the firm. Conversely, consumers also learn to discriminate and this information will be useful in working out different marketing strategies. Simply stated this learning model will help marketers to promote associations of products with strong drives and cues and positive re-inforcements from the consumers.

Psychoanalytical Model

This model is based on the work of psychologists who were concerned with personality. They were of the view that human needs and motives operated at the conscious as well as at the subconscious levels. This theory was developed by Sigmund Frued. According to him human behaviour (personality) is the outcome of *(a)* 'id' - the source of all psychic energy which drives to act, *(b)* 'super ego' - the internal representation of what is approved by the society, *(c)* 'ego' - the conscious directing 'id' impulses to find gratification in a socially accepted manner. Thus, we can say that human behaviour is directed by a complex set of deep-seated motives.

The psychoanalytical model is concerned with personality and says that human behaviour, to a great extent is directed by a complex set of deep seated motives.

From the marketing point of view this means that buyers will be influenced by symbolic factors in buying a product. Motivational research has been involved in investigating motives of consumer behaviour so as to develop suitable marketing implications accordingly. Marketers have been using this approach to generate ideas for developing products - design, features, advertising and other promotional techniques.

As per the sociological model, an individual buyer is a part of the institution called society, gets influenced by it and in turn, also influences it in its path of development.

The Sociological Model

According to this model the individual buyer is a part of the institution called society. Since he is living in a society, he gets influenced by it and in turn also influences it in its path of development. He is playing many roles as a part of various formal and informal associations or organisations such as a family member, as an employee of a firm, as a member of a professional forum and as an active member of an informal cultural organisation. Such interactions leave some impressions on him and may play a role in influencing his buying behaviour.

Intimate groups comprising of family, friends and close colleagues can exercise a strong influence on the lifestyle and the buying behaviour of an individual member. The peer group plays a very important role in acting as an influencing factor especially in adopting particular lifestyles and buying behaviour patterns. The group generally has an informal opinion leader, whose views are respected by the group. This leader is able to influence the individual member's lifestyle and buying decisions.

Similarly, depending on the income, occupation and place of residence etc., each individual member is recognised as belonging to a certain social class. As a member of a particular class, he may enjoy certain status and prestige. Further, each class has its own standards of lifestyle and buying behaviour pattern. So an individual member will adopt the role suitable to conform to the style and behavioural pattern of the social class to which he/she belongs.

The marketers, through a process of market segmentation can work out on the common behaviour patterns of a specific class and group of buyers and try to influence their buying pattern.

CONTEMPORARY MODELS

With the evolution of the consumer behaviour study, newer approaches were used to understand what influences consumer behaviour. (*Consumer Behavior,* D.L. Loudon & A.J. Della Bitta, 4th Edn., 2006). These were said to be contemporary models.

These contemporary models or views differed from the earlier models mainly because they focused on the decision process adopted by consumers and borrowed concepts from behavioural sciences field. Some of these models have been discussed hereunder. (The source of reference of the same have been mentioned under Suggested Reading).

THE HOWARD SHETH MODEL OF BUYING BEHAVIOUR

The Howard-Sheth model attempts to throw light on the rational brand behaviour shown by buyers when faced with situations involving incomplete information and limited abilities.

The Howard-Sheth model illustrated in figure 2.1 provides an integrating framework for a very sophisticated comprehensive theory of consumer behaviour. The model tries to represent the rational brand choice behaviour by buyers when faced with situations involving incomplete information and limited abilities. The model refers to three levels of decision making:

- **Extensive Problem Solving :** The initial stages of decision making when the buyer has little information about brands and has not yet developed a well defined and structured criteria to make a selection from the various products (choice criteria).
- **Limited Problem Solving :** In a slightly more advanced stage choice criteria which is well defined but the buyer is not clear and undecided on the set of brands which will best serve him. In this situation, the consumer is uncertain on the 'best brand' which will suit him (or her).

FIGURE 2.1

THE HOWARD-SHETH MODEL OF BUYING BEHAVIOUR

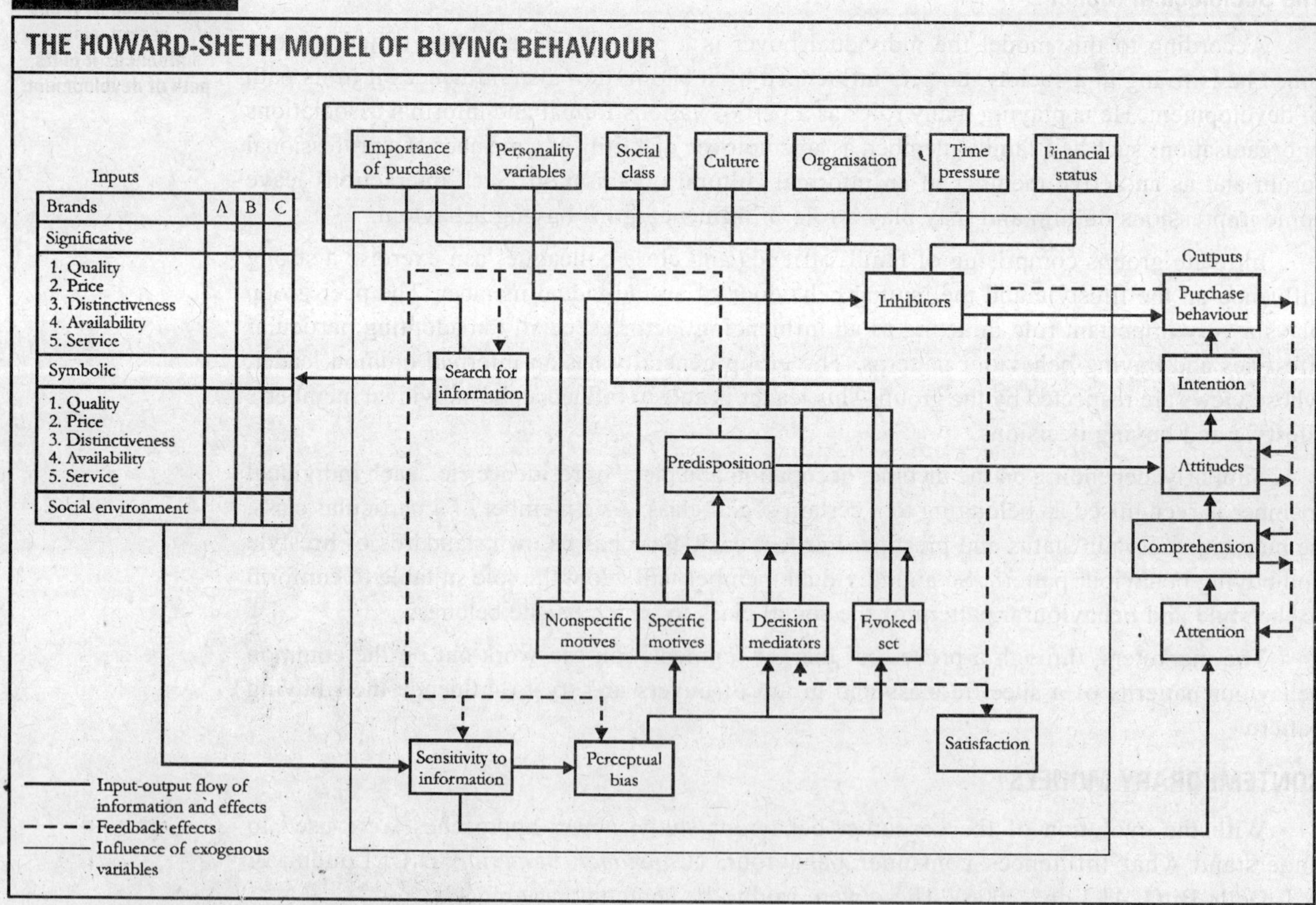

(*Source : Consumer Behavior*, D.L. Louden, A.J. Della Bitta, 4th Edn., 2006, pp. 608)

- **Routinized Response Behaviour :** The stage when buyers have well defined choice criteria along with strong predispositions towards one brand. In such a situation, there is hardly any confusion in the consumer's mind and he is ready to purchase a particular brand with little evaluation of alternatives.

The model has borrowed the learning theory concepts to explain brand choice behaviour when learning takes place as the buyer moves from Extensive Problem Solving to Routinized Problem Solving behaviour. There are four components involved in the model: (a) input variables, (b) output variables, (c) hypothetic constructs and (d) exogenous variables.

This model has borrowed the learning theory concepts to explain brand choice behaviour when learning takes place as the buyer moves from extensive problem solving to routinized problem solving behaviour.

Input Variables

Input variables are shown in the left side of the model (Figure 2.1) as stimuli in the environment. *Significative stimuli* are those actual elements of brands which the buyer confronts, whereas *symbolic stimuli* are those which are used by marketers to represent their products in a symbolic form (say through advertisements) *Social stimuli* are generated by the social environment such as family, friends, groups etc.

Output Variables

There are five output variables as shown in Figure 2.1, which are the buyer's observable responses to stimulus inputs. They appear in the sequence as shown here under:

- *Attention:* based on the importance of the buyer's information intake.
- *Comprehension:* the store of information the buyer has about the brand.
- *Attitude:* the buyer's evaluation of the particular brand's potential to satisfy his or her motives.
- *Intention:* the brand which the buyer intends to buy.
- *Purchase behaviour:* the act of actually purchasing, which reflects the buyer's predisposition to buy as modified buy any of the inhibitors.

Hypothitical Constructs

The model proposes a number of intervening variables which have been categorized into two major groups: 1. **perceptual** constructs which deal with information processing and 2. **learning constructs** which are related to the buyer's formation of concepts.

The *perceptual constructs* include:

- *Sensitivity to information* refers to the degree to which the buyer regulates the stimulus information flow.
- *Perceptual bias* means distorting or altering information
- *Search for information* involves actively seeking information on the brands or their characteristics.

The buyer's *learning constructs* can be defined as:

- *Motives* are general or specific goals impelling action.
- *Brand potential of the evoked set* refer to the buyer's perception on the ability of brands in his or her *evoked set* (those brands which are being actively considered) to satisfy his or her goals.
- *Decision mediators* are based on the motives. The buyer will have certain mental rules for matching and ranking the purchase alternatives.

- *Predisposition* means a preference towards brands in the evoked set which expresses an attitude towards them.
- *Inhibitors* refers to environmental forces like price and time pressure which may inhibit or put restrain on the purchase of a preferred brand.
- *Satisfaction* the extent (or degree) to which, post actual purchase will measure upto the buyer's expectation of it.

Exogeneous Variables

These are a list of a number of external variables (external to the buyer) which can significantly influence buyer decisions.

LIMITATIONS AND WORKING OF THE MODEL

The model makes a significant contribution to understanding consumer behaviour by identifying the variables which influence consumers.

As per the model, the process starts when the buyer confronts an input stimulus, to which his attention is drawn. The stimulus, on account of the influence of the buyer's predispositions, motives, decision mediators and evoked set could be subjected to perceptual bias. The modified information can influence these variables which in turn, can influence his or her predisposition to purchase.

The actual purchase gets influenced by the buyer's intentions and inhibitors (if confronted). After the purchase the buyers will evaluate his or her satisfaction from it, and satisfaction will increase the buyer's predisposition towards the brand. Once the buyer obtains more information about brands, he or she will be engaged in less external search for information.

Thus the model has not only identified the various variables influencing consumers but also on how they interact with each other. Further, it also recognizes the different types of consumer problem solving and information search behaviours. It also acknowledges that the outcomes of consumer's decisions go beyond purchases too.

The model has the following limitations:

- There is absence of sharp distinctions between exogenous and other variables.
- Some of the variables, which are not well defined, and are difficult to measure too.
- The model is quite complex and not very easy to comprehend.

➲ THE NICOSIA MODEL

In the past few years marketing scholars have built buyer behaviour models taking the marketing man's point of view. The Nicosia model is one such buyer behaviour model. It is also said to be a systems model, because the human being is analysed as a system, with stimuli as the input to the system and the human behaviour as an output of the system.

This model was developed by Francesco Nicosia, an expert in consumer motivation and behaviour. Nicosia was one of the pioneers, who attempted to bring into focus the more complex decision process undertaken by consumers rather than the act of purchase itself. (D.L. Loudon, A.J.D. Bitta, Consumer Behavior, Tata McGraw Hill, 4th Edn. pp. 605). The Nicosia model tries to explain buyer behavior by establishing a link between the organisation and its (prospective) consumer. The model suggests that messages from the first influences the predisposition of the consumer towards the product or service. Based on the situation, the consumer will have a certain attitude towards the product. This may result in a search for the product or an evaluation of the product attributes by the consumer. If the above step satisfies the consumer, it may result in a positive response, with a decision to buy the product otherwise the reverse may occur.

The Nicosia model, groups the above activity explanations into four basic areas-

Field one has two sub areas - The consumers attribute and the firm's attributes. The advertising message sent from the company will reach the consumer's attributes. Depending on the way, the message is received by the consumer, a certain attribute may develop. This newly developed attribute becomes the input for Area two.

The second area or area two- is related to the search and evaluation, undertaken by the consumer, of the advertised product and also to verify if other alternatives are available. In case the above step results in a motivation to buy the product/service, it becomes the input for third area.

The third area explains how the consumer actually buys the product.

And area four is related to the uses of the purchased items. This fourth area can also be used as an output to receive feedback on sales results by the organisation (refer to Figure 2.2)

The Nicosia model attempts to explain buying behaviour by establishing a link between the organization and its prospective customer. It analysis human being as a system with stimuli as the input to the system and the human behaviour as an output of the system.

FIGURE 2.2

NICOSIA MODEL IN BRIEF

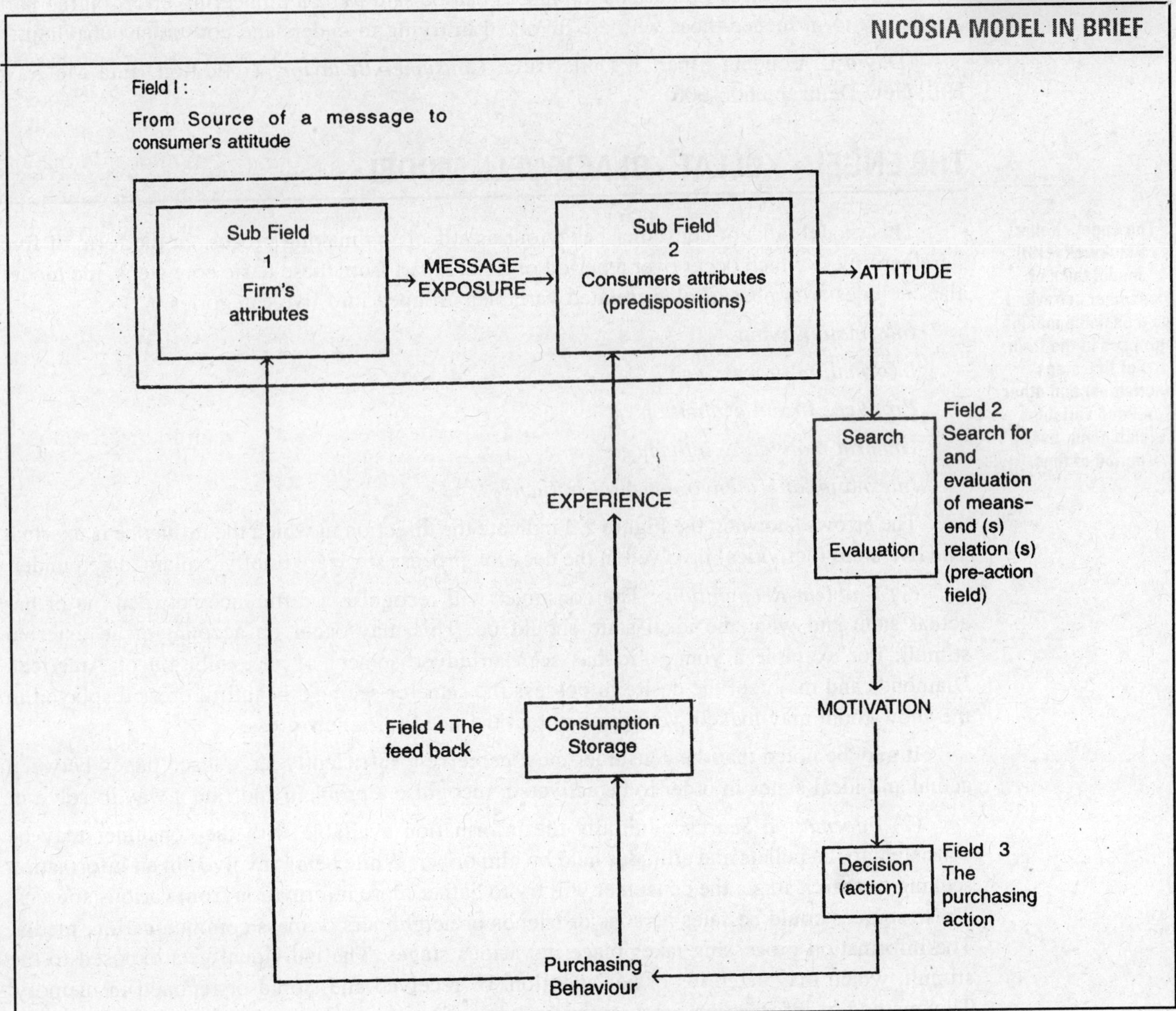

(*Source* : Francesco. Nicosia, *Consumer Decision Processes : Marketing and Advertising Implications*, Prentice Hall, Englewood Cliffs, New Jersey, 1996, p. 156)

Evaluation of the Model and its Limitations

The model can be said to be the pioneering efforts by Nicosia to identify the decision making process carried out by consumers. It is noteworthy to observe that the model has viewed consumers to be involved in an active role and that they move from general product knowledge towards specific brand information (knowledge), while being involved in a purchase behaviour.

However the model is said to have certain limitations. To mention a few:

Firstly, the flow is not complete and does not mention the various factors internal to the consumer.

Secondly, the assumption about the consumer being involved in the decision process with no predispositions about the various brands (or firms involved) is restricting.

And thirdly, the firm's attributes and consumer attributes mentioned in the model seem to be overlapping.

Inspite of the these limitations the model can be said to be a pioneering effort on the part of Nicosia to influence those who are involved in trying to understand consumer behaviour.

(David L. Louden, Albert J. Della Bitta; *Consumer Behavior*, 4th Edition, Tata McGraw Hill, New Delhi, pp.606-606)

THE ENGEL - KOLLAT - BLACKWELL MODEL

The Engel - Kollat - Blackwell (EKB) model talks of consumer behaviour as a decision making process in the form of five steps (activities) and other related variables which occur over a period of time.

This model talks of consumer behaviour as a decision making process in the form of five step (activities) which occur over a period of time. Apart from these basic core steps, the model also includes a number of other related variables grouped into five categories.

Information input

Information processing

Product - brand evaluation

General motivating influences

Internationalised environmental influences

The arrows shown in the Figure 2.3 indicate the direction in which the influence is exerted. The five steps (activities) involved in the decision process stage are briefly explained hereunder:

(1) *Problem Recognition :* The consumer will recognise a difference between his or her actual state and what the ideal state should be. This may occur on account of an external stimuli. For example a young girl has seen an advertisement of an exhibition of American Diamonds and may feel the desire to possess the same or seeing a beautiful dress displayed in the show-room may make a youngster to feel the need for a new dress.

It may be noted that the consumer must perceive a sufficiently large discrepancy between actual and ideal states in order to be activated, recognise a problem and find a way to solve it.

(2) *Information Search :* Initially the information available with the consumer may be consistent to the beliefs and attitudes held by him or her. While being involved in an information seeking or search stage, the consumer will try to gather more information from various sources. These sources could be sales persons or friends or neighbours or mass communication, media. The information processing takes place in various stages. The individual gets exposed to the stimuli, which may catch his or her attention, be received and stored or retained in memory. This method of information processing is selective in nature and the consumer will accept the information, which is conclusive to what is perceived by him.

FIGURE 2.3

ENGEL-KOLLAT-BLACKWELL MODEL

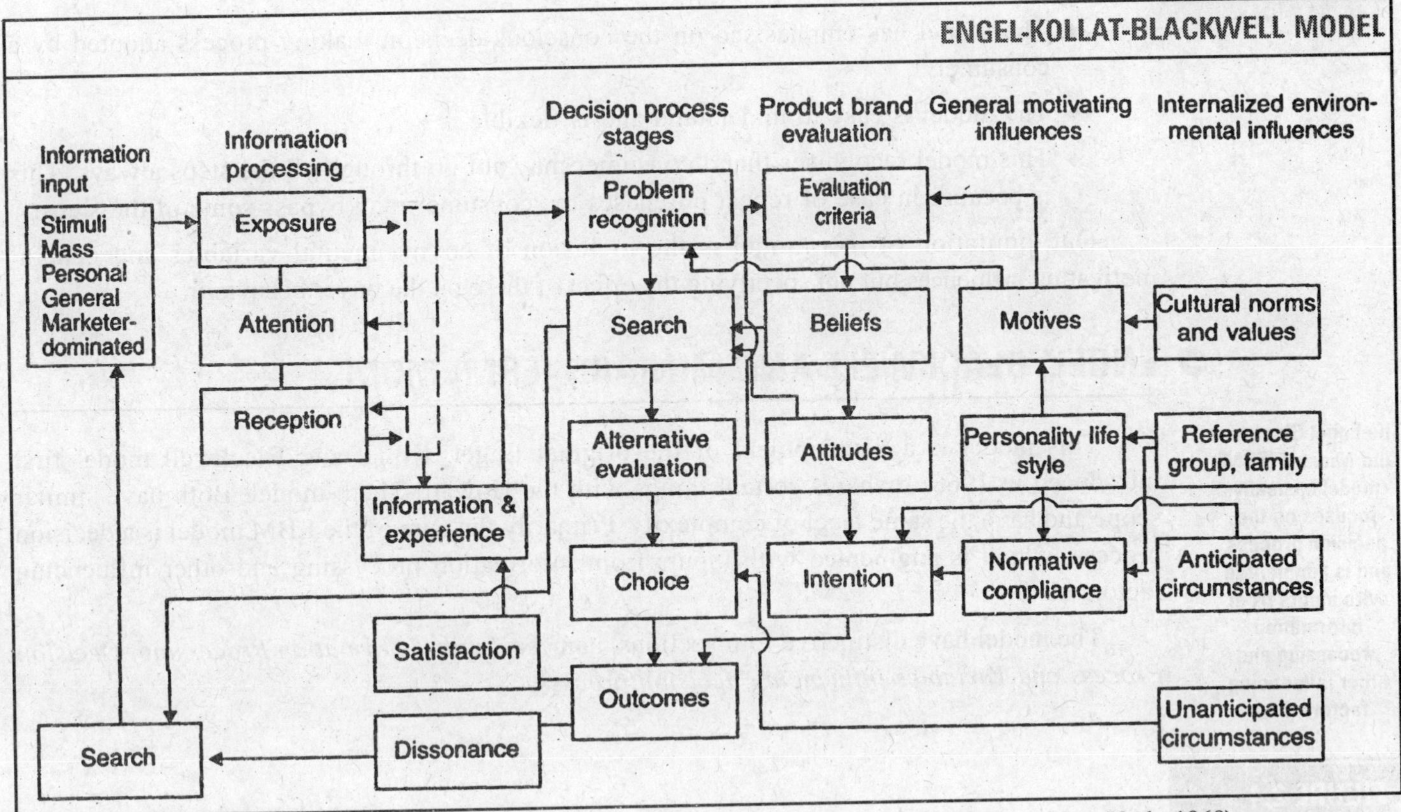

(*Source :* J.F. Engel, D.T. Kollat, R.D. Blackwell, *Consumer Behavior,* Dryden Press, New York, 1968)

The EKB model gives a lot of emphasis on the consumer's decision process stages which comprise of the problem recognition, search, alternatives evaluation, choice and outcomes.

(3) *Alternative Evaluation :* Now the individual will evaluate the alternative brands. The methods used for evaluating the various products will be dependent on the consumer's underlying goals, motives and personality. The consumer also has certain (predetermined) beliefs about the various brands in terms of the characteristics associated with them (different brands). Based on these beliefs the consumer will respond either positively or negatively towards a particular brand.

(4) *Choice :* The consumer's choice will depend on his or her intention and attitude. The choice will also depend upon normative compliance and anticipated circumstances.

Normative compliance relates to the extent to which the consumer is influenced by other people like friends, family members etc. Thus normative compliance and anticipated circumstances will attempt to influence the individual. The person's choice of the product can also be dependent on the sensitivity of the individual to handle unanticipated circumstances like losing one's job, funds diverted for another urgent cause etc.

At this stage, a purchase decision is likely to occur unless he or she is confronted by unanticipated circumstances. In case of the latter occurring, it could act as a barrier to the purchase decision at that point of time.

(5) *Outcome :* The outcome may be either positive or negative. If the end result is positive, the outcome will also be positive. Conversely, if there is dissonance, that is, a feeling of doubt experienced by the consumer about the choice made by him or her, the outcome will not be positive. If this occurs then the consumer will search for more information to support his or her choice.

The above mentioned Engel-Kollat-Blackwell model has taken into consideration a large number of variables which influences the consumer.

- The model has emphasised on the conscious decision making process adopted by a consumer.
- The model is easy to understand and is flexible
- This model recognises that a consumer may not go through all the steps always. This is because in case of repeat purchases the consumer may bypass some of the steps.

One limitation of this model is the inclusion of environmental variables and general motivating influences but not specifying the effect of these on the buyer behaviour.

➲ ENGEL, BLACKWELL AND MINIARD (EBM) MODEL

The Engel Blackwell and Miniard (EBM) model basically focuses on the decision process and is augmented with inputs from information processing and other influencing factors also.

This model is a development of the original Engel, Kollat and Blackwell model first introduced in 1968. It shares certain things with the Howard-Sheth model. Both have similar scope and have the same level of complexity. Primarily the core of the EBM model is a decision process, which is augmented with inputs from information processing and other influencing factors also.

The model have distinctive four sections, namely: *Input, Information Processing, Decision Process and Variables influencing decision process.*

FIGURE 2.4

ENGEL-BLACKWELL AND MINIARD MODEL

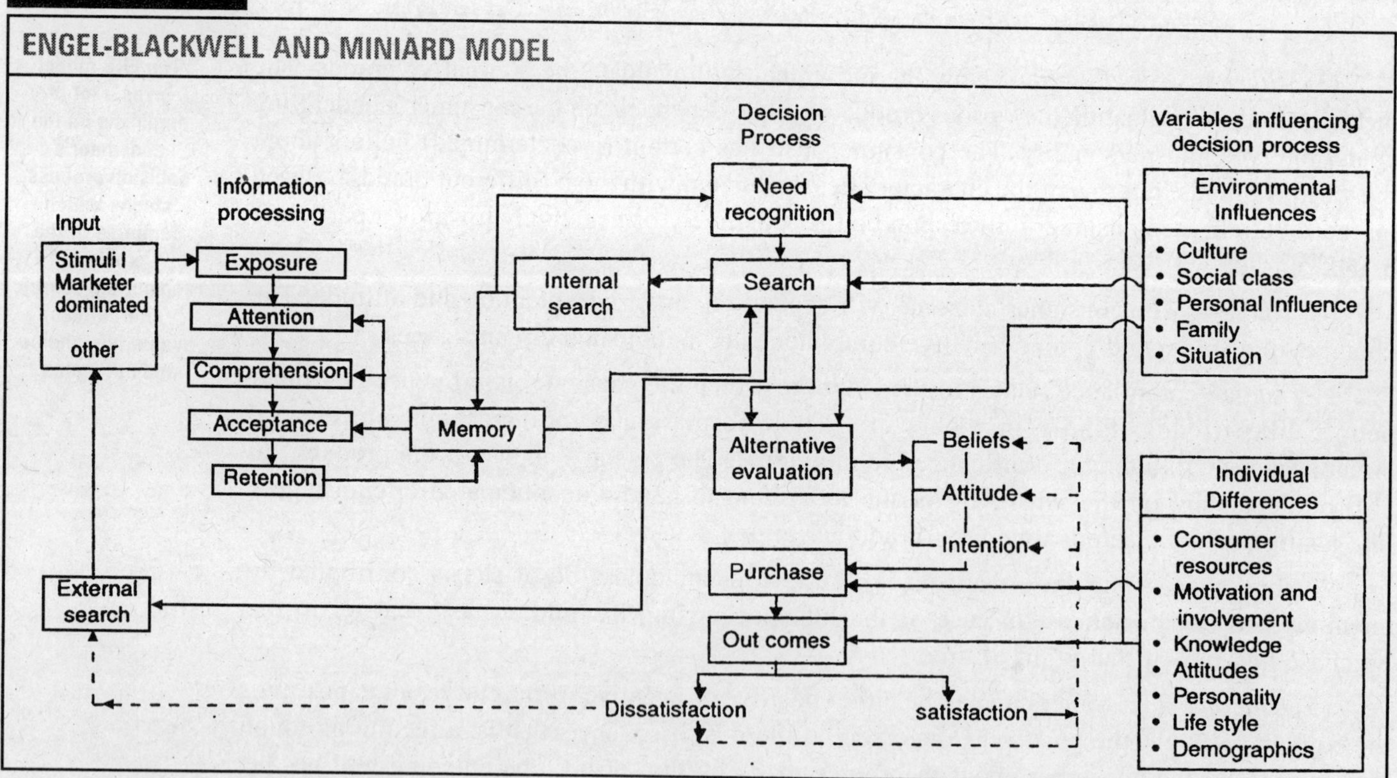

(*Source :* J.F. Engel, R.D. Blackwell and P.W. Miniard, *"Consumer Behavior",* (6th Edn.,) Hinsdale IL Dryden Press, 1990)

information Input

Information from marketing and non-marketing sources are fed into the information processing section of the model. The model also suggests additional information to be collected as a part of an external information search especially when enough information is not available from memory or when post-purchase dissonance occurs.

Information Processing

Before information can be used in the rest of the model, the consumer will first be exposed to the information processing. That is, the consumer must get exposed to the information, attend to it, comprehend or understand it, accept it and finally retain it in memory. Any selective attention or exposure mechanisms (which may occur in post purchase dissonance) would operate at this stage.

Decision Process **:** This process consists of five basic stages:

Need Recognition : This acknowledges the fact that there exists a problem. That is, the individual is aware that there is a need to be satisfied.

Search : When enough information is available in memory to take a decision, then only internal search will be required. If information is scarce, an external search for information is undertaken.

Alternative evaluation : Thereafter an evaluation of the alternatives found during the search is undertaken. We can see from the model, that this takes into account our attitudes and beliefs also.

Purchase : A purchase is made based on the chosen alternative.

Outcomes : The outcome can be either positive or negative depending on whether the purchase satisfies the original perceived need. Dissatisfaction can lead to post-purchase dissonance.

The EBM model when compared to the Howard-Sheth model is more coherent and flexible than the latter. Moreover, it also includes human processes like memory, information processing and considers both the positive and negative purchase outcomes.

Variables Influencing Decision Process

This section will consider the individual, social and situational factors, which influence the decision processes.

The EBM model is very flexible and more coherent than the Howard Sheth model of consumer behaviour. It also includes human processes like memory, information processing and considers both the positive and negative purchase outcomes.

However, the model has been criticized on two aspects. Firstly, on the somewhat vague definition of the role of the influencing variables. Secondly, it is felt that the separation of information search and alternative evaluation is somewhat artificial.

WEBSTER AND WIND MODEL OF ORGANISATIONAL BUYING BEHAVIOUR

This is a complex model developed by F.E. Webster and Y. Wind, as an attempt to explain the multifaceted nature of organisational buying behaviour. This model refers to the environmental, organisational, interpersonal and individual buying determinants, which influence the organisational buyer(s). These determinants influence both the individual and group decision making processes and consequently the final buying decisions.

The Webster and Wind model refers to the various organizational, interpersonal and individual buying determinants which can influence the organizational buying decisions.

The environmental determinants comprise of the physical and technological factors, economic, political, legal and socio cultural environmental factors. These are external factors which cannot be controlled, but an understanding of the same may be crucial to succeed.

FIGURE 2.5

WEBSTAR AND WIND MODEL ORGANISATIONAL BUYING BEHAVIOUR

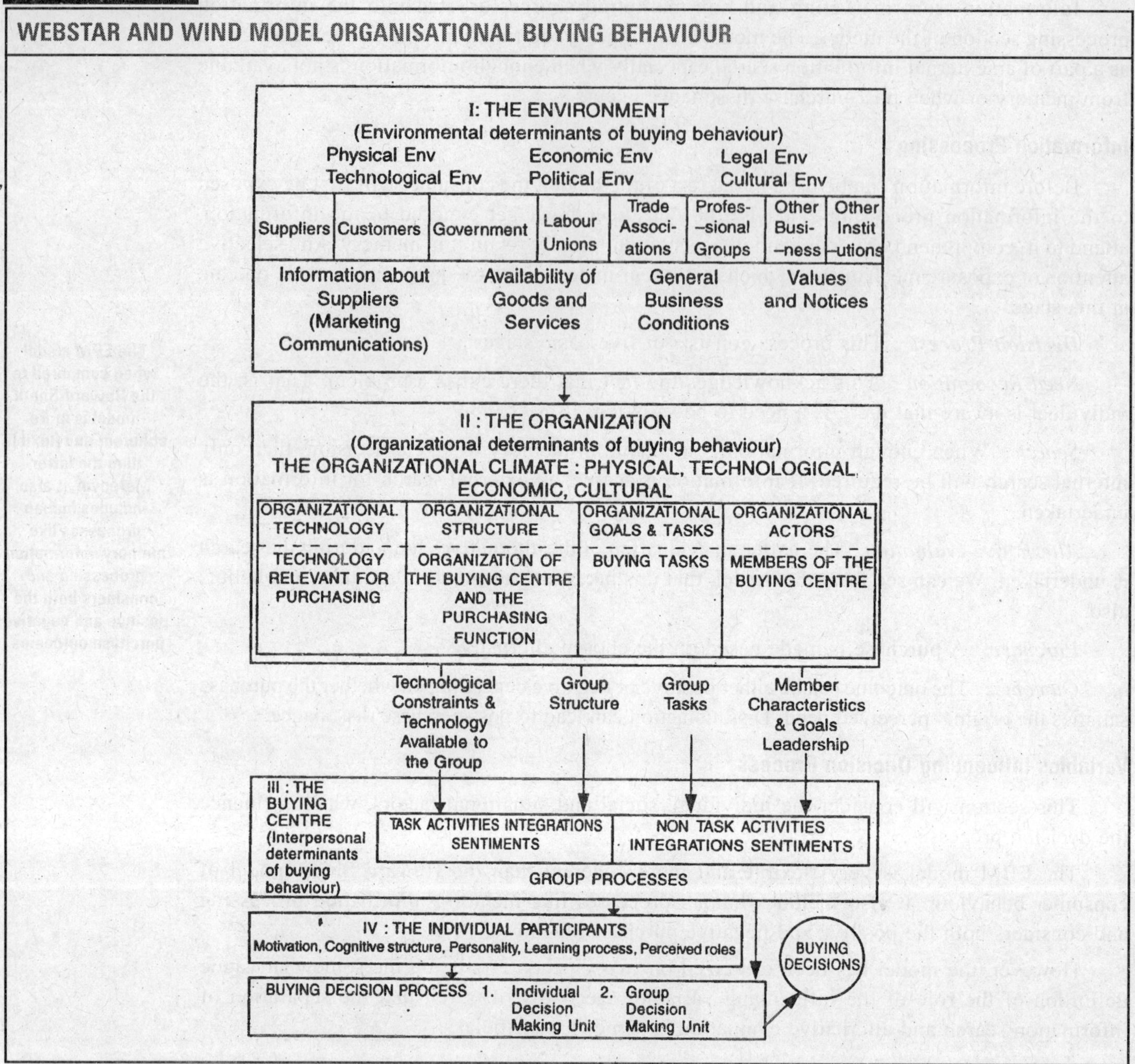

(*Source :* W. Webster and J. Wind," *Organization Buying Behavior",* Englewood Cliffs, Prentice Hall, 1972.)

An individual may be involved in one or more buying roles during organisational buying.

The organisational determinant is based on Harold Leavitt's four elements of buying organisation namely-people, technology, structure and task. (*Source :* The Organizational World W.R. Dill and H. Eyring, Harcourt Leavitt H.J., Harcourt Brace Jovanovich, 1973) This is seen in 'Buying Centre', mentioned in the figure 2.5. The buying concepts emphasise the fact that a number of people participate in the buying decision process including individuals and groups from the various functional areas in the organisation.

An individual may be involved in one or more buying roles during organisational buying These roles could be of:

(a) *Users :* The ultimate users who often initiate the buying process and help in defining specifications.

(b) *Influencers :* They may or may not be directly connected with the decision, but their views or judgments of a product or a supplier carry a lot of weightage.

(c) *Buyers :* People who negotiate the purchase.

(d) *Deciders :* People who take the actual/decision (they may be formal or informal decision makers).

(e) *Gate Keeper :* The person who regulates the flow of information.

This model is a valuable contribution and helps in revealing the whole range of direct and indirect influences, which affect the organisational buying behaviour. However, the limitation is that this model provides only a static representation of a dynamic situation.

THE SHETH MODEL OF INDUSTRIAL BUYING

This model concentrates on the purchasing process and highlights the importance of four main factors:

I. The expectations of the individuals making up the DMU (Decision Making Unit)

II. The characteristics of both the product and the organisation

III. The nature of the decision making process

IV. The situational variables

These factors are discussed more in detail:

I. Expectations within the Organisation

These elements are mentioned under (1). According to Sheth, every person in the DMU brings with them, his/her own unique set of attitudes and orientations. Their expectations will be conditioned by the *individual background* (1a) *education* (general or professional), *role orientation* (Accountant, Production Manager, Engineer etc.) *lifestyle.*

Their expectations will be influenced by:

- The various *sources of information* (1b) include (sales persons, exhibition and trade shows, direct mail, press releases, journal advertising, professional and technical conferences, trade news, word of mouth) and the process through which they have obtained the information.
- *Perceptual distortion* (1d) (could be as a result of the form of communication).
- The person's previous *experience* (1a) which will mediate the incoming information.
- The *active search* (1) can be carried out by anyone listed in the DMU - purchasing agents, engineers, users or others.

The Sheth model of Industrial Behaviour highlights four factors which play a role in the industrial decision making process. These are the expectations of the individuals who form the DMU (Decision making Unit), characteristics of the product and the buying organisation, nature of the decision making process and the situational variables.

II. Characteristics of the Product and the Buying Organisation

In the figure 2.6 of the model these elements are coded (2). Under this Sheth talks of the actual buying process and contends that it is affected by:

The Product Specific Factors (2a) such as :

- *Time pressure* : Group decision will take longer time as compared to individual ones.
- *Perceived risk* : When the decision involves risk, more members of the DMU will be involved.

- *Type of purchase :* If the type of problem is an extensive one, then more members of the DMU will be required. This will be unlike a simple repeat purchase, where a single individual can be asked to carry out the decision.

Company Specific Factors (2b) include :

- *Organizational orientation :* Is the firm sales and marketing oriented? Or is it technology dominated one? etc. Depending on how the organisation sees itself will determine the internal power balance and influence in the DMU.
- *Organization size :* Depending on the size of the organisation the type of group decision making will be determined. If the organisation size is small, it is more likely that a single buyer will possess all the relevant information. But if the organisation is a large one, it is more likely that there will be group decision making.
- *Degree of centralization :* Decentralized organisation's involve a lot of people in the decision making than centralized organisations, which will have a centralized buying function.

FIGURE 2.6

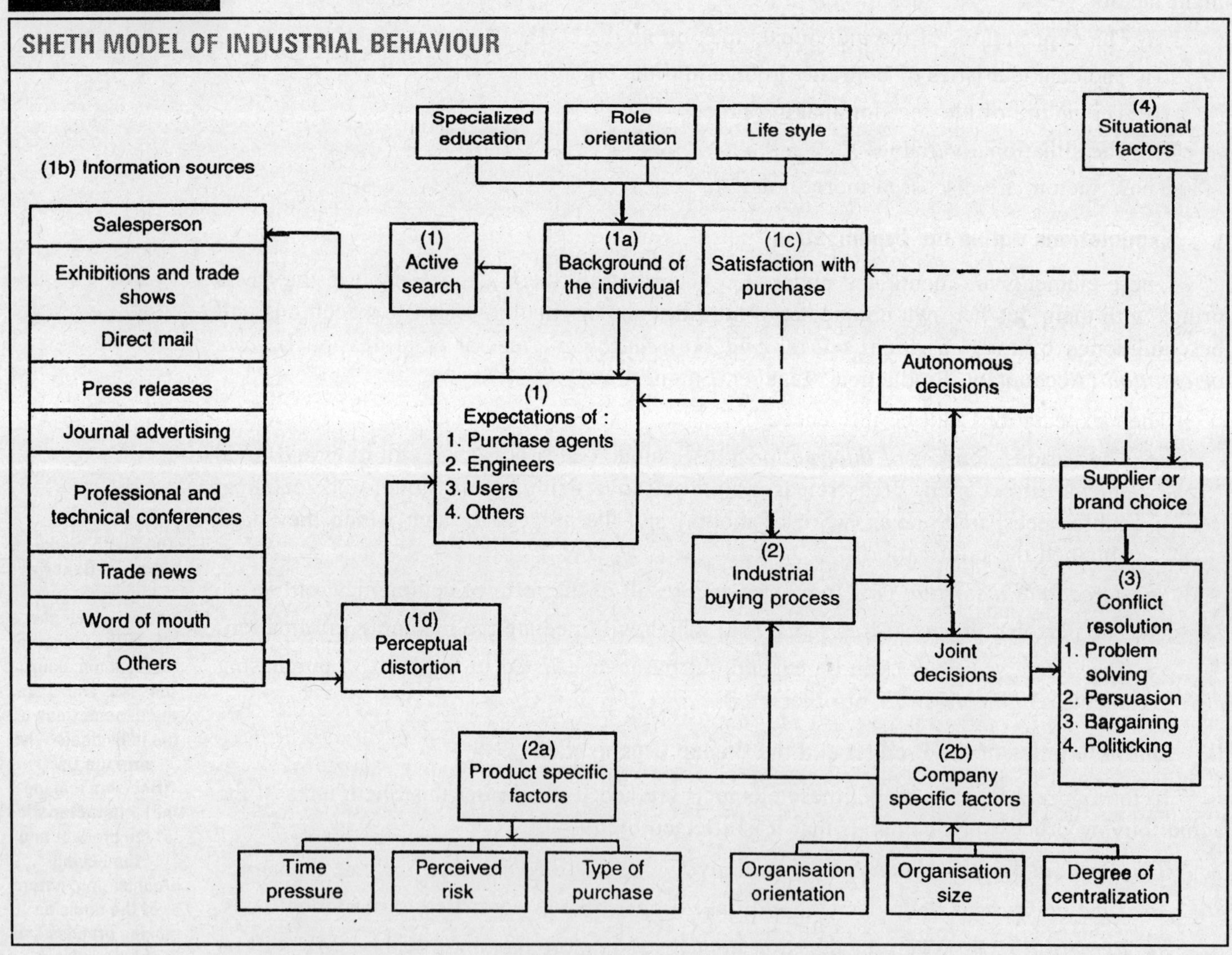

(*Source :* Sheth J.N, "Model of Industrial Behavior", *Journal of Marketing* 1973, 37(4), pp. 50-56)

III. Nature of the Decision-making Process

In the model, the elements are coded (3). Sheth has differentiated between autonomous decisions and those taken jointly by the DMU. When a decision is taken autonomously, it is usually (relatively) straight forward. However, when a group is involved in decision making, conflict is likely to arise because of the different goals and orientations with people within the group. The model also devotes a section (3) on how to solve the conflict:

- Problem solving
- Bargaining
- Persuasion
- Politicking

IV. Situational Variables

These elements are coded (4) in the model. Here Sheth has referred to unforeseen factors, those that fall outside the control of the DMU and could affect the purchasing organisation or the suppliers. For example - industrial relation problem, major breakdowns, cash flow problems, bankruptcy etc.

SUMMARY

The purpose of this chapter was to introduce the various models which are relevant to consumer behaviour and review their usefulness to marketers in different markets situations.

After an introductory case on 'Falafel's, a brief mention was made on the meaning of the term model'. The earlier models comprising of: the Economic model, Learning model, Pshchoanalytic model and the Sociological model were briefly discussed. These models threw light on how consumers would behave: in situations involving limited purchasing power, influenced by both innate and leaved needs, directed by a complex set of deep seated motives or are required to adhere to the expectations of the institution called society.

Some of the important specific contemporary models were reviewed. The Howard Sheth model is an important contemporary model. This model has clearly distinguished three levels of consumer decision making: Extensive problem solving. Limited problem solving and Routinised response behaviour, which were discussed. The Nicosia model analysis how organisations interact and establish a link with their prospective customers through communications taking the form of advertisement etc. The Engel-Kollat-Blackwell model refers to the consumer behaviour as a decision making process in the form of five step activities and other related variables which occur over a period of time.

Then Engel-Blackwell-Miniard model was reviewed. This model which focuses on the decision process is well augmented with inputs from information processing and other influencing factors, was also discussed.

Two models related to organizational buying behaviour were also reviewed. The first was a complex model developed by F.E.Webster and Y.Wind. This model spoke of the environmental, organizational, interpersonal and individual buying determinants all of which played a role in influencing the organisational buyer(s). Then the Sheth model of Industrial behaviour was reviewed. The four factors: expectations of those forming the DMU, characteristics of the product and the buying organisation, nature of the decision making process and the situational variables were also highlighted.

➲ CHAPTER QUESTIONS FOR DISCUSSION

1. What do you understand by the term 'model'? In what way will one gain by studying different consumer behaviour models?
2. Today when the recession is affecting markets world wide, marketers feel that the consumer decision making process will ultimately help understand the 'what' and 'how much' of the buyer behaviour. Do you agree? Why?
3. Write a brief note on the earlier models of consumer behaviour.
4. Briefly comment on the Nicosia model, Howard-Sheth model, Engel-Blackwell-Miniard model and the Engel-Kollat-Blackwell model.
5. Compare the Webster and Wind model with the Sheth model of industrial behaviour.

➲ SUGGESTED READINGS

1. Ashley. Coutinho., 'Bring them on, ready to serve', Brand Equity, *The Economic Times,* June 25, 2008.
2. John A. Howard and Jagdish N. Sheth, 'A Theory of Buyer Behavior' in Harold H. Kassarjian and Thomas H. Kassarjian and Thomas S. Robertson eds., *Perspectives in Consumer Behavior*, 7th edn., Scott, Foresman, Gleanview, IL 1973, p. 523.
3. W. Webster and J. Wind," *Organization Buying Behavior",* Englewood Cliffs Prentice Hall, 1972.
4. J.F. Engel, D.T. Kollat, R.D. Blackwell, *Consumer Behavior,* Dryden Press, New York, 1968.
5. Nicosia, P.M.," *Consumer Decision Processes: Marketing and Advertising Implications",* Englewood Cliffs, NJ, Prentice Hall, 1966.
6. J.F. Engel, D.T. Kollat and P.W. Miniard," *Consumer Behavior,* (6th Edn.,) Hinsdale IL Dryden Press, 1990.
7. Sheth J.N, *"Model of Industrial Behavior",* Journal of Marketing 1973, 37(4), pp.50-56.
8. Bennett Peter. D. and Kassarjan, *"Consumer Behavior",* Prentice Hall of India Pvt. Ltd., New Delhi, 1987.
9. David L. Loudon, Albert J. Della Bitta, *Consumer Behavior*, Tata McGraw Hill, New Delhi, 4th Edn. (Reprint) 2006, pp. 605-613.

CASE

BOOMING BATTER BUSINESS

Mrs. Gomathy Moorthy arrived in Mumbai (then Bombay) around 37 years ago, as a young bride alongwith a 'wet grinder' gift from home, which was considered to be a status symbol in South India then. While her husband was engaged in the restaurant business, she slowly settled down in the South Indian area of the Matunga East area in Mumbai and was kept busy at home by making idlis and dosas for her family. Around 1988, when the family was facing financial problems, a family friend, Navin bhai, suggested that if Gomathy Moorthy could make and pack idlis, he would sell them to many of the Gujarti traders who worked at the city's wholesale markets.

So in this way Mrs Moorthy started getting up at 4 A.M. to make idlis and pack them (four in a packet) along with some coconut chutney. She sold the packets to Navinbhai for Rs 3 and made a decent profit on that. At that time boiled rice cost Rs. 3 a kilo and urad dal Rs. 7 a kilo and a good coconut was available for just one rupee. Slowly the business started growing. Her husband, who had joined the business by then started helping her to make 200 packets a day from their 200 square feet house, would take to sell in the central Railway canteen. They started getting bigger orders and when the demand increased to over 1,000 idlis, Mrs. Moorthy realized that she needed a larger grinder. Under a women help scheme she got a Rs. 3,000 interest free loan from Syndicate Bank, which she used to have a machine made that could produce 50 kilos of batter. The business was so good that she was able to pay back the loan in six months.

Around 1996, when Mrs. Moorthy's husband died she started catering to many more customer requests and in this way she made Rs. 20 lakh in two years. Mrs. Moorthy took a break to go and spend some time with her daughter in the U.S. When she came back her catering business was in pieces due to many problems. That is when she started looking at the batter business seriously.

The demand for batter started coming from people such as Gujarati's and Mawari's who found it too hard to make the batter at home and would buy in small quantities from them.

So it was decided that Mrs. Moorthy and her son Venkatesh, who had joined his mother in running the business, would focus on supplying Khiru (the term used for batter in Mumbai) from a garage operation which they set up with wet grinders. The unique selling point (USP) used by Mrs. Moorthy was *convenience* and *quality* especially because no preservatives or baking soda was being used. She uses just pure rice and dal and water.

Gomathy Moorthy has successfully churned her everyday chore into a profitable business venture

Mrs. Moorthy's reputation is so good that she has customers coming from across the city to buy from her. At times customers even buy batter to take it to the UK or US or Hongkong. Though they are getting many offers to expand their business, they are preferring to stick to one outlet in order to maintain their reputation and the quality of their 'product'.

Competition is from other local producers (Jain & Iyer amongst other small players in Matunga) and a big threat from especially a large retailer *Magnet* who has a big hypermarket set up across 60,000 square feet in Matunga west. This hypermart offers clothes, home products, furniture groceries and tucked in a corner are a row of grinders, that are busy churning out fresh batter. Magnet sells around 400 kgs of batter in a day. They produce different types of batter for idlis, dosas, vadas and dhoklas, which has proved to be a useful differentiation point for Magnet.

Thus the batter business seems to be booming and fitting neatly into the changing lifestyles of consumers and the capacities of those who produce it.

(*Source :* Vikram Doctor & Nandini Ragavendra, *The Economic Times*, Bangalore, March 5, 2006)

QUESTIONS FOR DISCUSSION

1. Which Model according to you is being informally used when thinking about the target maket in the above case? Why?
2. Which variables can be said to be the major influences on consumer behaviour in the above case?
3. How will you use Howard-Sheth Model to explain rational routinised brand choice behaviour of consumers in the above case? You are free to make your own assumptions as well as borrow useful aspects from the model to justify your answer.

❑ ❑ ❑ ❑

UNIT II : INDIVIDUAL DETERMINANTS OF CONSUMER BEHAVIOUR

CHAPTER 3

CONSUMER PERCEPTION

- Case : **Tata Tea**
- Concepts underlying perception
- External and internal factors
- The Perceptual process
- Consumer imagery and marketing implications
- Perceived risk
- Summary
- Chapter questions for discussion
- Suggested readings
- Case : The working of two low cost airlines
  (a) From **Air Deccan** to **Kingfisher Red** (b) **Spice Jet**

CASE

CONSUMER PERCEPTION - TATATEA

Tea - it is said that world over, tea is the most commonly consumed beverage after water. In India too, tea is strongly embedded and very much a part of our daily rituals. In spite of strong competition from the other hot beverage coffee, tea is perceived to be the choice across generations both young and old. Tea is integral to our lives starting from the morning cup which helps to kick start the day, making one, ready to take the day's challenges to the evening cup which helps to bring on moments of sharing and togetherness with the family. In India, tea is perceived not just as a hot beverage but also as something which can intoxicate consumers with its heavenly fragrance and taste.

The manufacturers of **Tata Tea Premium** has been trying to match consumers passion for tea by producing fine quality tea. This is the reason why **Tata Tea Premium** has been proudly given the name "The world's no. 1 Tea" in all its communications.

The *Tata Tea Premium* was first launched in India in 1985, heralding the polypack revolution in tea, bringing the promise of 'Garden fresh tea' and the 'Asli-Taazgi' concept to consumers for the first time. The winning combination of a quality product and a great value proposition has helped Tata Tea to gain a big market share from the market leader Hindustan Lever. Tata Tea Premium has strived to keep in pace with the changing times and consumer needs by adopting a relevant and contemporary brand positioning. Over a period of time, the brand seems to have evolved itself from a transactional relationship (Asli Taazgi) to a more contemporary, deeper and emotional one (Energy to succeed).

Marketers of TataTea Premium wanted the consumers to perceive the brand to match their dreams. Today, Indians are exerting themselves to achieve and chase their dreams. The accent is on hoping and shaping one's own destiny rather than on coping with what is *fait accompli.* All segments of the society are dreaming a play of dreams big and small, where aspirations have no limits. The new communication strategy focuses on the line "Taste Kamyabi ka". This punch line is to encourage everyone to push themselves, face the future with confidence and conquer tomorrow. The marketers of Tata Tea Premium have positioned the brand so that it is perceived as a tea, which activates you to take on challenges-providing one the 'Energy to Succeed.' The ad film for this brand features Sania Mirza, then an emerging tennis player who endorses the brand as an individual who challenges life and triumphs as an achiever to conquer the world. Sania is the brand icon, for she is perceived by the youth as someone young and dynamic who has conquered all odds to become highly successful in her field. In her is imbibed a driving spirit. And she drinks TataTea Premium for that vitality. Such a communication was aimed at forging a stronger emotional connect with the consumer by bringing to face values which are relevant and foster greater empathy amongst them.

The rapid rise in the popularity of Sania Mirza (a youth icon) and her success in tennis in 2005, ensured that consumers perceived positive association with the brand, through her and the ad line 'Taste Kaamyabi Ka'. The success of TataTea Premium can be attributed to consumers acceptance of the brand, brand ambassador and the brand positioning — *Energy to succeed.*

The above example of Tata Tea Premium shows that irrespective of the objective reality of the product, what matter most is the consumer's perception of the product / brand.

As consumers, one's decision making process is greatly influenced by his or her perception of the product or brand and not necessarily the objective reality. Usually, consumer decisions will be based on the persons's individual needs, wants, values, personal experiences and perception of the extent to which the product or brand matches his or her requirement. Thus, it is very important for marketers to understand the role of perception in influencing consumers decision making processes.

In this chapter we have tried to examine the basic concepts, and factors underlying consumer perceptions, the perceptual process and the marketing implications of consumers' perceptual inferences.

CONCEPTS UNDERLYING PERCEPTION

Perception is defined as *the process by which an individual selects, organises and interprets stimuli into a meaningful and coherent picture of the world*. No two individuals are alike. Although two persons may be exposed to the same stimuli, and under the same environmental conditions, how each one of them recognises, selects, organises, and interprets the stimuli will be a highly individualised process. Often the perceptual process is based on each one's own needs, values and expectations. Marketers are interested in knowing how each of these variables will influence the perception process.

We start with discussing the basic concepts underlying the perception process.

Sensation

Sensation may be described as an immediate direct response of a physical sensory organ. The physical senses are vision, hearing, touch, smell and taste. These physical senses are continuously exposed to internal and external stimuli and human sensation occurs because of them. The sensation may be in the form of reaction of the eye to colour or mouth to taste and so on. Thus, sensation is related to a very elementary or basic behaviour which is based on physiological functioning. And sensitivity of the person to the stimuli will vary depending on the individual's sensory receptors and the intensity of the stimuli to which he or she is exposed.

Perception can be defined as the process by which an individual selects, organises and interprets stimuli into a meaningful and coherent picture of the world. Often, the perceptual process is based on each one's own needs, values and expectations.

Perception is something more than sensation. It co-relates, integrates and comprehends the various sensations and information received from the different organs of the body by means of which a person develops his sensitivity to various things and objects. Perception is determined by both physiological and psychological factors. This is because perception is developed based on previous experience (learning), feeling and motives. Whereas, sensation only activates the sensory organs of the body. Simply stated, activation of the ears to hear what another person is saying is sensation and the inference of what is heard is perception.

An individual's sensitivity will depend on the sensory inputs.

Absolute Threshold

The point at which an individual senses a difference between 'something' and 'nothing' is referred to as the *"absolute threshold'* for a particular stimulus. For instance, two friends after a long ride on the motor bike are hungry. When these two friends first spot a restaurant, it is said to be their absolute threshold. If both of them spot the restaurant at different times, they are said to have different absolute thresholds.

Under conditions of constant stimulation, *i.e.,* the individual gets continuous exposure to certain objects or events, then inspite of the absolute threshold increasing, due to the 'adoption' process, the stimuli will cease to make a positive impression.

This sensory adoption is a problem, which most of the advertisers try to avoid. If viewers are continuously exposed to the same ad for a long and continuous period, after some time they will no longer see the ad as it is. That is, they will no longer 'See' the ad such as to provide sufficient sensory input. It is due to this sensory adoption problem that many of the television advertisers, change their advertising campaigns after some time. If the advertisement, whether shown on T.V or in print media, loses its initial impact on the consumers mind and will cease to provide sufficient sensory input to be noted, it will be preferable to change the ad campaign. For instance the advertisement showing the evil cackle of the horned spokes Saitan (Devil) of *Onida TV* had been changed to a more humorous and synthetic announcement by an airhostess and now Onida T.V has after a gap of some time re-introduced the 'devil' in its ad.

With the emergence of new media, advertisers have realized the necessity of developing new advertisements, which will help to strengthen their brand building efforts.

For example, Magicbricks.com, Dainik Jagran (India's largest selling Hindi Newspaper), *SOTC Travels* have been buying a lot of advertising space in leading newspapers such as The Times of India to ensure that readers note their ads. *Big Bazaar* uses the rear side of public transport city buses to advertise their products, ensuring that people on the road will be exposed to the ad. At times, advertisers try to draw attention by decreasing sensory input, such as include a lot of space so as to accentuate the brand name or product illustration. Some times the T.V may use silence (no voice over or audio music) to generate interest among the viewers.

The point at which an individual senses a difference between 'something' and 'nothing' is referred to as the absolute threshold for a particular stimulus.

Maruti Suzuki is attempting at determining the relevant just noticeable difference or j.n.d to woo prospective customers

Marketers are seeking innovative ways in an effort to catch the attention of the consumers. Through usage of such non conventional sensory inputs, marketers want to ensure that consumers notice their products and induce product trails, brand preference and create a high set of positive perception and experience with it. For instance, *Tata-AIG Insurance* uses SMS and ring tones (like to Zandu Balm, Maggi etc.,) apart from regular telesales in order to reach out to its audiences faster and at lesser cost. Some marketers use specifically engineered fragrance product offerings. *Tide* detergent powder advertises about its Rose plus Jasmine fragrance associated with their product. Such attempts are made to determine the target customers absolute threshold and woo them to purchase the particular brand.

The minimal difference that can be noticeable between two similar stimuli is known as the differential threshold or the 'just noticeable difference' (j.n.d).

Differential Threshold

The minimal difference that can be noticeable between two similar stimuli is known as the differential threshold or the just noticeable difference (j.n.d).

This concept was developed by a German scientist named Ernst Weber in the 19th century. He observed that the just noticeable difference between two stimuli was not an absolute amount but was relative and dependent on the intensity of the first stimuli or stimulus. According to this *Weber's law*, if the initial stimulus is strong, more or additional intensity will be required for the second stimulus to be perceived as different (*Consumer Behavior,* L.G. Schiffman, L.L. Kanuk, 6th Edn., Prentice Hall of India, New Delhi, 1997, pp. 148-150). For instance, if the price of a colour T.V increases by Rs. 100/- This increase in price may not be noticed (because the increment was below the just noticeable difference). But if the domestic cooking gas price increases even by Re one, this will easily be noticed by consumers. This is because in case of cooking gas, this price increase is a significant percentage of the basic cost of the cooking gas and thus the consumers attention will be drawn to the price hike.

As per the Weber's law, an additional level of stimulus (equivalent to the just noticeable difference) is required for most of the people to perceive a difference between the resulting stimulus and the initial stimulus. Further, it is also said that Weber's law holds true for all the senses and for almost all intensities also

Weber's law has very good marketing applications. Marketers are using Weber's law to determine the relevant just noticeable difference for various reasons. In case of reduction made in product size, increase in product price or reduced quality, the firm would not want the public to notice the difference or when the firm has updated its existing products, or lowered the price, they would want the consumers to just notice the difference, without being wastefully extravagant. For instance, because of increasing costs, firms have to choose between increasing prices or reduce the quantity offered at the existing price. There are some marketers who have preferred to keep themselves in the consideration set of the consumers mind by making a change in quantity. For instance, Brooke Bond's **Red Label Tea** which used to be available in the sizes of 250 gms and 500 gms is now available at the retail outlets in the 245 gms, 490 gms quantity size packs. This attempt by Brooke Bond is to make consumers just not notice the difference in the quantity size.

As per the Weber's law, an additional level of stimulus (equivalent to the just noticeable difference) is required for most of the people to perceive a difference between the resulting stimulus and the internal stimulus.

In product categories like soap, toothpastes, tea, fast foods etc, marketers have realised that consumers are in a position to try out and choose a number of brands based on price, symbolic appeal or the 'value for money' proposition offered by the manufacturers. And consumer loyalty in this segment is not very strong because even a small change in price may upset the brand. That is why for such product categories, the firms are announcing various promotional schemes like free toothbrush with *Pepsodent toothpaste* or one plus one free offer of *Close-up Gel.* Even in the consumer durables category such as the colour T.V., exchange offers (or exchange value proportion) are being offered in order to motivate consumers to buy. Since the market is filled with brands glutter, marketers are working out planned attempts to gain a share of the consumers' mind.

In a period, when the market is crowded with many (consumer) products (especially in consumer non durables) marketers try to adjust the price of their products so that the consumers may not become aware of the just noticeable difference. For instance when the price of tea goes up, the retailers offering loose tea, will downgrade quality (by making a blend consisting of inferior quality of tea leaves mixed with many other ingredients), while not including the 'just noticeable difference'. Some companies are either decreasing the package but maintaining the earlier pack size and get charging the same price. But such tactics will not reveal the Invisible price rise' to the consumers. For instance, *Procter & Gamble* reduced the number of sanitary napkins in its '*Whisper Ultra size*' pack and *Kimberley-Clark* have reduced the number of diapers *'Huggies'* in their packages.

At times, marketers realising the impact of cumulative advertising built up over the years, for a particular brand, may only go for updating the existing packaging so as to not lose the recognition of the product by the consumers. For instance *'Grasim Gwalior* advertising has always been associated with the royal, Nawab of Pataudi. This trend was continued only with the emphasis, shifting to fall below the just noticeable difference with the inclusion of Saif Ali Khan, the son of the Nawab of Pataudi.

Medimix herbal soap has differentiated itself on the herbal plant more than two decades ago when there were only synthetic soaps available in the market. Inspite of many other brands having entered this product category, Medimix continued to communicate the benefit of the 'herbal' proposition through appropriate imagery.

Marketers are continuously engaged in trying to identify the consumer's differential threshold so as to determine the right amount of improvements to be made in the product, which would be readily perceived by the consumer's also.

Usage of sensory inputs by Pondicherry Tourism

A few decades ago *Horlicks* was positioned to appeal to convalescing people and other segments of consumers who need nutrition-professionals, dancers and children. The brand has not been able to maintain its consistency with regard to its user imagery but has been able to successfully sustain its 'nutrition' association. This brand has been re-launched a few times over the past few decades with an improved version of its offerings. Horlicks through its advertising imagery has continued to re-inforce its nutritive association by focusing on its 'Junior' variant (aimed at children), introduction of its cold shake (Targeting teenagers) — all in an attempt to match the changing needs of its consumers.

When *Whirlpool bought* the *TVS washing machine,* they entered into an agreement, where by they were entitled to use the brand name of TVS washing machine, initially for a short period. This was felt necessary because, Whirlpool realised that during the transition period, they would build up a brand name for 'Whirlpool washing machine and this gradual change in the brand name will fall below the just noticeable difference threshold.

Another popular soap in the sandalwood fragrance category is the *Mysore Sandal Soap* from Karnataka Soaps Detergents limited (KSDL). Over the years whenever the change in packaging of this soap was made, it was a very small one, so as to call in the just noticeable difference threshold level and also to retain its 'Originality'.

So, marketers are continuously engaged in trying to identity the *consumers' differential threshold* so as to determine the right amount of improvements to be made in the product which would be readily perceived by the consumers' also.

Subliminal Perceptions

There is a major controversy regarding consumer perception *i.e.,* whether consumers can actually perceive marketing stimuli below their absolute threshold. The process whereby stimuli which are too weak or too brief to be consciously seen or heard, although they may be strong enough be perceived to by one or more recepter cells and thus be below the threshold is known as the *subliminal perception.* Simply put, *Subliminal perception refers to the perception of a stimulus below their absolute threshold.* Thus perception below the absolute threshold is referred to as subliminal perception. It is reported that in an experiment conducted by Vicary in 1957 had indicated that exposure may occur without attention or comprehension (*Consumer Behavior,* L.G. Schiffman, L.L. Kanuk, Prentice Hall, 1997, P. 153). That is, even though consumers may not see the message, they may register it. In Vicary's text, two messages were shown "Eat popcorn" and "Drink Coca cola" in movie theatre for a very short time (much below the absolute threshold) at five-second intervals. Subsequently, the sales of popcorn increased by 58 per cent and coca cola by 18 per cent when compared to the time period when there was no subliminal advertising (*Consumer Behavior,* D.L. Louden, A.J. Della Bitta, 4th Edn., Tata McGraw-Hill, New Delhi, 2006, pp. 379). Ofcourse, later on there were controversies regarding the influence of subliminal advertising on consumer actions.

Nevertheless, evidence suggests that it will be very difficult to exert influence through subliminal stimuli. Further, due to variations among consumers in terms of their perceptual ability, the difficulty in implementing advertising themes at low threshold level and the lack of evidence to any effect of subliminal advertising on the purchasing behaviour of consumers, it is not often used as an effective marketing tool.

Perception below the absolute threshold is referred to as subliminal perception.

GRASIM GWALIOR ADVERTISING

The history of Grasim Gwalior advertising is closely interwoven with the history of advertising of Indian textile. Pre-independence suiting campaigns were mostly typographical advertisements combined with one or two line drawings in the layout. There were very few advertisements in the print media just as there were just a handful of advertisers and advertising agencies.

Post-independence suiting campaigns can be classified into three distinct developmental stages:

1. Technological development
2. Creative development
3. Development in the area of competition

Grasim pioneered celebrity-lifestyle advertising in the textile industry.

1. The lifestyle of the Pataudi family was chosen as the model. This theme gave Grasim Gwalior a distinctive image and placed it in a class apart from the rest.

2. Ever since, Grasim Gwalior's objective has been to keep its campaign leadership position intact.

3. The interest in the campaigns have been kept alive with constant updating and regular creative inputs.

4. In 1989, Grasim Gwalior completed four decades in the business of quality textile manufacturing.

5. Grasim's role in the history of Indian textiles has been very prominent.
On its 40th anniversary Grasim decided to adopt an emotional theme and introduced a series of campaigns which expressed this through the lifestyle of the Pataudis. The campaign 'Like the warmth in your heart, a range of emotions', registered a very high recall. It was widely appreciated.

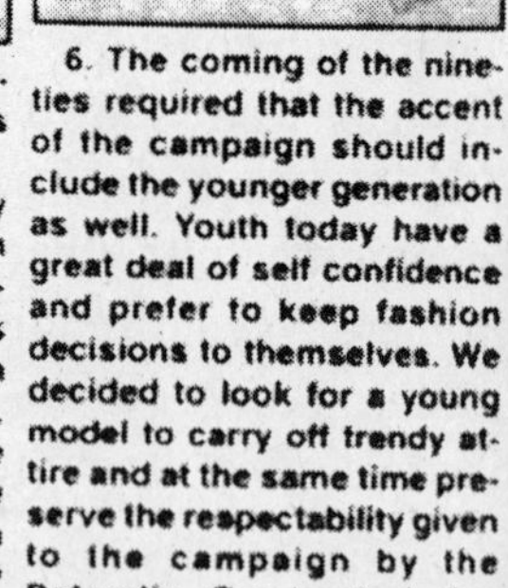

6. The coming of the nineties required that the accent of the campaign should include the younger generation as well. Youth today have a great deal of self confidence and prefer to keep fashion decisions to themselves. We decided to look for a young model to carry off trendy attire and at the same time preserve the respectability given to the campaign by the Pataudis. Our best choice was Saif Pataudi, the Nawab's own son.

7. Media explosion made television a highly competitive medium. Capturing viewer attention became a challenge to the creative pundits.

8. Entertainment became an essential part of classy advertising.

9. Liberalisation brought international brands marching in. At this juncture, Grasim decided to don the global mantle by bringing in 'Scabal'.

Sequential changes in the advertisement of Grasim Gwalior to ensure just - noticeable - difference

EXTERNAL AND INTERNAL FACTORS

The manner in which either a product or service is perceived will depend upon both internal and external factors. This is to say that both external reality and internal reality are intertwined. As hunıan beings, we carry all of our experiences in our mind and have our own selfish interests, needs, motives and expectations in the way in which we would like 'reality' to exist in the world.

Now-a days, no firm can make a strong claim about having brand loyal customers because researches conducted have revealed that for a number of products where there is strong brand loyalty and where taste would appear to have a strong influence on the buying decisions, there is little sensory difference between products.

As human beings, we carry all of our experiences in our mind and have our own selfish interests, needs, motives and expectations in the way in which we would like 'reality' to exist in the world.

This is illustrated in the following case. A blind test was conducted (*i.e.,* a test where the identity of the brand is cancelled) to determine the power of the sensory differences, values between 'Pepsi' and 'Coke' by a panel of consumers. The results of the above test are given here under:

- Prefer pepsi 51 %
- Prefer coke 44%
- Equal/can't say 5%

Then, the two brands were once again given to a matched sample, now with the true identity being revealed to the consumers. The results of this open test were as follows.

- Prefer pepsi 23%
- Prefer coke 65%
- Equal/can't say 12%

From the above illustration it can be concluded that the value added appeal of a brand lies in terms of that which is aroused in the minds of the consumers when they see a familiar brand name or logo.

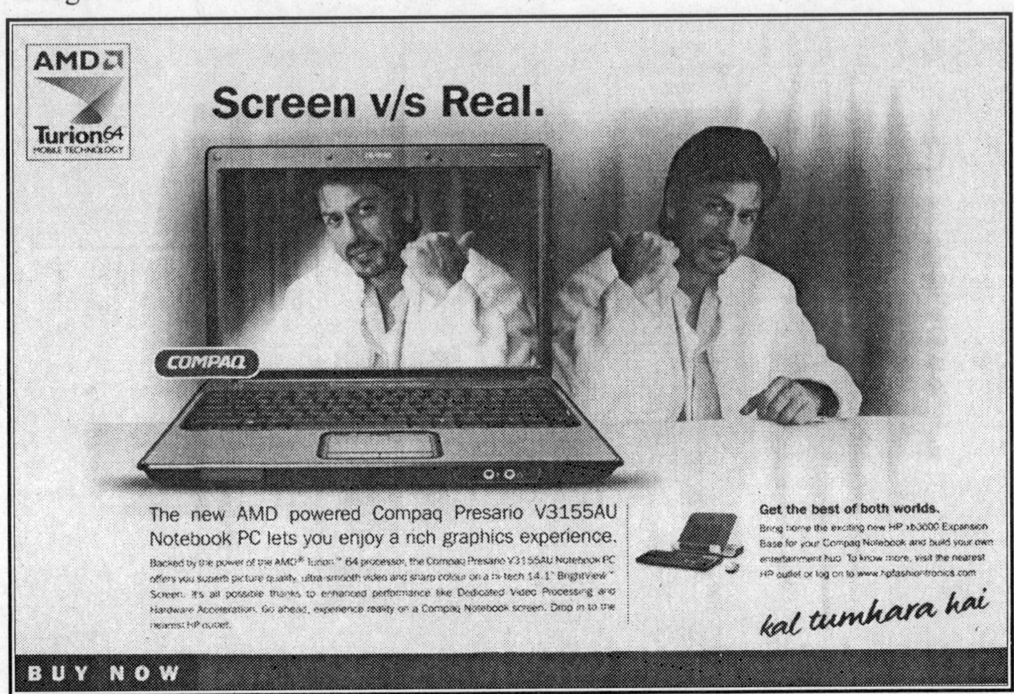

Ad conveys the difference between perception and reality

So, external factors can be said to be related to the physical character of the stimulus, while internal factors include our motives and expectations. Both the internal and external factors influence the way in which an individual perceives a product or brand.

External Factors Influencing Attention

Physical properties of the stimulus include intensity, size, position, contrast, novelty, repetition and movement.

Loud sound, bright colour and big banner especially when the atmosphere is otherwise serene will draw the attention of potential customers.

Intensity and Size : The brighter the sound (intensity) or more louder the sound, more likely that the person's attention is drawn to it. For instance, advertisers use this characteristic to draw the attention of the readers or viewers. Large sized advertisement in a newspaper or magazine will be noticed and also read more often than a small insertion given although the increase in size may not be linear. Prior to the launch of KINGFISHER AIRLINES, big advertisements were released in all leading newspapers to this effect in order to draw public attention. It is more likely that persons or readers notice an advertisement appearing on other pages of the newspapers than if it were to be given under the classified ads columns.

The various down line activities, organised as a part of the sales promotion campaign by various leading organisations are also used as a stimulant to attract the attention of potential customers. Marketers are using festivals to familiarize customers with their product or brand offerings. (For instance, *Chateau Indage* has tried to increase the mass popularity of its wine brand *Vino* by sponsoring festivals such as Ganesh Chathurthi pandals, put up banners and signages in high traffic areas of Mumbai.) *World Space* are advertising at festivals (it sponsored onam festival) venues via hoardings and occasionally even opting for ground promotions. Loud sound, bright colour and big banner especially when the atmosphere is otherwise serene will draw the attention of potential customers.

ON THE SAME WAVELENGTH: WORLDSPACE

THE RED, THE WHITE & THE SAFFRON: CHATEAU INDAGE

Worldspace and *Chateau Indage* use unique ways to draw consumer's attention.

Position : The position of display of the product or advertisement also is a determining factor of attracting attention. An advertisement placed next to a compatible editorial column of magazines, and newspapers is thought to attract more readership response. The even number pages in the newspaper or magazine is assumed to be likely to attract more readers than the odd number pages. In magazines more readership is obtained when advertisements are put on the cover pages or within the first 10% of the pages.

The *position* of display of the product or advertisement also is a determining factor of attracting attention. Similarly, human beings also have the ability to adapt to sounds, odours, pain, bright lights, neon signs and movements.

Similarly, positioning of point-of-purchase, placement of the products (*i.e.*, brands) at prominent places on the shelves at the retail outlet, rotating bill boards, hoardings at certain important points is more easily perceived by consumers and people.

For instance, the advertisements of organisations offering services such as Banks, Hotels, Airlines and Restaurants are prominently placed at airports.

Contrast : Human beings have the ability to adapt to sounds, odours, pain, bright lights, neon signs and movements. That is, human beings are able to use sensory organs to adapt themselves to various stimuli. This is where contrast will help in the perception process.

In the context of marketing, media planners also plan their advertisements keeping in mind the impact of contrast on perception. For instance,

- A black and white advertisement with a small spot is likely to attract attention because of the contrast *(ICICI Bank* uses the principle of contrast for its advertisements in magazines and newspapers).
- Advertisers consider colour advertisements to be more effective than black and white advertisement. (People have got a preference to seeing the 'colour films of the 60's and 70's rather than the black & white films of the pre-colour film's period).
- Some advertisers, alternatively make use of large and small sizes, loud and soft tones or primary and paster shades to attract more attention rather than using only one stimulus.
- A quiet commercial after a loud programme can attract attention. Say the advertisement of *'De Beers'* diamond after listening to a frantic rock music show shown on the television.
- Showing an object or product out of its normal setting will also attract attention, such as a car travelling across and dunes or along a beach. The print advertisement shows the luxury *Scorpio* car against the backdrop of a beach.

Marketers have observed that anything which is different from what are normally expected or a novelty tends to attract the attention of consumer's, say an unusual bottle shape or a perfume strip in a magazine etc.

Novelty : It has been observed by marketers that anything which is different from what are normally expected tend to attract attention like an unusual bottle shape or a perfume strip in a magazine and so on. For instance, *Frooti'* was the first to introduce the novel idea of soft drink being offered in a tetra pack or when *'Coca Cola and Pepsi'* were launched in small 'cans' during the World Cup. Likewise, Baron International was one of the first to start with the novel idea of exchange offers. *Videocon, Onida and Philips are* some of the brands which have created the perception among consumers that a second T.V means a smaller T.V.

Repetition : Advertisements are repeated more often to enable consumers for brand recall as well as stimulate them and create a strong desire for interest in the purchase of the product.

In the crowded category of consumer non durables, consumers may not be interested to search for specific information about the product and brand before taking a decision to purchase the product. This is where constant exposure through repetition of the ads, will help in linking the brand wise 'top of the mind' recall. Thus marketers must work towards ensuring that, while there are several brands in the same product category, their brand will convey a different value felt proposition and he or she will be geared up to make purchase choice accordingly. For instance, in the tooth paste category, some of the leading brands such as *'Colgate', 'Close-up',*

Advertisements are repeated more often to enable consumers for brand recall as well as stimulate them and create a strong desire for interest in the purchase of the product. Sometimes advertisers use bill boards or hoardings with movement so as to inject a feeling of movement into it.

'Dabur', 'Anchor' and *'Pepsodent,* have used repetition through mass media to ensure that the brand's proposition will make a significant impact on the consumer's purchase decision.

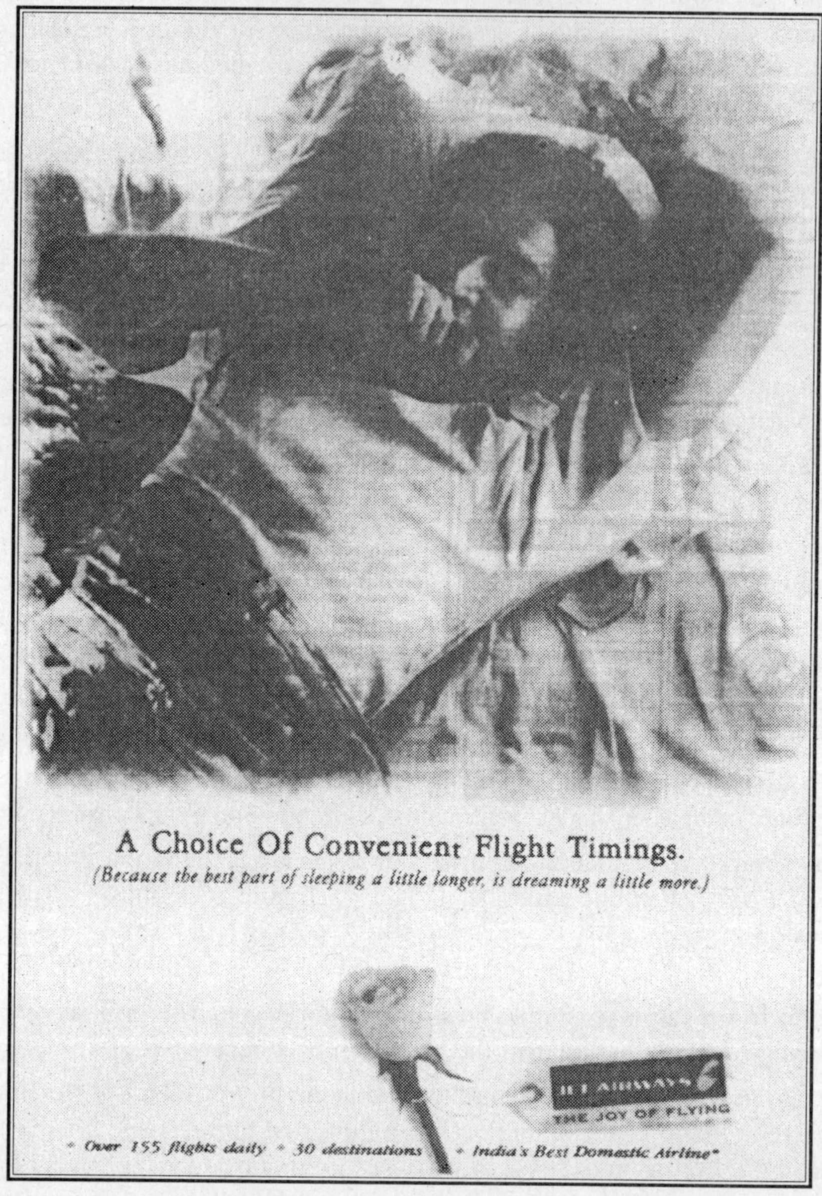

Ad of Jet Airways makes use of the contrast principle of perception

Movement : Advertisers have also started using billboards or hoardings with movement, mobile vans etc., so as to inject a feeling of movement into it. Many marketers are finding out smarter ways to reach out to the consumer by organising some movementful activities like holding free trials, demonstrations, exhibitions, mobile vans etc. Such exercises could also result in creating excitement and reinforce top of mind recall. *L.G. Electronics* had organised a summer strategy. L.G. hired vans and drove through select cities taking its refrigerators and washing machine to the consumer door-step. Similarly, *'Honda City* had also taken its car through the city, answered queries, allowed prospective customers to test ride the car and so on. It is assumed that such activities will not only help in easy recall of the brand but also stimulate the purchase decision and then go a long way in building long term relationship with their customers.

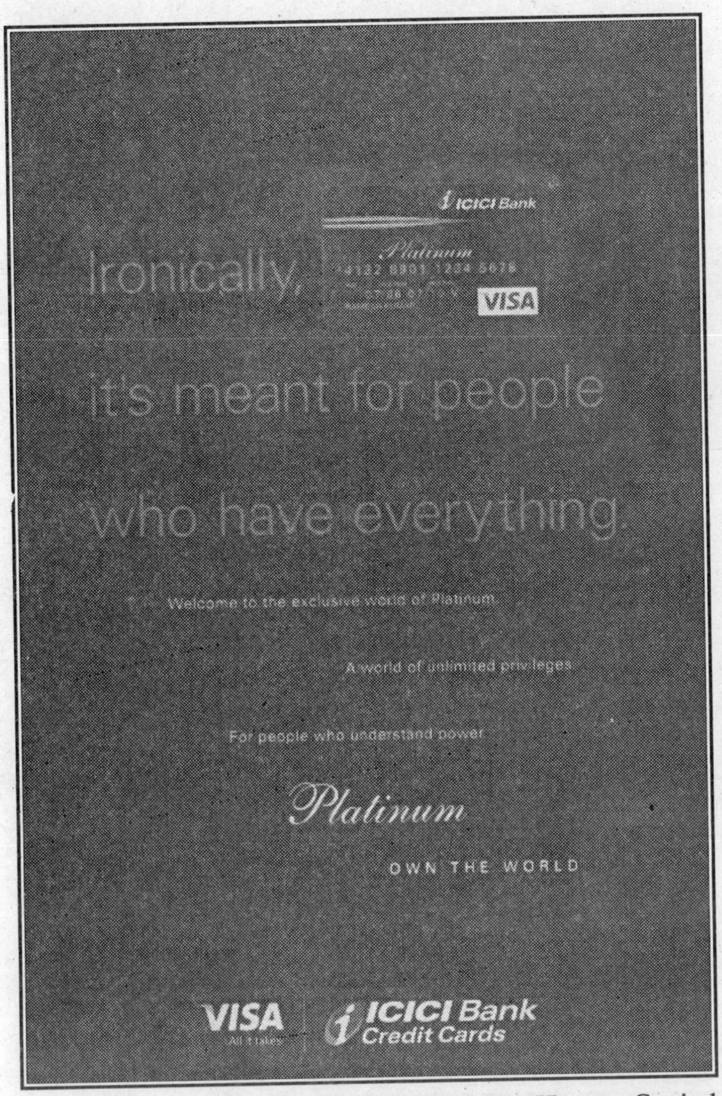

ICICI Bank and Adrenalin, Human Capital Management Software using the contrast principle to attract attention of customers

However, it is left to the respective marketer's to make efforts and find out the extent to which such tactics have really helped the brand in attracting customers.

INTERNAL FACTORS

Customers, may not receive the messages passively. Marketers are interested in knowing what is the impact of their usage of marketing mix elements on the minds of the consumers. The marketer has to constantly understand "What is going on in the consumers' mind there". Whereas, customers have the tendency to use the messages exhibited by the marketers and make their own meaningful interpretation of it and determine the brand's capability.

Marketers try to assess the impact of the use of marketing mix elements on the inner minds of the consumers. They are constantly involved in seeking answers to the internal factors which may affect the consumer's perception about the product or service (brands).

Consumer will typically associate his or her idea of the product or service with the brand name. It is not the organisation nor marketer but the brand which becomes the consumers's idea of the product or service. The consumer has got his or her own way of perceiving, interpreting and developing beliefs on the value of the brand. Because it is what customers perceive, interpret and believe the value of the brand to be, which plays a significant role at the market place. That is why organisations are working at developing a 'Brand Personality'. When a brand acquires a personality that is well recognised, even products with very little functional differences are seen as being different. Marketers are using marketing mix to develop differentiation strategy. Either of the marketing mixes can be used as a differentiating factor. A few of the more success examples in the Indian market on the basis of selected Superbrand India 2006-07 are :

• *Nirma*	• Economically priced, one of the largest selling single detergent brands in the world.
• *HSBC*	• Bank to give India its first ATM in 1987
• *Faber World Class kitchen appliances*	• First company to introduce a life time warranty on electric chimneys.
• *The Bournvita quiz contest*	• India's longest running national school quiz.
• *Airtel*	• India's largest mobile service provider and with 18,000 songs, 20 languages, retailing across 1,00,000 outlets, it is the world's largest vendor of music.
• *Oriental Insurance Company*	• An impressive record of 91.13% of settling customers grievances satisfactorily.
• *Dainik Jagran (newspaper)*	• Believes in reflecting,' the free voice of the people' – as per the National Readership Survey (NRS) 2005, it is the largest read daily in the world with readership of 21.2 million readers.

Thus marketer's are always involved in a search for a proposition that is unique and also sells. A good advertisement helps in the creation of a "Personality difference". And a brand personality can be linked to positioning also. So marketers are trying to assess the impact of the use of the marketing mix elements on the "inner" minds of the consumers. They are constantly involved in seeking answers to the internal factors which may affect the consumer's perception about the product or service (brands).

THE PERCEPTUAL PROCESS

Having discussed about the basic concepts and the external and internal factors affecting consumer perception, we will now try to understand the perceptual process. The perceptual process involves three components:

- Perceptual Selection
- Perceptual Organization
- Perceptual Interpretation

PERCEPTUAL SELECTION

Perception is a selective process. Usually, people are able to sense and receive only limited information from the environment and hence are characteristically selective.

The first, component of perception, *selection*, involves consumer being exposed to marketing stimuli and then he has to attend to them.

There is a tendency among people to consciously see and hear or be attentive to only certain aspects of the advertising message which is being communicated.

Perception is a selective process. Usually, people are able to sense and receive only limited information from the environment and hence are characteristically selective. During this process of selection, certain aspects of stimuli are screened out and others admitted. These aspects of the stimuli which are admitted remain and fall within the threshold of the person, while those which are screened out fall out or below the threshold limit.

Attempt at identifying internal factors influencing consumer behaviour.

FIGURE 3.1

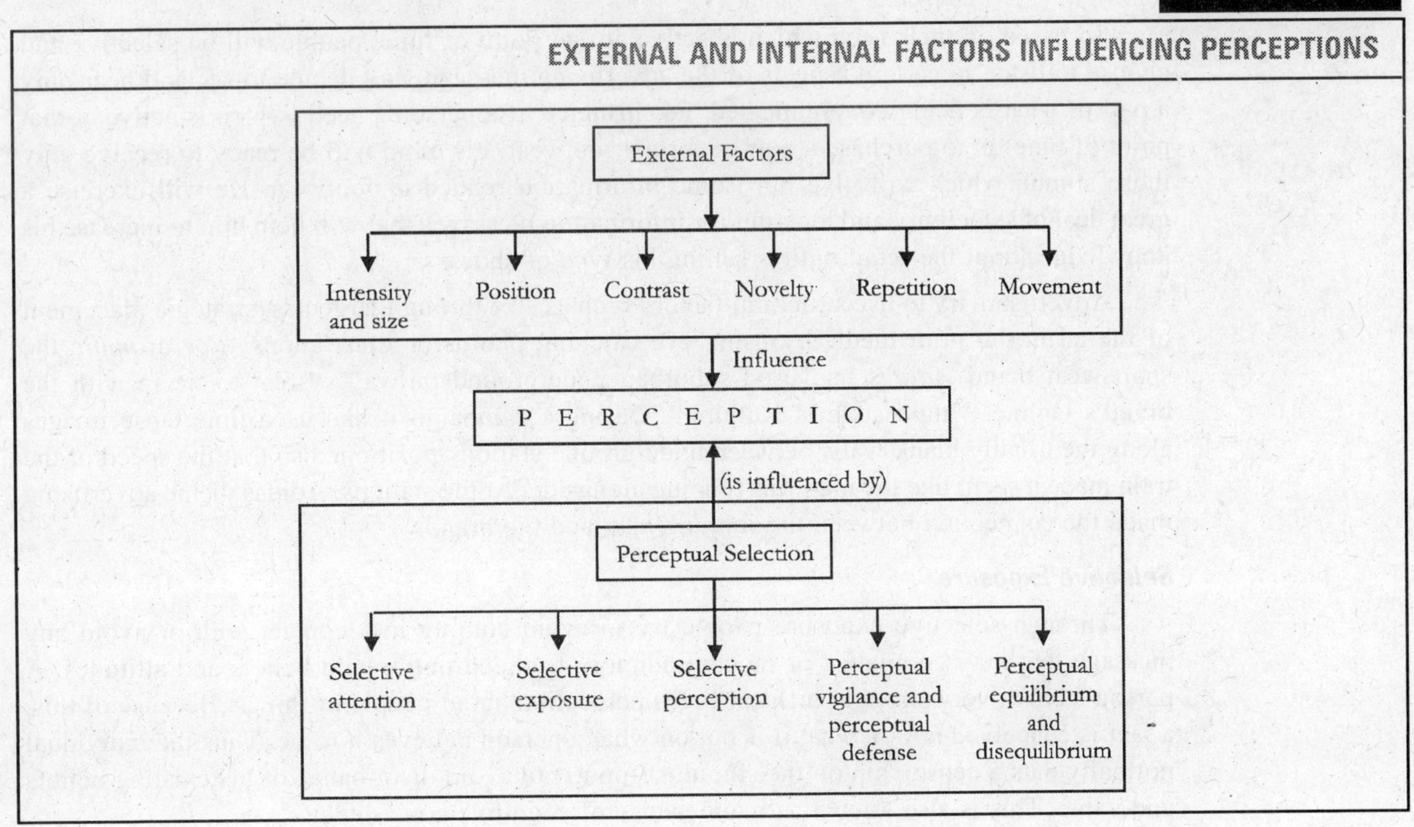

Consumers will identify and choose marketing stimuli based on their needs and attitudes. A consumer intending to buy a sports bike will be more attentive to motor bikes ad, a style conscious person will be more receptive to ads for fashionable clothes while another consumer who is a habital soft drink lover will be more attentive to advertisements potraying the various soft drink brands. In all the above instances the consumer will process stimuli selectively by picking and choosing them based on his by her psychological set.

For perceptual selection to actually take place, the consumer must first see or hear the stimulus and then respond to it.

For perceptual selection to actually take place, the consumer must first see or hear the stimulus and then respond to it.

There are three processes which define selection:

- exposure
- attention
- selective perception

Exposure and Attention

When a consumer's senses – sight, hearing, smell, taste, touch are activated by a stimulus, exposure is said to have occurred. But their interest and involvement with the stimulus will be reflected at the level of attention they devote to it. Attention is defined as the momentary focusing of a consumer's cognitive capacity on a specific stimulus. *For example,* when consumers take notice of a TV ad, a new product displayed in the retail outlet or a new vehicle in the company showroom, it is said that attention has taken place.

Selective Attention

People will be selective in their choice of receiving various kinds of information for different products or services based on what interests them rather than the message content and also selection of the media.

So based on their need which is active at that point of time, people will be selective and choose to listen to certain aspects of the advertising message, and decide to see and hear only a part of what is being communicated. For instance, if a person's need (which is active at that point of time) is to purchase a pair of formal footwear, his mind will be ready to receive only those stimuli which will give him some information related to footwear. He will exercise a great deal of selectivity and look out for information messages that will help him to increase his knowledge about the retail outlets selling his type of shoes.

Advertisers try to use structural factors such as size through large ads, strategic placement of the ad in the print media by using eye catching photos or illustrations. *For example* the sportswear brand *Adidas* had used suburban underground railway system to tie in with the brand's tagline. "Impossible is Nothing". During a campaign it had used time lapse images along the usually blank walls between underground stations-positioned so that the speed of the train made it seem like the man was running alongside. At the stations, Adidas theme advertising made the connection between the running man and the brand.

Selective Exposure

Through selective exposure people try to avoid coming into contact with or avoid any message that may go against or be contradictory to the strongly held beliefs and attitudes. A person's belief very strongly influences his perception about people or things. Because of this, a fact is conceived not on what it is but on what a person believes it to be. Thus the individual normally puts a censorship on the stimulus (inputs) to avoid disturbance of his existing beliefs and value. This is also known as maintenance of cognitive consistency.

Consumers also look out and seek messages that they feel are pleasant or which are sympathetic to their causes and action. They try to avoid painful or unpleasant messages or are against those which they perceive to be threatening in nature. This is also referred to as a part of the process of cognitive dissonance. If a consumer is dissatisfied or unsure after the purchase of a particular product he or she will try to reduce the dissonance. In the words of Leon Festinger, (L. Festinger, *A Theory of Cognitive Dissonance,* Harper and Row, New York, 1975) this drive is "to *establish internal harmony, consistency or congruity among his opinions, knowledge and values"* Such dissatisfied consumers will try to reduce the dissonance by seeking information that will reiterate the high value of the product purchased by them and avoid information which may speak against the (presumed high value) product. For instance, those people who have developed the habit of chewing paan or tobacco will avoid all information (including articles) which may link 'chewing tobacco' to cancer. Consumers will selectively expose themselves to advertisements that will reassure and reinforce them of the wisdom in their purchase decision.

Attention is defined as the momentary focusing of a consumer's cognitive capacity on a specific stimulus. So, based on their need which is active at a point of time, people will be selective and choose to listen to certain aspects of the advertising message and decide to see and hear only a part of what is being communicated.

In today's age of e-technology, when consumers are bombarded with a lot of information, it becomes humanly impossible to take in all of it. So, they indulge in selective exposure. In other words:

- People are more likely to get attracted to the stimuli which relates to the current need.
- It is more likely that people may observe the stimuli that they anticipate.
- People are more likely to notice a large deviation of the stimuli than the usual size of the stimuli (*For example,* a consumer who is interested in the purchase of a car is more likely to notice an ad offering Rs. 15000/- off the list price of an "A" brand than 'B' offering Rs 1500/- off the list price)

Selective Perception

Consumers will perceive marketing experiences stimuli selectively because each person will be unique in terms of her needs, attitudes experiences and personal characteristics. *Selective perception* means that different persons may perceive the same product, advertisement package in a different way. *For example,* one consumer may believe that *Tide* washing powder washes and makes clothes whiter than the other washing powders. Whereas, there could be another consumer who may not agree with this claim, for she may believe that all the washing powders are the same.

Through selective exposure people try to avoid coming into contact with or avoid any message that may go against or be contradictory to the strongly held beliefs and attitudes. Selective perception means that different persons may perceive the same product, advertisement package in a different way.

YAMAHA
Yamaha Festival Offer Continues
CRUX — Road Tax Free* — Save upto: Rs. 2500/-
G5 — Road Tax Free + Helmet free* — Save upto: Rs. 3000/-
Gladiator — Road Tax Free* — Save upto: Rs. 3500/-
or attractive minimum exchange offer upto Rs: 6,000 or check for attractive offer on cash purchase also
*Conditions apply. Offer is only for finance scheme. Finance at the sole discretion of the financier.
Prices shown are ex-showroom, Karnataka. Accessories shown in the above are not part of the standard fitment

An example of *Yamaha* trying to use *selective exposure* to attract the attention of prospective customers

FIGURE 3.2

THE PERCEPTUAL PROCESS

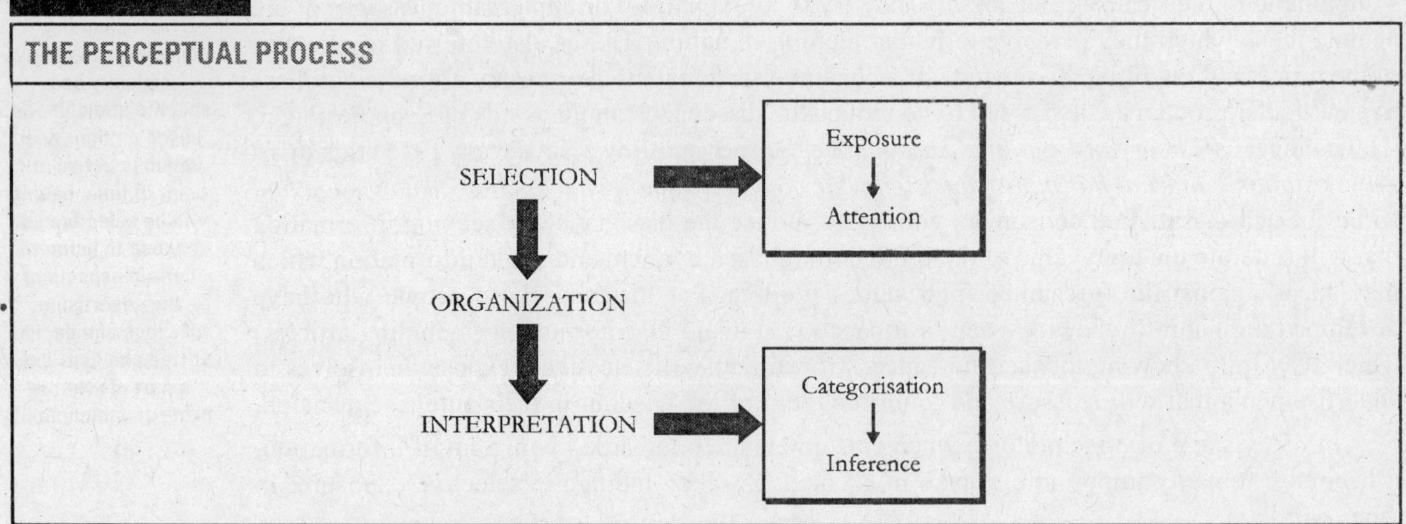

As seen from Figure 3.2, selective perception occurs at every stage in the perceptual process. *Selective exposure* takes place because each individual's belief will influence what she decides to read or hear. *Selective organisation* occurs because each person will organize information so that it is consistent to her beliefs. And *selective interpretation* will take place such that perception will conform to prior beliefs and attitudes.

For example, Oral B toothbrush claims that its toothbrush will indicate when the user has to purchase a new toothbrush. This, the marketer assumed would be consistent to the consumers beliefs that such a toothbrush will be helpful. However, dentists, in general, may not concur with the claim. Such consumers' perception can be influenced by brand name associations arrived at from advertising and social stimuli, where the association tends to conform to the consumer's current knowledge and past experiences.

Such selective perception can affect both high involvement and low involvement purchase decisions. In case of low involvement purchases, consumers will selectively screen out more information so as to avoid informational clutter and cognitive activity. Whereas, in case of high involvement, consumers' will selectively choose information so that :

- It helps them to evaluate brands which meet their needs
- They can select brands which conforms to their belief and predispositions.

Perceptual Vigilance and Perceptual Defense

Through selective perception consumers will receive information having relevance to her needs. Hence this process is also called perceptual vigilance. Perceptual defense refers to the individual being vigilant and screening out those stimuli or elements which create conflict or may give rise to a threatening situation.

Since selective perception will help the consumer to receive information having relevance to her needs, this process is also called *perceptual vigilance.*

During high involvement purchases, consumers, through perceptual vigilance obtain the necessary information which matches their requirement. For low involvement purchases, consumers will screen out and minimize information processing through perceptual vigilance. In such instances, the consumer tends to selectively screen out information.

Perceptual defence refers to the individual being vigilant and screening out all those stimuli or elements which create conflict or may give rise to a threatening situation. Consumers may subconsciously screen out the stimuli which is found to be psychologically threatening, even if the exposure has taken place. They may even perceive other factors to be present, which may not be a part of the stimulus situation.

Perceptual vigilance or defence can also be said in reference to the way in which people maintain their prior beliefs. For instance, going by the saying "The customer is always right", the restaurant manager will deal in a proper manner with the customer who is upset with the customer service, ignoring the fact that it was actually the customer who behaved badly. This example again emphasises that individuals unconsciously may distort information that is not consistent with their needs, beliefs, opinions or attitudes.

Perceptual-Equilibrium and Disequilibrium

Perceptual Equilibrium

The underlying principle influencing selective perception is that consumers seek perceptual equilibrium *i.e.,* consistency between prior beliefs they have about a brand and the information they receive about a brand. There are three theories which are based on the Principle of Selective Perception and Perceptual Equilibrium (*Consumer Behavior,* Henry Assael, 6th Edn., Thomson Learning, Singapore, 2004, P. 221).

Sherif's Social Judgment theory which says that consumers process information in order to ensure consistency by either rejecting contradictory information or by interpreting acceptable information such that it fits in more closely with their views.

Heider's Balance theory which states that when information received about an object conflicts with consumer's belief, they will try to achieve balance by changing their opinion about the object or the source of information or both. *i.e.,* consumers will try to get a balance in beliefs about the information and the object.

According to the *Cognitive Dissonance theory* when post purchase conflicts arise, consumers will try to seek balance in the psychological set by seeking supporting information or by distorting contradictory information.

Each of the above theories indicate that consumers are seeking consistency between consumer's perception of marketing stimuli and their belief and attitudes.

Perceptual Disequilibrium

Sometimes consumers would accept discrepant information about a selected product. If they did not, it will mean that every time a consumer was dissatisfied, he or she will try to rationalize the purchase and would never switch brands. There are two theories which predict different outcomes of customer dissatisfaction.

The underlying principle influencing selective perception is that consumers seek perceptual equilibrium *i.e.,* consistency between prior beliefs they have about a brand and the information they receive about a brand.

The learning theory suggests that when a brand does not meet expectations, consumers learn from the negative experience and will adjust their belief and attitudes accordingly. The outcome is a reduction in the probability of repurchase. *For example,* even though a majority of the non paan eating consumers accept the link between eating paan and cancer, only half of the heavy paan eaters could be in a state of perceptual disequilibrium. Many of such paan consumers may accept this dissonant information and try hard to stop eating paan *i.e.,* change their behaviour to conform to the information.

Cognitive dissonance theory suggests that when a brand does not meet expectation, consumers will disbelieve the negative information received. *For example,* the heavy paan eaters may disbelieve the link between cancer and eating paan and rationalize their paan eating behaviour.

Marketing Strategy and Selective Perception

Marketers can communicate messages which are clear cut or ambiguous. When consumers are engaged in perceptual defence, then ambiguous messages will be more effective because consumers are being given latitude to interpret their messages according to their belief about the brand. *For example,* advertisers use ambiguity in advertising when the product or service is important to consumers but its benefits are not clear cut. But since consumers are utilizing beliefs which are consistent with their needs, this can be referred to as perceptual defence.

For example Indian Oil's Ad asks

"Correct quality?
Correct quantity?
Special services?
Here's where you should be heading...."

Indian Oil uses ad to attract consumers engaged in perceptual defense

The above questions from the Indian Oil gives consumers enough reasons for using Indian Oil's products and services. This ad enables consumers to selectively perceive a range of application with a minimum of informational content and relate it to the ad.

When consumers are engaged in *perceptual vigilance*, clear cut messages are likely to be more effective, especially when the information is supportive or contradictory to the consumer's belief. When the product or service benefits are clear cut and it is targeted at a specific target market, marketers use an advertisement where the informational content dominates and ambiguity is at the minimum. *For example,* in case of industrial advertising, most of the ads are providing direct informational content to match the consumers needs of receiving straight forward information. Here the principle of perceptual vigilance is being used.

Chunking or grouping of information will help consumers to evaluate various brands of products by making use of a variety of attributes.

When consumers are bombarded with lots of information there is a general tendency to 'block out' some stimuli' from their conscious awareness, this is called 'perceptual blocking'.

Perceptual Blocking : Another aspect of perceptual selectivity is perceptual blocking. When consumers are bombarded with lots of information, there is a general tendency to 'block out' some stimuli from their conscious awareness. It will be noticed that when consumers are exposed to many advertisements together, they will automatically switch off, from their mental set, most of the advertisements. *For example,* popular T.V. programmes are sponsored by marketers of products with commercial viability. The advertisements of all the sponsored products are shown (at times even repeated many times) in short intervals of time during the time of telecast. But most of these ads are perpetually 'blocked out' by consumers due to over exposure of the same.

Ad suggests 'learning' through product re-inforcement

FIGURE 3.3

THE PRINCIPLES OF ORGANIZATION

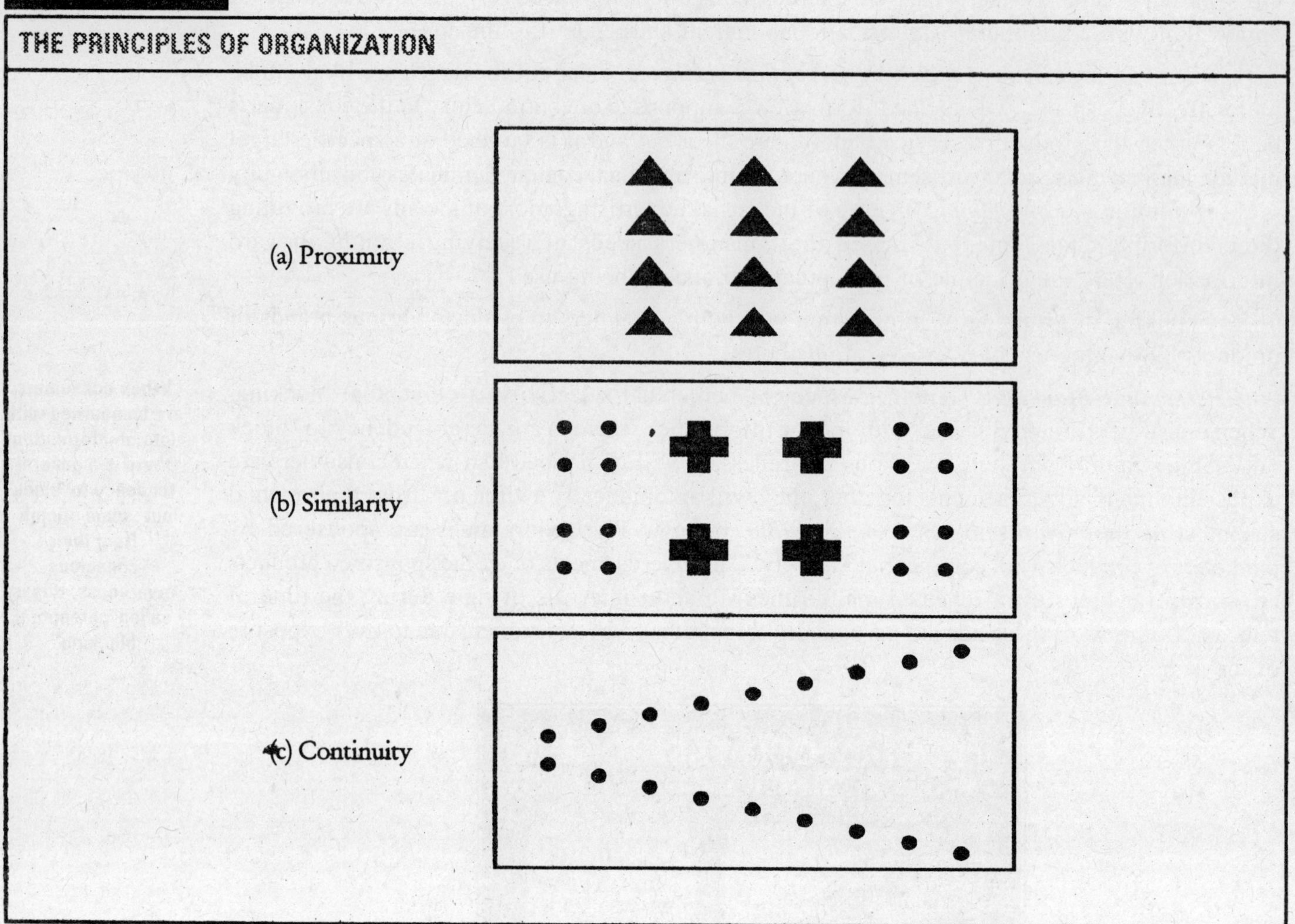

PERCEPTUAL ORGANISATION

People do not experience all the stimuli selected by them as separate and discrete sensations. They rather, organise this stimuli into groups and perceive them as a unified whole. This method of perceptual organisation enables individuals to view life in a simplified manner.

The underlying principles helping individuals in perceptual organisation was first developed by the Gestalt psychologists. (Gestalt, when translated from German means total configuration or whole pattern). These principles help in understanding perceptual organisations, which are primarily related to the physiological events occurring in the nervous system of the individual in direct reaction to stimuli by the physical objects. There are three basic principles used in perceptual organisation - grouping, closure and context.

In grouping, the perceiver groups the different stimuli based on the principles of similarity, continuity and proximity.

Grouping : In grouping, the perceiver groups the different stimuli based on the principles of similarity, continuity and proximity. This means all those stimuli which are grouped together are likely to be perceived as having the same characteristics. The perception of stimuli as groups of information will facilitate easy memorising and recall by consumers.

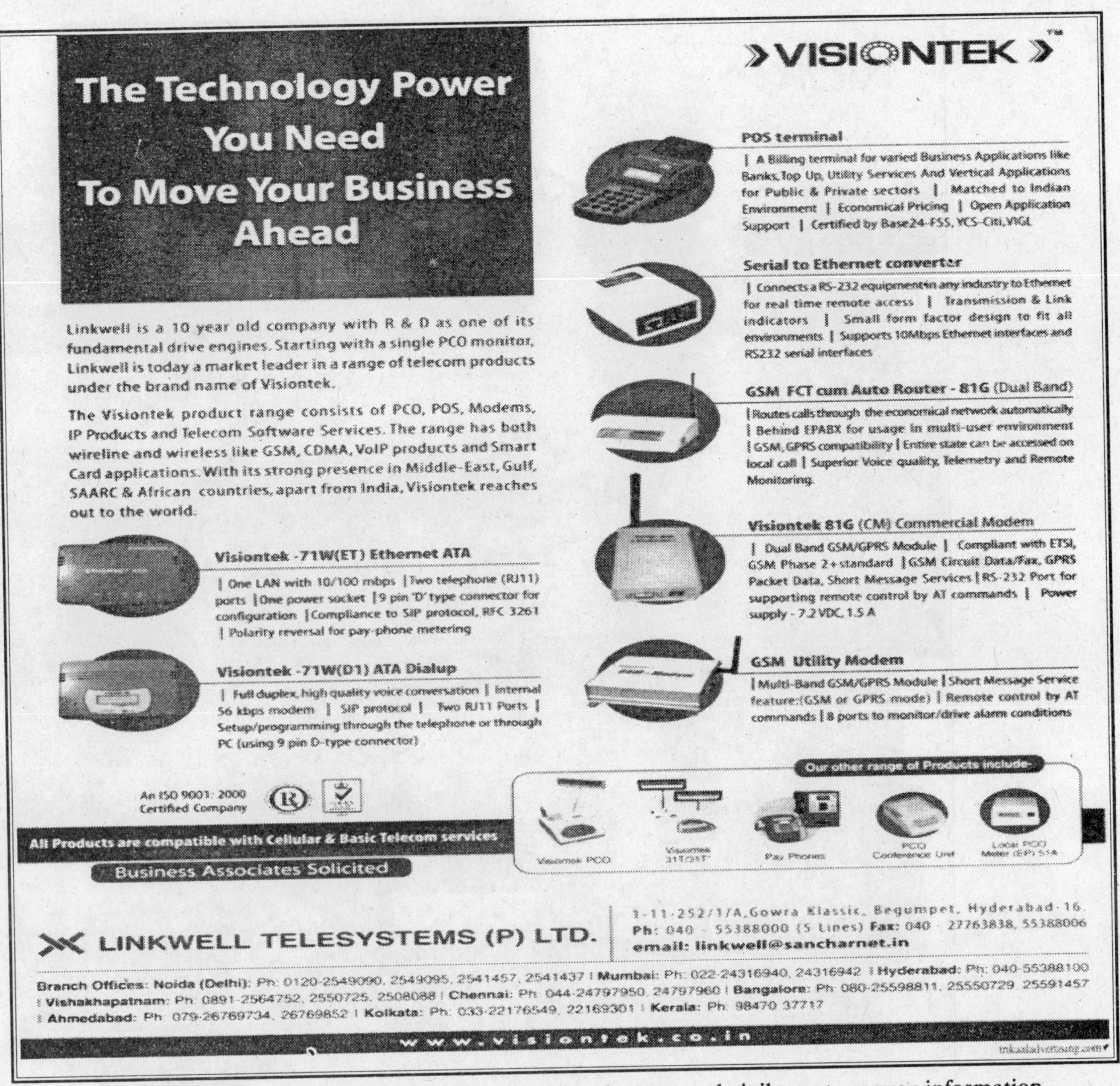

LinkWell TeleSystems (P) Ltd. uses the principle of perceptual vigilance to convey information.

People organize all stimuli selected by them into groups and perceive them as a unified whole. This method of perceptual organisation enables them to view life in a simplified manner. The principle of grouping suggests that all those stimuli which are grouped together are likely to be perceived as having the same characteristics.

Marketers are using this principle to enable consumers to get a unified picture and co-relate desired connection with their products. For instance, one of the commercials *for Cadbury* used to show an old grandfather blowing bubbles with his little grand children. Cadbury was promoting chocolates by associating with the natural spontaneous behaviour on the part of adults. The ad also conveyed the message "The real taste of life". This grouping will convey to the consumer that chocolates is a universal product to be enjoyed by all, irrespective of age barriers.

Through the ad of *Nokia N 91*, the advertiser is attempting to associate the brand with music and phone. The ad of *The Economic Times* (Now in Lucknow) tries to illustrate the concept of similarity through grouping the various editions of The Economic Times by providing different business news relevant to the particular city although it caters to the needs of the business news readers across the country as a whole.

"The ad of Nokia N91 positions mobile phone in proximity to earphones and picture of rock music enjoyers"

The principle of continuity can be applied to the ad of Microsoft software which says that it can be used by all the company's employees, where the transition is continuous. The software can be utilized by all people and also provides them the software to match their ambition to succeed far and wide equally.

"Use of the principle of similarity in the ad of 'The Economic Times'"

"Microsoft software tries to use the principle of continuity in its ad

Context

Figure and Ground

Consumers tend to perceive an object in the context in which it is shown. While organizing information, people have the tendency to keep certain phenomena in focus and some other phenomena in the background. This is said to be the working of the figure and ground principle. This is a very important principle of context.

According to Gestalt psychologists, when individuals organize stimuli into wholes, they will distinguish stimuli which are prominent (the figure that is generally in the foreground) from stimuli which is less prominent (those in the ground or background.)

According to Gestalt psychologists, when individuals organize stimuli into wholes, they will distinguish stimuli which are prominent (the figure that is generally in the foreground) from the stimuli which is less prominent (those in the ground or background).

Advertisers, usually try to ensure that the product is the figure and the setting is in the background. This can be seen in the ad of *Johnnie Walker* given below.

Closure : When faced with incomplete information, individuals have the tendency to fill in the gaps themselves so as to gain a more meaningful information. They feel ill at ease when faced with an incomplete picture. They prefer to organise their perceptions so as to form a

The closure principle suggests that when faced with incomplete information, individuals have the tendency to fill in the gaps themselves so as to gain a more meaningful information.

complete picture. In other words, if people are exposed to incomplete stimuli, they tend to perceive it as complete, by either consciously or subconsciously filling up the missing gaps. This may be done on the basis of his or her (the individual's) past experience, past information or on the basis of hunches. This concept of closure can be seen as the tension experienced by a person when a task is incomplete, and the satisfaction and relief that may be experienced on its completion.

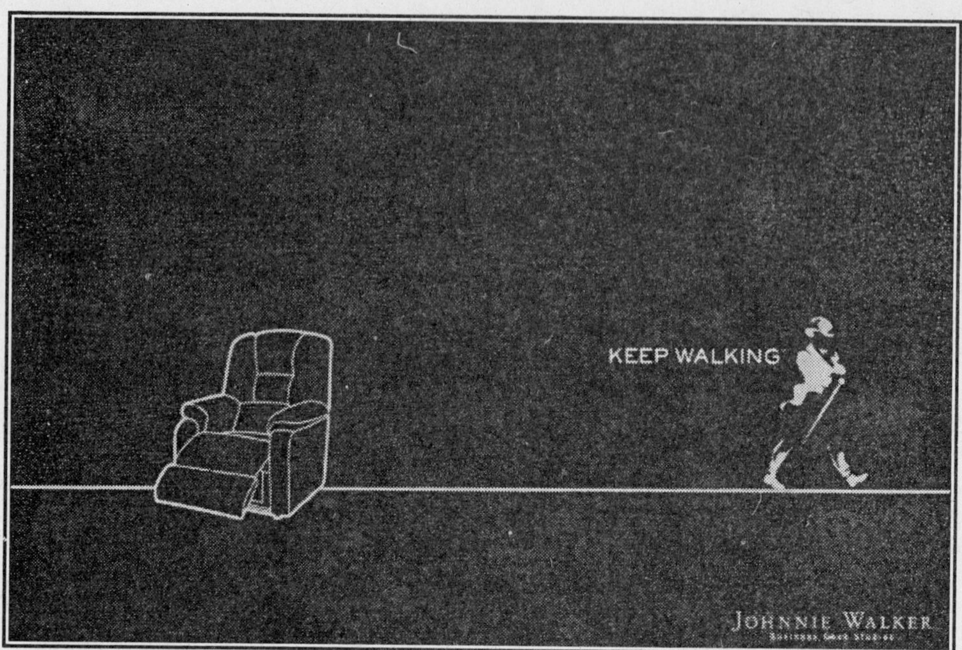

This ad uses the principle of figure and ground

At times, some of the advertisements are given in an incomplete manner, where broken lines are put, which have to be filled in with certain alphabets in order to convey some meaning. People usually fill up these gaps to get the picture or meaning.

PERCEPTUAL INTERPRETATION

We have seen that perception is a personal phenomenon. People have the tendency to interpret the meaning of what they have selectively perceived and organised on the basis of their own assumptions about the stimuli. This interpretation of the stimuli will be dependent on what the individual expects to see in the light of his previous experience, intuition, data received, motives and interests at the time of perception.

It is likely that the stimuli are highly ambiguous. Some stimuli may be strong while others may be weak. Moreover, based on the angles at which stimuli are viewed, varying distances and changing levels of illumination, it is likely that there may occur fluctuations in the stimuli. Due to the ambiguity of the stimuli, the individual will prefer to interpret the sensory inputs received by him or her, such as to fulfil their personal needs, interests and so on. Thus, we can say that the perceptual interpretations of the stimuli by individuals are also done in relative terms. So there are chances of misinterpretation. But in order to understand how close a person's interpretation is to reality, we will have to determine the clarity of the stimuli, the previous experience of the perceiver, the individual's motives (or needs) and interests.

Thus, after consumers have selected and organized stimuli, they interpret them. Consumers are able to interpret marketing information by making use of two principles:

(a) **Categorization :** This principle is with reference to the tendency of consumers to process and place information into their interpretation of logical categories. *For example,* "This new ad of mineral water must be probably just like 'Bisleri mineral water'".

(b) **Inference :** This principle refers to consumers reasoning out and developing an association between two stimuli. *For example,* consumers might associate herbal extracts in body care products with natural ingredients.

Perceptual Distortion

There are certain factors which could influence the individual, leading to perceptual distortion. These are briefly discussed below.

Sometimes perceptual distortion can occur due to certain factors such as Personality (or physical appearance), Stereotypes, Halo effect, Irrelevant cues, First impressions and Hasty conclusions.

Personality or Physical Appearance : Personality of the perceiver greatly influences the perception process. Researches have shown that people have a tendency to perceive others to be having the same attributes or qualities as themselves. People have the tendency to associate certain persons with others who may have certain attributes, irrespective of whether they consciously recognise the attributes or not.

This is why, advertisers give a lot of importance to the selection of models for advertisements. Potrayal of an attractive model to promote the product or service will have an added touch of persuasiveness. This can automatically induce the consumer to develop a positive attitude and behaviour towards the product. For instance, using celebrity, to endorse a product or brand is more appealing to the consumer's mind.

Example of celebrities endorsing certain brands are:

- Hema Malini — *Kent water purifier, Malabar Gold*
- Amitabh Bachchan — *Reid & Taylor, Boroplus Antiseptic tube*
- Juhi Chawla — *Kurkure snacks*
- Kajol — *Marie gold biscuits, Whirlpool washing machine, Asmi diamonds*
- Sania Mirza — *Tata Tea Premium*

Stereotypes : This term 'Stereotype' is used to describe 'biases' involved in perceiving people. This means that there could be a bias involved when the perceiver sees/perceives the person or individual on the basis of a single class or category to which he or she belongs. Stereotypes also convey another meaning, that is there is a general concurrence on the attributed traits and also the possibility of a discrepancy between attributed traits and actual traits. Accordingly, stereotypes may attribute favourable and unfavourable traits to the person being perceived. *For example,* statements such as :

"All salespersons are fast talkers and bluff a lot." Stereotypes indicate the expectations from certain specific stimuli and how these (stimuli) will ultimately be perceived.

Halo Effect : The term 'Halo effect' is used to describe a process, in which judges use the general impression (either favourable or unfavourable) to evaluate certain specific traits. Here 'Halo' acts as a barrier or screen to keep the perceiver away from actually seeing the trait he is judging. The broad difference between the halo error and stereotyping error is that - in stereotyping the person is perceived on the basis of a single category, while under the halo effect the person is perceived on the basis of one trait or event.

According to consumer behaviourists, 'halo effect' includes the evaluation of multiple brands (say a product line of a firm) by evaluating just one dimension (either the brand name or celebrity endorsement). Going by this perspective of halo effect, marketers can extend the use of a brand name associated with one line of products to another. The knowledge or familiarity

Personality can result in perceptual distortion.

which consumers have with the product or brand is likely to influence their perception of the brand and extensions, if any. *For example, Amul* with the 'Taste of India' tag line has successfully been extended to its ice creams. *Horlicks* brand name has been successfully extended to its horlicks biscuits also. The value of the brand as perceived by the consumer will be in terms of assurance of quality, reliability and acceptable price.

Irrelevant Cues : Sometimes, consumers form perceptual judgement based on their giving importance to irrelevant cues. In the case of purchase of automobiles, at times, consumers' purchase decisions are based on the importance given to the look, colour, leather upholstery etc. rather than giving due consideration to the mechanical and technical superiority.

First Impressions : There is a very old saying which goes as "First impressions tend to be lasting ones" However, this wisdom will depend on the context and also on the extent to which the perceiver is aware of the relevance of the stimuli considered by him or her.

It is reassuring to observe that often an individual's past experience may help in resolving stimulus ambiguity in a more realistic way, right up to the interpretation, in the perceptual process.

Firms have to exercise care, especially when launching new products and trying to create a good first impression on the minds of the consumers. If the product fails to make the desired 'first' impact, a 'second chance' to taste success may not occur. And, any subsequent attempts at communicating the advantages may not be sufficient to delete from the consumer's mind about its (unsuccessful) earlier attempts. For decades, Coca-cola company was known only for its *Coca-cola brand*. Later on the company tried to introduce other flavours and fruit juices and extend the Coca-cola name but consumers had learnt to perceive and link the brand name to the cola drink only. Finally they decided to advertise and support them separately.

Hasty Conclusions : Often people have the tendency to arrive at conclusions very quickly, before examining all the relevant evidence. This behaviour can be based on the person's attitude, motivation level, interest and past experience also. Consumers at times develop the attitude of drawing conclusions based on limited receipt of information. This factor will also act as a distorting factor and come in the way of his perceptual process. There is one ad which appears on the mass media, showing a spokesperson for 'consumer rights' cautioning consumers against blindly accepting the packaged product received from the shopkeeper. Consumers are advised that rather than jumping to conclusions about the verbal assurance of the contents, it is the consumer's right to ask the retailer to measure and verify the same in their presence.

Inspite of the above mentioned distorting influences, it is reassuring to observe that often an individual's past experience may help in resolving stimulus ambiguity in a more realistic way, right up to the 'interpretation' in the perceptual process. Moreover, it is only under changing stimulus condition situation that the individual's expectations may lead to wrong interpretations.

Perceptual Inference

Consumers draw inferences about brands, outlets, and associations. For instance, consumers may associate a *Tanishq* watch with quality. This inference could be drawn on the basis of word of mouth communication from peer group, friends or advertisements. We can understand this better by having a look at discussions, on product symbols and semiotics.

Product Symbols: Many of the symbols we see in the ads and packages are socially and culturally derived. *For example,* Air India's Maharaja symbolizes royal treatment, even the usage of orange, white and green colours on many of the packages can be associated with patriotism.

Symbolises - power due to fuel efficiency

Symbols can affect the consumption process. For example the advertisement of *Bajaj Discover DTS-i* can be associated with fantacy (computer graphics showing how the pipes follow the bike rider) and conveys the message that the bike is fuel efficient.

However, advertisers have to remember that consumers will perceive symbols selectively. *For example, Blackberry* may indicate the iconic status to some while there could be others who may find it too fanciful for usage.

Semiotics: The study which examines the role of signs and symbols in assigning meaning to objects is called semiotics. Semiotics tries to determine the meaning consumer's assign to symbols through three components:

- The object or product (say, Kent Mineral RO)
- The symbol associated with the object (water purifier)
- The interpretant or meaning of the symbol (domestic, pure and healthy water).

Microsoft provides informational cues to match the perceived product quality offering

For marketing purpose, semioticians view the symbol used in the packaging as a kind of culture or cusumption dictionary, where the entries are considered to be products which are culturally designed.

For marketing purposes, semioticians view the symbols used in the packaging as a kind of culture or consumption dictionary, where the entries are considered to be products, which are culturally defined (*Consumer Behavior,* Henry Assael, 6th Ed., Thomson Learning. p. 232). Now, going back to the example of Kent Mineral (RO), Water Purifier, assume that the associations mentioned are what the company wants the consumer to associate with the symbol (water purifier). In reality, if the consumers were to associate with the symbol positively (*i.e.,* as the company hoped to elicit), then it can be said that the consumer's perception matches with that of the company's symbolic representation. Under such circumstances, a positive perceptual inference has taken place suggesting that consumer perception has positively interpreted the said symbol. However, if the meaning many consumers associate with the symbol (Kent Mineral RO water purifier) does not match with what the company had hoped to elicit, the very purpose of using the symbol, by the company, is defeated.

CONSUMER IMAGERY AND MARKETING IMPLICATIONS

Consumers have a number of enduring perceptions or images, which are quite relevant to the study of consumer behaviour. Thus, it becomes very difficult to gauge the consumer's mind.

Generally, products, brands, other people, places and possessions have symbolic value and are judged on the basis of how they fit with the personal picture of themselves.

Brand Image and Self Image

An important aspect of self concept is the person's level of aspiration. Generally products, brands, other people, places and possessions have symbolic value and are judged on the basis of how they fit with the personal picture of themselves. The different types of self image are :

- Actual self image - How consumers see themselves.
- Social self image - Consumers' perception of how they are seen by others.
- Ideal self image - How consumers would like others to see them as.
- Expected self image - Consumers' expectations of how they would like to be seen as, at some specified time in the future.

Researches have revealed that consumer's prefer brands which relate to their self perception and to their subjective images of brands.

Brand image will indicate the overall perception of the brand and is based on how the consumer draws inferences about the brand. Brand image is influenced to a great extent by the company brand name too. Say Tata Steel or Bajaj Tempo travellers have established a certain brand image in the mind of the consumers.

A very important aspect influencing consumer's brand image is *product positioning*. Marketers try to position their brand such that it can meet the needs of the defined market segment. This is done by developing a product concept which will communicate, by using a suitable media, the desired benefit to the target market. Some of the brands which have succeeded due to the suitable product positioning are:

- *ICICI Bank :* Provide customers a large variety of products at affordable prices across a wide network of branches.
- *NOKIA 1100 India phone :* Innovative technology meant for rugged use.
- *SONY :* Technology innovation and premium quality in the field of high-tech entertainment.

But if the product is not positioned properly it may fail to capture the consumer's mind. *For example, Mountain Dew*, a lemon drink, with the USP "The Spirit of Adventure - Do the Dew" was launched in India. But this USP failed to position Mountain Dew as an adventure drink in the minds of the consumers. And the company had to think of a repositioning of the product.

Perceptual mapping is a technique used by marketers to know consumer's perception of their products or services in relation to competitors' brand on one or more relevant characteristics.

Perceptual Mapping and Product Positioning

Perceptual mapping is a technique used by marketers to know consumer's perception of their products or services in relation to competitor's brand on one or more relevant characteristic. This technique will enable them to identify and see gaps in the positioning of all the brands in a particular product or service class category.

This technique had been first introduced by Volney Steffre to marketing, in order to determine the share of consumer choices that a new brand will draw when introduced in the market, and also to ascertain the patterns of substitution and competition that is likely to occur after a new brand is made available in the market. Usually consumer's tend to perceive the brand on many dimensions such as quality, price etc. Perceptual mapping technique is multidimensional in nature, enabling the marketer to measure how may stimuli characteristics can influence product perception. Simply stated, the technique of perceptual mapping will help marketers to make an estimate on how their products or services will appear to the consumers in comparison to competitive brands based on one or more relevant characteristics. Such a technique will also help the marketer to position their brand in the particular product category. For instance, the publisher may find that consumers (or readers) perceive its magazine say *'Business Today'* to be similar in its editorial content to its closest competitor say *'Business World'*. Here the publisher can try to reposition his magazine by changing the focus of its editorial features. Another example could be related to the brand personality. To enable consumers to perceive the difference in their brand as compared to its competitors in the luggage category, VIP industries positions its '*VIP Sky bags*' with the *value-for-money* proposition.

Especially with many global brands available in the market, marketers need to think and concentrate on brand personality positioning.

The Perception of Quality

Consumers perception of quality is often based on his or her evaluation of a product's attributes. This in turn is determined by certain physical cues such as taste, smell, size and shape. But, in many instances, the consumer is unable to form a judgemental (perception) view, by merely going on the basis of the product's physical characteristics. This is because

- The physical differences that exist between competing brands are not sufficient enough to penetrate across consumer's sensory thresholds.
- The consumer may not be sufficiently experienced to determine which product differentiation is more important.

In the absence of first hand experience with the product, consumers tend to assess the product's quality on the basis of certain clues or indicators. At times, these indicators may be external, extrinsic to the product itself- such as price, brand name, promotion, display, P.O.P. (point of purchase) retail outlet and so on. For instance, many of the disinfectants are purchased on the basis of smell. Incense sticks (Agarbattis) are purchased on the basis of fragrance.

There are also intrinsic factors, related to the actual characteristics of the product itself- size, colour, feel and functional effectiveness. For instance, Laptop attached to LCD projector is preferred because of its functional effectiveness and size. The executive will find it to be very handy because of its size and functional utility.

Both intrinsic and extrinsic cues can affect the consumer's perception about the quality of the product and it's perceived value. Consumers perceive value in brand which are cost driven or products (brands) which have certain unique benefits which offset their premium prices.

Generally both intrinsic and extrinsic cues will affect the consumer's perception about the quality of the product and its perceived value.

In case of *services,* it becomes very difficult for the consumer to evaluate the quality of services. This is because of certain *distinctive characteristics* associated with services such as intangibility, variability, perishability. Moreover services are also simultaneously produced and consumed. These characteristics are not easily measurable, can vary from day to day, from person (employee performing the service) to another and from profession to profession.

In the absence of a method, whereby the consumers could compare the quality of services, they (the consumers) rely on *extrinsic or surrogate cues* to evaluate the quality of service provided. For instance, in evaluating a hotel's services, the consumer may look into the quality of furniture, interior decor, the services provided at the front office and reception, the availability of added services such as restaurants, swimming pool, the number of awards (if any) displayed, the cleanliness visible in the surroundings and so on.

This means marketers should aim at standardising and maintaining consistency with the quality of services provided. Consumer's use of surrogate indicators to make product or service choice means that research needs to be undertaken to find out those indicators or attributes which are used by consumers in making purchase decisions for particular products.

Price Perceptions

Consumers perceive value in brands when :

- They are cost driven brands, *i.e.,* the brand costs less as compared to competing brands offering similar benefits.
- The product brands have certain unique benefits which offset their premium prices *i.e.,* they are referred to as value added benefits.

MNC food and beverages major Pepsico, in the initials stages while trying to find a place in the Indian market for its juice brand *Tropicana* had to struggle. Till late 2005, the brand was seen only occupying the shop shelves, especially because of its premium positioning. Finally, Pepsico had to do a rethink on its positioning. It decided to introduce localized flavours such as 100% sweetened orange, guava, mixed fruit and others.

In the high end tech segment, brands such as *IBM*, *Hewlett Packard* and *Compaq* have been able to quote premium pricing position by offering certain specific features such as: more memory, higher CPU speed, LCD screens, DVD (read & write) etc. Such value added unique benefits offsets its premium price quoting. A very important link between consumer perception and marketing is related to the issue of price. Often, consumer's price perception will affect their perception of brand equity and thereby influence their purchasing behaviour also.

Due to the constant changes and intense competition at the market place, the Indian consumer with the *imaginary* remote control explores the various brands, evaluates them according to his or her concept of 'Perceived value' before purchasing the product or service. While taking purchase decisions , consumers will be looking at the *perceived value* aspect, which is a blend of quality and price. Thus, marketers need to understand what consumer's price perception will be based on:

- What their (consumers') expectations are about prices (price expectations).
- Whether the above expectation will or not be reflected in the actual prices quoted (Actual versus reference prices).
- Whether consumers perceive a price- quality association (price-quality relationship).

Price Expectations

Supposing a consumer is planning to replace an old Philips 21 inch colour T.V set, with a new 29 inch colour T.V. He may expect to pay around Rs. 18,000/- for the new set. This price is the consumer's reference price (also known as a standard price), *i.e.,* the price the consumer expects to pay for a certain item. The reference price can be defined as a reference point based on which consumers compare prices for alternative brands.

Generally, consumers have an acceptable price range, for a particular product, which shows a willingness to accept a range of prices. Marketers are concerned about the consumers' reference prices and the actual prices of the products or services available at the market place.

Apart from this, generally consumers have an *acceptable price range*, for a particular product, which shows a willingness to accept a range of prices. Marketers are concerned about the consumer's reference prices and the actual prices of the products or services available at the market place. Usually, there is a lot of difference between the consumers reference prices and the actual prices of items.

Sherif's Social Judgment Theory

> **Sherif's social judgement theory suggests three levels of latitude: A latitude of acceptance, A latitude of rejection and A latitude of no commitment and throws some light on the involvement of consumer's in the decision making process.**

Marketers are interested in knowing consumers' reaction to the difference between their reference price and actual prices. Sherif's social judgment theory will help to throw some light on the involvement of the consumers in the decision making process. Sherif had suggested three levels of latitude:

- A latitude of acceptance (the number of positions the individual accepts)
- A latitude of rejection (the number of positions the individual rejects)
- A latitude of no commitment (the positions towards which the individual is neutral)

A highly involved individual will have a definite opinion about an issue and would be willing to accept very few other positions. Such individuals will use more attributes to evaluate fewer brands. They also tend to agree with messages (within their latitude of acceptance) and interpret it more positively than it actually is. Such reactions of highly involved individuals is known as the *assimilation effect.* Such highly involved individuals with a definite opinion about an issue would not only accept few other positions but also reject a wide number of positions (narrow latitude of acceptance and wide latitude of rejection). The message which the individual disagrees with (within the latitude of rejection) will be considered to be more negative than it actually is. Such a reaction is referred to as the *contrast effect.*

For example, a young motorbike enthusiast who just bought a helmet and is very satisfied with the motorbike may recall some opinions passed out by a friend as more positive and encouraging than they were (assimilation). But , if very disappointed with the helmet, the motor bike enthusiast may recall the same comment by the friend to be more negative that it actually is (contrast). This shows that the highly involved individual is more likely to perceive messages selectively based on his or her preconceptions and biases.

In case of an uninvolved individual, he is likely to find more positions acceptable (*i.e.,* has a wide latitude of acceptance) or would have no opinion about the issue (*i.e.,* he or she has a wide latitude of non-commitment). Thus, such uninvolved individuals, are less likely to perceive the message selectively, and so an assimilation or contrast effect is less likely to occur.

Application of Sheriff's theory to consumer behaviour is illustrated in the figure 3 4.

FIGURE 3.4

APPLICATION OF SHERIF'S THEORY TO CONSUMER BEHAVIOUR

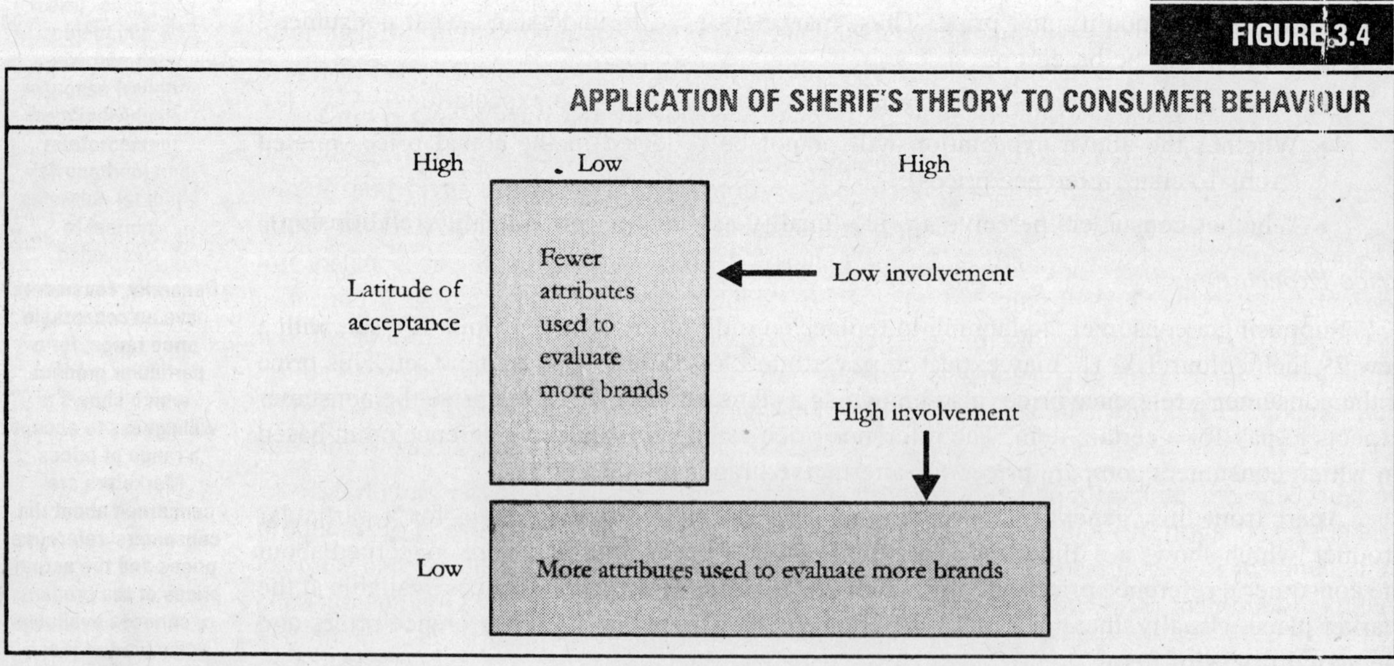

As seen in Figure 3.4, highly involved customers would be actively processing information though they may find fewer brands acceptable. Whereas, less involved consumers would be engaged in less information processing and would find many brands acceptable too.

Sherif's theory throws more light on the buying behaviour of passive or less involved consumers. Less involved consumers will consider a wider number of brands because of a lack of commitment to one or more brands. Due to their lack of commitment to any brand, they are not interested in spending time to interpret advertising messages or search for and evaluate brands. Such consumers will perceive advertising with little cognitive activity and adopt an easy way for purchasing goods. They will purchase the most familiar brand and also buy the same brand, repetitively.

Involved consumers will seek a more optional solution to their purchase decisions. They will use more attributes to evaluate fewer brands. This aspect has been illustrated in Figure 3.4 which shows that such consumers' latitude of acceptance is narrower and level of information processing greater.

A Comparison between Actual and Reference Prices

Researchers have taken the help of Assimilation Contrast theory (explained above) to understand consumer reaction. Going back to our earlier example, we presume that the consumer's expected price range for 29 inch colour T.V is from Rs. 14,000/- to Rs. 18,000/-, while the actual price may range from Rs. 16,000/- to Rs. 24,000/-. If the difference between actual and reference is within the consumer's acceptable price range, an assimilation effect occurs. Suppose our consumer evaluates three colour T.V. brands and finds that 29 inch T.V. sets are priced around Rs. 16000/-, Rs. 18,000/- and Rs. 19,000/-. Since these prices are within the acceptable price range, he is likely to shift his reference price from Rs. 14,000/- towards the actual price of one of the brands (say Rs. 16,000/- after making a comparison of the various brands. This implies that the consumer did not mind changing the reference price closer to actual prices as long as the actual price was acceptable.

A study by *Urbany, Beardan and Weilbaker* revealed that when consumers found actual prices not in the acceptable price range, a contrast effect is likely to occur. *i.e.,* they will reject brands priced higher than the acceptable price range.

A Price – Quality Relationship?

Generally it is found that when consumers do not have sufficient information about product quality, they are likely to use price as an indication of quality. If our consumer does not have sufficient knowledge about T.V. sets and feels that there are significant price quality relationships between the various brands, he is likely to use high price as an indicator of quality.

The consumer perception of prices are important for marketers, because it often influences their perception of quality, which in turn will influence their purchase behaviour.

Price is perceived to be an indicator of quality, if consumers have more confidence in the source of price information *i.e.,* wherever they felt that the source of information was reliable and trustworthy. Thus consumer perception of prices are important for marketers, because it often influences their perception of quality which in turn will influence their purchase behaviour.

For example, in case of high end products such as electronic items, computers, cars etc., where technological along with functional attributes counted, the Indian consumer behaviour, has been showing positive inclination towards top brands from *Toyota, Sony, Samsung* and *L.G.* This can be because consumers perceived these foreign brands offer a proven product delivery experience so there is more involvement from them. But in case of low priced products such as hair dye or hair oil, Indian market is dominated by brands such as *Godrej hair dye* and *Parachute hair oil.* Consumers feel they are receiving the same value proposition from these brands, so there is less involvement and the consumer may buy the same brand consistently as he is happy with the brand.

Corporate Image : A corporate image goes beyond the design of a company's letterhead. In reality, the corporate image will encompass a much deeper and broad view, *i.e.,* it will communicate the way a business enterprise will relate to its whole social and cultural context.

A corporate image carries an 'added value'. A corporate image goes a long way in its ability to enter into a relationship with its customers. Because consumers enter into a relationship not only with the brands but with the organisation also. Just as brands create an image in the minds of their customers, so do organisations both for its internal customers (employees) and for their external customers. To keep pace with the technology advancements, the firm needs to go for providing various services *i.e.,* a core service such as offering advice, or answering queries about product shipments, supplementary service such as to offer after sales maintenance for a machine and so on invariably involving interaction between customers and the employees. Further, recognising the human element in offering such services and the immense opportunity it provides for fostering customer (external) loyalty, has resulted in many corporate houses calling for broadening the marketing concept by emphasising on the customer contact employees relationship. This aspect is explained in the figure 3.5.

Jet Airways advertises about its services and price perceived benefit value

FIGURE 3.5

THE TRIANGLE MODEL OF MARKETING

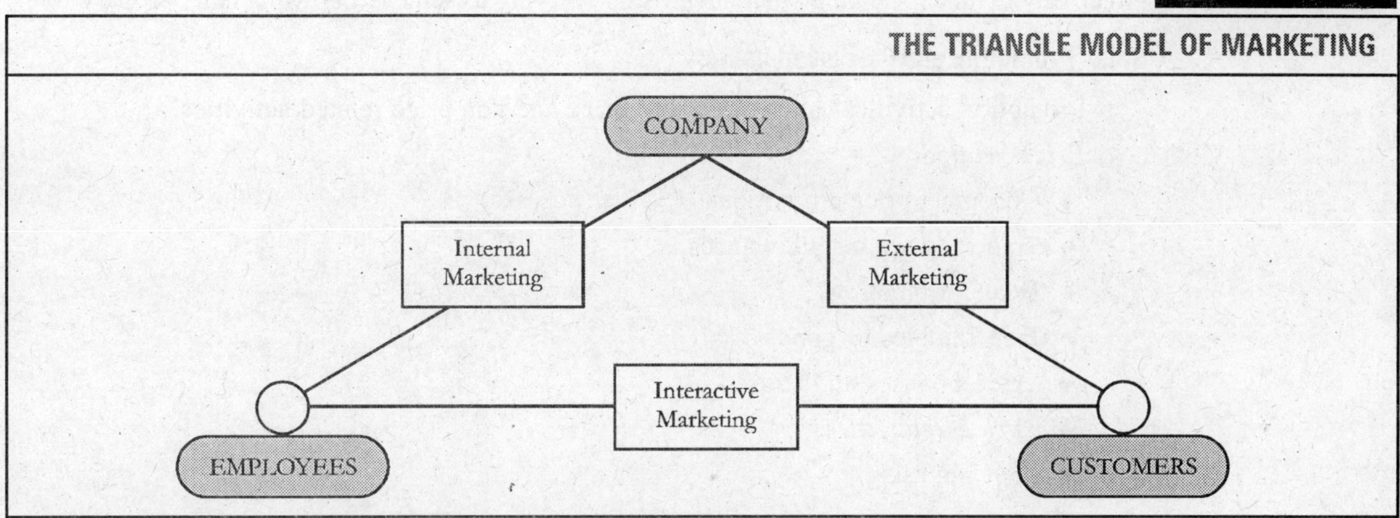

(Source : A Parasuraman "Augmented Marketing", Business Today, January 7-2, 1997)

Recognizing the human element in offering such services and the immense opportunity it provides in fostering customer (external) loyalty, has resulted in many corporate houses calling for broadening the marketing concept by emphasizing on the customer contact employees relationship.

If the employees or internal customers of an organisation are highly motivated and the firm is able to build a chain of loyal and very much involved internal customers and expose them to the external customers, the corporate house can blossom into an enterprise wide with the culture of customerisation. The pay off will be visible in "The values of customer service which will flow all over the Company" and in turn be passed on to the ultimate consumers. This will also enhance the perception or corporate image in the eyes of the consumers. The 'corporate image' of some established companies such as *Tisco, Tata Motors, Infosys, Wipro Technology* is well known. These companies have successfully created a positive image of themselves in the minds of people by adopting various means of customerisation.

Advertising and Perceived Benefit

The principle of competitive persuasion plays a big role in our decision making process. Advertising helps in the creation of images in consumer's minds. People have a lot of belief in the brand image of a product or service.

Advertising helps in converting a product into a brand by adding psychological intangibles and functional tangible value to it. The intangible values will be the self image, life style and benefits. Advertising helps in creating images and uses this image and feelings to create equity for the brand. Advertising helps to make an asset out of a product, with 'cash value'. It is through advertising that brands help in forming the basis of a company's assets and are valued on them.

Jim Young (Jim Young, How to become an Advertising Man', *Advertising Publications,* Inc. 1963) suggested five ways to make advertising work. These are :

1. By familiarising - bringing the product into common use.
2. By performing the function of 'reminding' the consumers about the product and its utility or usage.
3. By communicating or spreading news in the commercial field.
4. By overcoming inertia - the drag on human progress explained by the term 'Cultural lag'.
5. By adding value to the product through creativity.

Thus advertising helps in increasing the perceived benefit of the brand. And this can be done effectively by understanding what advertising is trying to achieve *i.e.,* what is its primary role?

Sales Promotion and Perceived Value

Promotion activities can be split into price and non price related activities.

Price related :

- Consumer price promotions
- Trade advertising allowances
- Dealer promotions
- Free samples or goods
- Trade bonuses and so on

Non price related :

- Merchandising
- In store displays
- Point of Purchase
- Coupons
- Competitions
- Premiums and so on.

Advertising helps in the creation of images in the consumer's mind. It helps in converting a product into a brand by adding psychological intangibles and functional tangible value to it.

Perceived value promotional offers from Big Bazaar

As mentioned earlier in the chapter, care should be taken that in case of price reductions, efforts are also made to re-inforce the belief of the positive worthiness of the brand by highlighting its attributes.

Further, continuous, indiscriminate and badly executed price cutting may also result in creating a negative image in the minds of the consumers. For instance, some retailers always have sale promotion programme, offering 20% or 40% discount on their products, throughout the year.

Nevertheless to ignore the role of normal price and the impact of a short term price reduction, would also be foolish or dangerous, especially when very often, for certain products, consumers make purchase decisions at the point of sale. *For example,* during festival seasons consumers may be in the mood to spend more than what they would do usually. So ideally speaking, firms have to determine beforehand their long term strategic decisions (especially in the event of wanting to beat competition) and on short term tactical pricing decisions to encourage new buyers or persuade lapsed buyers to return to you.

The role of promotion is to encourage purchase by temporarily improving the value of the brand. So value-added promotions must be used to enhance consumer's perception of the brand.

Public Relation and Perceived Value

Every firm strives to have a good relationship within the environment in which it operates. Public relation is a marketing tool used by firms to add value especially to the organisation. Public awareness and relation influence opinion of those who have a stake in the business, such that they are happy to support it.

The role of promotion is to encourage purchase by temporarily improving the value of the brand. Public relation is used to add value especially to the organisation. Personal selling through sales force is used to create and keep customers.

Personal Selling and Perceived Value

Personal selling through the company's sales force is another effective marketing tool used by the firm to create and keep customers. Few of the specific advantages that can increase the perceived value through personal selling are :

- Due to direct communication the salesperson can use this to build a more intimate relationship with the customer.
- The sales person can personalise and tailor make the offer.
- The sales person can help the customers articulate their requirements more clearly and also modify the offer so as to fit the perceived needs of the customers.
- Whenever objections are made and if it comes in the way of the perceived value of an offer, the sales person will be able to deal with them at functional as well as emotional levels.

Thus firms should make use of various marketing techniques to add value to a brand and alter or improve its perceived value.

PERCEIVED RISK

Perceived risk can be defined as the uncertainty experienced by consumers due to their inability to foresee the consequences of their purchase decisions.

The above definition talks of two relevant aspects of, perceived risk, namely 'Uncertainty' and 'Consequences'. Though consumers examine all aspects of a purchase decision *i.e.,* what to buy, how to buy, where to buy and so on, they cannot be absolutely sure about the consequences of their purchase decision. Due to this uncertainty, consumers perceive some degree of 'risk' in their purchase decision.

Perceived risk can be defined as the uncertainity experienced by consumers due to their inability to foresee the consequences of their purchase decisions. The perception of risk varies from person to person, depending on the individual, the type of product, the shopping method and the culture of the country.

The major types of 'risk' perceived by consumers when making purchase decisions are :

- *Functional risk:* The perception that the product may not function well as expected
- *Financial risk:* The risk that the product may not be worth its cost.
- *Physical risk:* The risk related to the physical characteristics or features of the product.
- *Social risk:* The risk of the product not being accepted by the society as a good choice.
- *Psychological risk :* The risk that the product choice may result in hurting and bringing down the morale and ego of the consumer.
- *Time risk:* The risk combined with the fear that the time spent in product search may be in vain if the product does not perform as expected.

The perception of risk varies from person to person, depending on the individual (his or her tolerance limit) the type of product, the shopping method and the culture of the country. The amount of risk perceived can be based on whether the consumer falls under the *high risk perceiver category* (who will make a product choice from limited choices of products) or *under the low risk perceiver* category (who will make their choices from a wide range of alternatives).

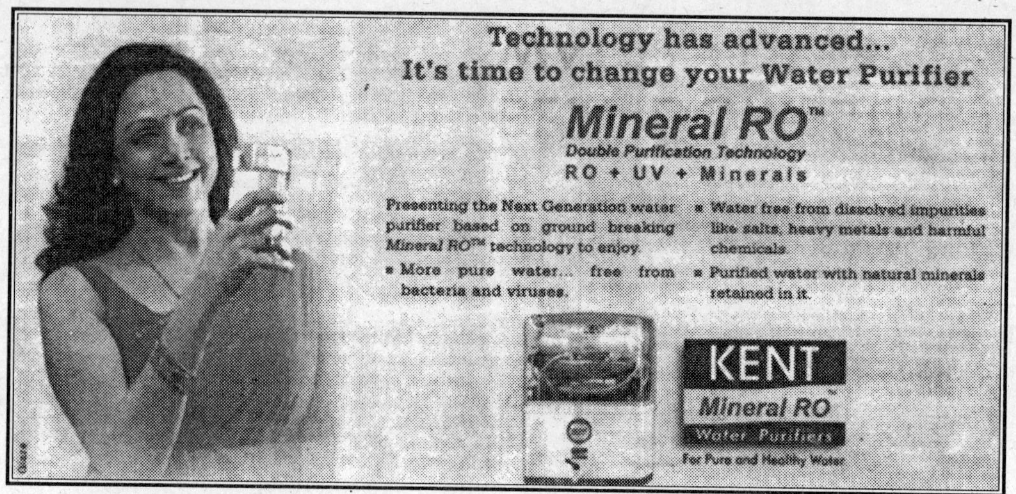

Kent Mineral RO **water purifier provides more information to reduce consumers' perceived risk**

With product categories also, consumers are likely to perceive a higher degree of risk with the purchase of higher priced products with more functional benefits than with products which do not have many technical features. The type of shopping method used by the consumer also influences his or her notion of "perceived risk", *i.e.,* direct shopping from a retail outlet or by teleshopping, catalogues, personal selling etc. In the absence of direct experience with the product, consumers tend to perceive risk in mail order shopping. But now with many channels, having introduced the consumers to the benefits of tele shopping, there is less perceived risk being associated with such shopping experiences. Each country follows it own unique culture and accordingly its people will also display varying degrees of perceived risk.

Risk Reduction Strategies Adopted by Consumers

Consumers usually develop their own strategies for reducing perceived risk. These strategies could be one of these :

Consumers Seek Information : Under this, consumers are engaged in a search for more information about the product from various sources of information (world of mouth, family, friends etc). This method is quite straight forward and logical because with more and more information available the consumer becomes more confident about his product category and brand choice thus reducing his perceived risk.

Consumers usually develop their own strategies for reducing perceived risk which could include seeking information, continuing with the same brand, going by brand image (or store image) buy the most expensive product and seeking reassurance.

Continuing with the Same Brand : Consumers try to reduce the perceived risk by avoiding changing the brand and going for new brands. Here, the consumer prefers to be loyal to the brand with which he is familiar rather than going for a change in brand.

Going by Brand Image : Marketers spend a lot of money in promoting their brands by enhancing on the perceived quality of their products and thereby creating a favourable brand image. When consumers are required to make a choice from a particular product category, they tend to place more trust and favour the product which is a well known brand. For, with a well known brand, consumers are assured of the quality, functional performance etc., which will help to reduce the perceived risk associated with the brand.

Consumer's perception of "Time Risk".

Going by the Store Image : Retail outlets also carry store image. Store image will communicate about the quality of products sold by them, assurance about good after sales service, privilege to return in case of dissatisfaction and so on. For instance, a customer may decide to make purchases from the *'Park Avenue'* outlet because he is assured of the quality of the products sold there going by the store image. This in turn will also help in reducing the concept of perceived risk if he were to buy the same from a new retail outlet (say).

Buy the Most Expensive Product : There is a perception among people that high price is an indicator of high quality *i.e.,* consumers tend to equate price and quality. Thus by going for purchasing the most expensive product, consumers will perceive that the risk factor is reduced.

Seeking Reassurance : Seek assurance by adopting the various schemes offered by companies. These schemes may include money back guarantees, warranties, samples etc.

The concept of perceived risk has many implications especially in case of new products as well as high priced goods. Thus, it is important for marketers to provide consumers with opportunities to reduce the perceived risk associated with the product, and thereby gain their confidence in the brand.

➲ SUMMARY

Perception has been defined as a process by which an individual selects, organises and interprets stimuli into a meaningful and coherent picture of the world. The basic concepts underlying the perception process such as sensation, absolute threshold, differential threshold and subliminal perception were touched upon. The external factors affecting perception are related to the physical properties of the stimulus *i.e.,* intensity, size, position, contrast, novelty, repetition and movement. Whereas, internal factors which affect an individual's perception process are related to their motives and expectations. The perceptual process involving the three components: Perceptual Selection, Perceptual Organisation and Perceptual Interpretation were discussed in detail.

Consumers have a number of enduring perceptions or images which are quite relevant to the study of consumer behaviour. It is seen that consumer's prefer brands which relate to their self perception and to their subjective images of brands. In the absence of first hand experience with the product, consumers assess its quality on the basis of certain clues which may be extrinsic or intrinsic. While taking purchase decisions, consumers will be looking at the *perceived value* aspect, which is a blend of quality and price. *Price* is perceived to be an indicator of quality, if consumers have more confidence in the source of price information. *Advertising* helps in converting a product into a perceived beneficial brand by adding psychological intangibles and functional tangible value to it. Sales promotion, Public Relation and Personal selling can help to increase the perceived value.

Perceived risk can be defined as the uncertainty experienced by consumers due to their inability to foresee the consequences of their purchase decisions. Generally, consumers develop their own strategies to reduce the perceived risk.

CHAPTER QUESTIONS FOR DISCUSSION

1. Why is important for marketers to understand the role of perceptual process in marketing? Briefly discuss the basic concepts underlying the perception process.
2. Do you feed subliminal perception works? Explain giving reference to any advertisement where you feel that subliminal perception is being used for marketing the product or service.
3. Divide the class into groups of five members each. Each group is asked to collect information on advertisements which use *Position, Novelty, Repetition* and *Movement* techniques to influence consumer perception. Discuss in class, the effectiveness of these techniques for each advertisement.
4. Briefly explain the three principles of grouping, closure and context used in perceptual organisation.
5. Interact with ten individuals (five of whom are in your age group and the other five who are at least 5 years elder to you) and determine their views on the role of perceptual distortion, quoting specific advertisements. What is your conclusion based on the interactions, in relation to age, gender or education of the sample?
6. Explain the role of consumer imagery in marketing giving suitable examples.
7. With economic recession having set in and consumer's postponing purchase decisions (unless very necessary) due to the perceived risk factor, discuss ways in which marketers of consumer durables can overcome this problem.

SUGGESTED READINGS

1. www.tatatea.com
2. L.M. Prasad " *Organisational Behaviour*', Sultan Chand & Sons, New Delhi, 1996.
3. Bennett. D. Peter, Kassarjan," *Consumer Behavior,* Prentice Hall of India Private Limited, New Delhi, 1987.
4. Kotler Philip, *Principles of Marketing,* Prentice Hall of India Private Limited, New Delhi, 1985.
5. Henry Assael, *Consumer Behavior and Marketing Action*, 6th edition, Thomson Asia pte, Ltd, Singapore, 2001, p p. 141-174.
6. *Ibid.* p.p 206-238.
7. Jagdish N.Sheth., Banwari. Mittal., *Customer Behavior A Managerial Perspective*, Thomson South Western Learning, Singapore, 2003, pp. 128-136.
8. Strategic Marketing vol III issue V, September October 2004.
9. *The Economic Times,* 'Super Brands, Bangalore, Wednesday 22, November 2006.
10. Brand Equity, *The Economic Times,* Bangalore, 13, September, 2006
11. Jagdeep Kapoor, A switch in time, *Strategic Marketing*, Jan-Feb 2006, pp. 24-27

CASE

THE WORKING OF TWO LOW COST AIRLINES

(A) FROM AIR DECCAN TO KINGFISHER RED

The initial period

Air Deccan, a pioneer in low cost flying in India, was a business unit of Deccan Aviation Pvt Ltd, a very big (India's) private helicharter company. This venture was the outcome of the hard efforts put in by its then Managing Director, Capt. G.R. Gopinath. It started its operations in August 2003, with one aircraft and four fights a day. Air Deccan's objective had been to provide offordable, reliable and speedy heliservices for company charters, tourism, medical evacuation and offshore logistics. As an airline, it had also wanted to provide better connectivity to the common man by linking various small and big sectors across the country.

In order to make air travel offordable, reliable and accessible to the common man, the airline had positioned itself as a low cost, no frills airline, where in there is no free food service, no business lounges, single economy fare for all, no frequent flier mileage etc.

Air Deccan, had revolutionized air travel in India by enabling large number of people who had never travelled by air to opt for flying by air. In fact through good route planning, it had been able to provide air connectivity to many small cities across the country. The airline had estimated to earn a decent modest profit by the last quarter of 2006.

However, the global recession had a big impact on the aviation industry, with people opting to travel by other cheaper modes of transport like the train/bus etc. This drastically affected the profitability and expansion plans of *Air Deccan*. Though, Air Deccan had learned that there is an untapped market in India, for low cost airlines, due to the economic slowdown it could not capitalize on this demand for long.

Post merger with Kingfisher Airlines

In December 2007, Air Deccan merged with Vijay Mallya's *Kingfisher* Airlines. It was felt that the combined entity, post the merger would help in cutting costs as well as increase the profitability. Then the low cost carrier was renamed (or given the brand name) 'Simplify Deccan'. Further, the trademark Kingfisher bird was added to the Deccan Logo of two hands along with the Kingfisher Airlines signature colour of red being incorporated into the Deccan aircraft, replacing it's earlier colour of yellow and white. It was decided, after the merger, that the low fare service would be available under the *Deccan brand* and premium services under the *Kingfisher brand.*

In September 2008, since Deccan had completed the stipulated five years of operation required to start flight services on international routes, it was officially announced that the name Deccan Aviation Ltd would be changed to Kingfisher Airlines. Thereafter, Kingfisher thought of adopting differential positions for using its brand to fly: *(a)* international routes and *(b)* domestic routes.

The company then announced that for all the international routes it would offer full services which the airline claimed would be the luxurious experience. Whereas, for the domestic routes, the Kingfisher brand would operate under two models *(a)* a full service carrier and *(b)* a more upgraded low cost carrier service.

Due to the global economic environment and the near recession conditions prevalent in many of the western countries, the aviation industry flight operators like Kingfisher airlines had to take a re-look at its operative plans. Kingfisher Airlines had a second rebranding for the original 'Air Deccan', which has come to be known as *Kingfisher Red.* As the term indicates, the low cost carrier arm *i.e.,* Kingfisher Red splashed it's carriers red with suitable modifications made both within and on the exteriors of the aircrafts, to clearly convey the style of the Kingfisher Airlines. From December 2008 onwards, the low cost Kingfisher has started serving hot meals and juices to its passengers at no extra cost. Kingfisher Red officials claim that *they are offering a compelling value when flying kingfisher Red.* (*The Economic Times*, 1 December 2008, P.4) This is very much unlike the other low cost airlines such as Indigo & Spice Jet which do not serve on-board meals despite charging the same fares on similar routes. The airlines has also introduced frequent flyer programme.

Thus, Kingfisher Red flyers get to enjoy more than what a typical low budget airline would offer.

(B) SPICE JET

Spice Jet is another low cost, no frills airline of India. On 7th February, 2005 *Royal Airways* (a re-incarnation of Modiluft) which was a listed airline company in India, inducted a modern fleet to launch its new low fares, no-frills brand- *'Spice Jet'*. On may 4th 2005, Royal Airways Ltd announced the name change to Spice Jet Ltd, after obtaining the due clearance from the Register of Companies. The new name was selected keeping in mind the new brand identity of the airline which is a me'lange of modern, cosmopolitan outlook and Indian ethos. Spicejet's mission statement indicated that it wanted to become India's preferred low cost Airline, delivering the lowest airfares with the highest consumer value to price sensitive customers.

Efforts to promote Spice Jet

The airline has tried to incorporate various ways to make customers get interested in flying Spice Jet.

- Spice Jet has adapted the Navitaire's software which permits direct internet distribution and ticketless travel. Spice Jet's Internet site enables passenger's to price shop, manage bookings and even select shops in advance at the time of booking.
- During the time of its launch, Spice Jet had introduced its "Ret Hot Special fares" starting at Rs. 99/- for the first 99 days of its operation. In fact within nine months of its launch *i.e.,* on 10th February 2006, Spice Jet flew its one million th passenger on its Pune-Delhi route.
- Spice Jet has integrated its unique reservation system along with various online travel service providers (make my trip. com, cleartrip.com and travelguru.com) to empower the consumers to compare and buy tickets across various low cost carriers and full service airlines. It was felt that such tie-ups or integrated service with the online service providers would help Spice Jet to penetrate various market segments with the help of the travel service companies growing customer base. Moreover, such integrated service would help the customers to "make travel simple" also.

Spice Jet is a typical low budget airline and does not offer on-board meals. More Indians are traveling for business and pleasure and yet want to save on both time and money. Spice Jet's aim has been to address these needs and also fulfill everyone's dream of flying. To ensure pleasure in flying by Spice Jet, the airlines has a new generation of aircraft fleet (with contemporary interiors, modern graphics and vibrant colours) flown by experienced pilots with an efficient crew and ground staff who make sure that customers are comfortable and feel good at the end of a flight arriving on the destination-fresh and on time.

Recognition on performance

- Spice Jet's on time performance is amongst the best in India, at 82% coupled with a Technical Dispatch Reliability of 99.6%, making it an airline with least cancellations.
- Spice Jet was recognized as Best Low Cost Airline for 2007 by TAFI (Travel Agents Federation of India) –Abacus, awarded at Kota Kinabalu, Malasia.
- Spice Jet was voted the Best Low Cost Airline by a reader's survey conducted nationally by India's Leading travel magazine, Outlook Travels (Feb 2008).
- In September 2008, Spice Jet was ranked amongst the top 10 budget airlines in Asia, by *Smart Travel Asia Magazine* based on a surveyed commissioned "Best in Travel Poll" on the low cost carriers.
- In November 2008, Frost & Sullivan, London bestowed its prestigious award *2008 Emerging Company of the year award for Indian Commercial Aviation*, on Spice Jet.

Unique marketing strategies

Spice Jet's marketing focus has been on generating positive word-of-mouth, ably supported by print and Internet media initiatives. To further build up the brand value, Spice Jet introduced on board (as well as through company's website) merchandise sales of products such as goggles, airplane models, perfumes, caps and watches.

Innovative pricing has tremendously contributed to the airlines success. Spice Jet started off its services with a revolutionary pricing of Rs 99 for the first 99 days (mentioned earlier in the case). This was followed by air tickets priced at Rs 500 and Rs 999- a pricing strategy which is continuing to be used. This, has often resulted in the airline's prices competing with first class Indian railway fares.

In October 2008, Spice Jet announced Spicy Hot Fares starting at Rs. 99 across its operating network and was to be made available till it runs out and bookings were to be open till march 2009. The airline felt that their Spicy Hot Fares would encourage more people to resume flying by air as before. In the words of Samyukth Sridharan, Chief Commercial Officer, Spice Jet Ltd" We realize that the times are difficult and challenging for industries across the globe. We want to encourage people to continue to fly in these hard times to close their business deals and visit their families and friends".

(*Source :* www.kingfisherairlines.com, www.spicejet.com)

QUESTIONS

1. In the above case of Deccan Airways (Now Kingfisher Red), do you think the company went wrong in understanding the customer's perception on traveling by low cost-carrier before its merger to Kingfisher Airlines. Why?
2. What factors do you feel have contributed to Spice Jet's perceived acceptance by customers' as "India's most preferred Low cost carrier"?
3. In view of the global economic slowdown, (which is having its repercussions on an individual's decision to travel by air), according to you what steps should be taken by Low Cost carriers to build up customer's perception that it is worthwhile traveling by low cost airlines, when compared to the other modes of transport?

CHAPTER 

CONSUMER – LEARNING

- Case : **Star Plus** – Kaun Banega Crorepati
- Defining learning
- Elements of learning process
- Types of learning processes
- Classical conditioning
- Consumer memory
- Operant or Instrumental Conditioning
- Cognitive theory
- Observational Learning or Modeling
- Low involvement theory
- Habit
- Brand loyalty
- Customer loyalty
- Summary
- Chapter questions for discussion
- Suggested Readings
- Case : **Luxor Writing Instruments Pvt. Ltd.**

CASE

STAR PLUS - KAUN BANEGA CROREPATI

In the entertainment arena, Star TV's **Star Plus channel** had been able to aggressively increase its market share, especially during the primetime right from the time it had launched its Kaun Banega Crorepati (KBC) game show. Viewers or consumers had **learned** to accept those programmes (not channels) from which they feel they are receiving high **perceived value.** Seeing the popularity of the KBC game show, the other channels such as **Sony** and **Zee** had also made an attempt at repacking the offering (Kamzor Kadi Kaun etc) - advertising about the respective game show being hosted by other popular cine stars and with bigger prize money too. However, these programmes could not gain a significant market share, probably because the viewer (and consumer) felt that they were gaining more enjoyment and satisfaction from watching KBC. This show had been so popular that consumers continued to associate the brand name KBC programme. They had learned to derive higher perceived value, enjoyment and satisfaction with cine star Amitabh Bachchan. After a time gap, the game show was relaunched as KBC-II in 2004-2005, again hosted by Amitabh Bachchan and with double the amount as prize money. The show continued to be popular though due to the host's indisposition (illness and surgery) the programme had to be withdrawn prematurely.

In the third season of **Kaun Banega Crorepati (III)** Super star Shahrukh Khan had replaced super star Amitabh Bachchan. Star India was hoping that the KBC III show, with a new host would help bring back the fragmented audience *i.e.,* a brand switch from Zee TV to Star Plus apart from maintaining its image and status value. Star Plus channel had thought that viewers or consumers will learn to associate KBC III and Shahrukh Khan and bring them back on to the star network. However, this marketing strategy of Star Plus channel did not work for long. The consumers (viewers) of Star Plus who had learned to associate Kaun Banega Crorepati (KBC-I) to Amitabh Bachchan did not continue with their loyalty in the successive game shows. There could be many arguments or views on why KBC-III did not match the popularity of the KBC-I. However, the fact remains that it is difficult to understand the 'how', 'what' and 'why' of consumer learning.

Nirma was able to secure a huge market share from HLL's Surf in the 80's by introducing a low priced detergent power Nirma to the mass market. Then Nirma tried to extend the product to the premium segment soap (**Nima**), market. But they could not replicate the success of the Nirma detergent powder because consumers were now required to learn to associate the name 'Nirma' (lower priced product) to that of a premium product Nima. The knowledge, image or familiarity that consumers have with a brand is likely to affect their purchase behaviour, or acceptance of extended products. Another product which consumers did not learn to accept is the **Kelloggs biscuits** which had bombed in the Indian market although Kelloggs cornflakes had gained wide acceptance among the Indian children.

Learning as a concept is of great interest to marketers because an insight into an individual's learning process will throw light on the what, where, how and why decisions of their consumption behaviour. This information will help them to plan marketing strategies and teach and inform consumers about their products (product attributes and benefits), where to try them, how to use them, maintain them, dispose of them and differentiate them from competitors offerings. Marketers want consumers to learn about their products (or services) through suitable communications campaigns, worked out by them. These could include direct (through advertisements) and indirect [product visibility (appearance), packaging labelling, price, and distribution] channels.

Although, we as human beings are continuously learning throughout our lives, there is not a single universal theory on how people learn. In this chapter we try to understand the role of consumers as learners. We start with discussing the various elements of learning, and then try to understand the different mechanisms of learning including consumer memory. The chapter concludes with discussions related to how habit and brand loyalty work on the principles of consumer learning.

DEFINING LEARNING 

Simply stated learning can be defined *"as a relatively enduring change in behaviour due to experience"*. But, since learning theorists do not agree on how learning takes place, it will be difficult to come up with a generally acceptable definition of learning. However, from a marketing perspective, consumer learning can be said to be *"The process by which persons acquire the purchase and consumption knowledge and experience that they apply to future related behaviour."* There are a few important aspects in both the above definitions worth noting:

The process by which persons acquire the purchase and consumption knowledge and experience which they apply to future related behaviour is called consumer learning.

- Learning involves a change in behaviour, though this change is not necessarily an improvement over previous behaviour.
- Learning is a process which continuously evolves and changes as a result of newly acquired knowledge. This consumer learning can occur with increased knowledge based on getting information from reading magazines or articles or books, through observation, from thinking or from discussions.
- The behavioural change is based on some form of practice or experience. This newly acquired knowledge and experience serve as a feedback to the person and also forms the basis for future behaviour in similar situations.

From the above definitions we can see that learning is based on two vital aspects-behaviour and experience. Though it must be remembered that all learning is not deliberately sought. Because learning can be intentional (*i.e.,* it is acquired after a deliberate attempt at a careful search for information or learning can be incidental (*i.e.,* it is acquired by accident without much effort). Intentional learning occurs when the individual is deliberately searching for information on the utility, benefits etc., of a brand, before he or she purchases the product. While incidental learning is said to have occurred when individual's learn about the brands, say, Coke, Pepsi, 7-Up etc., even though he may not have consumed the same. This could have occurred accidentally when the consumer learns of the brand, probably because of hearing about (brand) sponsored programmes on the television. This accidental learning is said to have taken place through 'hearing' the brand name, even though the individual may have been engaged in another activity say, reading a book or magazine.

➲ ELEMENTS OF LEARNING PROCESS

An individual receives a variety of stimulus inputs. When specific stimuli become associated with specific responses in a sufficiently permanent manner, the occurrences of the stimuli tends to bring out a particular response, then we say learning has occurred. But to understand the learning process, we have to consider the various components or elements of the learning process. These components are : Drive, Motivation, Cues, Response, Reinforcement and Retention.

Drive : Learning occurs because of the presence of drive. *Drive is said to be any strong stimuli that impel action.* The drive arouses in an individual an urge to respond to the stimuli and thus forms the basis of motivation. There is a lot of difference between a motive and a drive.

A motive is based on needs and goals, *i.e.,* a motive is purposeful or directed towards the specific goal while drive refers to an increased probability of activity without actually specifying the nature of the activity.

Motivation : Motivation is also an important concept for learning theory. Learning occurs because of motivation. Motivation acts as an incentive to learn. For instance, a young working executive is interested in the purchase of a (time saving) fully automatic washing machine–so she (the executive) will be motivated to get all information related to a washing machine – the features (whether it is preferable to go for a top loading washing machine, or a front loading washing machine), the various brands available, prices, quality of performance and the time saved in case of the various types of washing machines. The degree of involvement will be dependent on the consumer's level of motivation which will be seen in the way she searches for more information and tries to increase her knowledge about the product or service.

The learning process includes components such as drive (a strong stimuli that impels action), motivation (an incentive to learn), cues (any object in the environment), response (reaction from individuals), reinforcement (strengthen) and retention (stability of learned behaviour)

Drive as mentioned above will be the presence of any strong stimulus which impels action. *For example,* seeing a new washing machine at her friend's place or having seen advertisements of many new washing machines, must have acted as the "drive," for the above mentioned product *i.e.,* washing machine. So the task before the marketer is to motivate consumers by using various marketing mix elements. They can also involve the consumer's in a learning process whereby they learn to associate their (consumer) motives with the product or service offerings. But in the first place, marketers much understand that to predict consumer behaviour, they will have to establish those drives which will stimulate consumer's the most.

Cues : Cue stimuli can be any object existing in the environment, as perceived by the individual. If motives stimulate the learning process, it is the cues which serve the purpose for stimuli and gives direction to these motives. So marketers have to determine the conditions under which a stimulus (or cue) will increase the probability of eliciting a specific response. For instance, seeing advertisement for 'a package tour deal to important destinations' may act as a cue for an executive, who may suddenly realise that by going for the tour package deal, he will be able to fulfil his long cherished dream of visiting important destinations and enjoying holiday vacations with his family. Marketers attempt at using many advertising, packaging, styling, POP displays etc., to act as cues and help consumers fulfil their needs in product-specific ways.

Marketers have to take care that the cues used by them to stimulate the sale of their products are consistent with consumer expectations from the product offerings. They have to exercise care so that the cues do not to fall below consumer's expectations. For instance, high class consumers expect high priced products such as designer clothes, with matching jewellery and other accessories to be available in certain exclusive retail outlets only. Further, they also

Consumer learn to associate 'cues' with product offering.

expect the advertisements for such products to be displayed in certain elite class magazines. If such consumer expectations are not adhered to, then the product may not act as a stimuli to elicit the desired response from the target market.

We can take the example of *Lakme,* which has been able to capture a major market share of the organised cosmetics market. Lakme understood the desire of women to look ***stunning,*** young and confident with an energetic individuality. Realising this Lakme communicated about its Lakme Beauty Salons where professional beauty services are provided, through various print media. In these ads, women who look stunning with their fruity, juicy make up convey the message about energy and individuality. Any women would linger at the ad page and visualise herself to be wearing the first shack make up but she may not be familiar with all aspects of make up and beauty treatment, for which she could visit the Lakme beauty salons. The salons were the cues used by the company to motivate consumers and strengthen the brand name by working at customer contact through valuable service experience. In fact, *Lakme India Fashion Week* provides the top tier of the brand communication structure.

Response : The stimuli will result in responses. How people react to a drive or cue, *i.e.,* how they behave constitutes their response. The response may be in the physical form or may be in terms of complex phenomena such as attitudes, familiarity, perception, etc. Learning can take place even when the responses are not over.

Studies by various marketers have revealed that women (working and non working) are actively involved in purchasing or the decision making process. From automobiles to financial services, white goods and home improvement products etc., women are influencing buying

Learning can take place even when the responses are not over.

Ad uses cues to motivate consumers

decisions. So manufacturers have also learned to respond by offering women specific products and services, designed to woo this new, financially independent discerning target market.

For instance, *Hero Honda* revolutionised the Indian two-wheeler industry with the launch of its' why should boys have all the fun? Scooter *'Pleasure'*, customised for women with the focus on manageable bikes. The company claims *Pleasure* is fuel efficient and has distinct features like the tuff-up tube – a technology which offers an immediate remedy in case of a tyre puncture by secreting an antipuncture sealant gel. Further, the company also has an exclusive showroom for women customers of Pleasure called *'just 4 her,'* which offers special facilities to women customers besides after sales service. Women customers response to all the above cues was very positive and the brand has been successful in the market.

Psychologists have suggested measuring of learning process in behavioural terms, that is responses must be operationally defined and preferably physically observable. The stimuli or a need or motive may evoke many responses. As mentioned earlier cues will provide a sense of direction. But the problem arises when there are many cues competing for the consumer's attention. During such times, the response from the individual consumer will be dependent on his or her previous learning and this in turn, may depend on which responses were reinforced in the past.

Reinforcement : Re-inforcement is a very basic condition of learning. Without re-inforcement, we cannot observe any measurable modification of behaviour. Re-inforcement is closely related to the psychological process of motivation. *Re-inforcement refers to those environmental events, which increases the likelihood of specific response occurring in the future as a result of particular cues or stimuli.* The role of re-inforcements in learning has been highlighted by Edward L. Thorndike – who opines that of several responses made to the same situation, those which are accompanied or closely followed by satisfaction (reinforcements) will be more likely to recur. Those responses which are accompanied or closely followed by discomfort (negative re-inforcement or punishment) will be less likely to re-occur.

For example, suppose one is going to have a masala dosa at an Udipi restaurant. Assume a new joint has recently opened near to your college. You visit this new joint with certain expectations based on your previous experience (re-inforcements) of having a masala dosa at an Udipi restaurant. If your past experience with regard to the taste, size, ambience, service, sitting arrangements etc., had been positive, you may continue to patronice the brand, otherwise not.

Domino's Pizza have been able to create positive re-inforcement through their claim and delivery of the Pizza (ordered by the customer) in 30 minutes. Customer expectations are build up through the various promotional schemes used by the company. So when Domino's Pizza is delivered in 30 minutes, the customer will be satisfied with it. For, the customer learning takes place, especially since his or her past experience has been positive and very satisfying.

Retention : *The stability of learned behaviour maintained by the individual over a period of time is called retention.* Retention is a well learned response which is achieved with the passage of time. Thus, under repeated conditions of positive re-inforcement, there is a tendency for the conditioned response to continue for a long period of time. When a consumer is very much satisfied with a particular product or brand, he or she will learn to positively re-inforce using the product. *For example,* when a lady receives a very good response on visiting a particular retail outlet for the fist time, she will learn to positively respond by visiting this retail outlet again whenever the need arises. If she continues with this store patronage over a period of time, this learned behaviour is known as retention.

There are two types of learning processes (a) routines and (b) a more elaborate learning process.

TYPES OF LEARNING PROCESSES

Learning processes can be of two types–routines and a more elaborate learning process.

Routines : Many of the consumer behaviour occurs without the involvement of extensive consideration and reflection like – shopping in a departmental store, have a snack at the restaurant, going out for a movie with friends and so on. Such forms of consumption are routine in nature. On the other hand, the consumption behaviour involved in the purchase of a Television, a Home theatre system etc., will involve an extensive information search. Routine consumption involves a learning process, where the thinking process and actions involved are very short. Appropriate script or scheme is worked out as soon as a purchase need is felt. Such learned scripts and schemes are used when purchase decisions are made on a routine basis.

As customers we are bombarded with a multitude of products and services at the market place. But one learns to adapt and respond to the environment through the various mechanisms of learning.

We will take an example which will help to differentiate between routine and problem solving purchase decisions. In India, for most of the people, purchasing a loaf of bread is a routine process. It will involve a number of sequential steps or actions (scripts). Take money, go to the bakery, place order, pay for it and bring home the bread. But the same decision (to purchase a loaf of bread) in Japan, will become an extensive problem solving situation involving a more ***elaborate learning process***. In this situation, the consumer will be involved in obtaining information such as: Is there a bakery from where a loaf of bread can be purchased? Where is it situated? How much yen will be needed for this? Does bread exist in Japan? What is the Japanese name for bread? Is there a particular system to be followed for purchasing a loaf of bread in Japan? Will there be a difference in taste between the bread available in India and Japan and so on.

Routines help to ensure efficient consumer behaviour in the purchase of routine products. But there are different learning processes which influences purchase behaviour. These can be understood better by having a look at the "Mechanisms of Learning".

MECHANISMS OF LEARNING

As consumers and customers, we are bombarded, with a multitude of products and services at the market place. But one learns to adapt and respond to the environment through the various mechanisms of learning which are discussed below.

- Cognitive learning
- Classical conditioning
- Instrumental conditioning and
- Modeling.

There are mainly two schools of thought in understanding the process of consumer's learning: the cognitive and the behaviourist. The *cognitive school* treats learning as problem solving and concentrates on the changes in the consumer's psychological set (their attitudes and desired benefits) as an outcome of learning. Looking from this context, the cognitive school describes learning within a framework of complex decision making. But the concepts are more relevant to habit especially because complex decision making can lead to routinised purchasing when the consumer is satisfied with brand and continues to purchase it over a period of time.

The *'behaviourist school'* as the term indicates is more concerned with observing changes in the way an individual responds on account of exposure to stimuli.

Behaviour psychologists have developed two categories of learning theories :

- Classical conditioning.
- Instrumental conditioning.

Classical conditioning considers behaviour as a result of a close association between a primary stimulus (social success) and a secondary stimulus (particular brand of personal care products, clothes and accessories)

While, *instrumental conditioning* advocates that behaviour is a function of the consumer's assessment of the extent to which purchase behaviour can lead to satisfaction. Satisfaction can result in re-inforcement and an increase in the probability of repurchasing.

PAVLOV'S EXPERIMENT WITH CLASSICAL CONDITIONING

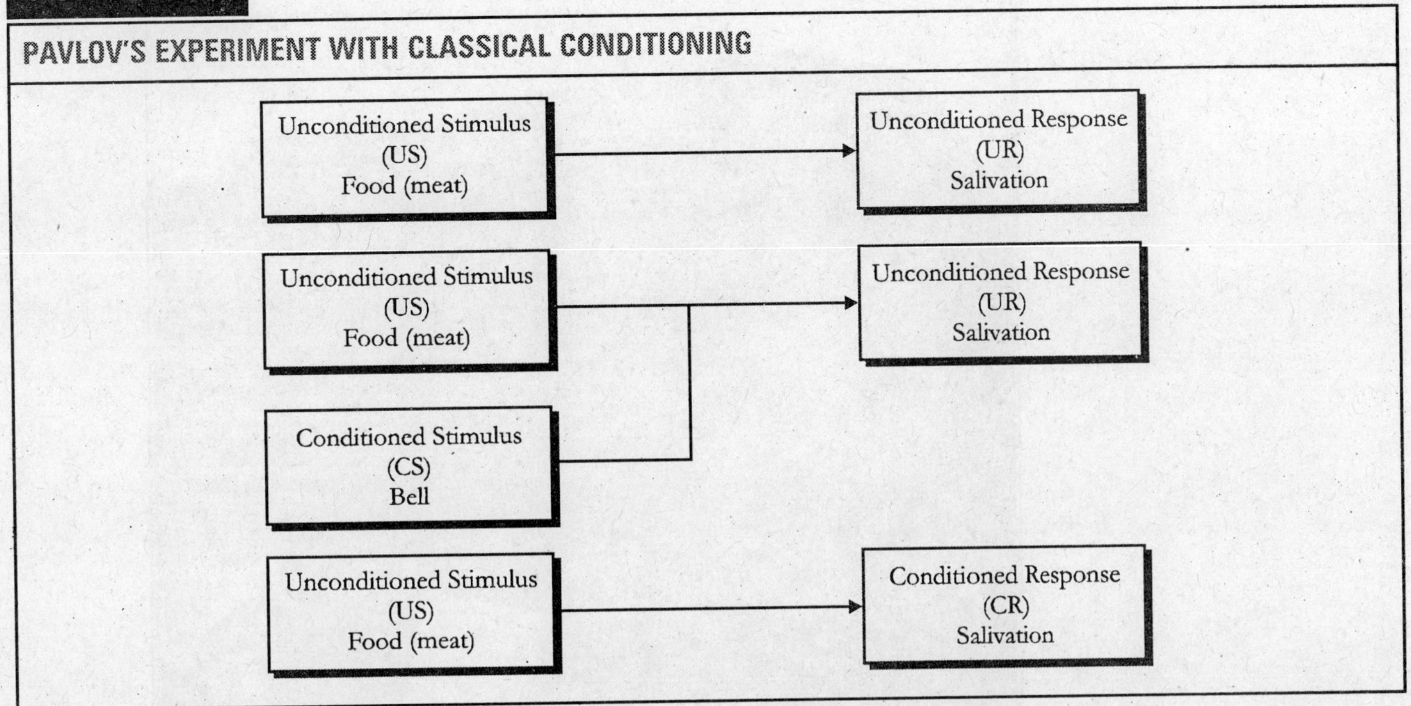

CLASSICAL CONDITIONING

Definition : *Classical conditioning is a process in which a previously neutral stimulus acquires the ability to elicit a response by repeated association with a stimulus that naturally produces a similar response.*

Thus the starting point of classical conditioning is the presence of an unconditioned stimulus (US) which results in a natural spontaneous reaction : the unconditioned response (UR). The Russian physiologist, Ivan Pavlov, was the first to suggest "conditioning" as a general model in describing how learning occurs. Classical conditioning describes behaviour as a learned process, by repetitive association between a stimulus and response (S-R. Association). Pavlov demonstrated the classical conditioning on a dog, who upon seeing food (US) starts to salivate (UR.). This phenomenon of salivation was originally studied by Pavlov as a reflex action. The classical conditioning process is shown in figure 4.1. In the experiments, when Pavlov presented a piece of meat (unconditioned stimulus) to the dog, a great deal of salivation was noticed (unconditioned response). On the other hand, merely ringing the bell had no effect on the salivation of the dog.

Classical conditioning describes behaviour as a learned process by repetitive association between a stimulus and response.

In the next step Pavlov presented meat along with ringing of the bell. To this, the dog salivated. This experiment was repeated many times. After this, Pavlov rang the bell without presenting the meat. To this the dog salivated to the bell alone (This was a neutral stimulus in the beginning of the experiment). But in the new situation, the dog becomes classically conditioned to Salivate (CR Conditioned Response) to the sound of the bell (CS).

We can see that the dog learned to associate between the signal of the approaching food and hence the reflex. The development of this dependency or association in the learning process is known as the classical conditioning. As one can observe from the above discussion, after a while,

Much of our consumer behaviour is learned under the influence of classical conditioning.

Ad uses spokesperson to provide information on the product, which can lead to associate learning

the dog started to salivate (CR) to the sound of the bell (CS). Further, unlike the unconditioned response (UR), the conditioned response can be activated without seeing the food (US).

The Pavlovian example is visible in some of the advertisements. For, instance, the visual showing children playing (or helping to clean) in the soil (US) can easily be associated with brands such as *Lifebuoy* and *Dettol,* which claim to be weapons to be used by mother's for today's inevitable battle against germs.

Long back, Ad Agency, Lintas had used an imagery and concept of a bikini clad model bathing under a water wall. The idea had been to help Indian house wives to associate the soap, *Liril* with freedom towards a world of fantasy from her mundane surrounding. Bathing or getting wet under a waterfall can also be associated with purity and closer to nature concept. Thus, both intentional and desirable associations were made for the *'Liril'* brand.

Much of our consumer *behaviour is learned under the influence of classical conditioning.* After a few visits to the *McDonalds,* one may learn to react to their logo (salivation-C.R) without necessarily even seeing any of the 'fast food items', even if one were not hungry. In consumer behaviour context, brand names and logos play the role of the conditioned stimulus (C.S). Associations are built between US (unconditioned stimulus) and CS (conditioned stimulus) through advertisements.

Information Processing and Associate Learning

Consumers process the information received based on their *cognitive ability* and the complexity of the information to be processed. They will process product information on the basis of its attributes, brand names, comparing competing brands or a combination of the above factors. *I.e.* consumers with higher cognitive ability will seek more product information and are also capable of integrating information on several product attributes when compared to consumers with lesser cognitive ability.

Consumers process information based on their cognitive ability and the complexity of the information to be processed.

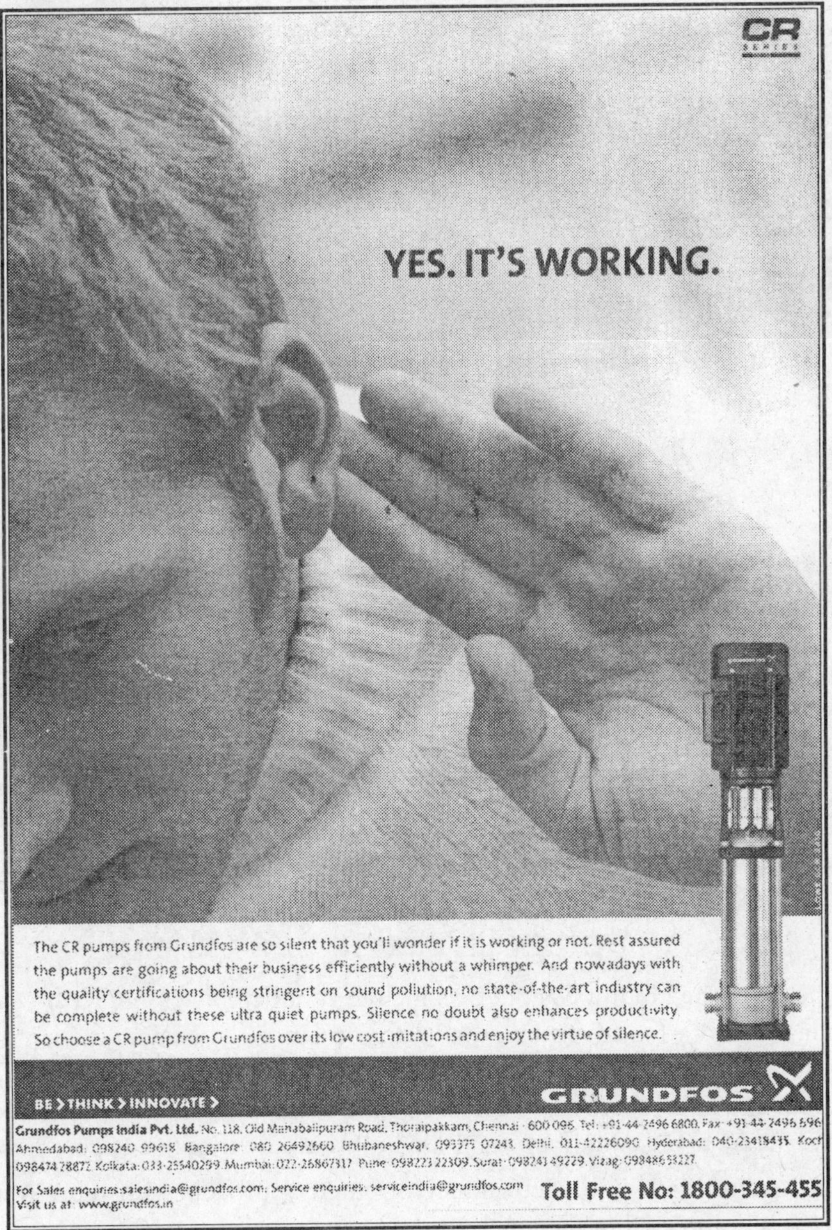

Providing product information increases cognitive ability and learning

Consumers may also vary in terms of *imagery i.e.,* their ability to form mental images which in turn can influence their ability to recall information. When a consumer has more experience or is more familiar with a product category, it increases his cognitive ability and learning during new purchase decisions.

Strategic Applications of Classical Conditioning

A brief look at the history of Indian advertising, will show that there was only a limited private sector advertising before our independence. For instance, TOMCO (Tata Oil mills Co.) launched its *Hamam Soap* in 1931, mainly by playing on the swadeshi wave. The slogan for Tata products was *'Made in India with Indian capital and management.'* But the trend had been usually to place an ad in a publication. One of the first ad campaigns to come out with a distinctly Indian flavour was the *'Dalda Vanaspati Ghee'* made into a 10 minute film. The film shows a bride's father worrying over whether he could afford to use pure ghee for her wedding feast and switching to Dalda (ad emphasizes the economics of using vanaspati ghee). Other successful ads with humour being the central theme featured mascots such as the maharaja (identified with *Air India)* and the *Amul girl* who morphs and made her sharp observations on the Indian scenario. Consumers remember the jingle *'Utterly Butterly Delicious Amul'* which made the brand very popular. Consumers learnt to associate the above brands with the theme (Maharaja Identified as the Air India Airline) or Jingle' (as in the case of Amul butter).

Consumers learnt to associate mascots (Amul Girl and Maharaja) with the respective brands Amul and Air Inida

Marketers have been using T.V. as a medium to communicate, through ads, about their brands, to consumers.

Today, with competition having increased manifold, the criteria for measuring ad effectiveness has moved from measures of association (or ad recall) to measuring a change in the consumer's psychological set.

During the 60's when Indira Gandhi became the Prime minister and Radio (Vividh Bharati Service) became a media for advertising and later on the T.V, consumers learned to associate popular brands with memorable Jingles. Some of the popular ones are : *Tandurusti ki raksha kartha hai* Lifebouy *(Life bouy Soap)*, Chehre par lao apne Hamam se nikhar *(Hamam Soap)*, Sona sona naya Rexona *(Rexona Soap)* and Dodh ki Safedi Nirma se aaye *(Nirma Soap)*

T.V. as a medium, adopted a consumer oriented approach with more variation in the advertisements being directed to the concerned consumer segment. Now, apart from repetition of ads, measures of recall are also being used to evaluate ads and determine whether basic brand associations have been established. Having entered the e-age and with the usage of computers, the advertising industry has received a boom. Electronic media (including computers) are used for special effects in TV ads while hi-tech printing ensures a good reproduction of the ads.

Today, with competition having increased manifold, the criteria for measuring ad effectiveness have moved from measures of association (such as recall) to measuring a change in the consumer's psychological set *i.e.,* brand perception and attitude change. Advertisers are also attempting to associate their brands with positive symbols and images. Few examples of ageless brands which have positive symbol association with the consumers are – *Dabur* (the proven goodness of age old Ayurveda)

Canara Bank – (serving to grow, growing to serve – motto). Some time back the Devil symbol had worked for *Onida* T.V for a long time. Then this symbol was withdrawn for some time because the marketers felt that the magic of the Devil had begun to fade. Subsequently Onida Devil had to be brought back in a new avatar in the late 2004.

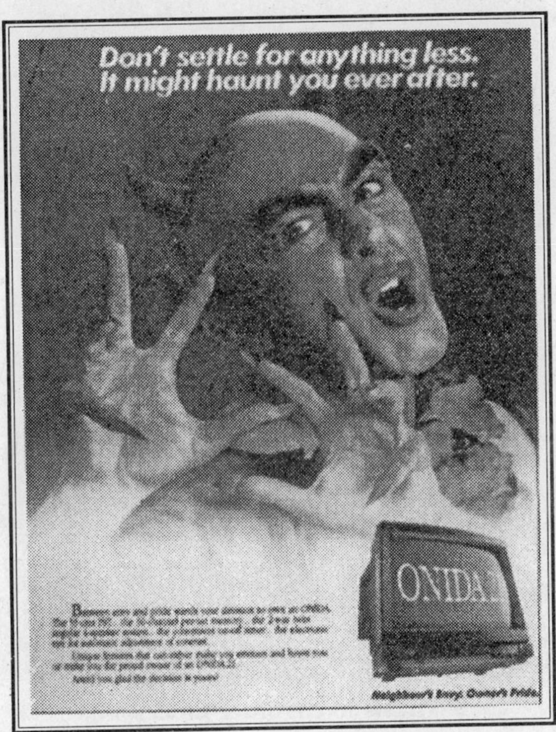

'Consumers' symbolic association with the Onida's devil

CONSUMER MEMORY

The importance of processing information can easily be linked to **consumer memory.** Marketers are interested in consumer memory since it will help to answer certain questions:

- What do consumers do after the receipt of information on products and services?
- What do consumers do after perceiving the information received?
- What is the role of consumer memory to bridge the gap between receipt of information and actual purchase?

Marketers are interested in learning about human memory because it will help them to know how consumers process information and then act upon it while taking purchase decisions.

Ad helps in cognitive processing

Merely perceiving information is not enough, marketers, also want consumers to think about the information they perceive. Usually there is a time gap between acquisition of product information and when the consumer will act upon it. This gap between information acquired and information used will be taken care by the human memory. Human memory also comprises of a multiple memory system.

In order to work upon the information or process it, the relevant information has to be retrived from inactive long memory and brought into active short term memory.

Human beings can store a huge amount of inactive memory traces, (or information) in long term memory. But in order to work upon the information or process it, the relevant information has to be retrived from inactive long memory and brought into active short term memory. We are consciously aware of information (under active consideration) and held in our **short term memory.** Since consumers are consciously aware of the contents of short term memory), they are able to perform many of the cognitive functions such as – thinking, reasoning, judging and deciding. However, the short term memory has only a limited capacity to process information. Whereas, information held in inactive long term memory is not under conscious consideration and hence cannot be used in thinking (about the price of the product) or evaluating and rating products (reasoning processes).

FIGURE 4.2

HUMAN MEMORY AS AN INFORMATION PROCESSING SYSTEM

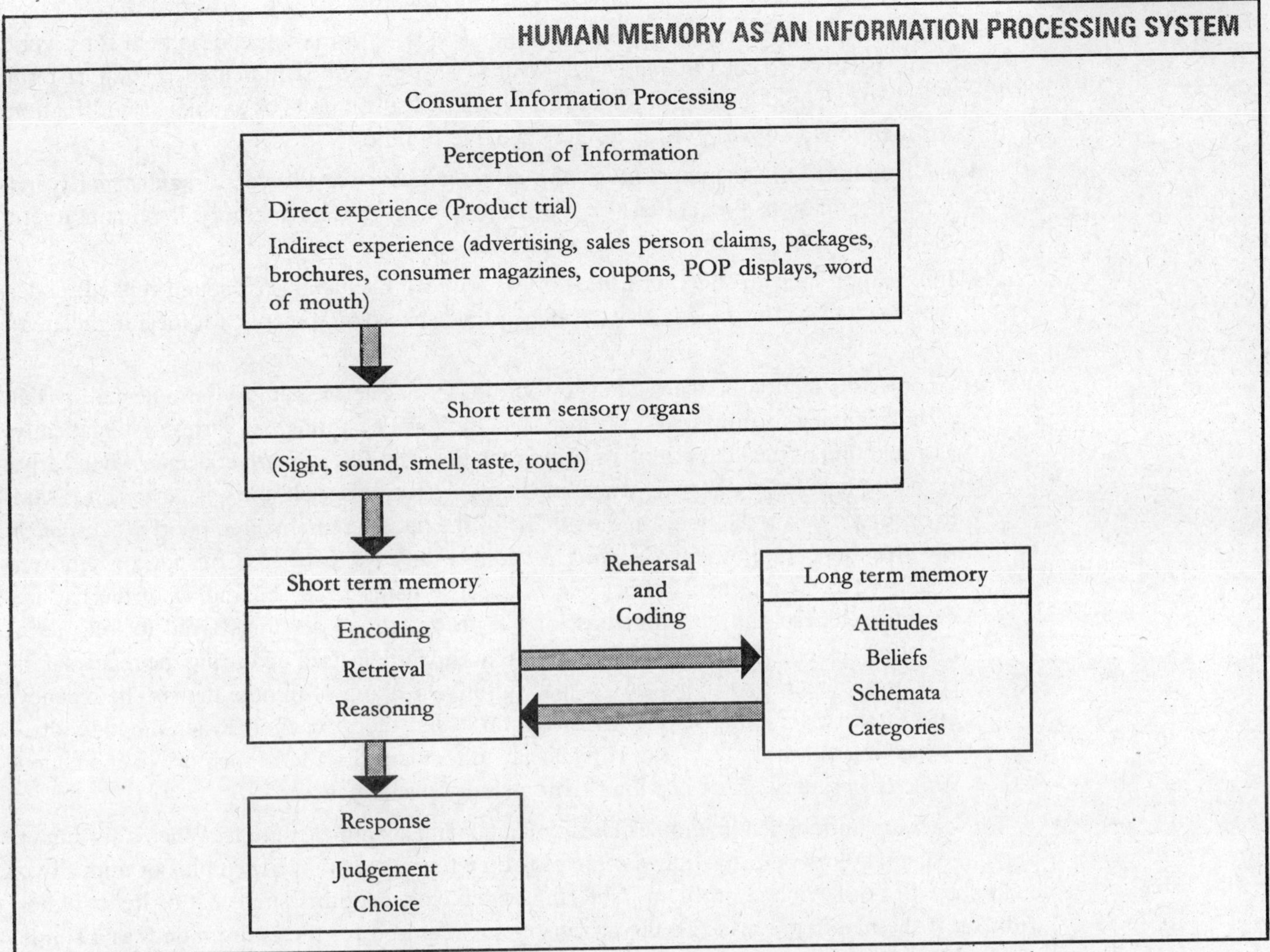

(*Source : Consumer Behavior and Managerial Decision Making,* Frank R. Kardes, 2nd Edition, Prentice Hall of India Pvt. Ltd., New Delhi, 2002, pp. 53)

As per the information processing model, information is first perceived and transferred to the sensory register. From here a part is transferred to the short term memory.

Frank Kardes says that, human memory can easily be conceptualised as an information processing system as shown in figure 4.2. He informs that most of the information processing models are build upon the Atkinson and Shiffrin 1968 model. According to this model, information is first perceived and transferred to the sensory register. Some part of the information stored in the sensory register is transferred to short term memory, which is controlled by the **attentional process**. Generally, people tend to have a limited cognitive capacity to attend to information. Consumers need to attend to product information (obtained either directly or indirectly) in order to become knowledgeable about products. Kardes has informed that at a time, people are able to attend to and process only about seven (plus or minus two) chunks of information. Further, arousal and alertness of the individual can also affect the amount of information, he can attend to. Some of the information stored in short memory is transferred to long term) memory, which in turn is controlled by **rehearsals** and **coding** process, where

- *Rehearsal means repeating information over and over again in one's head.*
- *Coding involves relating (or moving) information stored in short-term memory to information stored in long term memory.*

Characteristics of Short Term and Long Term Memory : Given below are few differences between short term memory and long term memory.

- In *Short term* memory as the term itself suggests, information can be held for a very small period of time. In fact, G.A. Miller's Study (1956) indicated that short term memory can hold information up to an average of seven units or chunks of information (as mentioned above), with a range from five to nine.
- Unlike short term memory, *long term memory* has a very large storage capacity and once information is encoded (or transferred) to long term memory it remains there permanently, unless physical damage occurs to the brain.
- Information held in short term memory is based on semantic (or sound related) code, whereas information held in long term memory is based on semantic (or meaning related) code.
- Another distinction between the short term and long term memory is indicated by the recall accuracy for information provided in the form of a long list varies systematically as a function of the position of an item in the list. The *Primary effect* occurs when early, items are recalled well, while when late items are recalled well, the *recency effect* is said to occur, however, the items in the middle of the list are remembered poorly (*Consumer Behavior and Managerial Decision Making,* Frank R. Kardes, 'Consumer Memroy', 2002, P. 55). The primary effect occurs because items in the beginning of the list are easy to rehearse and later on most of this information gets transferred to long term memory. Nevertheless, much of the cognitive capacity is used up during the rehearsal of early items, thereby leaving little capacity for rehearsing of middle items. The recency effect takes place because late items are still in short term memory when the individual is carrying out the recall task. This recency effect is a short term memory phenomenon while the primary effect is a long term memory phenomenon.

Short tern memory phenomenon can be explained with a simple example. When a consumer goes to the neighbourhood provision shop to pick up a few things (say seven plus or minus two items) she will not have any problem in storing or remembering this small list of items in her head. But if she had to purchase all the grocery items required for the entire month as a single purchase decision, then the safest way would be to write it down in the form of a grocery list.

Key Principles of Long Term Memory

The long term memory has a very large storage capacity and, information transferred remains there for a long period of time.

Various studies have indicated that long term memory has a very large storage capacity. Besides, once information is transferred into long term memory it remains there for a very long period of time (or permanently) unless the brain gets physically damaged. But, if information can be stored in long term memory permanently, then why does forgetting occur? Forgetting is not due to information loss but because one is not able to find the information desired during the memory search. *For example* students, inspite of knowing the answer to a difficult exam question are unable to recall the same while writing the examination. More the information which is stored in memory, more difficult it will be to locate one specific information. Certain instances when it becomes more difficult to locate the information from memory is when:

- One does not understand the material or
- The material was encoded into memory in a disorganised manner.

That is why it is necessary for students and managers to understand how memory operates and develop suitable strategies for studying and improving memory performance, which can help deal with forgetful consumers.

There are *three* key principles which deal with long term memory: the organization principle, encoding – specificity principle and the association principle.

The Organization Principle of Long Term Memory

Organization can be said to be the process of grouping or chunking individual pieces of information into larger units on the basis of a specific relationship between the pieces. If the pieces are in some way related, they can be grouped together and memory for the individual pieces will be greatly improved.

Various studies have indicated the importance of organization and memory. These studies demonstrated that when individual pieces of information (like words in a sentence or items in a list) which are related can be organised in some manner, the memory performance will be enhanced. Whereas, random words, items and ideas are incomprehensible and difficult to remember.

The marketing implication of the organization principle is that organised product displays will help consumers in their decision making process.

For instance, at retail outlets and supermarkets, one is able to see the organization principle in practise. At most of these outlets one gets to see similar products grouped together – say all personal grooming products (soaps, deodorants, shampoos, moisturising creams etc.) are displayed or located in the same aisle. Such organised displays will enable consumers to find the, items (or products) they need easily and quickly.

The Encoding – Specificity Principle of Long Term Memory

Long term memory is dependent on contextual clues or background. When people encode (or learn) information they wish to remember, whatever is irrelevant gets encoded alongwith whatever is relevant. The specificity principle states that memory performance is better when the same contextual cues were present during encoding and retrieval than when the encoding and retrieval environments are different.

The long term memory is based on the working of three principles namely: Organisation principle (grouping of individual pieces of information in a specific way), Encoding – specificity principle (encoding of information based on contextual clues) and the Association principle (information is stored in memory through associations between nodes)

It is possible to measure memory performance by:

(a) Asking multiple choice questions and the person is supposed to recognise the correct answer *i.e.,* through *recognition* questions.

(b) Fill-in-the-blank questions or *cued recall* questions *i.e.,* cue is given and the person is required to supply (or complete) the rest.

(c) Essay type questions where no cues are given and all information must be retrieved by the individual. *i.e.,* the *free recall tests*.

A very simple example of the memory performance based on the encoding – specificity principle can be explained by having a look at the studying style and examination hall. Students who are used to studying in a quiet room alone or in a library (people seated around quietly and reading) will be able to remember whatever studied and learned well when writing the examination in a quiet room filled with other people (say class room). This is probably because the lectures and examination are given in the same environment.

Implications for Marketing

Marketers can use the encoding specificity principle to bridge the gap between watching television commercials (or advertisements) and making purchases or shopping. Organisations

Consumer's store information in the long term memory in the form of a long list.

are using various point of purchase displays, ad in various print and mass media to provide information on specific products which will help customers remember and draw the link between the ads and shopping for those products at the retail outlet.

The Association Principle of Long Term Memory

The association principle of long term memory says that each concept or idea or piece of information is stored in memory in the form of a node (or idea) and each idea is connected to other nodes by links referred to as associations (J.R. Anderson, *Rules of the Mind*, Hilsdale, New Jersey, Lawrence Rrlbeum Associates, 1993). All the nodes and the associations between nodes together form a complex associative network, where-in all the pieces of general knowledge are interrelated with the other pieces.

For instance, if one were asked to think of *Sundrop oil,* the first thing that comes to mind is the tingle *"the healthy oil for healthy people."* The health benefits on consumption of Sundrop super refined oil are used by ITC in the form of a rational appeal in its advertising. If one were to think a little longer, other closely related ideas would occur to us. Say-the health benefits emphasised by Sundrop (easy food absorption, energy, healthcare and vitamins) are also highlighted by the other related brands such as *Gemini, Nutrela* etc. The competing brands also talk of similar benefits. Thus not only a single but there could be a string of associations between 'Sunflower oil' and healthy benefits' such as less fat content and good for the family.

Studies were carried out to understand the associative network structure of long term memory. It was seen that response time differences between propositions containing closely related versus distantly related ideas will help researchers to draw conclusions [about the precise nature of the structure] of an associate network in long term memory. It is said that merely thinking about two concepts frequently or deeply increases the strength of the association between the two concepts. Thus, when one concept is activated from memory, the other concept is also activated quickly and automatically. Further, the response speed also increases as the distance between two concepts decreases. (Frank Kardes, Consumer Behavior, 2nd Edn., 2002, PHI pp. 63).

Amul Food Festival 2007

Jawab batao,
Maharani ban jaao...

Amul MAHARANI CONTEST

TO PARTICIPATE IN THE CONTEST, PLEASE FILL IN THE CONTEST FORM BELOW
OR CALL 011 30813250* (FROM 8 AM TO 10 PM)
OR SMS 'AMUL' TO 676787*
OR LOG ON TO www.amul.com

WIN GOLD WORTH Rs.3 LAKHS

1st PRIZE GOLD WORTH Rs. 1 LAKH
2nd PRIZE GOLD WORTH Rs. 50,000 EACH
3rd PRIZE GOLD WORTH Rs. 35,000 EACH

ALSO WIN 100 AMUL GIFT HAMPERS
LAST DATE FOR RECEIVING ENTRIES: 15TH FEBRUARY 2007

Amul tries to enhance consumer memory performance through contests involving cued recall questions

Storing Information in Long Term Memory

Information is stored in long term memory in the form of *images* which could be a reflection of our memory of past events *(episodic memory)* or in the form of words or sentences which reflect facts and concepts remembered by us *(semantic memory)*.

Consumers memory of any brand is in the form of words and images. The word *Rasna mango* may evoke words such as *soft drink* concentrate and the highly popular line *'I love you Rasna'*. It can also evoke images learned from past experience and advertisings such as sense of taste (Fresh and juicy), and happy children. Another example is of *Cherry Blossom shoe polish*. The words and images that are associated in the long term memory with Cherry Blossam polish (a node) are Charlie Chaplin, easy to use and quick shine.

Amul Doodh – Images or nodes consumers associate with Amul Doodh are milk, health and happiness.

Information is stored in consumer memory in the form of images or words, which are associated with the brand.

Or take the example of *Garden* Sarees (a node) which consumers can associate as sarees, that can make one look sensuous youthful and with full vitality. The nodes associated with a particular brand represent beliefs about them (Rasna, Cherry Blossam polish and Garden Sarees in the above examples). Such a clutter of beliefs is called a schema, which in the context of memory processes occuring when a particular node (or brand) elicits a cluster of other nodes.

Consumer memory of *Garden* is that it's sarees convey a feeling of sensuous, youthfulness with vitality

The consumers, on the other hand find it hard to select the most satisfactory products due to the small differences between the products and brands. So they feel that by paying close attention to these differences, stimulus discrimination can be achieved. Sometimes, a small difference (deduction) in price may be large enough to be discriminated or distinguished by consumers. It is observed that discount offerings of less than 10% are not seen as real advantages by consumers. Simply stated, firms must ensure that 'special offers' are seen as a price or value improvement above the level as perceived to be improvements in the eyes of the consumers.

Retrieval of Information

According to Henry Assael, consumers filter information through short term memory and store it in long term memory, from where it can retrieved (refer to figure 4.3). While retrieving information from long term memory, consumers will briefly store it in short term memory and use it for evaluating brands. In the process of evaluating, they will activate some key pieces of information.

Consumers filter information through short term memory and store it in long term memory from where it can be retrieved and used for evaluating brands.

There are **three factors** which will help to retrieve information from long term memory: Activation, placement and transfer.

- **Activation :** For retrieval to take place, the linkages between nodes have to be activated. Marketers try to provide positive linkages to a brand by going for repetitive advertising. Repetition will help strengthen the linkages between nodes over a time period and also reinforce a positive brand image.
- **Placement :** The second process necessary for retrieval is placement which will determine the other nodes to which consumers, will connect the activated node. A college student buying a digital camera may connect *Canon* to processing quality picture on the basis of information received.

FIGURE 4.3

A MODEL OF INFORMATION PROCESSING

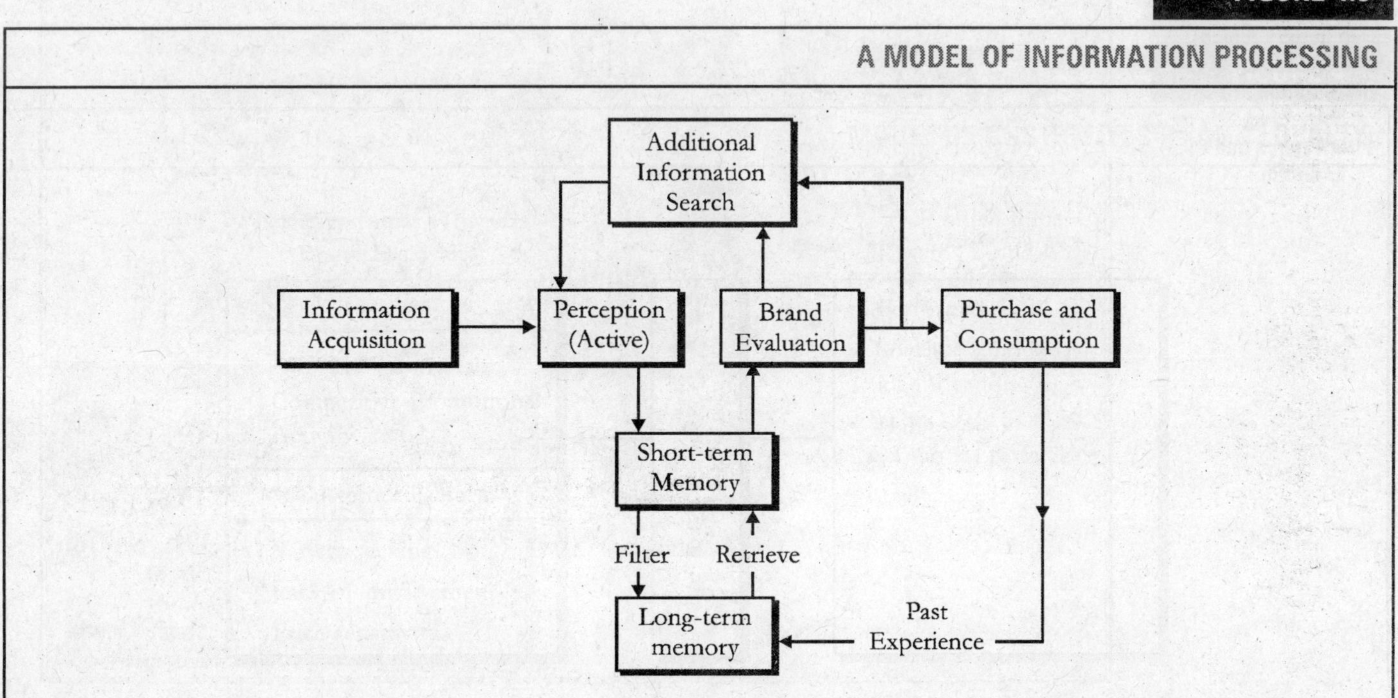

(*Source : Consumer Behavior and Managerial Action,* Henry Assael, 6th Thomson Learning, Singapore, 2001, pp. 53)

- **Transfer :** The third factor required for retrieval is a transfer process which will determine the information consumers will retrieve from long term memory and put in short term memory. Usually, consumers will transfer information which has the highest potential utility and is important in making a decision.

Simultaneously, there are also three factors which inhibit retrieval : Forgetting, Interference and Extinction.

- *Forgetting* refers to the inability of the consumer to retrieve information from long term memory for a period of time. Moreover, in such instances any subsequent attempt to retrieve information may also fail.
- *Interference* takes place when related information node will block the recall of the relevant information. For instance, an advertisement by *Subhiksha* for discounted prices of grocery may cause a consumer to lose the connection in long term memory between discounted prices and *Food Bazaar* because of the strength of price discounts – *Subhiksha* connection.
- *Extinction* refers to changes in linkages in long term memory: *For example*, we assume that a consumer reads somewhere that in Food Market store vegetables, artificial pesticide is used and this reduces the real nutritional value. For this consumer, the linkage between Food Market store and, "grown organically" is broken, and this brand could easily face extinction from the consumer's long term memory.

The three factors which help to retrieve information from long term memory are Activation, Placement and Transfer. Simultaneously, the three factors which inhibit retrieval of information are Forgetting, Interference and Extinction.

Related information from *Food Bazaar* and *Subhiksha* could inhabit retrieval of information from long term memory.

OPERANT OR INSTRUMENTAL CONDITIONING

Definition : *Operant conditioning is a type of learning in which the consequences of Behaviour lead to changes in the probability of that behaviour's occurrence.*

American psychologist Furrhus Skinner is known as the discoverer of operant conditioning. According to him, the process of operant or instrumental conditioning rests on the unconditioned stimulus (US) after certain behaviour is shown. The unconditioned response is said to be the positive or negative re-inforcement of the performed behaviour. The effect of operant conditioning is based on the strengthening or weakening of the performed behaviour. A positive stimulus (reward) increases the chances of the given behaviour being performed again (strengthening). On the other hand, a negative stimulus (punishment) reduces the chances of a given behaviour being repeated again. According to Skinner, most of the learning takes place in a controlled environment, wherein the individuals are rewarded for the selection of an appropriate behaviour. While analysing consumer behaviour, it can be said that as per instrumental conditioning, consumers learn through a trial and error process, in which some purchase behaviour can have favourable outcomes or rewards while other purchase behaviours may not have such favourable outcomes. So a favourable experience is instrumental in encouraging the individual to repeat the purchase behaviour.

While analysing consumer behaviour as per the instrumental conditioning it can be said that consumers learn through a method of trial and error, in which some purchase behaviour can have favourable outcomes while others may not be so favourable. And it, is such favourable experiences which is instrumental in encouraging the individual to repeat the purchase behaviour.

Any lesson on instrumental learning will not be complete if we don't mention about skinner's work. Let us have a brief glimpse of the work carried out by the Father of behaviourism, Dr. B.F. Skinner. Skinner advocates that behaviour occurs because it is re-inforced or rewarded. Skinner, in his experiment, had placed a pigeon in a box (Skinner Box) equipped with a key (or switch) which is wired to a data recorder along with a food dispenser. Each time the pigeons pecked the switch, a premeasured quantity of food was dispensed. Once the pigeons' realised this contingency they would consistently display this pecking behaviour each time they were in a state of food deprivation. Skinner argued that the pecking behaviour displayed by the pigeons was because of "external" re-inforcements or rewards and thus there was no need to invoke "internal drivers and states". Similarly, Skinner stated that human behaviour can be shaped or modified by rewarding that behaviour. Simply put, human beings can be made to learn a behaviour by providing re-inforcements or rewards.

Instrumental conditioning in the marketing context can be explained with an example. We presume a person can behave in three ways, A, B or C (as shown in the figure 4.4 below)

FIGURE 4.4

THREE TYPES OF RE-INFORCEMENT IN OPERANT CONDITIONING

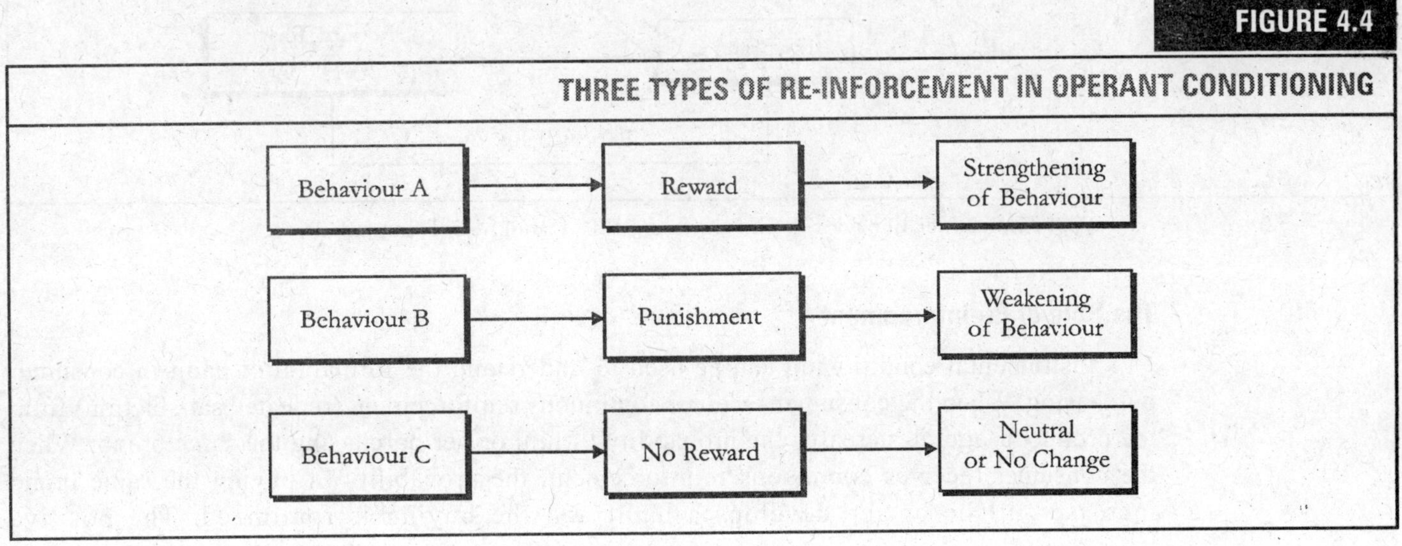

For example, a teenager may use a '*Elle 18*' range of nail polish and receives many compliments for it. She will therefore start using this nail polish more often. This is behaviour A, which is followed by a reward and is therefore strengthened. Now one evening she may try out another nail polish, for which she is mocked at or laughed at by her friends. This will result in 'B' type behaviour; This incident will weaken her desire to use this nail polish again in the future. And in case of the third type of behaviour 'C' there is no reward or punishment and so her behaviour will not be strengthened or weakened.

Instrumental conditioning requires the development of a link between a stimulus and response. Usually, the consumer (or individual) will select the response which provides him or her the greatest satisfaction.

The purchase behaviour is influenced by operant conditioning say a college student may try out many after shave lotions before deciding on a particular one that he feels will suit his personality (positive re-inforcement). The student is said to be engaged in instrumental learning. And if he is appreciated for his ruggedness and choice of after shave lotion, he will continue to purchase this product. This model of instrumental conditioning is shown in figure 4.5.

Thus instrumental conditioning requires the development of a link between a stimulus and response. The individual will select the response which provides him or her the greatest satisfaction. So, there is no previous stimulus-response connection and the response is based on the conscious control of the individual. Ads communicating about the adverse effects of consuming tobacco or betal nuts work on the principles of instrumental conditioning by linking their consumption to cancer. Such a link is conveyed to create an avoidance of consuming (such) harmful products.

FIGURE 4.5

A MODEL OF INSTRUMENTAL CONDITIONING

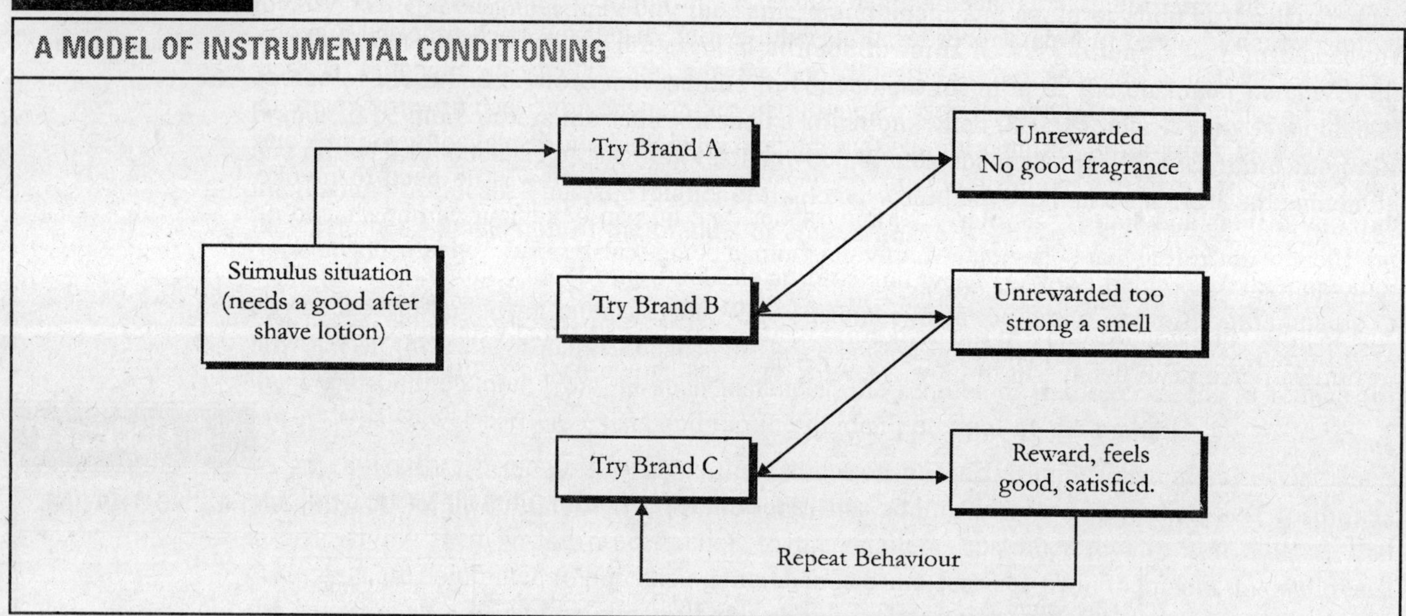

(*Source:* Consumer Behavior, L.G. Schiffman, L.L. Kanuk, 8th Edn., p.222)

The Role of Re-inforcement

Instrumental conditioning can be used to understand the formation of habit in consumer purchasing. When the consumer receives continuous reinforcement (repeated satisfaction) from the product usage, it increases the probability of him or her purchasing the same brand. When the consumer receives continuous re-inforcement, the probability of buying the same brand increases till he or she develops a habit and the buying is routinized. The positive re-inforcers can range from the products (brand name), positive word-of-mouth from friends /neighbours/peer group or reputation of the dealer, quick and good after sales service etc.

However, if the consumer is not satisfied with the product then the subsequent behaviour would lead to the consumer ceasing to buy by habit. This could result in a process of **extinction** (elimination of the link between stimulus and expected reward) or **forgetting** (when the stimulus is no longer repeated or perceived). These two terms have already been discussed earlier in the chapter.

Timing of Rewards

In the operant conditioning process, it is not necessary to reward the behaviour each time. This is based on the fact that a reward given occasionally is more effective than giving one each time.

When consumer receives continuous re-inforcement,the probability of purchasing the same brand increases till he or she develops a habit and the buying is routinized. In the operant conditioning process, timing of rewards (given for the behaviour) can also influence the purchase behaviour.

If a reward is given for some behaviour, it is referred to as a ratio reward. The ratio reward can be either a fixed ratio re-inforcement or a variable ratio re-inforcement. Whenever, rewards of stamps or sales coupon are given for a fixed time schedule, it is called a fixed ratio schedule. Such schemes can also result in strengthening brand and store loyalty. Rewards for answering quiz questions, lotteries etc. have a chance of reward factor involved, thus they form a part of variable ratio schedule.

More often, the time schedule rather than a ratio schedule of re-inforcement is followed. This fixed time schedule like *Bata's* or *Arvind store's* sale *i.e.,* factory seconds sale or the new year discount offers which generally attract bargain hunters who may not return to shop until the next sale. The variable time schedule can be offerings of small rewards. For instance, during exhibitions of consumer durables, some of the participating consumer firms may announce every tenth customer who walks into their stall will receive a free gift. Under the fixed ratio schedule every customer gets a coupon. A variable ratio schedule is less expensive as compared to a fixed ratio schedule.

Positive and Negative Re-inforcement

In operant conditioning process, Skinner talks of two types of re-inforcements which can increase the chances of a response being repeated. These are:

- *Positive re-inforcement :* This communicates the positive response and the likelihood of a specific behaviour in the positive direction.
- *Negative re-inforcement :* This is an indication of a negative or unpleasant response in the form of a specific negative behaviour.

In operant conditioning, there are two types of re-inforcements which can increase the chances of a response being repeated. These are positive reinforcement (positive response indicating the likelihood of a specific behaviour in the positive direction) and Negative re-inforcement (unpleasant response in the form a specific negative behaviour).

Using of a herbal anti bacterial disinfectant and pore cleanser such as *Nomarks* or *Eraser* which minimizes the re-occurrence of pimples is a positive re-inforcement and increases the likelihood of a repeat purchase. Fear appeals in ad messages are examples of negative re-inforcement. The fear of aversion from peers and friends due to body odour or using fairness cream meant for the fairer sex. Ad of *Lifebuoy plus soap* or the *Fair and Lovely fairness cream* for men uses negative re-inforcement to illustrate the effectiveness of the above product brands. Other examples of negative re-inforcement can be the advertising of '*Saffola Oil*' (fear of losing your husband), as well as the advertisements of most of the life insurance companies such as *LIC, ICICI-Prudential, HDFC standard life, Tata AIG* and *Aviva.*

Ad acts a positive re-inforcement for individuals undergoing stress

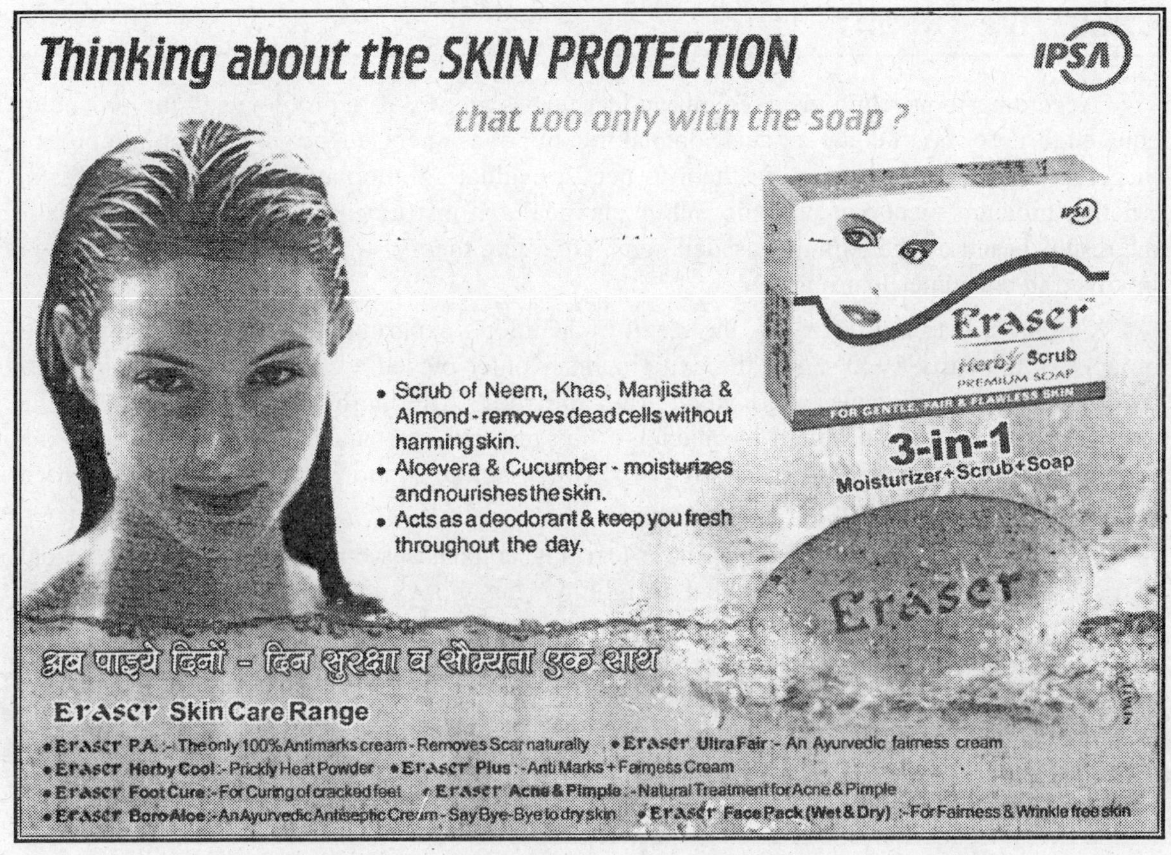

Ad suggests use of *Eraser skin care range* of products, a positive re-inforcement to protect one's skin.

Marketers use either positive or negative re-inforcement to drive home a point and elicit the desired response.

Critics have opined that a considerable amount of learning can also take place in the absence of direct re-inforcement.

Instrumental learning theorists have opined that learning takes place through a process of trial-and-error due to habituation on the basis of rewards received for certain responses or behaviour. So a consumer, over a period of time is able to identify the retail outlet selling the brands preferred and then he will soon develop store loyalty (positive re-inforcement).

There is some criticism on this theory, that is the critics have opined that a considerable amount of learning can also take place in the absence of direct re-inforcement. They have observed that individuals also learn by observing the behaviour of others. Like teenagers observe the lifestyle of their idols and youth icon (their dressing style etc.) and then also try to imitate it.

TATA AIG LIFE INSURANCE

'Ad indicates a connection between thinking ahead and living the life of one's dream post retirement with Tata AIG Life Insurance'

Of course, now life-insurance is no longer a sober, serious, investment driven by necessity, security needs and fear. It is a combination of both positive and negative re-inforcement. *i.e.,* apart from taking care in case of one's untimely death, it is also a positive empowered choice and decision to grow one's wealth and have a fun filled life. The ad on *Tata AIG Life Insurance* reflects shade of this learned shift in consumer behaviour.

COGNITIVE THEORY

According to psychologists, cognitive learning is viewed as a problem solving procedure and equated to the process of complex decision making.

According to psychologists, cognitive learning is viewed as a problem solving procedure equated to a process of complex decision making. For consumers, cognitive learning is a process of perceiving stimuli, associating them to needs, evaluating alternative brands and assessing whether products meet expectations. While classical and instrumental conditioning emphasize the results based on the stimulus associations' cognitive theory stresses on the thought process involved in consumer learning.

Cognitive learning theory is, the result of 'Kohler's experiments which were carried out on apes in the early 1920's. For the experiment, Kohler placed a chimpanzee in a cage with several boxes, and bananas were hung from the roof. After failing to reach the food, the chimpanzee solved the problem by placing a box under the bananas. Thus, it was concluded that learning was not a result of contiguity between stimulus and response or re-inforcement but the result of thought process and insight.

As shown in figure 4.6 the cognitive learning emphasises on the recognition of a goal, purposive behaviour to achieve the goal, insight to bring about a solution and goal achievement. Re-inforcement is very much a part of cognitive learning as there must be an awareness of goal achievement for learning to take place. Further, the nature of the goal is understood from the beginning and the reward (*for example* eating banana as revealed in the experiment) is also anticipated.

FIGURE 4.6

COGNITIVE THEORY WITH EMPHASIS ON PROBLEM SOLVING

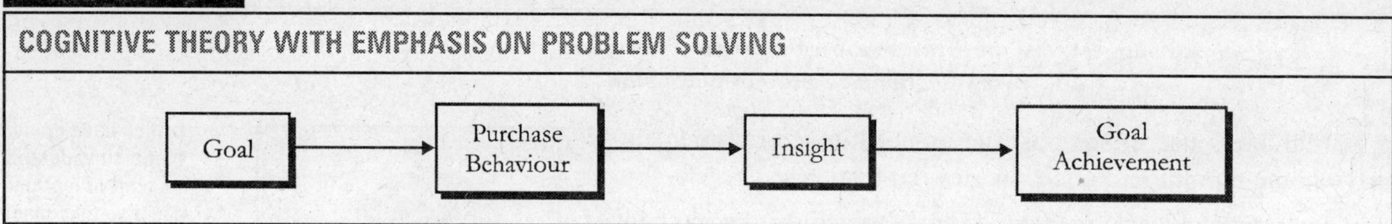

(*Source : Consumer Behavior and Managerial Action,* Henry Assael, AB, Singapore, 2001, pp. 108)

OBSERVATIONAL LEARNING OR MODELING

The learning processes under classical and operant conditioning are more or less mechanical. In cognitive learning it has been discussed that considerable amount of learning takes place because of consumer thinking and problem solving. There is another form of learning which is based on the social aspects and the imitation of other's behaviour, as a 'model'. This means that the model person serves as an 'ideal' and their behavioural pattern will be the goal for others to follow. Psychologists Neal E.Miller and John Dollard have tried to explain this type of imitative behaviour or modeling. They opine that individuals try to imitate the behaviour of those who are (seen as being) rewarded because they themselves would like to be rewarded by imitating (or adopting) that behavior, either by the concerned person (model himself) or by those who admire the model (Customer Behavior, Jagdish Sheth, Banwari Mittal, Thomson South Western, Singapore, 2003. pp. 141-142). This is also referred to as vicarious learning.

According to observational learning, a lot of emphasis is based on the imitation of the behaviour of the model. As per our Indian culture, elders have always been respected and emulated. But now there seems to be a change in the trend. There seems to be a preference to imitate the behaviour of those occupying a higher social status. For instance this aspect of modeling is visible when, the middle class consumers try to imitate the behaviour of the upper class (or rich).

Ads depicting how consumers learn by observation

Observational learning or Modeling is based on the social aspects and imitation of other's behaviour as a model. *i.e.,* the model person serves as an ideal' and their behavioural pattern will be the goal for others to follow.

Marketers have realized the significance of consumer's imitative behaviour and tried to influence it through usage of models in the advertisements such as *Gilette Vector Plus*, *Hero Honda Super Splender*, *Kellog's, Mrs. Marino* etc., It is assumed that such advertisements may result in the optimal use of a product. Instructions on how to use the product or demonstrations suggest to follow or imitate the behaviour of the person demonstrating the same. Demonstrations in case of consumer durables like vacuum cleaner (*Eureka Forbes*) or washing machines (*Whirlpool*) have followed the principle of imitation. Similarly, persons who are good at culinary art, *e.g.,* Sanjeev Kapoor have released a videotape of cooking course to enable the buyers to imitate the behaviour of the model. It has been observed that the learning process takes place faster through imitation than when compared to following the trial and error method.

Through observational learning or vicarious learning, people try to imitate the behaviour of others by observing them. Of course, the consumer should feel that the behaviour of the person being observed is worth imitating. *For example,* consumers fond of diamond jewellery should feel it is worth, purchasing **Nakshatra jewellery**, endorsed by film star Aishwarya Rai, then only would they purchase the same. Consumers (including children) observe how other persons behave in response to certain stimuli (or situations) and the resulting re-inforcements, and then emulate or imitate the positively reinforced behaviour when required to respond in a similar situation. *For example,* beyblades had some time back become an obsession with children.

This is because fast spinning tops that are activated by pulling hard on an attached rip cord, 'beyblades' was the weapon of choice of online hero Tyson in the Cartoon Network's popular show *Toonami*. Thus, Funskool's *beyblsades* created a massive interest and demand among children who wanted to emulate the actions of the animation hero Tyson.

When attractive models or users are shown having experience with the products or services such as cosmetics / jewellery / perfumes or personal care products, it will communicate social success and thus gain acceptance among consumers. At times, typical customers are shown providing testimonials for certain products such as *Sparsh* baby soap, *Kellogs cornflakes, Bournvita, VLCC, Whisper Ultra, Dove soap, Gillette Vector Plus Shave* etc. In all the above examples, the target consumers will learn to associate the actions of others to some positive consequence and then emulate those actions.

On the other hand there could also be situations *i.e.,* negative outcomes of certain actions, resulting in others avoiding them. *For example* the social embarrassment of not using a proper tooth paste *(Closeup)*, unkept rough hair *(Sunsilk Shampoo)*.

Certain features which consumers accept while observing 'models' who are worthy of imitation include: suitability, relevance, consistency and re-inforcement.

(A) (B)

Ads convey the negative outcomes when one doesn't take care of oral hygiene (Colgate Active Salt) and insurance (ICICI Prudential).

There are certain features which consumers accept while observing 'models' who they feel are worthy of imitation.

- **Suitability** of the model endorsing the product is worthy of imitation Example : mother's concern for baby *(Johnson & Johnson baby care products*).
- **Relevance** of the model in the social learning process. *For example*: 'Sports stars' Shewag and Sachin Tendulkar talk of the sporty and supplementary *Energetic drink - Boost*.
- **Consistency** in the behaviour of the model. There should be consistency in the behaviour of the model which helps in the learning process (*Bajaj* lights has been consistently used throughout the model's life cycle).
- **Re-inforcement** behavioural response is very often conditioned by re-inforcement (Rewarding experience of patients using Dr. Batra's medicines).

'Consumers learn to imitate the behaviour of models'

Television advertising does not involve extensive information seeking and processing. Here through repetition of the ad, learning can take place in the form of low involvement and unnoticeable steps.

LOW INVOLVEMENT THEORY

Television viewers and print media readers may not be consciously processing the information received from the advertisements seen by them because these are presented to them in an uninvited manner. So the question is – Do consumers learn anything from the advertisements, when there is no involvement from their side? The answer to this would be sometimes 'no' sometimes 'yes". The reason for this can be understood by having a look at the low involvement learning theory.

Television advertising will not involve extensive information seeking and processing. Within a span of less than a minute the advertiser's aim is to bring about a positive brand awareness and attitude towards the product. Through repetition of the ad, learning can take place in the form of low involvement and unnoticeable steps.

Many advertisers go for three exposures of the same advertisement. They believe that the level of involvement during message processing plays a crucial role in determining which route of persuasion is likely to be more effective. During the *first exposure* of the ad to the consumer, an attempt is made to form an identification and assign the message to the product category. The advertiser tries to build up the likeability of the product. On the *second exposure*, the consumers' may feel the message is becoming personally relevant. That is, the consumers' involvement increases and so they are likely to form their attitudes or choices on the message contents. It is on the *Third exposure* that the consumers really see the product and get the real meaning or message of the advertisement. After this, further exposures will serve as reminders. For simple messages, one exposure is enough but if complex messages are to be communicated then more exposures may be necessary. So depending on the contact frequency and the target audience, a suitable strategy on exposure has to be worked out.

From the marketing point of view it can be seen that consumer's involvement is related to their purchase decision. That is, there is high involvement from consumer's when the purchases are very important to them (say, if the *perceived risk* factor is high) for them they are likely to be engaged in an extensive problem solving (information processing) situation. *For example,* the purchase of a car is a high involvement purchase decision because of the perceived high financial risk involved. Whereas, the purchase of products such as washing powder, toothpaste etc. are low involvement purchases holding little relevance and less perceived risk, resulting in very limited information processing.

From the marketing point of view, consumer involvement is related to their purchase decision. *i.e.,* when the purchases are important there is high involvement where as, in the purchase of routines, due to less perceived risk there is little information processing.

This low involvement theory is also known as the ATR Hierarchy (Awareness, Trial, Re-inforcement/Repeat). One of the effects of low involvement learning is that it may attain a passive registration in the mind. This could be to say that the consumer may not remember the commercial or even think about it but may recognize the brand in the shop. In this case, the consumer may purchase the brand and the learning process will only begin after he or she starts using it. Thus prior product knowledge or formation of attitude is unlikely to take place before the product usage. If positive usage experience takes place, then it can be called as operant conditioning. Because favourable experience can be rewarding and may lead to repeat purchase, while unfavourable experience will be seen as 'punishments'. Advertising can help in the confirmation of favourable experiences. These are briefly put in the Figure 4.7 showing classical conditioning (associations between brand name, people and situations), observational learning (consumers imagining to behave as the model after observing the latter) and operant conditioning (reward after favourable product experience or punishment after unfavourable experience).

➲ HABIT

Habit can be defined as repetitive behaviour resulting in limited or no information seeking and evaluation of the brand choices. Over a period of time when consumer satisfaction is experienced, learning leads to habitual purchasing behaviour with hardly any information being sought for brand evaluation. This habitual behaviour can also be defined as routinized decision making.

When consumers make purchases by habit, since they are involved with the product, it reduces the risk of product failure. Incidentally, when limited information is available, consumers buy the most popular brand as the safest choice. Habit also facilitates decision making by minimizing the need for information search which results in routinised decision making.

FIGURE 4.7

LEARNING HIERARCHY UNDER LOW INVOLVEMENT

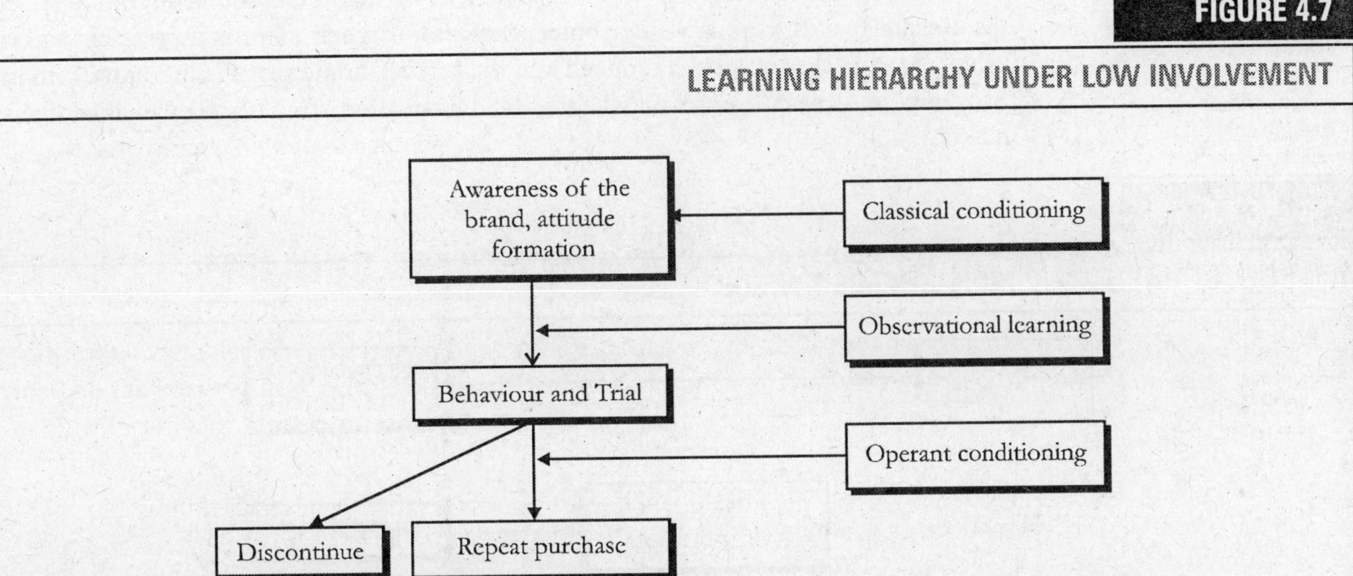

A Model of Habitual Purchasing Behaviour

A model showing the process of habitual purchasing behaviour is shown in figure 4.8. We will understand this process by taking the example of a consumer who has become a regular purchaser of **Pepsi**. This choice decision is based on past experience and satisfaction. Say, the need arousal may occur simply because the consumer is feeling thirsty and realises that he is out of stock of Pepsi.

Recognition of a need (thirst) is likely to directly result in an intention to buy, with limited information processing. Probably being out of stock of that brand may be a sufficient reason to include Pepsi to the shopping list or say, the consumer may be reminded of Pepsi when he sees it during a trip to the super market. Being a prepackaged product, it ensures standardization. The consumer evaluates the brand after purchase and expects to receive, the same satisfaction as experienced previously. Continuous satisfaction will increase the probability of the repurchase of the brand.

Over a period of time when consumer satisfaction is experienced, learning leads to habitual purchasing behaviour with hardly any information being sought for brand evaluation. Such behaviour can be said to be similar to routinised decision making.

However, there is another possibility that the brand does not meet the consumer's expectations, resulting in extinction of the link between brand usage and positive awards. *For example,* we presume that a consumer does not like the taste of a reformulation of a brand of cookies, then the consumer will decide to evaluate alternative brands, thus initiating a process of decision making.

There could be other factors other than dissatisfaction which may cause *extinction* and a change from habit to complex decision making.

- Say a new product has been introduced in the market, which the consumer comes to know and considers purchasing, initiating information search and brand evaluation.
- Receipt of new or additional information could ignite a change in needs and a decision making process. Say, information on the negative effects of consuming cigaratte (cancer) may prompt a frequent consumer of cigaratte to reassess the particular brand of tobacco.
- Monotony resulting from continuous consumption of the same brand (or boredom) can make the consumer try to seek and search for something new and a different brand.

- Extinction may occur in the following instances - when the brand is out of stock, (then the consumer will evaluate other brand choices) or when there is a price change (*i.e.,* price of competing brands is reduced and the regular brand price is increased). In these two situations, the consumer may be involved in an alternative brand evaluation decision making.

FIGURE 4.8

A MODEL OF HABITUAL PURCHASING BEHAVIOUR

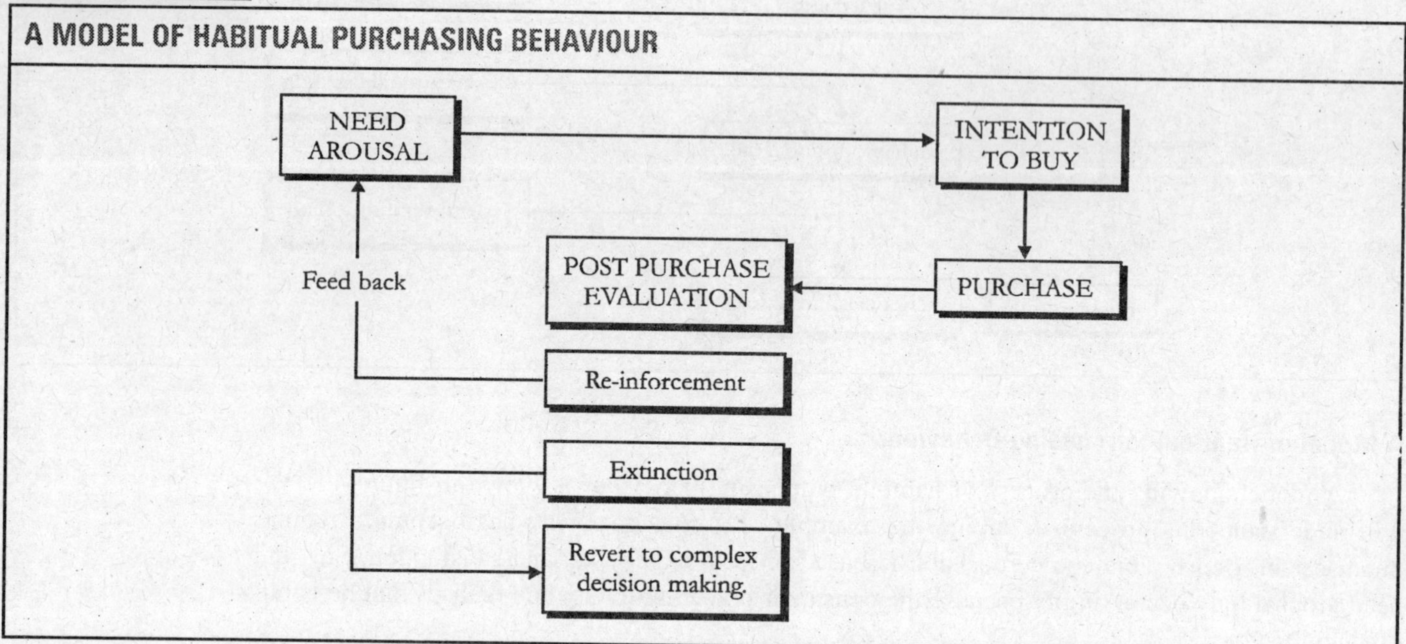

(*Source* : ***Consumer Behavior and Marketing Action,*** Hency Assael, 6th Edn., pp-123)

Habit and Marketing Management

The habitual behaviour of consumers can lead to brand loyalty. Marketers are interested in understanding the habitual behaviour of consumers, for, it is seen that through repeated use or habit, they develop preference for certain brands.

There exists a close link between learning, habit and brand loyalty. Consumers learn that a particular brand can satisfy their needs which results in brand loyalty.

The habitual behaviour of consumers which can lead to brand loyalty is of interest to marketers. Through repeated use or habit, consumers acquire preference for certain brands, generally due to three reasons :

- When consumers become familiar with a brand, they feel comfortable with it. (One prefers to stick to the same doctor or visit the same fast food outlet or coffee house or beauty parlour).
- Through habitual purchase, one gets conditioned and develops a taste for the brand. (*For example,* in the beginning, one may not like Chinese food but after repeated consumption, he or she may learn to enjoy it and even crave for it. Even usage of particular (brands of) colognes, deoderant or perfumes or type of music enjoyed by one, are all examples of habitual tastes developed through conditioning.
- Consumers accustomed to usage of a particular brand in the family home right from childhood is likely to consider it as a testimony to the brand's goodness.

The strategic implications of habitual usage for marketers can include:

Products : Products purchased habitually are frequently purchased. Generally packaged goods involve few service requirements and little direct selling. Whereas, a complex decision making involves purchasing products which are technically more complex (say a computer) and personal selling is more important.

Habitual purchases involve hardly any information seeking or evaluation of various brands.

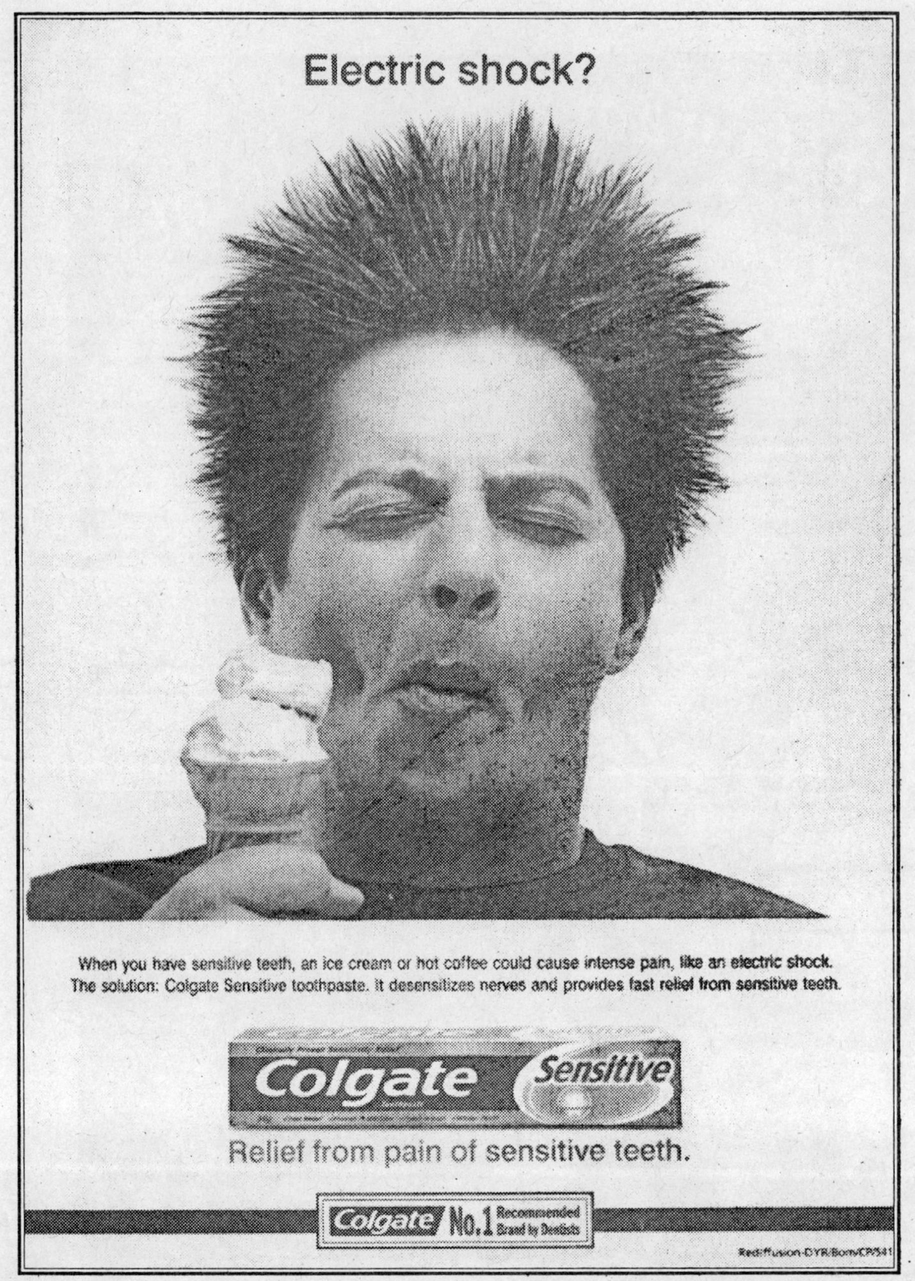

Advertising to inform and remind consumers

Distribution : For products purchased habitually, widespread distribution is necessary, because seeing the item will remind purchasers to buy it. While for products involving complex decision making, selective or exclusive distribution is required.

Pricing : For habitual purchases, consumers are price sensitive. So marketers can go for price deals or free sample offers.

Advertising and in-store Promotions : For products which are purchased frequently, marketers need to advertise and remind consumers about the same. Similarly, in-store promotions also help to draw the attention of consumers once they are inside the store. However, in case of products involving complex decision making, marketers will be required to selectively advertise and convey information based on the specific customer requirement.

BRAND LOYALTY

According to George S. Day (Professor, Wharton School) Brand loyalty can be defined as **consisting of repeated purchases prompted by strong internal disposition. (*i.e.*, favourable attitude).** In the above definition, internal disposition refers to the attitude which is expressed in terms of overall liking and predisposition.

There exists a close link between learning, habit and brand loyalty. Consumers learn that a particular brand can satisfy their needs which results in brand loyalty. Thus, brand loyalty indicates a positive attitude towards a brand resulting in consistent purchase of the brand over time. This approach to brand loyalty can be said to be **cognitive**. Professor Day has opined that consumers might continue to buy the same brand as other brands are not easily available or a brand offers a long series of price deals or consumers may want to minimize decision making. In such situations, **spurious loyalty** is said to exist and it doesn't indicate commitment.

Brand loyalty when measured considering the *behavioural aspect*, simply indicates a consumer's repurchase of a brand consistently. For instance, if the consumer purchases the same brand of product (say toothpaste, soap, shampoo etc.,) every time, then he is considered to be a brand loyal consumer in that product category. Such a measurement of brand loyalty only based on past behaviour can be misleading and may not reflect consumer's positive re-inforcement towards the brand. This means that measurement of brand loyalty has to be multidimensional with a clear indication of consumer's commitment to the brand.

The model of brand loyalty speaks about certain positive factors which induce brand loyalty and certain (other) negative factors which will work against it.

A Model of Brand Loyalty

While trying to understand what makes a consumer brand loyal, through this model we will have a look at certain positive factors which induce brand loyalty and negative factors which will work against it. The degree of brand loyalty will be the net outcome of these positive and negative factors.

FIGURE 4.9

A MODEL OF CUSTOMER'S BRAND LOYALTY

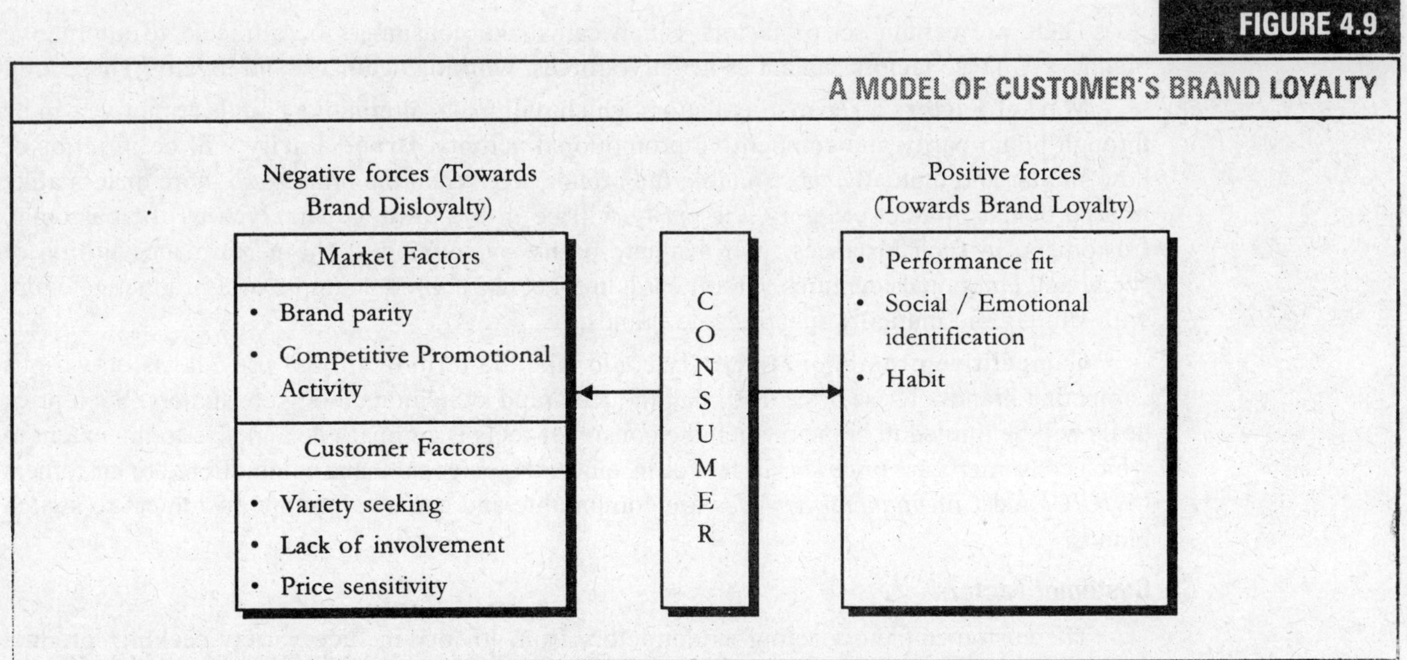

(*Source : Customer Behavior,* J.N. Sheth, B. Mittal, 2nd Edn., Thomson Learning, Singapore, 2003, Pp 393-398)

Positive Factors

The three major positive factors which contribute to brand loyalty are perceived brand performance fit, social and emotional identification with the brand and habit combined with a long history of using the brand.

Perceived Brand Performance Fit

Perceived brand performance fit, social and emotional identification with the brand and habit (and history) are the positive factors while certain market factors and customer factors are negative factors. Both these factors can affect brand loyalty.

Consumers will prefer brands which will meet their needs and wants well. If they have a positive usage experience, they will want to purchase the same brand again. Brands may differ in terms of the quality of their performance as well as the specific performance dimensions. Moreover consumer's will have different needs for specific performance features (*e.g.,* soap for dry, normal or oily skin). Thus, brand loyalty will depend not merely on whether a brand performs on what it is intended to do but also on the degree of fit between the customer's specific performance requirements and the brand's performance capability.

Another very important measure of customer's brand loyalty is it's (brand's) performance and perceived brand quality. Sony, L.G. Nokia and Tata are few examples of company brands well known for their quality and hence have loyal users for their products.

Social and Emotional Identification with the Brand

Brands come to be known through certain social images acquired through marketing communications and or by names of those using the brand (Aishwarya Rai *Nakshatra Diamonds*), *Reid and Taylor,* Amitabh Bachchan). Such brands reflect social self concept (the kind of person you like to be seen as). Emotional identification with the brands is another aspect. Sometimes consumer's enjoy using the brand such that they get psychologically attached to it.

Habit and History : As already discussed earlier in the chapter, customers get habituated to using a particular brand and prefer to continue doing it. This could be because they are familiar and comfortable using the brand, develop a taste through conditioning and view the long history of usage of the brand by parents as a testimony of good brand.

Negative Forces Acting against Brand Loyalty

There are certain set of factors which can make consumers be attracted to alternative brands. *i.e.,* these factors can act as negative forces, working against brand loyalty. These are :

Market Factors : The market factors which will make alternative brands attractive can be through brand parity and competitive promotional activity. **Brand Parity** will be in terms of how similar and mutually substitutable the brands are. When the brands are more or less alike in a particular product category, the parity will be in the form as perceived by the customer. Customers, in such instances, will evaluate parity by looking at the performance utility, or social and emotional identities. Credit cards market are a good example of a product category with similar and mutually substitutable brands.

Competitive promotional activity could take the form of special price deals on various competing brands. These price deals can induce brand switching among consumers. Such price deals will be limited to brands which the consumer feels is comparable and also to the extent to which consumer's are price sensitive. For instance, the personal loans being offered to customers by *ICICI* and *Citi-financial Services* are comparable and can also prompt customers to switch brands.

Customer Factors

The customer factors acting as detractors from loyalty include variety seeking, product involvement, price sensitivity, multi-brand loyalty, withdrawal from the product category and change in needs.

- Some consumers are always **backing variety** in order to avoid boredom, using the same brand, so they are less brand loyal.
- Product involvement refers to the extent to which the consumer considers the product is important and how involved he/she is to it. For products such as clothes, cars, hairstyles etc., consumers are very much involved and thus are usually committed to the brand.
- Consumers vary in their price sensitivity. Those who are more price sensitive are likely to change brands and are not brand loyal.
- Consumers may purchase more than one brand in the same product category regularly (say tooth paste) and thus are not completely loyal to any brand. At times consumers may discontinue using the product (say stop eating non veg food) and thus will permanently withdraw from eating non-veg food at the particular restaurant they were patronising. Even when the consumer moves through his life cycle, (say – young to middle age) there will be a change in his needs and wants and accordingly loyalty to brands may also change.

BRAND EQUITY VERSUS BRAND LOYALTY

Brand equity is the value of the brand to the consumer when compared to other brands. Brand equity reflects the greater confidence that consumers have in a brand, which translates into customer preference, resulting in brand loyalty and even a willingness to pay a premium.

The concepts of brand equity and brand loyalty are related and are also distinct. Brand equity reflects the greater confidence that consumers have in a brand, which translates into customer preference, resulting in brand loyalty and even a willingness to pay a premium.

The concepts of Brand equity and Brand loyalty are related and are also distinct. Brand loyalty is a consistent repurchase of the brand due to a favorable brand attitude. While, customers who perceive a higher brand in a brand (a mental concept of the superiority of the brand) should logically purchase the brand. Brand equity is based more on specific brand associations and the value it generates.

In a study carried out by Marketing Professors Walfried, Banwari Mittal and Arun Sharma, five dimensions of brand equity were identified:

- **Performance** – a customer's view on a brand's flawless and long lasting performance.
- **Social image** – the esteem with which the consumers' reference group views the brand.
- **Value** – the brand's perceived utility when compared to its cost.
- **Trustworthiness** – the extent to which the customer finds the brand trustworthy in terms of its performance and quality.
- **Identification** – the degree to which consumer's identify or feel attached to the brand.

Since brand equity, for the consumer, will be the perceived relative superiority of a brand name, it is highest when the brand scores well on all five components.

CUSTOMER LOYALTY

Sheth and Mittal have defined customer loyalty as "*a customer's commitment to a brand, store or supplier based on a strong favourable attitude and manifested in consistent repatronage.*"

The above definition of customer loyalty includes both behaviour and attitude, which can result in four possible situations as shown in figure. 4.10.

FIGURE 4.10

BEHAVIOUR AND ATTITUDE ASPECTS OF LOYALTY

		BEHAVIOUR	
		Strong	Weak
ATTITUDE	Strong	Loyalty	Latent Loyalty
	Weak	Spurious Loyalty	No Loyalty

(*Source: J.N. Sheth and B. Mittal,* Customer Behavior, *Thomson South Western Learning, 2003, p. 404.)*

Customer loyalty can be defined as a customer's commitment to a brand, store or supplier based on a strong favourable attitude and is manifested in consistent repatronage.

When both attitude and behaviour are weak, it means no loyalty exists; weak attitude indicates the customer may not have any liking for the brand or stores. While weak behaviour means that the purchase of the brand or visiting the stores is sporadic. When the attitude and behaviour are strong, it means that the customer has a strong brand or store loyalty. The remaining two situational cases are interesting.

When the behaviour is high but attitude is low, it can be said that the customer has spurious loyalty, *i.e.,* the customer may buy the same brand again and again or shop at the same store regularly but may not have a preferential attitude towards it. Very often in such instances the choice of the brand or store may be due to convenient location or the customer perceives all brands to be more or less the same. In such a situation, when the customer loyalty is incidental and not well founded, he or she may easily switch brands/change stores if given more choice or interesting price deals. Thus, the retailer or marketer would have to make efforts at strengthening the customer's perception of the brand's or store's image.

In the quadrant with strong (or high) attitude and weak (or low) behaviour, the customer can be said to be having latent loyalty. The customer likes the brand or store but is unable to buy or visit the same probably because the price is too high or he (or she) lacks accessibility to the brand or the store. Thus, in such instances, the retailer or marketer needs to reduce (or lower) whatsoever barriers exists and tap the hidden potential of the market.

Retailers are beginning to focus their attention on encouraging customers to visit their outlets, treating them to attractive promotions, thus adding more value to their best customers and satisfying them in the process. For, to the retailers, customer loyalty will indicate that customers are committed to purchasing merchandise and services from them and this will resist the activities of competitors attempting to attract their patronage. Of course, one of the basis, for retailers to gain competitive advantage is through having dedicated employees, unique merchandise and providing extraordinary customer service-all of which will go a long way in building a solid, loyal customer base.

VARIABLES INFLUENCING STORE LOYALTY

Consumers can be loyal to stores just as they are to product brands. *Store loyalty can be defined in a number of ways. Store loyalty behaviour can be operationalised to be :*

- A sequence of purchases at the same store.

- The proportion of purchases or expenditure that a particular store takes in the retail sector.
- The frequency of *repeat patronage.*
- The duration of patronage or store allegiance.

Despite the assumptions that these different measures have certain common basis, they tend to show weak associations. For instance, a customer may regularly purchase from store 'A' but may spend more money at store 'B'. Here it can be said that the buyer is loyal to store 'A' on a duration of patronage criteria but can be said to have low loyalty when measured by a proportion of purchase criterion. Thus, we are actually trying to accommodate two different concepts:

(a) the proportional use of the store in the shopper's store portfolio,

(b) the duration of patronage.

It is difficult to know how much these two different forms of behavioural loyalty move together. It is possible that they may be driven by the same motivations or there could be other factors which could make them diverge.

Understanding store loyalty through the 'What' and 'How' factors

Marketers are interested in the revenue earned when consumers' visit their store again and again. This is possible only if they gain consumers' store loyalty. Marketers can work on developing the store loyalty by understanding the 'what' factors and the 'how' factors.

Marketers can work on developing the store loyalty by understanding the 'what' and the 'how' factors.

What Factors :

The 'what' factor requires the marketer to examine what products and services the customer gets at the store. Specifically put, the quality of merchandise available at the store. If good quality of merchandise is available at the store, it is more likely that customers will develop loyalty towards that shop. The store's assortment in terms of the number of different product categories it carries can also influence a customer's patronage. Consumers prefer to purchase merchandise from stores, where they feel that they are being offered **low price** for a given **quality of merchandise**. Customers are attracted to store label brands, which when compared to national brands seem to be exclusive in value or in performance or features and are available only at the specific store chain.

How Factors :

The how factors try to examine store loyalty in terms of how favourable the shopping experience was for the customers at a particular store. This can be assessed by verifying: the **ease of merchandise selection** (well planned in-store layout facilitating easy accessibility to merchandise, and makes shopping at the store an enjoyable experience), availability of credible in-store information (about the merchandise displayed and assistance from sales personnel who are knowledgeable, credible and trustworthy), **ideally located** store (conveniently located, with ample parking facility and quick checkouts), **smooth complaint handling** (store which follows a reasonable return policy) and **personalisation** (pleasant and positive in-store employees behaviour).

If marketer's try to examine the various 'What' factors and 'How' factors mentioned above, the question as to what makes a customer loyal to a store can be understood.

TYPICAL FEATURES TO BUILDUP STORE LOYALTY

Customers are constantly changing and their expectations also rising. Consumer behaviour in the organised retail industry has altered drastically in the last few years. The retail market is growing not only in terms of numbers but also in terms of stature, image and class. Alongside with Indians becoming world class consumers they also expect and demand world class service. So, it becomes vital for retailers to pay attention to every little detail in order to be successful. This can be done by providing a good brand and store experience. For this, in general, the retailer will have to look into various aspects such as:

- The timings of the store
- The in-store design and layout
- The 'welcome' the customer receives
- The ability to browse easily
- The behaviour and product knowledge possessed by the sales persons
- The facility for making payments
- The attractiveness of the loyalty programmes
- The packaging and the exit.

All the above aspects are crucial for the consumer to experience delightful shopping at the outlet. If not handled well, it could result in a disgruntled consumer, who will spread a bad word-of-mouth.

'SKODA Enjoys Brand Equity'

SUMMARY

Learning as a concept is of great interest to marketers because it provides an insight into the consumer's decision making process. Consumer learning can be said to be the process by which persons acquire the purchase and consumption knowledge and experience that they apply to future related behaviour. The learning process can be understood better by taking a look at the various components namely drive, motivation, cues, response, re-inforcement and retention.

The various mechanisms of learning *i.e.,* Cognitive learning, Classical conditioning, Instrumental conditioning and Modeling were discussed. There has been an elaborate discussion on the role of consumer memory and how it can be linked to processing information. The low involvement learning theory was also briefly touched upon.

Habit has been defined as repetitive behaviour resulting in limited or no information seeking and evaluation of the brand choices. When consumers purchase by habit, it facilitates decision making by minimizing the need for information search. Marketers are interested in learning more of the habitual behaviour of consumers which can lead to brand loyalty. Brand loyalty can be defined as consisting of repeated purchases prompted by strong internal disposition *i.e.,* favourable attitude. There was a brief discussion on the model of customer's brand loyalty; where - in the positive forces (which work towards brand loyalty and negative forces, which work towards brand disloyalty) were viewed. The chapter concludes with discussions on 'customer loyalty', which is defined as a customer's commitment to a brand, store or supplier based on a strong favourable attitude and manifested in consistent repatronage.

CHAPTER QUESTIONS FOR DISCUSSION

1. Define learning. Why are marketers interested in understanding consumer learning?
2. Which mechanism of learning (classical conditioning, instrumental conditioning, modeling or cognitive learning) would explain consumer behaviour in the purchase of:
   a. A face wash pack
   b. A home theatre stereo system
   c. Cigarettes
   d. Jewellery
   e. A new car

   Give reasons while explaining the above.
3. What is habit? Explain how an understanding of consumer's habitual behaviour can help marketers?
4. Assume, as a part of an assignment, you are required to help a company selling electronic goods, to prepare a list of features, on the new model of cellular phone, they are about to launch in the market. What and where would you place the most important features (which you want consumers to remember) in the list? Why?
5. Why are marketers interested in the study of customer brand and store loyalty? Explain taking the example of any consumer durable product.
6. Make a list of any five brands of products or services to which you feel you are loyal. Ask five other classmates to prepare a similar list. Compare all the lists. Which are the common brands identified? Find out the reasons for the brand choice, does it match your answer?

7. Talk to two customers in your neighbourhood, who are loyal to store brands and another two customers who do not purchase store brands. Give a brief description of these customers in terms of their personality, perception of store and the reasons for being loyal (or not loyal) to store brands. Use this information to relate it to the concept of brand equity.

➲ SUGGESTED READINGS

1. Leon. G. Schiffman & L.I. Kanuk *"Consumer Behavior"* Prentice Hall of India Private Limited, New Delhi, 2005, pp. 205-249.
2. Rosemary, Phipps Craig Simmons.' *Understanding Customers* 1996-1997, 'Butterworth Heinemann, Oxford, 1996.
3. Henry, Assael., *Consumer Behavior and Marketing Action,* 6 edition., (AB) Thomson Learning, Singapore. 2001, pp 103-139.
4. Frank. R. Kardes., *Consumer Behavior and Managerial, Decision Making,* 2nd edition, Prentice Hall of India Private Ltd, New Delhi, 2005, pp 50-77.
5. Jagadish N.S. Sheth, Barwari Mittal, *Customer Behavior : A Managerial Perspective,* Thomson South Western Learning, Singapore, 2003. pp. 141-142.
6. Harshikaa Udasi, Customer is queen, *The Week* December 3, 2006, pp 38-47.
7. Greg. Anderson, 'Off the Beaten path,' Edmund's *Automobile Buyer's Guides*, Summer 1997.
8. S.A. Chunawalla., K.C. Sethia., *Foundations of Advertising Theory and Practice,* 1997, Himalaya Publishing House, Mumbai.
9. Babar-Zaidi, Vikram Doctor, Turning it all to good account, *Business World*, 22 June, 1997, pp 110-117.
10. Wolf gang Kohler, *The Mentality of Apes*, Harcourt Brace and World, New York, 1925.
11. Priya Srinivasan, Rahul Sachitanand and Archana Shukla' The Tween Economy.' *Business Today*, January 1, 2006, pp 53-56.
12. George S. Day, "A Two-Dimensional Concept of Brand Loyalty," *Journal of Advertising Research* 9, September 1969, pp. 29-36
13. Alan S. Dick, and Kunal Basu, "Customer Loyalty: Toward an Integrated Conceptual Framework," *Journal of the Marketing Science,* 22, No.2, 1994, p. 101.
14. Walfriend Lassar, Banwari Mittal, and Arun Sharma. "Measuring Customer-Based Brand Equity," *Journal of Consumer Marketing* 12, No.4, 1995, pp. 11-19.

CASE

LUXOR WRITING INSTRUMENTS PVT. LTD.

The Beginning

Luxor Writing Instruments Pvt. Ltd (LWIPL) was started way back in 1963 by Mr. Davinder Kumar Jain (or D.K.) in Delhi. In the year 1963, at the tender age of 19, D.K. Jain started a small assembly shop in Sadar-Bazaar (New Delhi) where he started manufacturing fountain pens under the name **Luxor Instruments Pvt. Ltd.** During those days there were only two types of writing instruments:

- Wooden Pencils
- Fountain pens with rubber grips and metal levers.

Although, it may seem that there is nothing much which goes into the manufacturing of a pen, in the early 1970's, it was a Herculean task. For, every small part which goes into the making of a pen had to be imported from various corners of the world. Mr. D.K. Jain had a clear vision when he started assembling the fountain pen – to produce only truly home grown pens using backward integration and absorbing emerging technologies.

Learning about the Market and Customers

Luxor had imported technology in order to convince consumers about the superiority of its own home grown technology. It has also taken many bold initiatives like foreign collaborations and technical tie ups at the time when Indian business was severely restricted by Government policies. It has aimed for mass appeal by powerful quality brands to help Indian consumers experience the pleasure of writing. In keeping up with the market expectations LWIPL has constantly innovated and reinvented its product range to meet every writing need of the Indian consumers – be it school children, college students, executives or the corporate world.

The Brand 'Luxor'

The usage of imported technology in order to convince consumers about its own home grown technology has worked and Luxor today enjoys the leadership position in the Indian writing Instruments Industry. It has remained the unmatched leader in the market by offering a writing instrument for everyone in the widest possible range of quality and price. The Luxor brand enjoys an appeal that is universal and the preference of every age group. The *Luxor* brand is registered in more than 110 countries in writing instruments category. It is the only Indian brand of Indian writing instruments to export to countries such as Austrialia, The European Union, Russia, CIS, East European countries, Africa, Middle East and the U.S. The name Luxor, today commands respect and awe from competitors and consumers as a company which provides value for money to its customers.

The many first's of LWIPL

LWIPL, as a company has many milestones to its credit. The many of its 1st initiatives include:

- In *1971*, Luxor pioneered the manufacturing and productions of *Fibre Tip Colour Pen Sets* in India. Later on it introduced *Micro Tip and 3-D Roller Ball Pens.*
- In 1975, an exciting and mesmerising range of products for children were launched. These included *Sketch pens, Plastic pens, Crayons, Colour pens, Tatoo markers, Dual colour pens* and *Magic pens.* These pens were available in various styles and types to explore the imagination of children.
- In *1978,* Luxor introduced the *roller ball pens.*
- In *1984,* pilot Hitech needle point pens were launched in India, in association with Pilot Corporation of Japan.
- In *1986*, Luxor introduced *Permanent Markers* and *Florescent Hi-Lighters*, followed by the launch of the French brand *Waterman* range of writing instruments.

In the year 2003, French brand, *Waterman* range of writing instruments were launched in India. Today, Luxor is the largest manufacturer of writing instruments in India, producing over 1,000,000 pens per day.

Awards and Recognition

LWIPL has earned itself many recognitions and laurels.

- Mr. D.K. Jain has earned the distinction of being awarded *'The President of India Award'.* LWIPL, has been awarded the coveted *"Number One Writing Instruments Exporter"* consecutively for three years and hence has been given the exclusive right of manufacturing and distributing four international brands in India, *Viz., Pilot, Papermate, Parker* and *Waterman.*
- Luxor was awarded the coveted **'Super brand'** award (2004).
- BSi, has awarded the company ISO:9001:2000 certification, acknowledging its commitment to quality.
- Luxor is the only ISO 14001 and OHSAS 18001 certified company in writing instruments category for Environmental Management System (EMS) and Occupational Health and Safety Assessment Series (OHSAS).

Competition

The other competitors in the industry could include brands such as, **'Cello'** and **Reynolds** (India).

Future Plans :

Luxor has been credited with the status of being the first organized player in a largely unorganized section. Having established itself as a leading consumer products company using advanced technology to meet the ever-changing needs of consumers across key markets such as North America, U.K, Germany, Russia and Australia, LWIPL wants to expand its market. In the next few years, the company's vision is to position itself as a world leader in the existing categories by focusing on three main areas:

- geographical
- technological innovation
- productivity gain.

(*Source :* www.luxorparker.com)

QUESTIONS FOR DISCUSSION

1. Comment on the consumer's buying behaviour for high priced pens.
2. According to you which theory of learning (Instrumental or observation or cognitive) will best explain the consumption behaviour of Florescent Hi lighter pens? Why?
3. Do you feel a better communication package can be worked out for marketing Luxor pens to college students? Why and How if yes?

CHAPTER 5

PERSONALITY AND LIFESTYLE INFLUENCES

- Case : **Reid & Taylor** and **Amitabh Bachchan**
- Meaning of Lifestyle, AIO and VALS frame work
- Changing lifestyle trends of Indian consumers
- Personality (meaning and properties)
- Theories of Personality.
- A Business Today - Synovate study.
- Personality influences and consumer behaviour
- Certain inter-related consumption and possession personality traits.
- Self concept or self image
- Summary
- Chapter questions for discussion
- Suggested readings
- Case : **Britannia Industries Limited**

CASE

REID & TAYLOR AND AMITABH BACHCHAN

If one were to understand the 'why' of consumer behaviour, we will need to take a look at the personality and lifestyle of the individual. **Personality** can be defined as **patterns of individual behaviour which are consistent and enduring.** Lifestyles can be referred to as consumer's mode of living as reflected in their attitudes and opinions.

Marketers have tried to communicate to consumers about their product offerings by referring to their personality characteristics. This, they feel will influence their purchase decisions in terms of 'what', 'when' and 'how' consumers buy. Marketers and advertising personnel have always attempted to incorporate specific personality traits to their brand ambassador who endorses their brand. For instance, take the personality match between **Amitabh Bachchan** and **Reid & Taylor.** Reid Taylor started manufacturing premium range of fabrics in India, in 1988 at a state of art fabric plant in Mysore. The company claims that Reid & Taylor is the first brand in India to offer both fabrics and apparel, under one label. By offering fine international quality garments and sharp styling, duly endorsed by Amitabh Bachchan, the Reid & Taylor brand has been able to create a unique space for itself in the Indian consumers' mind. The company sources claim that Reid & Taylor is the finest cloth that is available in the country today and also the second largest suiting brand in the luxury segment. Amitabh Bachachan is Indian cinema's great actor and voted super star of the millennium. He is recognized as a charismatic style icon, whose outfits create a trend, often leading to a fashion revolution. Mr. Bachchan with an enigmatic persona, huge global fan following has been synonymous with style and acknowledged as a constant-trend setter in fashion.

Reid Taylor, premium apparel designers have been using Amitabh Bachchan as the legend, who **Bonds With The Best**-to endorse their brand. Through Mr. Bachchan, Reid & Taylor conveys about its-premium suits, shirts, trousers, chinos, Jackets and knit area accessories which spells style quotient in terms of a unique style which reflects elegance and dignity. This brand appeal is reflected in its endorser, who is considered to be a fashion phenomenon, loves comfort and style with an unmatched, distinct dressing sense and a constant (fashion) trend setter. Thus, Reid & Taylor has successfully depicted specific (legendary) traits of their brand ambassador in their advertising messages. *For example,* "There are those who make a statement and those **who are** a statement (Amitabh Bachchan). Style is one rare indefinable, quality, and not everyone has it."

In this chapter, we start with a brief discussion on lifestyles, AIO, VALS framework and trends which are affecting strategic marketing decisions. Next we will have a look at personality variables which are relevant for understanding the underlying motives involved in purchase decisions. In the chapter we have also attempted to discuss about the relevance of various personality theories affecting consumer behaviour. The chapter concludes with a short discussion on the concept of self image.

Lifestyle variables can be described in terms of certain quantifiable psychographic variables defined on the basis of how people spend their time (Activities), what they consider important in their environment (Interests) and what they as well as the world around think of them (Opinions).

MEANING OF LIFESTYLE, AIO AND VALS FRAMEWORK

Lifestyle variables can be described in terms of certain quantifiable psychographics variables defined on the basis of how people spend their time (Activities), what they consider important in their environment (Interests) and what they as well as the world around think of them (Opinions).

Joseph Plummer has described certain variables which define lifestyle. These are presented in Table 5.1. These lifestyle variables are defined by how people spend their time (activities), what they consider important in their environment (interests) and what they think of themselves as well as the world around them (opinions).

TABLE 5.1

VARIABLES DEFINING LIFESTYLE

Activities	Interests	Opinions
Work	Family	Personal relations
Hobbies	Home	Social issues
Social events	Job	Politics
Vacation	Community	Business
Entertainment	Recreation	Economics
Club membership	Fashion	Education
Community	Food	Products
Shopping	Media	Future
Sports	Achievements	Culture

(*Source :* Joseph T. Plummer, *Journal of Marketing,* 1974).

Understanding of life-style variables will help marketers in two ways:

- Broad lifestyle trends (working couple) have altered the habits, tastes and purchasing behaviour of Indian consumers.
- A knowledge of lifestyle can be used on a product-specific basis by marketers. Say VLCC can work on developing an inventory of activities, interests and opinion specially designed for the health conscious consumer market.

Measuring Lifestyle Characteristics

Marketers need to measure lifestyle characteristics specific to certain product's and consumer categories in order to market to them. We will discuss two ways to measure lifestyles.

Develop an AIO Inventory : A very common method of measuring lifestyles is by developing an inventory of activities, interests and opinions. (An AIO inventory). There can be two types of AIO inventories:

(a) **A Generalized Inventory :** which can be applied across to all product categories and given under broad segments such as housewives, trend conscious consumers or gadget savvy consumers.

(b) **Product Specific AIO Inventory :** which will be specific to a particular product category. *For example,* a lifestyle inventory to describe health conscious consumers, purchasers of lifestyle accessories or online purchasers.

The AIO framework attempts to distinctly lifestyle groups on the basis of a questionnaire designed to measure Activities, Interests and Opinions (AIO).

Both the above inventories are developed by formulating many questions related to consumer activities, interests and opinions and then selecting a smaller number of questions which will best define the consumer segments. Box 5.1 throws some light on the change in lifestyles of working women and housewives, on the basis of a survey, (carried out by The Knowledge Company, an initiative from the team of Techno Park, a management consulting firm) of 50 centers representing 784 urban areas covering seven town classes and a sample size of more than 25000 consumers.

BOX 5.1

HOW THE COOKIE CRUMBLES?

Research has shown that a typical working parent spends just 21 minutes a day looking after their children.

With guilt pangs twanging away, more and more working women are opening up their wallets as compared to their stay-at-home sisters.

Spending patterns: The researching team noticed an interesting trend variation between single income families and dual income ones.

Even though the difference in average annual spends between dual income households and single income households was just Rs. 12.621, (the minuscule difference in annual income comes to barely Rs. 1,000 more per month), the knowledge that there is a second bread-winner in the family seems to change the way that multiple-income families feel about money All of this necessarily impacts and changes their lifestyle.

The research paper covered seven consumer life stages from school going children to retired individuals for their share of the wallet.

The study showed that working women with dependent kids tend to spend more (Rs. 17,061) than at any other life stage—working singles, working married without children, working married with dependent children, working married with independent children and the retired.

The next highest individual spending, that of housewives with dependent children, amounts to Rs. 15,819, just Rs. 1,500 less than that of her working counterpart.

However, working women with dependent kids buy more on credit. They spend more on repaying loans, almost to the extent of Rs. 2,620, than housewives who spend around Rs 2,000. If the kids are on their own and not dependent on the mother, this amount is actually halved.

Working women with independent Kids pay Rs. 992 as loan repayments, as compared to housewives with independent kids who shell out Rs. 533 as loan repayments.

The research highlighted another interesting fact: Working women with dependent kids spend substantially more on car loans (Rs. 1,973) than housewives with dependent kids (Rs. 70). This could reflect a dual car, ownership status in, most households.

Munching time: Eating out is clearly indulged in more by double income families, as they spend more on this activity. Working' women with dependent kids spend Rs. 500 more on eating out as compared to housewives with dependent kids. The former also spend about Rs. 335 more on ordering in.

Eating out or ordering in could be a lifestyle choice for working couples. For the working woman, ordering in from the choicest restaurants could assuage some of the guilt. Concerned with a fast and convenient checkout, working woman frequent stores where they can avail of this facility. Both incidentally consider high-quality produce, high-quality meats and a clean, neat store to be the top three factors when choosing a primary supermarket, another study has shown.

The survey threw up other interesting findings. The dual income household is a softer target for financial services and indulges more in lifestyle expenditure However, the proportion and the amount allocated on education is higher for single income families as compared to dual income ones. Expense on books, stationery and music, toys and gifting and recreation are also somewhat higher by single income households.

However, the percentage allocated on fuel and transport as well as on communication is higher by multiple income households, and also the percentage allocated to household help.

(*Source :* Amrita Nair - Ghaswalla, How the Cookie Crumbles?, *The Times of India*, Bangalore, January 8, 2007)

The AIO Framework

The AIO framework is broadly similar to the concepts of VALS system, in that it also attempts to classify distinctive lifestyle groups. This is done on the basis of a questionnaire designed to measure Activities, Interests and Opinions (AIO).

Such a classification will enable the marketer to identify the specific group of consumers at whom the product or service is targeted and then work upon the suitable marketing mix elements. For instance, in the early 1980s, Levis Strauss had used the AIO framework while developing a new range of clothes, when the company took the decision to diversify away from their core business of denim jeans. Even though the new line had eventually proved unsuccessful, their research had identified five basic lifestyle segments, each of which had revealed specific characteristics. These were :

- Q_1 *Main Stream Traditionalist* (19% proportion of population). This category of customers were over 45 years, a typical department store shopper, conservative, who prefers to shop with wife and values her opinion and could easily be the main target for Levi action slacks and action suits (*i.e.*, semi smart casual wear).
- Q_2 *Classic Independent* (20% proportion of population). Such customers were aged between 20–60 years, typically a specialist store shopper, who dresses traditionally although not unfashionably. For such customers looking 'right' is important. They prefer to shop alone and spend more on clothes when compared to other groups.
- Q_3 *Utilitarian Jeans Buyer* (26% proportion of population). In this category consumers can belong to all ages, typically are department store shoppers who don't care much about clothes, preferring wearing jeans for work and play, *i.e.*, a Levi Loyalist.
- Q_4 *The Trendy Casual* (19% proportion of population). These customers are aged between 16–45 years, shop at department and specialist stores, like to be noticed, may or may not wear jeans for work but definitely will wear them for play.
- Q_5 *Price Shopper* (15% proportion of population). Such customers belong to all ages, are department and discount store shoppers looking for bargains. For them appearance is only important within certain parameters.

The Vals Framework

The original VALS (Value and Lifestyle) framework was developed in the United States by Arnold Mitchell of the Stanford Research Institute, using the answers of 2713 respondents to 800 questions to classify the American public into nine groups, namely, survivers, sustainers, belongers, emulators, achievers, I-am-me, experimentals, societally conscious and integrated. The original VALS system was specifically designed to understand the dynamics of societal change and later on adopted as a marketing tool.

The original VALS (Value and Lifestyle) framework system was developed and specifically designed to understand the dynamics of societal change and later on was adopted as a marketing tool.

However in 1989 a revised VALS system was developed with the intention of using it to understand consumer purchase behaviour. The current VALS framework classifies American population into eight distinct sub-groups (or segments) on the basis of consumer responses to 35 attitudinal and four demographic questions. Figure 5.1 gives a brief description on VALS classification alongwith details of the consumer traits in each of the segment. This revised VALS grouping is worked out on the basis of two dimensions: (a) Self Orientation, (b) Resources.

The major groupings (in the Figure 5.1, from left to right) are defined in terms of three major *self orientations* alongwith a new definition of *resources* which are :

FIGURE 5.1

CLASSIFICATION OF CONSUMER TRAITS BASED ON VALS (REVISED)

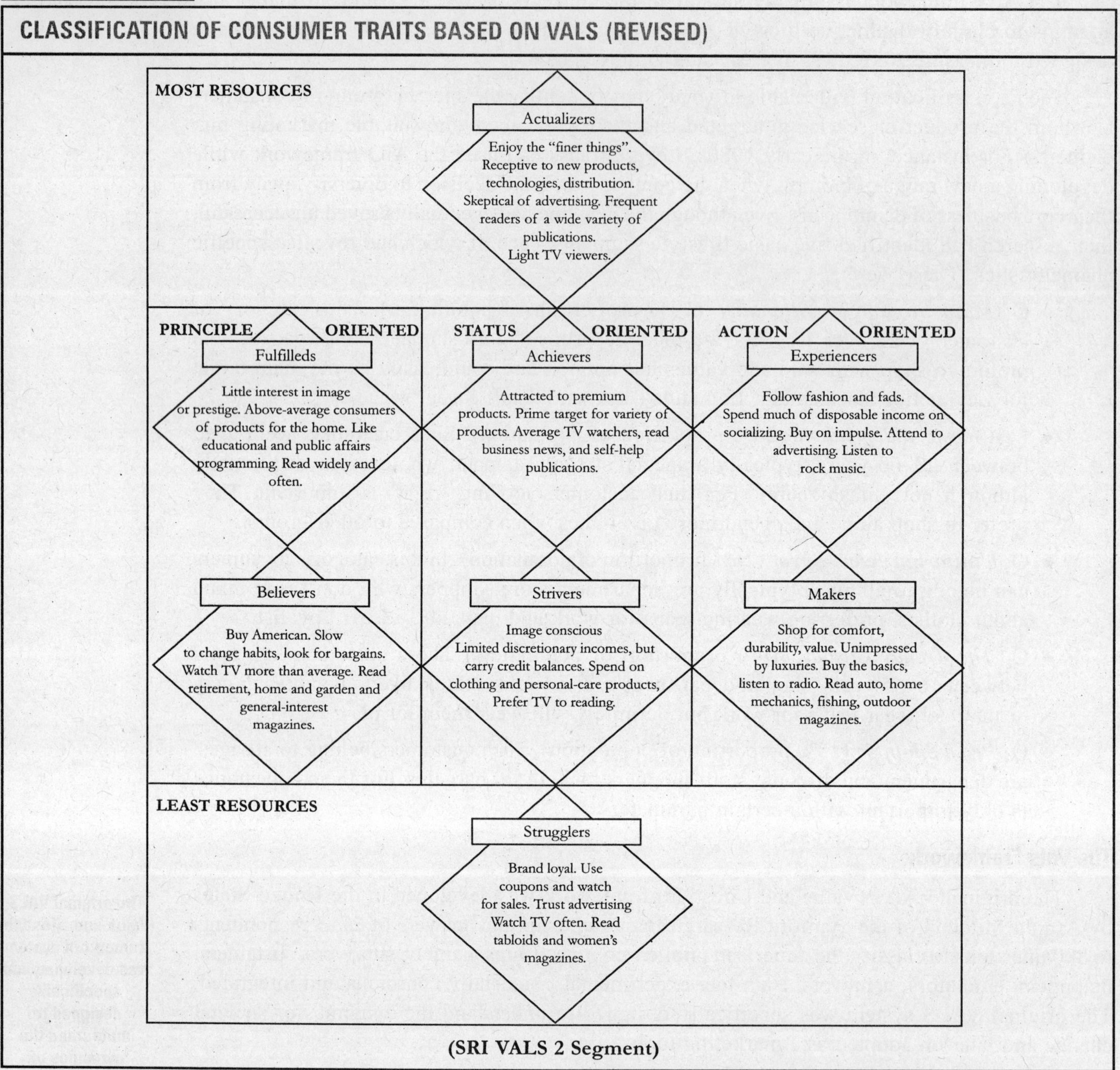

(SRI VALS 2 Segment)

(*Source :* Henry Assael *Consumer Behavior and Marketing Action*, Thomson Learning, Singapore, 2001, pp. 441)

The current VALS framework classifies American population into eight distinct sub groups (or segments) on the basis of consumer responses to 35 attitudinal and four demographic questions.

The principle oriented refers to consumers whose choices are motivated by their beliefs rather than by desires for approval. Such consumers choices are based on abstract or idealised criteria rather than on emotions or desire for approval from others.

The status oriented refers to those consumers whose choices are guided by the actions, approval and opinions of other people. They prefer products and services which will convey their success to others.

The action oriented are those consumers who are motivated by a desire for social or physical activity.

Each of these major self-orientation describes clearly perceptible (distinct) attitudes, lifestyles and decision-making style of individuals.

Resource (from most to least) refers to a range of psychological, physical, demographic and material means and capacities of the consumers which includes education, income, self-confidence, health, eagerness to buy and energy level. In terms of consumer characteristics, all the eight VALS 2 segments differ in certain important ways. *For example,*

Marketers are interested in investing in an emerging market such as India, where the challenge lies in trying to gauge and understand on how to meet consumer needs in such a diverse market.

Believers have a tendency to purchase American made products and are also slow in changing their consumption related habits.

Actualizers are attracted to top-of-the-line and new products. *i.e.*, They can easily become early adopters of new products especially if it involves a new innovative technology.

VALS system have been used by American marketers to understand the traits affecting consumer purchase behaviour and decisions.

Ad talks of the growing clout of the contemporary woman buyer

They have used VALS to develop market segmentation, media and advertising strategies. India, has slowly started emerging as an upcoming economy, developing at a fast pace. Marketers are interested in investing in such an emerging market, where the challenge lies in trying to gauge and understand "how to meet consumers needs" in such a diverse market. *The Future Group* (formerly *Pantaloon* Retail) realized that they are targeting a complex group of consumers with different profile, requirements and aspiration. So, in order to address the consumers needs, the Future Group decided to have a finger on the consumers' pulse and understand the consumption trends. For this, they carried out surveys and sifted through an enormous data and compiled it into trends which helped to make informal strategic decisions. The future group have invested to understand the diversity at the bottom of the pyramid – study communities, (their sensitivity of income and consumption), infrastructure, access and distribution (to ensure better (suitable) products to cater to every region's cultural and local consumption needs) and efficient financial services (to help smooth the income shocks).

For instance, through a group company, *Future Capital,* the company identified a *'Project Money Bazaar'* for the manufacture and retailing of financial products. The format was to focus on tapping the middle and mass end of the consumption market with a retail credit plan, which will offer everything from credit cards, auto and consumer durable finance, mutual funds, insurance, money transfer, financial planning micro finance and mortgages. The researching team used a mix of anthropology and economics to map the consumption trends and behaviour and also suggested different strategies for different cities. *For example,* the company planned to have specialized kiosks to tap the urban poor, in Asia's biggest slum at Dharavi (Mumbai).

Forester's Model

Forester's research model on life-style segmentation talks of two dimensions: on the horizontal axis are shown primary motivations, family, career, entertainment and status; while the vertical axis speaks of attitude towards technology and disposable income.

Forester's research has also contributed to lifestyle segmentation. This model speaks of two dimensions:

(a) On the *Horizontal axis*, are shown primary motivations, family, career, entertainment and status.

(b) The *Vertical axis* conveys about attitude towards technology (optimistic or pessimistic) and disposable income.

The segments also include consumers who are :

- **Career focused** with high disposable income but are technology pessimists.
- **Entertainment focused couch potatoes** with high disposable incomes and proponents of technology and
- **Status oriented** cyber snobs, with high disposable income but are optimistic about technology.

Forester opines that consumer's who are *fast forwards* and *techno strivers* make rational decisions while purchasing technological products and so can be targeted for products which connect to superior performance. *For example,* cell phones and computer connections.

Generally, knowledge about such categories can help marketers to address consumer segments with specific needs such as those who are inclined towards technical products and services.

CHANGING LIFESTYLE TRENDS OF INDIAN CONSUMERS

Changes in the lifestyles of Indian consumers is partly due to changes in their demographic characteristics and partly due to changes in their values. Some of the visible changes in the lifestyle trends are given below:

This new financially independent and discerning target are found to be actively involved in buying decisions which were once considered to be predominantly male dominated.

Changes in the Traditional Male/Female Purchasing Roles

There have been changes accruing in the demographic lifestyle of Indians. Various studies (like the Technopack Study and Census) have indicated an increase in the number of women working outside the home, which is a shift away from the traditional roles of a working husband and housewife households. Now with double income households very common in urban India, unlike the earlier popular saying where 'customer is king' featured , the shift is now towards the 'queen'. This new financially independent and discerning target market are found to be actively involved in buying decisions which were once considered to be predominantly male dominated areas right from automobiles to financial services, white goods and home improvement products.

Lifestyle change – women are actively involved in decision making.

THE WEEK/C-Voter Opinion Poll (from November 20 to 22, 2006 in 10 metros) was carried out interacting with 1,218 women while they were shopping. The poll findings revealed that 68 per cent of them are major decision makers in their household, 73 per cent are more confident purchasers than their previous generation and a (huge) 80 per cent of them said that they were ready to spend more for better quality. In fact for decisions involving children's education, or buying clothes or even an apartment, women were consulted by their male counterparts and sometimes they even take the final decision.

In India there is seen a change in the male and female purchasing roles. There is more acceptance of equality between the sexes and males do not feel the need to conform to the earlier 'macho' image.

Men are also seen to be actively involved in parenting with accompanying children for shopping, entertainment and visiting malls and eating joints. This is the reason why mall owners and retailers are trying their best to woo the entire family by providing *'value addition'* in terms of customer care initiatives, special offers, events and promotions and make the shopping a wonderful experience.

The changing role of man has even extended into changes in male values also. There is more acceptance of equality between the sexes and males do not feel the need to conform to the earlier 'macho' image. Men are more willing to purchase products which was once dismissed as exclusive feminine skin care products, cosmetics, jewellery etc. For instance, exclusive *Fairever* cream for men are also available in the market. A new concept of the sensitive man

Changing purchasing roles of the traditional roles of males and females

Source : The Week, December 3, 2006

has emerged, as one who is equally vulnerable as the women of today. The ad for *Krack Cream* (the forgetful husband remembers to purchase Krack Cream for his wife, who has cracked heels) or the nurturing father who purchases *Dabur Baby Oil* for his baby son or the caring father who looks after his sick child *(Vicks Vaporub)* while his wife has gone out of station. All the above advertisements convey the message of more involvement of men in family and home making activities.

These lifestyle changes, which is an offshoot of better earnings is playing a big part in the purchasing roles of women. In the words of Ms. Abha Shukla (Additional Commissioner, Nagpur, Revenue division), "There is an overall change in lifestyle, especially in urban areas. With improved financial status, people prefer to make their lives easier by using an array of electronic gadgets. It also means women take active participation in the decision-making process".

The present day, working woman is sharp, educated, value and price sensitive and thinks a lot before making up her mind. Now, women are displaying greater affluence, independence and self confidence than in the past. The change is visible across all age groups. In fact, surveys (like the week/c-vder) have shown that spending from one's pocket is a thrill even reflected in smaller towns where there are fewer working women. Marketers are trying to match the changes seen in the women purchase roles by making suitable offerings. *Trent* started the hypermarket star India Bazaar in Ahmedabad, where "store credit cards" were introduced. While the ratio of men owning the in-store card was higher, about 30 per cent women owned it. Well known apparel manufacturer selling *Van Heusen* and *Provogue,* essentially men's brands are branching out to cater to women. *Reebok,* has gone to the extent of creating a knit salwar kameez for the Indian women. *Tata Motors* has designed and marketed four wheelers to women. *For example,* the advertisement of *Tata Sumo Victa,* shows the nonsense lady driving her sleeping family in the car or the group of girls singing Dumb Dumb Dumb… in the *Tata Indica Xeta* commercial.

More Conscious and Inclined Towards Health and Nutrition

Alongwith education and financial independence, Indian consumers (both males and females) are also showing a concern towards maintaining a fit and healthy lifestyle. This awareness is affecting the consumer purchase pattern. Indian food, traditionally has been using a lot of oil content, now consumers are switching over to oils which have lesser cholesterol content like sunflower oil *(Gemini, Fortune, Nutrilite),* dairy products with low fat content (*Britannia's* 33% less fat cheese slices or *Amul's low fat* cheese spread etc.,) or *Nestle's Everyday slim tea whitener.*

Along with education and financial independence, Indian consumers (both males and females) are also showing a concern towards maintaining a fit and healthy lifestyle.

Calcium Sandoz has positioned itself as a calcium supplement targeted at growing children and women (especially in the menopausal age group). Spas such as *Kumarakom* (Kerala) or *Kenilworth Beach Resort and Spa* (Goa) advertises about massages, treatments, therapies and beauty baths, gym and diet meal and low calorie dishes being served for health conscious customers. Even food and Beverage companies are positioning their brands so as to appeal to the health conscious, customers. *For example, Maggi's healthy soup, ITC'S Sunflower oil.*

Alongside, because of the self indulgent lifestyle adopted by the people, at times they also become victims of obesity and related health problems. Marketers of various products are trying to take care of this problem through offers *(Sugar free, VLCC)* which can address these concerns.

Ads which will appeal to the health conscious customers

The Lifestyle Changes of the Emerging Consumption Community

People belonging to the middle class are more educated, better exposed to the global lifestyles and with constantly growing aspirations reflected in their consumption pattern and standard of living.

Post liberalization, the middle class has made several significant developments in the marketing scenario and emerged as the 'consumption community' of the country. People belonging to this class are more educated, better exposed to the global lifestyles and with constantly growing aspirations which is reflected in their consumption pattern and standard of living. There are also certain socio-cultural factors which has affected their lifestyle pattern. Broadly these can be categorized into three:

- The rapid growth of urbanization
- The earlier existing joint family system giving way to the nuclear family setup.
- More women taking to work and the domestic help becoming scarce and/or costly.

All the above have acted as precursors for bringing about rapid changes in the middle class consumption pattern. The dual income households are able to purchase household appliances, due to changes in lifestyle and increase in affordability.

Products such as *Whirlpool Washing Machine* with water saving facility, or *Haldiram* instant ready to eat eatables are examples of products which, are sold on the positioning of – *saves time/ makes the job easy* — all of which will suit the lifestyle of the neo rich middle class family.

The role of today's women in decision making

***Source : The Week*, C Voter Survey, December 3, 2006.**

Further, research (Grey Worldwide) has shown that a majority of consumers in the metro cities, being exposed to the best global consumption culture have no qualms about indulging themselves and get a feel of better lifestyle. According to the National Council of Applied Economic Research (NCAER), in mid 80's, India's middle class constituted less than 10 per cent of its population but today it comprises over 30% of the total population. The transformations at the social level like a younger population which has tasted financial independence at a much earlier age, the rise of nuclear families, increased media exposure and broad acceptance of the credit culture-have all contributed to the growth of the middle class. Naresh Gupta, National Head (Account planning) Grey Worldwide, points out that a recent research on young Indian consumers revealed that they were very confident and assured about their future and well being and not too apologetic about their indulgence and expenses. Broadly what Indians spend on, is presented in Table 5.2.

TABLE 5.2

SPENDING PATTERN OF INDIANS

Spending Pattern	Percentage
Food & Beverages	42%
Transport & Communication	15%
Rent, Fuel & Power	12%
Health Care	8%
Clothing & Foot wear	5%
Furniture & Fixtures	4%
Recreation & Education	3%
Miscellaneous	11%

(*Source : Business Today*, January 14, 2007)

Adapting to Greater Time Pressures, Growing Self Awareness and More Value Oriented Approach

In order to cope up with the fast paced lifestyle, consumers are giving increased emphasis to buying time saving conveniences and with an increase in personal disposable income, they are adopting more self aware lifestyle purchase decisions.

In order to cope up with the *fast paced lifestyle* consumers (as mentioned earlier in the chapter) are giving increased emphasis to buying time saving conveniences. With working couples on the rise, the woman of the house is required to do 'multitasking' *i.e.,* she has to devote and manage time between home and career. Such consumers will appreciate various marketers' products and service offerings such as *Kellogg's breakfast* offerings, Instant food mixes *(Mother's choice, Maggi, MTR, Haldiram's)* snack bars or fast food outlets (such as *McDonald's , Domino's, Subway, Nirula's, Pizza Hut* etc.)

Even organizations offering services in the form of financial services, tourism, (or travel) auto purchases etc., have launched online services (e-ticketing, travel.com etc.,) to enable customers facing paucity of time to avail of the convenience of online service offerings.

Ad could appeal to consumers facing paucity of time.

With an increase in personal disposable income, consumers are keen on adopting a more *self aware lifestyle. i.e.,* they are interested in the purchase of products and services which convey a feeling of personal achievement such as well known branded clothes, cars, personal care products, home appliances, cars etc. These consumers are also technology savvy and often plan and lead their lives through the use of technology. This also seems to be a global trend, where consumers find information on the web and are able to communicate and connect with other consumers having similar interest. Thus, this e-age has given rise to consumers who are more interconnected and knowledgeable.

With increased buying powers consumers have adopted a value oriented lifestyle and purchase products which signify a certain level of quality. Consumers, who use the internet, surf the set for entertainment, socializing and enjoyment.

In fact studies (The Economic Times) have indicated that internet access is changing the consumers' lifestyles (spending significantly less time on reading or watching television) because of more time spent on the web.

Big Bazaar helps consumers, seeking a value oriented lifestyle

To keep pace with economic developments, with increased buying powers consumers have adopted a value oriented lifestyle.

To keep in pace with economic developments with increased buying powers, consumers have adopted a *value oriented lifestyle.* Consumers are interested in the purchase of products which signify a certain level of quality. They are looking out for affordable quality. This value orientation has resulted in loosening of brand loyalties, increase in the purchase of private labels and economically priced products. The growing popularity of retail outlets such as *Big Bazaar/Food Bazaar* etc., can be attributed to the value oriented lifestyle preferred by today's consumers.

Internet & Lifestyle Patterns

Today, access to the internet has also brought about a change in consumers' lifestyles. It is seen that consumers who are addicted to the internet, spend fewer time reading books (or other reading material), watching television or socializing. Thus, internet usage is changing lifestyles because total involvement with the network, makes consumers surf the set for entertainment, socializing and enjoyment. Such consumers (or individuals) are completely focused on the activity at hand and managing their skills to match the online environment challenges. In fact, they are less conscious about what is happening in the world outside the internet. But health specialists have suggested that rather than adopting of such compulsive internet addicted lifestyle, a more healthy lifestyle should be followed which includes or integrates internet surfing along with other interests and activities.

➲ PERSONALITY

As seen in the beginning of the chapter, personality has been defined as patterns of individual behaviour which are consistent and enduring. An individual's personality also represents a set of characteristics which will help to understand consumer behaviour better. Understanding of personality characteristics can work as valuable guides for marketers. *For example* Health Food Drink Market in India is dominated by popular brands such as *Horlicks, Boost, Maltova, Viva, Bournvita* etc. All these brands have been scientifically developed to specially cater to the nutritional needs of the varying consumer segments. It was observed that these drinks were mainly consumed by children who were strong influencers in the family purchase decisions. Studies revealed that this category of customers who had the highest supplementary requirements were also more enthusiastic about sports and cricket in particular. The makers of *'Boost'*, consequently repositioned the brand such that it associates growing kids with cricket. It is said that *Boost* was one of the first in the HFD category to have used celebrity endorsement to convey its energy proposition and there by differentiated itself from the other brands. *Boost* has been successfully endorsed by India's most famous cricket stars, especially those who had a humungous fan following among children, starting with Kapil Dev the most charismatic cricketer of his time in the 1980s and then with Sachin Tendulkar in the 1990s. Sachin has continued to remain steadfast in his support for Boost, with Virendar Sehwag joining him as a brand (*Boost*) ambassador in 2001.

The personality of the Boost brand is now designed to be distinctly sporty and energetic and everything from the tone of communication to packaging is done to reflect this vibrant energy.

In fact today, the colour red and the tagline *"Boost is the secret of my energy"* have become synonymous with the brand.

The personality of Boost is distinctly sporty and energetic reflecting the personality characteristics of its consumers-children

Personality has been defined as patterns of individual behaviour which are consistent and enduring. An understanding of personality characteristics can work as valuable guides for marketers.

Properties of Personality : In the study of personality, one should be aware of three distinct properties.

- *Personality will reflect individual differences :* No two individual's are alike because their inner characteristics will be unique and relevant to that individual only.
- *Personality is consistent and enduring :* Generally, an individual's personality will remain almost the same throughout his or her life. We often hear older people commenting "He has been of the same nature "very quiet" since the time I have known him". Such statements support the contention that personality is both consistent and enduring.
- *Personality can change :* Certain specific events can bring about a change in the individual's personality, *for example-* marriage, birth of a child, a significant career promotion etc.

THEORIES OF PERSONALITY

We will briefly discuss three major theories of personality: (1) *Trait theory* (2) *Psychoanalytic theory (Freudian theory)* and (3) *Neo-Freudian theory.*

TRAIT THEORY

The trait theory is primarily quantitative in nature and focuses on the measurement of certain specific characteristics or traits. A trait is defined as "any distinguishing, relatively enduring way in which one individual differs from another" (J.P.Guilford, 1959).

Trait theorists advocated that personality tests will indicate the individual differences in terms of specific traits.

Trait theorists would make up personality inventories and ask those included in the sample to give their response to many terms, which could take the form of:

- agreeing or disagreeing to certain statements or
- indicating a liking or disliking for particular situations or certain types of people. Thereafter, these items are statistically tested and analysed and worked out to indicate few personality dimensions.

The trait theory is primarily quantitative in nature and focuses on the measurement of certain specific characteristics or traits. Marketers can use personality traits to segment different markets.

Marketers can use personality traits to segment different markets. *For example,* there are some personality tests based on a single trait personality (which measures only one trait - say self confidence) being specifically used to analyse consumer behaviour. Such tailor made personality tests are specifically used to measure consumer traits like:

- Consumer innovativeness (to what extent a person is receptive to a new buying experience)
- Consumer susceptibility to interpersonal influence (SUSCEP) (To understand how consumers will respond to social influences).
- Consumer materialism (To ascertain the extent to which consumer's are attached to worldly 'material' possessions).
- Consumer ethnocentrism (CETSCALE) (The likelihood of consumer accepting or rejecting foreign-made products).

PSYCHOANALYTIC THEORY OR FREUDIAN THEORY

Psychoanalytic Theory goes beyond studying the traits of groups of people. This theory is based on indepth study of individual personalities. Psychoanalytic theory developed by Sigmund Freud at the beginning of the twentieth century has been a major contribution to psychological thought especially on the term 'Personality'. This theory has been developed on the premise that unconscious (biological) needs or drives are all root forces determining human motivation and personality.

The psychoanalytic theory of Freud emphasises on the fact that human personality is made up of three main interdependent forces - the Id, the Ego and the Superego. And human behaviour is dependent on the interaction of these three systems.

FIGURE 5.2

PERSONALITY TRAITS

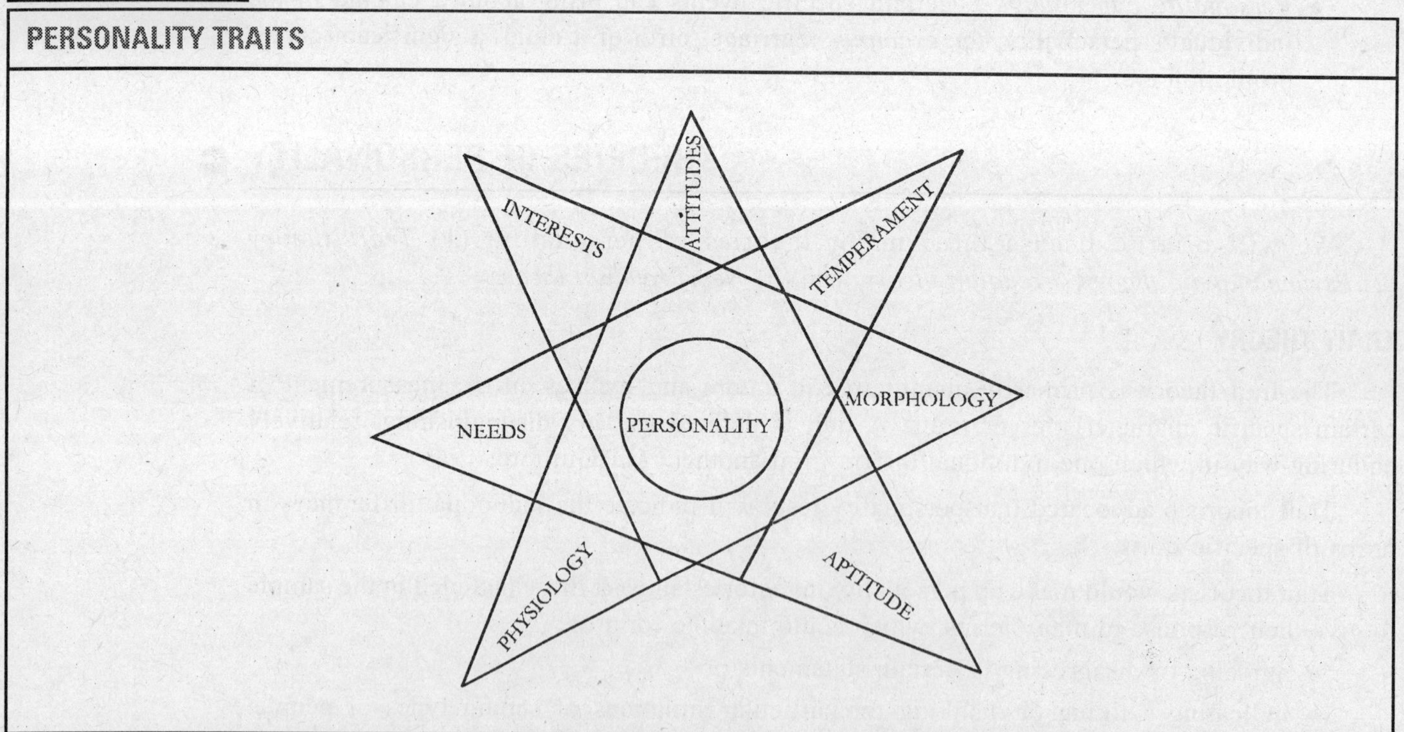

(*Source :* E.R. Hilgard, *Introduction to Psychology*, Harcourt Barce, Jovanorich, New York, 1962. p. 452)

Ad potrays the working of the *id* status of the individual's mind

The psychoanalytic theory of Freud emphasises on the fact that human personality is made up of three main interdependent forces- the Id, the Ego and the Superego. And, human behaviour is dependent on the interaction of these three systems.

Id : The id is referred to as the source of all its driving psychic energy (the libido). All the instinctive carvings, needs, desires which demand immediate gratification - all have their origin in id. The human being will seek immediate satisfaction without much concern for the specific means of satisfaction. However, it is not possible for man to express his basic impulses or animalistic nature in society because then it would mean going against rules, mores and values. Thus this makes it necessary to have a second system of personality.

Super Ego : It is the internal representative of the traditional values and the ideals of society. The function of the super ego is to restrict those impulses (which are condemned by the society) of the id. The super ego can be conceptualised as the moral arm of the personality. The super ego's role is to ensure that the individual satisfies his needs in a manner which is acceptable to the society.

Ego : There could be conflict between 'id' and 'Super ego'. Ego is the individual's conscious control. It will act as an internal force to control and re-direct the id-impulses and the sociocultural restraints exercised by the super ego. Figure 5.3 shows the inter-relationship between the Id, Super ego and Ego.

FIGURE 5.3

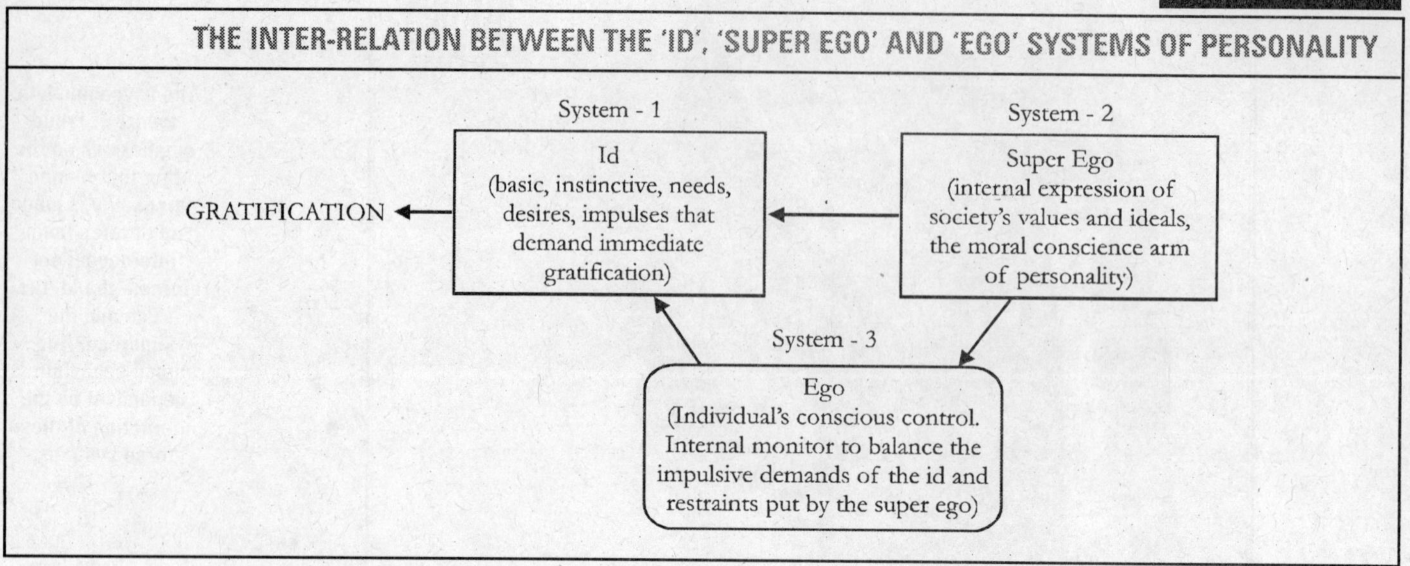

Ad conveys the ego status or that the individual's conscious control is working.

FREUDIAN THEORY AND CONSUMER BEHAVIOUR

Going by the premise that human drives are largely unconscious and usually consumers are unaware of the true reason for buying various goods and services, researchers are applying Freud's psychoanalytic theory to the consumer purchases or consumption situations by considering them as an extension of the consumers' own personality.

Brand Positioning and Brand Personality

The concept of product positioning was introduced to the marketing world around four decades ago. But it has come a long way and today it is used to emphasise 'brands' and brand differentiation. Positioning is adopted by marketers so as to carve out a distinct and valued slot in the consumer's mind, for their brand. Marketers will try to match the attributes of their brand with the consumer's needs.

Since human drives are largely unconscious and usually consumers are unaware of the reason for buying various goods and services, researchers are applying Freud's psychoanalytic theory to the consumer purchases and consumption situations by considering them as an extension of the consumer's own personality.

Consumers have a tendency to assign certain psychological and symbolic values to the brand. They prefer to look beyond the functional value and performance and look at 'it' with human description. Marketers have often used 'brand personality' as a metaphor to convey the emotional relationship that exists between a consumer and a brand.

Marketers are using psychographic base to describe the personality traits of the target market. A well known example can be of the *Garden Vareli* dress material for women. The *Vareligirl* was projected as a younger woman, whose personality was different from the usual Indian women (who preferred wearing a saree). Vareli was targeted at women whose aspirations ran high. She had a unique combination of being universal and yet unpredictable. The Garden Vareli girl was keen to venture and explore new territories and also do exotic things. Thus *'Garden Vareli'* was given a feminine persona to match the consumers' view at the market place.

Consumers may not only assign personality traits to products and services but they also tend to associate personality factors with specific colours. Union Carbide has associated its *Red Eveready Batteries* - with red colour, which connotes excitement ("Give me Red"). In the detergents market, 'White or Blue' - is associated with superior quality. *Rin Shakti, Surf Excel Blue, Ariel or Tide.* Pearl, Silver, Gold colours suggest something with premium price or royal, wealthy - like *'Nakshtra/DTC'* Diamond, *Tanishq watches and* so on. Green colour signifies close association with nature - *'Hamam soap', Nirma lime, Vim lime bar soap, Dabur Vatika, Brahmi oil* etc.

To gain a better insight into consumer acceptance, researchers use a variety of qualitative research measurement techniques observation, depth interviews, projective techniques and so on.

Marketing applications of psychoanalytic theory is known as *motivational research techniques.*

It is believed that the deep rooted purchasing motives can be understood in an indirect manner by researching a small number of consumers in motivational research. The two most frequently used techniques in marketing – depth interviews and projective techniques is discussed here.

Depth and Focus Group Interviews : The foremost proponent of depth and focus group interviews was Earnest-Diether, the father of motivational research.

Through depth interviews, individual consumers are encouraged to talk freely in an unstructured interview and their responses are interpreted carefully so as to reveal motives and the likely purchase inhibitions. An offshoot of the depth interview is the *focus group interview,* wherein 8 to 10 consumers are, under the guidance of a moderator, brought together in order to discuss issues which may reveal the unconscious or deep rooted motives. A *big advantage* of this focus groups is that the group context is likely to prompt open discussion and also convey individual consumer's thoughts and motives which the depth interview may not do so.

Projective Techniques : Projective techniques, like depth interviews are designed to determine motives which are difficult to identify. Say, sometimes consumers may not be aware

Marketing applications of psychoanalytic theory is known as motivational research techniques. The most frequently used techniques in marketing are in-depth interviews and projective techniques.

of their motives for buying, then researchers cannot ask direct questions which the consumers may not be able to answer. So, to tackle this problem, consumers are given a situation, a cartoon or a set of words and asked to respond. It is seen that they will project or convey their feelings and concerns about products when the situation is found to be less threatening or involving.

Other projective techniques may take the form of:

- Asking consumers to complete sentences "Someone who buys Brand A is......
- Father talking to his son on the play ground with a bubble over the head (to complete the bubble) indicates he is saying something.
- Personify brands (*Horlicks*-helps to fight Exam ghosts, *Tiger biscuits* gives the strength of a tiger).

In each of the above cases, the consumer is projecting his or her feelings about a product or situation without a direct question being asked.

NEO FREUDIAN PERSONALITY THEORY

Neo Freudian theorists felt that social relationships played a vital role in the formation and development of personality. They disagreed with Freud's rigid adherence to consider only the basic biological or instinctive traits as determinants of personality.

There were several Freud's colleagues who disagreed with his rigid adherence to consider only the basic biological or instinctive traits as determinants of personality. According to these neo-Freudian's, social relationships played a vital role in the formation and development of personality. Alfred Adler, for instance, was of the opinion that the basic drive of man is to *Strive for Superiority.* So all efforts of the individual will be aimed at perfecting one self and to overcome the feelings of inferiority. A unique aspect of personality is that each child is born in a different world and hence will learn and adopt different behaviour patterns for striving.

Eric Fromm another neo-Fredian speaks on man's goal *to escape from his bonds* (loneliness) and seek, love, brotherliness and security. Yet another Neo Fredian, Harry Stack Sullivan was the one to stress on man's need for *inter-relationships with other men.* He opined that people continuously looked for establishing significant and rewarding relationships with others. He gave a lot of emphasis on the individual's efforts to reduce tensions, such as anxiety.

Another social theorist, Karen Horney also felt that the main drive of man was to cope with anxiety. She gave importance to the *parent-child relationships* on how an individual's personality can develop life long patterns of behaviour as he learns to cope with his *anxieties* and strives to reduce them.

Horney's views have been expressed well in a research project by Joel Cohen. Horney had proposed to classify three personality groups of individuals, in coping with anxiety:

- Compliant type of individuals. (C)
- Aggressive individuals. (A)
- Detached persons. (D)
- The compliant individuals are those who desire to be included in activities of groups. They desire to be loved, want appreciation and want to experience the feeling of being needed.
- The aggressive individuals seek to cope with anxiety by going against others. They try to achieve success, prestige and administration. They desire to excel and see others as competitors.
- The detached persons attempt to put emotional distance between themselves and others. They prefer to have independence, self reliance, self sufficiency and to be free from obligations.

Although the Neo Freudians did not have influence in the field of marketing, many of the advertisements indicate that marketers have been using neo Freudian theory intuitively. Ads depicting products or services which provide an opportunity to belong, be appreciated by others or social group setting are being potrayed as compliant individuals.

For example, advertisements of *Close-up confidence, Rexona deodorant, Fair & Lovely Cream, Denim after shave, Old Spice deodorant, Axe, Garnier Colour Naturals* etc. help in creating self confidence or in reducing anxiety.

A personality test based on Horney's theory known as CAD (mentioned above) has been developed and tested to study consumer behaviour. It helped to uncover a number of tentative relationships between college students and their products and brand usage patterns.

Jung's Personality Types

Carl Jung of Zurich was a contemporary and colleague of Freud. He had said *"Personality is the supreme realisation of the innate individuality of a particular living being"* (Kanuk & Schiffman, 6th Edn., PHI, p. 113). He had undertaken systematic investigations of the unconscious dynamics with the association test. He had given more attention to the question of personality type in the association test. And based on the typology of the personality, he had grouped them into two fundamental types.

1. Extrovert
2. Introvert.

The Extrovert was very much interested in building a social relationship. While the introvert was found to be pre-occupied with his own inner world of fantasy and body activity and was relatively incapable of outgoing social interactions. This conception was further elaborated by going for a sub division of the mental operation into four fundamental activities :

- Sensing
- Feeling
- Thinking
- Intuiting.

Carl Jung was a contemporary and colleague of Freud and had undertaken systematic investigations of the unconscious dynamics with the association test. He felt that personality is the supreme realization of the innate individuality of a particular living being.

These four psychological functions of grouping personality are very often used for gathering and evaluating information. According to Jung, individuals are strong either in 'sensation' or 'intuition' when gathering information, and while evaluating the information they are strong either in 'thinking' or 'feeling'.

Carl Jung's theories and personality types are very relevant to consumer behaviour. Marketers are benefited by using Myers-Briggs type Indicators that measure the following pairs of psychological dimensions:

- Sensing - Intuiting
- Thinking - Feeling
- Extroversion - Introversion.
- Judging - Perceiving.

Each of the above four pairs show two distinct different personality characteristics which offer a picture of how consumers respond to the world around them. In order to avoid complexities with too many combinations of personality types, a consumer researcher suggested to investigate consumption relevance with two pairs of dimensions.

- Sensing - Intuiting
- Thinking - Feeling.

As mentioned above, sensation and intuiting will help consumers to obtain and find out about things and products. Whereas, the thinking and feeling dimensions can be related to the decision styles adopted by the consumers. Such psychological inventory indicators will help in learning about the four personality types impact on consumer information processing, their decision making process and other consumption related issues that will enable marketers to satisfy consumer needs in a better manner.

For instance, we presume four individuals were faced with a situation when they had to take decision regarding whether and how much of, to purchase new public issue shares. Both the Sensing-Thinking (ST) and Sensing-Feeling (SF) types will try to gather all information related to the company coming out with the new issue, read magazines such as "Data Quest" etc. and secure all the relevant facts. Though, the ST types may arrive at their own decision and purchase the new shares directly from the market. As against this, the SF prospective investor is likely to include the recommendations of others before finally purchasing the new issue shares through a full service broker. The intuitive - thinking (IT) and intuitive - feeling (IF) consumers are likely to purchase the shares using their gut feeling or hunch. The IT consumers would rely on their imaginations and carefully think over the option. Although IF would also rely on their imagination while making a choice, their ultimate decision can be influenced by the information received from other people such as comments expressed in a social gathering and so on.

Some of the advertisements have been communicating consumer targeted messages which may be said to be of the Jungian personality types say *HDFC Post Retirement* (schemes).

TABLE 5.3

FEW CHARACTERISTICS OF SELECTED JUNGIAN PERSONALITY TYPES

Sensing - Thinking (ST)	Intuitive - Thinking (IT)
• Logical, empirical and rational in decision making • Risk avoider, will search in depth for decision making information • Price sensitive and materialistic in considering motives • Short-term consideration in decision making	• Takes a broader perspective of the situation and world • Thinks, uses logic and imagination in taking decisions • Considers many options while taking decisions - speculative • Takes long term view while taking decisions
Sensing - Feeling (SF)	**Intuitive - Feeling (IF)**
• Considers personal values rather than logic - empirial viewpoint. • Makes decision after considering others-subjective orientation. • Status conscious and materialism reflects the impact on other persons. • Short term consideration in decision making.	• Takes a broader perspective of the situation or world. • Considers various options for decision making. • People oriented and subjective oriented in decision making. • Least price conscious, are venturesome and novelty seeking. • The time period is indefinite while taking decisions.

A BUSINESS TODAY-SYNOVATE STUDY (BT-SYNOVATE)

A BT-Synovate study was carried out by Business Today (with the help of Market Research firm Synovate) in order-to understand how many different kinds of tweens are there in India. The study was conducted (involving both quantitative and qualitative exercises) across six cities namely-Delhi, Mumbai, Chennai, Kolkata, Hyderabad and Bangalore. The target audience were *8-12 year olds* who belonged to households in the higher socio-economic classification Sec- A and Sec-B. The study was carried out in two stages. *In the first stage* 563 respondents across the six cities were administered *an in-depth questionnaire* in order to understand their lifestyle, aspirations and influences, attitudes and values, involvement in purchase decisions, media habits and consumption pattern.

In the second stage, focus groups were conducted to understand attitudinal and behavioural facets of tweens, which would not be possible to obtain through quantitative exercises. Based on both sets of findings, the study arrived at a conclusion that there are four tween segments, although each segment is unique in some ways and the same in some others. These segments include:

- **Tween Type I – The All Indian Jock / Cheerleader (15.2 percent of tweens)** who can be described as brash, spoilt *not academically oriented* and prone to tantrums. This type of tweens receive the most pocket money and freedom of space from their parents. However, they are not involved with big-priced purchases as expected. They receive an average pocket money of Rs. 421.86 per month.
- **Tween Type II – The Traditional Reticent (11.8 percent of the tweens)** can be described as quiet, ambivalent to most things and a *traditionalist at heart.* These tweens do not really seem to care about most things, nor do their parents have high expectations of them.

  It was also found that this segment has the least influence, when it comes to big or high priced product decisions at home. This segment on an average receives Rs. 287.69 per month.
- **Tween Type III – The Dependent Diffident (25.38 percent of the tween population)** can be described as toeing the parental line and still clutching on to the apron strings. This segment of tweens tend to be highly involved in the purchase of high priced products for home. Although this segment of the respondents expressed views of their parents, they received the least pocket money (Average being Rs 192.18 per month), probably because they get their parents to buy almost everything for them and so do not feel the need to have money of their own.
- **Tween Type IV – The Righteous Angel (47.51 per cent of the tween population)** can be described as home birds with an active outside life, good at school and *with a strong value system* ingrained in them.

The tweens from this segment have an inherent goodness and never push for anything. For instance, they do not mind missing out on fun and games if it means securing the top rank in an examination. However, they feel that the system has too many exams for their liking and also do not like being pushed. They receive on an average pocket money of Rs 245.09 per month.

The researching teams concluded that children in the 8-12 years age group, although from similar backgrounds tend to think and behave alike sometimes and very differently at some other times.

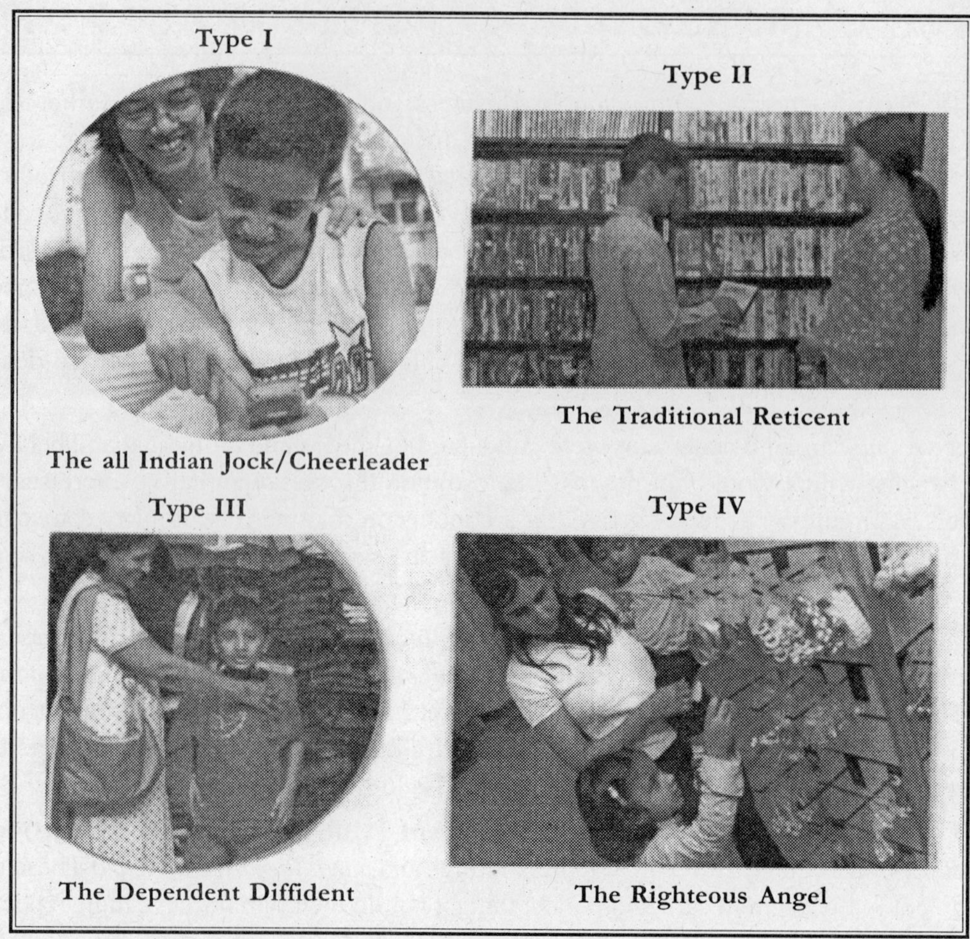

(*Source : Business Today*, January 1, 2006)

Since the study covered only the metros and two major cities, it cannot be said to be conclusive and a representative of the entire country. Nevertheless, since these children (in the age group of 8-12 years) are more aware of lifestyle changes due to media exposure, marketers could try out unique ways to communicate their product offerings and through interactive ways get them more involved in purchase decisions.

PERSONALITY INFLUENCES AND CONSUMER BEHAVIOUR

There are certain personality traits which can influence consumer acceptance of new products and services. Availability of this information will enable marketers to work out suitable market segmentation and other communication programme.

Marketers are interested in knowing how personality can influence consumption behaviour. Availability of this information will enable them to go for suitable market segmentation and then target these consumers with appropriate communication programmes. There are certain specific personality traits which influence consumer acceptance of new products and services.

Especially while trying to analyse the likely market response for new innovations, marketers are interested in knowing the personality traits which can be useful in differentiating between consumer innovators and non innovators. Schiffman and Kanuk (Consumer Behavior, PHI, 2005, pp. 126-131) have referred to the personality traits (behaviour) as:

- Consumer innovativeness.
- Dogmatism.
- Social character.

- Need for uniqueness
- Optimum stimulation level.
- Variety - novelty seeking.

Consumer researchers have developed various measurement instruments to understand the level of consumer innovativeness specially the personality trait which provide insights into the nature and boundaries of a consumer's willingness to innovate.

Consumer Innovativeness : Innovation always has an element of risk, because there will be easy accepters of the new products and services only if both the marketers and consumers are to equally gain from the right innovation. Consumer researchers have developed various measurement instruments to understand the level of consumer innovativeness, specifically the personality trait which provide insights into the nature and boundaries of a consumer's willingness to innovate.

Recent researches have indicated about the positive relationship that exist between purchasers of online products and the innovative use of the internet. The personality of internet users can be described as people who are confident about themselves and in their ability to control their own future and in using the internet to seek out information, enjoy change and are not afraid of uncertainty.

Gray and Starke have identified sixteen source personality traits, which are presented below in Table 5.4.

TABLE 5.4

SIXTEEN SOURCE TRAITS

1. Reserved / Introvert	Vs	Outgoing/Extrovert
2. Less Intelligent	Vs	More intelligent
3. More Emotional	Vs	Emotionally more stable
4. Submissive	Vs	Dominant
5. Serious	Vs	Happy go lucky
6. Expedient	Vs	Conscientious
7. Timid	Vs	Venturesome
8. Tough minded	Vs	Sensitive
9. Trusting	Vs	Suspicious
10. Practical	Vs	Imaginative
11. Forthright	Vs	Shrewd
12. Self-assured	Vs	Apprehensive
13. Conservative	Vs	Experimenting
14. Group dependent	Vs	Self-dependent
15. Uncontrolled	Vs	Controlled
16. Relaxed	Vs	Tense

(*Source :* Jerry *Gray and Frederick A. Starke, Organizational Behavior, Concepts and Applications McMillan Colombus,* 1980. p. 77
Re-adopted: *Dr. Niraj Kumar, A Genesis of Behavioural Science, Prashant Prakashan, Lucknow,* 1995)

Dogmatism : Dogmatism is the personality trait which will indicate the degree of rigidity individuals display when confronted with something which is unfamiliar to them or towards information which is contrary to their own established beliefs. The person who is high on dogmatism will approach the unfamiliar defensively and decide on the worthiness of the products or services. On the other hand, those who are low on dogmatism will willingly consider unfamiliar or opposing beliefs.

Personality traits can influence dressing style.

Consumers with *low dogmatism* (open minded) display more acceptance of innovative products than to established or traditional alternatives. Whereas, highly dogmatic *(close-minded)* consumers display preference for established rather than innovative product alternatives.

Optimum Stimulation Level : Consumer researchers have examined the relationship between personality traits and differences in the stimulation which, in turn, may be related to consumer behaviour. Researches have indicated high optimum stimulation levels (OSLS) with consumers who display more willingness to take risks, try new products, be innovative etc.

Researches have indicated high Optimum Stimulation Levels (OSLs) with consumers who display more willingness to take risks, try new products, be innovative etc. OSL reflects a person's desire for the level of lifestyle stimulation.

It is also suggested OSL reflects a person's desire for the level of lifestyle stimulation. Accordingly, if consumer's actual lifestyles are equivalent to their OSL scores, then they are likely to be quite satisfied. Whereas if their OSL is more than their current reality, they are likely to be restless or bored, while if their (lifestyles) or OSL is below their current reality, they are likely to seek relief. This conveys that consumers will make their choice of products or services depending on the OSL. An over stimulated person is likely to seek for rest in a quiet, isolated place or holiday (Examples can be of various Resorts/Vacation halts etc. which seem to be invitations for over stimulated persons).

For instance, *S Kumar's Nation Wide* (SKNL) has used cine star Sushmita Sen to endorse its new brand *Carmichael House.* This brand offers total solutions in the home textile segment including bed linen, table linen, kitchen linen, curtains and upholstery. The brand offers unique and latest trends for the home and the personality of the brand endorser (Sushmita Sen.) as an icon, stands for international styling. Research had indicated that women, who will be the primary market segment look up to her on style issues. While men, who comprise the secondary audience admire her style. Thus, the brand is trying to appeal to customers whose lifestyles will match their OSL scores.

Variety or Novelty Seeking : As the term itself indicates there are certain types of customers seeking variety or novelty in their consumption behaviour. This variety seeking behaviour can be:

- *Exploratory purchase behaviour* (exploring newer brands).
- *Vicarious exploration* (consumer obtains information about new alternatives and contemplates about the new option) with caution and reservation.
- *Use innovativeness* (Already using a product in a new or novel way)

The use innovativeness trait is more relevant to products which are technological or electronic products such as home appliances (home stereo system, washing machine etc.) In case of such products there could be certain product models with additional functions or features while some other models with only the essential features. Consumers who are high on variety seeking are more likely to be attracted to product brands which offer novel features or have multiple applications, unlike consumers who score low on variety seeking, who may not do so.

Ad of Zipouch will appeal to those who display low dogmatism trait

Social Character : The personality trait depicting social character is closely related to socio-cultural environment or sociological research. Here the reference is of two types of personality traits -inner *directedness* (consumers who rely on their 'own' intuition or standards or values while evaluating new products) and *other directedness* (These are consumers who look to others for directions or guidance, especially in case of new products). The former category of consumers are more likely to be innovators.

The personality trait depicting social character is closely related to socio-cultural environment.

The inner-directed consumers have a preference for ads which stress product features and personal benefits thus enabling them to self evaluate and use the product in an innovative or novel way. Whereas, other directed people prefer ads which convey social acceptance and this can influence their purchase decisions.

Need for Uniqueness

One must have come across people who seek to be unique. Such people do not like to be in conformity to other's expectations or standards either in appearance or in terms of possessions. In a study undertaken to explore the circumstances under which persons who are high on the Need For Uniqueness make (or do not make) unconventional choices, it was revealed that these individuals were more open to making unique choices when they were not concerned about being criticized. (L.G.Schiffman, L.L. Kanuk, *Consumer Behavior*, 8th Edn., PHI, 2005, pp. 129). So, it would help marketers to carry out researches to measure this trait in the context of consumer behaviour, while introducing new products in the market.

Thus having knowledge of various personality traits and differences is essential for the marketer to design suitable market segmentation and other promotional strategies for their product or service.

Ad of Prerana will appeal to consumers depicting a social character.

Cognitive Personality Traits

Consumer researchers are also keen to understand the role played by cognitive personality factors in influencing various aspects of consumer behaviour. Here the discussion will be related to two cognitive personality traits.

- Visualizers Versus Verbalizers
- Need for cognition.

Consumer researchers are interested in the role of cognitive personality factors (visualisers versus verbalizers and need for cognition) in influencing consumer behaviour. Visualizers stress on visual information while verbalizers refers to verbal information on products.

Visualizers vs Verbalizers : Cognitive personality researchers have classified consumers into visualizers and verbalizers. *Visualizers* - who stress on the visual information and visual products, for example membership of a CD/DVD cassette shop. *Verbalizers* - are those (consumers) who prefer verbal information on products. For example membership in books or magazines shop. The privilege card issued by *Sapna Book House* (Bangalore) is a written information. Thus marketers try to attract their target market by categorising them as above.

The ad *(A) Cancer patients aid association* speaks on a unique and refreshing way of looking at it for smokers. In ad *(B)* for *The Indian Association for promotion of Adoption and Child Welfare* the transparent sheet in the middle with the child's picture was conveying about how changing some one's life could be as easy as turning a page. Both these ads communicate a lot visually and makes one think hard as the truth jolts you.

(A) (B)

These ads (A) related to antismoking and (B) adopting some one makes one think really hard and help in acting as visualisers

In case of the *Cadbury Dairy Milk*, it works as a verbalizer because the central idea of the ad revolved around 'Celebrate the joy of Pappu passing the exams with a *Dairy Milk.* This message was further, appropriated at the precise moment when Pappu passed and he was given a congratulatory message from Cadbury Dairy Milk. In fact, this message was flashed out 39 million times in a span of three months and was also well received by the target audience.

Need for Cognition : Need for cognition (NC) is another cognitive personality characteristic which is related to the individual's thinking process and measures a person's craving for something. The information on consumers' *need for cognition* will enable the advertiser to decide on the creation of advertising messages with the right combination of colour mix.

Need for Cognition is another personality characteristic which is related to the individual's thinking process and measures a person's craving for something.

This ad is a verbalizer integrating the message around celebrating the joy of pappu passing in Exams with a Dairy Milk'

Researches have shown that consumers who are high on the 'need for cognition' will be more receptive to an ad giving, such rich product related information. While those consumers seeking less need for cognition will be more attracted to the peripheral background or model or the celebrity endorsing the product in the advertisement.

Long back the ad *of Maruti 1000 cc* car had evoked some strange and yet irresistible attraction, echoes of which linger in the haunting melody of Monalisa. The ad had show a car with a celestial aura with a heading "The lady with the mystic smile". This ad is an example of an appeal to those consumers who are less on the need for cognition.

A similar intriguing charm was built up in the series of ads for the *'Taj' group of hotels and* is an example of an ad which will appeal to consumers who are high on need for cognition. The setting of the ad (both in print as well as on television) takes the form of a lady moving about ethereally and purposefully in a grand manner. When the commercial was first revealed it had an element of mystery evolved around it with the viewer puzzled as to what the advertiser had in mind. The voice over could be heard saying things like. "She plays a host to celebrities. She receives you just as graciously. She is not your business manager, your secretary, your this and that...... but she values efficiency".

The puzzle is solved when it is announced *"She is the Taj",* she runs luxury hotels that has epitomize, elegance and a whole lot virtues. The closing line says *"Nobody cares so much".*

Sony Entertainment Television (SET) had before the launch of its popular serial *'Jassi Jaissi Koi Nahin'* tried to create hype and a need for cognition among the target audience about its launch.

The *primary objective* was to fuel curiosity about Jassi and build endearment for her as a character by giving the TV viewers different facets of personality –all without revealing her. During the pre-launch period of Jassi, the consumers (audience) were fed pieces of (bits of) information on Jassi's persona even allowing the viewer to create a personal image such that this character (Jassi) sounded real and identifiable.

The *campaign messages* and various elements were used so as to fuel the curiosity around and after the launch. The media mix included host of unconventional media vehicles such as

Ad of 'Sparkle mustard oil will appeal to consumers who are high on the 'need for cognition'.

Researches have shown that consumers who are high on the need for cognition will be more receptive to an ad giving rich product related information, while those who are low on cognition will be more attracted to the peripheral background or model endorsing the product.

sms, flash mobs, airport placards, leaflets designed specially for traffic junctions, shop trains etc., apart from the conventional T.V radio, outdoor and print media. At the media launch, SET presented the entire cast of the show *(except Jassi)* further increasing the curiosity and intrigue among the media.

Sony Entertainment Television (SET) had before the launch of its popular serial "Jassi Jaisi kio Nahin", tried to create hype and a need for cognition among the target audience about its launch.

The *communication strategy* started with building attributes which personified Jassi. The next step involved anonymous people talking about Jassi, then the campaign moved on to characters from the show talking about Jassi (her parents, her boss and her peers) in their inimitable ways. Once sufficient momentum was generated and the initial feedback from critics, media and viewers was very positive, the next place of communication the *Shaher Shaher Mein Charcha* campaign was launched, which had people from all walks of life voicing their opinion about Jassi. This move continued to fuel the buzz on T.V and billboards, when the channel embarked on another unusual activity-it created a *Jassi's Pals Club*. The purpose of the club was to help in the creation of a community of Jassi fans who would become apostles and advocates for the show. Simultaneously Jassi merchandise was now being made available-the first in a series of items to be launched was the ring tone download.

All the efforts and initiatives were taken by the channel to maintain the interest, of the audience and build viewer affinity to Jassi and the show. In the final place, since Jassi had been kept hidden all the while, it was decided that the time was right to get the viewers interact with the Jassi character and further drive up the connect and emphathy. All efforts had been made up to build up the consumers' (audience) need cognition around Jassi. Finally, the channel took Jassi to Delhi where she became the talk of the town. She was interviewed live in the studios of Aaj Tak and the FM. There was a lot of excitement on seeing her, which is similar to that reserved for film personalities.

In fact, what started as a buzz turned into a roar, with the Jassimania taking the country by storm. The serial went on to command very high TPR ratings during the primary viewing time, winning many T.V awards and was even hailed by all (media, critics and audiences) as the new refreshing and popular face of Indian Television.

Personality traits showing self assurance and tenseness in two persons

➲ CERTAIN INTER-RELATED CONSUMPTION AND POSSESSION PERSONALITY TRAITS

Consumer researchers have identified certain consumption and possession traits which influence consumer behaviour. They are as follows:

Consumer Materialism : 'Materialism' refers to the attachment people have towards (material) possessions. When considering materialism as a personality like trait, it differentiates between person's who identify themselves and others on the basis of the material goods possessed by them. As against this there are certain people for whom possession of material goods is secondary.

When considering materialism as a personality like trait it differentiates between persons who identify themselves and others on the basis of the material goods possessed by them.

Researchers have made the following characteristic observation about materialistic people:

- They give undue importance to acquiring and displaying their worldly possessions.
- They crave for possessing 'lots of things'.
- They are usually self centered and selfish.
- They like to possess things irrespective of whether they derive greater happiness or satisfaction from possessing the same.

Ad is meant to attract materialistic consumers

Fixated Consumption Behaviour : Lying between being materialistic and addictive regarding buying or possessing objects is the fixated consumption behaviour. Fixated consumers not only are interested in purchasing objects or things but also enjoy displaying them and are known for their involvement with others who share a similar interest.

Fixated consumers are not only interested in purchasing objects or things but they also enjoy displaying them and are known for their involvement with others who share a similar interest.

The characteristics profile of fixated consumers are as follows :

- A very deep interest displayed for a particular object or a product category.
- A dedicated search for additional examples of the object or the particular product category.
- Willingness to spend a considerable amount of their discretionary time and money in searching for the product or object.

Under this category, we can put the various people who are vigorously involved in collecting (or have a hobby) various objects like stamps, coins, antique articles etc. These fixated consumers become totally involved in the process of acquiring the object.

Compulsive Consumption Behaviour

Compulsive consumption is abnormal behaviour. Consumers who display this type of behaviour are sometimes said to be having abnormal behaviour. Their compulsive actions reveal an addiction, whereby their actions are out of control and could result in causing harm to themselves or to those around them. Some of the problems associated with this type of behaviour are: uncontrollable consumption of liquor, gambling, drug addiction and so on. Such problems can be handled by going for clinical therapy treatment.

Some research studies have indicated that certain actions such as self gifting, impulse buying etc. are compulsive actions adopted by few consumers to manage their moods, which may indicate "I am feeling down, so I will go and purchase something, then I will feel better".

Consumer Ethnocentrism

This term is used to measure the consumer responses to foreign made products. Under this, there can be two types of consumers – consumers who are highly ethnocentric and who feel it is inappropriate to purchase foreign made goods. In India, sometimes the term 'swadeshi goods' is used. If such individuals are in reality highly ethnocentric, they would exclusively go for the purchase of 'Indian made' products - like khadi clothes etc. In contrast, those consumers who are low on ethnocentrism may have more attachment or affinity for made in U.S.A., Japan, etc., labelled products. This could probably be one of the reason's for the flourishing of the so called "Burma Bazar's, China Bazar's and so forth in many cities, where many imitation products manufacturers sell similar goods by affixing false labels like made in U.S.A., made in Taiwan etc. on them.

➲ SELF CONCEPT OR SELF IMAGE

Consumers tend to purchase products or services, which according to them have symbolic images closely related to their self image. Researchers have proposed that instead of considering an individual as a 'single self', it would be more appropriate to think of the consumer in terms of multiple selves.

Individuals have a specific perception and image of themselves. These self concept or self images are closely connected to the personality of the products or services patronised by them. This means that consumers tend to purchase goods or services, which according to them have symbolic image closely related to their self image.

Multiple Selves

Researchers have proposed that instead of considering an individual as a 'single self', it would be more appropriate to think of the consumer in terms of a multiple self. This is because the behaviour of an individual at a particular time will be dependent on the person with whom he is interacting and the social setting or social role which was prominent at that time. From this the marketer must infer that they have to market their product and services to suit the context of the 'consumer's self image'.

Self Image

Each individual has an image of himself or herself as that of being a certain kind of person, with certain personality traits, habits, possessions, behaviour and so on. Each individual's self image will be a unique one based on his or her background and experience, and knowledge gained from various persons' over a period of time.

According to various researchers, an individual can possess any of these self images:

- *Actual self image* (how they actually see themselves).
- *Ideal self image* (how they would like to see themselves).
- *Social self image* (how they feel the society sees them).
- *Ideal social self image* (how they would like the society to see them)
- *Expected self image* (Their expectation of how they see themselves at some specified future time).

All the above self images will be useful for the marketer's. But the 'ideal self image' and 'expected self image' will be of more relevance to the marketer. This is because consumers may be induced to purchase goods or services to improve their actual self image *i.e.,* to reach their 'ideal self image'. And expected self image conveys that consumers may look out for opportunity to change their 'self. This can be used by marketers to manufacture products projecting the above opportunity for consumers.

Consumers have a preference for those products and services which match their personal images. Thus a knowledge of the various types of self images of consumers, will enable marketers, work out marketing strategy programmes. For instance, the marketer can work on market segmentation programmes on the basis of the relevant consumer self image and then position their products or services to match the consumers social status and lifestyle, in various product categories.

Extension of Self Image

Researchers are convinced of the relationship between consumers ownership of goods (or possessions) to their self images. If a young son were to receive a stylish high priced wrist watch from his father, after faring well in the examination, the gift will serve as an enrichment to the son's self image. The son *will* feel enriched and see himself as a more hardworking, confident and successful and 'include' the stylish wrist watch to his inventory of self enhancing possessions.

This only goes to show that human emotions are related to valued possessions. Researchers have identified possessions which can extend the self in a number of ways such as:

It is seen that human emotions are related to valued possessions. Researchers are convinced of the relationship between consumer ownership of goods (or possessions) to their self images *i.e.,* extension of self image.

- *Motivate the individual* to do things; which otherwise would have been difficult (*For example,* buying a personal computer to add to the status, may force the housewife to learn to operate the PC).
- *Through symbolic representation,* make the person feel better and bigger. The contestant receiving cine star Shah Rukh Khan's wrist watch on not earning much on the KBC reality show.
- *By conferring status or rank* (For instance, M.F. Hussian being given a unique status by art lovers because of masterminding and possessing a unique masterpiece of painting.
- *By bestowing upon someone close, and handing over a priced possession.*
- *By perceiving the receipt of a 'gift'* from someone *as a 'good luck charm' for you.*

Cine star Amrita Rao while endorsing D'damas diamonds also communicates about the expected self image

Altering the Self Image

Going by human psychology of wishing to change themselves to enrich oneself with an 'improved self image', marketers of various products and services are working at this. Consumers have the desire to project a new self, or maintain the present self, or extend the self - all with the intention of expressing their individualism or uniqueness. Firms marketing products or services related to clothes, cosmetics, jewellery, hair styles, membership to certain clubs, other personal care products, beauty saloons etc. are working out marketing plans so as to help the consumer gain an inflated and enhanced view of their physical appearance or self image.

Firms marketing products or services related to clothes, cosmetics, Jewellery, hair styles, membership to certain clubs, other personal care products, beauty salons etc., are working out marketing plans so as to help the consumer gain an inflated and enhanced view of the physical appearance or self image.

Jewellery brand marketers are working at innovative ways to woo the consumers and induce them to alter their self image. Well known brands are associating themselves with Bollywood films where they are endorsed by celebrities shown using signature jewellery ranges. For instance, the audience are exposed to seeing Aishwarya Rai show off *Nakshatra Diamonds* in Guru, the large star cast of Salaam-e-Ishq sparkle with *Ira* diamond jewellery, Woh Lamhe film featured a fashion show of *Orrq* and in Vivah, Amrita Rao is shown wearing *D'damas* diamonds. Later on D'damas came out with a Vivah range of jewellery and Bollywood Gold (a range of contemporary Indian jewellery).

Asmi brand of diamonds prompts consumers to alter their self image

Attempting at altering one's self image.

Keeping in mind the emergence of the new, modern, multi tasking women of today with disposable cash to indulge herself in, marketers are making attempts to come out with suitable products to match their altered self-image. *For example, Electrolux* came out with a premium brand range called *"affirmation of the self". Idea Cellular* launched the first ever women's card available on both prepaid and postpaid connections packed with value add ones such as tips on beauty, fashion, health and safety alerts to near and dear ones.

➲ SUMMARY

Personality can be defined as patterns of individual behaviour which are consistent and enduring. Lifestyles can be referred to as consumer's mode of living which is reflected in his attitudes and opinions. An understanding of lifestyle variables can help marketers to learn more of the purchasing behaviour of consumers and then work out the product specific marketing plans.

The VALS (Value and Lifestyle) system framework was initially developed in the United States by Arnold Mitchell of the Stanford Research Institute in order to classify the American public into nine groups. Subsequently, in 1989 a revised VALS system was developed with the intention of using it to understand consumer purchase behaviour, on the basis of two dimensions:

- Self orientation
- Resources

The AIO framework, is broadly similar to the concepts of VALS system and attempts to classify distinctive lifestyle groups using a questionnaire designed to measure Activities, Interests and Opinions (AIO).

Some of the visible changes in the lifestyle trends of Indian consumers include: changes in traditional male/female purchasing roles, more conscious and inclination towards health and nutrition, lifestyle changes in the emerging middleclass consumption community, adapting to greater time pressures, growing self awareness and more value oriented approach and impact of the internet on the lifestyle pattern.

Three major theories of personality namely, the Trait theory, Psychoanalytic (Freudian) theory and the Neo-Freudian theory were discussed. An over view of the BT-synovate (Business Today-Synovate) study helped to learn more on the different kinds of tweens in India, their lifestyle, aspiration and influences, involvement in purchase decisions, media habits and consumption patterns.

There are certain personality traits which are useful to analyse the likely market response for new innovations. These personality traits include consumer innovativeness, dogmatism, social character, need for uniqueness, optimum stimulation level and variety novelty seeking. Consumer researchers are keen to understand the role played by cognitive personality traits (visualizers versus verbalizers and need for cognition) influencing various aspects of consumer behaviours. They have also identified certain consumption and possession traits such as consumer materialism, fixated consumption behaviour, compulsive consumption behaviour and consumer ethnocentrism, which can influence consumer behaviour. The chapter concluded with a discussion on the 'self concept or self image, which are closely connected to the personality of the products or services patronized by consumers.

CHAPTER QUESTIONS FOR DISCUSSION

1. Why is an understanding of consumer personality necessary for marketers selling consumer products?
2. Do you find a difference in the lifestyle variables used by individual's of the current generation and those belonging to the earlier generations? Explain with examples how you arrived at the conclusion.
3. Briefly bring out the importance of the Freudian and Neo-Freudian theories by quoting examples of products you feel are using these concepts.
4. Interact with your peer (friends, neighbours or colleagues) and try to identify the personality traits of those who prefer foreign brands and those who purchase Indian brands of products. Make a table to chart out the differences in the personality traits of these two categories of consumers.
5. Explain with giving examples, why is it necessary for marketers to identify the difference between consumers self image and ideal self image while analysing the purchase behaviour of individuals?

SUGGESTED READINGS

1. www.bondwiththebest.com
2. Clifford T. Morgan and Richard A. King *"Introduction to Psychology"*, McGraw-Hill Company, NewYork, 1966, p. 460.
3. Henry Assael, *Consumer Behavior, A Strategic Approach,* (Indian Adaptation) 6th Edn., Biztantra, New Delhi, 2005, pp. 278-308
4. Joseph T. Plummer, "The Concept and Application of Lifestyle Segmentation", *Journal of Marketing* 38, January 1974, pp. 33-37.
5. Roopa. Purushothaman, Where the Future Lies, *Strategic Marketing,* July-August, 2006, pp. 48-51
6. Harshikaa Udasi, Customer is Queen, *The Week,* December 3, 2006. pp. 38-47.
7. V.S Ramaswamy, S. Namakumari *'Marketing Management, Planning, Implementation and Control,* MacMillan India Ltd., (3rd Edition) New Delhi 2002. pp. 238-245
8. Archana. Shukla, Aman. Malik, The Market Makers, *Business Today,* January 14, 2007, pp. 145-152.
9. Super Trooper-Boost, *Business Today,* March 14, 2004. pp. 116-117.
10. A BT- Synovate Study, *Business Today,* January 1, 2006. pp. 60-71.
11. Jerry Gary, Frederick A. Starke, *Organizational Behavior – Concepts and Applications*, MacMillan, Columbus, 1980.
12. Dr. Nirajkumar, *A Genesis of Behavioural Sciences,* Prashant Prakashan, Lucknow, 1995.
13. Bhanu Pande, Homing: in Sushmita to endorse S Kumar's, *The Economic Times,* Bangalore, 1 April, 2006.
14. Global Attitude, Brand Equity, *The Economic Times,* Bangalore, 16 August, 2006. pp. 2-3
15. Albert Almedia, Sunil Lulla & Nina Jaipuria, Jassi Jaissi Koi Nahin?- Case Study, *Strategic Marketing,* July-August, 2004, Vol. III, Issue IV, pp. 57-62.

CASE

BRITANNIA INDUSTRIES LIMITED

A BRIEF HISTORY

The business for biscuit making started in 1892, with an initial investment of Rs. 295, in central Kolkata when biscuits were manufactured in a small house. Later, this business was acquired by Gupta brothers and operated under the name of V.S. Brothers. In 1918, C.H Holmes, an English businessman in Kolkata was taken as a partner and 'Britannia Biscuit Company Ltd.' (BBCo) was launched. In 1924, the Mumbai factory was set up and Peak Fream of UK acquired a controlling interest in the company. During World War II, biscuits were in great demand and this helped the company to increase its sales. In 1968, after celebrating its Golden Jubilee, the company changed its name to the current Britannia Industries Limited in 1979. In 1982, *Nabisco Brands Inc.,* U.S.A. became a major foreign shareholder. In 1992, Britannia Industries Limited celebrated its platinum jubilee . The following year, the Wadia Group acquired a stake in ABIL, UK and thus became an equal partner with Group Danone in Britannia Industries Limited.

BISCUIT MARKET AND PRODUCTS (BRANDS)

Studies have indicated that the biscuit segment enjoys one of the most developed markets for any item of mass consumption, there by covering over 90 per cent of the overall potential market. This is also an indication that the market is very huge, with over 900 million Indians who buy and consume biscuits in varying frequency during the year.

Britannia is existing in the market since so long that as a brand it is synonymous with the rise and growth of the biscuit industry in India. During this process it has displayed an uncanny intuition about emerging popular tastes for biscuits. Britannia has a structured portfolio of products in an attempt at redefining and strengthening the Indian biscuit market. It has an optimum range of brands to meet the key needs of the Indian consumer across various age groups and diverse consumption situations

'Eat Healthy Think Better' - Brand Value

All of Britannia's product offerings reflect a health dimension. Earlier, the biscuit industry was traditionally driven by taste alone. However, in 1997, Britannia introduced a brand slogan *'Eat Healthy, Think Better',* which was an instant hit. This concept was quickly embraced by the entire industry, which came up with similar promotional campaigns showing biscuits to be an epitome of a healthy, happy diet. By emphasizing on the key premise (or principles) of a lifetime menu where a Britannia product exists for every stage in a person's life.

(a) The biggest *consumption group* of biscuits are *children*, for them Britannia offers:

- **Milk Bikis-** With all the 'goodness of milk' required by younger children.
- **Tiger-** Provides children in the age group of 7-14 years of age, with the exuberant health required by 'winners of tomorrow'.
- **Treat-** A range of delicious cream biscuits, meant as a treat for children during fun times.
- **Little Hearts-** A snack of sweet biscuits meant for teenagers and kids

(b) *Other consumption groups* of Britannia biscuits include:

- **50-50-** a biscuit snack for young adults with its sweet-salty duality.
- **Time pass-** a savoury biscuit meant for young adults.
- **Britannia Marie Gold-** for health conscious urban adults a venerated tea time offering packed with 'wheat energy'.
- **Good Day-** a cookie filled with rich ingredients, a healthy everyday treat for the entire family.
- Britannia also has a **range of bread and cakes** (vanilla, orange etc., flavour) entrenched in the fresh bakery segment.

In the past two years, Britannia has come out with new products and package combinations, such as:

- **50-50 pepper chakkar, chutkule-** Britannia's first venture in snacking.
- **Sugar-Out-** a sugar free cream range under Nutrichoice.
- **Tiger Tikki-** a pack of four biscuits for Rs 2, targeted at the value conscious rural consumer (a bite sized variation of *Tiger*).
- **Anlene-** a highly specialized health drink targeting people with osteoporosis (available in the cities of Kolkata and Chennai initially)
- Pile packs, priced between Rs. 3 and Rs. 5, are a step up between sachets (or tikki packs) include Jam Treat, Bourbon, Marie and 50-50. The company also has presence in the dairy business (Britannia cheese slices etc.,) from a decade ago.

COMPETITION

In all the segments of biscuits, Britannia Industries faces competition from rivals such as **Parle Products, Surya Foods and Agro** (Makers of Priya Gold) and **ITC's** Sunfeast range of biscuits (Graph will give picture of BIL (Britannia Industries) limited and its competitors)

In the diary business (apart from the unorganized players), Britannia has direct competition with cooperatives or companies which own the entire supply chain such as the Gujarat Cooperative Milk Marketing Federation *(Amul)* and National Dairy Development Board *(Mother Dairy)*. Apart from them, there are well-entrenched players in virtually every state-*Verka* in Punjab, *Parag* in U.P and *Aawin* in Tamil Nadu.

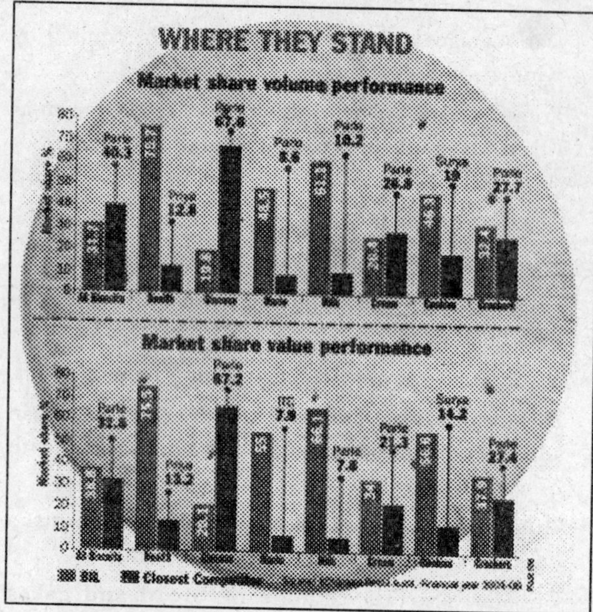

Graph : Market share volume and value performance

As per AC Nielsen Audit, Britannia also faces competition from regional players such as:

In the East-there are some 350 brands like *Biskfarm, Anmol, Nezone* and *Champion.*

PERFORMANCE WISE-BRITANNIA INDUSTRIES LIMITED

Britannia's market share in biscuits form 92 per cent, bread constitutes 4 percent and in cakes and rusks 2 per cent. In 2004, BIL'S market share fell from 40.2% in 2003 to 35.8% in 2004. In the financial year 2005-2006. the market share continued to fall to 31.7% (As shown in the graph). In 2004, tobacco major *ITC* entered the biscuit market with its *'Sunfeast'* range of biscuits in all the seven segments. Sunfeast with its big bang advertising and better quality not only managed to capture a share of the consumer's mind but also 8 percent of the market. Parle reacted with price cuts of 10-14 per cent.

These moves by competitors left Britannia at a weaker position. In the Rs 4,500 crore biscuit market, it still leads in five out of seven categories although this figure was six in 2004. But in two of these categories, the competitors are fast catching up.

- In the glucose segment (the largest by volume), Parle has three times the share of Britannia.
- In the crackers segment, there is just 5 percent gap between the Parle & BIL

Even the regional players (from East and North) have managed to capture a major share of Britannia and Parle's markets.

To *counter competition*, Britannia has during the past year (2006) tried its hand at product innovation and a drive towards offering new products and package combinations. Among these are *50-50 Pepper Chakkar Chutkule* (Venture into Snacking) *Sugar out* (a sugar free cream range under Nutrichoice) and a bite sized avatar of *Tiger* biscuit.

It forayed into the health segment with *Anlene.* Britannia also introduced pile packs priced between Rs. 3 and Rs. 5 which act as step up between sachets (or tikki packs) for *Marie, Jam Treat, Bourbon* and 50-50.

Britannia's marketing strategy is to *penetrate distribution channels.* This is being done by stocking pile packs of *chutkule* and *chota Tiger* at their smaller multi brand outlets. The company is ensuring that 'Tiger's own cream offerings don't affect its pile packs by having no flavours in common.

Britannia is attempting to *break down sub categories that exist* largely in the minds of the company and do not reflect the way the consumer thinks. For instance, Britannia *Treat* is being positioned as a range of delicious conspiracies which will help in the brand's passage into *"The Kid's indulgence space".* In this market segment, Britannia is presently having only 2%-3% of the entire indulgence space market.

Britannia is continuously trying its hand at *innovation* at various levels. *For example,* the *Fruit Treat* variant was the outcome of a consumer research which showed that mothers were upset at children merely eating the cream of a biscuit and leaving the shell behind. Thus the solution a product where the shell cannot be separated. The brand is currently rolling out 'Masti Ka Boss' which celebrates mischief.

The long term challenge is to maintain its earlier market leader position. Simultaneously, it has also got to maintain prices even as all the ingredients that go into biscuit making has been increasing significantly.

(*Source:* Nandini Vaish, 'Wither Britannia', *Business World,* 29, May 2006, pp. 40-42; Ravi Balakrishnan, 'Britannia 90 not out', Brand Equity, *The Economic Times,* 31 January, 2007; www.britanniaindustrieslimited.com)

QUESTIONS

1. Competitors like ITC, Priya Gold etc., have entered into other products like ready-to-eat, pasta's, juices etc. Should Britannia also increase product lines and build-up its brand personality. Discuss.
2. Do you feel developing a different brand name for dairy products and biscuits will help BIL in market positioning? Why?

CHAPTER 

ATTITUDE AND BEHAVIOUR

- Case : **Frito Lay India**
- Attitudes (definition and characteristics)
- Nature of consumer attitudes
- A simple model of the relationship between Attitudes and Behaviour
- Attitude measurement
- Attitude change
- Factors involved in attitude formation or development
- Theories of attitude
- Models of attitude
- Strategies for attitude re-inforcement and change
- Summary
- Chapter questions for discussion
- Suggested Readings
- Case : **Handling of Down Age Syndrome**

CASE

FRITO LAY INDIA

Most of us at some point or the other have been asked what we 'think' or 'feel' about a particular object, issue, activity or person. We have also responded to such questions with an expression of our attitudes. That is, our responses would have indicated whether we generally like or dislike the object, issue, activity or person under discussion.

Social psychologists have viewed attitudes as a major, basic construct leading to behaviour. That is, attitudes have been considered as a major factor affecting behaviour. Attitudes affect and influence the perception of products, brands, people, exposure to and comprehension of information, choice of friends and so on. The concept of learning and understanding attitude has been emphasised by social psychologists very early, from 1920s onwards. Though after world war II there was a growing concern about the role of attitude in understanding prejudice and thereafter more emphasis was given to the measurement of attitude and how to bring about attitude changes.

World over, Fortune 500 companies such as Disney, Pontiac, IBM and Virgin Atlantic are using various marketing tools such as blogs and podcasts to reach out to consumers. Blogs form part of the online tools available to all IBMers, to enable faster sharing of information, answers and views in public and widely accessible places. Blogging has a lot of potential as a new medium of communication and collaboration between employees, business partners, clients and members of other community activities. Globally IBM is also doing internal and external podcasts with a pod casting strategy to expand its communication and marketing and even post podcast on its investor relations website.

Going by the positive attitude of the tech savvy youth of today, Indian companies are also trying to reach out to their consumers' in unique ways. For instance, *Frito Lay India* had launched its Lay's *'Latino Style'* music featuring Bollywood star Saif Ali Khan through a video pod cast. This move by the company was an attempt to connect with the youth because of their positive attitude towards pod casting. This was a part of the communication support plan for the new Lay's Latino style special edition flavour in the market. It was felt that the youth of today are always on the net, pod casting away, interacting and expressing via blogs, so they will have a positive attitude towards brand such as Lays.

Companies such as ITC and MTR Foods Ltd. have seen the change in consumer attitudes towards the ready-to-eat food and other packaged food. (or convenience food), especially due to rising disposable income and both the spouses working. This led to the launch of ITC Ready-to-eat and MTR ready-to-eat brands, which have gained acceptance among consumers. The above are examples of the 'changing attitudes of today's consumers.

As consumers we have developed certain attitudes towards products, services, advertisements, other media of communication and choice of retail outlet. Marketers are also interested in analysing and understanding the consumers' attitudes towards their products and services. This information about the prevailing attitude amongst their consumers will help them to devise suitable marketing programmes.

In this chapter we start by discussing the meaning of Attitudes, their characteristics and nature. Then we will try to understand how a simple model of the relationship between attitudes and behaviour works. We will then discuss about the factors involved in attitude formation and the concept of attitude change. We will also have a look at the various theories and models of attitude. The chapter concludes with discussions on the strategies for attitude reinforcement and change.

ATTITUDES (DEFINITION AND CHARACTERISTICS)

Attitudes have usually been associated with the notion of 'liking' or 'disliking' someone or something. That is, attitudes are inner expression or feelings that reflect whether a person is favourably or unfavourably predisposed to a product or brand or establishment.

Long ago a psychologist, Gordon Allport had given a classic definition of attitudes, which says

"Attitudes are learned predispositions to respond to an object or class of objects in a consistently favourable or unfavourable way".

Attitudes are usually associated with a notion of liking or disliking someone or thing. Attitudes are said to be resulting from a combination of beliefs, values and opinions.

There could be several implications of this definition.

- *Attitudes are learned:* This means attitudes get formed on the basis of some experience with or information about the object.
- *Attitudes are predispositions* and reside in the mind of the individual.
- *Attitudes cause consistent response:* This means attitudes precede and produce behaviour.

Martin Fishbein has defined 'attitude' in a way that it can be useful in predicting behaviour. As per this definition a person's overall attitude towards an object is said to be the function of (a) the strength of each of a number of beliefs the person holds about various aspects of the object and (b) the person's evaluation of each of the belief's held by him as he relates it to the object.

From a marketer's point of view, this definition is helpful, for it implies that consumer's will perceive a product (or object) to be having many attributes and accordingly, may develop beliefs on each of the attributes. *For example,* a consumer may strongly believe that *Vicks VapoRub* provides fast and long lasting relief from the six symptoms of cold namely: blocked nose, cough, body ache, headache, muscle stiffness and breathing difficulty. Since this consumer evaluated all of these attributes as favourable qualities, as per the definition, she has a strong favourable overall attitude towards the brand. However, if there was another consumer who may not believe *Vicks VapoRub* to possess all the above mentioned attributes, she may not evaluate all attributes as favourably as the first consumer. Accordingly, her overall attitude towards the brand would be less favourable.

Ad of *Vicks VapoRub*

Attitudes, Opinion and Belief

Attitudes are said to be resulting from a combination of beliefs and value and opinions. Terms such as opinion and belief are often used quite closely with attitudes. Attitudes tend to be generalised predispositions to react in some way towards objects or concepts, Whereas, opinions tend to be focused on more specific aspects of the object or concept. Earnest J. Me Cormick and Joseph Tiffin have opined " *The measurement of attitudes is generally based on the expression of opinions. But we should distinguish between attitude scale which, like a thermometer or barometer, reflects the generalised level of individual attitudes towards some object or concept, and opinion surveys, which typically are used to elicit the opinions of people towards specific aspects."*

Belief can be defined as *"an enduring organisation of perceptions and cognitions about some aspects of an individual's world'.* (Krech and Crutchfield, 1948) This means beliefs could be hypothesis and are based on one's judgement regarding the probability of the nature of the objects. Simply stated beliefs are the body of knowledge we hold about the world (may be incomplete or inaccurate). Beliefs are often expressed in sentences where the word 'is' appears. *For example,* the information that *"Complan is good for you"* has been presented as a fact (endorsed by the health and nutrition specialist in the ad clipping) in the cleverly designed advertising campaign. As a result, this view now forms a part of many peoples' (especially mothers) belief system.

Value – is very often viewed as an attribute possessed by an individual and considered to be desirable. According to psychologist Milton Rokeach, values are centrally held and enduring beliefs which guide actions and make judgments in specifics situations. They may induce one to respond (or adopt specific behaviour) which can help or come in the way of attainment of some values (David Louden & A.J.D.Bitto, Consumer Behavior, Tata McGraw Hill, 4th Ed., pp. 88-89)

From the above definition we can see that values involve an individual's judgement on what is right, good, desirable and worthwhile. Unlike beliefs, these are usually ideals to which we aspire and may be expressed in sentences which includes words like 'should be'. *For example,* the Government's pulse polio statement – "India must be eradicated and free from polio" is an expression of the *value of the principle of social justice.*

Values involve an individual's judgement on what is right, good, desirable and worthwhile. While, beliefs are usually ideals to which we aspire and may be expressed in sentences which includes words like 'should be'.

The differences between attitudes, opinions and beliefs and values exist only on a conceptual basis. The relationship between them is a complex one. It is usually said that people have thousands of beliefs and opinions about the world, hundreds of attitudes although probably fever than fifty values.

Interestingly, advertisers have used these values to sell products. Typically, a product is associated with a particular value dimension to give it an appeal.

For instance :

Brand		*Value*
Dove	–	The moisturising effect
Tide washing powder	–	The stain-busting power
Shoppers Stop	–	A complete fashion and lifestyle store
Vicks VapoRub	–	Gentle, Quick Relief medication from cold
Bank of India	–	Relationships beyond banking

So firms try to sell their products by using the dimension of truth. At times they support this with the presentation of facts and figures or graphs or professionals in related areas endorsing the brand.

The relationship between attitudes, opinions, beliefs and values is a complex one and exits only on a conceptual basis.

	Total readership	SEC A readership	15-34 year readership	Readership among households owning cars
TOI + VK	52,60,000	7,45,000	29,70,000	4,07,000
DH + PV	39,06,000	4,64,000	21,80,000	3,65,000

Presentation of facts with figures can reinforce the belief of the consumers' faith in the brand.

For instance, Star chef Sanjeev Kapoor endorses that it is possible to make tasty sweet (Gajjar Ka Halva) by using *Sugar Free* or when he opines that it is possible to make healthy and tasty (with less fat and cholesterol content) snacks by using *Saffola Gold cooking oil*. Similarly, *Jawed Habib*, Hair stylist & Grooming expert, states the goodness of using *Sun Silk Shampoo* (helps the hair to remain conditioned, smooth and silky).

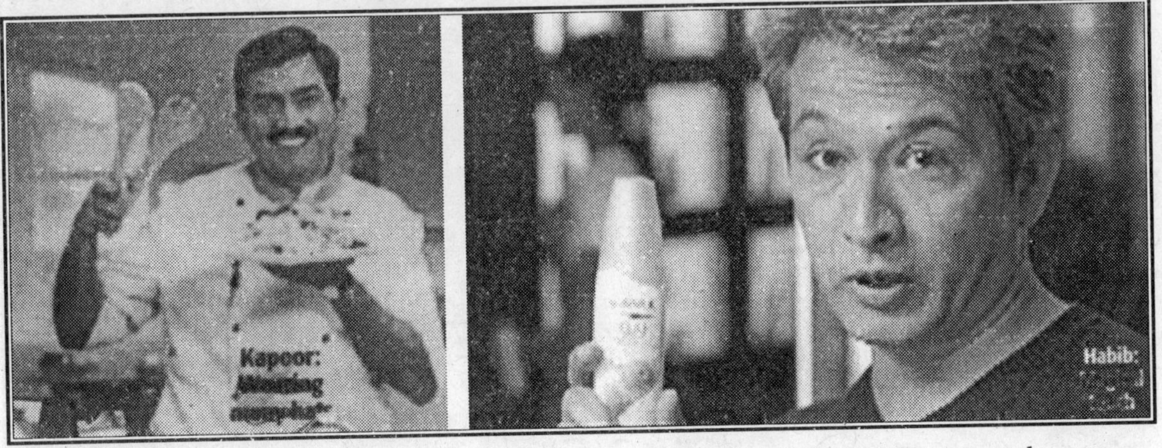

Experts in their relevant area of profession (A) Star chef Sanjeev Kapoor and (B) Hair stylist and specialist Jawed Habib give their opinion on the benefit of using Saffola Gold cooking oil and Sun Silk shampoo, respectively.

Characteristics of Attitudes : Individuals hold different attitudes. The following are generally referred to as characteristics of attitudes :

Marketers are trying to understand attitudes, modify them and turn positive attitude towards an object or product into an action resulting in the purchase of the item in question.

- Attitudes can be held about any object, person, issue or activity - referred to as the attitude object. For instance, if as a researcher one is interested in knowing about consumer attitudes towards major brands of mobile phones (object) then the study will include Airtel, Hutch and Reliance.
- Attitudes may be strongly or weakly held. An attitude is an assessment based on continuous evaluation.
- Attitudes are learned : We acquire attitudes in much the same way we acquire culture, through classical and operant conditioning and social interaction. Attitudes having relevance to purchase behaviour may have been formed (or learned) through direct experience with the product, word-of-mouth, from ads (or other mass media advertising, from retail outlet leaflet, internet etc.) Such learned predispositions will lead to attitude formation and the subsequent purchase behaviour.
- Attitudes are dynamic and can change. We no longer have the same attitudes as we did when we were younger. We are constantly modifying attitudes based on our experiences and acquiring new attitudes as we encounter new attitude objects. Sometimes, attitudes occur within and are affected by the *situation* also. By situation, we are referring to

Display of positive attitude towards the brand.

events or circumstances at a particular point of time which can influence the relationship between an attitude and behaviour.

- Some attitudes are more fundamental than others and more resistant to change. Certain opinions stay with us throughout our lives, while others may change from week to week.

Marketers are more concerned with *understanding attitudes* (for instance, does a brand have a favourable or unfavourable image), *modifying attitudes* (to make consumers more favourable toward certain attitude object and or less favourable towards others), and *turning positive attitudes towards an object* or product *into an action* resulting in the purchase of the item in question.

Marketers are trying to understand and meet consumer demands by trying to match products with the situational requirement. *For example,* consumer preference may vary, in terms of eating situations, if one were to look at outlets such as *McDonalds, Pizza Hut, Nirula's, Coffee Café Day or The Indian Coffee House*. So accordingly Coffee Café Day may be preferred by young, trendy executives working in the IT sector. While middle age, price conscious customers may prefer to eat at the Indian Coffee House. Examples of how situations can influence attitudes are given in the Table 6.1.

TABLE 6.1

SITUATIONAL EXAMPLES WHICH CAN INFLUENCE ATTITUDES

Product/Service	Situation	Attitude
• Moov	Severe back pain	"I need to get immediate relief from severe back pain"
• LIC	Financial planning	"Even after my husband's death I am able to fufill a mother's duties due to his investing the money properly"
• Sanifresh Germ Kill	Germs and bacteria problem	"I need to keep the toilet disinfected from germs and bacteria"
• Pantene Pro.V Shine	Hair fall	"I need to use a shampoo which controls hair fall and also keeps it smooth and shining"

NATURE OF CONSUMER ATTITUDES

Brand attitudes are based on the schema of a brand consumer's store in long term memory. *For example,* say a schema of Ambassador car as being a dull and old fashioned car has led to many of the younger generation customers selecting other trendy cars. The older consumers are likely to have certain attributes such as reliability, security and good after sales service associated with Hindustan Motors (the makers of Ambassador). Due to this belief that the older consumers have of Ambassador they are likely to make a positive evaluation of the car. Consequently, brand beliefs (Ambassador is reliable) can lead to brand evaluation (I like Ambassador) and thus can lead to the intended behaviour (I am planning to use Ambassador for a long term period).

The nature of consumer's attitudes can be understood by having a look at the three: cognitive, affective and conative components of attitudes. They are expressed in terms of brand beliefs, brand evaluation and intention to buy.

The Three Components of Attitudes

In order to understand the nature of consumer attitudes, we will briefly discuss the three components, cognitive, affective and conative components of attitudes. These components can be defined in term of brand beliefs, brand evaluation and intention to buy.

FIGURE 6.1

THE THREE COMPONENTS OF ATTITUDES

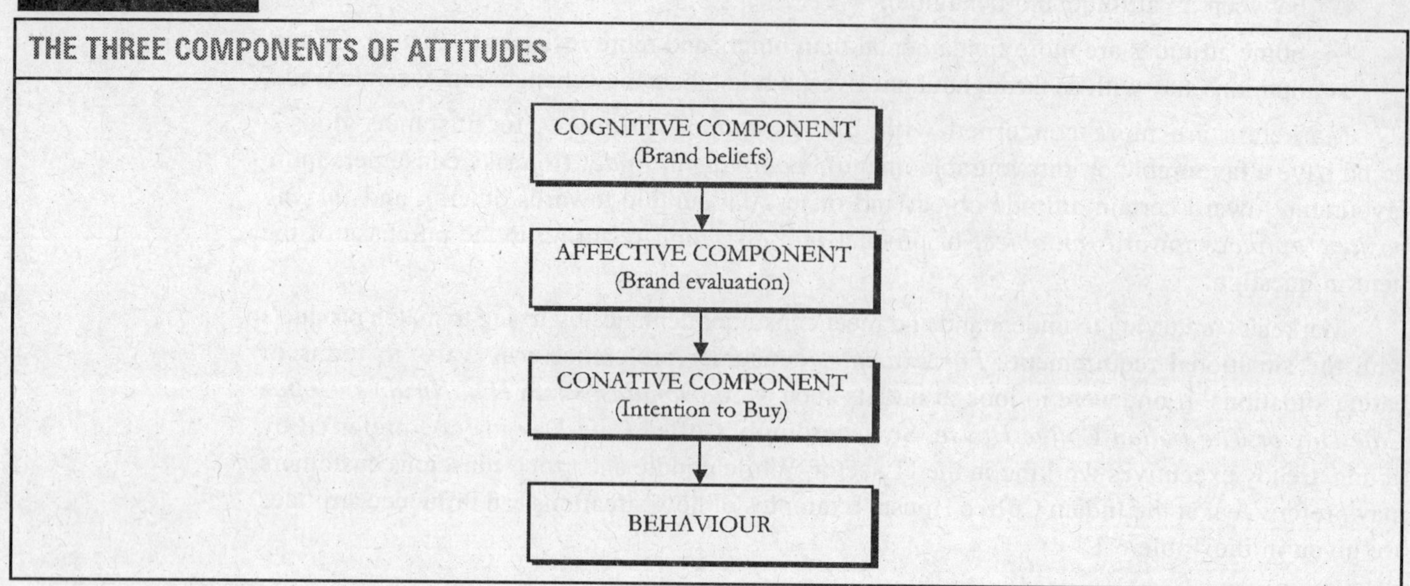

Brand Beliefs : Brand beliefs are the cognitive components of attitudes. These could be in terms of the consumer's beliefs about a brand and the characteristics they ascribe to it. Marketers, through marketing research can interact with consumers and ask them to rate brands utilizing the vocabulary of product attributes developed by them. Then the marketer must determine the value consumers place on the various attributes based on the benefits they feel they will derive from it. Descriptive beliefs connect an object or person to a quality or outcome. *For example,* "this train is always late" is a descriptive belief an individual may have of that train.

This evaluative component of attitude will help the marketers to understand whether the consumer has a positive or negative attitude towards the brand and segment the market accordingly. Such evaluate beliefs connect an object to personal likes or dislikes or perceptions. Say a consumer states "the service in this store is poor".

Brand beliefs are relevant only to the extent that they influence brand's evaluation, the primary determinant of intended behaviour. There are also normative beliefs which invoke moral and ethical judgements like "It is wrong to advertise about cigarette smoking being enjoyable".

Brand belief refers to the consumer's beliefs about a brand and the characteristics they ascribe to it. The consumers overall brand evaluation can be measured by rating it from 'poor' to 'excellent' or from 'prefer least' to 'prefer most'. Consumer's tendency towards an object is measured by looking at the 'intention to buy'.

Overall Brand Evaluation : The affective component is the second attitude component and represents a consumer's overall evaluation of the brand. Beliefs about a brand are multidimensional because they represent the brand attributes consumers perceive. The affective component, is one-dimensional. That is consumer's overall evaluation can be measured by rating the brand from 'poor' to 'excellent' or from 'prefer least' to 'prefer most'. From brand evaluation, it can be said that it conforms to the definition of brand attitudes which says it is "a tendency to evaluate brands in a favourable or unfavourable way".

Intention to Buy : The Behavioural Component : Brand beliefs influence attitudes and attitudes influence intention to buy *i.e.,* consumer's tendency to act towards an object. Measuring buying intent helps in the development of a marketing strategy. Marketers generally try to test elements of the marketing mix such as ad packages, brand names etc., to determine what is most likely to influence purchase behaviour. *For example,* consumers viewing alternative ads are asked about their intentions to buy after experiencing these marketing stimuli. Marketers will regard the alternative producing the highest buying intent as the best choice in the absence of actual buying behaviour. Unlike brand evaluation and beliefs marketers can try to influence this third component of attitude. For, a sharp reduction in price or a special coupon can work out to be inducements for consumers to try a less favoured brand. Table 6.2 gives examples of the three attitude components against two services. The relationship between the three components of attitudes is known as the *hierarchy of effects*.

TABLE 6.2

EXAMPLE OF LIKELY MEASURES OF THE THREE COMPONENTS OF ATTITUDE FOR TWO SERVICES

Attitude Component	UPS (United Parcel Services) for shipping a business's small packages	Booking Airline Tickets on the internet
• COGNITIONS OR BELIEFS	• UPS is very reliable in its Service • UPS is able to customise its service to my shipping needs	• I find it convenient to book tickets on the internet • While booking airline tickets I am able to get a comprehensive set of airlines and flight options.
• AFFECTIVE OR FEELINGS	• I feel secure when I ship by UPS. • I am happy to use UPS for my shipping needs	• I feel booking airline tickets on the internet is enjoyable • I feel it comfortable booking tickets on the internet.
• CONATIONS OR ACTIONS	• I use UPS for my shipping more than I use other carriers • I often recommend UPS to other business associates	• I have even recently purchased airline tickets on the internet • I often search the internet for planning travel itinerary.

The High-Versus Low Involvement Hierarchy

The hierarchy of effects works as a sequence in the consumers choice process and can be distinguished between a high and low involvement hierarchy. The high involvement hierarchy involves a "think before you act" process while low involvement hierarchy is described as an "act before you think" process. These are briefly described in terms of the three components of attitudes. When consumers get involved, they will first develop beliefs about the brand through a process of active information search. Based on this they will evaluate the brand, develop definite brand attitudes and make a purchase decision accordingly. Marketers have found that attitudes were more closely related to purchase intentions for the motivated group as compared to that of the unmotivated group. *For example,* a consumer tries out a new paper tissue and decides that it is not as good as her regular brand and so she is not likely to purchase it again. Such overall evaluation provides important information for the marketers even though the consumer is not very involved with the brand.

The Hierarchy of effects works as a sequence in the consumer's choice process and can be distinguished between a high and low involvement hierarchy. The experimental hierarchy is mainly concerned with a consumer's emotional response to a brand.

The Experimental Hierarchy

The experimental hierarchy is mainly concerned with a consumer's emotional response to a brand. From the Table 6.3 it can be said that consumers first evaluate a brand on an overall basis treating it on the basis of their feelings, emotions and fantasies. It is only after this that their beliefs, about the attributes and characteristics of a brand may be formed. Consumer's primary purchase motive is the anticipated experience of enjoying the brand and not the projected performance of the brand based on evaluative product criteria. Since experimental hierarchy considers consumer's emotional involvement, they are likely to search for stimuli such as symbols and imagery on an on going basis which could affect their feelings about a brand. Many marketers use this hierarchy by advertising product features and benefits to influence beliefs.

TABLE 6.3

THE THREE HIERARCHIES OF EFFECT

Types of Hierarchy	Sequence	Nature of Information Processing
• HIGH INVOLVEMENT	Beliefs Evaluation Behaviour	Active, purchase specific processing
• LOW INVOLVEMENT	Beliefs Behaviour Evaluation	Passive, purchase specific processing
• EXPERIENTAL	Evaluation Behaviour Beliefs	Active, on going processing

➲ A SIMPLE MODEL OF THE RELATIONSHIP BETWEEN ATTITUDES AND BEHAVIOUR

Figure 6.2 represents a simple model of the relationship between attitudes and behaviour.

FIGURE 6.2

A SIMPLE MODEL OF THE RELATIONSHIP BETWEEN ATTITUDES AND BEHAVIOUR

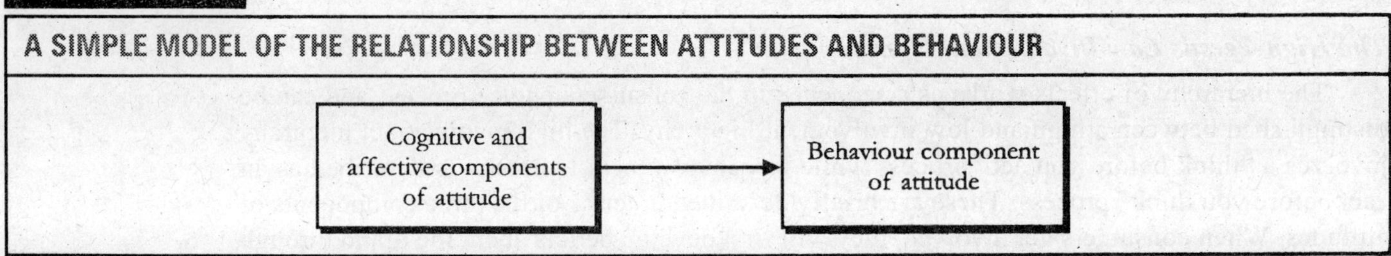

A simple model can be used to show how the cognitive and affective components of attitude can lead to a behaviour component of attitude.

As seen from the above figure of a simple model, positive cognitive and affective perception of an object leads to positive behaviour and vise versa.. But, unfortunately various psychological researches have proved that there is no clear relationship between measured attitudes and behaviour. This may be true because, very often our behaviour could be the outcome of many external factors, which are beyond our own control. For instance, an individual would like to purchase the newly launched car diesel version of the *Sonata Embera*. The individual may be favourably inclined towards the idea, but there may be a number of reasons which may be coming in the way of his actually buying the car. Few of these external influences might be:

- Lack of sufficient money or finance to book the car.
- Want of time, to enquire about the various available 'finance' schemes.
- The initial bookings confirmed by the company are already over and no more fresh bookings were being undertaken.
- A family member is ill and urgently needs financial help.

Another problem can be related to measurement. For instance, merely by observing a person buying a product, we cannot infer that he or she is buying the product because they are favourably inclined towards that product. It may be that, the particular outlet was close to their

Ad uses Experimental Hierarchy to convey the product features residence or the non availability of any other brand, may have prompted the consumer to buy a particular product (brand).

There are many experiments carried out by psychologists and sociologists to determine the factors which provide the link between attitudes and behaviour. A very interesting and famous experiment known as the Travelling Chinese Experiment' carried out by a sociologist, 'Richard La Piere' is given below in the Box 6.1.

BOX 6.1

LA PIERE'S INFORMAL EXPERIMENT

In the early 1930s strong feelings existed against the Chinese in the United States. Around this time Richard La Piere, a sociologist, took a Chinese couple on a tour of America. The trio stopped at 250 hotels and restaurants during their trip. On only one occasion were they refused entry. After returning from his trip, he wrote to each of the establishments he had visited asking them whether they would accept Chinese patrons. Somewhat surprisingly, of the half that responded to his letter, 90% said they would not.

This experiment demonstrates a rather large gap between what the various proprietors said they would do and what they actually did. In other words, their attitudes (as secured by letter) were strikingly different to their behaviour (as demonstrated by La Piere's visits).

There are a number of methodological problems with La Piere's informal experiment. *For example,* was the same person that answered the letter been in a position to refuse service. But nevertheless the results are strongly suggestive of a real discrepancy between attitudes and behaviour.

(*Source :* Understanding Customers 1996-97, *"Attitude and Behaviour"*, Rosemary Phipps & Craig Simmons, Butterworth Heinemann, Oxford, 1996, Page 191).

This ad can influence brand belief

Ad influences brand evaluation

ATTITUDE MEASUREMENT

For the purpose of developing marketing strategies, the components of attitude have to be measured reliably. Since these components are qualitative variables, marketers usually develop rating scales in order to identify: the degree to which they think a brand has certain attributes (brand beliefs).

- to identify the attributes which make the consumers go for their ideal brand (attribute evaluation)
- to identify the degree to which they prefer certain brands (brand evaluations)
- to obtain the percentage of consumers who indicate a firm intention of buying the product (buying intentions)
- try to measure consumers' behaviour by asking attitudinal related questions.

With the help of the components of attitudes which are qualitative variables, marketers usually develop rating scales in order to identity the degree to which they think a brand has certain attributes or brand beliefs.

Attitudes are subjective attributes of people. They are also regarded as constructs in the sense that they are conceptualisation of human qualities which are formed based on either rational consideration or on the basis of statistical evidence. This means individuals may vary along a number of attitudinal dimensions. Psychologists have devised numerous methods for the measurement of attitudes. The most significant ones are :

- Thurstone type of scale.
- Likert scales.
- Semantic differential.
- Kelly's repertory grid.

Thurstone type of scale was developed by L.L. Thurstone and E.J Chave by collecting a large number of statements relating to the areas in which attitudes were to be measured. (The Measurement of Attitude Change, L.L. Thurstone, E.J. Chave, University of Chicago Press, Chicago, pp. 929) The statements relating to the attitude object are both favourable and unfavourable and are placed in 11 piles with most favourable statement placed on pile 1, to the most unfavourable ones being placed in pile 11.

The scale is then presented to the respondent who will make his selection based on his choice of the statement. His attitude score will be worked out based on the average or median scale of the statements that he has checked.

Likert Scales : Likert's attitude scale uses five points. The statement relating to the measurement of attitudes is given to the respondent, who is then asked to check one of the five points given for every statement. These points show degree of agreement or disagreement with the given statements. A positive aspect of the Likert scales is that in this scaling technique, it will be possible to make numerous statements because for every aspect only one statement is required, which will have both positive and negative degrees.

Semantic Differential : This attitude scaling technique was developed by C.E. Osgood, G.J. Suci and R.H. Tannenbowm (Organisational Behaviour, L.M. Prasad, Sultan Chand and Sons, New Delhi, 1996, pp. 110). This technique calls for successive allocation of a concept to a point in the multidimensional space by selection from among a set of given scaled semantic alternatives. It consists of several or many pairs of opposite adjectives or phrases, with scale values in between. While using this scale, the respondent will mark the position along each scale that reflects his or her attitude to the attitude object. The scale values (often ranging from 1 to 7) are associated with the different responses. The individual's score is usually the sum of the values.

The typical scales used for measuring attitudes include the Thurstone type of scale, Likert scales, Semantic differential and the Kelly's repertory grid.

Repertory Grid : The personal construct theory, developed by George Kelly has been considered to be of relevance to the study of perception, personality and attitudes.

The underlying notion of Kelly's theory is the belief that people are fundamentally inquisitive and will explore and explain the world using what he calls 'constructs'. These constructs are, essentially, definitions of the parts of the world - a way of dividing it into various compartments - to make sense of it and predict what is likely to happen in the future.

The repertory grid technique developed by Kelly for the measurement of constructs is frequently used in marketing in the comparative study of attitudes.

In the original repertory grid format, Kelly had presented a series of cards (known as elements) with various occupations written on them. The respondents were then required to pick any three occupations and describe the way in which any two were different from the third. The resulting response was used as a construct. The respondent is free to describe the differences between the elements in any way he likes. The generation of construct is repeated using any other three elements and repeated till either no more constructs can be originated or a predetermined limit has been reached.

Thus, such a technique can be applied to a number of marketing problems, involving the comparison of one or more products and services or brands. For instance, the Rep Grid can be used in comparing the various types of cars.

Say the respondents will be given a grid and asked to title the columns with brand names of the types of car. If we are to consider *Pajero, Sonata and Cedia* brands of cars, here say, the respondent may describe Pajero and Sonata as "*Power packed, smooth speed machines*", when compared to a Cedia. This description is then used as a row title and each of the other brands are rated accordingly.

FIGURE 6.3

REP GRID FOR CARS WITH THREE CONSTRUCTS

Constructs	Elements		
	Pajero	Sonata	Cedia
Power packed, smooth speed machines			
Comfortable			
Luxury			

So by repeatedly selecting and describing three ways in which a consumer perceives the product brand the market is found. It is emphasised that constructs are a very personal thing and no two individuals will have the same perception. After three constructs are generated, the grid may look like the Rep Grid shown in Figure 6.3.

Based on the information obtained from the various (individual) respondents, the firm could plan for a promotion programme, identify the attitudes associated with established products and the gaps in the market. Simply stated, Rep Grid technique can be used by marketers for market segmentation, brand comparison and identification of marketing branding opportunities.

Functions of Attitude

Thus an individual's behaviour is not a simple stimulus - response relationship. Apart from the individual, the situation as interpreted by him, and the attitude of the individual play an important role in interpreting the situation. The response (or behaviour) of the individual will be based or dependent totally on his own attitudes and on how he interprets the situation. Daniel Katz had proposed to consider attitudes to be performing four functions, which in turn will affect the individual's behaviour. (Daniel Katz, "The Functional Approach to the Study of Attitudes", Public Opinion Quarterly 24 (Summer 1960, pp. 163-204))

The various functions of attitude: Utilitarlian or instumental, Ego defensive, Value orientation and knowledge, can help the individual to interpret all the information coming to him and then adopt a behaviour suitable to the situation.

These functions are:

1. *Utilitarian or Instrumental:* Attitudes usually are formed to reach a particular goal or may be to avoid an undesired one. Instrumental attitudes are formed because of the activation of certain needs or cues which are associated with the attitude object (product) resulting in the arousal of favourable or unfavourable feelings.
2. *Ego defensive :* This ego-defensive function is associated with psychology. Ego defensive attitudes may be formed by the individual to protect herself or himself from internal or external threats or frustration or to build up resistance or suppress impulses, and suggestions from authoritarian sources. Based on the individual's perception of the situation, he or she will develop certain attitudes, which will affect their behaviour.
3. *Value orientation :* The value - orientation function takes into account and considers those attitudes which express the person's value or enhances his or her identity. These attitudes emphasise the person's self image and help in highlighting the person's salient value oriented attitudes.
4. *Knowledge:* The knowledge function will help the person to organise and form a meaningful structure against which he will evaluate the various aspects of his world.

These functions of attitudes will help the individual to interpret all the information coming to him or her and then adopt a behaviour suitable to the situation.

ATTITUDE CHANGE

Various studies have indicated that re-inforcing users' positive attitudes of a brand was more successful in increasing its consumption than when compared to efforts at changing consumers' attitudes. Nevertheless, marketers have realized that they must attempt at making attitude changes to survive and compete in the market. This is visible in the fact that a significant portion of the advertising budget is used in executing advertisements which convey the desired (or additional) information on the brand through persuasive appeals.

Certain principles which can help to develop marketing strategies that can help to bring about attitude changes are given below:

- **It is Easier to Change belief Rather than Desired Benefits :** Marketers could try to change the existing brand beliefs and the benefit being sought to, by changing the value consumers place on brand attributes. For instance, a manufacturer of detergent powder may produce a brand which consumers may regard to be harsh on the hands with strong odour but helps to remove stains from clothes. However, most consumer's may put more value on the benefit of a mild, yet effective stain removing detergent. So, accordingly, the manufacturer, could try to convince consumers through advertisements where more emphasis is laid on the strain removing ability along with additional information to convey that the detergent is not harsh on hands. Through this marketing strategy marketers can try to bring about a change in brand beliefs within the consumers existing value structure.

Zydus, while advertising for its *Nutralite Margarine* as a product better than butter, had claimed that it was 100% fat free. Gujarat co-operative milk marketing federation (GCMMF) which sells two butter based brands *Amul butter* and *Amul lite* – a butter based low fat bread spread had objected to this claim. But in spite of the former's claim, consumers consumed more of the Amul brands. Thus Nutrilite margarine found it difficult to bring about a change in consumers' desired benefit attitude.

Various studies have indicated that re inforcing user's positive attitudes of a brand was more successful in increasing its consumption when compared to efforts at changing consumer's attitudes.

- **It is Easier to Change Brand Beliefs than Brand Attitudes :** Through advertising, marketers follow the principle that belief are easier to change because advertising generally communicates about the attributes of the brand. People did not have a positive attitude towards the performance of the *Karnataka State Road Transport Corporation (KSRTC)*. In order to change this brand belief it undertook many initiatives- KSRTC increased the strength of its luxury fleet (Rajahamsa, Volvo etc.), introduced the electronic ticket machines (ETMs) on all its buses giving concessional passes (to students, freedom fighters, to the disabled etc.) made strides with regard to operational efficiency, commissioned the electronic driver testing track among others. All these efforts helped in bringing about a lateral shift in passengers from private vehicles to KSRTC-registering almost a 20 per cent growth.
- **In Case of Hedonic Products, Attitudes are the more Relevant Strategic Vehicle for Change :** When consumers purchase products based on emotion or fantasy, they are relying more on attitudes rather than beliefs.

When consumers purchase products based on emotions or fantacy, they are relying more on attitudes rather than beliefs.

KSRTC was able to bring about a change in brand belief

Earlier, Indian consumers had the attitude that any product well maintained can be used for a life time. They had the attitude which conveyed the feeling, "yeh to accha khaasa toe chal raha hai". But now with a large per capita income, falling interest rates, easier consumer credit, increased mobility, exposure to newer markets and products, media exposure to global lifestyle etc. have brought about a change in consumer attitudes. Now products such as a mobile (or celluler) phone are not purchased for its utility value only. In fact the added features are inducing and also changing the consumer attitude towards the mobile phone which is used even as a hedonic (pleasure giving oriented) product.

- **It is Easier to Change Attitudes, when there is Low Level of Involvement with the Product :** When consumers are having a high level of involvement with a product, they will accept messages only if the messages agree with their beliefs. Similarly, when the involvement is low, consumers are more likely *to accept communication (or message) even if it does not agree with prior beliefs.*

Typically people have a poor opinion of the performance of the political party in power. This could be visible in the poor turnout of voters during the election poll. The Congress party was during the last election poll able to communicate about the anguish felt by the consumers.

The Congress party's *"Aam Aadmi"* campaign had empathy, humanity and connected well with the people. The advertising had a tone of voice which spoke to the deprived consumer "I am on your side." Because it represented a unique attitude, it connected, worked wonders and brought in the nation a change in political power.

- **Weak Attitudes are Easier to Change than Strong Ones :** Marketers have found that when consumer brand attitudes are not strong, it will be more easy to establish new associations with the brand. Every woman would like to get attention and looking young is her eternal desire. Many savvy marketers in the past understood this and tried to please them by creating women oriented. T.V soaps and movies, build and sell houses to women etc. But it was *Lakme* which through its printed advertisement, was able to communicate about the energy and individuality of women who look stunning in their fruity, juicy make up. In the ad, *Lakme* talks of its *Fruity shock* makeup for lips, nails, eyes or skin and is said to contain do-good fruit extracts. This message is conveyed by women who look stunning in their fruity, juicy makeup. Any woman would pause at the ad page and imagine herself with the Fruit shock makeup. But she may not be familiar with all aspects of make up and beauty treatment.

It is said that it is easier to change: weak attitudes than strong ones, when there is a low involvement with the product and also change attitudes held by consumers who have less confidence in their brand evaluation.

FIGURE 6.4

PRINCIPLES WHICH CAN HELP TO BRING ABOUT ATTITUDE CHANGES

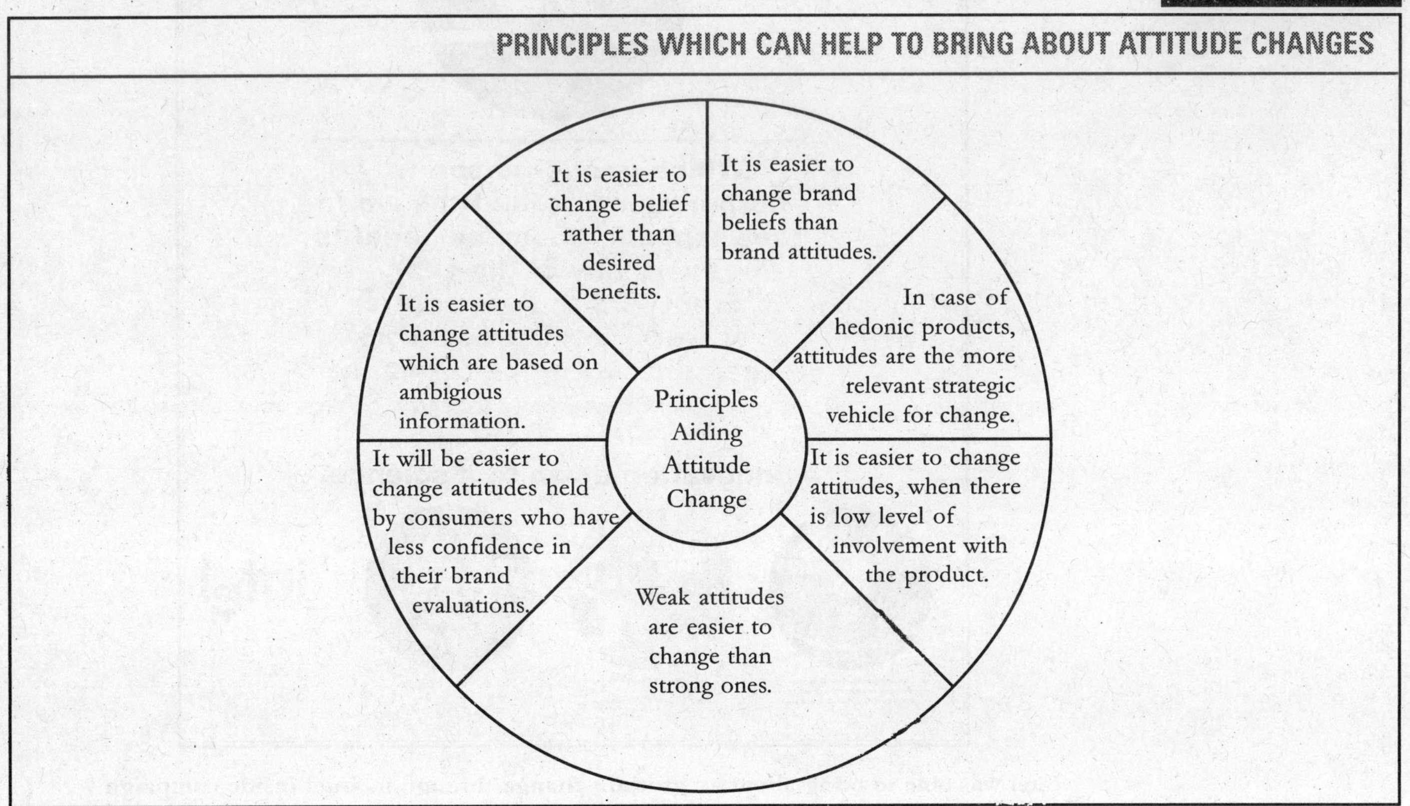

This is the reason why since 2000 Lakme has been setting up Lakme beauty saloons across the country where professional beauty services are provided. Such saloons apart from providing services, also help to strengthen the brand by complementing customer contact and experience. Thus Lakme has been able to create a strong attitude towards its products by communicating that Lakme through its ready mix, (which few women can ignore) are able to show women the way to fashion and feel good about herself. In fact Lakme India Fashion week provides the top tier of the brand communication.

- **It will be Easier to Change Attitude Held by Consumers who have Less Confidence in their Brand Evaluations :** In India with increasing life expectancy on the one hand and rising inflation and medical expenses on the other, the need for planning one's retirement was emerging as an important one. However, it was found that only around 11 per cent of India's total working population was adequately covered for post retirement life. This can be attributed to low awareness of and attitudinal barriers with respect to these issues among consumers.

Another principle used by marketers to bring about a change in consumer attitudes is that it is easier to change attitudes which are based on ambiguous information.

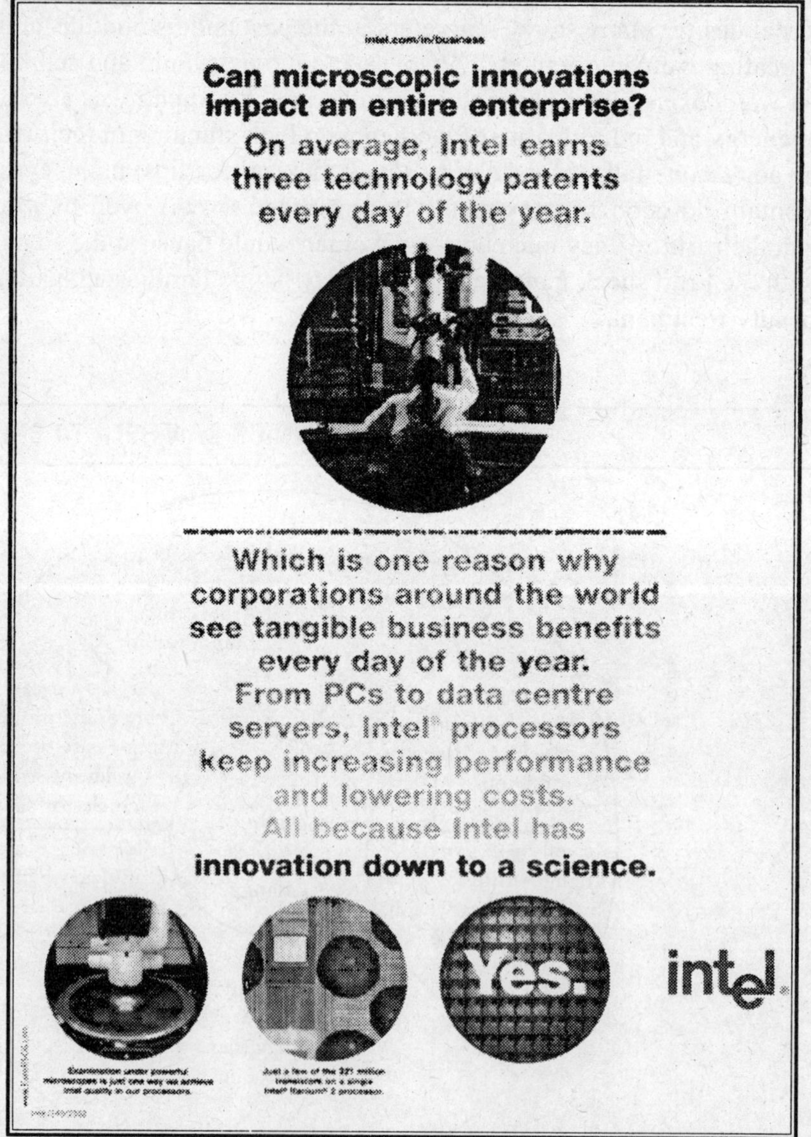

Intel was able to bring about an attitude change through its intel inside campaign

A research carried out by **ICICI** indicated a lot of barriers :

- Low awareness of the need for early retirement planning among consumers.
- Belief among consumers that planning for retirement starts only when one is in one's 50s.
- The word 'retirement' itself brought to mind a lot of negatives associated with old age, loss of independence (social, financial and physical), leading to avoidance or deferment of decisions regarding the same. However, ICICI through its multidimensional creative strategy which advertised **Retire from work-not life** was able to bring about a change in attitudes. It had a communication strategy which conveyed *'ICICI Prudential Retirement Solutions'* will help you plan early (among the 30-40 years age group) for retirement, ensuring that you will continue to live life the way you always wanted to. The end result was the well known success story of the brand ICICI prudential.

◆ **It is Easier to Change Attitudes which are based on Ambiguous Information :** When purchase of certain products involve highly technical information which needs to be clarified, it could lead to an attitude change if the same is provided for. For instance, Intel has been able to establish itself in the corporate sector through its *Intel inside* campaign. At that time very few people were aware of the fact that it was Intel's chip which was being used inside the PC (Personal Computer). It was through the above campaign that the brand's popularity increased with users specifically asking for Intel's chips.

FACTORS INVOLVED IN ATTITUDE FORMATION OR DEVELOPMENT

Attitudes are learned, though there are different approaches on how learning works and is acquired by individuals. Generally it is viewed that people learn things from the environment in which they interact. Thus for attitude formation, we have to consider all those factors from which people learn. Broadly, these factors could be analysed in the form of group (factors) and personality (factors), personal experience, direct marketing and mass media.

Attitudes are learned though there are different approaches on how learning works and is acquired by individuals.

Group Factors

The influence of groups on the attitudes of individuals is inversely proportional to the closeness of the group with the individual. From this point of view, there are three types of groups which affect the attitude of the individual differently.

1. **Family :** The term family can include the immediate family members and also the extended family which means along with immediate family (father, mother, sister and brothers) the extended family (relatives and close friends). Thus the family plays a very important role and is an extremely important source of influence on the formation of attitude. In fact it is the family which provides the individuals many of the basic values and a wide range of central beliefs. And the family mediate the influence of larger social systems on the individual's attitudes, values and personality characteristics. Thus as an individual interacts with other family members, he simultaneously both influences the personality characteristics and attitudes of others and in turn is influenced by others.
2. **Reference Groups :** Reference groups also play a role in influencing consumer's attitudes or behaviour. The reference groups serve important inputs to a consumer's learning of his attitudes and awareness of alternative behaviours and lifestyles. In this

Generally it is said that people learn things from the environment in which they interact. And thus attitudes are formed. This can be understood by considering all those factors: group, personality, direct experience, direct marketing and mass media.

process of socialisation, the consumer will learn the value system, norms, the desired behaviour patterns of the society etc.

3. **Social Factors :** The social classes also influence a consumer's attitudes. The social classes perform the important task of transmitting cultural behavioural pattern to specific groups and families. They define the expectations of society from groups of consumers as well as from the individual consumer. So consumers within a particular social class will be influenced by the value pattern and attitude formation of members in the same social class.

Personality Factors

Personality factors are important in attitude formation. However, many personality factors/ characteristics are themselves determined by group and social factors. Many research studies show positive relationship between a consumer's personality variables and particular attitudes. But since a consumer's personality is influenced by various groups and social factors as well as heredity factors, in understanding attitude formation, these factors particularly the former ones have to be analysed.

Direct Experience

Very often attitudes towards goods and services are formed through the consumers' direct experience with the product or service. Realising this marketers have frequently attempted to stimulate trial of new products by offering samples, discounts and other sales promotion offers. For instance, the various shampoo's like, *Pantene, Heads & Shoulder, Sunsilk,* etc. are available in sachets form in the market. The marketers' objective is to induce consumers to try the product and evaluate its performance. If the product proves to be satisfactory, then it is more likely that consumers will form a positive attitude and go for repurchase.

Direct Marketing

Consumer's prefer direct experience with the product before developing an attitude.

Marketers are increasingly using highly, focused direct marketing programmes to target 'consumers' with products and services that fit into their interests and lifestyles. Marketers very carefully build up customer information through the creation of a huge data base (as done by organisations like the Reader's Digest, Citibank and the LIC). On the basis of the customer's demographic, psychographic or geodemographic profiles, they are approached with personalised product offerings (vacuum cleaners, Tupperware products, Amway India's home care products, etc.), which convey the message that the company understands their special needs and comforts. Thus such direct marketing efforts help in creating a positive attitude in the minds of the consumers.

Tupperware through direct marketing makes customised product offerings.

Exposure to Mass Media

Marketers also use mass media to communicate and provide information to the consumers at large, about their various product offerings. Thus consumers are constantly exposed to newspapers, other print media and television, through which they get introduced to new ideas, products, opinions and advertisements.

Such mass media communications apart from proving to be important sources of information, can also influence in the formation of attitudes.

Marketers are using highly, focused direct marketing programmes to target consumers with products and services that fit into their interests and lifestyles. They also use mass media to communicate and provide information about their product offerings to the consumers at large.

Mass media communication can influence attitude formation

➲ THEORIES OF ATTITUDE

A number of theories have been proposed to understand the formation of attitude and how attitudes change and adapt to changing circumstances. These theories have been organised into major groupings on the basis of the psychological processes postulated to underlie formation and change of attitude.

Some theories are based on the assumption that people seek consistency in their attitudes. In this context there are four prominent attitude theories :

- Balance theory (F. Heider, 1958).
- Congruity theory (C.E. OSgood and RH. Tannenbaum, 1955).
- Cognitive dissonance theory (L. Festinger, 1957).
- Affective Cognitive Consistency Theory (M.J. Rosenberg, 1960).

The above theories are based on the assumption that an individual cannot simultaneously hold two contradictory beliefs. For instance, a family friend may recommend a showroom for the purchase of a two wheeler, which you may subsequently visit and find disappointing. According to consistency theorists, one cannot simultaneously presume that the friend is reliable and yet his recommendation was wrong. Thus, according to them, you would be 'forced' to change the opinion about the friend or make some excuse to cover up the performance/or service provided at the showroom.

A number of theories have been organized into major groupings in order to understand the formation of attitude and how attitudes change and adapt to changing circumstances.

Balance Theory : This theory has been developed by F. Heider. It is mainly concerned with the transfer of information between people. That is, it is concerned with consistency in the judgement of people and issues that are linked by some form of relationship. There are three elements in the attitude formation : The person, other person and the 'object' or impersonal entity. It is said that there are two generic types of relationship which exist between the elements *(a)* linking or sentiment relations and *(b)* unit relations.

- Linking relations - includes all forms of sentiments or effects.
- Unit relationships - it perceives that two elements belong together.

Both the unit and linking relations can be positive and negative also. In a three element system, balance will exist if all three relations are positive or if two relations are negative and one is positive. Conversely imbalance exists if all three relations are negative or if two relations are positive and one is negative. People have a tendency to perceive others and objects linked to them such that the system is balanced. This means that if a person likes a source (another person) who supports a certain position on an issue, the balancing process will induce the former to favour that position too. But the problem arises when there are imbalanced states, which may result in the rise of the psychological tension, which in turn will motivate the individual to restore balance cognitively by changing the relations. So we can say that a person's attitude towards an object will depend on his attitude towards the source, which is linked to the object.

This theory will be useful to marketers investigating ways in which to communicate recommendations as well as negative information.

Suppose a person 'A' receives information from another person 'B' concerning an attitude object. Depending on whether the information is positive or negative, there are four possibilities. The interactions are given in the form of triangles, the nature of the communications are positive [favourable or (+)] or negative (unfavourable or (–)]. [Refer to Figure 6.5]

The triangle [I] is balanced. Both the persons A & B have a positive attitude, towards each other as well as the object. There is no inconsistency.

Triangle [II] is unbalanced. This is because although their views of the object are consistent (both positive) their views of each other are negative. This is inconsistent.

Triangle [III] is balanced because both the persons A and B have a positive attitude towards each other and also share the same (negative) attitude towards the object thus there is no inconsistency.

The balance theory is concerned with the transfer of information between people and the consistency in the judgment of people and issues that are linked by some form of relationship between the elements involved in attitude formation.

Triangle [IV] is unbalanced because both the persons have a positive attitude towards each other but their attitudes towards the object are different, resulting in inconsistency.

According to the Balance theory, (as mentioned above) whenever there is inconsistency as in situations [II] and [IV], this must be resolved either by changing the attitude to a person or the object. We can illustrate this with a hypothetical example. Suppose a sales person from a company ABC Ltd., approaches you and tries to sell you a 'Personal computer'. Initially, the salesman will try to sell to you the benefits of the personal computer (his view) by showing you the brochures. So to start with, you (the prospective customer) will go by the trust you place in the salesman (Figure 6.6).

FIGURE 6.5

INTERACTIONS AND ATTITUDE FORMATION

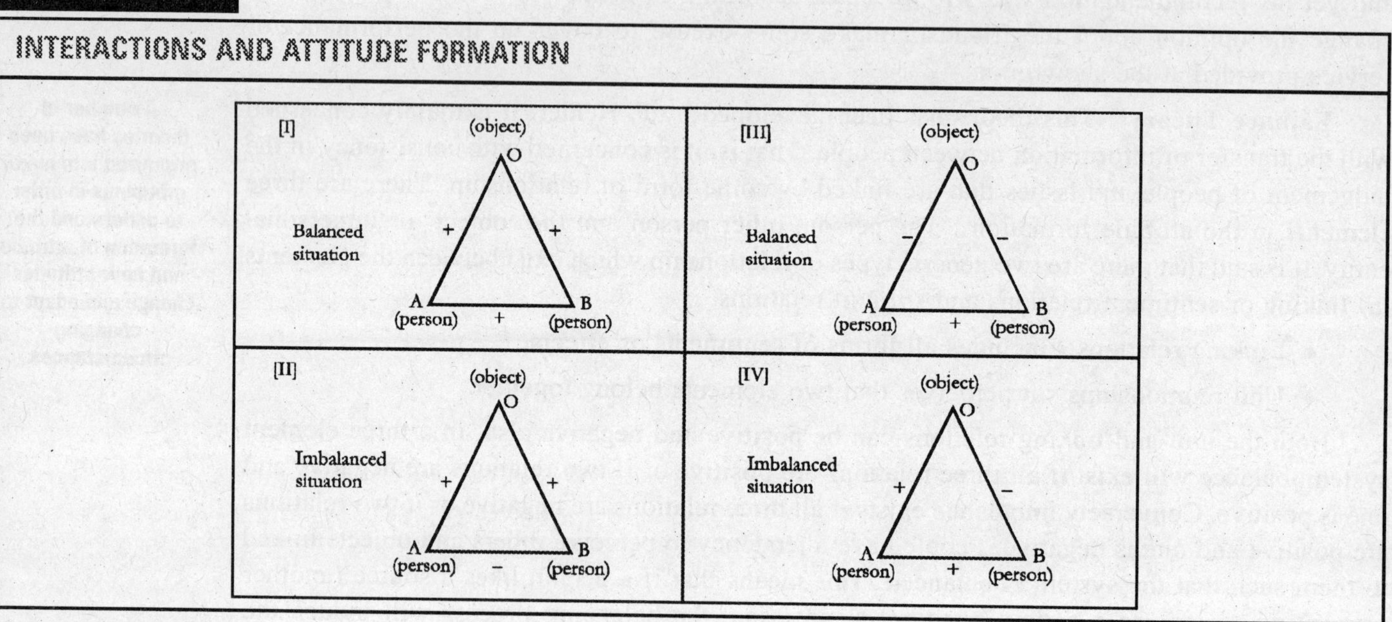

FIGURE 6.6

INITIAL BALANCE TRIANGLE

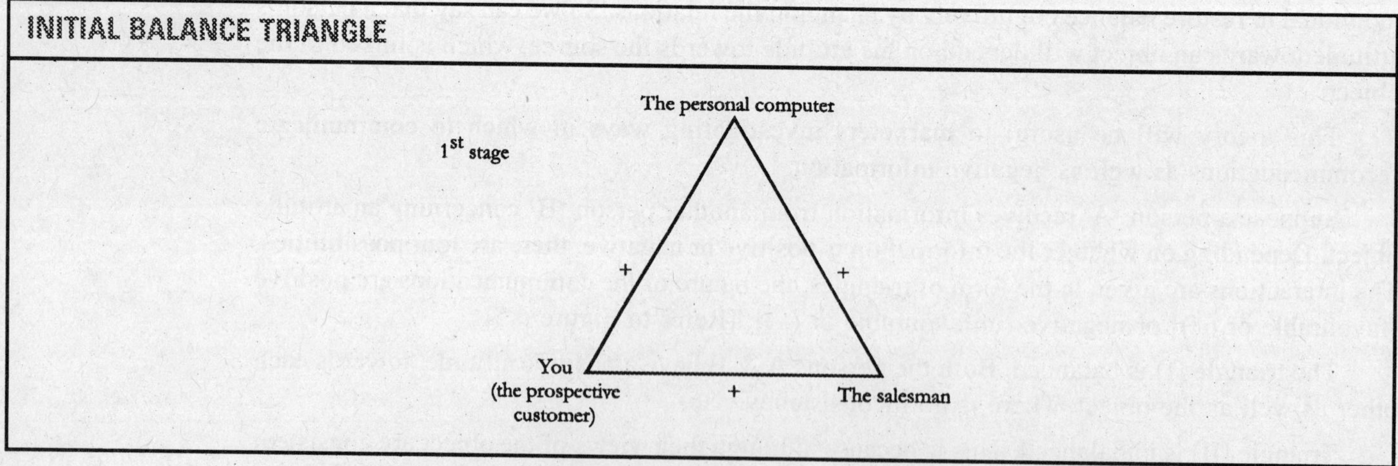

During the sales talk of the salesman, you will undoubtedly develop either a favourable attitude towards the salesman (as shown in fig. 6.7), or if you do not feel favourably disposed towards him, the most likely situation is shown in fig. 6.8.

FIGURE 6.7

FAVOURABLE TOWARDS THE SALESMAN, SO TO BE CONSISTENT, YOU ARE MOST LIKELY TO FEEL FAVOURABLE TOWARDS PERSONAL COMPUTER

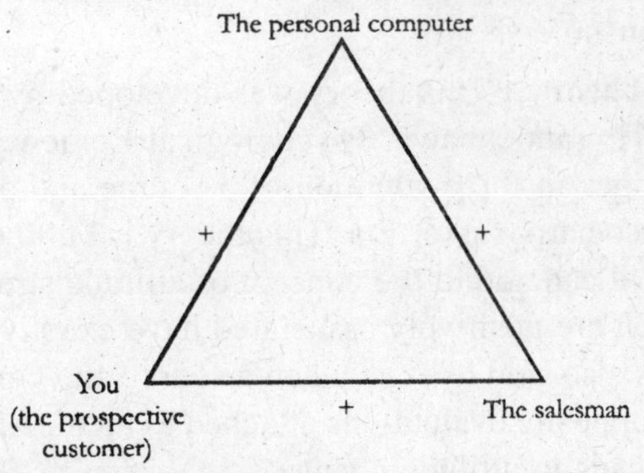

FIGURE 6.8

UNFAVOURABLE TOWARDS THE SALESMAN, SO TO BE CONSISTENT, YOU ARE MORE LIKELY TO FEEL UNFAVOURABLE TOWARDS THE PERSONAL COMPUTER

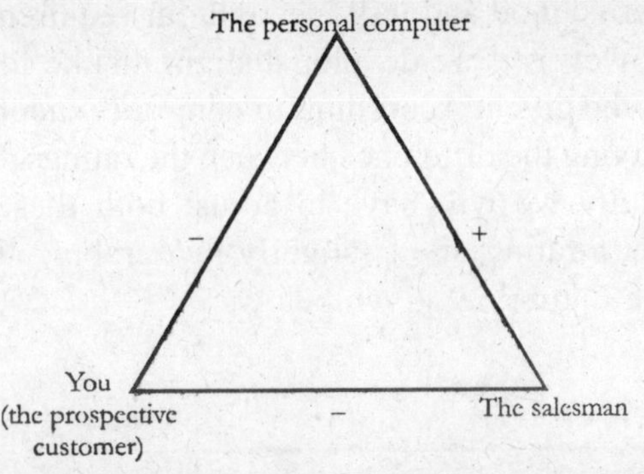

Similar marketing situations could occur, whenever the customers do not have direct contact with the product and are dependent on indirect information through the intermediaries.

The basic model of F. Heider has been criticised on some grounds. For instance, the theory does not consider the extent or degree of linking or unit relationship. It also does not consider the relevance of the elements and relations to the person (or perceiver). As a result, there is no mention of the degree of balance or imbalance. Thus, it is not possible to make quantitative predictions about the degrees of attitude change.

As an extension to the balance theory, R.P.Abelson has suggested four methods (denial bolstering) differentiation and transcendence) by which a person can resolve imbalance in cognitive structures.

As an extension to the balance theory, R.P. Abelson (R.P. Abelson, 'Modes of Resolution of Belief Dilemma', *Journal of Conflict Resolution*, No. 3, 1959, pp. 343-352) has suggested four methods by which a person can resolve imbalance in cognitive structures : denial, bolstering, differentiation and transcendence.

- *Denial* : When imbalance occurs, to deny the relationship.
- *Bolstering* : Add another element or issue to the main structure.
- *Differentiation :* Breaking up or splitting one of the elements into two elements such that they are related in opposite ways to other elements in the system but negatively related to each other.

- *Transcendence* : Combining elements into larger, more superordinate units from a balanced structure.

These processes will occur in a hierarchy, wherein the person will try to resolve the imbalance by attempting the least effortful resolution first. Through this theory marketers are able to understand how to use persuasive communication and interpersonal relation to change the attitude of consumers.

Congruity Theory : This theory was developed by C. E. Osgood and P. H. Tannenbaum (C.E. Osgood, P.H. Tannenbawn, Psychological Review, No. 82, pp. 42-55). The focus of the theory is on changes in the evaluation of a source and a concept which are interwined by an associative or dissociative assertion. This theory is build on the notion of positive and negative attitudes and that it can add to the concept of attitude strength. Congruity exists when a source and concept which are positively associated have exactly the same evaluations. Congruity is a stable state and is also said to exist when a source and concept which are negatively associated have exactly the opposite evaluations attached to them. And when incongruity exists, according to the theory, it leads to attitude change.

The congruity theory focuses on the changes in the evaluation of a source and a concept which are interwined by an associative or dissociate assertion. While the affective cognitive consistency theory refers to the consistency between persons overall attitude towards an object and on his beliefs about its relations to his more general values.

Congruity theory helps to rate attitude towards an object from - 3 (highly unfavourable) to +3 (highly favourable) with a middle zero point. Here, in order to obtain congruity, one should take into account not only the direction of the attitude (as in balance theory) but also its strength. To illustrate this, let us return to our personal computer salesman.

Suppose we are convinced based on the information received from the salesman that the personal computer is good and will meet all our requirements, a rate of +3 (highly favourable) may be given. However, if we develop a slight dislike for the salesman, a rating of -1 (slightly unfavourble) may be given. According to congruity theory, the final attitude towards the object is calculated by having the difference between the ratings. So in the case of the personal computer, to achieve congruity we will have to adjust both these ratings. Therefore we will give the personal computer a rating of +1 (slightly favourable), the mid point between -1 and +3. This can be seen in the Figure 6.9 given below.

FIGURE 6.9

CONGRUITY THEORY

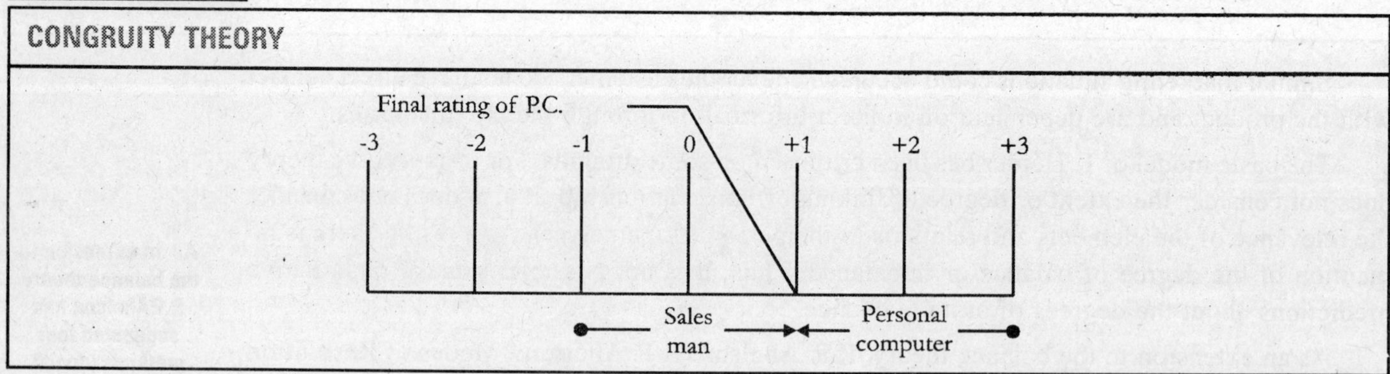

Affective Cognitive Consistency Theory : This theory which is developed by M.J. Rosenberg is about the consistency between a person's over all attitude towards an object and on his beliefs about its relationship to his more general values. According to this theory, attitudes are related to one aspect of cognitive structure (- means - end relationship) between the object and the achievement of desired and undesired values or goals. This theory is also referred to as structural because it considers what happens within an individual when attitude changes.

This theory postulates that a person's effect over all attitude object tends to be consistent with this cognitive structural component. This theory suggests that changes in the affective component will produce changes in the cognitive component so as to bring about consistency between the two. This theory also suggests that through persuasive communication one could change the attitudes resulting in attainment of the desired ends or in a re-evaluation of the goals themselves.

Cognitive Dissonance Theory : Cognitive dissonance is a motivating state of affairs just as hunger impels us to eat, so does dissonance which impels a person to change his opinions or his behaviour. (L. Festinger, 1957)

This theory considers the third component of the attitudes - behavioural tendency, with cognitions. This theory states that there are three types of relationships between all congnitions dissonance, consonance and irrelevance.

- Congnitions are dissonant when they are opposed, to one's experience about the relationship of events.
- Cognitions are consonant when one follows the other on the basis of logic or experience.
- Cognitions are totally irrelevant when two events are not interrelated.

The cognitive dissonance theory considers the behavioural tendency with cognitions and also states there are three types of relationships between all cognitions, dissonance, consonance and irrelevance.

For instance, say two pieces of information A and B, in a person's mind can be related in one of the three ways :

1. They can be consistent or consonant, then A implies B.
2. They can be inconsistent or dissonant, then A implies opposite of B.
3. They can be unrelated or irrelevant, then A is not related to B.

For example, two pieces of information *'I like icecream'* and *'Icecream can make me fat'* are dissonant. This means, one does not want to become fat and yet one wants to eat icecream. On the other hand, *I like green salad'* and *'Green salad is good for you'* are consonant pieces of information. The presence of dissonances gives rise to pressures to reduce or eliminate the dissonance.

The aim of cognitive dissonance theory is to reduce the amount of dissonance, often defined as 'mental discomfort'. Dissonance can be reduced by three methods : changing a behavioural cognitive element, changing an environmental element or adding a new cognitive element.

This theory can be applied to marketing so as to reduce post-purchase dissonance in consumer purchase decisions. Say for instance, when information about an accepted or rejected item is received subsequent to or after a purchase decision is made. At this time, positive information about a rejected item will generate dissonance. Similarly, negative information about an accepted item will lead to dissonance.

Suppose an individual is required to choose from 'Kashmir' and "Ooty" as the two alternative summer holiday destinations. We presume that the individual will finally settle on 'Kashmir'. Just after making the necessary booking arrangements, he may meet someone who has just returned after a visit to Kashmir. A negative opinion and report from them is likely to generate dissonance, as well a positive opinion expressed by recent visitors to Ooty.

The extent to which dissonance will be felt will depend on the following factors :

The Significance of the Decision : If the individual has spent a lot of money on the holiday, the dissonance would undoubtedly be greater.

The Attractiveness of the Rejected Alternative : If the decision had been a negative one then positive information from one of the rejected options is likely to create greater dissonance.

The Number of the Negative Views of the Choice Made : If the selected destination is seen as having a number of positive aspects, then a disappointing report about the weather, for instance is less likely to create dissonance.

The Number of Options Considered : The more rejected choices, greater the dissonance. Trying to choose a holiday destination from more alternatives makes it more likely that one of the rejected options would have turned out better.

Commitment to Cecision : If the decision can easily be reversed then less dissonance is likely to result.

Choice (Voluntary or Forced) : If the choice is 'forced' rather than voluntary, then lesser the dissonance.

Here also, a person experiencing dissonance will try to reduce the discomfort by adopting either of the following ways. The individual may:

Marketers can use the dissonance theory to include post-purchase positive reinforcement in the product, offer try and buy schemes and anticipate and address dissonance in the advertising message and product branding.

- Change his decision.
- Selective exposure or actively seek positive information about the chosen alternative.
- Selective attention or concentrate on positive information about the chosen alternative.
- Change the attitude.
- Selective avoidance, that is, avoid information likely to cause dissonance.
- Selective interpretation, that is, dismiss ambiguous information about the choice made.

In case of our above example, 'I like icecream', and 'ice cream can make me fat'. Dissonance resulting from this information can be reduced by adopting one or more of the following. The individual may

(a) Stop taking ice cream (change the decision).

(b) Take a decision that ice cream does not cause fatness (change of attitudes).

(c) Try to convince oneself that relishing an icecream was worth the risk of putting on a bit of weight (selective attention).

(d) Have doubt about the connection between taking icecream and putting on weight (selective interpretation).

(e) Take an ice cream and then avoid all information sources which suggest that icecream was bad and may lead to putting on weight. (Selective avoidance).

(f) Take an ice cream and then seek information sources which suggest that ice cream was good (selective exposure).

Marketers can use dissonance theory in the following ways:

Post Purchase Re-inforcement : The firm will continue to provide the purchaser with positive information about the product even after purchase and thus reduce post purchase dissonance. This will also help to build brand and corporate identity. For instance, this is usually done by various car manufacturing companies.

Try and Buy Schemes : Offering limited trials, re-inforced by various sales promotion techniques. This will help in creating a firm commitment and positive attitude towards the product, which will increase the likelihood of the purchase of the product. This may also help to avoid dissonance when the product is returned. Companies like *Coca-cola, Pepsico* etc. operate in this way.

Anticipating and Addressing Dissonance in the Advertising Message and Product Branding : For instance, HLL, was accused *by Fena* for including 'Lemon Power' on the packaging of *'Wheel'*, (washing detergent), especially in the absence of 'lemon' in its washing powder. So to avoid any dissonance in the consumers mind HLL was forced to change the packaging to 'cleaning power' and 'lemon perfume' instead of 'lemon power'.

MODELS OF ATTITUDE

In order to understand the relationship between attitudes and behaviour, psychologists have suggested the use of various models that will help in understanding the underlying dimensions of an attitude.

Given below are few important attitude models :

(A) Tricomponent Attitude Model

The Cognition Component : The first component of the tricomponent attitude model will be an individual's *cognitions.* This means that the knowledge and perception that are acquired either due to direct exposure to the attitude object and or from the information received from various sources will lead to cognition. This may give rise to consumer beliefs, that is the consumer believes that the *attitude object* possesses certain attributes and that specific behaviour will lead to specific outcomes, especially in case of consumer aspirants.

The Affective Component : The affective component of an attitude refers to a consumer's feelings or emotions towards a particular brand or product. Consumer researchers consider such feelings or emotions as evaluative statements. That is, the extent to which an individual will rate the attitude object as 'good' or 'bad' and 'favourable' or 'unfavourable'.

Researchers have also stated that the consumers' emotional state of mind is also likely to affect the shopping experience. That is, the emotional state of the individual at the time of shopping, will result in him or her experiencing a positive or negative feeling at the outlet. Further, subsequent recollection of this experience will be seen in the way they act. If a person has been joyous at the positive response he received from a particular retail out, he will persuade his friends and relatives to visit the shop and will even plan a revisit himself.

The Conative Component : Conation, the final component of the tricomponent attitude model is used to understand the likelihood of the consumer undertaking a specific action or behaving in a particular manner with regard to the attitude object.

When consumer researches are undertaken, usually buyer intention scales are used to ascertain the likelihood of a consumer purchasing or behaving in a particular manner.

Thus from the tricomponent model we can see that it consists of three major components a cognitive component, an affective component and a conative component. And an understanding of how these components are interrelated, will help determine the behavioural attitude of an individual consumer.

The tri component model consists of three major components: a cognitive component, an affective component and a conative component, which are interrelated and will help to determine the behaviour attitude of individual consumers.

FIGURE 6.10

THE TRICOMPONENT ATTITUDE MODEL

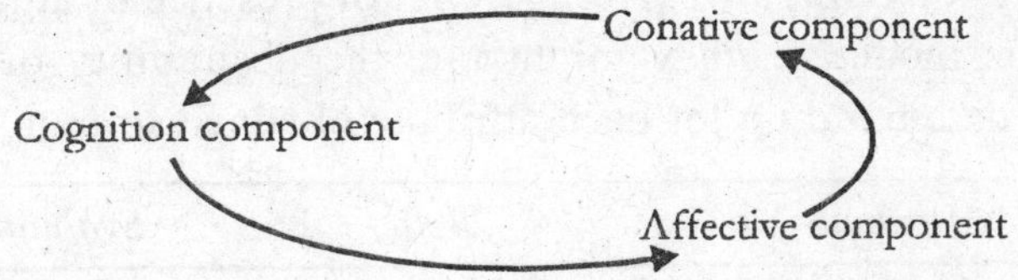

(B) Multi Component Model of Attitude

This model can help to predict attitudes from an evaluation of their component parts. This model was developed by Martin Fishbein. According to Fishbein, an attitude towards an object is dependent upon:

- Strength of the belief that object has certain attributes.
- The desirability of these attributes.
- The number of attributes.

(Attributes are those elements of an object which define it). For instance, few of the attributes of a vacuum cleaner may be :

- compact
- easy to handle
- has main cable storage
- can remove all dust from even odd, unreachable (by hand) places
- can clean up liquids and so on.

Fishbein Model

The multi component model of attitude was developed by Martin Fishbein. As per this model an attitude is dependent upon: the strength of the belief that objects have certain attributes and the number of attributes.

According to this model if a consumer believes strongly that an object has many positive, desirable attributes, then it will be rated favourably. This model can be explained with the help of a formula:

$$\text{Attitude towards an object} = \sum_{i=1}^{n}(bi\ ei)$$

Where

n = number of attributes

bi = strength of the belief that object contains 'i' attributes.

ei = evaluation of the desirability of attribute 'i'

Thus attitude towards an object can be described as the sum of the multiplication of the beliefs and evaluation for all attributes.

Usually 'b' is rated on a scale of 1 to 3, that is from (1) strong belief of presence of attribute to (3) uncertainty of the presence. And evaluation of desirability of the attitude on a 1-7 point of scale, that is from (1) highly desirable to (7) undesirable.

For instance, suppose we are asked to assess attitude towards a particular brand of 'camera'. There may have among others, the following attributes :

- Quality of picture
- Digital, Auto focus, easy to handle
- Reasonably priced

Based on the above attributes, the marketer can ask a sample of potential purchasers on their opinion of these attributes. If they strongly believed that the quality of pictures was good, they may give it a rating of 1 (strong belief of presence of attribute). If they find the quality of the picture as moderate, they might rate the desirability of it as '4'. We shall consider a hypothetical data build up for each attribute obtained from a single individual.

Attribute	*Belief (b)*	*Evaluations (e)*	*b × e*
Quality of picture	1	4	4
Digital, Auto focus, easy to handle	3	2	6
Reasonably priced	3	3	9
Total			19

The attitude score for the particular brand of camera is 19. The higher the figure, the less favourable the attitude towards the product or object. The worst possible score can be calculated by multiplying the number of attributes by 21 *i.e.,* 3 × 21= 63.

This method will help marketers to make brand comparisons.

Extended Fishbein Model

As discussed earlier, attitudes do not necessarily lead to corresponding behaviour. So in an attempt to improve the accuracy of Fishbein's original model, Williams in 1981, modified the model so that the ratings would refer to the behavioural outcomes of taking a particular action, unlike the above model where the ratings were given with reference to the object. Statistically, the formula will be the same as above, though the meaning will be different.

$$\text{Attitude-towards the behavioural action} = \sum_{i=1}^{n}(bi\ ei)$$

Where, n = number of outcomes;

bi = strength of the belief that action will lead to a particular outcome;

ei = evaluation or desirability of outcome.

So, if a consumer believes that purchasing a product will lead to a large number of desirable outcomes, then she or he is more likely to purchase it.

For instance, an individual may buy 'A' brand of a motor bike not only because of its speed but because of the outcomes of the speed. That it, due to the speed, he will be able to reach the ultimate destinations faster, easy to overcome other vehicles on the highway, to impress friends and so on.

Attitudes do not necessarily lead to corresponding behaviours. So a modified version of the Fishbein's original model called the Extended Fishbein model was developed by Williams. This Extended model suggests that we can predict the behaviour of the consumer accurately only if we rate these outcomes rather than rating the attributes.

According to the extended model, we can predict the behaviour of the consumer accurately only if we rate these outcomes, rather than rating the attributes of the vehicle. Thus if marketers are interested in knowing the link between behaviour and attitudes, this model is likely to give more reliable results.

Attitude Towards the - Ad Models

In order to understand the impact of advertising or some other promotional method on consumer attitudes towards particular products or brands, the attitude towards the ad models have been developed.

As shown in the Figure 6.11, consumers develop various feelings (affect) and judgements (cognitions) after being exposed to the ad. These feelings and judgements in turn will influence the consumers' attitude towards the ad and also develop certain beliefs about the brand and this will affect his or her attitude towards the brand.

While trying to assess consumer attitudes towards the ad, consumer researchers have suggested the importance of measuring *cognitive evaluations of* the ad (judgements as to whether the ad is humorous, informative etc., and the *affective responses from* the exposure to the ad.

Various researchers have also tried to examine the various underlying elements of attitudes towards the Ad model. Few of these have been reproduced here. One group of researchers (Mackenzie, Lutz and Belch) had felt that in *high involvement situations,* more of the *"central"* factors like the information content of the ad etc. will influence the consumers. Whereas in case of *low involvement situations,* it will be more *"peripheral* factors like the use of celebrities etc. which will affect the consumers response behaviour. Other researchers (Lord Lee and Saver) had felt that there were research studies which had indicated that both central peripheral factors

Marketers can try to re- inforce positive attitudes among existing users by continuously communicating about the goodness of their brands and also try to build up a long term relationship with them.

play a significant role in the formation of the attitude towards the ad, across different levels of consumer involvement. The above researcher's views indicate that marketers have to take care of the message contents to ensure that favourable perceptions and attitudes is created both in high involvement and low involvement situations.

Another researcher had drawn the attention to consider the nature of the attitude object in assessing the potential impact of advertising exposure. Still another view suggests the importance of assessing a wide variety of both positive and negative feelings when one is studying the influence of ad exposure.

Thus all the above researchers have made an effort to examine the influence of advertisements on the consumers attitude towards the product or brand.

FIGURE 6.11

THE RELATIONSHIP AMONG ELEMENTS IN AN ATTITUDE TOWARDS THE AD MODEL

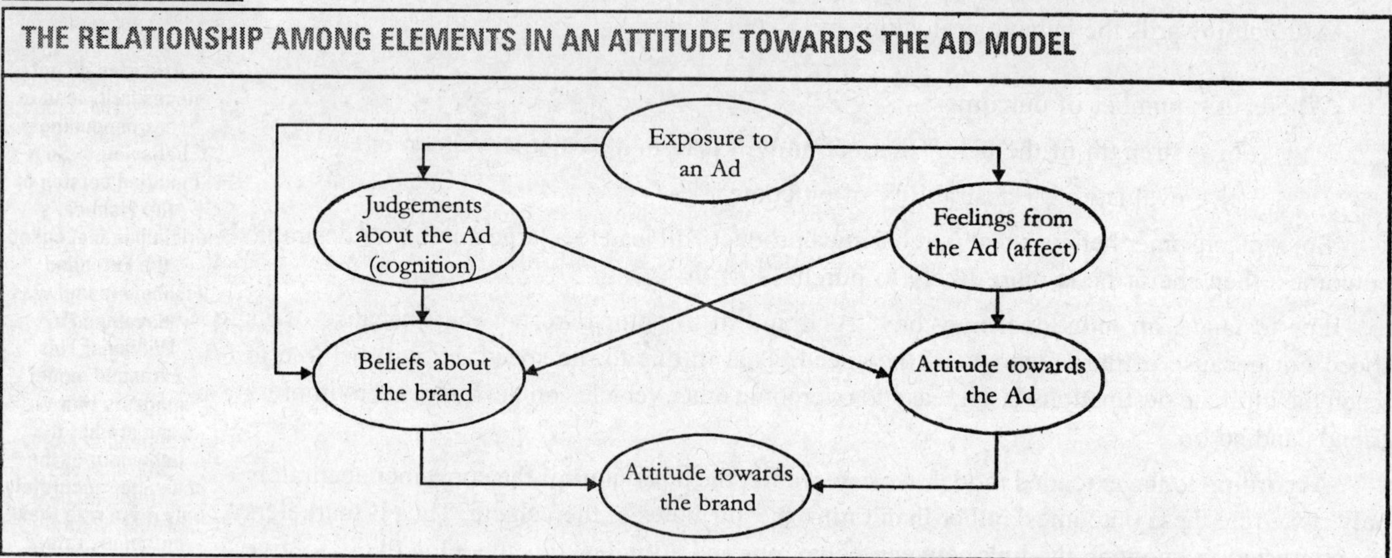

(Source : Consumer Behavior L.G. Schiffman, L.L Kanuk, 6th edn, 1997, page 251.)

➲ STRATEGIES FOR ATTITUDE REINFORCEMENT AND CHANGE

So far we have studied the various aspects of attitude, now we will have a look at the different types of strategies which will help to re-inforce existing attitudes or change them.

◆ **Attitudes Re-inforcement Strategy :**

Such strategies require the marketers to:

(a) Re-inforce positive attitudes among existing users.

(b) To an existing brand, attract new users

(c) Attract new users to a new brand.

◆ **Reinforce Positive Attitudes Among Existing Users :**

Marketers can advertise and re-inforce the consumers' (or users) positive attitudes towards their brand. In the long run this move can also help to build up brand loyalty. *Knorr soup* frequently advertises about variants of soup tomato, mix vegetables etc. *Maggi noodles* also advertises about the various categories of noodles, *Magi vegetable atta* noodles, the *Maggi rice noodles*. The marketers of the above product brands are re-inforcing the goodness of their brands and convince users to continue their positive attitudes towards it.

Another way of reinforcing positive attitudes is by building a *long term* bond or *relationship with* them. This can be done in the form of a company making efforts to build a long term relationship with every customer on a one-to-one basis. Such efforts are made through direct mailers, regular contacts from company sales representatives, via the internet, etc. Organizations offering various financial services such as the *Citibank, HDFC, HSBC, State Bank of India, Tata AIG Insurance, ICICI Prudential* etc., through their ongoing communications attempt to maintain customers' positive attitudes towards their company as well as the services offered.

- **Try to attract new users to existing products** by indicating that their products can deliver desired benefits in a better way. *Lifebouy care soap, Vaseline intensive care body lotion/ aluovera* or *Banjara's* (Multani mitti, chandan powder, henna, amla shikkakai) products are various brands which fall in the personal care category. All the above mentioned brands are brand extensions used by the marketer as a mean of optimizing relationship with the customer through a positive attitude on the brand image. Even *Amul* with its *'Taste of India'* tagline was successful in extending its brand name to its other products like ice creams.
- **Attracting new users to New Products :** When marketers try to identify opportunities in new and emerging areas then there arises the need to attract new users and communicate a positive attitude about their product offerings. They need to develop communication campaigns which will emphasise on the quality aspects, brand attributes and the imagery which will be associated with the brand.

Marketers can try to attract new users to existing products by indicating that their products are able to deliver desired benefits in a better way.

Many studies have found that there is a direct effect between the fit perceived by the consumers and the acceptance of the new or extended brands. The two components which count are the similarity between the new product(s) and the existing products of the company and the consistency between the new product and the parent brand. Ponds India has always offered products such as *Ponds* (cold and moisturizing) *creams, Ponds talcum powders* (with many variants), *Ponds anti aging product range* etc. All these products are catered to beauty conscious consumers who could choose from the range of face care, get fresh, skin care and natural care products.

Attempting at attracting new users to develop a positive attitude towards the brand.

Femina is attempting at re-inforcing positive attitudes among its customers through it's specialised offering

When marketers try to identity opportunities in new and emerging areas then there arises the need to attract new users and communicate a positive attitude about their product offerings.

Vaseline Intensive Care, offering, Ad tries to convey the bonding with the consumer and its positive brand image

Ponds trying to build a positive attitude for its new 'Ponds Age Miracle Products from new users

In the recent past Ponds India launched its new revolutionary anti-ageing skin care solutions range called the Ponds Age Miracle Range. The uniqueness of Ponds Age Miracle range is the key ingredient- Conjugated Linoleic Acid or CLA, which the company claims helps to reduce the appearance of age spots, rejuvenates the outer cells and increases the renewal rate of skin. Today when there is an increasing awareness of looking young, products such as Ponds Age Miracle Range (in a six pack through products) is definitely able to attract new consumers, especially since the parent brand Ponds is associated with a positive brand image.

Strategies to Change Attitudes

Marketers try to bring about a change in consumer attitudes generally when they want to reposition an existing brand or enter a new market with an existing brand. Through such strategies, marketers want to communicate about the set of attributes and benefits associated with the brand and influence consumers' purchase behaviour.

Tackling Change in Attitudes of Existing User

Marketers try to bring a change in consumers attitudes when they want to reposition an existing brand or enter a new market with an existing brand. They try to communicate about the set of attributes and benefits associated with the brand and influence consumers purchase behaviour.

Marketers have realized that there is a change in consumer attitudes and interest towards the premium market segment. Earlier most of the consumers who were exposed to the truly high end niche products used to be frequent travelers abroad. And very often they would purchase such products on foreign trips or through direct selling networks. But today, changes in consumer attitudes are acting as catalysts for the premium market revival. There are the mass market consumers who are still extremely value conscious about the everyday items but will display a willingness to spend a lot more on new products and categories.

Ashok Venkataramani, V.P. Skin and Care, HLL comments "With the boom in the BPO industry coupled with the explosion in the mall culture, there is a surge in the first jobbers' young adults between 20 and 30 years who are willing to spend. The two areas where there has been immense growth is skin, especially in the facial cleaning and the sun protection segment, both of which are growing, consumers are willing to pay an amount, depending on whether they see an actual value there". Accordingly, Hindustan Lever Limited has shifted focus to the top end for its *Lux brand,* upgraded *Lifebouy* and *Dove soaps* and has reasonably been successful in positioning its *Lakme brand* as a premium product.

L'Oreal, a market leader in most of the countries it is present in, had entered the Indian market more then ten years ago with a range of skin care products with the focus on the super premium category. Now in order to meet the rising aspirations of various segments, has come out with product offerings which can be said to be occupying the whole price range between the super premium and the affordable. Its very popular (key) brand is *Garnier* (separately for men and women), which is priced slightly lower then the L'Oreal, professional range. All the above brands are doing well. In fact L'Oreal positioned its premium products in a sharp, convenient and aspirational way different from its other popular offerings.

'L'Oreal offers an expanded product line to conform to consumers' changing attitudes

Changing Attitudes of Nonusers : In an attempt to attract non-users or consumers, marketers are using various methods to bring about a change in their attitudes. For example during the first three-four years Diamond Trading Company (DTC) had only focused on research in order to know what consumers' different need states were and how they see jewellery as. Then through mass media advertising of their product's salient features, they were able to arouse consumers interest, culminating into positive purchase behaviour. DTC also builds relationships by constantly interacting with its sight holders (world wide)-providing value added services like market research, and conducting branding and fashion seminars.

For many years Gold had been the popular jewellery, with not much awareness about platinum jewellery even though it has been available in India since 2001 onwards. So Platinum

Guild International (PGI) decided to educate the consumers by initiating tailored contact programmes, allowing them to interact with jewellery designers, learn the value of platinum jewellery and experience it first hand. Thus thematic ads helped in building image and aspiration and reaching out to prospective consumers. PGI also runs annual training sessions for jewellers and its sales people and has also instituted the Platinum Excellence Awards aimed at acknowledging the efforts of its best sales staff.

All such efforts by marketers will not only help to convert nonusers to users but also gain mind share by making its presence known in an already cluttered market.

'DTC focuses on research for understanding the attitudes of non users.

SUMMARY

Attitudes are inner expressions or feelings that reflect whether a person is favourably or unfavourably predisposed to a product or brand or establishment. Marketers are concerned with understanding attitudes, so as to modify them (and make it more favourable towards their brand) and turning positive attitude towards an object or product into an action resulting in the purchase of the item in question. The nature of consumer attitudes can be understood better by viewing the three components (cognitive, affective and conative), which can be defined in terms of brand beliefs, brand evaluation and intention to buy.

Since attitudes are subjective attributes of people, psychologists have devised certain methods for measuring attitudes by using the Thurstone type of scale, Likert scales, Semantic Differential or Kelly's Repertory Grid.

Studies have indicated that re-inforcing user's positive attitudes of a brand was more successful in increasing it's consumption. While trying to understand how attitudes are formed, one has to consider all factors namely: the group (factors), personality factors, personal experience, direct marketing and mass media.

Four prominent attitude theories which work on the assumption that people seek consistency in their attitudes were discussed. They were the Balance Theory, Congruity Theory, Cognitive Dissonance Theory and the Affective Cognitive Consistency Theory. Psychologists have suggested the usage of various models that will help in understanding the underlying dimensions of an attitude.

Two of the attitude models (Tricomponent Attitude Model and the Multi Component Models of Attitude) were discussed. Marketers have to use various strategies to re-inforce positive attitudes (among existing users) as well as to change the attitudes of non users.

➲ CHAPTER QUESTIONS FOR DISCUSSION

1. What do you understand by the term 'Attitudes'? Explain with an example, why marketers and consumer researchers are interested in learning about the link between consumer behaviour and attitudes?
2. Briefly explain the nature and characteristics of attitudes. Meet ten fellow students from your college and another ten students of a neighboring college (belonging to the same age group) and find out their attitude on wearing a helmet while driving a two wheeler? What conclusions are you able to draw from the study?
3. Write a short note on the various theories of Attitude.
4. Generally, it is accepted that 'Smoking is injurous to health' but it is still too early to say that everyone who used to smoke cigarettes has quit smoking. Suggest strategies by which you can change the attitude of those who smoke.

➲ SUGGESTED READINGS

1. Peter D. Bennett, Harold H. Kassarjian, *"Consumer Behavior"*, Prentice Hall India Pvt. Ltd., New Delhi, 1987.
2. Leon G. Schiffman, Leslie Lazor Kanuk ; *"Consumer Behavior"*, Prentice Hall of India Pvt. Ltd., New Delhi, 2005, pp. 251-286.
3. Rosemary Phipps, Craig Simmons, *"Understanding Customers"* 1996-97, Butterworth-Heinemann, Oxford, 1996.
4. Samidha, Sharma, Marketing in the New Age, *The Economic Times,* Bangalore, July 2006.
5. Suchi. Vyas; 'Expert advice, Brand Equity, *The Economic Times,* Bangalore, 26 July, 2006
6. Henry. Assael, *'Consumer Behavior and Marketing Action'* 6th Ed., Thomson Learning, Singapore, 2001, pp 281-338
7. Jagdish N. Sheth, Banwari. Mittal, *Customer Behavior A Managerial Perspective,* Thomson South Western Learning, Singapore, 2003, pp 198-229.
8. Rakesh Prakash, On the Road to Progress, *The Economic Times,* Bangalore, 10 February, 2007.
9. Prasoon Joshi 'Utility Value of Use and Throw, *The Economic Times,* Bangalore, 6 February 2007.
10. Skin deep - The Art of Marketing to Women, *Strategy Marketing,* July-August 2004, Vol. III Issue IV, pp. 49-52
11. Sussan. Verghese, It's your life (ICICI Prudential) *Strategic Marketing,* January- February 2005, pp. 57-61.
12. Sampa Chakrabarty. Lahiri, Extending Brands, *Strategic Marketing,* July-August, 2004, pp. 27-31.
13. Suchi, VyaS, 'The Topping Point-High on price, Brand Equity, *The Economic Times,* 16 August, 2006.
14. N. Shatrujeet, An Ear to the ground, Brand Equity, *The Economic Times,* 16 August 2006.
15. Anna. Robledes, Spoiled for Choice, *Business World,* 19 February 2007, pp 64-65
16. Ashish. Kapur 'Only Brands Sell Most in Retail, *Economic Times,* Bangalore, 15 February 2007.

CASE

HANDLING OF DOWN-AGE SYNDROME

The middle age consumer's attitude of "staying young"

The Indian society is witnessing a new behavioural paradigm shift across urban India, with people in their 40s and even 50s displaying a propensity to defy age. This is visible in their attitude to adopt a different lifestyle and behaviour in an attempt to look young and they view age not only in terms of a number but as a milestone which demands fundamental and frequent changes in behavioural pattern. The staying young phenomenon can be attributed to changes in the mental make up of the individual. In the past, people, as they pass new milestones in life, would tone down their behaviour and appearance accordingly. *For example,* individuals would change their style of dressing immediately after they start working undergo another change in attitude post marriage and so on.

The demographics profile is definitely influencing psychographics of individuals. Unlike the previous generations, which were mainly dominated by a single bread earner, today the house hold scenario has changed. Now a day's most of the homes are dual or more income households with the money (or income) inflow combining both the parents' salary along with the take home (salary) pack of the young adult children. In fact the average age of the workforce in most of the offices is around 24years. So, all those in their 40 plus age group are under greater pressure to turn the clock back and feel 'included' by the younger generation. Hence, in a quest to look, feel and think young, those in their forties are also changing their language and clothes to match that of the majority. They have become more conscious about physical fitness with many middle aged customers quietly opening accounts on Facebook, updating, status messages on an hourly basis and using fun applications, which five years ago they would not have taken seriously. Even wearing t-shirts and jeans has, by default become the dress code, especially since it has a strong 'youthful' imagery. At the office there are many persons who rise to the top echelons of power by their early forties. One of the factors that seem to have played a significant role in down aging is the new found belief in the advantage of looking young. In the words of Simeran Bhasin, Marketing head, Titan industries. "The 40-plus crowd has the confidence to carry around their young looks. And there is no guilt about indulging like an 18 years old". Further, the 'grow young' trend is not only restricted to personal grooming or fashion but is seen in the purchase of technology related products.

A-study to understand purchase behaviour

In Target Groups Index (TGI) India a study by IMRB International, involves more than 300 products categories, covering individuals in all urban India of SEC A/B/C households, in the age group of 15-55 years, the following information was revealed:

- The ownership of premium mobiles or mobiles with radio and MP3players was found to be equal among older (41 to 50years) and younger (15- 19 years). This could partly be because of the change in the parent – child equation (parents becoming more of their children's friend) and with the young advising the forty plus group on picking up the handsets.
- For decisions regarding taking holidays to off beat destinations, the study revealed that while 43percent of respondents in the 41-50 years age bracket preferred to take to offbeat destination, only 44 per cent of the 15- 19 years olds preferred to get adventurous with their holidays.
- Nearly 41 per cent of respondents belonging to the 41 to 50 years thought that "it is important to be attractive to the opposite sex", where as 42 per cent of respondents belonging to the 15 to 19 years age shared the same feeling

Consumer's Attitudes (Percentage agreeing with the statement)

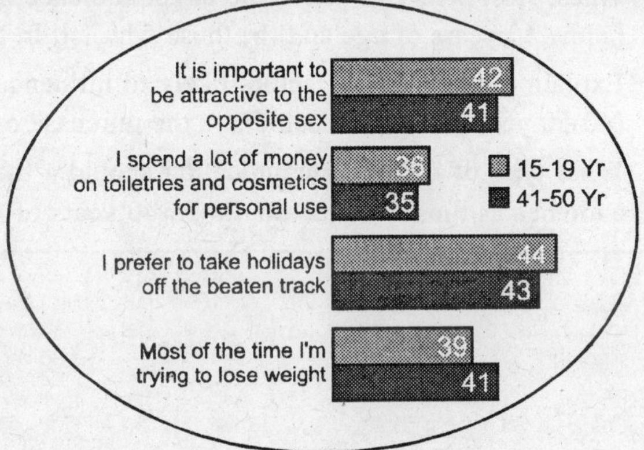

Personal Products Usage (Percentage used in last 12 months)

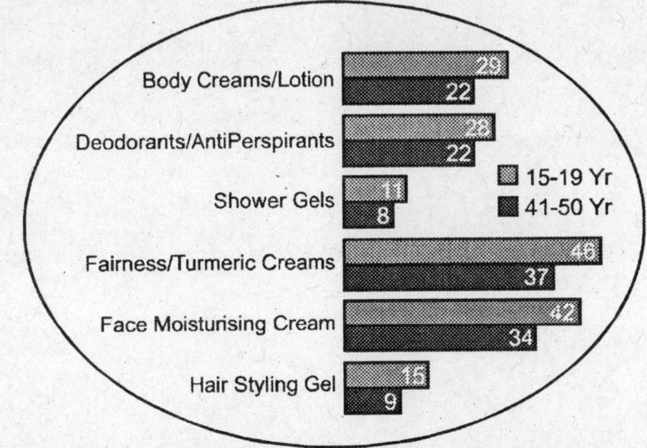

(*Source :* TGI India, IMRB International, 15-55 years, SEC A/B/C individuals in All urban India, * *The Economic Times*, Bangalore, January,2009, pp. 1 - 2)

The Expected Trends

As the consumption pattern continuous with the change in attitude of the 40plus customers, the challenge before the marketers who targets 'The young' as well as the 'young at least', will be to ensure that they adopt suitable sub-segmentation and micro-segmentation Strategies. Marketers have expressed their view on the marketing implication of these type of trends.

Rajeev Sharma, National Brand Planning, **Leo Burnett,** feels that this trend will result in the youth striving hard to search for exclusivity in product brands. He says "As older consumer start looking at traditionally youth dominated categories like denim and mobiles, youth will look for extreme youth fashion that older people won't or cannot imitate" Sharma's prediction of the expected trend is that youth influence can lead to demand of products which may not necessarily be targeting the youth. He feels design in particular will emerge as extremely important across categories.

According to Shyam Sukhramani, Marketing Director, **Levi Strauss India,** companies will have to concentrate more at segmentation in greater detail, develop more products to cater to sub segments, the marketing mix and deliver products which cater to every segment.

Says Harit Nagpal, (**Vodafone Essar**) "Target definitions need to be even tighter when consumption trends are converging" He opines that even if both the 40-50years olds and 15to 19 year olds use MMS as a service, it would be incorrect to assume that both are using it for the same purpose. So it is very necessary to clearly define and understand target markets motivations.

Markets have made changes to match the requirements of those belonging to the 'Down- aging syndrome' category. The tagline of ICICI- Prudential probably has conveyed their understanding of their targets audience's sentiment *"Retirement, sirf kaam se"*.

(*Source :* Prasad Sangameshwaran, Down the Ages, *The Economic Times*, Bangalore, January 7, 2009, pp. 1 - 2)

QUESTIONS FOR DISCUSSION

1. Suppose a real estate developer is planning to construct houses, which comprise of premium and super premium villas. How will you define the target audience, keeping in mind the motivations of consumers belonging to (a) the below 40 years of age and (b) those who fall in the 40 plus age group?
2. Explain the situational factors likely to influence the attitudes of the young (25-40 years of age) and not so young (40-50 years of age)consumers in the purchase of luxury cars.
3. What type of brand communication should a marketer of luxury watches work out, if he has identified his target audience as those who belong to 25-40 years of age?

CHAPTER 7

MOTIVATION

- Case : **Asian Paints**
- Differences between Motives, Motivating and Motivation
- Needs and Goals
- The Dynamic Characteristics of Motivation
- Various Theories of needs (Maslow's, Mc Clelland's, Alderfer's, Vroom's)
- Motivational research
- Summary
- Chapter questions for discussion
- Suggested Readings
- Case : **HDFC**

CASE

ASIAN PAINTS

Since long, psychologists and consumer researchers have concluded that there is a diversity in consumer behaviour with most individuals experiencing the same kind of needs and motives, although it may be expressed in varying degrees by them. This is why marketers are putting all efforts to understand human motives so as to be able to predict human behaviour and make suitable product offerings accordingly. An understanding of human needs – consumer needs are the essence of the marketing concept.

Let us have a look at how *Asian Paints* has established its leadership since 1968 (in India) in the paints industry driven by its strong focus of understanding consumer needs and innovating itself accordingly. Asian Paints had a humble beginning in 1942, when four friends started running the company on a partnership basis.

The customer centric approach with all retail initiatives evolved around the concept 'going where the customer needs go' has earned it lots of customers' satisfaction. In the early 90s, for the first time in the paint industry, Asian Paints offered the consumer over one hundred and fifty shades. This concept was extended to the dealer shops through the *Colour World*, in the mid 90s, providing the consumers – a service interface, where they can choose from one thousand shades and colours in 5,300 outlets around the world. The company sources claim that Asian Paints USP (Unique Selling Point) lies in the fact that only a limited number of base colors are sent across to its outlets. Thereafter, at the retail outlets, tinting machines are used to add various colours and colorants in predetermined ratio's so as to create any shade of the customer's choice. They even have a photometer, and customers can bring any mug or tee shirt and walk out with a shade close to it.

Asian Paints has carried out intensive research with interior designers, architects and the fashion community to arrive at the trend movements of colour in each year. This study has helped consumers to get an insight into the latest trends and happening colours and make a choice accordingly for furnishings, floorings and home accessories.

Understanding the importance of painting kids rooms, Asian paints launched *'Kids World'*, wherein, painting designs are offered for kids' rooms as well as kids' corners. This was a maiden attempt to invite the customers to get into a Do-it-yourself mode with these designs. *Royale Play* was another innovative concept – a collection of innovative and ready to use special effect finishes for interior walls, comprising a range of special effects which will offer interesting colour combinations.

Asian paints, in 2001 also introduced *a toll free help line,* which customers can use to make their paint related queries. They also have the *Asian Paints Home Solutions,* which along with providing paints also provides customers with painting services. In the words of P.M. Murthy, President, Decoratives "Home Solutions has helped us build the Asian Paints brand further and provides good insight into what the consumer needs and requires".

The above case on Asian Paints shows that even for the consumer's need of getting his house painted, the company's understanding of the underlying motives, through unique service offerings were able to satisfy the consumer's choice of colour.

In this chapter, the discussions are evolved around the role needs and motives play in consumer behaviour. Various theories on motivation have also been studied to understand their impact on consumer behaviour.

DIFFERENCES BETWEEN MOTIVES, MOTIVATING AND MOTIVATION

Before going for an in-depth discussion on needs and goals, we will understand the distinct connotation between the three interrelated terms, motive, motivation, motivating. All the three terms have been derived from the Latin word 'moyere' meaning to move.

Motive – give directions to human behaviour. A motive is an inner state that energizes activates, or moves and directs or channels behaviour towards the goal. Motives could be the "whys" of behaviour. Motives will not only arouse and maintain activity but also determine the general direction of the individual. Sometimes **motives** are referred to as needs wants, drives or impulses within an individual and they work towards achieving the goals.

Motivating – implies an activity engaged into by an individual, by which he or she will channelise the strong motives in a direction that is satisfactory. The ability or willpower or motivations of the individuals will depend on the strength of his motives.

A psychologist has described *the study of motivation as covering all those things which are biological, social and psychological and that they defeat our laziness and move us, either eagerly or reluctantly, to action.* So simply stated we can say that the study of motivation is concerned with why people choose to behave in a certain way.

It can be said that all the activities of human beings are caused and behind every action there is a particular need or motive. Needs can be a feeling or desire for something which is lacking and through performing various activities to get the feeling of lacking removed and thus become satisfied. Thus human behaviour is caused by motives or needs and motivation is the process of inducing persons to experience needs for a certain goal or behaviour. So we can say motivation is concerned with :

Human behaviour is caused by motives or needs and motivation is the process of inducing persons to experience needs for a certain goal or behaviour.

Needs - the most basic human requirements.

Drives - tells how these needs translate into behaviour.

Goals - what these behaviour's aim to achieve.

Emotional Versus Rational Motives

Consumer behaviourists have also made a distinction between *'rational motives'* and *'emotional* (or non- rational) *motives'*. Traditionally the term rationality is associated with persons who carefully weigh the pros& cons of all the alternatives and then choose the one that gives them the greatest utility. In the marketing context we can say that consumers who are *'rational'* will select the goals after ascertaining various objective criteria such as size, weight price etc. As against this *emotional motives* are those goals which are selected on the basis of emotion's involvement. Usually such goals are selected purely on personal or subjective criteria such as desire for recognition of status, fear, pride, esteem, love etc.

HSBC Bank communicates about its human face (rational motives) to banking. Its power vantage account ad communicates that it understands its customers' dilemma on financial planning and rational decision making. Another ad from *HSBC Bank* using the 'Different People,

Different Views' campaign tries to influence upon customers through the potrayal of the mother sewing up a teenager's fashionably torn jeans or the other situations shown in the ad. This ad has got an emotional appeal conveying that it understands its customers' point of view without going into the regular banking used phrases.

Motivation can be positive or negative. If an individual experiences a driving force towards an object or person or situation it is called positive motivation. Whereas, a driving force compelling the person to move away from someone or something will be known as negative motivation.

Though it may be argued that those who take purchase decisions based on emotional motive do not maximise utility or satisfaction, need not always hold true. For it may be counter argued that they (such consumers who are influenced by emotional motives) also make selection with a view to maximise satisfaction. Moreover, 'satisfaction' is a personal process and will vary from person to person based on his or her need structure, past experience and learning. Therefore, it is improper to distinguish between rational and emotional motives.

Potrayal of rational and emotional motives by HSBC Bank

Positive or Negative Motivation

Motivation can be positive or negative. If an individual experiences a driving force towards an object or person or situation, it is called positive motivation. Whereas a driving force compelling the person to move away from someone or something will be known as 'negative motivation'.

Though there is a difference between positive and negative motivational forces, in terms of both the physical as well as emotional activity, both are similar i.e. *both initiate and sustain human behaviour.* This is why researchers refer to motives (or drives) as needs, wants and desires.

We can understand better the difference between a positive and negative goal with an example. Say, a young executive male gets promoted and is transferred to a new place. This man (executive) will join the 'local club' *(a positive goal)* so as to gain social recognition and make new friends. The executive's wife may join the kitty parties held by the other executive's, wives to avoid a *negative goal* - rediculed by others as an unsociable person. In the above example, we have seen that both positive and negative goals can motivate an individual's behaviour.

Unfulfilled wants, needs or desires can induce individuals to set goals which can be positive if the behaviour is directed towards it (approach object). A goal is said to be negative, if the behaviour is directed away from it (avoidance object).

Unfulfilled wants, needs or desires can induce individuals to set goals which can be positive if the behaviour is directed towards it and accordingly it will be referred to as an *approach object*. On the contrary, a goal is said to be negative if the behaviour is directed away from it and thus it comes to be referred to as an *avoidance object*. Both the approach and avoidance goals can be said to be the outcome or results of an individual's motivated behaviour. For example a young woman may have a positive goal of 'looking good' and may regularly go to the gym and visit the beauty saloon. Her friend may view eating junk food as a negative goal, since she is aspiring to join the modeling industry. So she will avoid eating junk food and also exercise at the gym to maintain herself and be fit for a modeling career. In the former case, the young woman's actions and behaviour are designed to achieve the positive goal of 'looking good' and in her friend's case; her (friend's) action's are designed to avoid the negative goal of eating junk food.

Ads of VLCC and Castrol GTX Extra can induce positive and negative motivational behaviour respectively

Marketers also try to project their product or service offerings such that it conveys an approach motive or avoidance motive. For instance **VLCC** conveys an approach motivation to individuals who have a positive goal of fitness. **Castrol GTX Extra** Engine oil uses the avoidance motive, informing customers to avoid any other engine oil which could spoil the car engine and only use Castrol GTX Extra which has an advanced international quality formula.

Motivational behaviours called psychological reactance is seen when people get aroused by a felt threat of or fear of elimination of behavioural freedom.

There is another motivational state referred to as *psychological reactance.* This motivational behaviour is seen when people get aroused by a felt threat of or fear of elimination of behavioural freedom. The concept of super market is gaining popularity in the major cities, one of the reasons for this is "the freedom to make a product choice without the fear of undue influence from the retailer".

Hull's Drive Reduction Theory

One popular theory which links needs and drives with goals is that of Hull. Hull's drive reduction theory attempts to explain both motivation and learning. This theory is based on principles which may be of general interest, though Hull was mostly concerned with the operation of primary needs. Hull's theory is illustrated in the Figure 7.1 given below.

FIGURE 7.1

A SIMPLE VIEW OF HULL'S DRIVE REDUCTION THEORY

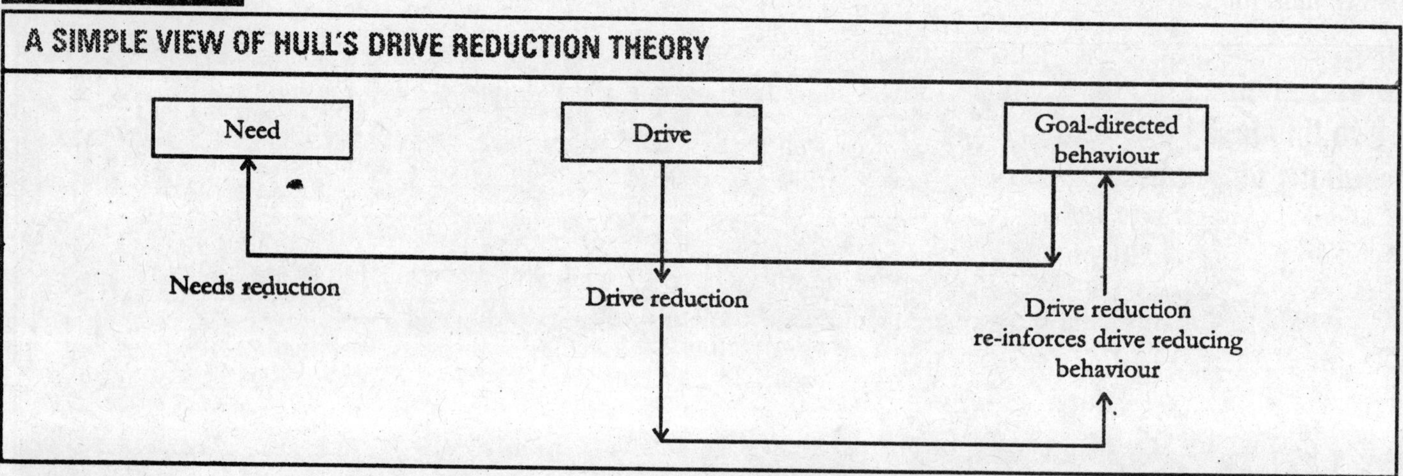

Hull's drive reduction theory attempts to explain both motivation and learning and is a popular theory which links needs and drives with goals.

As mentioned above a need will give rise to a drive and the resulting behaviour will be aimed at reducing the drive and thereby the need. According to Hull, the drive reduction act (or act of reducing the drive) re-inforces the drive reducing behaviour whereby it is likely the behaviour be repeated again in case of recurrence of the need in future.

Suppose, a salesman during the course of performing his work feels *thirsty*. His behaviour will be to seek and find out the nearest source of *refreshment*, a small restaurant perhaps. Going by Hull's theory it is most likely that the individual will prefer to have a cool drink which has satisfied his thirst in the past, 'Sprite' for instance. If this was not available, he may go for something in the same category *(7-UP)* or try something new. If this new option is found to be satisfactory, then it is likely to be selected next time the salesman is thirsty.

In the above example, we have discussed about positive motivation, similarly people can also experience negative motivations or prefer avoidance of certain items or situations. Since the above salesman is thirsty he is likely to avoid salty things, which can make him even more thirsty. Suppose, a tourist is visiting the various historical places in North India, but he is allergic to spicy food. So he will avoid taking spicy food items (avoidance of spicy food approach) and may prefer to take a bland diet (approach bland food).

Based on the above, we can classify objects or products as either approach objects (contact with whom will satisfy our need) and avoidance objects (contact with whom or those which will take us further away from our need).

Individuals are engaged in a tension reduction behaviour, which they presume will help in fulfilling their needs and thus reduce the tension (or stress felt by them).

Thus, (motivation) the driving force is the outcome of a state of tension, which arises because of unfulfilled needs and desires. Individuals are consciously and subconsciously engaged in a tension reduction behaviour, which they presume will help in fulfilling their needs and thus reduce the tension or stress felt by them. Of course the selection of the specific goal and the action undertaken to meet the goal will be based on the individual's thinking and learning processes. This can be illustrated with the help of a model of motivation process given in figure 7.2. From the diagram we can see that motivation is seen as a state of need induced tension that will exert pressure on the individual to be engaged in a behaviour which will satisfy the need and thus reduce the tension.

FIGURE 7.2

A SIMPLE MODEL OF MOTIVATION PROCESS

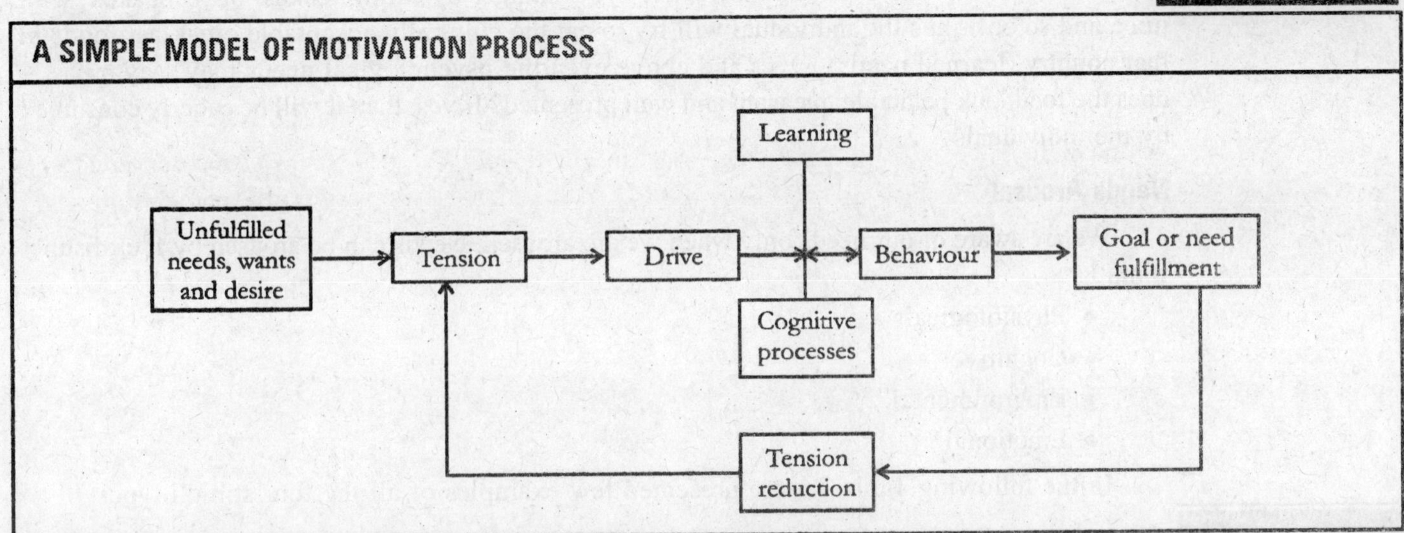

(*Source :* L.G. Schiffman, L.L. Kanuk, *Consumer Behavior,* Prentice Hall of India, 2005, pp. 88)

We can see that both the 'Hull's Drive Reduction theory and the 'Model of motivation process' are similar. In both the cases, the concerned individuals are engaged in a behaviour to reduce the drive (or tension). In the above model, it is emphasized that the specific behaviour adopted by the individual and the specific goals selected will be influenced by his or her thinking process (cognitive process) and previous learning. This goes to show that only those marketers who understand motivational theory can attempt at influencing the consumer's decision making processes.

NEEDS & GOALS

NEEDS

Every individual has needs. These needs could fall into three broad categories:

Physiological (or primary) Needs : These are referred to as innate needs or biogenic needs. These are the needs that sustain life. That is why these needs are considered as primary needs or motives also. They include the need for food, air, sex and self preservation.

Needs can broadly be categorized into physiological (or primary needs), psychological needs and learned (secondary or cultural) needs. These different categories of needs are related in complex ways.

Psychological Needs : These are the needs that relate to our competence to deal effectively with the outside world or environment. In simple terms they are also termed as personal competence.

Learned (Secondary or Cultural) Needs : These are also known as acquired needs. Learned needs are those needs which arise as a result of our socialization. They are acquired from the individual's subjective psychological state and relationship with other persons. As the name suggests, they are learned and are dependent on the culture we grow up in. Some cultures may give more value to power and status while others to humility and a structured life. These are all learned needs.

These different categories of need are related in complex ways. *For example,* food to eat is a primary need for all persons but the food a consumer purchases will depend on secondary needs. If you are hungry at breakfast time in India you are most likely to eat 'aalu paratha' or 'idli sambar' with 'tea' or 'coffee'. If you are in the U.K., you are most likely to eat 'cereal' and 'toast' while in the U.S. you may satisfy your hunger by eating 'cakes' or 'pancakes' with juice and so on. Thus the individual will try to eat the culturally acceptable breakfast foods in that country (learned needs). Over and above even the psychological needs may play a part – does the food look palatable, pleasant and well presented? If yes, then it will be eagerly consumed by the individuals.

Needs Arousal

We are aware of our needs only when we are aroused. Needs can be aroused by four distinct stimuli:

- Physiological
- Cognitive
- Environmental
- Emotional

In the following Table 7.1 are presented few examples of all the four stimuli types:

TABLE 7.1

INTERELATIONSHIP BETWEEN STIMULUS & NEED AROUSAL

Type of Stimulus	Mechanism	Need aroused
Physiological	• Fall in the blood sugar level	Hunger (primary)
Cognitive	• Remembering daughter who is staying far away	affection
	• Seeing an ad which reminds you to wish a friend on her wedding anniversary	social
Emotional	• Elderly couple staying alone have a fear of being burgled	security
Exterior or environmental	• Finding a dream house to match your budget and convey your prestige and status	success prestige

We are aware of our needs only when we are aroused. Goals are known as the sought after result of motivated behaviour.

GOALS

Goals are known as the sought after result of motivated behaviour. That is, they are the end points of motivation behaviour. Goals may be generic or specific. If you are thirsty you may opt for any liquid or you may want a specific brand of drink.

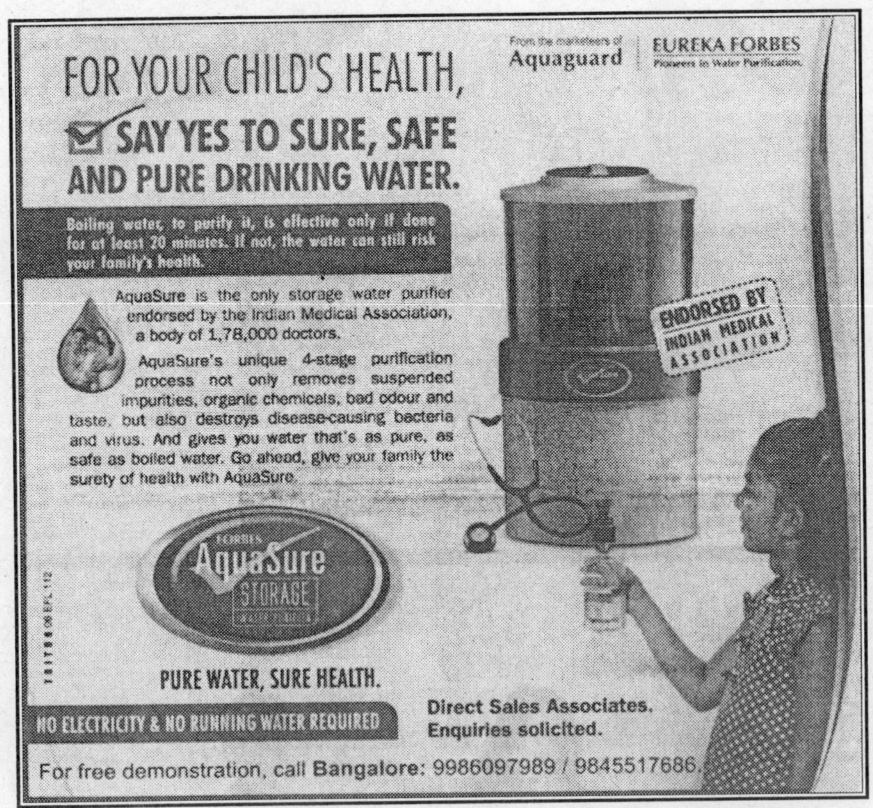

Emotional appeal to take care of safety needs

Ad takes care of primary need (hunger)

Environment as a stimulus can arouse the need to enjoy success (Purvankara Ad) and socialise (United Spirits Black)

Satisfying security needs can act as goal directed behaviour

FIGURE 7.3

GOALS ON A CONTINUUM OF GENERIC – SPECIFIC

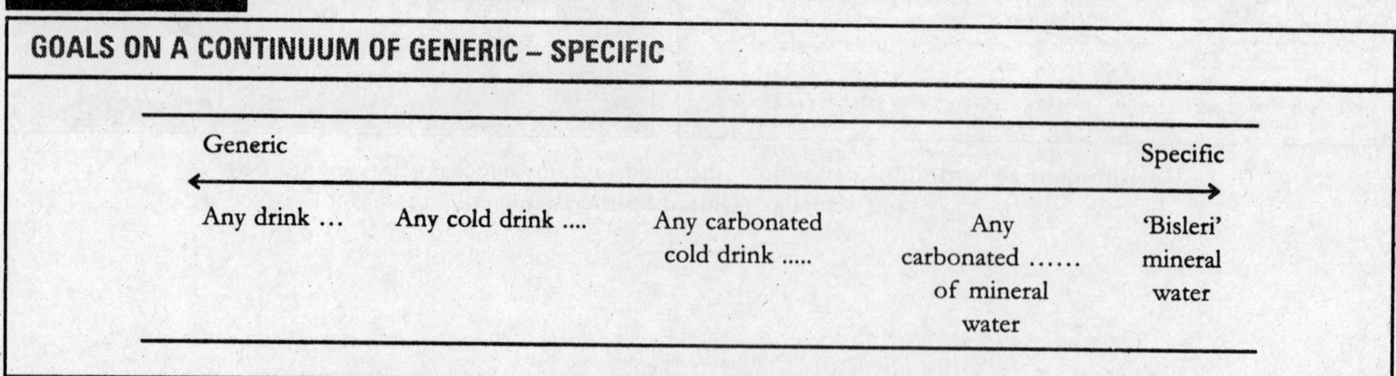

(*Source* : Rose Mary Phipps, Craig Simmons, *Understanding Customers*, 1996-97)

From the above Figure 7.3 we can see that consumers may try to fulfil their need for thirst with a generic goal or they could be product – specific (brand) goals. Some psychologists distinguish between wants and brands. According to them specific wants are the object of desire (Bisleri mineral water in the above case) and goal as the behaviour adopted by the individual to acquire it.

Selection of goals by an individual will depend on a number of factors such as personal experience, social and cultural norms and values, personal norms and values, physical and intellectual capacity, accessibility of goal and self image.

Marketers are interested in making consumer goals specific to their brands. But different levels of specificity exist for different types of products. The emergence of supermarkets has motivated consumers to make their everyday purchase of vegetables from these outlets. So even for a fairly generic goal (purchase of vegetables) consumer's are motivated to make their choice from *Reliance Fresh, Food World, Fab Mall, Food Bazaar* and so on.

Selection of Goals

For a given need, choice of the goal to satisfy it will depend on a number of things such as: personal experience, social and cultural norms and values, personal norms and values, physical and intellectual capacity, accessibility of goal and self image.

Personal values can affect an individual's consumption decision.

Personal Experience : If the consumer's past experience in satisfying the goal selected had been positive then it is more likely that the same goal is selected again. This aspect was seen while discussing the Hull's Drive Reduction Model - For instance, if a housewife has been satisfied with the *Surf Excel* detergent purchased by her, in all likelihood she will continue to patronise this brand in future also.

Social and Cultural Norms and Values : The social and cultural environment also affects consumer behaviour. Public display of love among adults or taking one's family to the dancing dias or public bar is not a part of our culture. Accordingly, people will avoid such behaviour which is treated as a taboo in our culture.

- *Personal norms and values :* An individual's own personal norms and values possibly religious or ethical can also affect the selection of the goal to achieve a particular need. For instance if a person is very much concerned about the killing of animals and birds' and 'green minded' he will avoid non vegetarian food and may prefer to purchase products which are environmentally friendly/or produced using organic materials.
- *Physical and or intellectual capacity :* At times some goals are unachievable due to personal limitations. Suppose a person is very fond of consuming tea but has got an acidity problem then he or she will have to go for an alternative goal. Similarly, an individual's intellectual capacity will influence his purchase behaviour and choice of goal. *For example,* a rural farmer's purchase of a computer to take care of his everyday transactions may be a personal computer with the basic functions. Whereas, a computer engineering student's purchase of a computer, will involve a goal, where his aim is to purchase a computer system which will have many complex functional utilities.
- *Accessibility of goal :* At times selection of a goal is made on the basis of accessibility. *For example,* the housewife may want to purchase only '*Tata salt*' but in the vicinity of her house only '*Annapoorna salt*' is available in the retail shops. Thus she is 'forced' to buy Annapoorna salt.
- *Self image :* A person's own perception of himself or herself also affects the selection of specific goals. Each person is likely to select or purchase products which closely reflect or are congruent with the person's own self image. Thus a man who perceives himself as 'young' may drive the '*Bajaj's Pulsar*' while a young woman who perceives herself as 'rich' and 'upwardly mobile' will ride a '*Corolla*'. Thus human beings often choose goal objects which will symbolically reflect his or her self image along with satisfying their specific need.

➲ THE DYNAMIC CHARACTERISTICS OF MOTIVATION

According to economists, needs and goals will continuously influence an individual's buying behaviour. This is because once individuals attain their goal, new ones emerge.

Motivation is a highly dynamic process. It continuously changes, to adapt to the changing life experiences of the individual. Under the dynamic constructs of motivation there are broadly three aspects which will be discussed:

- Role of needs and goals to adapt to the changes in motivation
- Frustration and defence mechanism in the needs – satisfaction chain
- Arousal of motives and motivation

Role of Needs & Goals to Adapt to the Change in an Individual's Motivation

Whenever there are changes in an individual's physical condition, environment (or situation), experience etc., his or her needs and goals will change accordingly. According to economists needs and goals will continuously influence an individual's buying behaviour. This is because once individuals attain their goal, new ones emerge. And in the event of them (individuals) not-being able to attain their goals, they will continue to strive for the goals or may opt for substitute goals. Some of these characteristic features of needs and goals are:

- *Needs are never fully satisfied* : Most of the human needs are not fully or completely satisfied. A very simple example is the basic need – hunger. Even after having a hearty breakfast, the individual is likely to experience hunger after a few hours. Man prefers to dress well and attend social gatherings to satisfy his social needs. An individual on his first promotion may purchase an *Alto LX* Car. He is satisfied initially till the euphoria exists. But thereafter he starts feeling that now he should strive for higher position in the company then he will be eligible for a *Ford Fiesta*. Thus in this case the individual is not adequately satisfied with the need (purchase of Alto) and makes an attempt to strive harder and work towards satisfying the need more fully.
- *New needs emerge as old needs are satisfied* : Motivational theorists like Abraham Maslow believed there exists a hierarchy of needs, with new needs of higher-order emerging as lower-order needs are satisfied. For instance once a person has built a house (*physiological need*) of his own he would have a lavish house warming ceremony with celebrations. This is to take care of his *social needs* as well as to gain recognition and increase his *self esteem*.
- *Success and failure influence goals* : Various researchers through studies conducted by them have concluded that individuals have the tendency to adjust their levels of aspiration on the basis of how successful they have been in achieving their goals. That is, once they (the individuals) have successfully achieved a particular goal, they will set new and higher goal for themselves *i.e.,* they raise their *levels of aspiration*. On the contrary, if they are not able to reach their goals they will lower their level of aspiration. Thus it can be said that success and failure influence goals.

For example, a 12th standard student on failing to get admission in a good medical college may, change his goal and decide to become a dentist or microbiologist.

Different product (brands) offerings to satisfy the changing consumer needs

An individual's behaviour towards reaching out to goals is very often influenced by his expectations of success and failure as well as his past experience. *For example,* a person may take to photography as a hobby. When he is appreciated by others, he gets motivated to undertake a course in photography and later on even purchases equipments to open a studio because now he is confident of achieving his goal.

An individual's behaviour towards reaching out to goals is very often influenced by his expectation of success and failure as well as his past experience.

An individuals's personality – his or her nature and persistence level also plays a role in building up their expectation level which in turn will affect his (or her) success or failure in reaching certain goals. This expectation will be based on past experience as mentioned above.

This particular aspect has got strategic implications for marketers. Advertisers should communicate about goals which are attainable. The advertisement should not promise more or exaggerate about the utility or performance of the product because if the product fails to perform as expected, (which is built up due to the impact of the advertisement) it is less likely that the purchase be repeated. For instance, a health club (gym) may advertise that it will help in reducing weight of the individual by 15 kg within a month's time. After going to the gym for a month if an individual finds that he or she has been able to shed only 3 kg weight, they may re-think about going to the gym thereafter. Thus creating unrealistic expectations for their products or services may result in causing consumer dissatisfaction, which, if taken care of, can help in reducing the gap between customer expectation and product's performance.

- *Substitute goals :* When an individual is unable to achieve or attain a specific goal, then his or her behaviour may opt to go for a substitute goal. This substitute goal will help in reducing the tension experienced due to the deprivation of the primary goal. For instance an individual who is very keen to purchase a "Zen Estillo" but cannot afford it may have to opt for an Alto by convincing himself that Alto suits his image better. In this instance we could also refer to the behaviour of the individual going for a substitute goal as a defensive reaction to avoid frustration.

Frustration and Defence Mechanism in the Needs - Satisfaction Chain

Frustration is the feeling experienced by an individual when he or she fails to achieve a goal. Individuals learn to handle frustrating situations differently. While some may go for substitute goals others may adopt a defense mechanism like behaviour to protect their self esteem or self image.

Frustration is the feeling experienced by an individual when he or she fails to achieve a goal. There are various reasons which come in the way of an individual attaining the goal. Inability due to limited financial resources or the goal is not in concurrence to the social and cultural environment and so on. Irrespective of the cause individuals learn to handle frustrating situations differently. While some may go for substitute goals, others may adopt a defence mechanism like behaviour to protect their self image and self esteem.

While taking a defensive reaction to frustration the individual may react in different ways. The defence mechanism may involve aggression, compromise or rationalization, regression, withdrawal, projection, autism, identification or repression.

Aggression : Individuals while trying to cope with frustration may resort to aggressive behaviour in an attempt to protect their self esteem. For instance the individual frustrated by his inability to make it to the finals of the quiz competition may dump his general knowledge book in the corner of his book shelf. In marketing context when consumers are unhappy with the product purchased from a particular retailer, they may boycott the latter till he returns the money paid by the buyer or offers another product at no additional cost (to the buyer).

Rationalisation or compromise : At times individuals try to rationalize by inventing plausible reasons for not being able to achieve their goal. He will be ready to compromise (with himself) by self convincing that it (goal) is not really worth pursuing. He will opt for reasons which will convince himself that he has really not lost by not being able to achieve the goal.

FIGURE 7.4

NEEDS – SATISFACTION CHAIN

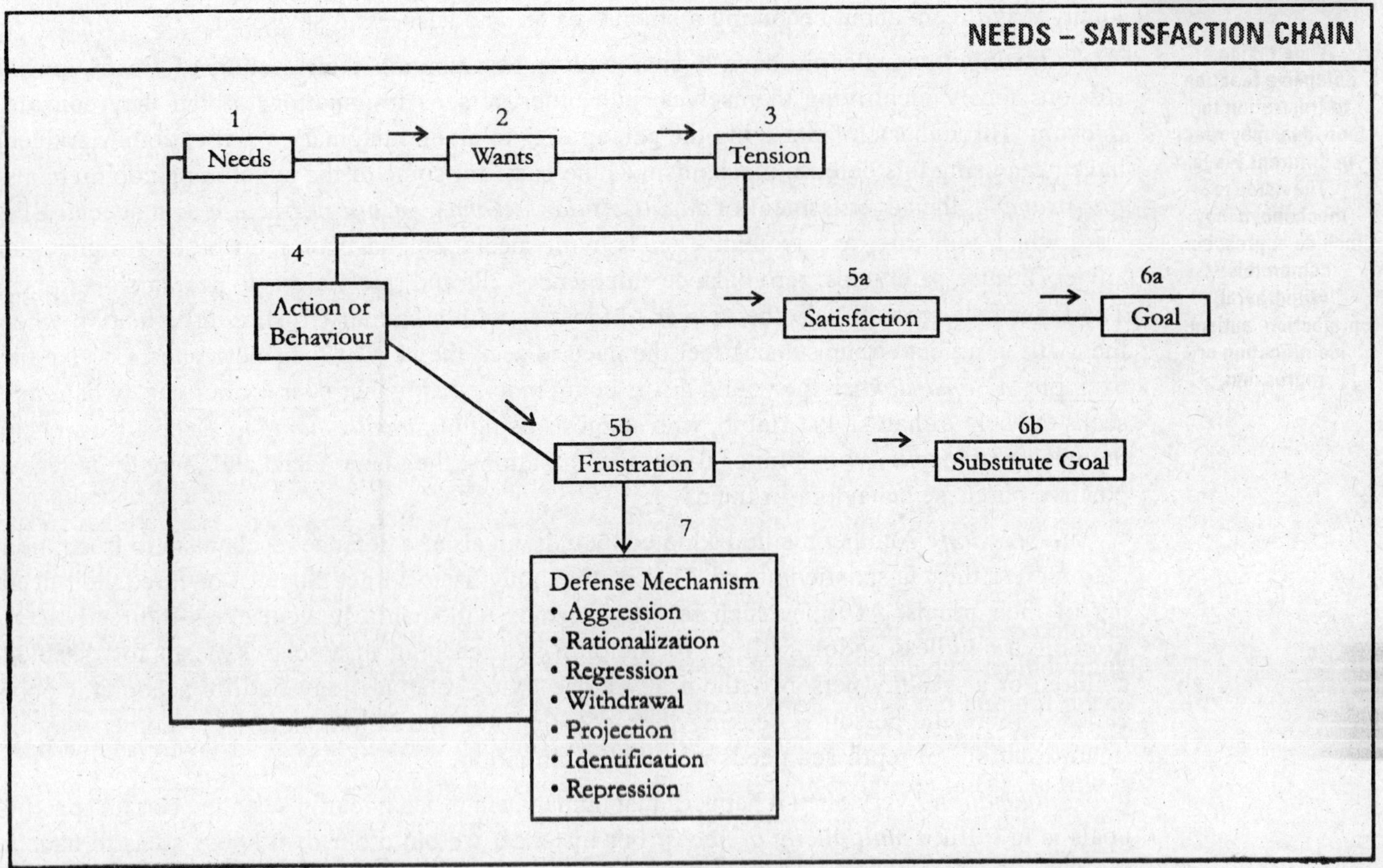

Regression : Sometimes people react to frustrating situations with childish behaviour. For instance, during the sales exhibition, a consumer may refuse to accept that the particular clothing liked by him is bought by another customer. In the process, due to frustration he will deliberately tear or cause harm to the product rather than giving it away to the other person.

Withdrawal : A person may try to handle frustration by slowly withdrawing from the situation. A person who was expecting a promotion to a higher status and being denied the same will put in his papers and quit the organisation. He will also rationalise his decision by deciding that the organisation was not worthy enough for him and that he can use his time more constructively.

In the market situation when the above customer realises that the particular clothing liked by him is purchased by someone else, he will leave the shop. Further, he will rationalise his decision by reasoning that the outlet was not well stocked and he can patronise another shop where he will get the products of his choice.

Projection : Under this an individual may redefine a frustrating situation by projecting blame (or putting blame) for his or her drawback or inabilities on other persons or objects. Thus, if a student does not get slected in the college cricket team he may put blame on favouritism shown by the selectors or bad pitch due to which he could not prove his worth.

If the customer returns a product which is not found to be of the desired quality, the retailer may assign cause to faulty packaging or blame the salesman.

Autism : Autism or autistic thinking refers to fictitious thinking evolved around needs and emotions with lesser association with reality. A person who is basically shy, an introvert and lonely may dream about becoming a smooth caller and successful salesman.

While taking a defensive reaction to frustration the individual may react in different ways. The defense mechanism may include aggression, compromise, withdrawal, projection, autism, identification or repression.

Identification : People have been found to be resolving their feeling of frustration by subconsciously identifying themselves with other persons in situations which they consider relevant. Through such fantasizing the person tries to attain imaginary gratification. Marketers have been using this defence mechanism as the basis for some of the advertising commercials. *For example*, the advertisement of *Idea Cellular's Women's Card* portrays it as a special SIM Card which will cater to a woman's needs, with special emphasis on alert based features like advice, beauty, safety tips, zero balance emergency cells and safety alerts to near and dear ones. The latter features will help the viewer to identify with a similar (frustrating) situation when they will in urgent circumstances feel the need to seek the help of their near ones. Or take the example of *Sunsilk,* when the young girl is being mocked at by her peer for her unruly hair, and seeks the help of hair stylist Habib, who suggests using of *Sunsilk shampoo*. Such ads can help the viewer to identify with similar frustrating situations; they have faced and there by induce a positive purchase behaviour in them.

Repression : Another method adopted by individuals as a defence mechanism to frustration is to repress their unsatisfied needs. That is, they may try to forget the need or force their need out of their minds. At times such repressed needs will manifest themselves indirectly. *For example* a childless widow will go for helping and teaching in a school meant for disabled children or a wealthy person without any close living relatives may build a school for poor children (here the person is seeking the need for love and belongingness). Another way of 'manifestation' of repressed needs is called sublimation.

Sublimation : Very often it happens that human beings behaviour in selecting certain specific goals is to fulfil *a multiplicity of needs*. For instance, we build our own house so as to have a shelter over our head but along with this our house will be constructed keeping in mind the desire to fulfil other personal (convenience) and social (design, size, decor etc.) needs. Consumer behaviour analysts have argued that there is a prepotent need which will supersede the other needs and is primarily responsible for initiating behaviour. A young woman may want to use cosmetics and skin care products because she feels concerned about her allergy of skin to certain type of cosmetics, wants to look more stylish and be included in the 'gang' of smart teenagers in the college. It is the combined effect of the above three needs which may prompt the girl to try out the *Lakme's* skin care cosmetics. But just one of the above reasons (to be included in group of smart teenagers in the college) can also motivate the girl and act as the *prepotent need.*

Because needs and goals may vary from individual to individual, it is not possible to infer about motives from the behaviour of individuals. Persons with different needs seek to fulfil them through selection of the same goal. A person may join a club as it is mandatory for an executive to become a member of the club, another person may join the club to fulfil his social needs of meeting new people, while another person may join the club because he feels he is likely to meet influential people who will help him in career advancement, still another person may join the club to enjoy the status accorded to members of the club.

Similarly, persons may try to achieve the same need (say esteem needs) in different ways. A person may try to fulfil his esteem needs by buying a premium priced luxurious car Mercedes Benz-C, another person may purchase and display diamonds and jewellery D'damas and visit elite clubs, while another person may become an active member of the exclusive Page 3 club.

Arousal of Motives and Motivation

An individual's specific needs are dormant most of the time. The arousal of any particular need (or needs) may be on account of an individual's:

- Internal stimuli (Physiological, emotional or cognitive processes).
- External environment. (Environmental).

An individual's specific needs are dormant most of the time. The arousal of any particular need (or needs) may be on account of an individual's internal stimuli and external environment.

Physiological arousal: Individuals may be aroused by his or her body's physiological needs at that specific period of time. Most of the physiological needs are involuntary and make the person undergo tensions, till he or she is able to satisfy those needs. During summer an individual may experience a dryness in the throat, which will trigger the feeling of thirst. A fall in blood sugar level or stomach contractions will trigger the 'pangs of hunger'. This arousal of motive will continue to cause tension to the individual till he satisfies it.

There are advertisements of products such as : ice cream, Cadbury's chocolate, designer clothes, cool drinks etc., which could cause arousal of physiological motives in the viewers mind.

Emotional arousal : Very often emotional needs are aroused by autistic thinking. At times, individuals, when bored or frustrated while trying to achieve their goals, get involved in day dreaming (autistic thinking), where in they imagine themselves to be in various types of desirable situations. Such thoughts tend to arouse dormant needs which will make him or her feel uncomfortable and then induce him or her to be engaged in a 'goal directed' behaviour. A young woman may visualize herself as an Air hostess and will get enrolled in a recognised aviation training institute. A young man who dreams of becoming a defence officer may try to get through the NDA Exam.

Cognitive arousal : There are instances when random thoughts or personal achievement may lead to a cognitive arousal of motives. An advertisement which proves to be a reminder of home or friends will trigger an urge to speak to loved one's. *For example, Western Union Money* enable NRI's to send money to their loved ones at home, quickly. '*Archies cards*' has got a collection of greeting cards for all occasions. Advertisements of cellular phones stress on the ability to make calls anytime and at reasonable rates. Cellular phones such as *Black berry, Samsung p310* claim to have features which can lead to a cognitive arousal of motives conveying a sense of personal achievement.

Environmental arousal : Here specific cues from the environment will arouse the set of needs. Without these cues the needs may remain dormant. *For example* : the nice aroma from the restaurant, smell of freshly baked cake, the advertisement of pizza or other fast food, advertisement of noodles on T.V etc., can all act as the environmental cues resulting in arousal or feelings of hunger. Thus modification of the environment will help to reduce the environmental arousal tension experienced by the individual.

At times seeing the 'product' or an advertisement may aggravate the situation making the individual experience an overwhelming desire or need for a particular product. *For example* seeing an attractive dress displayed at the showroom may arouse a feeling to purchase the same. Or say, a woman purchases a top loading washing machine on seeing an ad for the same. This consumer had not been very happy with the performance of her existing washing machine and was contemplating on buying another one, when she sees the ad. This will further trigger a desire and the need for purchasing a new washing machine.

Today, the impact of information technology is visible with televisions having penetrated into every common man's home, the influence of advertisement is seen in consumer's behaviour.

Exposure to global lifestyles ignites in them a desire to possess certain products, which will result in tension creation, till that need is satisfied (as seen in the Hull's Drive Reduction Theory).

There is a difference between two schools of thought with regards the arousal of human motives. The *behaviour school* advocators consider motivation process to be a mechanical process and the relationship between stimulus-response behaviour, while the *cognitive school* advocators feel that all behaviours are goal achievement oriented.

There is a difference in view regarding the arousal of human motives between two schools of thought. On the one hand there are the *behaviour school advocators* who consider motivation to be a mechanical process and the relationship between stimulus – response behaviour. According to the S-R theory consumers cognitive thinking is limited and they merely react to the stimuli at the market place and not act on it.

On the other hand *cognitive school advocators* feel that all behaviours are goal achievement oriented. They feel needs, past experience affects the individual's attitudes & beliefs and act as a predisposition to behaviour. These predispositions will help a person to satisfy his needs and thus indicate the direction he will take to achieve the feeling of satisfaction.

Personal achievement can lead to cognitive arousal of motives

➲ VARIOUS THEORIES OF NEEDS

Psychologists have been interested in the study of human behaviour so as to understand the human needs or motives which influence their behaviour. Various people have used different approaches to understand what motivates people, resulting in the formation of a number of theories concerning motivations. These theories have been classified into various categories such as those associated with human needs (Theories by A.H. Maslow, F.L. Urwick, and C. Argyris) and theories concerned with the expectancy of individuals.

Marketers have also been interested in knowing about human motives which influence consumer behaviour. Here we have only discussed some of the theories of motivation, usually referred to in a marketing context.

- Maslow's Hierarchy of needs.
- Mc Clelland's Theory of Need Achievement.
- Alderfer's ERG Hierarchy of needs.
- Vroom's Expectancy Theory.

Maslow's Hierarchy of Needs

Dr. Abraham H. Maslow, a famous social scientist had developed a framework of needs and formulated a widely accepted theory of human motivation based on the notion that there is a hierarchy of needs which influences the person's motivation level. Maslow's theory goes by the notion that there are basically five levels of human needs arranged in their order of importance. It starts from the lower level basic (biogenic) needs and goes to higher level (psychogenic) needs. He suggested that needs have a certain priority and individuals try to satisfy the lower level needs and then only go to satisfy his or her higher level needs. The lowest level of chronically unsatisfied needs will tend to motivate the individual's behaviour. Once that need is fairly satisfied a new and higher level of need emerges which the individual is motivated to fulfil. When this new level of need is satisfied another higher level of need emerges and thus it goes on. However, if a particular lower level need is not fully satisfied it may become temporarily dominant again.

Dr. Absaham Maslow had developed a framework of needs and formulated a widely accepted theory of human motivation based on the notion that there is a hierarchy of needs which influence the person's motivation level.

Given below is Maslow's hierarchy of needs in a diagrammatic form.

FIGURE 7.5

MASLOW'S HIERARCHY OF NEEDS THEORY

Self Actualisation
(Self fulfillment)

Esteem Needs or Ego Needs
(Prestige, status, self respect)

Social Needs
(Affection, friendship, belonging)

Safety and Security Needs
(Protection, order, stability)

Physiological Needs
(Food, water air, sex, shelter)

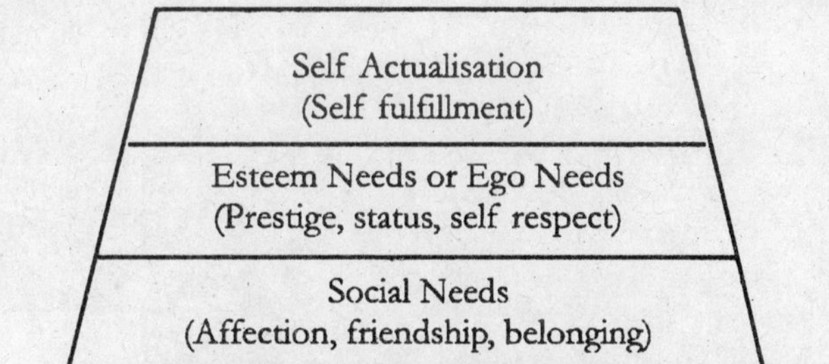

Physiological needs : In the hierarchy-of-needs theory the first and most basic level of needs are the physiological needs. These primary level of needs include all those needs required to sustain biological life – such as hunger, thirst, air, shelter, sex and clothing.

According to Maslow, the physiological needs will have highest strength and will be dominant until they are reasonably satisfied. Especially in a developing economy like India this physiological need will be dominant among all those people lying below the poverty line focusing entirely on trying to satisfy their biogenic needs.

Safety needs : Once the first level of needs are satisfied, safety and security needs will become the driving force behind an individual's behaviour. These needs are more concerned with personal needs and security. Health and wealth are of primary concern. People are concerned about the need for being free from physical danger or self preservation. They are more comfortable with the knowledge of having control over one's life and environment and certainity about the future (up to some extent).

According to Maslow, the physiological needs will have the highest strength and will be dominant until they are reasonably satisfied.

Ads which will appeal to physiological needs

Being a social being man feels the need to belong to and be accepted by various groups (Social need). The Ego needs are concerned with ego. They reflect an individual's need for self respect, self confidence, a feeling of personal worth, prestige, success etc.

This level of need is satisfied by opening savings account or taking insurance policies or by educating oneself and undertaking vocational training to be self sufficient. Further, such efforts will also satisfy their concern for safety and security to a certain extent.

Social needs : The third level of needs is related to needs such as love, affection, belonging and acceptance. Being a social being, man feels the need to belong to and be accepted by various groups. When this need becomes dominant, a person will strive for satisfying relations with others and are motivated by love for their families. People are now looking for relationships, affection and experiencing a feeling of belonging (or identification).

Esteem needs : When the social needs are more or less satisfied, the esteem needs gain importance. The esteem needs are concerned with ego. They reflect an individual's need for self respect, self confidence, a feeling of personal worth, prestige, success, power and control.

The satisfaction of esteem needs is not always obtained through mature or adaptive ways. Sometimes individuals while trying to achieve the ego needs may adopt disruptive and irresponsible actions and in the process their inability to satisfy esteem needs can also lead to frustration. The society thus can play a bigger role in trying to change the image of esteem needs especially in the eyes of such misguided youth through organising activities or camps or formal associations and programmes, where the impact reality (indulging in unprotected sex or adverse efforts of drinking / rash driving) can be communicated across.

Ad appeal to satisfy Esteem Needs

Maslow had also introduced two more categories of enabling needs which can provide the channels through which the five categories of needs can be achieved. Freedom of enquiry and expression needs and knowledge and understanding needs.

Self actualisation needs : This refers to the need to maximise one's potential (personal potential) – *i.e.,* he or she can desire to become everything he or she is capable of becoming. As Maslow say's 'what a man can be he must be'. Though Maslow also said that most people are not able to satisfy their esteem needs sufficiently to move up to the fifth level of needs – self actualisation. This is because self actualisation needs imply control over environmental factors both physical and social and achievement.

Maslow also introduced two more categories of 'enabling' needs which can provide the channels through which the five categories of needs can be achieved.

Freedom of enquiry and expression needs : This means the social conditions must exist to provide free speech and encouragement of justice, fairness and honesty.

Knowledge and understanding needs : These needs will provide and help in gaining knowledge of the environment so as to be able to explore, learn and experiment.

Thus Maslow's theory or hierarchy of needs theory postulates of the hierarchy of prepotent needs. This theory also emphasizes that only when the lower level needs are sufficiently satisfied, will a higher level of need act as the motivating or driving force.

Marketing Applications of Maslow's Hierarchy of Needs : This hierarchy of needs has proved to be useful to marketers enabling them to devise suitable advertising appeals depending on the need level for a particular product. This theory has been useful in applying a more behaviour oriented structure to the market. Further, marketers have used it for market segmentation and brand or product positioning also.

Each product or service always addresses a natural needs hierarchy. Some of the products like food stuff address the very basic and physiological needs for sustenance. At times the advertising appeals can address one or more level of needs. For instance soft drink ads such as *Fanta, Maaza, Dabur Real fruit* etc., satisfy two level of needs simultaneously. They help satisfy the thirst (physiological need) of the individual as well as the need to share good times with friends (social needs). Thus if marketers are able to position products to appeal to just any category of needs, then this can also be broadened and used to build a brand image.

TABLE 7.2

EXAMPLES OF PRODUCTS WHICH WILL APPEAL TO VARIOUS LEVELS OF NEEDS

Levels of Needs	Product Appeal in the Category
• Physical Needs	Coffee Cafe Day, McDonalds, Pizza Hut Product – Services offerings to take care of physiological needs of food and water.
• Safety and Security Needs	ICICI's Home insurance policies, Acqa Guard's water purifier, Godrej's security equipments – to appeal to one's concern for safety and security.
• Social Needs	Park Avenue's formal wear, Weekender's kid's wear, Nokia mobile phones, Canon camera – are products which help keep in touch with one another through informal or formal meets when these product offerings will be used.
• Esteem Needs	American Express Card, Nakshatra Diamonds, Benz Car etc. – are offerings which will appeal to esteem (or egoistic) needs.
• Self Actualisation	Manorama year book 2007 (Material to prepare for competitive exams), Art of Living's workshop, specific courses to improve one's knowledge in the area of operation etc.

Maslow's hierarchy of needs has proved to be useful to marketers enabling them to devise suitable advertising appeals depending on the need level for a particular product.

Product Positioning : Marketers go for product (or brand) positioning as it helps in easy recall, differentiate it from products which fall in the same product category and finally lead to an increase in sales. The product positioning statement should be clear enough to differentiate between two brands and also match with the consumer perception of the brand offering. When the customer perception matches the marketer's unique selling point, the product positioning can act as a bridge between the manufacturer and the user. If satisfied with this product positioning, it can lead to a long term loyalty from the customer's end. To quote a few of the product positioning differentiators.

- **Parachute Hair Oil :** Shudhata (pure, the goodness of coconut oil, healthy for hair and when used, takes care of social needs).
- **Vicks Vapo Rub :** Effective and Gentle, Quick cold relief medication to be used especially at night (focus on children), takes care of safety needs.
- **Ray-Ban Sun Glasses :** The exclusive collection which can change your view, takes care of style and esteem and ego needs.
- **Life Insurance Finance Ltd. :** takes care of one's financial plan to own a house (physiological and security needs).
- **Swift Car :** Small, stylish car, an affordable luxury (social needs).

Thus needs can also be translated into benefits which may form the basis of benefits segmentation. Marketers have also been using this hierarchy needs theory for psychographic segmentation.

SWIFT – AN Affordable luxury, an appeal to social needs

Evaluation of Maslow's Hierarchy of Needs

Maslow's theory has got a lot of intuitive appeal. If one is desperately looking for food it is unlikely that he will be concerned about socialising or improving self potential. And it is very useful in that Maslow has evolved all his suggestions and ideas around what 'drives' individuals. However, the theory does not fully explain certain things and there is lack of evidence to support the following:

Inspite of few objections, Maslow's work has provided a framework which is easy and useful for marketers. Marketers have been using this hierarchy needs theory for psychographic segmentation.

- It is not necessary that physiological and safety needs will be the predominant factors in determining behaviour.
- Some people have been unhappy due to the absence of money from the list of needs.
- Self actualisation and esteem needs will be dependent on each individual's self perception.

Inspite of the above objections or problems, Maslow's work has provided a framework which is easy and useful for marketers.

Some psychologists have a firm belief in the existence of a trio of basic needs : the needs for power, for affiliation and for achievement. These needs can be included under a particular classification within Maslow's Hierarchy needs theory.

Display of High Achievement Need.

- **Need for Power :** The power need is with reference to an individual's desire to control his or her environment. This can be similar to the ego needs, *i.e.*, individuals may feel the need to experience increased self esteem, when they display power over objects or other people.
- **Need for Affiliation :** This desire for affiliation may prompt people to display a behaviour which makes them socially dependent on others. Such people desire for friendship, for acceptance and experience a sense of belonging when with others.
- **Achievement Need :** Some people consider personal achievement as an end in itself. Such individuals are more self confident, enjoy taking calculated risks, search the environment for value feedback etc.

The first systematic approach to the understanding of non-biological human needs was seen from the research carried out by psychologist Henry Murray who gave a detailed list of 28 psychogenic needs.

Henry Murrays's List of Psychogenic Needs

For years together, all those interested in human behaviour have made attempts to develop an exhaustive list of human needs which are diverse in content as well as length. It can probably be said that the first systematic approach to the understanding of non-biological human needs was seen from the research carried out by psychologist Henry Murray who gave a detailed list of 28 psychogenic needs. According to Murray everybody has the same basic set of needs although there could be individual variation in terms of how they rank them. Murray looks at needs very minutely, so that each one is more focused, narrow as well as specific, whereas in Maslow's theory of needs they are more broadly defined with lesser number of categories.

Murray's list include's many motives such as acquisition, achievement, recognition etc. which can easily be used to have a better understanding of consumer behaviour. In Table 7.3, are given Murray's list of psychogenic needs.

TABLE 7.3

MURRAY'S LIST OF PSYCHOGENIC NEEDS

NEEDS ASSOCIATED WITH INANIMATE OBJECTS	**NEEDS CONCERNED WITH HUMAN POWER**
Acquisition	Dominance
Conservancy	Deference
Order	Similance (suggestible attitude)
Retention	Autonomy
Construction	Contrariance (to act differently from others)
NEEDS THAT REFLECT AMBITION, POWER, ACCOMPLISHMENT AND PRESTIGE	**SADOMASOCHISTIC NEEDS**
Superiority	Aggression
Achievement	Abasement
Recognition	**NEEDS CONCERNED WITH AFFECTION BETWEEN PEOPLE**
Exhibition	Affiliation
Inviolancy (inviolate attitude)	Rejection
Inavoidance (to avoid shame, failure, humiliation)	Nurturance (to nourish, aid or protect the helpless)
Defendance (defensive attitude)	Succorance Play (to seek aid, protection, or sympathy)
Counteraction (counteractive attitude)	**NEEDS CONCERNED WITH SOCIAL INTERCOURSE (The needs to ask and tell)**
	Cognizance (inquiring attitude)
	Exposition (Expositive attitude)

(*Source : Consumer Behavior*, L.G. Schiffman, L.L. Kanuk, 8th Edn., Prentice Hall of India, 2005, pp. 101-102)

McClelland's Theory of Need Achievement

Mc Clelland and his colleagues began to experiment with TAT (Thematic Apperception Test) in order to determine if it was sensitive enough to ascertain changes in motivation.

Shortly after world war II, a group of psychologists, Mc Clelland and his colleagues began to experiment with TAT (Thematic Apperception Test) in order to determine if it was sensitive enough to ascertain changes in motivation which were caused by simple attempts to change the individual's attitude. To simplify the task, Mc Clelland and group decided to use only a particular motive for intensive analysis. Mc Clelland considered and recognized three types of basic motivating needs. These motives were classified as need for power (n/PWR), need for affiliation (n/AFF) and need for achievement (n/ACH) (Organizational Behaviour, L.M.Prasad, Sultan Chand & Sons, N. Delhi, 1996, pp. 124-126)

- *Needs for power :* This relates to have control over other people and objects in the environment (Similar to Maslow's Ego needs).
- *Need for affiliation :* This relates to desire to belong to, be a part of a group and to have friends. (Similar to Maslow's social needs).
- *Need for achievement :* This relates to the need to achieve something (Close to ego and self actualisation needs level in Maslow's hierarchy).

An appeal to power needs

Achievement – needs persons will strive hard to achieve their goal. Today's competitive environment forces people to develop an ever increasing need for achievement-all to become something in life. Cricket is a very popular sport and widely followed by an enterprising target audience, children aspiring to be good cricketers in future. It is due to this reason that marketers of *Boost* roped in celebrities Sachin Tendulkar and Virendra Sehwag, who typified the achievement oriented aspiration of youngsters involved with cricket. These celebrities synergised with the personality of the brand and are able to motivate the target segment through the statement "Boost is the secret of our energy". Similarly, advertisers of Bournvita, Horlicks, Complan and Viva also lay stress on the presence of vital vitamins, carbohydrates, minerals and other supplements which will help their consumers to sufficiently satisfy their achievement needs.

The achievement need is closely related to both esteem needs and self actualization needs. Individuals who have a strong need for achievement will treat personal achievement as an end in itself.

The achievement need is closely related to both esteem needs and self actualization needs. Persons with high need for achievement are found to be self confident, look out for various ways to do self evaluation, enjoy being speculative or taking calculated risks. Individuals who have a strong need for achievement will treat personal achievement as an end in itself. They will prefer to handle situations, wherein they can take the responsibility of finding solutions. Accordingly, marketers must provide suitable appeals directed at consumers with high achievement.

Ad reflects Standard Chartered's focus on the achievement need

Incase of power needs, the individual desires to have control over other people and various objects. Affiliation need relates to man's social concern for socializing to gain friends, desire for being accepted and for belonging.

In case of power needs – the individual desires to have control over other people and various objects. Such persons will be interested in products like vehicles which highlight the feeling of power.

Affiliation need relates to man's social concern for socialising to gain friends, desire for being accepted and for belonging. Such persons opt for purchase of products which will have social acceptance. They prefer to make purchase decisions which meet the approval of friends and peers. This behaviour is reflected in the way teenagers and college goers who hang around with friends at the college canteen, go for movies, various music shows etc. in the company of their peers.

In the above theory we have seen that individuals with 'specific needs' tend to be receptive to certain types of products. Thus awareness of such needs will provide marketers information on what basis to concentrate or focus on while segmenting the markets.

Alderfer's ERG Hierarchy of Needs

As per the ERG theory, the **existence needs** are related to the need for survival, the **related needs** focuses on the interpersonal and social relationship and the **growth needs** are more concerned with the person's intrinsic desire for personal development. Alderfer had indicated about a continuum of needs and yet suggested that it was not necessary for an individual to fulfill a lower level of need to move on to a higher level of needs. Clayton Alderfer extended the work carried out by Maslow and Herzberg, when he put forward the need category model by grouping the core needs into a hierarch of three needs — Existence, Relatedness and Growth, hence it is called ERG theory. Though it is similar to Maslow's theory in many ways Alderfer has introduced another useful notion of frustration. He says in the event of a need not being satisfied it can result in frustration which in turn may lead to other behaviours.

As per the ERG theory, the existence needs are related to the need for survival, the related needs focus on the inter personal and social relationships and the growth needs are more concerned with the person's intrinsic desire for personal development.

In the marketing context it can be said that when consumers are not satisfied with a particular purchase they may either opt for an alternative brand or may resort to complaining about what (product) they have purchased. Thus accepting that frustration is a defence mechanism adopted by consumers, marketers must plan on how to handle their consumer's frustration (if any).

Ad appeals to the affiliation need of consumers

Vroom's Expectancy Theory

This theory is very strongly related to the extended Fishbein model of attitudes. The above mentioned theories are also referred to as the content theories of motivation, since they try to identify what motivate individuals. Whereas, the Victory Vroom's Expectancy theory is known as a process theory because it tries to identify the cognitive aspects which go into what motivates individuals. This theory is based on the concepts of valence, instrumentality and expectancy. **Valence** refers to the strength of an individual's preference for a particular outcome. Instrumentality is the first level outcome in obtaining a desired second level outcome. Expectancy relates to the probability that a particular action or effort will lead to a particular first level outcome. Vroom's theory proposes that individual's will be motivated to do things to the extent that they expect certain actions on their part will help them to achieve the goal. To put it simply, here it is believed that an individual's motivation will be based on the expectation from a particular behaviour. It is based on the premise that a behaviour will lead to a certain outcome and the preference (or valence) for that outcome.

For instance, if an individual is planning to go for a holiday to a certain place say 'Egypt' then he or she will first work out on the outcome expected from the holiday (to visit foreign country, opportunity to see the pyramids, a long deserved holiday with family and so on). Then the individual will work out a value (or valance or V) for each outcome (+ 1 if he likes them, O if neutral and, – 1 if he dislikes them). Then he will estimate the probability of attaining each outcome (this value will be E – the expectancy). In the last step the individual will calculate ExV for each outcome. The final score 'F' is obtained by adding up all the values of ExV. This 'F' will be the motivational value of the holiday.

From a marketing view point, it can be said marketers must work at increasing the perceived value of the product/services in the eyes of the consumer. This will increase the motivation of the consumer to buy and also raise the expectancy of satisfaction which will result from the purchase of the product or service.

MOTIVATIONAL RESEARCH

Motivational research is carried out to identify the reasons or motives for a person's behaviour. It is very difficult to determine consumer motives. However, realizing that consumer motives play a crucial role in influencing their purchase behaviour, marketers are using motivational techniques to identify the purchasing motives. Since the focus is on uncovering people's unconscious motives motivational research involves application of Freud's psychoanalytic theory to marketing. The two most frequently used motivational research techniques in marketing are the depth interviews and projective techniques.

Depth Interviews

Motivational researchers using this technique carry out interviews with consumers who are allowed to express themselves feely in an unstructured interview. The responses of consumers are interpreted by the interviewer and is said to reveal their real motives and the potential purchase inhibitions. An offshoot of the depth interview's are the focus interviews, which are informal open-ended group discussions carried out under the guidance of a trained moderator who will ensure that the discussions will be centered around the topics of interest to the concerned marketing firm. The focus group interview involves 8 to 12 consumers, who are encouraged to stimulate discussion, which may reveal their deepseated needs or unconscious motives, in the presence of a moderator.

Realising that consumer motives play a crucial role in influencing their purchase behaviour, marketers are using motivational techniques to identify the purchasing motives.

The father of motivational research, Ernest Dichter, was a psychoanalyst, trained in Vienna in the early part of the century and a foremost proponent of depth and focus group interviews. (Customer Behavior, J.N. Sheth and B. Mittal, Thomson, South Western Learning, 2003, pp. 166-167). On the basis of in-depth interviews with consumers, he had identified a set of motives/needs which he believed played a significant role in people's consumption related decisions.

Project Techniques

A projective technique is another motivational research method used by marketers to determine consumer's underlying motives which are difficult to identify. Since consumers may not be aware of their motives for buying, researchers do not ask them direct questions related to their purchase behaviour. However, researchers indirectly ask them to respond to a given situation, a cartoon or a set of words. Based on how the consumer's project their feelings, views and concerns regarding the product in such less threatening (or involving) situations will help the marketers to discover and identity the target consumer's buying motives.

Evaluation of Motivational Research

Motivational research has being criticized for the qualitative nature of the technique. So, the results greatly depend on the ability of the researcher's qualitative judgment's without any hard data. Some concern was expressed about how generalizations for the total market could be drawn from samples which were small. Some other theorists have criticized the application of Freudian theory to the study of consumer behaviour. They opined that Freudian theory was

Carrying out depth interview as a part of motivational research.

used to know more about the behaviour of 'disturbed' individuals, so how can it explain the behaviour of "typical consumers"? They also questioned the time period in the social context *i.e.,* the Freudian theory was developed in the early part of the century whereas motivational research in the 1950's since there is time gap the social changes affecting individuals should also be taken into consideration.

Nevertheless, the motivational researches were one of the first to put forward the fact that consumers are complex, behaving in a cunning way to get what they want, not easy to please and driven by forces of which they are unaware. So in this respect, marketers wanting to know about the underlying motives influencing the consumer's purchase behaviour are using the motivational research techniques.

SUMMARY

A motive is an inner state that energises, activates and moves or directs or channelises behaviour towards goals. Since human behaviour is caused by motives, motivations can be said to be the process of inducing person's to experience needs for a certain goal. Motives can be distinguished as being rational, emotional, positive or negative. A popular theory that links needs and drives with goals is the Hull's Drive Reduction Theory. Human needs can be categorized as being physiological, phychological or learned and are inter-related in complex ways. Goals are the sought after result of motivated behaviour. Selection of goal by an individual will depend upon a number of factors such as personal experience, social and cultural norms and values, physical and intellectual capacity, accessibility of goal and self image.

The dynamic characteristics of motivation were discussed with reference to (a) the role of needs and goals to adapt to the changes in motivation (b) frustration and defense mechanism in the needs-satisfaction chain (c) arousal of motive and motivation. Various people have used different approaches to understand what motivates people, resulting in the formation of various theories of motivation. However, in the chapter only a few of the theories, namely Maslow's Hierarchy theory of needs, Mc Clelland's theory of need achievement, Alderfer's ERG Hierarchy of needs and the Vroom's Expectancy needs were discussed.

Motivational research is carried out to identify the reasons or motives for a person's behaviour. The two most frequently used motivational research techniques by consumer researchers in marketing are Depth interviews and Projective techniques.

CHAPTER QUESTIONS FOR DISCUSSION

1. Why is motivation said to be a complex process, for marketing purpose? Explain with giving suitable examples.
2. Explain briefly the dynamic characteristics of motivation.
3. Discuss the Abraham Marlow's Hierarchy of needs theory, Mc Clelland's theory of need achievement, Alderfer's ERG Hierarchy of needs and the Vroom's Expectancy needs theory.
4. Why do marketers use the motivational research? Write a short note on the popular techniques used for research purposes.

➲ SUGGESTED READINGS

1. www.apaints.com
2. Asian Paints step by step, *Business Today,* March 2006 pp. 68-77.
3. Rosemary Phipps and Craig Simmons, "Understanding Customers 1996-97". Butterwoth. Heinemann, Oxford, 1996.
4. Leon G. Schiffman, Leslie Lazar Kanuk, *"Consumer Behavior"*, Prentice Hall of India, New Delhi, 2005, pp. 85-117.
5. Jagdish N. Sheth, Banwari Mittal, *Customer Behavior A Managerial Perspective,* Thomson South Western Learning, Singapore, 2003. pp. 159-196.
6. Abraham H. Maslow, "*A Theory of Human Motivation*", Psychological Review 50, 1943, pp, 370-96., also Abraham H. Maslow, Motivation and Personality (New York; Harper and Row, 1970).
7. Paul Hersey, and Kenneth H. Blanchard, *Management of Organizational Behaviour*, Prentice Hall of India, New Delhi, 1978.

CASE

HDFC

The Beginning

HDFC was incorporated in 1977 and was promoted with an initial capital of Rs. 100 million. The primary objective at that time was to meet a social need of promoting home ownership to households by providing them long term loans (finance). HDFC's aim has been to help Indians experience the joy of ownership, and enhance residential housing stock.

HDFC's Product-service Offerings

The offerings from HDFC include :

- A range of hassle free home loans and property related issues.
- Specialised financial services to customers based on partnerships with some of the best financial institutions world wide. Each institution offers financial services fine tuned for a specific market apart from offering the highest standards of quality in product design, facilities and services.

The Key Drivers or Factors Motivating the Demand for Houses

Way back in the 80's, HDFC had been the only company to offer home loans and related range of products. But during the last decade, especially the impact of liberalization and opening up of the Indian economy has seen a rise in the average income across households and thereby a desire and need to own a house.

The most crucial aspect of this 'shift' in the consumer's mindset can be due to the 'Generation Next' or young who are more in charge of their lives. This generation is independent, self reliant and nuclear, with an eagerness to succeed fast. This eagerness to succeed acts as a motivating factor, fuelled with the drive to own what one desires the most : a home, car and a healthy lifestyle. This change in consumers mindset, can mainly be attributed to the term 'loan', which used to be treated as a stigma, is no more considered so now. Further, the consumer has now got the extra freedom to make a well informed choice. He can also be more flexible with the availability of customised finance options.

HDFC's Efforts to Attract and Retain Customers

HDFC has adopted IT initiatives which have been service driven and predicted by customers requirements. Their IT system includes a state of– the–art automated loan processing system, which helps them to respond swiftly to the ever-changing customer needs. Customer's are notified through SMS and email about the state of their loan approval and disbursement. Advance intimation is sent before the post – dated cheques are banked. Customers have access to multiple channels (through call centre, internet, email, visits) for their service requirements. HDFC's deposit section delivers all the services across the counter, thereby increasing customer satisfaction. Security of the data is taken care of. All their records are stored with back ups so that in case of any mishaps there is no loss of data and work would not come to a halt. HDFC also carries out data mining. Its data base includes over 2.5 million customers, 1.1 million depositors, 1.25 million share holders and 50,000 deposit agents.

Brand Positioning of HDFC

Until the early 80's, HDFC had enjoyed a virtual monopoly in the field, without any real need to advertise. The brand equity kept growing through word of mouth from satisfied consumers and this resulted in HDFC becoming a trusted brand name synonymous with integrity, transparency and quality service.

To keep in touch with changing times, HDFC positioned it self as an 'organisation that one could trust. Their crucial baseline "with you right through" was evolved in the mid 80's. The entire service model and the delivery mechanism was based on the inverted pyramid with the customer at the top. This inverted pyramid is broken into two parts – the top portion (by far the largest in numbers) as the frontline, who meet and serve customers and the rest as the back office who support the front line.

HDFC's mission statement says *"if you are not serving the customer directly make more sure you are serving those who are."* This statement has helped HDFC to listen, understand, innovate and support their customers both with a wide range of products and services.

As a premier Housing Finance Institution, HDFC was the first to introduce products that supported housing loans on the basis of age and customer requirements. In 1999, anticipating market conditions on floating rate loans to go down and again on facing the same problem in 2002, HDFC came up with the option of '2 in 1' loans, which is part fixed and part floating, in order to help customers hedge their risks in an uncertain-environment.

With many industries migrating to smaller towns, HDFC is trying to tap the market which is likely to emerge with rural development.

Competition

In the 80's HDFC had been the only company to offer home loans and related range of products. But with RBI's (Reserve Bank of India) guidelines for commercial banks to earmark three per cent of their incremental deposits for housing finance resulted in the entry of Commercial Banks like Corporation Bank, State Bank of India, Canara Bank, ICICI Bank, etc. into this sector.

All the banks have gone all out to address the increase in demand for home loans. With this, there has been an increase in the number of distribution channels like DSAs (Direct Sales Agents). They even offer freebies on offer – from free insurance to products with fixed interest rates (though fixed for a certain period only). But looking to the demand for housing finance in the country, today, the challenge for HDFC will be to continue to innovate and offer customised solutions to its customers.

(*Source :* www.hdfc.com, Strategic Marketing, February, 2005)

QUESTIONS FOR DISCUSSION

1. **Can you suggest ways by which HDFC can motivate rural customers to invest in home finance?**
2. **What ways should be developed by HDFC to reinvent itself and ensure its leadership position in the market?**
3. **In a market like home finance, since product differentiation is almost neligible, what steps should be adopted and maintained by HDFC to ensure a long term relationship with its customers?**

CHAPTER 8

DEMOGRAPHICS, SOCIAL CLASS AND CULTURE

- Case : **STRAPS, AOS** and **RED-TAPE**
- Meaning of Social Stratification and Social class
- Nature of Social class influences
- Social class characteristics
- The growing Indian middle class - A Study
- Social influence on consumer behaviour
- Culture (definitions and meaning)
- Traditional and changing Indian values
- Sub-culture
- Cross-cultural marketing analysis
- Summary
- Chapter questions for discussion
- Suggested Readings
- Case : Tata's **"Gold Plus Jewellery"**

CASE

STRAPS, AOS AND RED-TAPE

Demographic Characteristics such as one's age, income, size of the family, employment status etc., are all objective in nature and can affect a consumer's decision-making process. *For example,* Adish Oswal, the third generation entrepreneur of the Oswal group and son of the Chairman, Ashok Oswal, had realized the potential of the emerging retail industry in the virgin category of women lingerie by studying the demographics and changing lifestyle of the Indian women. Studies indicated about the changing lifestyle trends, a growing brand consciousness, more income at their disposal, self confidence, and the evolving needs of the Indian women. The company realized that intimate apparel in India was being marketed more like a commodity rather than on a comfort or a luxury basis. To take care of this untapped market (with only a few unorganized local players) the Oswal group launched two identities **STRAPS** (a second skin store multi brand retail platform offering a complete range of intimate wear for women) and **AOS** (smart, casual brand for Men and Women). Thus, by clearly identifying the demographic characteristics of its target market, the Oswal group was able to offer suitable product offerings via the STRAPS and AOS stores.

Both the brands have received exceptional response from the customers with STRAPS having 16 stores across India and AOS with 20 stores across India.

Social class, which refers to one's ranking in society on the basis of power and prestige is primarily defined by demographic characteristics such as occupation, income and education.

Mirza International, in 1996 had launched premium footwear *Red Tape* with an average pricing of Rs.1,800 and a European flavour. Red Tape has positioned itself as a lifestyle product, targeted at the young and socially fashion conscious consumers and has tasted stupendous success too.

Cine star Salman Khan was brought in as the brand ambassador three years ago since his fashionable image matched with the brand image. Further, keeping in mind this social class's image, apart from the usual (traditional media) the brand has done cross promo tie-ups with other brands and also actively participated in all the major college fests. For instance, along with *MTV* and *Axe*, Red Tape co-sponsored the world's longest party at Fireball Club, Gurgaon in 1999, which was entered in the Guinness Book of World Records. The makers of *Red Tape* were able to offer premium footwear which matched the aspirations of the cash rich, high disposable income households resulting in creating a niche for itself in the product category.

Many sociologists, consumer economists and consumer researchers, have suggested using of social class as a meaningful characteristic to understand and predict consumer behaviour.

Man as a social human being, is a member of the most inclusive, dominant and complex type of social organization – the society. Society is created through social interactions between its members through the transmission of ideas or communication. Through such interactions, individuals over a period of time, automatically become participants of a social organization and will change their individual activities from a relatively independent social element to activities which are acceptable to the broader social organization – the society. This is visible in the way men create new relationships or join previously existing patterns of social order. The social class or society plays a major role in influencing the buying behaviour or consumption pattern factors, which will influence his purchase decisions. So, marketing decision makers have to understand how social class influences the consumer behaviour of the target market. For analysing this, they have to understand the role of 'opinion leaders', culture and subculture, which are the underlying determinants of the consumer behaviour in the society.

In this chapter, we start with defining social class, understand its nature and characteristics and how social class attitudes and behaviour can influence consumer behaviour. We will also look into how culture and sub culture can affect consumer behaviour.

MEANING OF SOCIAL STRATIFICATION AND SOCIAL CLASS

It is a common aspect noted throughout the world that human beings exist in a socially stratified environment. This may give rise to the question "What is the meaning of the term social stratification"?

"Social stratification is the division of members of a society into a hierarchy of distinct status classes, so that members of each class have relatively the same status and members of all other classes have either more or less status" (Consumer Behavior L.G. Schiffman & L.L. Kanuk, 6th Edn., 1997, pp. 376)

Man lives and breathes in a society, he also gets influenced by it and at times even influences its course of development.

Social class is the relative standing of the members of a society so that a higher position implies a higher status than those in the lower class. The determinants of a social class is decided by the income, occupation, place of residence etc., of the individual members of the society.

Social class is the relative standing of the members of a society so that a higher position implies a higher status than those in the lower class. The members of a particular social class will enjoy more or less the same status and prestige in the community.

The members of a particular social class will enjoy more or less the same status and prestige in the community. Although income is an important factor in deciding a person's social class, even one's education and profession can be used for determining one's social class. For instance, social class depends considerably on one's education and occupation so if an individual draws relatively low income but is highly educated or has a prestigious occupation then he or she will be accorded a higher social class in the society. The vice versa also holds true.

An appropriate example to explain the above will be the 'role' of 'doctors' and 'nurses'. There is no doubt that public health requirements of the society make both the roles of the 'doctors' and 'nurses' a very important one. However, there is a general tendency on the part of individual members of the society to value the roles on a comparative basis as higher or lower. Typically, the 'doctor' is accorded a higher status when compared to that of the nurses. Consequently, the society also expects better services of a higher level from a doctor than from the nurse. These two characteristics of our society of – deliberately differentiating and evaluating the roles of the individuals based on the role performed and status are the basis for stratification.

In India also we have a stratified society. This can be seen from the unequal distribution of income and wealth among the people. The principle of inequality is visible from the fact that wealth is concentrated in the hands of a few, resulting in a clear distinction between the rich and the poor or 'haves' and 'have nots'. There is a ranking of individuals in society from high to low in terms of social status. Further, all the people do not have the same power and prestige, similar possessions, share the same value system and also act discriminately with individuals of the low social class having lesser power, prestige and status.

There are certain symbolic identifications by which individuals accorded higher status are distinguished from those occupying lower status. These status symbols are:

(a) *Insignia* – Mark of qualitative identification differentiating people of different status.

(b) *Titles and designations* – People are identified based on the various titles and designations they carry with them. A person who falls into the high-class society will adorn herself with a **Rado** watch and platinum/diamond jewellery, wear high designer clothes and move around in a luxury car (**Mercedes** Benz).

(c) *Pay and perquisites* – Generally organizations award their employees salary and perquisites based on their job functions. So it is natural that a person occupying a higher grade will enjoy higher status and certain special perquisites due to him based on his higher-level status as compared to a person occupying a lower grade in the organization. The CEO of a company will prefer to fly Business class, while the executive may fly economy class or opt for the frills free airlines.

(d) *Physical facilities* – Status of people can be distinguished on the basis of various facilities provided to them by the company at work place and at home. Top executives of companies or people who are regarded as occupying high status in the society are provided at place of work exclusive rooms with excellent furnishings, exclusive parking places, etc. They are also allocated luxury manors, membership to elite clubs, etc., to take care of their home needs.

Social stratification is the ranking of people in a society by other members into higher and lower positions so as to produce a hierarchy of respect or prestige. Homes, clothes, cars, jewellery etc. are the indicators of the possessions of the particular social class. Social mobility refers to the movement or shift of an individual or household from one level to another.

The members of a given social class will enjoy more or less the same status and prestige in the community. They share a common lifestyle and behaviour pattern. They even prefer to do their shopping in a particular mall or shopping area and patronize selected shops which will suit their class image. Although differential preferences may exist among the members, in a buying situation when objective standards are not available to guide them, they may conform to certain 'class norms.' An understanding of such social class groupings can help the marketer to identify and segment the target market accordingly.

Studies have indicated every social class develops its particular lifestyle and behaviour standards and that the class members in their purchase behaviour are guided by their own class norms. Nevertheless, the extent of social class influence on its members will depend on the extent of attractiveness the group holds out to them. Greater the attractiveness more will be the behavioural conformity.

➲ NATURE OF SOCIAL CLASS INFLUENCES

The nature of social class influence on consumer behaviour can be understood if one has a look at social stratification, status symbols and social mobility.

Social Stratification

As mentioned earlier in the chapter, social stratification is *the ranking of people in a society by other members into higher and lower positions so as to produce a hierarchy of*

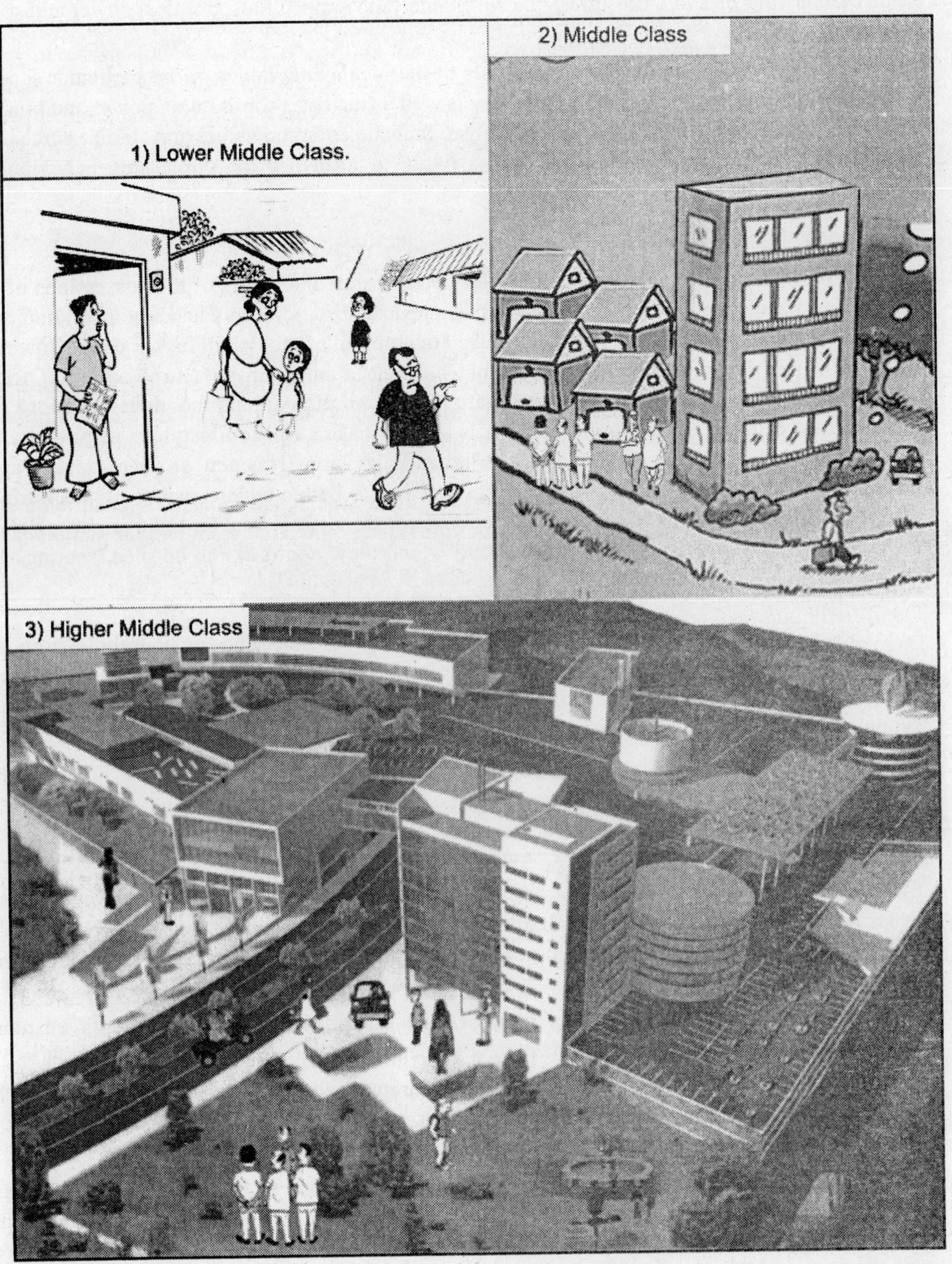

Type of houses based on social satisfaction.

respect or prestige. When we talk of the Indian society, it implies that certain members of the society are ranked higher than others on the basis of income, education, profession (or occupation) and other intangibles like lifestyles, one's influence and connections, political power and social service.

Social stratification occurs on the basis of the ideals and values of the particular society. Accordingly, the composition of social class as well as the basis for defining power and prestige will also vary. The social class status is likely to indicate common values and similar purchasing patterns. Thus, social class stratification is likely to influence the purchasing behaviour of consumers in a particular social class.

Symbolic Representation of Status

Typically, homes, clothes, cars, jewellery etc., are the indicators of the possessions of the particular social class. Indians have always had a penchant for jewellery and buying of diamonds was treated to be the exclusive previlege and status symbol of the rich or higher class. However, today, diamond manufacturers such as Mehul Chokshi (Gitanjali Group) and Vijay Jain (ORRA) diamond company) have discovered that there is an aspiration among individuals to move to a higher class of buyers. This new consumer is a homemaker, whose lifestyle is inspired by the fashionably attired 'bahus and betis' of the Indian Television. This new group of buyers, apart from easy accessibility and lower price have gained a better understanding of the intrinsic value of diamonds. Such consumers are looking for trendy, affordable, lightweight jewellery which can be worn on multiple occasions and which they would like to be seen wearing.

Social Mobility

Social mobility refers to the movement or shift of an individual or household from one level to another. This social mobility is visible in the shift of individuals from rural to urban and metro cities. Aspiring for a better lifestyle and standard of living, have prompted many youngsters to move to well known cities with better jobs prospects and with good jobs and pay packets, such individuals and households are moving up in the social ladder.

SOCIAL CLASS CHARACTERISTICS

The characteristics suggest that social class: have rank ordering, are relatively permanent, internal homogeneity, intergenerational class mobility, and consider determinants other than income.

As mentioned earlier in the chapter, social class is a relative standing of the members of a society such that those occupying higher position are accorded a higher status than those in the lower social class. A few of the characteristics of the social class concept are given below:

- **Social Class Suggests Rank Ordering :** Social class differences are given ranks on the basis of the social prestige accorded to a particular social class.
- **Social Classes are Relatively Permanent :** Social classes are relatively the permanent characteristics of the family. An individual's family's social class does not change from a day to day or from a year to year basis.
- **Social Classes have Internal Homogeneity :** The social class may remain homogeneous within each strata. It is observed that all those belonging to the same social class tend to be similar in terms of the kind of occupation, the residencial area occupied by them, their eating habits, socializing etc.
- **Social Class can have Intergenerational Class Mobility :** Although we have mentioned above about relative social class permanence, it is possible for an individual

to move out of the social class of his or her birth and shift to a higher or lower class. This could be obtained by him or her acquiring the values, resources and behaviours of the new class.

- **Social Class Considers Determinants other than Income :** Even though income is an important determinant of social class, there is no one-to-one correspondence between the two. The other determinants such as educational qualification, occupation and personal tastes can also be associated with the social class. Because of these determinants it will not be uncommon for a person with a relatively middle income to be accorded the upper social class status and visa versa. A person having political clout (though not very educated) may command prestige and status disproportionate with his income earnings.

The typical social class characteristics having relevance to marketing are elaborated here under:

Characteristic Features having Relevance to Marketing

Be it a developed economy or a developing economy like India, the society has certain characteristics, which will distinguish it from other societies. Analysis of the characteristic features of the social class, will help the marketer to gain a better understanding of its target market and thereby the consumption pattern adopted by the particular social class. Following are some of the major characteristics of the social classes relevant to consumer behaviour.

1. Persons within a given Social Class tend to Behave more Alike : Social classes are relatively permanent homogeneous divisions of the society with each social class showing similar lifestyles, values, status, prestige, interests and behaviour pattern. Marketers have observed that there was existence of shared attitudes and behavioural pattern among members within a particular social class and differing behavioural patterns, values and attitude between social classes.

For instance, a person belonging to middle class, when going to purchase an automobile, would prefer to make a choice between *Alto, Indica, Santro, Getz* or any other economically priced car, which will fit within his budget. Whereas, a person belonging to the higher class, intending to purchase an automobile, would prefer to make a choice from either a *Corolla 'Opel Astra'*, '*Mercedes*', or any other highly priced cars – which will indicate a higher status, value and prestige in the eyes of the society. Such differences in the buying pattern is even seen in case of products like shoes, mens/ladies formal wear, cigarettes, etc. This information can be used by the marketer in manufacturing products which meet the lifestyle, status and prestige of a particular social class.

2. Social Class is Hierarchical : Persons are ranked as occupying inferior or superior positions according to their social class or status held by them in the society. As discussed earlier, social class is decided by income, occupation, education and place of residence. Broadly speaking, in India, we have got at least three social classes – Upper class, middle class and lower class. Here each social class has similar lifestyles, values, interests and behaviour. Members of a specific social class perceive members of other social classes as having either more or less status as compared to them.

Social class characteristics relevant to marketing indicate: persons within a given social class tend to behave more alike, it is hierarchical and is measured as a weighted function of one's occupation, income, wealth, education, status, prestige etc.

It has been observed that shoppers in the various strata seek out retail outlets that reflect and cater to that particular class. *For example,* the elite class or higher class may prefer to buy designer sarees which conveys a status, style and prestige of the higher order. In case of a middle class customer, she may prefer to purchase silk sarees at any ordinary shop because here she is looking for making a choice from economically priced sarees. This results in a retail structure which conveys social class or social prestige characteristics. These differences are, ofcourse, relative and more noticeable with some class of products than with others. The elite or upper class may be willing to buy certain products like LCDTV, home theatre, refrigerators, etc., from company showroom where the brand name is the indicator of quality. However, where taste or style is important, as with furniture, dress materials, jewellery, high priced watches, etc., the upper class would prefer to shop at exclusive show rooms or retail outlets which the lower class people would generally avoid.

3. Social Class is not Measured by a Single Variable but is Measured as a Weighted Function of one's Occupation, Income, Wealth, Education, Status, Prestige, etc. :

The upper class consists of a very small percent of the population – the prominent "Social-register" families with wealth inherited from two or more generations. The members of this class have the benefit of going to "right" schools – Doon School, etc., occupy the executive positions in the family owned businesses, leading professionals like business managers,etc. The values inculcated by these people include living graciously, upholding the family reputation, reflecting excellent 'breeding' and displaying a sense of community responsibilities. *For example,* children of the Ambani's, Birla's, Wadia's etc.

The middle class people comprise of a very high percentage of the population. This social class is growing enormously. This class consists of families drawing income which is better than average and from various sources. It could include moderately successful business managers, owners of medium sized businesses, various professionals like doctors, lawyers, etc., middle level managers of public sector undertakings, etc. Their income is derived from salaries, profits and professional fees. Their drive is to earn professional success and membership into the upper class is very strong. They, with their limited income try to copy the lifestyle of the upper class and this can be seen in their choice of clothing and home furnishings.

Social class is continous, with individuals able to move into a higher social class or drop into a lower class.

The lower class also constitutes a reasonably large percentage of the population. This group comprises of skilled, semi skilled manual labourers, lower level supervisors, clerks, etc. Some of them have seen the light in schools while others not. They draw either meagre salary or wages. These people have limited sense of choice making and do not have money to "waste" on luxury items.

4. Social Class is Continuous rather than Concrete, with Individuals able to Move into a Higher Social Class or Drop into a Lower Class :

This mobility either up or down can take place most often with more industrialization or degree of urbanization as mentioned earlier. There are successful men who have moved up to the higher class due to increasing awareness to strive harder and harder, sheer determination and hard work. Examples would be of the successful story behind **'N.R. Narayana Murthy'** of the *'Infosys Technologies'* or of the Karsanbhai Patel's **Nirma** or late Dhirubhai Ambani's **Reliance**.

At the time when Indian economy opened up in the early 1990's, economists, planners and the marketers woke up to the concept of the "Great Indian Middle class".

➲ THE GROWING INDIAN MIDDLE CLASS – A STUDY

It was during the time that the Indian economy opened up in the early 1990's that economists, planners and marketers woke up to the concept of the "Great Indian Middle Class." However, the size of this clan continues to be a matter of debate. There are several indicators, which have implied that the Indian 'middle class is actually growing. However, for a variety of reasons, this rise has not been noticed.

1. The ground level numbers about the Indian Middle Class are not easily available and even if it is, it may not always reflect reality. For instance, Indian households tend to underquote income when approached with a questionnaire. Moreover, there is no income on agricultural income. Further, traders, business men and professionals are able to avoid most of their tax burdens.
2. The Middle Class's growth was not noticed earlier because its purchasing power was held tightly due to decades of socialistic planning and strict government control over the amount of goods to be produced in any category and the level of competition. Thus with not much to choose from goods and services to buy, the middle class's money and purchasing power was not manifested in any market place.
3. Although the middle class has been defined in many ways (cultural, education, consumption patterns and psychographics), income classification has perhaps been the most objective criterion. But, there is a great dearth of reliable longitudinal data on household income in India.

But NCAER'S publication called **The Great Indian Middle Class** and its MISH studies has helped in recognizing the phenomenon of the Indian Middle Class and in giving an estimation of its numbers.

Table 8.1 gives a view on the size of the Indian Middle Class.

TABLE 8.1

SIZE OF INDIAN MIDDLE CLASS

Class	Annual household income (at 2001-02 prices)	Distribution of households (Mn) 2001-02	Distribution of households (Mn) 2009-10	Distribution of households (%) '01-'02	Distribution of households (%) '09-'10	Share of rural (per cent) '01-'02	Share of rural (per cent) '09-'10	Annual growth (%)
Deprived	Below Rs. 90,000	135.4 (731)	1114.4 (618)	71.9	51.5	81.8	84.2	–2.1
Aspirers	Rs. 90,000 – Rs. 200,000	41.3 (221)	75.3 (405)	21.9	33.9	48.5	61.2	7.8
Middle class	Rs. 200,000 – Rs. 1000,000	10.7 (58)	28.4 (153)	5.7	12.8	35.2	33.4	12.9
Rich	Over Rs. 1000,000	0.8 (4)	3.8 (20)	0.4	1.7	22.9	22.2	21.4
Total		188.2(1014)	221.9(1195)	100.0	100.0	71.6	68.8	2.1

Source : "The Great Indian Middle Class", NCAER Publication   Note : Figures in ( ) are population in million

The Middle Class, has been defined as households earning Rs 2-10 lakhs annually. It was seen that between 1995-96 and 2001-02, the total middle class homes grew twice in size-from 4.5 million households to 10.7 million and by 2009-10, they are expected to rise to 28.4 million.

The middle class has been defined as households earning Rs. 2-10 lakhs annually.

At the bottom of the middle class tier, was found to be the category, which the study defined as 'seekers' who just moved into the middle class bracket earning Rs 2-5 lakhs and formed a bulk of this genre. There were close to 9 million of such households and they have grown by a little over 15% annually between 1995-96 and 2001-02. This category forms a primary market for most durable goods and services. Though they can easily afford an entry level car, less than one in three such households own one. Almost 70 per cent of such households have basic durable goods like colour televisions and refrigerators, but AC penetration is a low 13%.

The **upper tier** of the Middle Class are referred to as the 'strivers', with an annual income of between Rs 5-10 lakhs, numbering to over 1.7 million households and with a clear

The NCAER's study of the Great Indian middle class, found that the two key drivers for the growing economic prosperity was a robust GDP growth and a higher propensity to purchase products and services. Between 1995-96 and 2001-02, the economy grew at the rate of 6.1 per cent annually.

and distinct profile when compared to their lesser cousins. This category of households is growing at a faster pace of 18 per cent annually. A large majority of them own cars (one in two households) and other luxury goods. Marketers can try to influence this category as they (the consumers) will be interested in upgrading to a higher class. This class can be targeted as upgrade market for 29-inch CTVS, more loaded cars, larger apartments and higher volume refrigerators and washing machines.

The study found that the two key drivers for growing economic prosperity was a robust GDP growth and a higher propensity to purchase products and services. Between 1995-96 and 2001-02, the economy grew at the rate of 6.1 per cent annually. The growing prosperity and the increase in the middle class households and in the number of rich is visible not only in major cities and towns but also in other cities like Nagpur, Surat, Vadodara, Ahmedabad and Vijayawada too. Such a growth will have a far reaching impact and it is predicted that by 2010, the share of the lowest income will fall steeply from 72 percent (in 2006) to 52 percent in 2010.

This shift implies that marketers can create a market wherein those who can't afford most consumer products could become potential buyers of entry-level durable goods and services.

Social class is measured on the basis of one's residential location, income, status, prestige etc.

COLMEAN-RAINWATER'S SOCIAL STANDING HIERARCHY

We will have an overview of the social hierarchy which used to exist in the American society. A combination of certain socioeconomic factors such as occupation, income and education were used to indicate the individual's social status and define (a consumer's) his social class. The most widely used index of social status had been W. Lloyd Warner's **Index of Status characteristics** developed in the early 1940s. Two sociologists Richard Coleman and Lee Rainwater in 1978 tried to update the data and came out with another grouping known as the **Coleman-Rainwater Social Standing Hierarchy**.

This grouping, although similar to Warner's index, more directly reflects the power and prestige associated with each group when compared to the former. Another advantage is that it distinguishes between a middle class and a working class which is again reflected in the values of group as well as in the occupation.

Table 8.2 gives an overview of Coleman Rainwater Social Standing Hierarchy and other details in terms of their norms, values and lifestyles:

TABLE 8.2

SOCIAL CATEGORIES AS PER RICHARD COLEMAN AND LEE RAINWATER

Class Upper Americans	Middle Americans	Lower Americans
• **Upper-Upper** (The "Capital's society" world of inherited wealth aristocratic names) • **Lower-Upper** (The newer social elite, drawn from current professional corporate leadership) • **Upper-Middle** (The rest of college graduate managers and professionals, lifestyle centers on private clubs, causes and the arts.)	• **Middle Class** (Average pay, white collar workers and blue collar friends live on the better side of town, try to do correct things.) • **Working Class** Average pay, blue collar workers, lead lifestyle whatever the income. School background and job.)	• **A lower group of people but not the lowest** (Working not on welfare, living standard is just above poverty, behaviour judged 'crude trashy) • **Real lower-lower** (On welfare, visibly poverty sticken usually out of work (or have the dirtiest Jobs)

(*Source :* Consumer Behavior, Henry Assael, 6th Edn., Thomson-Learning' Asian Books Pvt. Ltd., New Delhi, 2001, pp. 411)

The markets in America use the above mentioned three socio economic indicators-occupation, income and education to identify a consumer's social class. In American society people are ranked on the basis of a hierarchy of upper, middle and lower classes based on their power and prestige, which depends upon the individual's occupation, income and education. (Consumer Behavior, Henry Assael, 2001).

The social hierarchy will be useful in the sense that the values, norms and lifestyles of each group will be reflected in what they buy, what they wear and who they interact with. Social clan is measured on the basis of one's residential location, income, status, prestige etc.

Marketers have been using the Cole man-Rainwater Social Standing Hierarchy, which helps them to understand how social stratification, status symbols and social mobility can influence their consumer's purchase behaviour.

As in any other market economy, the American society governed by its social class also affects its consumer's purchasing behaviours. So, marketers there have been using the Coleman-Rainwater social standing Hierarchy, which helps them to understand how social stratification, status symbols and social mobility can influence their consumer's purchase behaviour. Ofcourse, now with the economic recession greatly affecting the American market, only time will tell how this could affect the social class purchasing trends, resulting in changes in the social stratification and social mobility.

Ad is targeting the higher social class

➲ SOCIAL INFLUENCE ON CONSUMER BEHAVIOUR

The buyer maintains a constant contact with others ranging from members of his family, or colleaques, sales persons and sometimes a complete stranger also, who can influence his purchase choice.

The buyer whom we are studying does not function as an entity independent of those around him. He maintains a constant contact with others ranging from members of his family, or colleagues, sales people and at times a complete stranger also. Sometimes a casual comment like "what an attractive dress" or "Ah! That jacket really adds to your personality", from any of the above mentioned individuals will boost up his morale and influence his buying choice. Consequently, the next time while on his shopping spree, the buyer will spend more than the share of the money he had thought of putting aside for shopping.

Man as a social being, believes in having constant interactions with the various organizations because it serves many of his needs like socialization, feeling secure, a feeling of belongingness, etc. These constant interactions have an impact on him. While formulating purchase decisions, a person refers to the behaviour of another person **or group** and tries to conform to it. Such interactions may often also have a bearing on his day-to-day life.

We will briefly have a look at: (1) Reference group influence (2) Opinion leader influence (3) The role of communication and (4) The influence of social class on saving and buying attitudes of individuals

1. THE REFERENCE GROUP INFLUENCE

There are broadly three types of intimate groups in society which can influence the buying behaviour of individuals. These are:

Broadly there are three types of intimate groups in society, which can influence the buying behaviour of individuals: groups which serve as comparison points, groups to which the individual aspires to be a member and group whose perspectives are assumed by the individual irrespective of whether he aspires for its membership or not.

***(a)* Groups which Serve as Comparison Points :** There are certain groups which serve as points of comparison and are used to evaluate the individual's status. It has been observed that today's unpredictable consumer gets influenced by people with whom he perceives as sharing similar traits, psychological quirks, behavioural peculiarities and this automatically gets imprinted on his mind and influences his buying behaviour. Marketers are helping consumers in their decision making by providing relative groups for comparison purpose. Such moves will re-inforce the familiarity of the brand in the minds of the consumers. Further, it also provides a reassurance against any perceived risk which prospective customers may experience before going for purchasing. At times celebrities are used for endorsing, which also helps in easy association with the brand. For instance, in the past, Mansoor Khan Pataudi, the cricket celebrity with the regal touch, had endorsed *Royale* an up market brand from Asian Paints. Now the same brand is endorsed by his children Saif Ali Khan and Soha Khan. Royale brand targets up market consumers and using of celebrity will help to serve as the point of comparison. Another example can be of *Cadbury's Chocolates*. Cadbury had realized that there is a child in every adult. Hence the advertisement had spoken about experiencing "the real taste of life" which was targeted at the adult buyer. Thus the firm (Cadburys) wanted to transfer an experience by rediscovering the carefree, unself-conscious, pleasure-seeking child within each adult. Here the point of comparison is an adult to a child. These two examples reveal how certain groups can serve as a point of comparison irrespective of their status.

However, estimate of the status may vary according to the group with which the individual compares himself. A customer ideally will make the choice of a product/service between two ideal combinations of price and value.

Says Krish Iyer, CEO and MD Piramyd Retail, "With respect to consumer preferences, every customer, irrespective of income, affordability and age have two kinds of attitudes- one is that of fashion and the other of price." The lower or lower Middle Class customers could behave like a bargain hunter or price conscious informed customers who are looking for value for the money spent on the product along with the benefits offered. Such customers would prefer to shop at the **Big Bazaar**, **hypermarkets**, since such outlets serve as a point of comparison by providing basic necessities.

The other category of customers are those who look upon celebrities or high society person's willing to make fashion statements. They tend to spend more irrespective of their income just to imitate the buying behaviour of the group which serves as a point of comparison. Such customers prefer to do lifestyle shopping at outlets like *Piramyd Megastore, Globus, Westside* etc., These consumers are aspiring to occupy a higher social class of those whose behaviour they are imitating.

***(b)* Groups to which the Individual Aspires to be a Member :** Very often individuals imitate the behaviour of the group they aspire to be a part of. HLL has always used Hindi film stars to endorse *Lux beauty Soaps*, *Head & Shoulder Shampoo* (Priety Zinta) *Clinic anti dandruff Shampoo* (Shahid Kapoor) They are trying to help consumers connect with the brand, through celebrity endorsements. Social class influence through celebrity usage, to induce positive consumer behaviour is being attempted at, although there may not be face to face contact between the groups. *Pepsi's* association with cricket players is well known. The brand personality can be defined as vibrant, for fun loving, young, lively and adventurous. The target segment is the younger generation for whom cricket is a popular sport. This segment is able to associate Pepsi and the endorser's with cricket in terms of their accomplishments, attitudes and lifestyles, which they (the target consumers) are aspiring for.

The reference group can influence the consumer behaviour by affecting the level of aspiration and through establishing conventional patterns of personal expenditure.

***(c)* Group whose Perspectives are Assumed by the Individual Irrespective of whether he Aspires for its Membership or not :** With the market in the urban areas getting stagnated, marketers have woken up to the fact that there is a big rural market potential waiting to be tapped. This is because the rural customer is looking out for value and quality in the product and subconsciously he too wants to upgrade his living standards. Realizing this, '*Velvets International*' Pharma products caught on the aspiration led need of the lower class or low income consumers and started offering them shampoo, in a sachet pack at an affordable price. Likewise many companies have also succeeded in penetrating this lower income consumer segment with products such as 'detergent powder', 'pan masala' and even digestives like '*Hajmola*' being offered in the sachet form.

The above mentioned three types of groups are referred to as the reference groups – people who will act as references and could influence the buyer's purchase decisions. The reference group can affect the consumer behaviour broadly in two ways:

1. The reference group could *affect the level of aspiration* of the individual consumer thereby making the person experience a feeling of satisfaction or frustration. *For example:* A young boy may be aspiring to be a good badminton player and gets enrolled in a coaching class conducted by professionals. Inspite of vigorous practice if he is not selected to play in the match, it may lead to frustration.
2. The reference group can affect the behaviour of the individual through *establishing conventional patterns of personal expenditure,* thereby producing either conformity and contentment or discontentment. It has been observed that in case of products like cigarettes or vehicles, the reference group makes a significant impact on the consumer behaviour. *For example,* college going boys are very often seen using mobile phones and moving around on two wheelers/cars. The choice of both the product and brand in this case will be dependent on their selection of the reference group. The individual consumer will continue to use the specific (brand) mobile phone as long as he considers it to be the choice of his reference group, which may comprise of friends and classmates.

Thus, 'reference group' is a term used to designate the type of group an individual consumer uses as a 'point of reference' in determining his own judgments, preferences, beliefs and behaviour.

II. ROLE OF OPINION LEADERS IN CONSUMER BEHAVIOUR

Opinion Leaders: Marketers have spent lots of money in trying to identify those factors which affect consumer behaviour. However, it is often seen and said that "word-of-mouth advertising" has more influence on the success of the product rather than the money that is poured into advertising. Informal, reliable sources of information are given by opinion leaders.

The opinion leader will provide solicited as well as unsolicited information after seeking latest facts in detail from various sources. All this information is deliberately obtained in order to enhance his or her 'expertise status,' which is sought to in a particular product category. Consumers value the opinion leader's recommendation and suggestions because of their belief that the former does not receive material gain from the recommended actions. Consequently, the opinion leader's advice will be seriously considered.

The beliefs, preferences, actions and behaviour of the leader sets a trend and pattern for others to follow in a given set of situations, he is a reference individual.

Opinion leader advocates the goodness of using mustard oil.

"Opinion leadership refers to the degree to which an individual influences others in a given choice situation i.e., those who possess a disproportionately large amount of this trait". The beliefs, preferences, actions and behaviour of the leader sets a trend and pattern for others to follow in a given set of situations, he is a reference individual. Various research studies have revealed some distinctive characteristics of opinion leaders. The original study

says that marketing leaders are found in about equal numbers in the various levels of social status. The two strongest factors in favour of marketing leaders were the stage in life cycle and gregariousness. *For example,* in case of products related to home, current experience counted the most. Here, women with grown up children and those who had used the product would act as a leader. However, a significant factor to be noted is that, the more gregarious women are, the more likely they are to be marketing leaders.

Opinion leaders get involved in social activities. They are more gregarious, self confident and are very often found to be innovators of products also. They always enjoy being in the lime-light. They are always interested in gathering additional information of the products especially if the media helps them to exercise their leadership. Being an opinion leader, his/her advice is very often sought on issues at hand. This is because it is believed that with wider exposure, he/she is more knowledgeable than others and so they have to "live up" to their image as their advice is being sought.

Characteristics of the Opinion Leader

Marketers are of the opinion that the opinion leader can influence consumers **within a product category**. However, it will be difficult to identify opinion leaders across various categories. Yet certain traits identified among opinion leaders can be put as:

Though the opinion leader cannot directly influence the day-to-day purchase decisions of an individual member of the group, they can indirectly influence the group members by voicing their opinion and adopting a lifestyle, which is attractive enough to the group member so as to motivate him to purchase the particular product.

- Opinion leaders are knowledgeable about the product category.
- Opinion leaders are more involved in the product category.
- Opinion leaders are active to receiving communication about the product from various personal sources.
- Opinion leaders are interested in new products.
- Opinion leaders read magazines and other print media relevant to their area of product interest.
- Opinion leaders are self confident in their appraisal of the product category.
- Opinion leaders are more socially active, which is a reflection of their willingness to communicate with others.

Since opinion leaders play a major role in influencing individuals, marketers are interested in knowing if there is a connection between opinion leadership and innovativeness.

It has been observed that the opinion leaders and the people with whom they interact are able to influence, typically those belonging to the same primary or intimate groups of family, friends, close colleagues and small close knit organizations. Such a group and the leader generally have a common social background and also belong to the same age group. The opinion leader's judgmental views on lifestyle and fashions are heard to with a lot of respect. Though the leader cannot directly influence the day-to-day purchase decisions of an individual member of the group, they can indirectly influence the group members by voicing their opinion and adopting a lifestyle, which is attractive enough to the group members so as to motivate them to purchase the particular product.

Because of the role adopted by them, such opinion leaders are acceptable to new ideas and new products and if convinced they also act as propagators of these new product ideas and products. This has resulted in marketing managers making efforts to identify such opinion leaders, who can provide the necessary 'word-of-mouth advertising' and help in pushing the product into the market with the right type of motivation.

Opinion Leaders and Marketing

Marketers have realized that women evolve mentally, physically and socially just as the society around them. Accordingly, they have portrayed such women as opinion leaders in their advertisements. To quote a few examples:

- The advertisment of *Rin*, where a woman comments on another woman's white clothes **"Bhale uski Kameej Meri Kammej se Safed Kaise?"**
- *Surf's* Lalitaji (a smart housewife) who knew the difference between buying cheap and buying value. Her opinion statement **"Surf Ki Kharidari me he samajdari hai,"** was appreciated by the women (masses).
- The social change, with young girls no longer feeling guilty about indulging themselves was reflected in the opinion (or theme) **"I don't care"?** This statement was made by the young college girl in the *Lifebuoy Plus TVC* in the late 1990s.

The above examples indicate that marketers are trying to stimulate word-of-mouth communication through advertising or other direct identification of opinion leaders.

Another example is that of the *'Asian Paints'* company, when it had launched its 'Utsav' range of paints in the rural market, during the pre-Diwali season. At that time they had asked their salesmen to seek the help of opinion leaders to communicate with the villagers about their product. The salesmen of 'Asian Paints' selected the opinion leaders in the villages and painted the village post office/library/the house of the Mukhiya to demonstrate that the paint did not peel off. Over and above they also invited the village's painters for meets organized at the local dealer's place.

Social class acts as an important variable in segmenting the market. A knowledge about the various media will help the marketer to understand how best to reach out to these target markets.

Though the opinion leader may vary from product to product, marketers having realized the important role played by them and are trying to reach out to their customers through a medium (opinion leaders) that is palatable to them.

III. THE ROLE OF COMMUNICATION

Another important aspect of consumer behaviour related to social class is that of the exposure of individuals to the media of communication. Social class acts as an important variable in segmenting the market. A knowledge about the various media will help the marketer to understand how best to reach out to these target markets. Today consumer is living in the age of information overkill and is bombarded by commercials, unsolicited product information and pursued by hardsell media. . So, it is the responsibility of the marketer to get the consumers' attention, evoke their comprehension, gain their acceptance and then extract retention, alongside competing with thousands of other units of communication also trying to do the same. Thus, depending on the particular target segment, the marketer has to communicate and identify the path to penetrate the consumers mind through the media (mass print, outdoor, etc.) which is most suitable to them.

The Changed Social Scenario in India

For over more than a decade, along with a more liberalized economic policy, there are various transformations taking place at the social level. For instance, we have a younger population which has tasted financial independence at a much earlier age (when compared to the previous generations), rise in the number of nuclear families and an increased media exposure which has given rise to a new consumption culture in the country.

TABLE 8.3

DATA OF NEW CONSUMPTION CULTURE

Durables/ Parameters	Year	
	2000	2005
1. Television penetration	35 per cent of the total population	50 per cent of the total population (more than 60 per cent were cable and satellite connections)
2. Refrigerator penetration	9.4 per cent of the population	12 per cent of the population
3. Telephone connections	6.5 per cent of the population	12 per cent of the population
4. Average age of home owners	40 years	28-30 years.

(*Source :* Business Today, January 14, 2007)

Over and above the information provided in Table 8.3 it was seen that there were around 130 million mobile phone users and the internet population had stood at 40 million.

Credit card penetration has grown ten times between 2001 and 2005, although it is still low at around 2 per cent.

Research by Grey Worldwide revealed that the young Indian consumers were very much assured about their future and well being and also not too, apologetic about their indulgence and expenses. It is assumed that the consumer psyche apart from more indulgence, have a focus towards technology, more purchases with credit cards and a higher and global lifestyle orientation. Simultaneously, the pressures of modern life, especially lack of time is having an effect on their lifestyles. To make up for this, they are seeking leisure activities and products. In fact, in metros such as Delhi, Mumbai and Bangalore, even for mundane services, outsourcing seems to be an attractive option. Extended nuclear families seems to be common. Healthcare and psychographics shift seems to be towards down aging. Accordingly, consumers are spending more on self grooming and beauty care products.

With more spending power and disposable income in hand, consumers are showing more orientation towards personalization of entertainment through i-pods, web casting, and audience interaction on television programming (reality shows). Thus, when the consumer has access to so much information from various media (or sources), marketers will need to look beyond the conventional mind. They will need to work out a suitable media based on:

- The role advertising has to play.
- The advertising spends in the product category.
- The consumer behaviour pattern.
- The allocation of funds or budget estimated and asked for.

Studies indicate that even as the middle class consumers are thriving and able to afford many consumer durables, roughly 35 per cent of the population gets by with less than Rs. 45 a day and another 45 per cent lives on Rs. 45-90.

The Picture of the Rural Sector : It is estimated that in India there are about 630,000 villages. Studies indicate that even as the middle class consumers are thriving, and able to afford many consumer durables, roughly 35 per cent of the population gets by with less than Rs 45 a day and another 45 per cent lives on Rs 45-90. In order to help this social class grow, it is necessary that the poor or strivers as defined by NCAER (National Council of Applied Economic Research) gets enough to eat, an education, clean water and hygienic living conditions. If this is accomplished they will be able to graduate to the next level of the aspirers, as C.K. Prahalad's Theory of "The market at the bottom of the Pyramid", suggests.

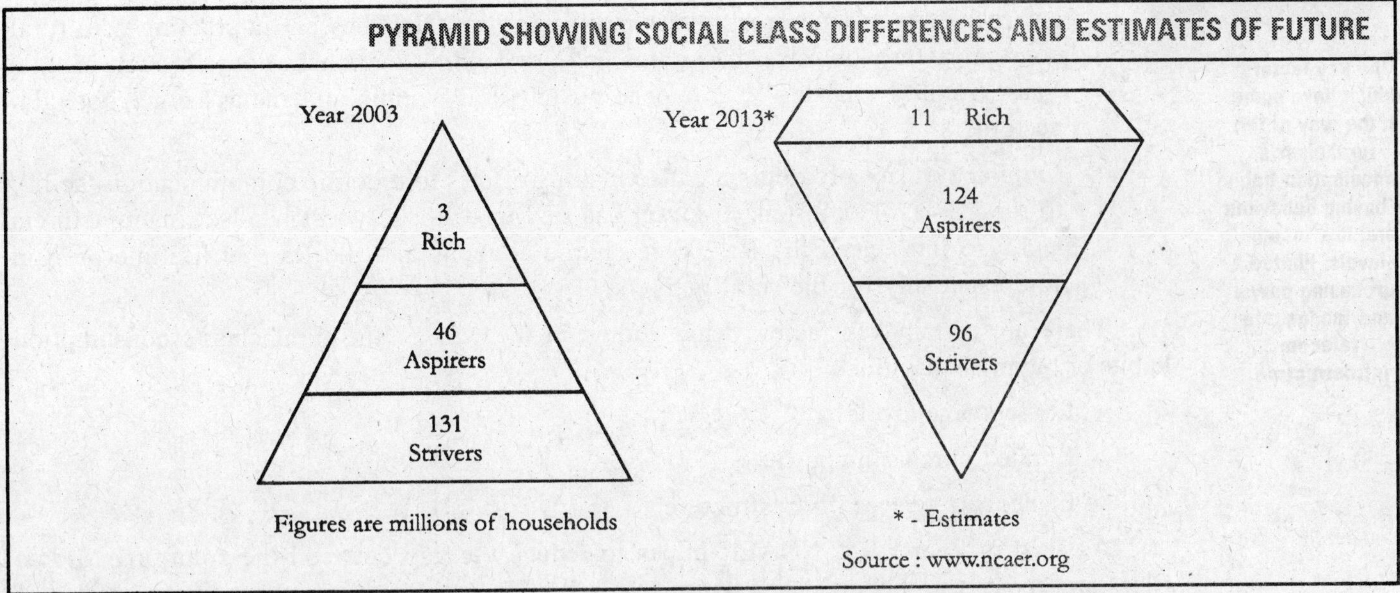

Efforts are being made by the various organizations to penetrate into the rural Indian market.

Efforts are being made by the various organisations to penetrate into the rural Indian market.

- Microsoft India has started some key programmes like **Project Shiksha,** for accelerating IT literacy, **Project Bhasha** to promote language computing, **Project Jyoti** for empowering women and rural communities, **Project Sakshan** a Kiosk-model initiative for a strong IT ecosystem and **Project Vikas** to enhance the global competitiveness of India's small and medium enterprises.
- **Philips India** is working on a project called **Disha** where the company is testing the possibilities of providing mobile, affordable access to healthcare.
- **Hindustan Lever Limited (HLL's) Project Shakti**, where it employs rural, local women to become direct-to-consumer distributors and tap the remote village market for its affordable products (especially for the poor) like shampoo sachets at 50 paise, soaps and detergents at Rs.5 and toothpastes at Rs 10. This project enables its women distributors to earn a decent income of upto Rs 10,000 per month. This project also comprises of shaktivanis, who are trained to communicate the brand's attributes and also educate the rural women folk on the virtues of health, hygiene and basic healthcare.

  Thus the rural womenfolk are enjoying the benefits of woman empowerment and HLL, on its part is able to increase consumption and penetration of the care products in its portfolio, in the rural areas. **ITC'S e, Choupals,** connect farmers with large firms and global markets. This alongwith reducing poverty levels it also increases the income levels.
- Cable and Satellite (C&S) TV is easily available in urban and towns but in rural areas their accessibility is not there largely because it is difficult to lay cables in the remote corners of the country. However, there has been a paradigm shift in TV viewing with the emergence of Direct-to-Home (DTH) satellite T.V such as **Dish TV** (from Essel group) **Tata Sky,** which have been able to take information and 'entertainment (infotainment) even to the remote rural areas.

Tata sky currently has 275,000 subscribers and in order to reach the million mark by the end of the year has brought in **ITC e-Choupals, Godrej Aadhar** (the rural services and retail arm of Godrej Agrovet) and the **Indian Oil.** They are interacting with rural consumers through Kissan Kendras and are holding demonstrations through Mobile Vans. Similarly, Dish TV is depending on rural mandis and melas to get potential customers.

- Cellular services providers are also making efforts to redefine communication facility to rural areas. For instance, **Airtel** has tied-up with low cost handset manufacturers and also introduced the Rs.200 re charge coupons and the Rs 999 lifetime prepaid card especially for the rural markets.

The key factors which have come in the way of the rural class's consumption habit or buying behaviour are: low income levels, limited purchasing power and inadequate telecom infrastructure.

There are certain key factors which come in the way of the rural class's consumption habits or buying behaviour

- Low income levels
- Limited purchasing power
- Inadequate telecom infrastructure

As seen in Figure 8.1, NCAER hopes to reduce the gap between the splurging Middle Class and today's no hopers. They estimate that by 2013, the strivers (those at the bottom of the pyramid) will gradually come down from 96 million households, with the aspirers in the middle rapidly rising from 96 million to 124 million households.

Marketers, as discussed above are making all efforts to create self sustainable scalable models that will help to make consumers out of the poor. Such efforts will provide opportunities to raise the income level of the rural consumers and then help them to save a part of it as disposable wealth to be used for purchasing products and services.

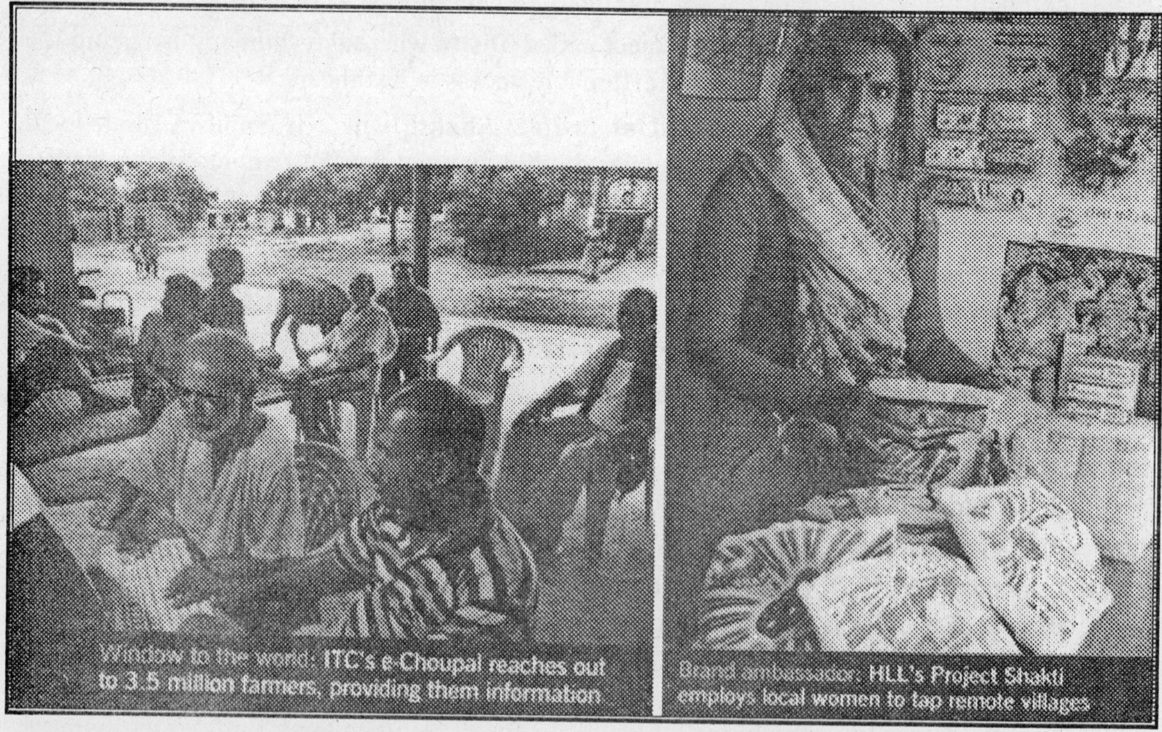

(Source : Business Today, January 14, 2007).

Use of Multimedia Mix

Today, most of marketers prefer to use multimedia mix, as a vehicle of communication at various levels of marketing. Advertising is a very important tool of communication and it is very necessary for marketers to work on the effectiveness of the ad. Once the ad effectiveness parameters are laid down and the ad budget worked out, the media manager has to understand how media delivers results. **Lodestar Media,** the media arm of FCB Group has developed a Threshold Grid applicable for different media, different products and different consumer segments. The Threshold Grid lays down the minimum media input needed to create an impact. Simply put, the model lays down:

Advertising is a very important tool of communication and it is very necessary for marketers to work out on the effectiveness of the ad. Depending upon the product or service offering and on how best to reach the target consumers, the advertisers work out a suitable media strategy which will ensure the best way to communicate with their target consumers.

- The Minimum length of advertising burst: 5 to 6 weeks
- Minimum amount of GRPs: 100-120/week (30 sec. Equivalent)
- Reach and OTS levels: 50%, 3+

In 1998-99, Lodestars had used newspapers almost to the exclusion of every other media to launch *Tata Indica.* At that time competitors *Santra, Matiz, Uno and Zen* were all using multiple media including TV to reach the target consumers. In the case of Tata Indica, the strategy was to go well above threshold level on one media and also ensuring that media reach and media OTS parameters were not sacrificed. The launch was a tremendous success. On the other hand, *Whirlpool* had used TV with very little newspaper advertising, whereas many of the other durable marketers were deploying the biggest part of their ad budget in print.

Studies to Understand Media Multiplication in India

In 1997, The Times Group had commissioned a study on "Measuring the Multiplier Effect" of print and TV through IMRB. The study used respondents in a controlled environment and exposed them to TV and print advertising of four FMCG products. The study found that synergistic effect of print and TV was more evident in terms of competitive imagery shift and brand recall, than in terms of preference shift. Print alongwith TV had a greater impact than only print or only TV.

Another more elaborate study done by INS through IMRB in 2002-03 was an attempt to replicate real market situation using live campaigns. Five leading brands in different product fields were co-opted to use only TV in one city while using TV and print in another. Even in terms of advertising recall, creative recall and brand recall, all five brands showed bigger shift in the media mix area compared to the TV only area on all or some of the various recall measures.

The brand where the difference was the smallest was the one where the creative elements across TV and print (or press) were very much apart (TV used film star, press used a cartoon).

Thus depending upon the product or service offering and on how best to reach the target consumer, the advertisers work out a suitable media strategy which will ensure the best way to communicate with their target consumers. Often, consumer's purchase decisions as well as the choice of the media are influenced by his social status. For instance, even if a person is not educated much but being rich he may have a high social status. Such an individual may have more preference for a LCD T.V and not necessarily the print media.

The media selected should be such that it will penetrate the mind of the customer with a matching significance between message and product.

For instance, during the T.V coverage of the *Wills* World Cup, *Britannia Industries',* co-related their 50-50 brand of biscuits with the third umpire replays, when viewers were eagerly waiting the verdict of the third umpire, with a message *"Gaya Ya Bach Gaya"* (out or not out): *Britannia 50-50*. It was assumed that such an advertisement will be easily retained by the viewers and could have a positive influence on the mind of the consumers when they go to buy biscuits.

Social class also affects the savings and money borrowing attitudes of the members belonging to a particular class. Even the use of technology has impacted the lifestyles and quality of life of consumers.

Another emerging market has been identified as the rural market consumers. The rural consumer is also facing media explosion with information about new products and services received right inside his home on one side and on the other side information trickling back from those who left the village in search of better prospects to the city. Here also the rural customer is vying with his better off urban cousin, by trying to improve upon his living style and consumption pattern so as to match his counterparts in the city.

Thus the marketer has to know the differences among the classes in their media choice behaviour. For this he will have to do analysis of the media and programmes watched by the target customers, the significant characteristic factors of each media and programme, which will be keeping in tune to the attitudes and values of one class as compared to another class.

Rural class's consumption gets affected by their income levels, purchasing power and infrastructure facility.

IV. INFLUENCE OF SOCIAL CLASS ON SAVING AND BUYING ATTITUDES OF INDIVIDUALS

Social class also affects the saving and money borrowing attitudes of the members belonging to a particular class. In a study conducted by Pierre Martineau, on 'Social classes and spending behaviour', Martineau had asked people to suppose their incomes were doubled over the next ten years, and to explain what they would do with the increased income. And he found that *'higher the social status, the more likely people are to save rather than to spend'*-

(*Source : Consumer Behavior* - Bennett, Kassarjian, P. 122, 1987*)*. Martineau's study reveals that unlike the usual assumption that only people belonging to the lower social class prefer to save rather than spend, the same holds true often in case of higher social class also. Martineau also noted that higher the status, the more likely is the individual to specify how he will save his money. This shows how elaborately financial planning is done by the consumers belonging to the higher social class in the society. With regards to the lower social class- consisting of individuals who are barely able to make two ends meet, their consumption pattern will be evolved around purchasing only the basic necessities of life. Consumers belonging to this social class are less likely to consider decisions related to investment or saving.

In the past decade or so, the Indian society has been witness to many changes occurring in the social class standing of individuals. This could be because of the focus on education, more job openings (compared to earlier times) with attractive salary, better purchasing power and so on. We will try to understand the influence on social class on consumer behaviour by viewing: impact of IT, taste of clothes, fashion and shopping, choice of recreational activities and middle class "consumption community".

Impact of IT

In the IT (Information technology) age today, there is seen a mad rush of people from all walks of life to become computer literate. Even youth belonging to the lower social class feel that a working knowledge of computors will help them to get a job.

In fact, the use of technology has impacted the lifestyles and quality of life of consumers. It is felt that understanding of computers is a necessary tool to be competitive as well as an indicator of success. Consumers are comfortable to carry out buying transactions over the internet, the popularity of websites such as indiatimes.com, amazon.com, etc., is an indication of this trend. The young upward mobile trendy individuals earning decent (surplus) salary use e-ticketing for air and rail travel.

Taste of Clothes, Fashion and Shopping

Marketers of clothing have long back recognized the need of consumers to wear clothes to fit their self image which may be in tune to emulate (more often) persons who have more purchasing power than them.

Even members belonging to different social classes wear fashionable clothes suitable to their class. For instance, middle class would prefer to purchase reasonably priced branded clothes such as *Peter England, Ruff & Tuff Jeans, Big Bazaar* made etc. These customers prefer clothes which will give them a decent identification and quality should match the price of the branded clothes. The upper social class will not be price conscious. They will prefer branded exclusive designer wear such as clothes from *Park Avenue, Westside, Reid & Taylor* etc, where the make itself spells exclusiveness.

Social class is also an important variable in determining where a consumer prefers to shop. Customers will not have a preference for shops which is frequented by consumers belonging to another class. For instance middle class consumers have two kinds of attitudes: one is oriented towards fashion and the other towards price. *I.e.,* this category of customers are seeking shops or retail outlets where they can get the value for the money spent on the (branded) product along with the benefits. They being bargain hunters may prefer to shop from **Fabmall, Trumart supermarket (Fresh & More), Margin Free, Food Bazaar, Big Bazaar, Star Bazaar** etc. In higher middle class category there may be classic customers who are willing to pay any price for the image or brand of the product. Such informed category of

Social class is also an important variable in determining where a consumer prefers to shop. Customers will not have a preference for shops which is frequented by consumers belonging to another class.

Advertisements which appeal to the upward mobile, I.T. Savvy young consumers

classic customers may prefer to patronize *Globus, Shoppers Stop, or Westside* outlets. In contrast, the rich class will prefer to purchase brands which are of the premium status these could be brands such as *Louis Phillip, Reid & Taylor, Rado* watch, *Piaget Cartier, Carbon (jewellery)* etc. For the premium product there are exclusive outlets catering to the rich class.

Some retailers have gone for outlets which cater to different, class category of customers. *For example,* the Future group runs **Big bazaar** outlets for the bargain hunting class, it also has **Pantaloon** retail outlets where vast branded product offerings, superior quality, genuine price, convenience, and ambience is available for the higher middle class customers.

Choice of Recreational Activities

There could be differences in the choice of recreational activities depending upon the social class. The rich (upper class) consumers are likely to attend Page 3 parties, socialize with the elite, attend concerts or theatre, play bridge billiards or Golf, have drink parties, and go abroad for shopping and pleasure. The upper middle class persons take membership in clubs, plan pleasure trips abroad with family, go shopping and entertainment with family in well known malls, watch live cricket matches, reading, go swimming etc. The lower class consumers may enjoy watching movies on TV or visit friends and relatives during festivals.

There would be differences in the choice of recreational activities depending upon the social class. The rich (upper class) consumers are likely to attend page3 parties and socialize with the elite, the upper middle class take membership in clubs, and plan pleasure trips abroad while the lower class may enjoy watching movies on T.V and visit friends and relatives during festivals.

The trend of joining clubs for recreation and entertainment is picking up among the middle class consumers.

In case of the middle class there is seen a trend of spending more on activities involving the family members. Especially the trend of joining clubs for recreation and entertainment is picking up among the middle class consumers.

Middle Class 'Consumption Community'

Marketers have realized that it is the middle class, as per the social stratification which is emerging as the consumption community for all types of goods and services. The behavioural pattern of this class shows that they want to live up to the image of the social class they belong to as well as rise to a higher class.

Marketers have realized that it is the middle class, as per the social stratification, which is emerging as the 'consumption community' for all types of goods and services. The individuals belonging to this class are better educated/professionals, exposed to the lifestyles of the rich/upper class and with high flying aspirations. The consumption pattern of the middle class includes instant food/beverages, toiletries, cosmetics (premium brands) readymade garments, home appliances and quality furniture. With the breaking up of the traditional joint family system and emergence of nuclear family set up, the middle class homes comprise of a working couple together ensuring an increased flow of income to the family. This has resulted in changed lifestyle and increased affluence of the middle class and also an open attitude to invest in the stock market. There is a change in their buying behaviour shown in their keenness to purchase products and especially home appliances conveying a message of 'save time' or 'makes your job easy'.

Various surveys have revealed that the desire to acquire credit cards is very high among the middle class consumers especially in the age group of 19-30 years. The initial misconception associating *'Credit Card'* as a status symbol has long since disappeared due to *'Citibank'* who was able to convincingly communicate to the target consumers the convenience of using the *Citibank* credit card. The target consumers were educated on the benefits of using a credit card-ability to withdraw cash from their ATMs and making purchases on the credit card. The taboo associated with "credit" has started disappearing with the phrase of *"buy now even without instant cash"* fast catching up, with the middle class buyer. The middle class person is also actively participating in the money market. He is seen investing in stocks and mutual funds which he feels will earn him good dividends. He is also interested in real estate, purchasing land in the hope to sell it off when the price of the land has increased substantially. The above mentioned behavioural pattern is because the middle class consumer wants to live up to the image of his social class. Simultaneously he is trying to rise to a higher class with more purchasing power in his hands.

Thus, the task set before the marketing decision maker is to identify the behaviour of the social class to which his target market belong. They have to strive to influence the buying behaviour by understanding the intimate group influences on the consumers, the opinion leader who can motivate the buyer and design suitable media for communicating with this target market.

➲ CULTURE (DEFINITIONS AND MEANING)

Culture can be said to be a set of socially acquired values that society accepts as whole and transmits it to its members through language and symbols. (Consumer Behavior, Henry Assael, 6th Edn., Thomson Learning, 2001, pp. 459.)

Cultural values are more deep rooted than lifestyle values. *For example,* a person may be defined as a lover of music, who regularly attends all music concerts. This could also be said to be a component of his or her lifestyle. A more deep seated cultural value may be that he comes from a family of music lovers and it is the desire for continuing with the tradition and involvement which takes him to attending music concerts. Thus culture reflects a society's shared meanings and traditions.

Howard and Sheth have defined culture *"as a selective, manmade way of responding to experience, a set behaviour pattern"*. Thus, culture consists of traditional ideas and in particular the values which are attached to these ideas. It includes knowledge, belief, art, morale, law, customs and all other habits acquired by man as a member of society. An accepted concept about culture is that it *includes a set of learned beliefs, values, attitudes, habits and forms of behaviour that are shared by a society and are transmitted from generation to generation within that society.*

In India we have our own shared beliefs, values, customs which distinguishes us from the rest of the world. Influences from various institutions and elements of the society combine in various ways, which will give rise to the resultant culture and customs.

In India, we have our own shared beliefs, values, customs which distinguishes us from the rest of the world. The uniqueness of our culture can be seen from the joint family system prevalent in many states, the caste system, the living style, customs, rituals, etc., followed by the people at large. These habits and forms of behaviour have been in practice for so long, that they are very often taken for granted. Our culture also includes mores or fairly strong cultural norms (respect for elders, patriotism, etc.) and these, if violated are likely to earn the condemn of the society.

From the Figure 8.2 we can see that culture can be graphically represented. Influences from various institutions and elements of society, such as Education, Politics, Religion etc. combine in complex ways, which will give rise to the resultant culture and customs and this, in turn, can be seen in our attitudes and behaviour.

Keith Williams (Behavioral Aspects of Marketing, 1990) has suggested five main characteristics of culture:

- Culture exists to serve the needs of the society.
- Culture is acquired from society, throughout our life time.
- Culture is learned through interactions with other members of the culture.
- Culture is transferred from generation to generation with new influences constantly being added to the cultural 'soup'.
- Culture will be adaptive to the needs of the society.

FIGURE 8.2

CULTURE - REPRESENTED BY INFLUENCE OF VARIOUS INSTITUTIONS IN SOCIETY, ON THE ATTITUDES & BEHAVIOUR

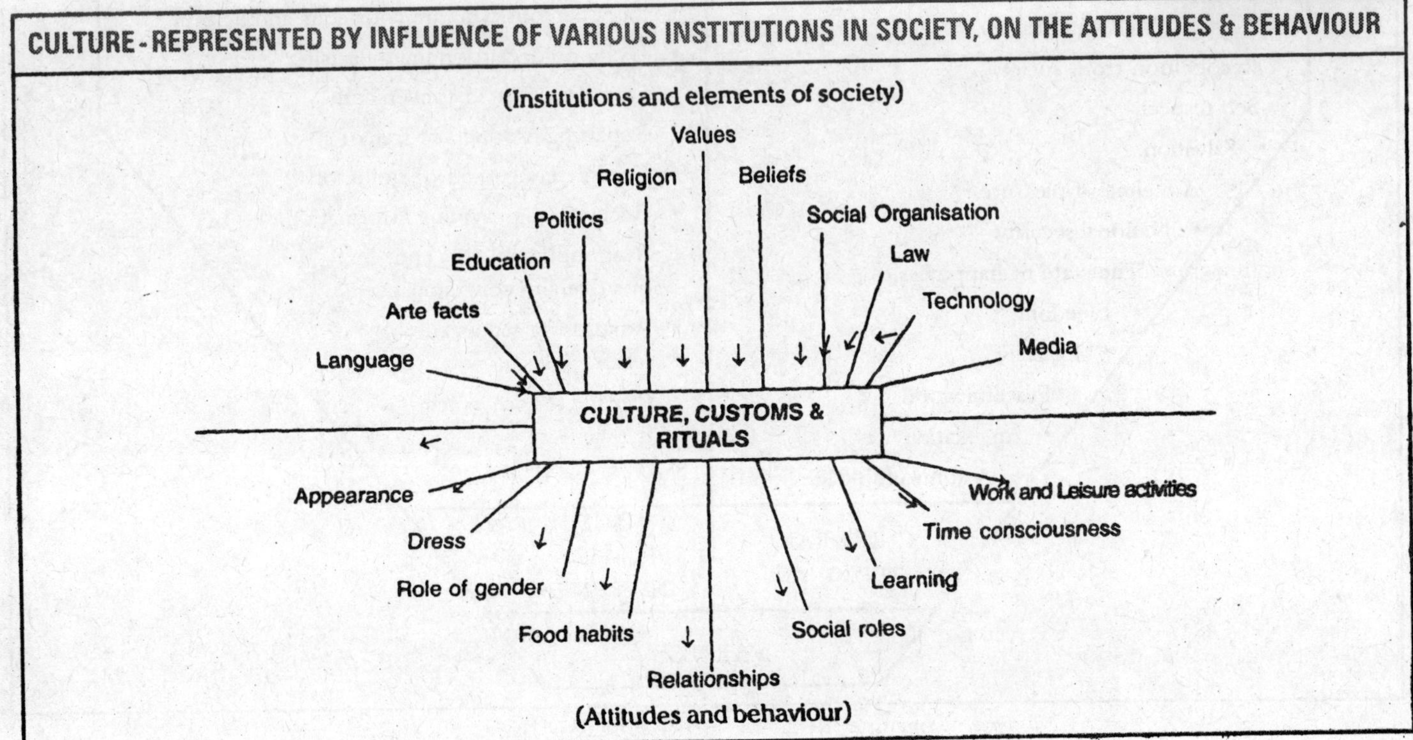

CULTURAL VALUES

According to Rokeach cultural values are terminal values or goals to be attained, while, instrumental values are the means of achieving the desired goals.

Milton J Rokeach has defined **cultural values** as beliefs that a general state of existence is personally and socially worth striving for. Figure 8.3 shows cultural values as defined by Rokeach. Value systems are the relative importance which cultures place on the values. *For example,* Indian culture has for many generations valued family togetherness (joint family system) and inner harmony as a part of our value system. While in America or the Western culture more emphasis or value is placed on individual accomplishment.

Rokeach has considered cultural values as **terminal values** or goals to be attained or developed. He has also defined another category of values, **instrumental values** which are the means of achieving the desired goals.

Rokeach's classification of cultural values can be used for studying purchasing behaviour. It may be said that terminal values are the ultimate purchasing goals and instrumental values are consumption specific guidelines to attain these goals. So in terms of consumer behaviour:

- Product attributes are the means of attaining goals
- Instrumental values are consumption specific values or vehicles for attaining goals.
- Cultural specific terminal values are the ultimate purchasing goals.

FIGURE 8.3

ROKEACH'S CULTURAL VALUES AND CONSUMPTION SPECIFIC VALUES

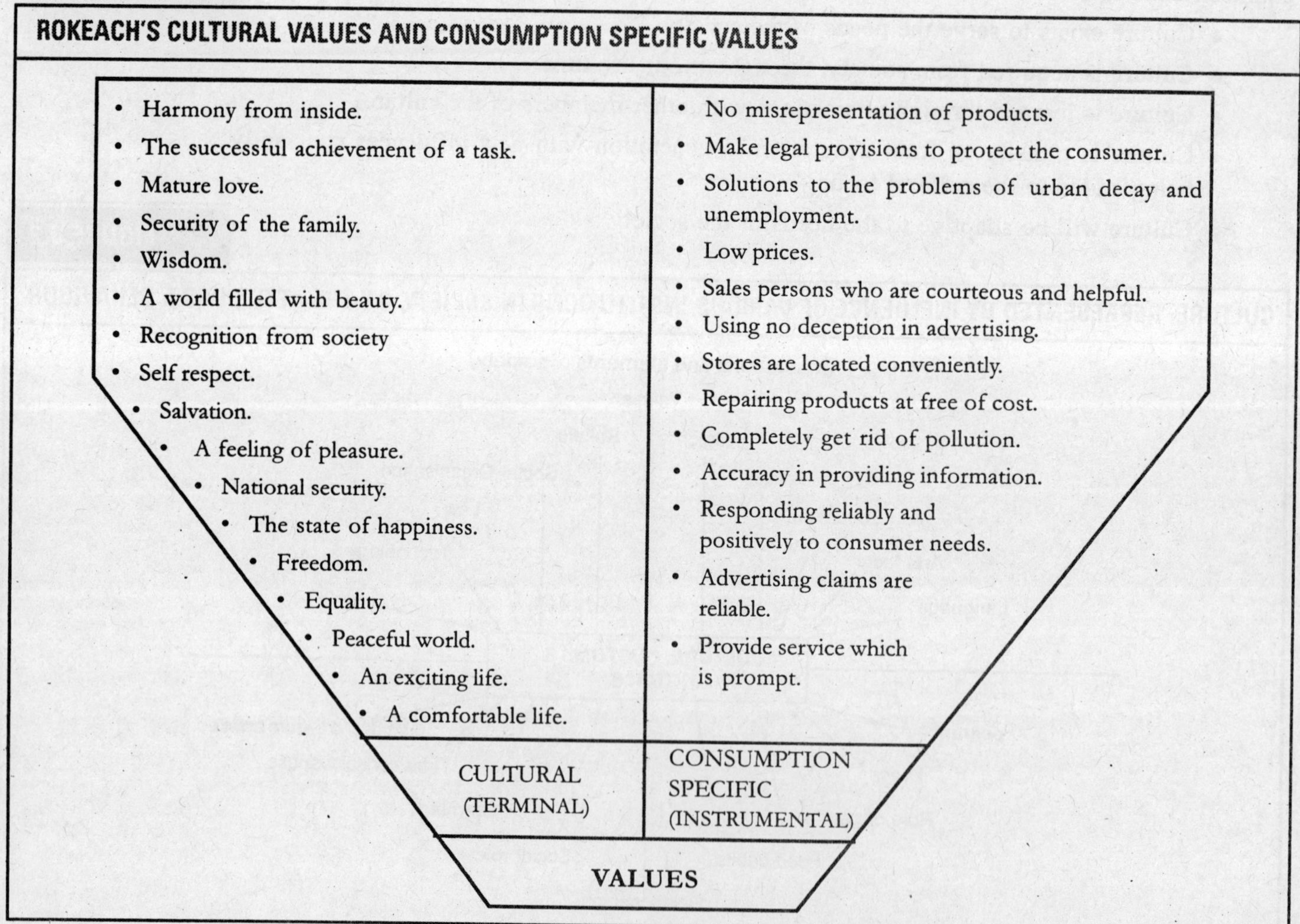

(*Source :* Consumer Behavior, Henry Assael, 6th Edn., pp. 462)

To a certain extent cultural values will help marketers to plan the marketing strategy. Cultural values are more likely to influence broad purchasing patterns. *For example,* a better understanding of the motivation behind brand purchases can be worked out by having a look at the culturally derived purchasing values.

Measurement of Culture

Because of the multifaceted nature of culture, certain techniques can be used for its measurement, these are:

Since cultural values are more likely to influence broad purchasing patterns, they will help the marketer to plan the marketing strategy.

- *Projective tests :* These tests are helpful in assessing individual's motivation and personality.
- *Attitude measurement tests :* These tests will be useful in determining beliefs and values.
- *Depth interviews and group discussions :* These methods can be used to discover the emerging cultural characteristics.
- *Observation :* Through this method it is possible to gain valuable insights into more obscure aspects of culture which may not be amenable to direct questioning (some of consumers' behaviours are ritualized which will be noted through observation).
- *Content analysis :* This technique uses an analysis of past and present media to know the cultural changes. This analysis can be carried out on a cross-cultural basis also.

Characteristics of Culture

(1) Culture is a Learned Response : As a human being living in the society, the consumer is required to behave in a particular way as desired by the socio cultural environment. Consumers/individuals learn to behave through experience. The cultural field represents a set of stimuli and a set of responses appropriate to the stimuli. The individual will be either rewarded or punished, directly or indirectly for adopting responses to relevant stimulus situations. This procedure continues till the individual learns to match his set of responses to the cultural ideology.

Right from his childhood, a person has observed his parents showing respect to elders and maintaining a respectful distance while talking to them. This custom gets imprinted in the mind of the child and is carried over even when he becomes an adult.

(2) Culture Includes Inculcated Values : Cultural norms and values are inculcated and passed on from generation to generation by specific groups and institutions. Much of our behaviour is determined by culture. There are various institutions like an individual's family, institutes imparting education, religious organizations, customs, traditions, etc., which help in transmitting cultural values, beliefs, traditions and customs from generation to generation.

Because of the multifaceted nature of culture, certain techniques such as Projective tests, Attitude measurement tests, Depth interviews and Group discussions, Observations and Content analysis are used to measure it.

For instance, in South India, young girls by tradition are required to learn classical dance and music. In rural areas North Indian girls traditionally dress up in Salwar Kameez, whereas, the South Indian girls are mostly found wearing 'skirt and blouse or sarees".

These traditionally inculcated values and beliefs are also reflected and seen in the behaviour and consumption pattern of the individual related to his/her eating habits, style of dressing, etc.

(3) Culture is a Social Phenomenon : An individual's way of thinking and behaving is governed by the society and the group he interacts with. The process of rewarding normative behaviour and punishing deviant behaviour is the outcome of the acculturation (learning a culture of which one is not native) and socialization (learning one's own native culture). The society punishes individuals with deviant behaviour or non conformers by:

Examples of instrumental and terminal values

- staring at the person who may walk on the public road with an arm around his girlfriend's shoulders and make the couple feel uncomfortable or
- stare and comment on a young woman who may attend her friend's marriage wearing a shirt and pant rather than the traditional silk saree or Salwar Kameez.

Drinking is considered as a 'taboo' and condemned by the society. If a young boy takes to drinks, the society will condemn the parents of the boy saying "you have not done an adequate job of socialization!"

Nevertheless, today with India being recognized as a global economy, some of the typical social acceptance of an individual's behaviour have undergone changes. This could probably be attributed to the mingling of various cultures. For instance, women are working as top executives earning on par or more than their male counterparts, traveling around on official work and so on. With exposure to global lifestyles and culture, there could be changes observed in her style of dressing.

Thus, more than an individual's way of thinking and behaving, it is the group (society) behaviour which constitutes culture.

(4) Culture is Gratifying and Continues for a Long Time : The society rewards people whose behaviour are gratifying for its members. In India, people have a lot a faith in the preachings of various religious heads. These religious heads are able to communicate and speak about the customs, traditional values and beliefs to the public through religious discourses. Such people are given due importance and recognition for contributing to the welfare of the society. The respect and gratification for those who continue this practice goes down from generation to generation. This is also a part of our culture.

The characteristics of culture indicate that it is a learned response, a social phenomenon, inculcates values, is gratifying, are similar and yet different and prescribes certain ideal standards of behaviour.

(5) Cultures are Similar and yet Different : All the cultures across the world will address certain common (or similar) aspects. *For example,* a few of the elements found in most of the societies could be a calendar, cooking, education, family, body gestures, rituals, customs etc. However in each society there could be variations in the nature and practice of these elements. An understanding of these elements can help marketers in analysing the consumer behaviour of the particular society.

(6) Culture Prescribes the Ideal Standards of Behavior : Each culture prescribes certain specific do's and dont's of behaviour which members of that society are ideally supposed to follow. These could take the form of norms, guidelines or sanctions. Style of dressing, consumption of food and drinks etc. These will to a great extent act as a guide to the prescribed culture.

FIGURE 8.4

CHARACTERISTICS OF CULTURE

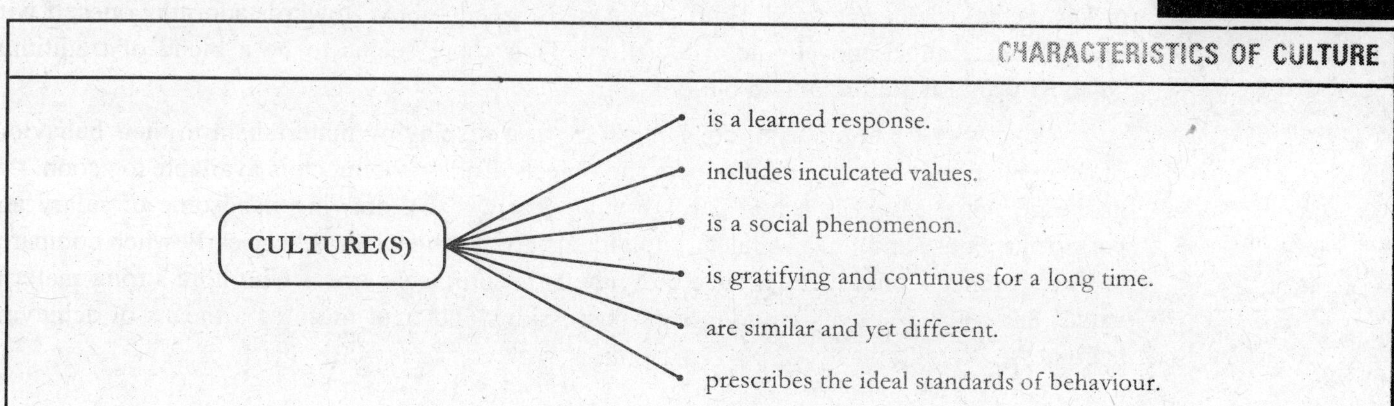

As seen above culture is responsible for inculcating a particular behavioural pattern in an individual. Thus, an understanding of the role played by the culture in shaping a person's behavioural pattern will help the marketing manager to cope with the non rational aspects of consumer behaviour.

TRADITIONAL AND CHANGING INDIAN VALUES

With the passage of time, India has been witness to changes occuring in some of the values practiced. These are briefly discussed below.

Diversity in Religions, Culture, Customs

In India, we have people belonging to various religious groups-Hindus, Muslims, Christians, Sikhs, Buddhists, Jains and Parsis. Alongside there are also various sects, sub sects, castes and sub castes. Each religion has its own customs, rituals and practices which are followed for generations together. Even there are diversities in the languages spoken across the various states alongwith hundreds of dialects. Few of the changes can be seen in the form of amalgams of languages that have risen due to floating population

With the passage of time, India has been witness to changes in some of the values practiced. These are seen in the form of: diversity in religions, culture and customs, traditionalism and materialism, orientation towards youthfulness, importance of self-fulfillment and 'mindset of scarcity', giving way to consumerism'.

As mentioned earlier in the chapter almost every religious community has its own traditional style of dresses, ornaments and jewellery. Of course, with the changes in demographics, many of the rituals have undergone changes. For instance, traditionally wearing heavy jewellary was the trend. However, now light, trendy designed jewellery is preferred, keeping in tune to the changing times.

Even in the case of food habits, rice is the staple food in the Southern states while, wheat is consumed more in the Northern states. Of course, there is seen visible changes in food consumption with people in Southern cities consuming wheat products as co food items and certain South Indian delicacies becoming popular in the North.

Traditionalism and Materialism

Traditionalism refers to more emphasis on family patriotic values and work culture. Indians have always been family oriented. Even when far away from home, we have tried to integrate the family values and the new lifestyles and this is extended even to the work-culture. The family values of respect for seniors, women and the importance of family togetherness is kept in mind while reaching out for personal development and self actualization.

The ads of Club Mahindra Holidays, Cox and Kings Travel etc. emphasize family outings together. The belief that purchase of Gold and Jewellery on specific days (like Akshaya Tritiya or Dhanteras) is still practiced. While there is also seen a move-towards adorning oneself with light, delicate and trendy branded jewellery. Thus there seems to be a blend of traditional customs with a more pragmatic outlook.

Along with traditionalism, consumers are also displaying materialism in their behaviour of accumulation of wealth and products and objects. Today, too much is available too soon. *i.e.*, goals are achieved easily when one is young (early 20's), drawing handsome of salary and perks (plus house and four wheeler). Individuals are tasting success very early when compared to their parents. Consequently, such individuals become consumers who hold strong material values and place a lot of importance to possessions and treat these as a means of achieving happiness.

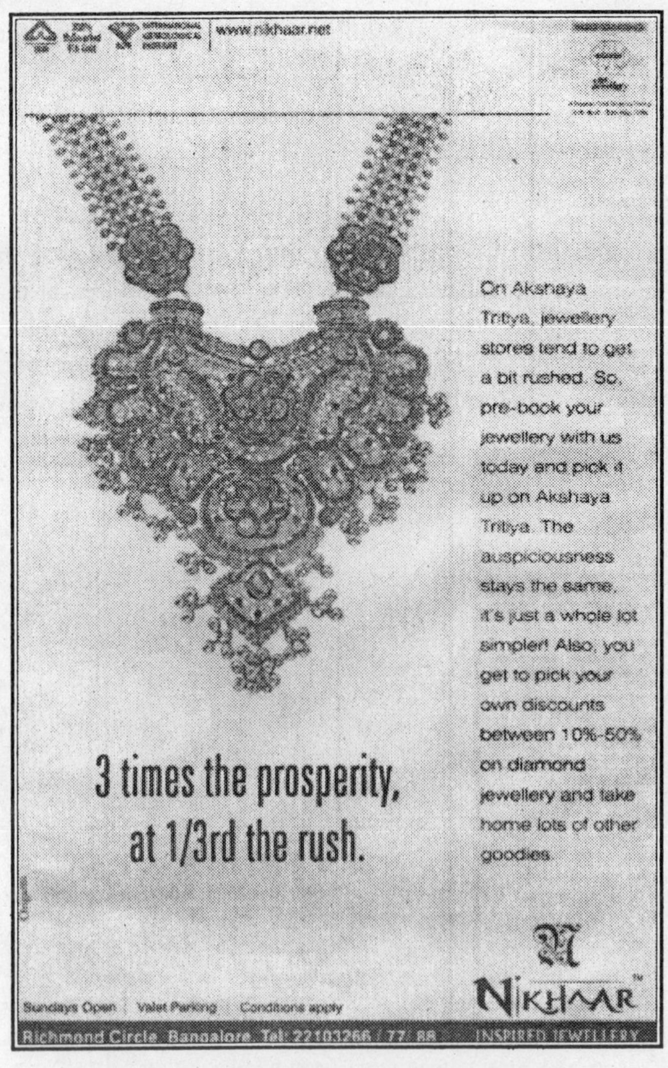

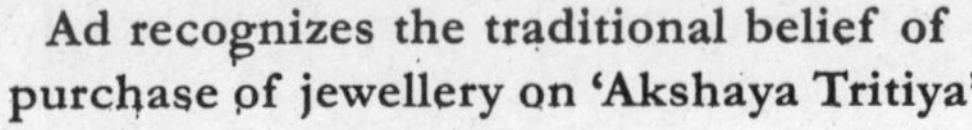
Ad recognizes the traditional belief of purchase of jewellery on 'Akshaya Tritiya'

Ad shows concern for 'family togetherness'

Orientation Towards Youthfulness

With exposure to global lifestyle, some of the western values seem to have caught on with the Indians. We have always in the past revered the elders and their suggestions and experiences used to be accepted with great respect. However, now there is a mature market (acknowledged by marketers) who have developed a passion to look younger and fitter than their biological age.

Importance of Self-fulfillment

Earlier anything that was material, be it containers or disposables had value. Today materiality is no long viewed as a mortal object and 'Disposability' is gaining acceptance as a concept.

As more individuals have been able to fulfill their dreams either through opportunities abroad or by pursuing it here, now there is seen a desire in them towards self- fulfillment. They have tasted worldly success through purchasing material goods and enhancing their lifestyle. Hence they are seeking a deeper satisfaction from their day-to-day living. More than the monetary aspect they are giving importance to personal enhancement and a meaningful life. For this, they are focusing on:

- Being physically healthy and fit.

- Alongwith work, healthy diversions by pursuing their hobbies, or get involved in other activities as an expression of self fulfillment.
- A yearning to learn more about one's culture and giving back something to the society by undertaking social work activities.

'Mindset of Scarcity' has given way to Consumerism

In the pre liberalization era, there existed a mindset of scarcity partly because of the 'socialistic leaning' that India had as a nation and partly due to the 'frugality' code *i.e.,* at that time consumers had little or no choice when it came to products. Hence consumers continued to use products long after they were out of vogue. In fact, Indian housewives were seen recycling Amulspray, Farex and Dalda tins, using them for storage since it (tins) had value.

Taste in clothes is also dependant on the specific cultural influence

However, the post liberalization scenario shows a move towards consumerism. Now the term 'value' can be said to be associated with the concept of disposability. Earlier anything that was material, be it containers or disposables had value. Today, materiality is no long viewed as a mortal object and *'Disposability'* is gaining acceptance as a concept. This can be attributed to a growing sense that they (consumers) can afford to spend today. Purchase of products or services has become a chronometer measuring instrument of success. There is a social status in newness. Consumers have developed the culture of disposability. Till around the mid 1990's the owner of a Bajaj scooter wouldn't want to part with it even after 15 years. But today consumers are willing to trade their cars at the first given opportunity. Even in case of buying houses, around a decade ago the house one bought was considered to be a once in lifetime purchase. Today, people buy a house, live in it for sometime and then sell it and buy a bigger one.

This ability to dispose off high priced products at regular intervals can be largely due to the growing purchasing power of the Indian middle class, easy availability of consumer finance, the steep drop in prices of most products and the firm belief that the next thing (new purchase) will be infinitely better.

SUB CULTURE 

Within the larger society there are specialties or subsystems of values resulting in a considerable variation in behaviour pattern, which exist within the total culture.

People generally try to avoid behaviour frowned upon by the society. Thus culture is universal in man's experience but each local manifestation of it is unique. However, within the larger society there are specialties or sub systems of values resulting in a considerable variation in behaviour pattern, which exist within the total culture. Rarely do we find perfect homogeneity in the content of melting pots. Similarly, we also find subcultures within a society.

Sub cultures can be said to be sets of learned beliefs, values, attitudes, habits and forms of behaviour that are shared by subsets of a society and are transmitted from generation to generation within each subset. Members of a subculture do conform to most of the norms of the dominant wide culture but deviate from those which are not compatible to the norms of the sub culture.

Marketers have begun to segment larger societies into smaller sub groups or sub culture groups that are homogenous in relation to certain customs and ways of behaving – say sociocultural or demographic variables. For instance in India, few of the sub cultural categories and their variations are shown in Table 8.4.

TABLE 8.4

SUBCULTURAL CATEGORY CLASSIFICATION BASED ON CERTAIN VARIABLES

Subcultural Category	Variations (Examples)
Religion	Hindu, Christian, Muslim, Parsi, Jain, etc.
Geographic location	North, South, East, West
Age	Elderly (old), teenage (young), middle age
Gender/sex	Male, female
Occupation	Service, Professionals, Businessman, etc.
Social class (status)	Upper, middle, lower

Though the above table shows a broad segmentation of the society into various sub cultures, any group that shares common belief, values and customs may also be categorized as a sub culture. For instance, college graduates, unmarried working women in a working women's hostel, etc.

Sub cultural Division and Consumption Pattern

The individuals belonging to a particular subculture may show different consumption pattern related to their lifestyle, functional ability, food preference reading habits, purchase of specific brands, purchase time etc.

The individuals of a particular sub culture may show different consumption patterns related to their lifestyle, financial ability, food preferences, reading habits, purchase of specific brands in a particular product category (brand loyalty), purchase time, store patronage, etc.

India presents a picture of varying styles and consumption pattern. Each state and religion has got its own traditional style of dressing, wearing ornaments, food preferences, etc. Certain communities do not accept non vegetarian food, while among the other communities, non vegetarian food is popular with slight differences – For the Muslims, eating pork is a taboo, while Christians find this a delicious food. Moreover, there are cultural taboos related to the consumption of certain products like liquor, etc.

There is also a lot of difference observed in the consumption pattern related to rural-urban sub cultural division. This is more visible in their tastes and preferences in food items, housing, clothing, home furnishing, transport vehicle used, recreation and leisure activities, saving pattern, etc.

Another visible sub cultural variation is the social class distinction based on the *economic status*. The social class can broadly be divided into three classes, namely, the upper or affluent class, the middle class and the lower class. The affluent class is only a negligible minority. Their consumption of real luxury items is more prominent as compared to their purchase of the necessary items. At the other end is the lower class or the poor sections of the society, who though large in size, have very little purchasing power. Their consumption pattern will not be of much significance because they are hardly able to make ends meet and hence will spend money only on the bare necessities of life. However, it is the middle class, whose consumption pattern is of interest to the marketers today. Marketers have noticed that it is the middle class which forms the demand basis for most of the products. A notable aspect of the middle class consumer is that inspite of the regional, linguistic and cultural diversities in India, they generally follow a common pattern of lifestyle and buying behaviour.

Some of the *middle class consumers* are security seeking or security conscious class. He/she wants social security along with economic and emotional security. He is receptive to new ideas and will welcome innovations only if convinced that these will satisfy his sense of security and help to improve his economic status and social relationships. The success stories of *ICICI Prudential, HDFC Life insurance* are because of the brand being able to create awareness towards planning for enjoying life after retirement. Usually, living on a fixed income and maintaining a reasonably good lifestyle, the middle class consumer is readily acceptable to the credit facilities made possible through the credit card. This consumer is also very *status/prestige* conscious and is always striving to rise higher in the social class. The middle class is also seen as a home loving person who enjoys indulging in purchasing products, which will add to the 'joy and comforts' of his family.

Thus, understanding of behaviour pattern of people based on sub cultural variations will enable the marketer to work out marketing programmes suitable to each sub culture category of consumers.

Ad appeals to consumers who want a blend of tradition and trend too.

Another sub cultural variation is the social class distinction based on the economic status. Accordingly there are three social class divisions: the upper or affluent class, the middle class and the lower class.

Sub cultural Effect on Advertising Media and Messages

As with social classes, sub cultures may be attracted to particular media often designed for that specific group. The advertiser chooses the advertising media to carry the advertising message depending upon the *desired reach, frequency and impact needed* to achieve the advertising objectives.

They usually use television while trying to reach out to housewives and teenagers. While for marketing home appliances like vacuum cleaners, cooking range, microwave oven, washing machines, refrigerators, etc. marketing decision makers like to use media which has the potential for demonstration, visualization, explanation, colour and believability. Since the sub culture category for the above products comprise of housewives, working spinsters, young married working couples, working bachelors, etc. – the most effective advertising media would be a combination of print, visual/mass communication along with demonstration. Television offers

Culture re-inforces values and the consumption pattern is influenced by it.

the perfect setting for eliciting the affective-or hot responses and the print media is better suited for appealing to rational or cold responses. For instance, *Titan Industries* had used television for its emotionally packed commercials on the theme of gifting a watch *Bandan Raga range* but switched to print media when it had to display the product and announce special schemes.

Another example can be of the *U.S. based lingerie maker, Lovable Inc.,* when it decided to enter the Indian market through a *joint venture with Maxwell Apparel.* This company discovered its sub cultural market comprising of the usage occasion and the stage in the women's life cycle -student, working woman, bride, mother, non working housewife, etc., played a crucial role in determining the choice of the lingerie. This information was used and various value media, relevant to each of the above sub culture market segments was used by the company to convey messages highlighting the need and experience of feeling thrilled at being noticed, the comfort, indulgence and functionality aspect of the product.

As with social class, subcultures may be attracted to a particular media often designed for that specific group. "The advertiser chooses the advertising media to carry the advertising message depending upon the desired reach, frequency and impact needed".

Marketers need to work out and identify consumer insight into what they desire. Long back, while wanting to be different, the *Onida Devil* had worked wonders for the brand, through its effective tagline 'Neighbour's Envy Owner's Pride. Subsequently this campaign had to be discontinued when it lost its charisma. Some time in early 2005 Onida brought back its devil in a new avatar.

Advertisers have to do a lot of proper planning in its media and communication strategy for the brand to succeed. Long back Real Value had launched *'Ceasefire fire extinguishers'* and communicated about the brand attributes through ad spends on television and print media. The product brand had been tremendously successful. However, when the same company launched another innovative product *'Real Value Vaccumised containers,'* it failed to click in the market. This was in spite of huge ad spends and massive advertising on T.V. This was probably because the company had failed to understand that for years together the Indian women preferred to store food in containers, just as her mother, so there was no real demand for Real Value's Product in the Indian Market.

Depending on the sub cultural category, the marketer will have to identify those who belong to the particular subculture, what are their reading habits, lifestyle, stage of family life cycle, preferences towards media, etc. This information will be required to break up each of the sub cultural group into smaller segments that can be reached through a specific media. Thereafter, needs of the market segments need to be communicated through a suitable media, so as to be able to build a brand image and also gain a competitive edge over rival firms.

CROSS CULTURAL MARKETING ANALYSIS

Today, various companies are going for cross cultural marketing or marketing in a big way. The reasons behind such a move are (1) pushed by poor opportunities in the domestic market (2) pulled by better and superior opportunities abroad. There are certain characteristic features of a firm going global:

Cross cultural marketing will facilitate marketers to understand the psychological, social and cultural aspects of foreign consumers they wish to target and design effective marketing strategies accordingly.

- Advantageous economies of scale.
- Access to marketing/manufacturing bases across global borders.
- Availability of resources and capability to absorb huge losses.
- Product/technology clout.
- Cost and differentiation advantages.

Inspite of the characteristic features of a global firm, there is a great element of risk involved in cross cultural marketing. We have so far discussed in this book, about the challenges faced by marketing manager within the domestic market, on account of various social, cultural, economic factors which govern an individual consumer's purchase decision. So one can imagine the dynamic world markets, where each country has got its own environmental, cultural, political legal and economic determinants! The dynamic markets of the various countries can be understood only by studying the respective people, their life pattern, their sensibilities, their social interactions, values, beliefs, their faith and fancies. Thus, one can easily say that it is the above socio cultural dimension of the global markets which contributes most to the complexity of international cross cultural marketing.

Although advances in modern sciences, technological improvement through effective modern communication network and logistics have helped in slowly bridging the gap between the different countries, the cultural diversity between countries still continues to exist. So cross cultural marketing analysis means getting to know a country's history, social and cultural heritage, beliefs, value systems and the code of conduct of its people carried forward from generations together. These are all components of a country's cultural environment.

Cross *cultural marketing* is defined as *"the effort to determine to what extent the consumers of two or more nations are similar or different". (Consumer Behavior, L. G. Schiffman, Leslie Lazar Kanuk, 1997, pp. 474)"* This will facilitate marketers to understand the psychological, social and cultural aspects of foreign consumers they wish to target, so as to design effective marketing strategies for each of the specific national markets involved.

As we have seen in the above discussion earlier, culture is alive, moving and ever changing. Cultural influence is deep rooted and has far reaching consequences which can be seen in the pattern of decision making and consumption of the individual consumer. Thus, sizing up the cultural diversity of various markets of the world is a mammoth task before the marketers. The way foreign consumers think about and use certain products must also be verified before going into the marketing programme fully.

Given below are a few of the differences in the behaviour pattern in the consumer markets over the world:

Sizing up the cultural diversity of various markets of the world is a mammoth task before the marketer. The way foreign consumers think and use certain products is to be verified before going into marketing programme fully.

- The average Frenchman uses almost twice as many cosmetics and beauty aids as does his wife.
- Women in Tanzania would not give eggs to their children for fear of making them bald or impotent.
- Italian children like to eat a bar of chocolate between two-slices of bread as a snack.
- The Germans and the French eat more packaged branded spaghetti than the Italians.
- Using the shampoo or hair conditioners had been a new concept for Russians, who washed their hair with soap. So when Procter and Gamble introduced their **Wash and Go**, a combination of shampoo with conditioner. Russians mistook the claim as 'air conditioner Wash' and got quickly popularised into a euphemism for washing down a vodka before heading out.
- Consumers in Peru and Bolivia cannot drink milk because they do not retain an enzyme enabling them to digest it, so they use powdered milk donated by the USA to whitewash houses.
- Venezuelan women use to wash their laundry by using slivers of bar soap they kneaded together to form a paste.
- In South East Asia, in some regions, people follow the custom of chewing betal nuts to achieve social prestige of darkly stained teeth. So toothpaste makers find it difficult to sell tooth paste by using the basic appeal-getting teeth whiter.

Similarly, business norms and behaviour also vary from country to country. For example:

- In the United States (USA) people put more pressure on results, want things to take place faster and believe in direct communication while taking business decisions.
- In the United Kingdom (UK) business talk is always from top to down and hierarchical. During business negotiations there is a tendency to avoid confrontations and disagreements. This could be one of the reasons whey they are indirect, reserved and tactical.

- In China, for business approaches, Chinese, emphasise on maintaining order and avoiding of chaos.
- In South America, all business talk is held in close physical proximity with the other members. Sometimes almost nose to nose. Whereas, American business executives prefer to keep a reasonable distance during business talk.
- In face to face communication Japanese business executives rarely say 'no' to an American business executive. Americans get frustrated and don't know where they stand. Moreover, Americans come to the point quickly, whereas Japanese business executives need time to mutually discuss the issue and take time before taking a decision. They (Japanese) instead of discussing profit tend to establish a long term business relationship that benefits all partners.

Thus, each country has its own tradition, culture, preferences, mores and taboos, which the marketers must understand before entering the global market.

FIGURE 8.5

A FRAMEWORK FOR DETERMINING STANDARD MARKETING STRATEGY

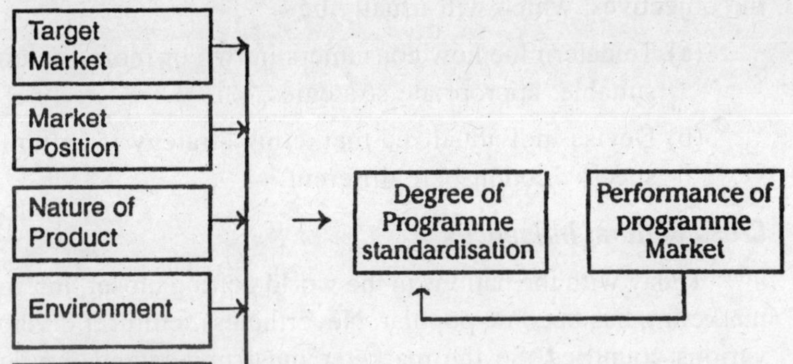

(1) Target market – geographic area, economic factors.
(2) Market position – market development, market condition, competition.
(3) Nature of product – type of product, product positioning.
(4) Environment (factors) – physical, legal, political and marketing infrastructure.
(5) Organizational factors – corporate orientation, Head office – subsidiary relation, delegation of authority.

(*Source : Consumer Behaviour* L.G. Schiffman & Leslie L. Kanuk, 1997)

A marketer will have to study various dimensions of the global market while formulating a suitable marketing strategy. For this he will have to study the target market, understand the market position, the nature of the product, the country's political legal environment and so on.

A marketer will have to consider various dimensions of the global market while formulating a suitable marketing strategy. He has at first to study the target market, *i.e.*, determine the wide geographical area to be covered, and the economic environment comprising namely its products and service requirements, income level, standard of living, employment level, etc. He has to understand the market position in terms of whether it is a growing market, the market condition, relationship between the demand and supply factors, the level of competition, etc. What is the nature of the product – is the product a new or an innovative product? If so how to position it so as to get a price advantage alongwith increasing demand? Along with the above factors certain equally important aspects have also to be considered. Firstly, the *environmental factors*. Nations differ greatly in their political legal environment. So the marketers have to determine –

how is the nation's attitude towards international marketing? (encouraging or hostile), Has the nation got a stable or fluctuating exchange rate? What is the government's attitude towards monetary regulations? Has the nation got a stable government who will continue for a longer period in the future? Has the foreign country got an efficient bureaucratic framework for assisting foreign companies? There are also other vital aspects to be considered by the marketer. Each individual firm's *corporate orientation* with regards to effective delegation of authority and relationship between the Head office and the subsidiary office also assumes importance before a company takes the decision to go for cross cultural marketing.

Cross Cultural Marketing Objectives and Policies

Before entering the global market, the company must determine its international marketing objectives and policies.

There are many options before a company planning to enter a foreign market. It can gain entry as a domestic exporter or as a foreign importer or as a foreign government – solicit the firm to sell abroad. At times the firm may think of entering the global market because it sees better marketing opportunities in other countries when compared to the domestic market or it might face over capacity, which they feel can be utilized for global marketing.

Since cultural diversity continues to exit between the various countries, the marketer must understand the cultural variances and nuances and respond to them in a way that is appealing to the consumer of that country.

Irrespective of the reason for cross cultural marketing way, the firm will have to work out the objectives, which will usually be :

(a) To determine how consumers in two or more societies are similar/different and devise suitable, appropriate strategies.

(b) Devise individualized marketing strategy if cultural beliefs, values and customs of a specific country are different.

Cross Cultural Influences

Today with the nations in the world getting closer, international marketing or cross cultural marketing has become popular. Nevertheless, cultural diversity continues to exist between the various countries. So the marketer must understand the cultural variances and nuances and respond to them in a way that is appealing to the consumer of that country. The success stories of companies such as *Hindustan Unilever Ltd, (HUL), Procter & Gamble, Colgate-Palmolive, Kellogs, Coca-Cola, IBM, Pizza Hut, Pizza Corner, McDonalds* etc. shows how they have identified the cultural variations and suitably modified their marketing strategy to suit Indian consumer's requirement. They typically need to '*Think Global act Local.*

Identify Cultural Variations Affecting Consumer Behaviour

Broadly we will discuss about six cross cultural factors influencing marketing strategies abroad:

(1) ***Consumer Customs and Values :*** Americans have a certain value system oriented towards achievement materialism, individual and youthfulness. However, in many Asian countries acceptance of one's place in society, is more important than individual initiative in influencing behaviour. Americans, while carrying out business deals structure their work schedule for the day and pleasure based on business. While, in European countries, people have the tendency to mix business with pleasure and arriving late for the appointment may be the norm. In India also it will not be unusual to find business transactions being carried out in an informal environment where business and pleasure are mixed. Hyundai motors when it launched *Santro* in India, had used 'the tall boy' image, with Shahrukh Khan endorsing and communicating about the car's features, which would suit a small family. This new design and car got a overwhelming response and even replaced Maruti800 as a first time car.

Vestas has been successful in its pursuit of international marketing.

Cultural Values Can Affect Consumers Product Preferences and Product Usage : In late 1990 on the one hand there were a lot of MNC fast food providers like *McDonalds, KFCs, Wimpys and Dominos* trying to woo the Indian housewife to their product launches. And on the other hand, the local Kirana shops' shelves were packed with the so called convenience food packets of tomato purees, garlic pastes, onion pastes, pre cooled pulao and the like from *'Kissan Dabur.'* The instant protein cereal mix *Kellogs* was also easily available at various outlets. However, the consumers' response to these convenience foods was far from satisfactory for the marketers. Research and insight into the lack of usage of convenience foods (to the extent it should) indicated the role of culture, values and lifestyle.

Cultural values can affect consumer's product preferences and product usage. Research into a country's language, its meanings and interpretations will help the marketers to have a better understanding of the cultural variances and nuances and respond with a suitable form of communication.

In the West, consumers prefer to use semi processed or processed foods due to the convenience factor. In India, traditionally, the wife manifests this aspect by spending time and effort in cooking nutritional fresh food for her family. Secondly, convenience food was perceived to have high status value and so only meant for the so called elite classes lifestyle.

Subsequently through appropriate communication strategy the companies were able to convince households the benefits of using convenience food. And today packaged food industry is doing very well. In early February 2007, Norwegian consumers goods giant *Orkla* acquired the Bangalore based *MTR*, which could give the former a strong foothold in the fast growing packaged food Asian Market.

(2) ***Language & Meaning :*** Language is one of the major aspects of culture. Research into the country's language – its meanings and interpretations will help the marketer to have a better understanding of the cultural variances and nuances and respond with a suitable form of communication easily understood by the consumer.

(3) ***Differences in Market Segmentation Opportunities :*** Even if a company has a superior product in terms of quality, cost, service, technology clout, financial muscle and a brand equity in the domestic market, understanding the marketing opportunities in the global market and doing a suitable market segmentation will help the firm to do well internationally. *For example,* Readymade garments is a segment where India has a strong competitive advantage in terms of low labour cost when taking into consideration the total cost of production of the readymade garments. To take advantage of this aspect, some of the Indian marketers have tried to establish their presence in global markets.

For example, Arvind Mills has established an international network for marketing garments. *Bhilwaras* have set up *Bhilwara Overseas* Ltd in Douglas UK, to market its products in Europe *Zodiac* is trying to market Indian brands such as Globe *Trotter* and *Mark Gibaldi* abroad. It has set up exclusive shops with wholesalers in India.

Cross cultural analysis reveals differences in the criteria for evaluating products and services and this aspect cannot be ignored by the marketer for cross cultural marketing. Across the world, one can find differences in the consumption pattern not only among various cultures but subcultures too.

(4) Differences in the Criteria for Evaluating Products and Services : India has tremendous scope in the 'Textile and readymade garment' category. This is because of the availability of quality natural fabrics at competitive prices. However, the 'quality' aspect is not given due importance by the Indian firms. This fact was emphasized by the 'Japan Apparel Manufacturers' Association'. The Japanese firms are very particular about quality assurance. However, a survey done by the above mentioned association revealed that there was a fundamental difference in the perceived evaluation of the products 'quality'. The report from the survey says" Apparel firms in India believe that the quality of the fabric determines the quality of the garment, whereas, the Japanese think that every aspect of the garment from sewing to packaging decides quality". The above example shows that cross cultural analysis reveals differences in the criteria for evaluating products and services and this aspect cannot be ignored by the marketer for cross cultural marketing.

(5) Differences in Consumption Pattern and Perceived Benefits of Products and Services : It has been seen that leather and leather products constitute an expanding category in India's exports. This has been because India has a competitive advantage in a durable product like leather. The reason behind this is that India has one of the largest livestock population in the world. Thus procurement of the best quality raw hides and skins is a big advantage for India. Another positive aspect is the availability of inexpensive skilled manpower. Moreover, leading global leather goods manufacturers such as Italy, South Korea and Taiwan were forced to curtail production due to rising cost of production and labour charges. Here again, India scored over her competitors because labour is comparatively cheaper here.

The consumption pattern in the world markets show that the demand for leather and leather products is rapidly increasing with footwear, belts, bags and wallets being considered as an inseparable part of the every day attire. However, for several years, India had been exporting her leather in the raw form to competitors, who made products out of them and sold in the same markets at cheaper prices. Since India had been exporting without a brand name, she was exporting only a commodity. It was perceived that India lags behind as far as adequate product design, quality of craftsmanship and inadequate supply base for handling large volumes were concerned. Thus, in order to assure its global customers about the perceived value added benefits received on buying Indian leather products, India could go for a tie up with well known companies with well known brand names and gain the benefit of ongoing brands and a ready marketing infrastructure.

Study by a Swiss software consultant found that there was great potential for Indian software exports to Switzerland, where the software market is estimated to be around SFr 6 billion. The consultant further reiterated that the market could be penetrated through a local partner only. *TCS* followed this route by tying up with a local company Teknosoft and won a contract from the *Swiss Securities and Exchange Agency* (SEGA).

Similarly, China has got a huge domestic, market in IT, but they want the software in their language. Seeing this as an opportunity, Infosys hired Chinese software personnel to penetrate the Chinese market.

(6) Differences in the Economic and Cultural Social Condition and Family Structure : Across the world, one could find differences in the consumption pattern not only among various cultures but subcultures too.

Professor W. Lloyd Warner of the University of Chicago, based on certain investigations carried out by him had divided the United States society into six social classes. (Consumer Behavior, Peter D. Bennet, Harold H Kassarjian, PHI, 1987, pp 113-115.)

Professor Warner had broadly divided the society into six social classes: Upper- upper, Lower –upper, Upper-middle, Lower-middle, Upper-lower and Lower-lower classes. The social class differences were worked out by taking into consideration parameters such as occupation, source of income, type of house, and neighbourhood. This study was carried out long back and many social changes must have occurred in the United States there after. Further, now with the recession affecting the global economy at large there could be many changes occurring in all cultures and sub-cultures across the world.

Nevertheless, marketers have found such social class differences to be useful in explaining consumer behaviour variations in relation to *(a)* preferences for products and brands *(b)* store patronage or shopping behaviour *(c)* exposure to promotion media and *(d)* saving and the use of credit for purchasing products.

Marketers have found social class differences to be useful in explaining consumer behaviour variations in relation to (a) preferences for products and brands (b) store patronage or shopping behaviour (c) exposure to promotion media and (d) saving and the use of credit for purchasing products.

Research has indicated that consumers prefer price-off and extra product free rather than getting a promotion item of the same value. Many MNCs have used this strategy in their promotional offers. Both *Coke & Pepsi* generally run the promotion in the summer on their 1.5 Lt. PET Bottles. The original 300ml bottle was the result of a consumer promotion by *Thums-up* offering *Maha Thums up* at the same price as 250 ml.

Fritolay carried out a successful promotion in foreign market, which was also replicated in the Indian market. Little Kids had gone crazy with round plastic coins (or Tazos) freely offered with *Frito Lays*. Although the monetary value was not much it had created brand awareness and tremendous excitement among the consumers. Similarly temporary tattoos were given with bubble gum brands like *Boomer*, which also created a similar impact on the children (users).

Keeping in mind the importance of a festival like, Diwali in India, in 2002, Samsung India came out with a *'Phir-se-Phod Ke Dekho'* offer, where the consumers got a coconut with each purchase of a Samsung product. There was a guaranteed prize along with a surprise gift inside the coconut (symbolizes cultural value). These gifts ranged from products of Samsung to all expenses paid trip to the cricket World Cup in South Africa.

During Mark Knopfler's tour to India, *Pepsi* ran a promotion where winners get to share a Pepsi with Mark Knopfler. This only added to *Pepsi's* trendy image something which the brand strives for.

Thus, while working out promotional activities to be carried out in international markets, marketers will need to develop a strong international trend spotting and consumer insight tracking mechanism to understand what will excite the target consumers of those countries.

This shows that the international marketer must be aware of the internationalized norms of the social class and the cultural issues prevalent in that country and then prepare marketing communications accordingly.

Apart from the above specific issues, the international marketer has to probe and find out about the market structure and conditions and also identify the marketing research possibilities in the international markets, where he plans to enter. In other words, there is an urgent need for a more systematic and conceptual cross cultural analysis of the psychological, social and cultural characteristics concerning the consumption habits of foreign consumers.

PROBLEMS IN CROSS CULTURAL MARKETING

The following are generally the problems related to cross cultural marketing:

Problems related to Symbols, Colour and Names Selection

In cross cultural marketing, there could be problems related to symbols, colours and names selection. For, usage of symbols can affect the consumer behaviour colours is another sensitive issue. Marketers will have to weigh the legal availability of a brand name as well as its acceptability.

Usage of **symbols** also affect the consumers' behaviour. For instance, the symbol of two elephants signifies bad luck in many parts of Africa. So *Carlsberg* was forced to add a third label for its Elephant Bees. In most of the Chinese ads a moon is shown as it symbolizes good luck in that country. In a country like India, which is God fearing, Maruti Suzuki uses the term and symbol of Maruti (God of Wind). While shooting for a film Aapka Suroor, (in which popular musician and singer Himesh Reshammiya debuted as an actor,) in Germany, the Bollywood had used a church in the German city of Cologne. The members of the diocese of Cologne had shown wide protests in the usage of the church as a film unit They argued that a church is a symbol of 'the house of God' and cannot be used as a function room.

Colour also is a sensitive issue. Pink is associated with femininity in the United States, while in many other parts of the world yellow is considered to be feminine. In India, Vastu Shastra influences choice of colours to a great extent. Blue indicates calmness or a cooling quotient, white signifies purity, yellow energies oneself and so on.

Most of the car manufacturers use different brand names that match the particular country's consumer segment's needs. Further, the auto brands are sometimes positioned in different segments across various (international) markets. So the brand name should be such that it fits in with the needs of that particular segment. For instance, GM's *Aveo* is positioned as a small car in America while India it is an aspirational mid level car.

While going for cross cultural marketing, marketers also weigh the legal availability of a brand name as well as its acceptability. For instance, Ford could not use the name *Everest* in India, so they used the brand name *Endeavor*. Accordingly Maruti's *Zen* in India is called *Alto* in Europe, Hyundai's *Santro* (in India) is called *Atos* in many European countries and *Getz* is called *Click* in Korea. Toyota Qualis (India) is known as *Kijang* in Indonesia and General Motors *Optra* becomes *Buick* in China and *Lacetti* in Korea.

Hyundai India's *Santro* and *Getz* are known as *Atos* in many European Countries and *Click* in Korea respective

The marketer going for cross cultural marketing has to select the customer/market not on the basis of the superficial similarities of age or income but by using the real motivating factors that prompt them to accept or reject products. They have to select products which meet local customs and tastes.

Arvind Saxena, Head Marketing Hyundai Motors India, says that situations where it becomes difficult to use the name of the launch country due to cultural sensitivities attached, then the company has to either pick a name from its global portfolio or come up with something totally new.

Problems Related to Product Selection

Under the fast changing socio economic environment, bringing with it its own psycho-cultural upheavals, the international customer is a truly moving target today. Thus the marketer going for cross cultural marketing has to select the customers/market not on the basis of the superficial similarities of age or income, but by using the real motivating factors that prompt them to accept or reject products. The customer's purchasing decisions are the outcome of the complex interplay of environmental factors like culture, social class, personal influences, family and situations and of individual differences in resources, involvement levels, knowledge, attitudes, personality and values. Today's customers are willing to try more products and brands. But the international marketers have to select products to meet local customs and tastes. This is more valid for consumer products such as food products, soft drinks, cosmetics and personal care items, since acceptability of these products depend on cultural characteristics. *For example,* the *Kellogg* of the U.S., a veteran of the global breakfast cereals market has realized that its initial reading of would be customers in India was incorrect. The firm needed to reanalyze how to drive the Indian consumer to accept readymade breakfast cereals in place of his hot, fresh, cereal based, fat free rice idli.

Similarly, when the Ford Escort car, a product of the joint venture between Ford Motors and Mahindra & Mahindra, during an experiment which involved draping the interiors of the Escort – as well as competitor cars in the Indian market had asked potential drivers to give their feedback on the size of the car. At that time the firm learnt that many potential users wanted the height of the roof in the rear compartment to be higher. This was because, unlike in the West – where the Escort is perceived as an owner driven car – in India, there is a high likelihood of the Escort being chauffeur driven. Due to the cultural diversity existing between various countries, the international marketer will have to examine the various cultural and environmental factors existing in a particular country. There could be differences in terms of food habits, dressing style, languages spoken, differences in interpretation of various features, product constituents, colour, etc. *For example,* the same colour may have a different meaning in various countries. The colour 'blue', in Holland conveys a feeling of warmth, in Iran 'blue' colour is associated with death, whereas in India 'blue' colour signifies purity.

Pizza Hut has positioned its product service offerings as an international brand with an Indian heart. It had to change its menu to suit the Indian customer's palate. Pizza Hut's menu includes Pizzas with added toppings such as barbecue, chicken and roasted cottage cheese, appetizers like garlic bread, soups, fresh salads, oven baked pastas and choices of ice cream sunders.

T.V. manufacturers or brands *Sony, L.G, Samsung, Sansui* among others were able to penetrate the Indian markets with their product offerings which had excellent quality, was innovative and premium in the particular market segment, with the ability to provide very good services in the field of high-tech entertainment.

Names such as *Nike, Benetton* and *Smirnoff* and *Reebok* are Global brands and the same international creativity has also gained consumer acceptance in India too. There are also other brands which though global had to adapt different positioning in the Indian market. For instance, the *Ford Escort* is at best, a mid-market brand internationally. However, in India it enjoys an extremely premium positioning status. Then there are certain other brands which are global and also positioned accordingly here. For instance, premium brands like *Piagot* and *Cartier,* which appeal to high class consumers who are aware of and aspire for a global high flying lifestyle. So marketers must not make the mistake of attempting to localize them.

So, it is the responsibility of the international marketer to develop products depending on the market conditions and ensure that these matched with the needs of the specific overseas market.

Problems Related to Promotion/Marketing Communication

In cross cultural marketing, the marketer has to interact and tackle unfamiliar target audience who speak a different language and communicate through an unfamiliar media. Thus, the marketing communication and message have to be adapted such that it will be consistent to the language and customs of the particular society.

In cross cultural marketing, the marketer has to interact and tackle unfamiliar target audience, who speak a different language and communicate through an unfamiliar media. He has to acquire a sound understanding of the demands made on him by the cultural dynamics of that market. Thus, the marketing communication and message have to be adapted such that it will be consistent to the language and customs of the particular society.

Media selection also requires international adaption because media availability varies from country to country. Moreover, apart from availability, cost and coverage of numerous ad media are some of the considerations while taking decisions related to advertising.

Usually, firms going for global marketing adopt a market oriented pricing policy. For instance, *Sony* of Japan while launching portable stereo *Walkman* priced it very low so that it is affordable to the youth world over. *Komatsu*, a Japanese earthmover equipment manufacturer had proved to be a formidable global competitor by using price, alongwith other marketing mix elements while taking on U.S mighty firm *Carterpillar Tractor*.

Established MNCs have realized that while entering a new market like India, quite contrary to their assessment, their high priced, high image brands may not sell in the same price bracket here. For instance, brands like *Nike,* and *Reebok* had to introduce products to suit the mid-price segment initially rather than focussing on the high priced product it sells globally. Even *Aiwa & Hitachi* had priced its HiFi systems and colour T.V using a low price strategy, when it had ventured in a joint venture with Baran Electronics in India.

Companies either adopt the same promotion strategy they used in the home market or change it for each local market. Because of the diversity in cultural dynamics, socio-economic setting and language, devising a suitable promotional strategy is an intricate job. The same colour, the same symbol, the same metaphor and the same brand name may convey different meanings to different cultures and their impact too may differ widely. So, not understanding the peculiarities of a particular country, and its customs and its language, could result in making a communication blunder. To cite a typical case, as narrated by David A. Ricks in his book 'Big Business Blunders'. A large MNC once made an attempt to sell its baby food in an African country. On the package of the baby food, it used the same copy used in the home market, the picture of a baby and a caption explaining the nature of the baby food inside the package. African consumers were horrified at the picture and the message. They thought the food inside was made of powdered babies. This shows that cultural dynamics and the specific buying motives of the target customers must be kept in mind while forming the promotional tool for a specific country.

Problems Related to Pricing

Basically, the techniques and principles used for pricing are more or less the same in domestic and cross cultural marketing. Firms interested in foreign markets have to take a long term view and adopt a market oriented pricing policy. They have to take into account the market conditions and each distinct market segment and formulate pricing policies suitable for each segment. Each country has its own method of deciding on the price front for foreign products. In some countries, the state administers the price for selected commodities, in some other countries, government agencies act as the sole buying and distributing agents and so on. So the marketer going for cross cultural marketing has to adjust his pricing policies according to the local economic conditions and customs.

Sometimes, marketers price their products lower in the foreign market because, they feel incomes are low so a low price is necessary to sell the products. Or the marketer may want to dump the goods *i.e.,* he may charge a lesser price in the foreign market than in the home market, since he feels that these goods have no market at home. This dumping of goods is not acceptable, and the country adopting this can also be levied a dumping tariff by the host country. The Zenith company had accused Japanese television manufacturers of dumping their T.V sets on the U.S. market.

Thus, it is always preferable for firms interested in cross cultural marketing to adopt a market oriented pricing policy suitable to the local economic environment.

Problems Related to Selection of Distribution Channels

Firms interested in marketing in foreign markets will have to take into account the market conditions and adopt a market oriented pricing policy. Further, as the distance between the producer and foreign consumer is very wide efficiency of the distribution channel becomes all the more necessary.

In cross cultural marketing, the marketer is also required to cope with problems related to selecting a suitable channel and also maintaining and motivating the consumers. Here as the distance between the producer and foreign consumer is very wide, efficiency of distribution channel becomes all the more necessary. An efficient distribution network can make up for the geographical separation.

Within a country, channels of distribution vary considerably. There are striking differences in the number and type of middlemen serving each foreign market. *For example,* to sell soap in Japan, longago Procter & Gamble had to work out a complicated distribution network.

P & G → General wholesaler → Basic product speciality wholesaler → Speciality wholesaler → Regional wholesaler → Local wholesaler → Retailers.

Having such a long distribution network may result in doubling or tripling of the consumers price over the importer's price.

Another difference lies in the size and character of retail units abroad. This difference is prominently seen in the developed markets and developing countries markets. In the U.S., most chains dominate the market. Whereas, in India there are many retailers who operate small shops or sell in the open market. Here the mark ups are high, but the real price is brought down through price haggling. However, with the liberalization policy of the government and opening up of the markets, many cultural and economic barriers have been broken, giving way to the concept of supermarkets, malls and large retail chains, especially in the major cities and metros of the country. Today, in the competitive and complex market place, the new crop of multi level marketing companies like Tupperware Amway & Oriflame are opting for an expensive but effective route of enlisting sales distributors (agents) from its customer base (direct marketing method).

Thus, companies interested in cross cultural marketing have to develop an effective organization and design a marketing programme by deciding the extent to which their products, promotion, price and distribution should be adapted to an individual foreign market.

➲ SUMMARY

Social stratification is the division of members of a society into a hierarchy of distinct status classes, so that members of each class have relatively the same status and members of all other classes have either more or less status. Social class is the relative standing of the members of a society so that a higher position implies a higher status than those in the lower class. The nature of social class influence on consumer behaviour can be understand if one has a look at social stratification, status symbols and social mobility. The characteristic features relevant to marketing indicate that persons within a particular social class tend to behave more alike, is hierarchical, not measured by a single variable but as a weighted function of one's occupation, income, wealth, education, status, prestige etc., and is concrete in nature.

There are broadly three types of intimate groups in society which can influence the buying behaviour of individuals: (a) Groups which serve as comparison points (b) Groups to which an individual aspires to be a member. (c) Group whose perspectives are assumed by the individual irrespective of whether he aspires for its membership or not. Opinion leaders are person's who have the ability to influence others in a given situation. The beliefs, preferences, actions and behaviour of the leader sets a trend and pattern for others to follow. Marketing Managers make efforts to identify opinion leaders who can provide the necessary 'word-of-mouth' advertising and help in pushing the product into the market with the right type of motivation. Today the consumer is living in the age of information overkill and is bombarded by commercials, unsolicited product information and pursued by hard sell media. So the marketer has to communicate and identify the path to penetrate the consumer's mind.

In the post liberalized era, there have been various transformations occurring in the social class scenario in India. We have a younger population which has tasted financial independence at a much earlier age, rise in the number of nuclear families and an increased media exposure which has given rise to a new consumption culture in the country. Another emerging market is that of the rural market consumer, who is comparing himself to his better off urban cousins, and attempting to improve upon his living style and consumption pattern so as to match that of his counterparts in the city. It is seen that the social class can affect purchasing behaviours, selection of recreation, the saving and money borrowing attitudes of the members belonging to a particular class.

Henry Assael has defined culture as a set of socially acquired values that society accepts as a whole and transmits it to its members through language and symbols. Milton Rokeach's classification of cultural values can be used for studying purchasing behaviour. India has also got her own set of shared beliefs values, and customs which distinguishes them from the other countries. Each culture has got sub cultures. Members of a subculture do conform to most of the norms of the dominant wide culture but deviate from those which are not compatible to the norms of the subculture. Marketers going for cross cultural marketing need to understand the psychological, social and cultural aspects of foreign consumers they wish to target and devise effective marketing strategies accordingly. There are certain cross cultural factors which can influence the cross cultural marketing strategies. Marketers also need to address certain problems in cross cultural marketing which can be related to: symbols, colours and name selection, product selection, Promotion/ marketing communications, pricing, and distribution channels.

CHAPTER QUESTIONS FOR DISCUSSION

1. What do you understand by the terms 'Social stratification' and 'Social class'?
2. Select any one social class category existing in India and briefly comment on the buying behaviour of the target consumers in relation to the purchase of consumer durables.
3. Categorise the big retail outlets in your city (or town) on the basis of your estimation of the social class of the customers who patronize the outlets. Comment on the differences in the marketing efforts put in by the outlets?
4. Do you feel social mobility can result in the reduction of social-class differences? Why?
5. As a part of a project, say you have been asked to work out a marketing plan and segment the market for (a) getting the health conscious urban consumer interested in the purchase of 'home exercise equipment' (b) get the rural consumer interested in 'package travel scheme plans'. How would you go about the assignments?
6. Do you think opinion leaders can influence the purchase of houses in planned real estate projects? Why?
7. Assume that a manufacturer of 'Oats' is considering targeting school going children and their mothers by positioning it as a healthy, nutritious breakfast food. What cultural values and appeals should the manufacturer use to get the target consumers interested in the product?
8. What do you understand by the terms 'Culture', 'Sub-culture' and 'Cross culture marketing'?
9. According to you which are the important sub-cultures existing in India? Explain with examples.
10. Suppose a retailer of designer sarees is planning to sell the same in the American market. Discuss what are the cross cultural analysis that the retailer has to undertake?

SUGGESTED READINGS

1. The Oswal Group, *The Economic Times,* Bangalore, 13 February 2007
2. Ashley. Coutinho, *Red Tape*, Brand Equity, *The Economic Times*, Bangalore, 28 February 2007.

3. Schiffman L.G., Kanuk. L.L., *'Consumer Behavior'*, Prentice-Hall of India, New Delhi, 2005.
4. Rosemary Phipps and Craig Simmons, *"Understanding Customers 1996-97"*, Butterworth Heinemann, Oxford, 1996.
5. Henry Assael, *Consumer Behavior and Marketing Action*, South Western College Publishing, Singapore 2001, pp. 382-418.
6. Aradhana Takhtani, 'Carving out New Markets', *Business Times*, June 20, 2006.
7. The Great Indian Middle Class, *NCAER*.
8. Ramesh Kumar, Celebrities and Consumer Behaviour, *Strategic Marketing*, July-August, 1999, pp. 46-50.
9. Pranesh Mishra, Women at work, *The Economic Times,* Bangalore, 8, March 2007.
10. Archana. Shukla, Aman.Malik., The Market Makers, *Business Today*, January 14, 2007, pp. 145-152.
11. Arvind. Singhal., The Liberalised Generation. A Different Consumer, *Business Today*, January 14, 2007 pp. 154-158.
12. Brian Carvalho, Anusho. Subramanian, Will it trickle down? *Business Today*, January 14, 2007, pp. 231-236.
13. M.G. Parameswaran, Eight Steps to Eighty Seconds, *Strategic Marketing,* August-September 2000 pp. 32-35.
14. M.G. Parameswaran 'The Media Multiplication mantra, *Strategic Marketing,* March-April 2005, pp. 22-27.
15. Harihar. Narayanswamy N. Shatrujeet., A Disposable Disposition, *The Economic Times,* (Brand Equity) Bangalore, 14 March 2007.
16. Aarti. Razdan., On a fast Track, *The Economic Times,* Brand Equity Bangalore, July 5, 2006.
17. V.S Ramaswamy., S. Namakumari *'Marketing Management' Global Perspective, Indian Context,* 3rd Edition, Macmillan India Ltd., New Delhi, 2005, pp.667-695.
18. Ishan. Raina., Suman. Srivastava., Just how global do you want to be? *Strategic Marketing,* July-August, 1999, pp. 22-26.
19. David .L. Loudon., Albert, J. Delta Bitla, *'Consumer Behavior'*, 4th edn, Tata McGraw-Hill, New Delhi, 2002.

CASE

TATA'S – "GOLD PLUS JEWELLERY"

THE RETAIL VENTURE

In 2005, Titan Industries launched its second retail, Jewellery brand 'GOLD PLUS' in order to capitalize on the opportunity in small-towns and rural India. **Gold Plus** is the jewellery retail venture (of Titan Industries) from the house of Tata's specifically targeted at the small town consumer. Unlike its well known brand 'Tanishq', which is the company's more upscale brand, Gold Plus is a lower end Jewellery brand meant for the mass market consumption.

Identifying the Opportunity

According to the World Gold council estimates, 60 per cent of the gold in India is purchased by customers in small towns and villages. Indian's have an insatiable appetite for the yellow metal. However, currently most of this gold market is dominated by the local mom and pop Jewellery stores. Such stores often do not have standardized equipment to ensure the desired (correct) weight and purity of the gold purchased. A research undertaken by BIS, a body of the Ministry of Consumer Affairs revealed that 90% of Indian consumers get adulterated gold (Under karatage varies anywhere between 12-36 per cent) (**The Economic Times,** Brand Equity, February 18, 2009 pp. 3). In this way, consumer's lose almost Rs. 7000 crore on a yearly basis. It was felt that in an otherwise fragmented and non transparent gold market, there was a big opportunity to herald standardization and buildup a customer-base. In the small towns and rural areas, often consumers are never sure of grammage and purity. This is where it was felt that a trusted name like that of the **Tata's** can help them to dominate this segment.

The Social Class Structure, Tastes and Needs of the Targeted Market Segments

Titan has set its sight on the lower end of the market through its 'Gold Plus' chain of Jewellery stores. So the target consumers for the Gold Plus brand are those who belong to the B and C income groups. This target segment's customers have different tastes, react to different triggers and so need to be communicated about the brand in a different way. Most of the target customer group comprise of people who are investing in the yellow metal (gold) *i.e.,* saving for their wedding or putting aside something for their daughter's trousseau, rather than buying it for immediate use. For such customers, purity of gold was more important than the variety of designs and quality of workmanship (which are important issues with the SEC A income group). The company sources felt that this was a market with huge potential because over 40 percent of the estimated industry wide an annual gold purchase of Rs. 70,000 crore was accounted for by the target group identified for Gold Plus Jewellery.

The marketers of Gold Plus felt that there is a need to educate the would-be buyers of gold on purchasing the 'real thing'. For this, it has installed carat meters at all its media campaigns and they also organized audio-visual shows and question-answer sessions at street corners. And the most important factor is the Tata name, which is conspicuously displayed on all Gold Plus hoardings and shop fronts (Research by the company showed that the Tata tag was more widely recognized and trusted).

Efforts at Wooing the Buyer

It was observed that in smaller towns, customers share a very strong bond with the family Jeweller, as from generations together, they had been buying gold from him (family jeweller). This relationship, from a long period of time, acts as a defacto for trust. Thus the big task before Gold Plus marketers was to distract the small town buyer away from his family Jeweller. Some initiatives at bonding with the buyer are given here under.

- Many of these buyers are accustomed to buying Jewellery from local goldsmith or family Jewellers, so in order to make them feel comfortable, the Gold Plus stores are designed to look traditional-either homelike or resembling temples.
- In order to encourage footfalls, the gold price points have been kept low. Customers can buy little as one gram of gold. Exchange of old gold for new one (a popular practice in south India) is allowed: at just two percent charge, when the market rate was six-eight percent. They also constantly bring out new designs because the customers are very demanding. Moreover, the preferences of customers for gold also varies from community to community.

Titan has used the direct approach in marketing (franchise model) and the store manager is required to play a key role in local involvement. He keeps a track of weddings and other social events by networking with local priests. He then sends a congratulatory card and token gift well in advance to the concerned family. In case they shop and spend for an appropriately large amount at the Gold-Plus outlet, the company sponsors banners at the wedding, and another round of gift is handed over to them. And because the manager is invited to the wedding, it gives him another opportunity to network further with potential customers.

Promotion Activities

Apart from using the conventional approaches of advertising by putting up hoardings, wall paintings and event sponsorships, other promotion activities are being attempted to. These include advertising on local cable channels as well as on the FM radio channels.

Below the Line Activities

The company decided to opt for below-the-line activities to promote the "Gold Plus" brand.

- Gold Plus introduced an initiative called the **'Golden Chariot',** which is a vehicle with a carat meter taken across to consumer hubs. The customers are encouraged to come forward and get the purity of the gold already owned by them tested on the carat meter. Further, they can also avail of services like cleaning and polishing their Jewellery, free of cost. Such a move can help to catch the attention as well as increase the awareness of the Gold-Plus brand among prospective customers.
- Another initiative was to create a promo which would attract attention. It created a gold bangle weighting 24.5 kilogram that gave it an entry into the Limca Book of Records and then took it on a road show of 17 towns. Consumers were asked to participate in a "guess the weight of the bangle" contest. The company also offered visitors a photo opportunity, with the option of mailing their photographs to five of their acquaintances.
- Other innovative promotions included distributing of gold paper slips to potential customers in a 3-5 kilometer radius prior to the inauguration of new stores.
- Similar promotions are conducted inside hotels when customers are given the bill along with an offering of a free sweet dish and the paper coin. Or people are given gold paper with flowers while leaving a temple.

The company has long term plans to reach out to customers across every corner in the country. However, the challenge is to make the brand 'Gold Plus' appeal to the many influencers (right from the grandmother to the aunt next door) who are a part of the gold purchase decision in India.

(*Source :* www.titanjewellery.com, Prasad Sangameshwaran, Precious Metal, *The Economic Times*, Bangalore 18 February, 2009)

QUESTIONS FOR DISCUSSION

1. **Can you suggest other promotional activities which can be used by the marketers of 'Gold Plus', if say, the brand is to be extended to include young and tech savvy target customer of the cities too?**
2. **Do you feel, the initiatives taken for the rural and small towns by the marketers of Gold Plus brand, could also be used for launching it in cities, targeting the middle class customer here? Explain with reasons.**

CHAPTER 9

REFERENCE GROUP INFLUENCES

- Case : Groups form a part of **"Nike's ad"**
- Factors relevant to reference group's exerting influence
- Reference group characteristics influencing consumer behaviour
- Types of reference groups
- Groups relevant to consumer behaviour
- Reference group and consumer conformity to the group
- Benefits of reference group appeal
- Marketing applications of reference group appeals.
- Summary.
- Chapter questions for discussion
- Suggested Readings
- Case : **Fashion Label-Gini Jony**

CASE

GROUPS FORM A PART OF NIKE'S AD

Groups form a part of the customer's personal context. **Groups can be defined as two or more persons who share, a common purpose.**

A very important environmental consumer behaviour influence is the face-to-face group. The influence of groups to a great extent is dependent upon the **reference group.** This group will be the reference point on the basis of which the individual will form beliefs, attitudes and imitate behaviour. By influencing individual behaviour, reference groups will serve as sources of norm, value and conduct. In this context, reference groups can be defined as persons, groups and institutions that individuals look to for guidance regarding their own behaviour and values and whose opinion they respect.

Global sportswear brand **Nike** just before the World Cup series, understanding the passion that Indians have for the game 'cricket' had created an advertisement using this as the reference point. Nike had succeeded in capturing the craze and chaos that go into the game in India in a two minutes commercial. Unlike the usual sweet neighbourhood-kids-playing-cricket formula, Nike's advertisement used the cricket formula as the reference group *i.e.,* cricket for what it is to most Indians. The reference group's cricket (shown as a hard tough game) is played by 15-to-17 year olds who can swing a mean ball or drive a bludgeoning bat in the gullies (bylanes) of India. The picture showing regard for the game is captured in all its grandeur with bats being flayed and balls being sprayed on top of buses in a typical Indian traffic jam. Since cricket is the game of reference, even in the commercial, the reference group is shown in the form of tough looking young Indians, cricket buffs (aspiring to be cricketers) who have the dare devilry to play in the crowded streets of the country. The above example of Nike illustrates how the marketer has attempted to influence the reference group to appeal to the target market.

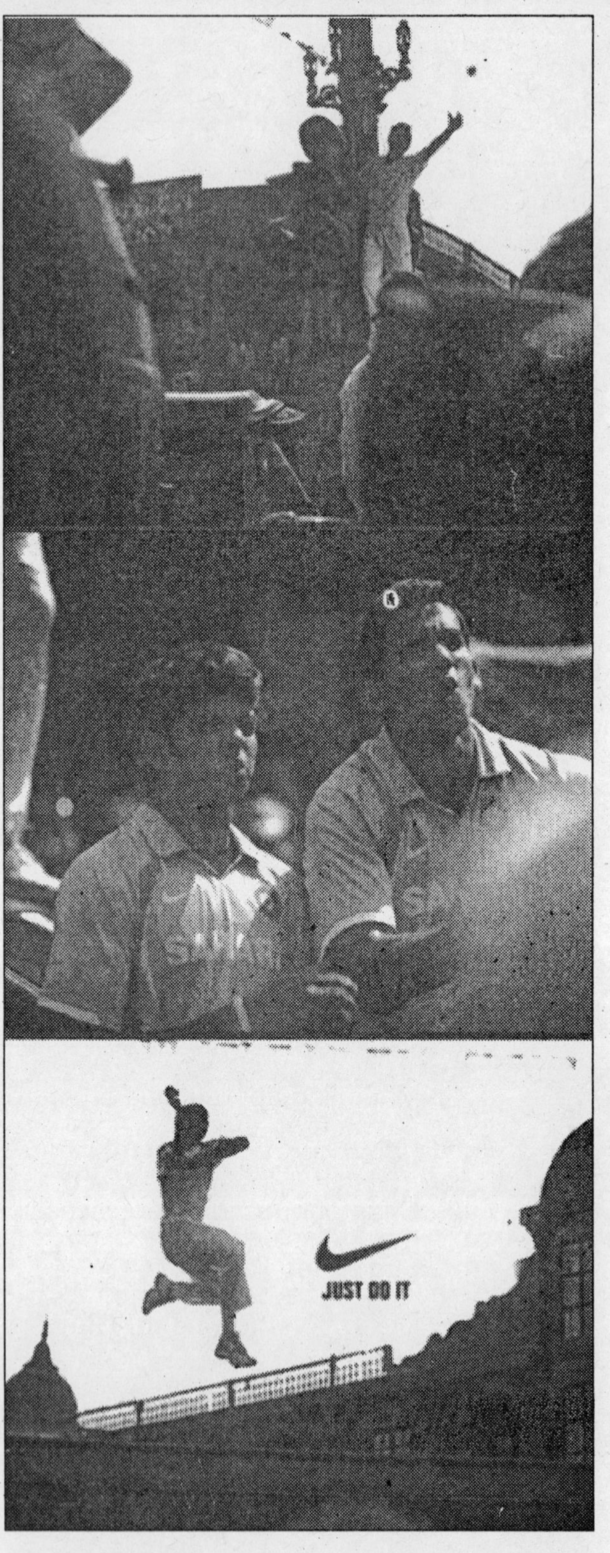

Nike trying to influence the reference group

Study of group dynamics when extended to 'consumer behaviour' will help the marketer to know and understand the impact of various types of groups on the individual's buying behaviour process. Each type of group with which the individual is associated serves important needs and functions for the individual. No single group can satisfy all the needs of an individual member, hence most of us belong to various groups. A family unit helps in biological maintenance, security and a feeling of belongingness. Whereas, sorority is purely social in nature and takes care of the other needs of the individual like helps in providing more educational information, in developing contacts for future employment, get associated through membership to other social organisations, provide information on purchase of speciality/shopping goods etc. For instance, an individual, a senior government official, may simultaneously be a member of the 'Gymkhana Club' and the 'Sports club'. This person may claim that his official duties and values are closely met by the Gymkhana Club, whereas, as a member of the Sports club, he gets a chance to improve his tennis skills by getting to play with professional tennis players.

Over and above, each group exerts a variety of influences on the individuals by putting pressure on him to conform to group norms and also guides his behaviour, be it related to going to the parlour or purchasing personal care products, or choosing a career and so on. In this chapter we are going to discuss the advantages of the groups and the role of the various types of groups which will affect the purchase decision of an individual.

FACTORS RELEVANT TO REFERENCE GROUP'S EXERTING INFLUENCE

Reference groups have certain roles and standards on the code of conduct which will have a direct influence on the individual's purchasing behaviour. *For example,* the family will influence the child's eating habits, the peer group will affect the teenager's T.V viewing and reading habits and the organizational group can exert influence on what the individual wears to office and his spending pattern.

In an attempt to adapt to group norms, we abide the values set by the family, peer group or the organization. This, in fact is very often used as a self concept, where reference group will work as the point of comparison.

Reference group have certain roles and standards on the code of conduct which will have a direct influence on the individual's purchase behaviour. There are three factors, based on which the group can exert influence: (a) the individual's attitude towards the group (b) the nature of the group (c) the nature of the product.

There are three factors based on which the group can exert influence on an individual's purchasing behaviour: (1) The individual's attitude towards the group (2) The nature of the group (3) The nature of the product.

When we talk of an **individual's attitude towards the group,** his or her purchasing behaviour will get affected if :

- The group is acknowledged as a credible source of information.
- The person gives due weightage (and values) to the views and reactions of the group members regarding purchasing decisions.
- Accepts the rewards / sanctions or punishment given by the group for appropriate or inappropriate behaviour.

Take for instance, the alumini formed by students who have passed out of a management college. The new students wanting to join the college may rely on the ex-students for information and advice regarding the faculty, library, internet facility, cafeteria etc., The more new the member is, more likely he or she will be to look to the seniors for advice and guidance. Moreover, usually there is a hierarchy of expertise in the group, with some members being relied upon more than others for information or help.

Nature of the Group

As for the nature of the group, reference groups are more likely to influence members if :

- They (members) are cohesive and have similar norms and values, so they are highly credible.
- They (members) interact frequently, so the group has the power to cause attitude changes.
- If the group membership is highly valued and considered to be distinctive and exclusive, it will be attractive for the individual.

Nature of the Product

The degree of influence a group has on an individual also depends on the nature of the product. *For example,* in case of products such as clothes, cosmetics, furniture or perfumes, they connote status and prestige to interact with group members.

The reference group's influence on purchase decisions will, to a certain extent depend upon how **visually or verbally conspicuous**, the product is to other people. Products such as a new car, jewellery, fashion accessories, designer clothes, branded home furniture are likely to be purchased keeping in mind the likely reactions from others.

➲ REFERENCE GROUP CHARACTERISTICS INFLUENCING CONSUMER BEHAVIOUR

There are certain reference group characteristics (or nature) which can exert their influence on consumers. Broadly they can be referred to as norms, values, roles, status, socialization and power.

- **Group Norms :** These are the undefined or not documented rules and standards of conduct which the group establishes and the members are required to conform to them. These norms may relate to the appropriateness of wearing (type) clothes, eating habits, type of cars (or mobiles), jewellery or brand of cosmetics.
- **Values :** These refer to the shared beliefs among group members as to which behaviours are desirable and those which are undesirable. Of course, as discussed in the previous chapter, values are largely defined by cultures and sub-cultures but could vary to a great extent depending upon, the family and peer pressure. For, say one family may give more value to social status while another family may find independent thinking and personal enhancement to be very important.

Reference group characteristics such as group norms, values, roles, status socialistion and power can exert influence on an individual's consumer behaviour.

Within the college campus, it will not be usual to find students valuing social status, moving around together, driving flashy vehicles, wearing branded designer wear or eating at the well known fast food outlets (like Café Coffee Day or Pizza Hut). There could also exist within the same campus another group of students who tend to give more importance to academic oriented activities as they feel this could lead them to achieve the personal goal desired by them.

Roles : These are functions that the group assigns to the individual, so as to attain the group objectives. Marketers try to identify specific roles performed by the group members in order to offer the best available brand or product category. In case of family decision making, the following roles have been identified, the influencer, the gate keeper (who controls the flow of information into the group) the decision maker, the purchaser and the user (or consumer).

Status : Status refers to the position the individual is accorded within the group. The symbolic representation of status is seen in the type of dress, ownership of certain types of products, membership to certain clubs and so on. Higher status implies greater power and influence when compared to one occupying lower status.

Sometimes consumers may purchase products to demonstrate a higher status in a broader societal sense, so that the message is conveyed of more wealth and implied superiority.

Socialization

When an individual learns the group norms and role expectations, socialization is said to take place. When a person takes up a new job he (or she) will learn the informal rules and expectations of the primary work group along with the organization's formal work rules and expectations.

Consumer Socialization : Consumer socialization refers to the process by which consumers acquire the knowledge and skills necessary to deal properly at the market place. Through the process of socialization, consumers will learn to understand the appropriate consumption behaviour from the various sources of information and media.

Ad shows referent power

Group members follow certain norms related to clothes, behaviour etc.

Consumers will to try emulate the behaviour of role models within the group

Power : The group is able to exert influence on an individual's behaviour. Although there are various sources of group influence, here we have discussed only three which are particularly relevant for marketing strategy.

(a) **Expert Power :** The consumer will treat a source of information (either friend or relative or the sales person) to have expert power only if convinced about the source's credibility or knowledge or experience with the product.

(b) **Referent Power :** As the term goes, referent power indicates the individual's identification with members of the group. More the similarity between the individual's beliefs and attitudes and that of the group members, more will be the referent power. The individual is either a member of a group or may aspire to be a part of a group because of common norms and values.

The consumer will treat a source of information to have expert power only if convinced about the source's credibility or knowledge or experience with the product. Referent power indicates the individual's identification with members of the group.

Nightclubs: The hottest destination for the young and hip

Reference group influence is seen in the eating habits, style of dressing and visiting night clubs of the young.

(c) **Reward Power :** This is with reference to the group's ability to reward a person associated with them. For instance, the employer (or organisation) can bestow reward on an employee via finance (monetarily) promotion and improved status. The family can reward an individual by providing moral support, praising and approval. Social groups can provide reward through complimenting the member on his (or her) purchase decision. Similarly the group which had displayed reward power also have coercive power over the member. For instance, the group may express disapproval by demoting the employee, or not supporting the family member or ignore the individual at social meets, respectively - for deviant behaviour of the member.

➲ TYPES OF REFERENCE GROUPS

1. Reference groups can be of many types. Reference groups that directly influence general or broadly defined values or behaviour are usually called **normative reference group**. *For example,* a child's normative reference group will be his family. The family inculcates certain norms of behaviour, which will be complying to "good values" and "belief". The family plays an important role in moulding the child's consumer behaviour and values. And this is reflected in the type of food he consumes, the selection of dress for specific occasions, the type of outlets where he prefers to shop etc.
2. Another reference group which will serve as a benchmark for certain specific or narrowly defined attitudes is called **comparative reference group**. Such a group serves as a point of comparison, especially for evaluating one's own status. Further, this estimate of one's status may vary according to the group with which one compares oneself. Consumers will compare their attitudes to those members of an important group and then work out whether the group will be supportive. For instance, people are interested in moving into residential complexes (areas) where they feel the neighbours are similar to themselves. This is because such neighbours will have similar social and economic characteristics as themselves. This could be the reason why consumers are seen seeking information from friends, who are perceived to be having similar tastes as themselves. This aspect is conveyed in ads like the (*Stayfree Lite* sanitary napkins, *Recova, Sunsilk Shampoo*) or a well informed sales person *(Eureka Forbes)*.

   The ads of *SBI Life*, where elderly folks' rediscover their childhood through a game of cricket is a comparison to how carefree one can be by investing in SBI Life insurance or the ad on the drastic effects if one doesn't bother about the cholesterol level and how this can be reversed by consuming *Saffola oil*.

Indirect reference groups could take the form of movie stars, sports personalities etc. who even in the absence of face-to-face contact are able to influence their fans.

Ads speak on comparative influence

   In college, sometimes students consider their peer group, who are seen wearing jazzy clothes, zooming past in cars etc. as a comparative reference group, who seem admirable and also worthy of imitation. Such a comparative reference group can influence an individual's dress code, lifestyle behaviour etc.
3. There could be **indirect reference groups** in the form of movie stars, sports personalities etc. The above mentioned categories /types of people generally have a large following in the form of fans. Though there is no face-to-face contact or interaction between the fans and the respective star, they are able to influence their fans. The fans admire their *hero/heroine* and try to imitate their hairdo, dress code, lifestyles, attitudes and behaviour also. Though the star may not be able to directly influence every fan on his day-today

purchases, their judgments on facts and fashions, or social messages etc. carry a lot of weightage and this is reflected in the consumer's purchase decisions. Since the star's views are heard with awe and respect, very often marketers use such personalities to promote their products.

4. **Informational Influence :** Consumers will accept information from a group, which is considered as a credible source of information and has expertise. Further, if he believes that the information will enhance his knowledge about product choices he may trust and believe this source. For instance, while purchasing consumer durables such as T.V., microwave owen, motor bikes or cars, consumers will regard personal sources of information as very trustworthy.

Consumers will accept information from a group which is considered as a credible source of information and has expertise.

There are two conditions under which informational influence is sought by the consumer.

1. When there is social, financial or performance risk involved in buying the product (say purchase of a car).
2. If the concerned individual has limited knowledge or experience regarding the product, informational influence is likely to be most important for him. (For instance, say technical products such as insurance policies, computers, printers or cellular phones).

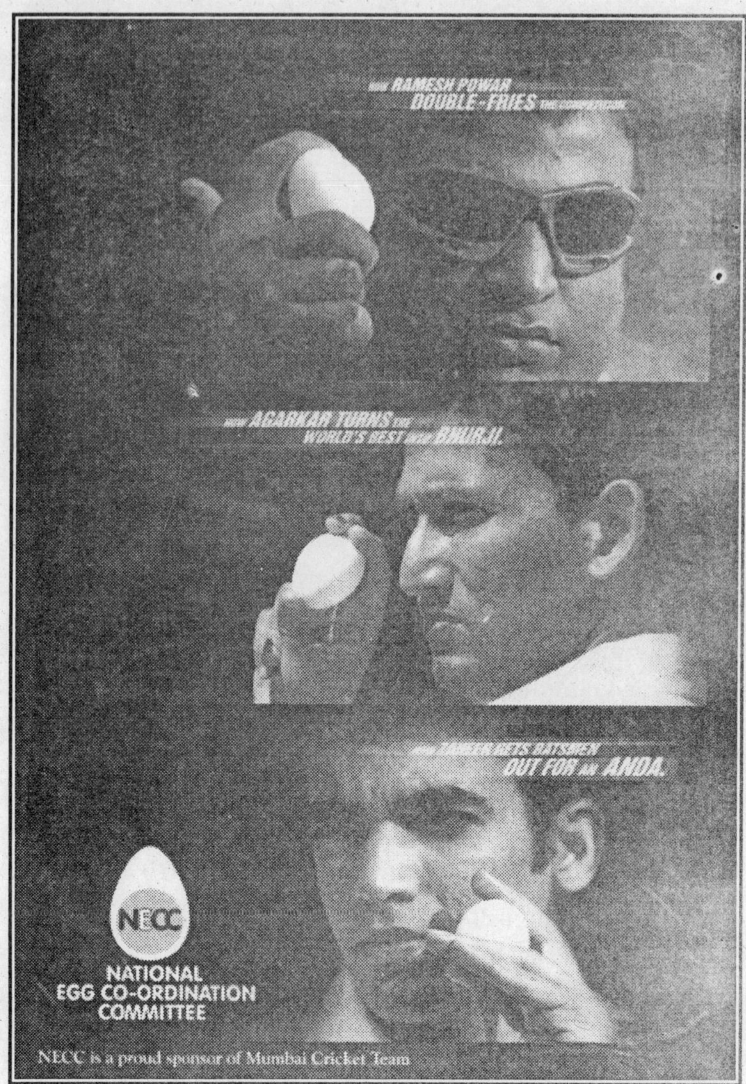

Ad acts as a indirect reference group

Studies have indicated that expert power (mentioned earlier in the chapter) can be based on the usage and experience of friends, neighbours or well as professional's expertise.

TABLE 9.1

TYPES OF INFLUENCE EXERTED BY REFERENCE GROUPS

Nature of Influence	Objectives	Perceived Characteristics of Source	Type of Power	Behaviour
Informational	Knowledge	Credibility	Expert	Acceptance
Comparative	Self-maintenance and enrichment	Similarity	Referent	Identification
Normative	Reward	Power	Reward or coercion	Conformity

(*Source* : Burnkrant. E. Robert and Cousineau Alain , *"Informational and Normative Social Influence in Buying Behavior"*, 1975)

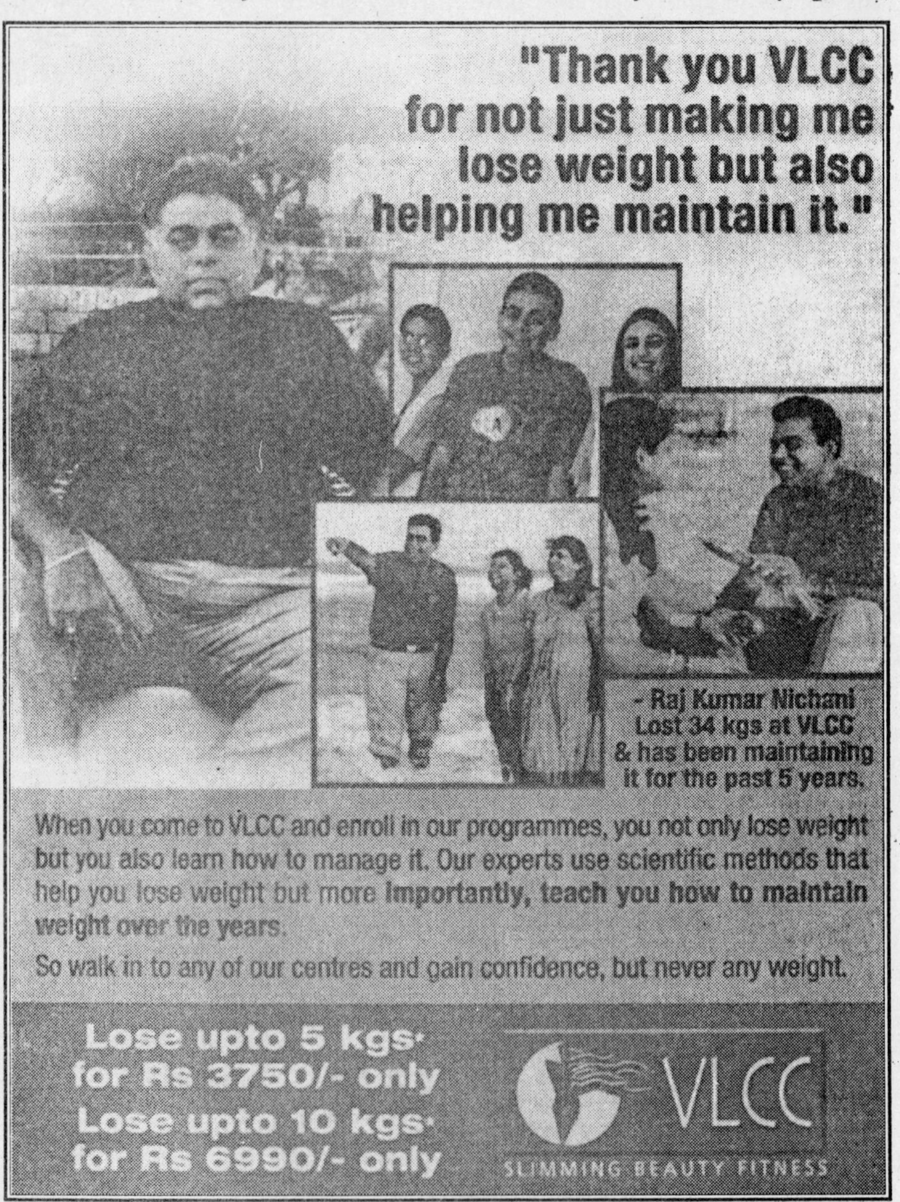

Ad acts an on informational influence

5. At times people get influenced by groups to which they do not belong. For instance, an **aspirational group** is one to which the individual wishes or aspires to belong. The individual may not have a formal membership and also does not have face to face contact, but he aspires to be a member. This aspiration acts as a positive influence on that person's attitude and behaviour. *For example,* a teen-age cricket player may hope to play some day for the country and he identifies with the Indian cricket team although there is no face to face contact. Thus his belief, values, attitudes and behaviour will be such, so as to match the ideologies of his aspirational group. Similarly, the consumer will select the product brand because of the personality it has attained, matches and expresses his own aspirations and self image. Personalities such as Aishwarya Rai (for *Lux International soap*), Priety Zinta. (*Heads & Shoulders Shampoo*) Shahrukh Khan & Priety Zinta (*Santro Xing Car*), Vishwanathan Anand (*Horlicks*) can all be referred to be aspirational group influences. Thus aspiration group can influence consumer behaviour in case of products like cigarettes, liquor, apparels, cosmetic products, automobiles and fashion.

At times people get influenced by groups to which they do not belong. For instance, an aspirational group is one to which the individual wishes or aspires to belong. At times the individual may not approve of the group values, attitudes and behaviour. So his behaviour will be opposite to the norms of that particular reference (or disclaimant) group.

TABLE 9.2

TYPES OF REFERENCE GROUP INFLUENCING CONSUMER BEHAVIOUR

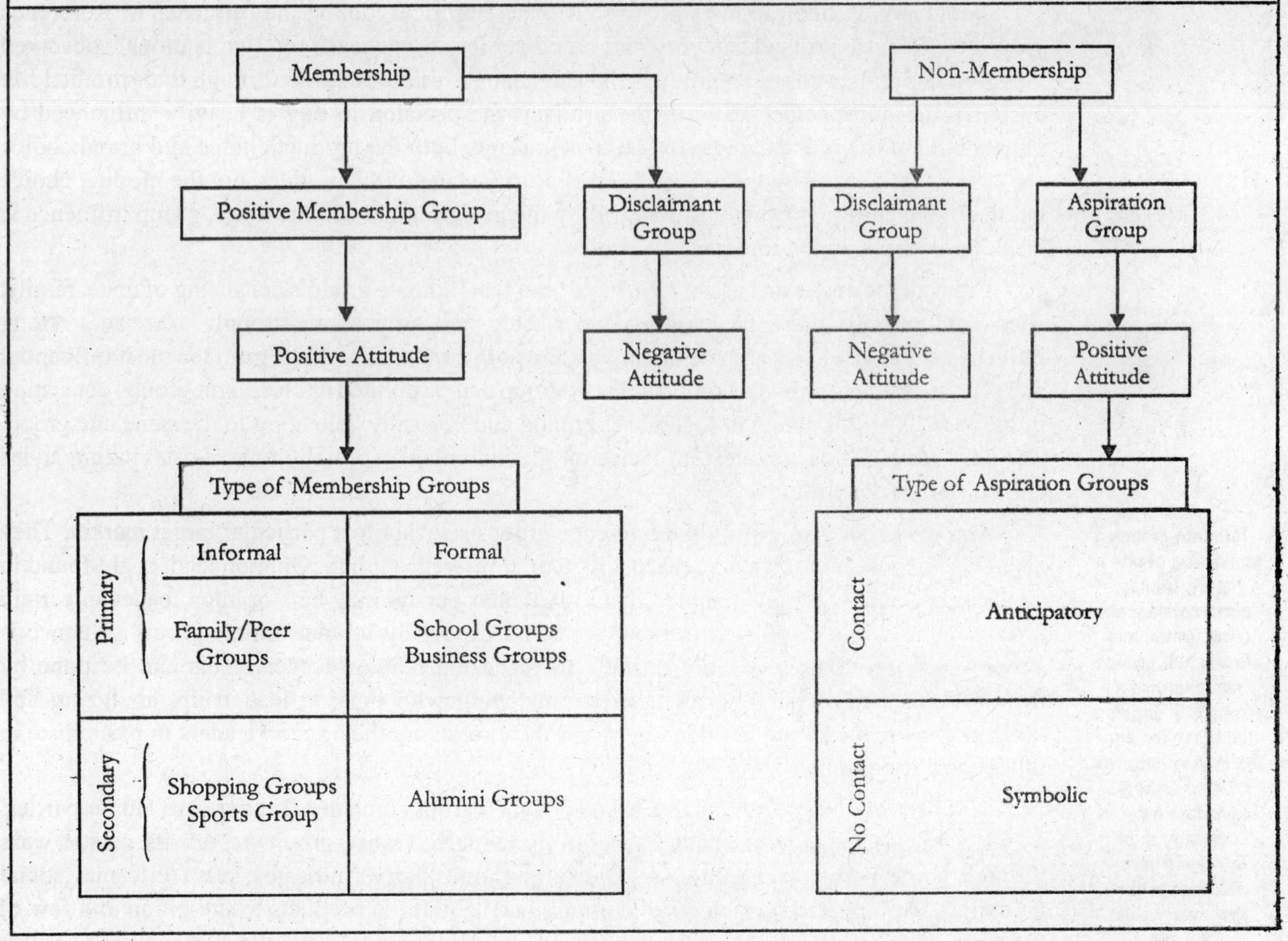

Membership → Positive Membership Group → Positive Attitude → Type of Membership Groups

Membership → Disclaimant Group → Negative Attitude

Non-Membership → Disclaimant Group → Negative Attitude

Non-Membership → Aspiration Group → Positive Attitude → Type of Aspiration Groups

Type of Membership Groups

	Informal	Formal
Primary	Family/Peer Groups	School Groups Business Groups
Secondary	Shopping Groups Sports Group	Alumini Groups

Type of Aspiration Groups

Contact	Anticipatory
No Contact	Symbolic

(*Source* : Henry Assael, Consumer Behavior and Marketing Action, Thomson Learning, 6th Edn., 2001, pp. 538)

6. Another type of reference group is the **disclamant group**. This is a group whose values or behaviour does not appeal to the individual. Here a person may have membership or face to face contact but he disapproves of the group values, attitudes and behaviour. So his behaviour will be the opposite or reverse to the norms of the particular reference group. *For example,* an individual's (teenager) family may be members of the 'Saibaba cult'. But, the particular teenager does not have faith in 'Saibaba' so his behaviour will be so as to oppose and avoid any claim of relationship with the followers of 'Saibaba'.

Avoidance group may be one to which the person may not hold membership nor have face-to-face contact but whose values, attitudes and behaviour he totally disapproves.

7. **Avoidance Group :** This may be a group with which the person may not hold membership nor have face to face contact and also of whose values, attitudes and behaviour, the person totally disapproves. Here the person will tend to avoid the group and will adopt values, attitudes and behaviour which will be in opposition to that of the group. A teenager may have no faith in the practices, values, attitudes and behaviour of the ISKCON or Hari Krishna cult group. So he will avoid any contact with the group.

It has been seen that the importance of group influence varies among products and brands. Donald W. Hendon, had done a study, involving two hundred consumers to describe which of their product and brand choices had been strongly influenced by others. The findings are given here below.

Donald W. Hendon in his study on "A New empirical look at the influence of Reference groups on Generic product category and brand choice: Evidence from Two Nations", observed that products choice based on group influence changes as products go through their product life cycle. In the introductory stage of the product, the decision to buy is heavily influenced by others, but not the brand choice. In the growth stage, both the product choice and brand choice are heavily influenced by the group. In the maturity stage of the product, not the product choice but the brand choice is heavily influenced by the group. In the decline stage, group influence is weak on both the brand and product choice.

From all the above discussions we have seen that intimate group's consisting of one's family, friends, close colleagues (peer group) and closely knit groups can strongly exercise a strong influence on the lifestyles and the buying patterns of its members. Apart from the most influential and primary group *i.e.,* one's family, the peer group can be defined as close-knit groups consisting of individuals with a common social background and normally belonging to the same age group. The peer group has the greatest influence on the individual especially towards stabilizing styles and behaviour patterns.

Intimate groups consisting of one's family, friends, close colleagues (peer group) and closely knit groups can exercise a strong influence on the lifestyles and the buying patterns of its members. Marketers have to identify the reference group relevant to the particular target market.

Marketers have to identify the reference groups relevant to a particular target market. They also have to look out for ways to reach a particular reference group. Opinion leaders are found in all strata of society. It may be noted that a particular person may be a opinion leader in certain product areas while a follower in other areas. So especially in areas where group influence is strong, marketers must work out on how to reach the opinion leaders. This can be done by identifying certain personal characteristics matching with opinion leadership, analyzing and determining the media preferred by them and then involving the opinion leaders to participate in influencing the group.

'Tupperware India Pvt. Ltd.', a branch of the parent company, Tupperware Home parties, a U.S A based company has been successfully using reference groups to sell its plastic ware through home party plan selling. As the term 'home party' indicates in an informal social gathering, the tupperware dealer will communicate about the products to the group and few of the guests may purchase some of the products just demonstrated, and the hostess will be given a commission on the sales made.

Style of dressing is influenced by peer group behaviour

TABLE 9.3

EXTENT OF GROUP INFLUENCE ON PRODUCT AND BRAND CHOICE

1. Strong product, strong brand influence		
- Automobiles	- Colour TV	
2. Weak product, strong brand influence		
- Magazines	- Furniture	- Clothing
- Instant coffee	- Aspirin	- Air conditioners
- Stereo	- Laundry detergents	- Microwave ovens
3. Weak-product, weak brand influence		
- Canned peaches	- Toilet soap	- Beer
- Cigarettes	- Small cigars	
4. Strong product, weak brand influence-none.		
- Nil		

(*Source : Principles of Marketing* - by Philip Kotler, Page 128)

The above example of Tupperware shows that the reference group introduces the person to new behavioural patterns and lifestyle. The reference group also influences the person's attitudes and personality, 'self image' and 'self concept' because he/she would prefer to purchase products which will match the preference of the group at large. Moreover, there is also group pressure to conform to the group norms, which will automatically affect the person's actual product and brand choices.

Ad shows family influence

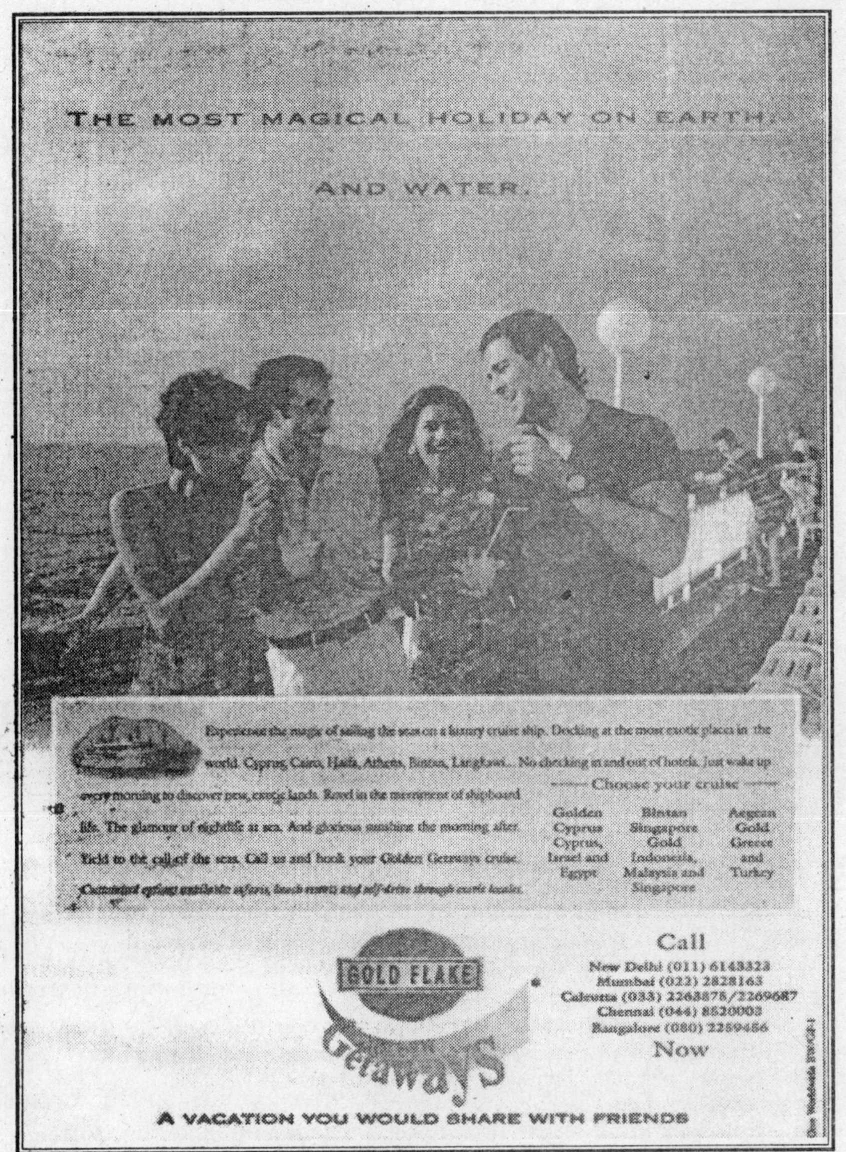

Ad shows group influence in the choice of vacation

GROUPS RELEVANT TO CONSUMER BEHAVIOUR

In the previous chapters in the book we have emphasised on various individual factors like perception, motivation, personality, learning and attitude. In this chapter, we have been discussing about an individual's behaviour in a group. This is because being a social human being, individuals always have contact with others like his immediate family and friends, fellow workers, fellow commuters, official customers and sometimes even strangers. All these interactions will affect the individual's behavioural pattern. So it becomes important for the marketing manager to understand and examine the influence of others on the individual, that is, both the influence of the group on the individual consumer and the personal influence exerted by an individual on another.

As a social human being an individual will have interactions with his family, peers, friends etc., which will affect his behavioural pattern.

To understand this, we will discuss about the various types of groups which are relevant to the consumer and who can also influence his decision making process.

FIGURE 9.1

GROUPS RELEVANT TO CONSUMER BEHVIOUR

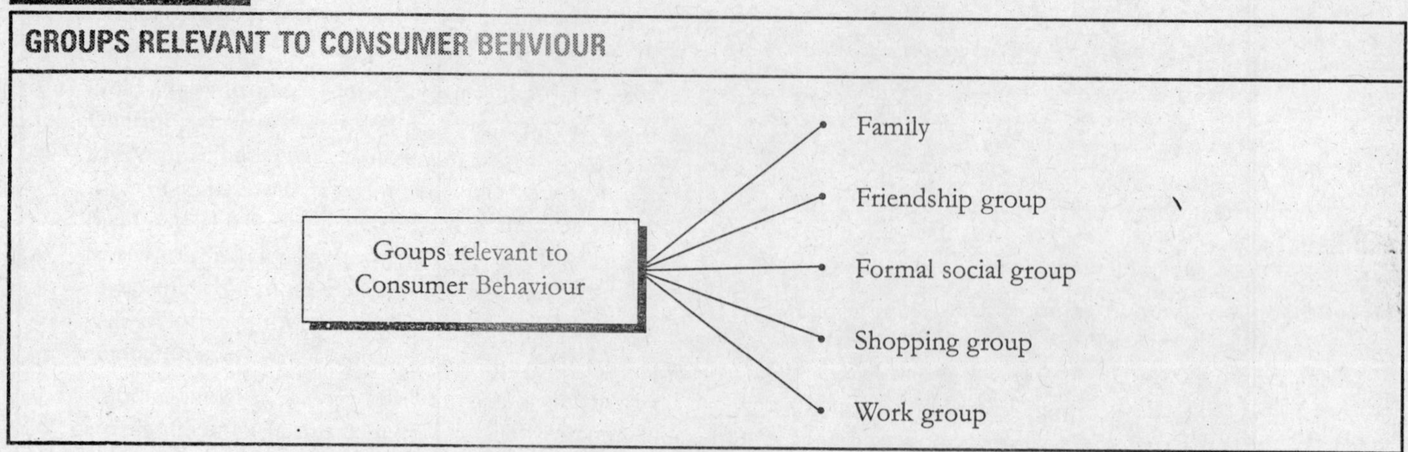

[A] THE FAMILY INFLUENCE ON CONSUMER BEHAVIOUR

Meaning of the Term 'Family'

The term **family** is a basic concept and is one of the most important primary groups to influence consumers' buying behaviour. Incidentally, it is with the family that most persons will have maximum interactions over a lifetime. *A family can be defined as two or more persons living together who are related by blood or marriage.*

Types of Family

The term family is a basic concept and one of the most important primary groups to influence consumer's buying behaviour. It is with family that most person's will have maximum interactions over a lifetime.

Family can come into existence **on account of orientation,** *i.e.,* it is the family a person is born into, consisting of one's parents, brothers and sisters and other relations such as grandparents, uncles etc. or the extended family. Such a family grouping has an established purchasing pattern which an individual is exposed to since childhood. So the person learns of the family's purchasing pattern right from her childhood. This gets imprinted in her mind and can lead to entrenched attitudes towards certain brands and suppliers. In fact, even selection of diverse products and services such as washing powders, instant or filter coffee/tea, banking services, health clinics, holidays etc. seem to be greatly influenced by family norms. In order to *generate new* customers. marketers have to design marketing programmes aimed at overcoming the reluctance of consumers to break these norms.

A family can also be referred to as a **family of procreation** which consists of a buyer's partner (or spouse) and children. This family has a more direct influence on everyday purchase decisions. All the members tend to influence different buying decisions.

There can also be **single parents with children below 18 years.** There could be such single parent households because of marriages ending in divorce or an unmarried parent with an adopted child under 18 years of age. In such a family, along with financial burden, the single parent will also have limited time to spend with his or her child. So such parent's are likely to spend more on their children, partly out of a sense of guilt. The outcome is that children in single parent households are likely to have more purchasing power and influence over a wide range of purchases.

In the recent past, there is visible, especially in metro cities, the emergence of households with **live-in couples**. Some heterosexual couples are choosing not to follow convention and remain unmarried though living together. Such live-in-couples are dual earning households and tend to have higher disposable income. Such households can easily become a good target for luxury goods, travel and entertainment. This calls for marketers to work out suitable marketing programmes to tap this market.

Benefits of Family

There are a few benefits which are applicable to a family member :

◆ **Financial and Economic Support :** A big family function is that it provides the necessary economic and financial support to its family members. In urban India, nuclear family set up is quite common, whereas in rural India, we can still come across joint families or extended families. In the cities, with most of the homes becoming dual income households (with more and more women taking to work) we can see the existence of extended family where a parent (or grandparent) is needed to do baby sitting and some minor household chores. In such dual income households both the husband and wife shoulder the economic and financial support well being of the family together.

◆ **Socialisation :** From a consumer behaviour point of view, family facilitates the process of socialisation. As a part of the socialisation process, right from one's childhood, each individual is taught the basic values and code of conduct expected from the society. All these are imparted so that one becomes a responsible citizen. Socialisation can take the form of direct interactions received from our parents and indirectly what we learn by observing the behaviour of others (parents, teachers, elders etc.) around us.

A big family function is that it provides the necessary economic and financial support to its family members. From a consumer's behaviour point of view, family facilities the process of socialization. Socialization is of interest to marketers because it is a two way process – a person gets influenced by his or her family friends, neighbours and others and in turn, also influences those who are socialising with him or her.

Marketers are interested in the consumer socialisation process. During childhood, parents are the role models for their children, so during this period, their consumption pattern (dressing, eating habits etc.) will be greatly influenced by the parents. During teens (or as college goers) it will be the peers and friends opinion and attitudes which will affect their purchasing decisions. Later on, after completion of studies when one starts working, our consumer behaviour can be influenced by our colleagues and working friends. After marriage, while setting up a new household one's consumption pattern and purchasing decisions will be greatly influenced by one's spouse. In this way, while moving along the family life cycle, the process of extended socialisation continues, with the changes occurring in one's life.

Socialisation is of interest to marketers because it is a two way process — a person gets influenced by his or her family, friends, neighours and others and in turn he or she also influences those who are socialising with them. Thus, the challenge before the marketer is to identify all those involved in the socialisation process and target them with suitable advertisements to influence their purchase decisions. For instance, these aspects are portrayed in the ads for different product categories such as : *Kellogs* (children and parents enjoy it together). *Liquid Surf Excel* (Bond between the newly married daughter and mother), *Vicks* suckable tablets (grandmother to grand children), *Allahabad Bank* (Son and Farther have preference for the same bank), *ICICI Bank (Husband and Wife), Whisper choice* (mother and daughter), *HDFC Standard Insurance* (Parents, son and his child) and so on.

◆ **Household Life Cycle :** The purchasing pattern or consumption behaviour will vary depending upon the age of household members, their marital status and whether or not there are children in the house. This is because of the changes occurring in the spending pattern of the family life cycle (FLC). Family lifecycle refers to the several phases people go through in their lives, *i.e.*, the process of family formation and dissolution. Each life cycle will differ from the earlier stage in terms of (a) family set up or structure (b) the financial status and requirement (c) products or services needed and preferences, and (d) consumption pattern and buying behaviours.

Benefits of family.

The purchasing pattern or consumption behaviour will vary depending upon the age of household members, their marital status and whether or not there are children in the house. Classification of families on the basis of stage in the family life cycle (FLC) will give valuable insights into the family consumption related behaviour.

'Patrick E. Murphy and William S. Staples (1979) had suggested modern family life cycle categories such as younger or middle age divorced couples and other married couples without children. An understanding of the FLC will help marketers to gauge the changes occurring in the individual's consumption pattern over his life time.

Classification of families on the basis of stage in the family life cycle (FLC) will give valuable insights into the family consumption related behaviour. However, with the many changes occurring in the contemporary family set up and lifestyle with the inset of the modern society, the traditional FLC stages have given way to the non traditional FLC stages. When households undergo status changes such as divorce, temporarily out of job, death of the spouse etc., the family as a consumption unit may undergo spontaneous changes in brand preferences. For instance, divorce may result in either or both the spouses trying to set up a new residence, obtain new landline phone connection, get membership to a good club etc. If divorced couples have children, then the concerned spouse will have to plan for additional entertainment expenses.

If the family unit comprises of young couple (dual income family) with growing children, they will have another life-style and with more purchasing power and are likely to spend more on durable consumables and entertainment. Thus marketers will have to pack their products and services relevant to the varying family lifestyles and FLC of the consumers. Recognising this need, Club *Mahindra* advertises about its family holiday offerings. It describes its family holidays as "A heady mix of family holiday experiences where every moment is special".

Tables 9.4 and 9.5 convey about the traditional family life cycle and non traditional household lifecycles of an American family. However, with the many changes occurring in the demographics, social and cultural, economic etc. environmental in India it may not be wrong to say that the traditional joint family system has given way to a similar family life cycle. This can probably take the form, as mentioned in Table 9.6.

TABLE 9.4

THE TRADITIONAL FAMILY LIFE-CYCLE	
1.	**Young Singles** Single people under the age of 35. Incomes are low since they are starting a career, but they have few financial burdens and a high level of discretionary - income.
2.	**Newly Married** Newly married couples without children. High level of discretionary income because the wife is usually working.
3.	**Full Nest I** Married couples with the youngest child under 6. Greater squeeze on income because of increased expenses for child care.
4.	**Full Nest II** Married couples with children from 6 to 12. Better financial position since parents' income is rising. Most children are "latchkey kids" because both parents are working.
5.	**Full Nest III** Married couples with teenage children living at home. Family's financial position continues to improve. Some children work part-time. Increasing educational costs.
6.	**Empty Nest I** Children have left home and are not dependent on parental support. Parents are still working. Reduced expenses result in greatest level of savings and highest discretionary income.
7.	**Empty Nest II** Household head has retired, so couple experiences sharp drop in income. Couple relies on fixed income from retirement plans.
8.	**Solitary Survivor** Widow or widower with lower income and increasing medical needs.

(*Source : Consumer Behavior*, Henry Assael, pp. 570)

TABLE 9.5

SEQUENCE IN NON-TRADITIONAL HOUSEHOLD LIFE CYCLES

Sequence I
- Young married couple with children
- Young divorced parent
- Single parent with older children
- Older, unmarried

Sequence 2
- Young divorced couple without children
- Middle-aged married couple without children
- Older married couple without children

Sequence 3
- Young married couple with children
- Middle-aged divorced parent
- Middle-aged married parent with children and step-children

Sequence 4
- Young unmarried couple without children
- Middle-aged married couple without children
- Older married couple without children
- Widow

(*Source: Consumer Behavior,* Henry Assael, 2001, p. 571)

TABLE 9.6

THE LIKELY FAMILY LIFE CYCLE IN INDIA

The family life cycle	Description
• Young Singles	: Single people in early 20's, starting a career, decent income with a high level of discretionary income
• Newly married couple	: Newly married couple with no children, dual income household with both the spouses working, so a high level of discretionary income.
• Young married couple with small child/children	: Double income household, additional expense towards childcare and daycare centre.
• Married couple with teenge/ grown up children	: Households where the father may be working in a senior position and earning a high salary. However, expenses may be incurred towards repayment of home loan and children's education.
• Middle age couple with Independent (working children)	: Working parents with independent and working children. Reduced expenses leading to more saving and a high discretionary income in hand.
• Post retirement	: With the household head having retired, a sharp drop in the monthly income. Though, now the couple rely more on pension scheme for fixed income.

Nature of Purchases

Purchase decisions are very often influenced by the family responsibilities or income constraints. *For example,* singles (who are young, unmarried drawing reasonable income) tend to spend more on clothes, personal care products, entertainment and vacations. Whereas, newly married couples (dual income) with significant discretionary income may spend more on setting up a new house, furniture, interiors etc. This consumption pattern and purchasing power will change once they have children, then later on when the children grow up and so on.

Thus, there are could be modifications which arise from the changes occurring in the living status—with a different set of needs relating to the household appliances, shopping expenses, and entertainment expenditures.

Family Decision Making

Although marketers have recognised the 'family' as the basic decision making unit, in order to get a complete picture of the consumption process, they like to examine the attitudes and behaviour of the user of the product or consumer and the major decision makers in the purchase decision. For this firstly they need to identify roles of the family members in their decision making process. In family decision making, the individual members can assume any of the roles specified in Table 9.7, depending upon the product or brand category. So, the marketer needs to identify the specific roles of those involved in the purchase decision process and direct marketing communication accordingly.

The marketer needs to identify the specific roles of those involved in the purchase decision process and direct marketing communications accordingly.

It may be noted that a family member can play one or more roles in the purchase decision process.

The number and the persons who may perform these roles may differ from family to family and from product to product also. At times, a single member will independently assume a number of roles. Say, the mother while passing the *Pizza Hut* on her way home, may pick up the attractive offer (multiple food items) for Rs. 75 only. Her decision does not directly involve the influence of other family members. She is the initiator, decider and buyer, she may or may not be the sole user (or consumer). Products may be consumed by a single family member (face pack, cosmetics, deodorant etc.) or consumed directly by many family members [*Dabur Real Juice, Fanta, Pepsi* — (1-2 litre packs)] or indirectly by the entire family (T.V, Fans, DVD player etc.) . Thus, depending upon the product or service and its utility value, the single role can be performed by two or more members. Or in certain cases one or more of these basic roles may not be required.

Another aspect of family consumption decisions of interest to marketers is whether the decisions are husband dominated, wife dominated, jointly taken or in solitary (or unilateral). Traditionally, husbands had dominated in decisions related to cars and insurance and wives for

TABLE 9.7

DESCRIPTION OF TYPICAL EIGHT ROLES IN THE FAMILY DECISION-MAKING PROCESS

Role		Description
• Initiators	:	Family members who take the initiative of putting across the idea to other family members about a product or service.
• Influencer	:	Family member who provides the necessary information to the other family members about a product or service.
• Deciders	:	Family member(s) who have the power to either unilaterally or jointly decide or determine whether there is a need to shop for, purchase, use or consume or dispose of a particular product or service.
• Purchasers/ Buyers	:	Family member(s) who actually go and make the purchase of the product or service.
• Preparer	:	Family members who transforms the product or service into a form, for consumption by other family members.
• Users	:	Family member(s) who are the real users or consumers of the product or service.
• Maintainers	:	Family member(s) who regularly maintain or service the product so that it continues to provide satisfaction.
• Disposers	:	Family members) who initiate the disposal or discontinuation of a particular product or service

food and toiletries. However, all the social changes occurring with women having taken to work and gaining financial independence, they are also actively involved in the decision making process especially for products such as automobiles, financial transactions, vacations etc.

So, it is necessary that marketers continue with their efforts at planning marketing strategies by understanding more on the family, roles played by the members and so on.

[B] FRIENDSHIP GROUPS

Apart from family, consumers also enjoy the company of their friends when purchasing certain types of goods. Such friendship groups are able to influence the consumer, especially for products like clothing, jewellery, cosmetics and personal care items, food items etc.

So far we have seen how important the role played by the family is in influencing an individual's buying behaviour. But an individual for his/her protection, self awareness and enhancement needs others around him/her. Leon Festinger in his *"A theory of Social Comparison Processes"* has claimed that there exists in the human organism a drive to evaluate his opinions and abilities. If objective, non social means are not available, people evaluate their opinions and abilities by making a comparison with the opinions and abilities of others (*Source :* Consumer behavior, Peter D. Bennett and Harold H Kassarjian). In other words, human beings prefer the company of others and these people's opinions also matter to them. Consumers also enjoy the company of their friends when purchasing certain types of goods. Such friendship groups are able to influence the consumer especially for products like clothing, fine jewellery, cosmetics and personal care items, food items etc.

If we were to segment the youth market based on age and sex, then the influence of the friendship group becomes more prominent. The youth market constituting of youngsters in the age group of 18-30 accounts for a reasonable percentage of the country's population and is of considerable marketing significance. The tastes and preferences of the youth market are greatly influenced by their friends' views and opinions. This youth market is fast emerging as a growing market today. This youth market generally comprises of about to graduate students, post graduates, executives, emerging professionals etc. A high intent to purchase products and services is found in this market. They easily get motivated to purchase reasonably rated and the high value products as perceived by 'their friends'. The influence of friends on the buying behaviour is seen in their desire to have access to credit cards, wearing men/women wear which fall in line to their friends' choice adopting hair style/using deodorant and personal care items according to the acceptance of their friends circle. Even people who are found to smoke, reveal that the smoking habit was introduced to them by their friends.

The influence of friends is also seen in the buyers' choice of food-habits and drinks. Marketers have realised the role played by friends in influencing the consumption pattern of individuals in certain category of products and have designed suitable marketing communication programmes.

Examples of a few advertisers using the friendship theme while advertising about their product brands include:

- *Sunsilk Shampoo, Dabur Vatika hair oil, Livon, Veet hair remover, Fair & Lovely cream* – brands in the personal care category
- *Pepsi - Cola, 7-up, Sprite, Moutain Dew* – brands in the soft drinks category
- *Cadbury Byte, Cadbury Eclars, Kitkat Lite* → brands in the snacks category
- *Colgate* and *Close-up toothpastes, Wringly's chewing gum* – brands in the tooth care and mouth freshner category.

[C] FORMAL SOCIAL CLUBS

Human beings are generally considered to be sociable in nature and spend much of their time in group situations. They like to be associated with formal social clubs like the *Rotary Club, Lions Club etc.* The reason for their getting associated with such social group may be to achieve a specific goal like making new friends, career advancement or pursuing a special interest or promoting a specific cause. Such formal social system generally comprises of three elements:

Human beings are generally considered to be sociable in nature and spend much of their time in group situation. Such social groups tend to develop expectations or norms that specify how people in a group might behave under certain specific circumstances.

Activities are the tasks that people perform. **Interactions** are the behaviour that occurs between people in performing tasks. And **Sentiments** are the attitudes that develop between individuals within the group. George C. Homans argues that these concepts though separate are closely related. A change in any of these three elements will produce some change in the other two.

FIGURE 9.2

THE MUTUAL DEPENDENCE OF ACTIVITIES, INTERACTIONS AND SENTIMENTS IN A FORMAL SOCIAL SYSTEM

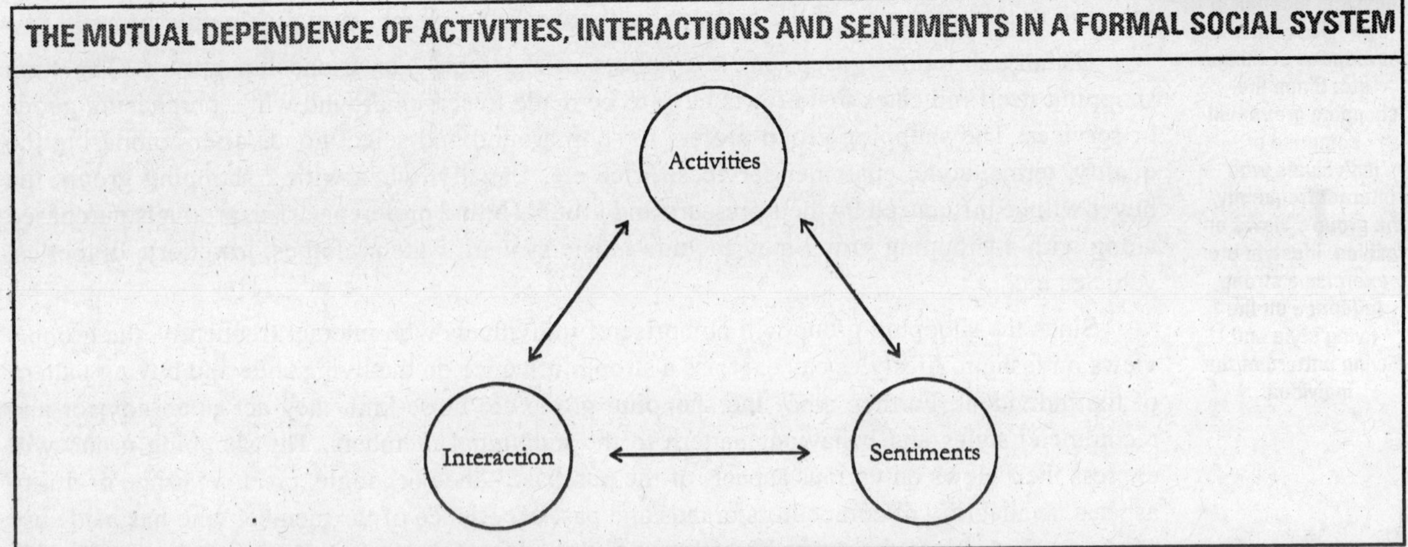

In a formal organisation set-up, job (activities) have to be done, that require people to work together (interactions). These jobs must be sufficiently satisfying (sentiments) for people to continue doing them. With more and more positive interactions with each other, more and more positive sentiments will be developed by the people towards each other. As this process continues, there is a tendency for the group members to become more alike in their activities and sentiments. The group now tends to develop expectations or norms that specify how people in a group might behave under certain specific circumstances. In other words, there will be group pressure to influence the perception and behaviour of the group members.

If an individual is elected as the secretary of the *Lions Club,* then according to the social status accorded to him he should proudly possess certain products / services like car, own house with good furniture etc. The initial thrust on joining the club as a member may have been to get acquainted with new friends, since he had recently arrived at the place. Now with his newly acquired status, he is influenced by the other club members and to keep up to the image as the secretary of the Lions Club, he has to maintain a lifestyle pattern adhered to by those occupying the seat before him.

In the same way, a Page 3 socialite may join the ladies club, so as to get admiration from like minded people who have already joined the club. All the members of the club are vying each other and in their desire to be appreciated by others, they furnish their houses with expensive furniture, wear fashionable and costly clothes and jewellery and drive expensive cars. Thus here as members of the prestigious club, they get influenced by the other members, to conform to group pressure and this is seen in the way they purchase various products.

Marketers realising the role played by the formal social groups on their individual members, can work out a suitable sales promotion and communication programme and deliver the same to its target segment.

[D] SHOPPING FRIENDS/GROUPS

Shopping groups can exist because friends or group members need to relate to each other mainly because of the physical location of people, similar perception of things etc. Since the shopping group will comprise of individuals who interact frequently, the group's views on fashion, lifestyle etc. exercise a strong influence on the living style and buying pattern of the individual.

According to psychology, 'group' refers to the number of people who interact with one another, are psychologically aware of one another and perceive themselves to be a group. In the same way, shopping groups can be assumed to exist because the friends or group members need to relate to each other mainly because of the physical location of people, similar perception of things, matching personality, styles, outlook etc. These factors are also responsible for the increase in the frequency of the interactions between the members of a shopping group.

Usually shopping groups are off shoots of the family or friendship groups. The term shopping itself indicates that efforts have to be made to search around while purchasing goods or services. The shopping group prefers to shop around and select goods after comparing the quality, terms, style, customer services, price etc. Usually, when with a shopping group, the buyer will be influenced by their pressure and group's brand preference. The products purchased along with a shopping group may include music system, watch, clothes, jewellery, draperies, vehicles etc.

Since the shopping group will comprise of individuals who interact frequently, the group's views on fashion, lifestyles etc. exercise a strong influence on the living style and buying pattern of the individual. Further, since the shopping group are close knit, they act as an advisor and recommend styles and behaviour pattern to the individual members. The shopping group will express their views on various aspects of the purchase - the cost angle, prestige, usage or utility aspects, availability of competitors brands and past experience of the member who has made use of the product. Since the buyer has a lot of faith and confidence in the views expressed by his shopping group, he will consider their view point before deciding on the purchase of the product.

For instance assume that the college going son in the family is interested in the purchase of an ipod. Usually, he is accompnised by his friends on shopping trips. Further, he gives due consideration to the suggestions and view points expressed by them. Brand name, unique features, how compact it is, price etc. could be some of the variables, the prospective buyer is weighing in mind. Finally, in all probability he will purchase the ipod brand recommended to, by his friends.

So depending on the product category and target market segment, the marketer should develop a marketing programme, keeping in mind, the shopping group who are likely to be involved in the decision making process and thus, able to influence the individual buyer.

[E] WORK GROUP

This group can comprise of formal work group and informal work group. The formal work groups are those which are deliberately created by companies in order to fulfil specific tasks or functions clearly related to the total organisational goals and objectives. Based on their duration, the formal work groups can be of two types.

(i) Permanent formal work group, *(ii)* Temporary formal work group.

The *permanent formal work group* are part of the top management team, work units in various departments of the organisation, staff groups providing specialised services to the line people in the organisation, permanent committees and so on.

Temporary formal work groups : are committees or task forces created for a particular purpose/mission. They may be created to study say review the salary policies, to suggest measures to improve the relationship between the union and management or to think of new products and services and so on. This temporary formal groups may exist till the task assigned to them have been completed. Very often the committee / temporary work group will comprise of members, who are already on the permanent payroll of the company. However, till the completion of the work assigned to the committee, there will be close interactions between the members.

Irrespective of whether the formal work group is permanent or temporary in nature, due to the close interactions between the members of the work groups at the place of work, the group can influence the consumption related attitudes of its members. In the formal work group setup, especially in a superior subordinate relationship, the superior (boss) is likely to influence the buying or consumption pattern of the subordinate. Very often the subordinate aspires to hold a higher position in the near future and so he will symbolically try to adopt the values, attitudes and consumption behaviour of the superior. This is also referred to as *aspiration based personality.* The theoretical version says that the consumer has a vision of himself as he wishes to be and also as he wishes the world to see him. So the product and brand he selects will be the best expression of his own aspiration and self image. In a formal work set-up, this will be reflected, especially influenced by his superiors and colleagues, in the individual's choice of FMCG products like *hard drinks* or *liquor* and more prominently seen in case of products like *automobiles and vehicles, apparels, personal use products, fashion and cosmetics.*

Irrespective of whether the formal work group is permanent or temporary in nature, due to the close interactions between the members of the work groups at the place of work, the group can influence the consumption related attitudes of its members.

Apart from the formal work groups existing in the organisations, if the ecology of the work area and the time schedule of the work permit, informal relationship will develop into informal work groups. Various studies have revealed that these friendships and informal associations are often based simply on the probability of one person's meeting another in the course of daily activities. In the informal settings the members of the informal groups develop a good two way communication path simply because of the probability of interaction created by physical proximity, similarity of interests or other fortuitous factors.

Under the circumstances, the informal group is able to influence the consumption behaviour of its members. This, influence is seen in their choice of products like eatables, soft drinks, credit card, television, refrigerators, other home appliances etc. A consumer buys certain FMCG brands not only for its functional benefits but for psychological gratification, For instance, the advertisement of *'Sunflame hot stove'* shows a housewife cum career woman saying "it (Sunflame) helps me to cope efficiently with my tasks as housewife while I get on with my career".

Marketers must realise that the work group also plays a very important role in promoting their products and work out marketing programmes to communicate information about their products and its usage to the work groups.

REFERENCE GROUP AND CONSUMER CONFORMITY TO THE GROUP

Marketers, being aware of the fact that an individual joins a voluntary (and informal) group because he agrees with the beliefs and value systems of the group, are interested in knowing the ability of the reference group to exert pressure on the individual consumer to encourage conformity and change his attitudes and behaviour.

The ability of the group to achieve conformity of its value system can be seen clearly in a marketing context in an experiment conducted by M. Venkatesh. Here subjects in groups of four were asked to choose the best of three identical men's suits. When three of the four group members were instructed by the experimenter to publicly choose a preselected suit, 22 of 42 critical subjects also choose that particular suit. However, when there was no group pressure, control groups selected the suits on a chance basis. *(Source : Consumer Behavior-Peter'D. Bennett, Harold. H. Kassarjian, 1987, pp. 99)*

The above study indicates the influence the group has on an individual can change his buying pattern.

There are certain methods adopted by a reference group to encourage conformity, that is to change the consumer attitudes and behaviour. To facilitate this, the reference group must:

In order to encourage conformity to the group, the reference group can adopt any of these methods: (a) inform or make the individual aware of the product (b) provide an opportunity to the individual to make a comparative study of her way of thinking viz-a-viz the attitudes and behaviour of the group (c) influence the individual to adopt attitudes and behaviour that are consistent with the norms of the groups (d) legitimize the individual's decision to experience the usage of the same product as that of the group.

(a) **Inform or Make the Individual Aware of the Product :** *For example,* A housewife may inform her neighbour about the availability of a new brand of washing machine, which can help in the washing of clothes. The neighbour is happy and convinced that she can wash clothes in the washing machine whenever the maid is absent.

Reference group will influence the choice of clothes of group members

(b) **Provide an Opportunity to the Individual to make a Comparative Study of her way of Thinking viz-a-viz the Attitudes and Behaviour of the Group :** The above mentioned housewife may invite her neighbour home to have a look at the new washing machine purchased by her. This will provide an opportunity for the lady to have a live demonstration and also understand the positive aspects of owning a washing machine.

(c) **Influence the Individual to Adopt Attitudes and Behaviour that are Consistent with the Norms of the Group :** The housewife may provide literature and more information about her brand of washing machine and also introduces her neighbour to some of the housewives who have had a positive and happy experience using the washing machine.

(d) **Legitimize the Individual's Decision to Experience the Usage of the same Product as the Group :** Finally, when convinced on the goodness of purchasing the washing machine, the neighbour who has initiated the purchase decision will now try to influence the housewife on her selection of the particular brand. This is attempted by talking to her about other friends' pleasant experience with using the same brand of washing machine.

Customers are looking out for products which will be accepted by the group with which they would like to be associated. Hence marketers are focusing their products at people/group with whom the target market identify as a user of the product/service.

FIGURE 9.3

WAYS TO ADD VALUE TO GROUP CONFORMITY

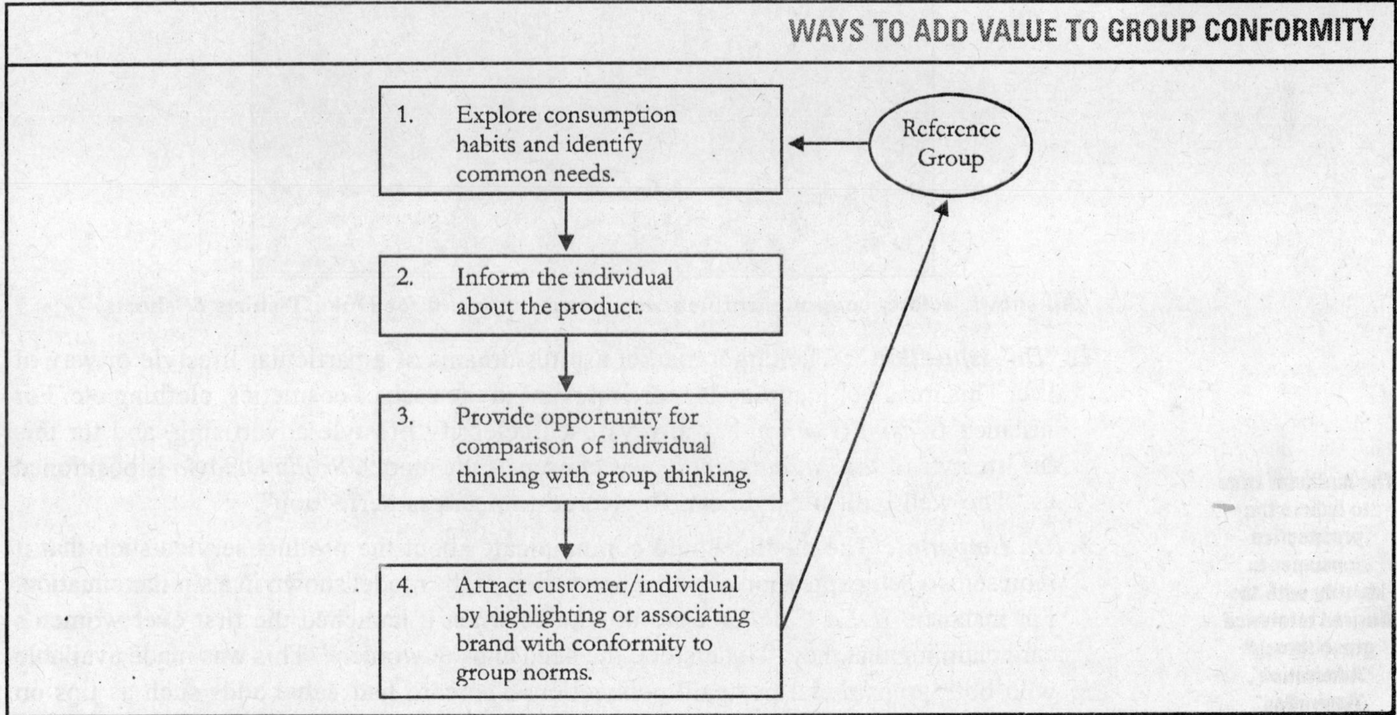

It has been observed by marketers that customers are looking out for products/brands which will be accepted by the group with which they would like to be associated. Hence marketers are focusing their products at people/group with whom the target market can identify as an user of the same.

This identification may be based on either of the following :

1. ***'Admiration'* :** The target market admires the personality and look up with awe at the person who is shown promoting a particular brand of the product. For instance, Amitabh Bachchan has been a brand endorser for companies like *Parker Pens* and *ICICI Home loans* to promote their products. Actress Deepika Padakone is seen endorsing brands such as *BSNL, Fiama Di Wills* and *Parashute Oil*. These personalities are admired and hence appeal to the target market.

Ad shows 'reference group' influences among the youth for Duke T-shirts & shorts.

The marketer tries to induce the prospective consumer to identify with the desired reference group through 'Admiration', 'Aspiration', 'Empathy', or 'Recognition'.

2. ***'On Aspiration' :*** The target market aspires/dreams of a particular lifestyle or way of life. This image or ideology is more relevant in the case of cosmetics, clothing etc. For instance *Grasim Gwalior* has always used celebrity lifestyle advertising, and for this the lifestyle of *the Pataudi family* was chosen as the model. *Skoda Octavia* is positioned as "The well built lifestyle car, Engieered to peerless perfection".
3. ***On Empathy :*** The media should communicate about the product/service such that it represents a self expression or portrays a vision of the model shown in a similar situation. For instance, *IDEA Cellular* used this mode when it launched the first ever women's card claiming that they "Understood the need gaps of women". This was made available with both prepaid and postpaid connection. The card had value adds such as tips on beauty fashion, health and safety alerts to near and dear ones.
4. ***On Recognition of a Similar Situation :*** Here the marketer will advertise showing or in recognition of a situation or a person (real or stereotype). A classic example would be the campaign used by *Hindustan Lever,* when it had launched *'Surf Excel'.* The focus was to get the real time customers/users involved in the advertising and be given a chance to test the product and also give a feedback which would be mass communicated. Further, the company had also used a money back offer for dissatisfied customers. The company had carefully chosen to represent the people that customers would identify with. Another advertisement is of *'Saffola cooking oil',* a product of *Marico Industries.* The commercial drives home the message of Saffola's product benefit "there are many things in your husband's life that you cannot control. Saffola-its your life insurance"-strikes up an immediate association of safety and relief.

Usually group decisions are made through meetings wherein members interact among themselves, persuade and influence other group members and put pressure to conform to group norms. So, an understanding of the factors which can guide and influence consumer's purchase decision can help marketers to work out a suitable marketing strategy.

BENEFITS OF REFERENCE GROUP APPEAL

There are certain positive aspects associated with groups in terms of better decisions, better commitment of the people towards decisions and especially better communication with increased brand awareness and reduced perceived risk. Some of these aspects are briefly presented below.

Benefits of reference group for the consumer is better communication and increased brand awareness along with reduction in perceived risk. Marketers have been using three types of groups influence (informational, comparative and normative) for developing advertising and personal selling strategies.

1. ***Better Communication and Increased Brand Awareness :*** Reference group acts as the source of learning through observation and hearing others experiences and also with more data and information available from other group members. The individual customer is able to communicate and interact with the group. He is able to learn more about the brand based on the views and facts expressed by the group. This constant interactions between the individual and group, influences his buying behaviour and consequently increases his awareness of the brand.
2. ***Reduces Perceived Risk :*** On the one hand the marketer is continuously involved in trying to identify consumer needs, her/his motives, buying habits, behaviour pattern and decision making process and accordingly manufacture and sell products matching such needs and desires. At the same time, the consumers also have to be convinced that the product/service being offered to them will satisfy their needs. There may be hesitation on the part of the consumer to immediately accept a product as it is because of the perceived risk associated with its utility aspect. This perceived risk is reduced with the customers association with the reference group. The group provides and shares the information about the product with the members in an open environment. Moreover, past experiences of other members with the usage of the product brand are also revealed. There is also group pressure to conform to group behaviour. All these will pave the way to remove whatsoever doubt the individual may have about the product and enable him to whole heartedly accept the product due to reduction in perceived risk now associated with the usage of the product.

MARKETING APPLICATIONS OF REFERENCE GROUP APPEALS

Marketers have been using three types of group influence (informational, comparative and normative) for developing advertising and personal selling strategies.

Advertising Strategies

While working out advertising strategies, group influence is portrayed through **informational influence** by using an expert spokesperson such as a doctors *(Lizol disinfectant)*, engineers *(ACC cement)* to communicate on the product features and performance. At times they also use celebrities such as sports persons, film stars (Filmstar Mohanlal on *Pankajakasturi* or *Parker Pens* and *ICICI Home Loan* by Amitabh Bachchan). Sometimes marketers request person's who have used the product brand to testify and speak on their experience. Nevertheless, all efforts will be put to ensure that the target consumers will view the spokerperson to be an expert and hence his or her opinion is credible in the product category.

Marketers focus their product brand at people or group with whom their target market can identify.

Ad portraying comparative influence by using actual typical referent consumer

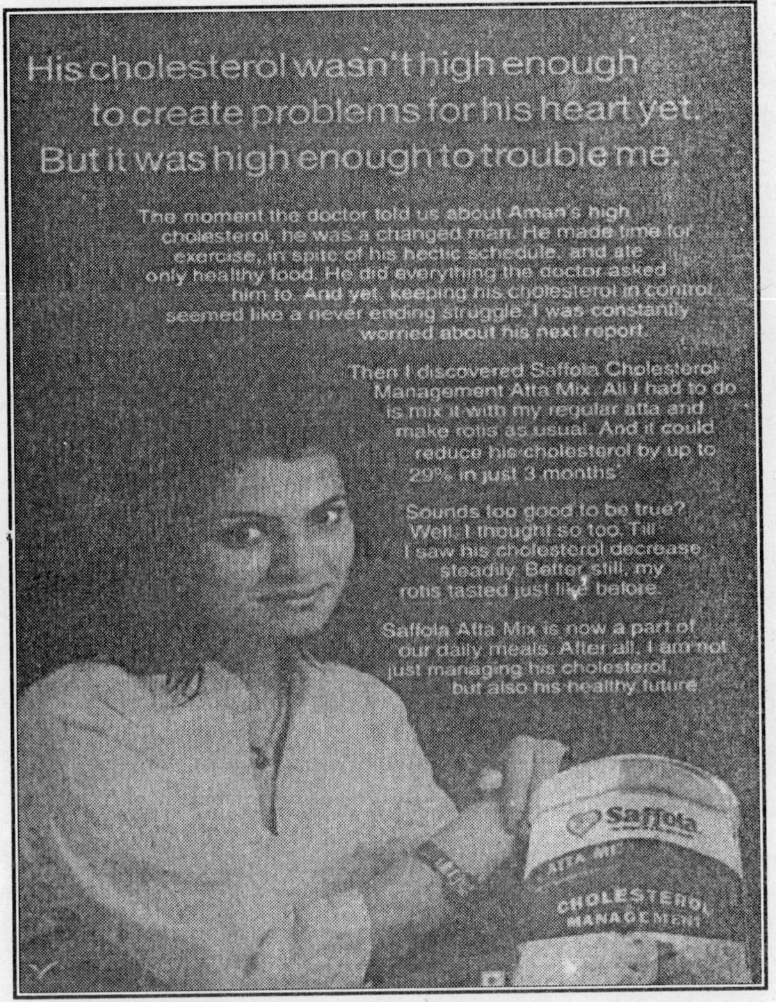

Ad conveys informational influence through using an expert spokesperson

Portraying Comparative Influence

Advertisers have been using comparative influence by using two types of referents.

(a) Actual referent or "typical consumer", who cite into common needs and problems which are portrayed as being similar to that of the prospective purchaser.

(b) Symbolic referent *i.e.*, a celebrity whom the consumer empathizes and identifies with, especially because this person (celebrity) is likeable or attractive. For instance Hema Malini is used as a symbolic referent to promote *The Bank of Rajasthan* and *Zero-B water purifier.* Or take the case of Simone Singh endorsing *Garnier Hair Dye* or Ajay and Kajal being used as referents for *Whirlpool Washing Machine.* In all the above instances, consumers would like to identify with the referents.

Portraying Normative Influence

Marketers have tried to use normative influence by showing group approval in advertising. Praise for the cup of tea or coffee *(Red Label, Bru),* glorious hair *(Sunsilk Shampoo),* tasty snacks *(Kurkure)* a smooth and comfortable ride *(Alto)-* are all examples of advertising's simulation of social (or society's) approval. In all the above advertisements, persons who are important to the consumer (spouse, in-laws, friends, neighbours) have shown approval of the consumer's choice.

At times, marketers have used normative influence to show the probable adverse results of not using the product. *Dr. Bhatra's Clinic* uses fear of social group's not acceptance due to excess hair loss or *Lifebouy Soap* and *Rexona Deodorant* demonstrates the fear of group obtracism due to body odour. In the above advertisements, it is indicated that use of the particular product changes disapproval to approval, which re-iterates the fact that coercive power and reward power are linked.

When the salesperson is considered to be an expert source of information, it reflects expert power. When the salesperson is able to re-inforce the customer's ego and social needs by demonstrating similar needs, concerns and predispositions, it reflects referent influence. Normative influence refers to the relative bargaining power of the buyer and seller to arrive at favourable terms of sale.

Ad uses normative influence, to show the potential results of not using the product services

Personal Selling Strategies

Marketers use three types of reference group influence while developing sales strategies.

(*a*) **Informational influence,** when the salesperson is considered to be an expert source of information. *For example, Acqua Guard* water purifier. Such influence reflects expert power.

(*b*) **Comparative influence,** when the salesperson is able to re-inforce the customer's ego and social needs by demonstrating similar needs, concerns and predispositions. Such influence reflects referent influence. The sales agents of *ICICI* or *HDFC* banks are able to demonstrate their expertise and knowledge in communicating about the variety of financial offerings that can be of interest to the customer. This is expert power in action.

However, price conscious or bargain hunting customers will prefer to shop at outlets such as *Big Bazaar*. The sales persons at this outlet are persons with similar needs and with low risk involved, they are able to regularly sell products to buyers. In this instance the sales persons are able to sell using the comparative (or referent) influence.

(*c*) ***Normative influence,*** which refers to the relative bargaining power of the buyer and sellers to arrive at favourable terms of sale. Of course, bargaining will take place only when the consumers' have the ability to bargain and this may have a direct effect on the sales outcome. This behaviour could be visible during the purchase of products such as cars, home appliances, furniture and second hand items. Studies have indicated that a big reason why some customers are able to obtain items for lower prices is because of their bargaining strength and knowledge.

SUMMARY 

Groups can be defined as two or more persons who share a common purpose. A very important environmental consumer behaviour influence is the face-to-face group. The group can exert influence on consumer behaviour based on three factors: (a) the individual's attitude towards the group (b) the nature of the group (c) the nature of the product: Reference group characteristics which can influence consumer behaviour include norms, values, roles, status, socialization and power.

The various types of reference groups which can exert influence on the consumer's behaviour are normative reference group, comparative reference group, indirect reference group, informational influence, aspirational group, disclamant group and the avoidance group. There are certain types of groups which are relevant to the consumer and can also influence his decision making process. These are the family, friendship group, formal social group, shopping group and the work group, Being aware of the fact that an individual join's an informal group because he agrees and believes in their beliefs and value system, marketers are interested in knowing about the ability of the reference group to exert influence on the individual consumer to encourage conformity and change their behaviour and attitude. Marketers are targeting their products at people or group with whom the target market identify as an user of the product or service. The identification may be based on admiration, aspiration, empathy or recognition. Group influence can benefit the consumer through better communication and increased brand awareness and reduction in the perceived risk factors. Marketers have been using three types of group influence (informational, comparative and normative) for developing marketing and personal selling strategies.

CHAPTER QUESTIONS FOR DISCUSSION

1. What is meant by the term 'reference group'? Can you identify the type of social groups which can influence an individual's choice of a health club?
2. As a college student, name two reference groups who are very important to you. What type of purchase decisions of yours have been influenced by your reference group appeal?
3. Divide the class into 4-5 groups, with each group required to collect information on the various advertisements where marketers have used reference group influence. Discuss on the type of group power influence and the factors which appear to support the particular reference group appeal.
4. Recall advertisements where you feel the advertiser is using spokesperson as a referent or an expert. Explain your reason for selecting the particular ad.
5. Explain with examples how marketers can use group influence for developing marketing and person selling strategies.

SUGGESTED READINGS

1. Jagdish N. Sheth, Banwari. Mittal *'Customer Behavior A Managerial Perspective'*, Thomson Learning, South Western Singapore, 2003, pp. 63-67.
2. Pallavi. Srivastava, Sultan of Spin, *Business Today*, March 23, 2007, pp. 54.
3. V.S. Ramaswamy, S. Namakumari, *Marketing Management - Planning, Implementation and Control* (3rd Edition), McMillan India Ltd., New Delhi, (Reprint) 2005.

4. Philip Kotler, *Marketing Management: Analysis, Implementation and Control,* (8th Edition), Prentice Hall of India Pvt. Ltd., New Delhi, 1994.

5. Paul Hersey, Ken Blanchard, *Management of Organizational Behavior :* Utilizing human resources (4th Edition), Prentice Hall of India Pvt. Ltd., New Delhi, 1985.

6. Peter D. Bennett, Harold H. Kassarjian, *Consumer Behavior*, Prentice Hall of India Pvt. Ltd, New Delhi, 1987.

7. Henry. Assael, *'Consumer Behavior and Marketing Action'*, 6th Edition., Thomson Learning, Singapore, 2001 pp. 552-560.

8. Jim Blythe, *The Essence of Consumer Behavior,* Prentice Hall Europe, Hertfordshire, 1997.

CASE

FASHION LABEL – 'GINI & JONY'

The Beginning

Gini & Jony had a very humble beginning, when the brothers Prakash, Jay and Anil Lakhani started the business in 1980 with a handful of machines and each of the brothers handling the various aspects of the business, namely procurement of material, production, deliveries or billing. The Lakhani brothers had initially got into children's garment business.

Mr. Anil Lakhani, the Managing Director (MD) of Gini & Jony, recalls the place (Crawford Market, Mumbai) from where they used to purchase the cloth way back in 1980, "The entire Crawford Market is a labyrinth of various markets intertwined into one another. One had to pass through lanes and by lanes of various wholesale cloth markets to reach the wholesale cloth market, from where we used to purchase cloth." Of course, in the course of traversing those lanes and by lanes, the brothers' journey has led them to the creation of a premier children's apparel brand in India, today.

Creation of the Brand Name

It was during one of Prakash Lakhani's overseas trip, that the idea of creating their own brand struck and thus Gini & Jony came into existence. Since they were already into children's garments business, it was decided to venture into retailing. For selecting the brand name, the idea was to have a name which would be easy to remember as well give a westernised look and feel to the brand. At the very outset it was decided that Gini & Jony brand would be retailed in only selective number of outlets. This move was to ensure that the demand is always there especially since the market was not bombarded with Gini & Jony brand offerings. Initially, the children's garments were imported, subsequently it was decided to use cotton to manufacture apparel for children. By 1994, when modern retail players like Shopper's Stop started operations, Gini & Jony also made their entry with their first shop-in-shop in Shopper's Stop outlets.

The Three Brands

In the organized kids wear segment, Gini & Jony boosts of a very modern approach to fashion and lifestyle, offering an array of collections spanning premium garments, trendy party wear, casual day wear and the right style for the right occasion.

- The thematic concept for kids was pioneered through the mother brand **Gini & Jony Freedom Wear** which was a phenomenal success. This brand is positioned as premium range offerings.
- One of the sub-brands of Gini & Jony is **GJ Jeans** Un limited. This brand comes across as a hip 'n' trendy range of denims for kids and teens under the age of 18 years.

  There is also another collection for girls and boys with jeans in the latest styles, washes and fabrics teamed up with trendy tops and matching accessories.
- There is also another sub-brand **palm-tree,** which specializes in everyday dressing and is inspired by a kid's dream holiday. The clothes are cool in fresh and bright undiluted colours, adding a twist of fun to the garments.

Plans for the Future

The makers of Gini & Jony have ambitious plans of investing heavily and opening exclusive Gini & Jony outlets for each of the three brands. While this focus is on the domestic markets, it

is also keen to tap the export market. Exports of the brand accounts to 8%-10% of the total business (figures as in January 2006), where the focus was in the Middle East. By the next year, the company planned to have exclusive branded outlets in Middle East as well as in Europe.

To promote the brand, the company had organized an exclusive fashion show of each brand in the presence of illustrious dignitaries from the fashion industry.

Competition

Gini & Jony specifically caters to the needs of the kids wear segment. Children or kids who form a part of this segment are actively involved in the decision making process. They are greatly influenced by their peers' style of dressing, views and opinions. They are fond of imitating the tastes and preferences of their peer group. Understanding this behaviour of kids there are some competing brands who also cater to this market segment.

To name a few of the competitors:

Pepe Jeans (London), Weekender Kids, K.G Denim's Trigger, Westside etc.

(*Source :* Gini & Jony Brand Launch, *Retail Biz,* March 2003, pp.40 and Rajiv, Banerjee, No Jony Come Lately, *The Economic Times,* Bangalore, January 25, 2006)

QUESTIONS FOR DISCUSSION

1. Since the children and youth of today are very fashion conscious, what methods should be applied by Gini & Jony to ensure that they have offerings to match the fast changing lifestyles?
2. Since youngsters have a penchant for fashion labels, what type of reference appeal can be used to promote the brands?

UNIT IV : CONSUMER DECISION MAKING, AFTER SALES AND RELATED ISSUES

CHAPTER 10

CONSUMER DECISION MAKING

- Case : Consumer decision making involved in **Pleasure, Scooty, ELLE-18** and **Candico**
- Meaning of Decision making
- Different views of Consumer Decision making
- Buying motives
- Types of decision making processes in buying
- Consumer Information processing
- Schiffman & Kanuk's Model of consumer decision making
- Types of households
- The household life cycle
- A Model of household decision making
- Summary
- Chapter questions for discussion
- Suggested Readings
- Case : **Gili – Gili India Limited (Gitanjali Group)**

CASE

CONSUMER DECISION MAKING INVOLVED IN "PLEASURE", "SCOOTY", "ELLE 18" AND "CANDICO"

The Indian market has witnessed, tremendous social changes and trends, with women, to a great extent, being actively involved in the decision making process. Women, whether they are working or housewives, in the age group 24-54 years have emerged as a potent force in the market place changing the way companies, design, position and sell their products. Although women may earn less then men, they are making 80 percent of buying decisions in their homes. In the words of the CEO Nagesh, **Shopper's Stop** "We have seen the rising purchasing power of women at our stores. "Approximately 40 per cent of the floor space is allocated to women based categories, up by 10 percent from just two years ago". Women roles have changed in the decision making from passive recipients to active participants. There is a new sophistication and confidence seen in the new women consumers of today, and this is reflected in the changing trends in her consumption behaviour.

Marketers are wooing the women like never before and addressing them with ads specifically targeted at them. Even though marketers have always targeted women for conventional categories like FMCG, personal care and consumer durables, now-a-days there is seen a subtle change in the way they look at women and communicate to them.

- Of the total gearless scooter market, according to industry estimates, women account for 80 percent of the market, which is estimated to be around 1 million units per annum. Given below are Hero Honda and TVS Motors efforts at addressing the needs of the women decision makes.

Hero Honda, known as a company selling masculine bikes, launched **'Pleasure'** an exclusive 100 cc scooter, specially targeted at the women customers. On conducting an in depth market research, it was found that specific to the scooter market, there were immense opportunities to develop a product customised for women, which led to the launch of Pleasure.

Another initiative from the company in order to aid and motivate the women customers is the opening up of the various 'Just 4 her' outlets, or the exclusive women's showroom for the scooter. Apart from offering products for women, Hero Honda offers services like emergency services, anytime pick up services personal accident insurance of up to Rs 1 lakh and a Lady Rider's club.

- **'Scooty'** is the brand name of the offering from TVS Motors, with features like mobile chargers, easy centre stand and also provides the benefit of power with the variant TVS **Scooty Pep**. It has been endorsed by cine stars Preity Zinta and Priyanka Chopra and had played upon the campaign which indicated that it was 'surprising powerful.'

TVS research had shown that there was a huge population of women seeking mobility with only around 3 percent of them being mobile.

This indicated that there was a huge market waiting to be tapped involving women decision makers.

- Marketers are trying to involve the customers and decision makers in certain product categories in creating marketing strategies. *i.e.,* marketers are inviting customers to co-create customised products for themselves. For instance, Hindustan Lever Ltd (HLL) once had got consumers to develop new colour shades for its **Elle 18** brand of cosmetics.

- Similarly, confectionary manufacturer *Candico India* had attempted to involve the consumers (children below 14 years) not only to devise new flavours but also to use their inputs to create marketing strategy. Some time in 1997, when Candico India had entered the confectionery market, it was felt that the market was highly penetrated inspite of the presence of established players. So the company decided to do something that would make a difference to the consumers. That was when the Young Consultant Programme (YCP) was worked out involving kids not older than 14 years, were appointed as brand ambassadors, they had to visit the company plant and give their opinion on everything. Nevertheless, although everything said by them was heard, only the feasible suggestions were implemented. The exercise of both HLL and Candico paid off very well. Elle 18 found a favourable response from its customers. While the YCP helped Candico to position its product differently in the market and its flavours like *litchi, imli* and *kaccha aam* were unique product offerings.

Thus marketers are trying out unique ways to get involved and help customers in their decision making process.

Customers decide to purchase products and services to satisfy their personal, social and environmental needs. This aspect has been illustrated in our examples of *Pleasure, TVS Scooty, Elle 18* and *Candico* discussed above. In this chapter, we are considering the consumer decision making process as the first step of the consumption process. Hence, an attempt has been made to examine the various models of man in terms of his consumer behaviour. We are also having a look at the buying motives, types of decision making and consumer information processing. The Schiffman and Kanuk's model has been discussed which provides an overview on the consumer decision making process. Finally, we have also briefly touched upon issues related to the types of households, the household life cycle and the model of household decision making.

MEANING OF DECISION MAKING

Everyday we are involved in taking decisions related to the various aspects of our lives. Usually such decisions are taken automatically without the involvement of any particular decision making process. For instance say a housewife goes to purchase a mid priced range of tea, her decision making merely involves making a selection from the various brands of tea like *Taj Mahal, Tata Tea, Red label, Yellow Label* and so on. *The process by which a person is required to make a choice from various alternative options is referred to as decision making.*

The process by which a person is required to make a choice from various alternative options is referred to as decision making. The changing market environment provides the impetus for a careful study of consumer decision making or buyer behaviour.

The marketing environment has been evolving, become competitive and more of a buyer's market, with each marketer trying to adopt unique strategies which can result in positive decision making from the consumer's side. While the customer gains from having to decide and select from a wide array of choices, the marketer will benefit from a substantial increase in sales when the consumer decides to purchase their brands.

Box 10.1 on the role of men and women in the decision making process, as discovered by Hindustan Lever's Prakash Tandon makes interesting reading.

BOX 10.1

FOR BETTER OR FOR WORSE

Often, the man makes the choice. But of course, it's the woman who tells him what to choose.

Indian marketers learned the importance of women early on. In his memoirs Prakash Tandon, the first Indian to head Hindustan Levers, recalled his experiences as the company's first Indian trainee in 1937, developing its first brands. Tandon was not convinced that Levers' classic strategy of targeting housewives would work in India's patriarchal society and told this to his boss, a perceptive Englishman named Thompson Walker: "I explained that our Indian housewife always deferred to her husband, for she had been brought up traditionally to look to him for decisions. I grew quite eloquent about the classical training of girls as future wives, the place of the husband as lord of the house, while she is *devi, grihalaxmi,* the goddess of the home, demure, submissive and deferential to her master." As proof Tandon pointed to their first door-to-door surveys where questions about who chose brands, was always answered by 'husband'.

Thompson Walker valued Tandon's local expertise, but was skeptical on this point. He asked their researcher Ada Rodrigues to probe further. "The result was funny and demolished me, "Writes Tandon ruefully." At the very first call Ada made, the housewife as usual said 'husband chooses'. Ada began to probe as instructed. Suddenly a light dawned on the woman's face and she said simply, "Oh I see what you mean. My husband chooses, but, of course, I tell him what to choose!".

That devastating reply firmly ensured the ascendancy of the Indian woman consumer. Some products like liquor and cigarettes were seen as male consumed, but for most FMCG categories, it was accepted that women called the shots. Yet reality was always more complex. Most Indian consumers do operate within the parameters of a patriarchal society which might allow women to choose the brands in the basket, yet was always likely to allow men to dictate which products are selected in the first place.

(By Vikram Doctor, The Economic Times, 14th August 2005)

DIFFERENT VIEWS OF CONSUMER DECISION MAKING

The changing market environment provides the impetus for a careful study of consumer decision making or buyer behaviour. The term 'model' generally refers to a general 'view' or perspective as to when and why individuals behave as they do. In buying and consuming a variety of goods and services, consumers are pursuing a sets of motives. Though need satisfaction is the underlying motive source of all consumption activity, an understanding of needs and processes that influence the formation and satisfaction of such needs will help the marketer to devise suitable marketing programmes. Here we will examine the various models of consumers in terms of the following four views:

An Economical View or Model

As per the economic view, consumer will allocate his expenditure over different products at given prices rationally so as to maximize utility. The passive view or model perceives consumers to be impulsive who take irrational purchase decisions influenced by the promotional offers of the marketers.

Traditionally, economics has been considered to be the mother discipline of marketing. Economists believe that consumers derive some utility (a feeling of satisfaction) from consuming a particular product and so their consumption activity will be directed towards pursuing maximisation of utility. That's why if given a certain amount of purchasing power, and a set of needs and tastes, a consumer will allocate his expenditure over different products at given prices rationally so as to maximise utility. Economists also postulate that the utility from the consumption of a certain product diminishes as the quantity of the product consumed increases (based on the Principle of Diminishing Marginal Utility). According to this model it is also possible to make a number of predictions about the behaviour of buyers in terms of the price effect, income effect and substitution effect. While these predictions are useful, questions are being raised on the assumption of rationality in the behaviour of buyers. The criticism by consumer researchers is based on a number of reasons. They argue that in reality, the consumer may not be (a) aware of the various product alternatives or (b) in a position to evaluate all the advantages and disadvantages related to the various product alternatives so as to rank them accordingly. Thus in the absence of all the possible sufficient, and accurate information, it will not be possible for the consumer to make the so called *rational or perfect decision.*

It has been criticised that the economic view is too idealistic and simplistic. It is being argued that consumers in reality behave very differently and do not maximise their decisions in terms of economic considerations such as price-quantity relationships, marginal utility or indifference curves. Very often the consumer will settle down for a 'satisfactory' decision and not necessarily the best one though it will be a 'good enough' decision.

The Passive View or model

Unlike the rational economic view of man, the passive view portrays the consumer as someone who is basically carried away by the promotional and self oriented efforts of the marketer. As per the passive view, consumers are perceived to be impulsive who take irrational purchase decisions and are influenced by the promotional offers of the marketers.

The passive model is criticized as it fails to take a pragmatic view of the consumers. It is argued that in a buying situation, the consumer will be involved in a decision making process wherein he seeks information on the product, evaluates all the alternative brands and then makes a selection based on the brand which provides him maximum satisfaction. At times the consumer's purchase decision is also based on emotions or moods. So it is wrong to assume that the consumer will be passive while taking purchase decisions.

A Cognitive View or Model

As a consumer, man is usually involved in thinking and problem solving. He is constantly involved in an active search for goods and services which will not only satisfy his needs but enrich his life also. As per the cognitive view consumers are involved in an information seeking and processing method. They try to gather all the necessary information from various sources, such as a trusted friend, or an expert and so on. Once he feels that he has sufficient information, so as to make a 'satisfactory choice decision', he will cease to gather more information and will ultimately decide on his purchase intention.

This model of man as a thinker, views consumer as an information processor. And all the focus is on the processes by which consumers seek and evaluate information about the concerned brands and the respective retail outlets.

The advertisement on *Panasonic* can work as a cognitive appeal to customers seeking information for purchasing high end television. The ad provides information on the technology benefits in terms of V-Real Technology, Advanced Smart Sound Speaker System and HDAVI control offered by the Panasonic brand of TV Series.

Panasonic is trying to appeal to the cognitive brand

Thus according to the cognitive model of consumer, the above mentioned ad will make the consumer think on the benefits of Panasonic. The consumer will finally take the purchase decision based on his satisfaction of the information received. In other words the problem solving view or model of consumer talks of a person who in the absence of the total information or knowledge of all the available product alternatives, would actively seek *'satisfactory information* and thereby attempt to make *satisfactory decisions* accordingly.

An Impulsive or Emotional View of Consumer

Another aspect of consumer decision making is that they can be emotional or impulsive while taking purchase decisions. Very often, we, as consumers are involved in purchases made on impulse or on a whim. For such emotional buying, the consumer may not undergo the usual process of carefully searching, evaluating and then deciding on the brand or outlet to purchase from. Rather he is more likely to purchase the product (brand) based on a whim or an impulse. Such consumer decisions are said to be *'emotionally driven'*.

As per the cognitive view, consumers are involved in an information seeking and processing method. Here all the focus is on the processes by which consumers seek and evaluate information about the concerned brands and respective retail outlets. Another aspect of consumer decision making is that he can be emotional or impulsive while taking purchase decisions.

Ad to induce the cognitive man's thinking process

For emotional or impulse purchases, in the absence of a search for pre-purchase information, it is the mood and feelings of the consumer which will decide on the emotional purchase decision. Emotional decisions could be rational to some extent also. That is, the consumer may take an emotional decision to purchase a product but he will be rational while deciding or choosing one brand over another.

This type of behaviour is displayed while making purchases of apparel, gifts, selecting holiday destinations or toys (for children). In all the above situations, the final decision may be made on the basis of emotion. Advertisers are projecting, their products or services in a way to appeal to the emotions of the particular target market. Such emotional appeals can be seen in the advertisements of *Johnson and Johnson baby products, Huggies diaper, Wipro Baby Soft, Fisher Price toys* and so on.

Moods play an important role in consumer decision making. It is often the mood of the consumer which influences his decisions related to when to shop, where to shop etc.

Related to consumers emotions and feeling is the 'mood' of the person. Mood may be defined as a feeling state or state of the mind. The basic difference between an emotion and a mood is that the former is a response to a particular environment, while mood is an unfocused, pre-existing state-already present, when the consumer gets motivated or experiences a positive feeling about an advertisement, or the retail outlet or brand or a product.

Moods play an important role in consumer decision making. Very often it is the mood of the consumer which influences his decisions related to when to shop, where to shop, in whose company to shop etc. It has been observed that even within the shopping environment, the interior decor, the attitude of the sales persons, the type of services provided etc. could affect the shoppers mood and influence the consumer's decision on how long to shop and on how often to go to that shop. Realising this now retailers and dealers are creating a positive store image. This is likely to have a positive impact and influence on the consumer's mood and decision to purchase.

Impulse purchases involve pre-purchase information search.

➲ BUYING MOTIVES

A consumer purchases a particular product or service because of a strong inner feeling or force which instils in him a strong desire to have possession of the same. A buying motive, can thus be said to be all the desires, considerations and impulses, which induces a buyer to purchase a given product. Marketers are interested in the understanding of buying motives because it would indicate about their attitudes and the 'why' of their purchase decisions.

A consumer purchases a particular product or service because of a strong inner feeling or force which instils in him a strong desire to have possession of the same.

Ad is trying to appeal to the 'emotional' consumer

Basically, buying motives are of two kinds:

1. Product motives, 2. Patronage motives.

Product is said to be a bundle of satisfaction to take care of consumer needs and desires. Then the questions before the marketing decision maker are - why does a person buy a product, a specific brand? And why does he not have brand loyalty or why does he change his brand from one to another? These questions can be explained by understanding his buying motives.

The impulses, considerations and desires that induce a person to be positively inclined to purchase a particular product are called product motives.

Product Motives

The impulses, considerations and desires that induce a person to be positively inclined to purchase a particular product are called product motives. Accordingly the product will be inclusive of the attributes *i.e.,* the colour, design, package, price and utility.

Ad is trying to appeal to the 'emotional' consumer

Emotional product motives are those impulses which persuade a consumer to purchase a product spontaneously without forethinking on the consequences of the action.

Emotional and Rational Product Motives

Product motives can be classified on the basis of the nature of satisfaction sought by the buyer. Based on this classification, we can have two categories of product motives.

(i) Emotional product motives, *(ii)* Rational product motives.

Emotional product motives are those impulses which persuade a consumer to purchase a product spontaneously without forethinking on the consequences of the action or decision. Evaluation of the pros and cons of the decision or logical reasoning analysis is not found behind such purchase decisions. Here the buyer lets the heart rule over the mind. That is, emotional product motives usually appeal to the buyer's sense of ego, to display his social status, tendency to imitate others or convey the feeling of love and affection to close friends and family members. For instance, a father may on impulse buy a saree for his wife and gift a toy to his little daughter.

Rational product motive involves careful reasoning and logical analysis of the intended purchase by the buyer. Patronage buying motives can be categorized into two: *Emotional patronage* motives are impulses which motivate and persuade a buyer to purchase from a specific shop, while, if a buyer solicits a particular shop after following a logical reasoning of the mind, these are called *rational patronage* motives.

Rational product motive, on the other hand, involves careful reasoning and logical analysis of the intended purchase. The buyer will work-on whether it is worthwhile to purchase the product, the purpose to be served by the intended product purchase, the various alternatives available to the buyer and so on. The buyer will think and work-out the valid and relevant reasons to justify the proposed purchase of the product. For instance, if a person is planning to purchase furniture for his house, he/she will work on various aspects like suitability to the home environment, durability, economics, etc. before purchasing the same. They will lookout, enquire about the furniture available at various outlets before taking the final decision on whether or not to buy the furniture.

At times the product motives may be a mixture of emotion and rationality. That is, a buyer may react quickly to a situation and make an impulsive buying decision but there could be some conscious reasoning behind such purchases. So a more logical way of classifying product motives is by adding two dimensions to the product motives — utility and prestige. In most purchase decisions, these two motives are combined to a certain extent. It is believed that a buyer gains satisfaction from the purchase of a product partly because of its utility to him/her and partly because of the social recognition he or she gets from the purchase of the product.

Patronage Buying Motives

Why do buyers purchase from certain *specific shops?* What are the considerations or factors which persuade the buyer to display such store patronage? These questions can be answered by understanding patronage buying motives.

FIGURE 10.1

THE TYPES OF BUYING MOTIVES

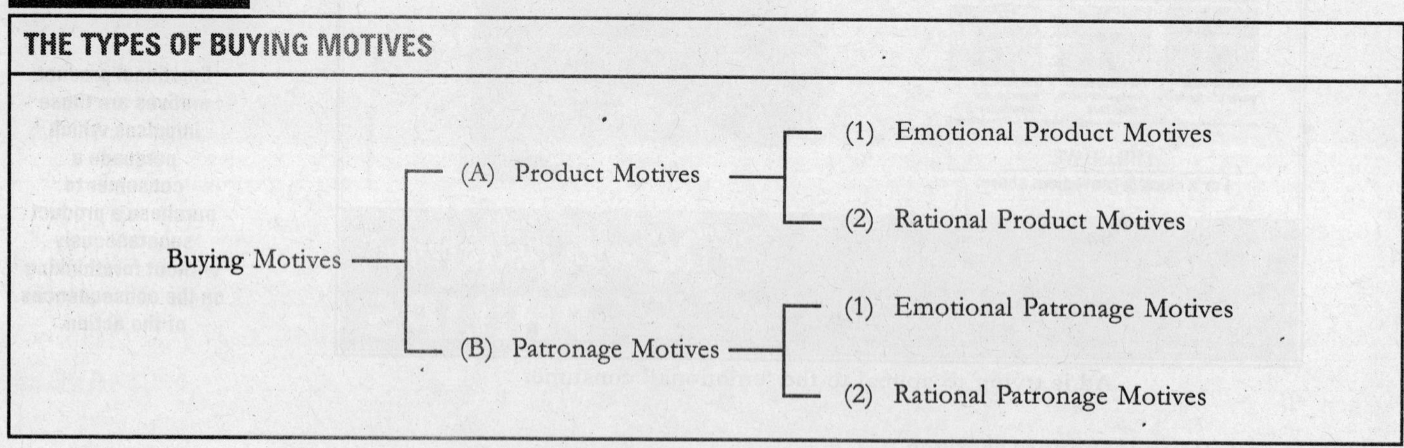

Patronage buying motives can also be categorised into two namely, emotional patronage motives and rational patronage motives.

Emotional patronage motives are those impulses which motivate and persuade a buyer to purchase from specific shops. There may be no logical reasoning behind his decision to purchase from a particular shop. He may simply decide to buy from his "most preferred" or "favourite" shop, based on subjective reasons. This is referred to as emotional patronage motives. Here also it may the urge to gain social recognition or urge to imitate others. which may have led to the buyer developing to patronage to a specific shop (s).

On the other hand, *if a buyer solicits a particular shop after following a logical reasoning of the mind, it is called rational patronage motives.* He/she may select a shop because it offers a variety of products, or stocks the latest designs and models or prompt delivery or assures good after sales service. Then we can say that the buyer is influenced by rational patronage motives. But, as mentioned earlier here also every patronage will be inclusive of a combination of rational and emotional motives. Knowledge of the product motives and patronage motives will help the marketers to devise or formulate sales promotion programmes such that the same product appeals to the different motives of the buyers. Marketers can also work-out strategies to attract and retain store patronage.

Consumer decision making is not a single process. While examining the extent of decision making, it can be said that consumer's take their decisions on the basis of undergoing a cognitive (thought) process of information search and evaluating the brand alternatives.

TYPES OF DECISION-MAKING PROCESSES IN BUYING

The success of *'Indica'* car and its variants is because Tata Motors was able to understand the importance of the decision-making process undertaken by compact car buyers who were looking out for quality at reasonable prices. But consumer decision-making is not a single process. Deciding to purchase a car will be different from deciding to buy a bathing soap. The consumer decision making processes can be examined at two levels :

- By examining the extent of decision-making
- By understanding the consumer's degree of involvement in the purchase.

FIGURE 10.2

TYPES OF CONSUMER-DECISION MAKING

	High Involvement	*Low Involvement*
Decision-Making Behaviour (Information search evaluation alternatives)	*COMPLEX DECISION-MAKING* (products such as automobiles, digital camera, ipod, T.V., computers etc.)	*LIMITED DECISION-MAKING* (breakfast items, coldrinks, snacks, seeing movies etc.)
Habit (Little or no Information search, considers only one brand)	*BRAND LOYALTY* (Groceries, sports shoes etc.)	*INERTIA* (tissue napkins, vegetables)

(*Source : Consumer Behavior*, Henry Assael, 6th Edn., 2001)

A look at Figure 10.2 will indicate that while examining the extent of decision-making, it can be said that consumer's take their decisions after undergoing a cognitive (thought) process of information search and evaluating the brand alternatives. However, little or no decision-making may take place if the consumer is satisfied with a particular brand which is purchased consistently (say the same brand of toothpaste or Talcum powder is purchased everytime). Here

In complex decision making consumers are involved in detailed information processing.

consumer decision-making can be seen in the form of a continuum *from decision making to Habit.*

The second angle of examining consumer decision-making is by looking at the degree of involvement. The level of involvement can be in the form of all continuum from high-to-low involvement purchases. *High involvement purchases* are very important for the consumer. This means it can be closely connected to his or her ego and self image and probably involving some financial, social or personal risk. For instance, the consumer is planning to purchase a new mobile phone, say. Now the consumer will channalise his time and energy to weigh the product alternatives before settling on a particular model which will suit his ego and self image.

When the consumer has to undergo *low involvement purchases,* the financial, social and psychological risks may not be very high. So the consumer may not feel it is worth spending considerable time and effort in searching for information, about the various brands or range of alternatives.

Decision-making versus Habit and Low versus High Involvement

If one were to *consider decision making* versus *habit* and *low* versus *high involvement, there* can be four types of consumer purchase processes.

(a) The *Complex decision-making* takes place when involvement is high. Say the consumer has decided to purchase a *LCD* T.V. Since this purchase is important to the consumer he will be engaged in taking time to search for information and process it in more detail. He will evaluate various brands by using specific criteria such as brand name, look, specific functions, price etc. before taking a final decision.

(b) When the consumer makes decision through low involvement, it is said to be a *limited decision-making process.* Sometimes, the consumer goes through a decision-making process, even if he is not highly involved probably because he does'nt have much experience with the product. *For example,* a consumer may on seeing a new line of snacks that can be prepared in the microwave oven, will read the package and purchase a smaller pack of the same on a trial basis. Since the consumer was not involved or aware of the product category, she may purchase a small pack to compare it with the regular snacks. In this case, the information search processing is limited and only a few brands are evaluated.

The complex decision making takes place when involvement is high. When the consumer makes decision through low involvement, it is said to be a limited decision making process. The degree of involvement and decision making is more dependent on the consumer's attitude towards the product than on the product's characteristics.

At times, limited decision-making may take place when low involvement is there and the consumer is also seeking variety, out of being bored using the same brand. *For example,* the consumer may decide to purchase *Sunfeast Cashew Biscuits* as she is bored with the continuous consumption of "Britania's *GoodDay* Cashew biscuits. Such decisions may not be preplanned and could easily be taken inside the shop.

(c) Limited decision-making or even complex decision making *may not take* place *everytime* the consumer purchases a brand. When the consumer makes the same choice repeatedly, he or she learns from past experience and with little or no decision-making may purchase the brand which is most satisfactory. Take for instance, the purchase of *Reebok* jogger shoes or *Complan.* In both the cases, the purchase was important to the consumer (*Reebok* are Comfortable Jogging shoes because he is health conscious; and he has Complan because of its nutritional value).

In the above instances of the decision-making processes, it is seen that they are all consumer oriented. That is, the *degree* of involvement and decision making is more dependent on the consumer's attitude towards the product than on the product's characteristics. One particular consumer may be involved in the purchase of Complan because of its nutritional value while another consumer may find all brands *(Bornvita, Boost, Horlics etc.)* to be the same and switch brands in a search of variety.

(d) The fourth choice in figure 10.2 is referred to as *inertia* or the stage where there is low involvement with the product and no decision-making. Here the consumer is only looking to the convenience factor. He is purchasing the same brand not because he is brand loyal but because he feels it is not worth the time and trouble taken to search for an alternative. Examples could be the purchase of vegetables or tissue paper.

Thus the various decision-making processes which may be of interest to the marketer can be categorised into three namely:

- Limited problem solving or Dissonance reducing buying behaviour.
- Complex buying behaviour or Extensive problem solving.
- Habitual buying behaviour or Routinised response behaviour.

CONSUMER INFORMATION PROCESSING

When we talk of consumer information processing it will have to be linked with the nature of consumer involvement. This is because it is seen that higher the level of involvement, greater is the search for information and visa versa. There are various theories explaining consumers low involvement decisions. When low involvement decisions are taken, consumer may not cognitively evaluate advertising messages. *(Krugman's Theory of Passive Learing)* or though consumers are willing to consider many brands, they are likely to consider only a few attributes while evaluating them *(Sherif's Theory of Social Judgement)* or uninvolved consumers are more likely to react to message stimuli in communications rather than the message itself (*Petty and Cacioppo's Elaboration Likelihood Model*). (*Source : Consumer Behavior*, Hentry Assael, 6th Edn., 2001, pp. 153)

In low involvement conditions when brand evaluation is minimal, consumers make decisions by following the principles of cognitive economy *i.e.,* they minimize the time involved and effort taken in shopping and decision making. During inertia, consumers go for repetitive buying of the same brand to avoid taking a decision.

For instance, let us take the example of the purchase of table salt by a consumer. We assume that the housewife felt the need to purchase table salt as she realised that the amount of salt in the house is running low. In this case it is unlikely that the consumer will undertake a process of information search to determine the brand characteristics. Nor will she evaluate brands to identify the most favoured one.

Instead of searching for information, the consumer will receive information. The consumer will buy *Tata Salt* because of the familiarity with the brand Say, the consumer is sitting in front of the television and sees the advertisement of Tata Salt, which emphasises on the technological tests carried out to ensure that *the* best quality of Tata Salt is made available. The consumer sees the brand on the store shelf, associates it with the advertising theme and immediately purchases it. She does not form an attitude or evaluate brands before purchasing *Tata* Salt. The consumer is not involved in an active information search and processing in such low involvement purchases.

Decision-making in Low Involvement Product Purchase

If brand evaluation is minimal in low involvement conditions, then how do consumers make decisions ? It is said that in such instances, the consumer follows the principles of ***cognitive economy*** *i.e.,* they minimise the time involved and effort taken in shopping and decision-making. For, in the Tata Salt example, the consumer may behave in any of the following ways :

- She may see Tata Salt on the stores shelf, recognise the name, associate it with the advertisement and pick it up.
- She may purchase Tata Salt as she had purchased it the last time and found it adequate.
- If, say, the consumer has few prior associations with the brands, she may pick up the least expensive brand.

Marketers must work at creating and displaying advertising messages which will help in passive learning and ensure brand familiarity.

Inertia

The above Tata Salt example can also be based on ***inertia.*** When such low involvement occurs, consumers form beliefs passively, make decisions with little information processing and then evaluate the brand after the purchase. During inertia, consumers go for repetitive buying of the same brand to avoid making a decision. Only after the first few purchases will the consumer think of brand evaluation. Moreover, if the brand achieves a certain minimum level of satisfaction, the consumer will repurchase it on a routinsed basis. That is why, sometimes this process is referred to as **spurious *loyalty.*** The repetitive nature of purchases will make it seem that the consumer is loyal to the brand when in reality such loyalty does not exist.

Studies have indicated that repetitive viewing of the advertising message can result in more favourable brand attitudes towards low involvement purchases (Rajeev Batra, Micheal Ray, Journal of Marketing Research, March 1986).

Limited Decision-making

Occasionally, low involvement purchases may involve some decision-making. *For example,* the introduction of a new product, a change in the existing brand or a desire for variety may prompt the consumer to switch from a routinised to ***limited decision-making.*** For instance, say a consumer has been consistently buying *Amul cheese slices. Britania* introduces the 33% less fat content variant of cheese slices. The consumer happens to see this product at a supermarket. Involvement with the category is low but introduction of the new improved version of Britania cheese slices is enough for the consumer's interest and curiosity to be aroused. This decision-making has low involvement as there is little information seeking and brand evaluation done by the consumer.

The marketer needs to remember that in limited decision-making, since many low involvement products are ordinary, it is due to boredom that the consumer seeks variety although he (or she) may be having a favourable attitude towards their existing brands. Marketers must work at *creating and displaying advertising messages* which will help in passive learning and ensure brand familiarity. Even for high involvement cases, advertising can be used to create awareness and continuity. The other elements that need to be focused on are:

Product Positioning. The marketer should aim for 'product positioning' of *low involvement products* such that it highlights minimisation of the problem. *Zip pouch* is positioned by highlighting the benefits of keeping the food fresh and intact; or say, the *Lizol* disinfectant liquid suggests the minimisation of the problem that could occur such as catching infections due to dirty floors usage etc. Even a product, such as the aluminium foil wrap can be positioned to emphasise on benefits *i.e.,* the protection it offers to food.

Price. Consumers purchasing low involvement products are likely to be highly price sensitive. So marketers can induce customers to purchase more by reducing the price or offering coupons.

Distribution. *In-store Stimuli and Product trial.* In case of low involvement products, marketers have to ensure its wide in-store availability. They could also use in-store stimuli in the form of coupons, displays or price deals and small packs (or samples) to induce product trial amongst its users.

High Involvement Decision-making

In limited decision making, since many low involvement products are ordinary, it is due to boredom that the consumer seeks variety although he (or she) may be having a favourable attitude towards their existing brands. In case of complex decision making, the consumer will be involved in an extensive search for information to evaluate brands.

During complex decision-making, consumers evaluate brands in a detailed and comprehensive manner. They seek more information about the brands and are more involved with the product. Such decision-making takes place for :

- High priced products.
- Products associated with performance risks (consumer durables, automobiles)
- Complex products (ipod, personal computers)
- Products associated with one's ego (clothing, cosmetics etc.)

In case of complex decision-making, the consumer will be involved in an extensive search for information to evaluate brands.

Henry Assael has suggested that consumer information processing involves the exposure to and perception of information and how it is retained in memory.

He says the consumer information processing starts with the need arousal. Once the *need* is recognised, consumers are more likely to search for and process information relevant to their need. Although they are exposed to many *stimuli,* it will be *selective* in nature. This *selective* stimuli exposure is driven by the need to reinforce existing brand attitudes and perceptions and seek additional information. Consumers will seek ads which will reinforce consumer beliefs and experiences. By *selectively perceiving stimuli,* consumers are striving to reach a state of psychological equilibrium i.e. a state that lacks conflict and avoids contradictory information.

Past information and experiences are stored in consumers' *memory so* that it can be recalled for future use. (in the Figure 10.3 this is indicated by double arrows).

Search for "additional information takes place when consumers feel that they do not have sufficient information, (say, alternative brands are considered to be inadequate, have insufficient information about the brands under consideration or receive conflicting information from other sources etc.).

FIGURE 10.3

CONSUMER INFORMATION PROCESSING

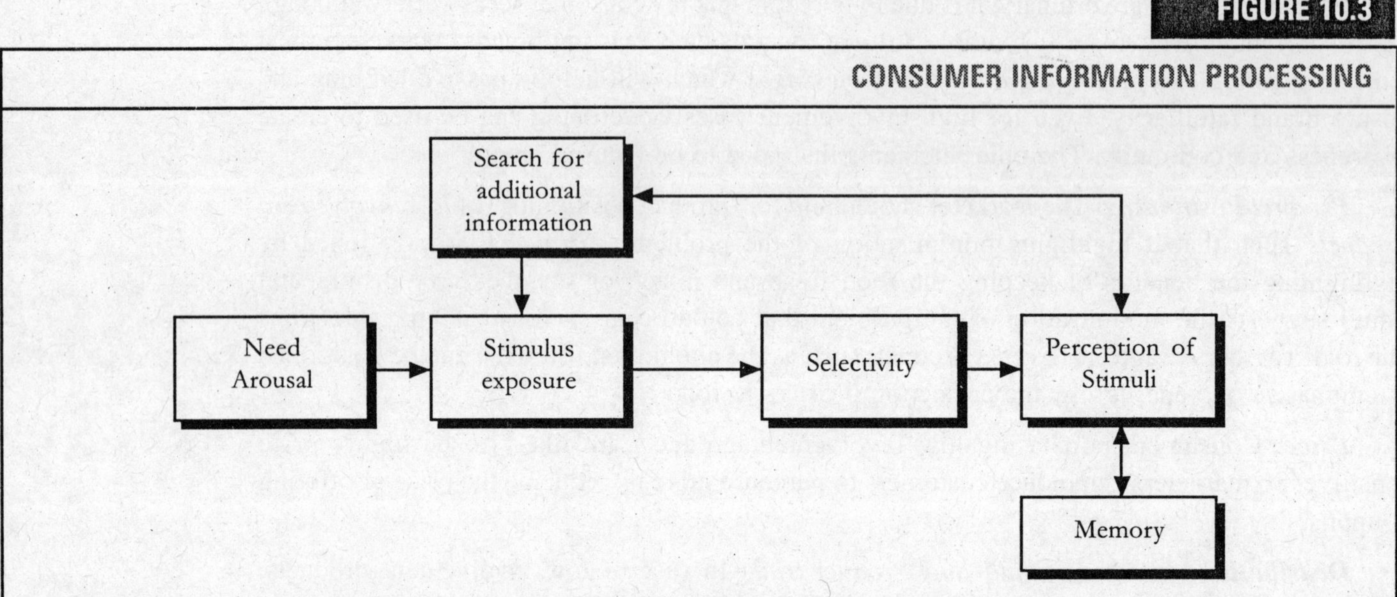

(*Source : Consumer Behavior*, Henry Assael, 6th Edn., 2001, pp. 84)

Studies reveal that consumers do not engage in an extensive information search unless they feel that the value of any additional information collected is worth the cost of obtaining it.

Of course, studies reveal that consumers do not engage in an entensive information search unless they feel that the value of any additional information collected is worth the cost of obtaining it. As shown in the figure 10.3, the search for additional information can go back as feedback to stimulus exposure and can stimulate further search.

We will try to understand the above terms using an example. Assume Vinit and Nanda are a couple in their 30s with two school going children. They live in a middle class locality of a metro city. Vinit works as a software engineer in a private company, while recently Nanda has taken to work in a BPO. They have been using a Maruti 800 car since the past 10 years. They have been using the car primarily on weekends and for shopping needs, and have been satisfied as it had served this benefit criterion.

Now, after becoming a dual income household, they feel or recognise the need to go for an additional car. The rise in income and status has prompted them or motivated them to develop a set of expectations regarding the new car. They have come to expect good service, a car that performs consistently (service dependability and performance) and comfort, in that order.

We have seen that Vinit and Nanda's (consumers) past *experiences* (with the existing Maruti Car), *consumer characteristics* their demographics, lifestyles and personalities will all play a role in influencing the benefits consumers seek and in their brand attitudes. Keeping all these aspects we assume that this family may think of cars such as *Indigo, Baleno, Ford or Accent.* The *motivational drive* will directly affect the specific benefit criteria Vinit and Nanda use to evaluate the various brands of cars. The benefit criteria in this case are a mix of size and style and economy (petrol mileage and service costs). The *environmental influences* could be — the individual family members (since it is a family decision-making unit), neighbours, friends and peers could also act as important sources of information. And finally, past marketing stimuli will be the information consumers seek about brand characteristics and prices from various sources such as advertising, in-store stimuli and the sales staff at the outlet. Thus, it was when the couple (Vinit and Nanda) recognised the need due to the disparity between their current need and the desired end state, they got involved in the information processing and brand evaluation stages. So need recognition and consumer characteristics can play an important role in the marketing strategy. **Maruti** and **Hyundai** have been using selective stimuli exposure to influence consumer's perception and memory and evaluation to make a positive decision in favour of Alto and Santro Xing as the small family's car.

SCHIFFMAN & KANUK'S MODEL OF CONSUMER DECISION MAKING

This model of consumer decision making developed by Schiffman and Kanuk is related to the problem solving consumer and to some extent the emotional consumer model. It provides an overview of the consumer decision making process. The model is made up of three major components: input, process and output.

INPUT

The input component comprises of the external influences, which are the sources of information used to make a positive influence on the consumer's product related values, attitudes and behaviour. The input component includes the *marketing mix elements i.e.* the various marketing stimuli used by the organisations and *the sociocultural environmental factors,* which will also act as a stimuli and influence the consumer's purchase decision.

Firm's Marketing-mix Efforts or Marketing Stimuli : Typically marketing stimuli will consist of the four P's Product, Price, Place and Promotion. Marketers are interested in knowing how consumers will respond to the various marketing stimuli. In the absence of direct contact between the consumers and the organisation, marketers make use of various marketing strategies and programmes to communicate with the prospective customers. These may be in the form of attractive product features, size, packages, suitable prices; mass media advertising, personal selling , direct marketing, other sales promotion measures and the selection of suitable distribution channels to ensure the availability of the product at the market place.

The Schiffman & Kanuk's model of consumer decision making is related to the problem solving consumer and to some extent emotional consumer model. The input components of the model comprises of the external influences which are the sources of information used to make a positive influence on the consumer's product related values, attitudes and behaviour.

Understanding how these marketing efforts have had an impact on the consumer's mind and to gauge the consumers' behaviour, many marketers are turning to consumer researches.

Socio-cultural Environment : The socio cultural inputs also play a major role in influencing the consumer's decision making process. The social cultural environmental factors can include the family, social class, culture and subculture, informal sources and all the other noncommercial sources. Generally stated the socio cultural inputs will consist of a wide range of non commercial influences.

The family members can exercise a strong influence on the buyer's behaviour. The family can also include a friend. Informal sources will include public's communication (comments expressed) via print media, comments of a friend and so on, these could be the specific noncommercial sources of information.

Social classes show distinct product and brand preferences in areas such as clothing, home furnishings, leisure activity and automobiles. Social class influences can be seen in their choice of the retail outlets, exposure to media etc.

By and large culture has the broadest and deepest influence on consumer behaviour. There are certain unwritten codes of conduct communicated and to be followed by each culture. These cultural norms will put restrictions or the 'do's and don't's on the buying behaviour of individuals. In this way culture also influences the buying behaviour of consumers.

Though it should be remembered that unlike the organisation's marketing inputs, the socio-cultural environment will only influence consumers decision to avoid a product; whereas, the marketing efforts will induce and motivate them to purchase the specific product.

It is the cumulative impact of the firm's marketing efforts and the socio -cultural environmental factors which will influence a consumer's decision making process. This is linked by a two handed arrows connecting the input and the process components of the model in the Figure 10.4.

FIGURE 10.4

CONSUMER INFORMATION PROCESSING

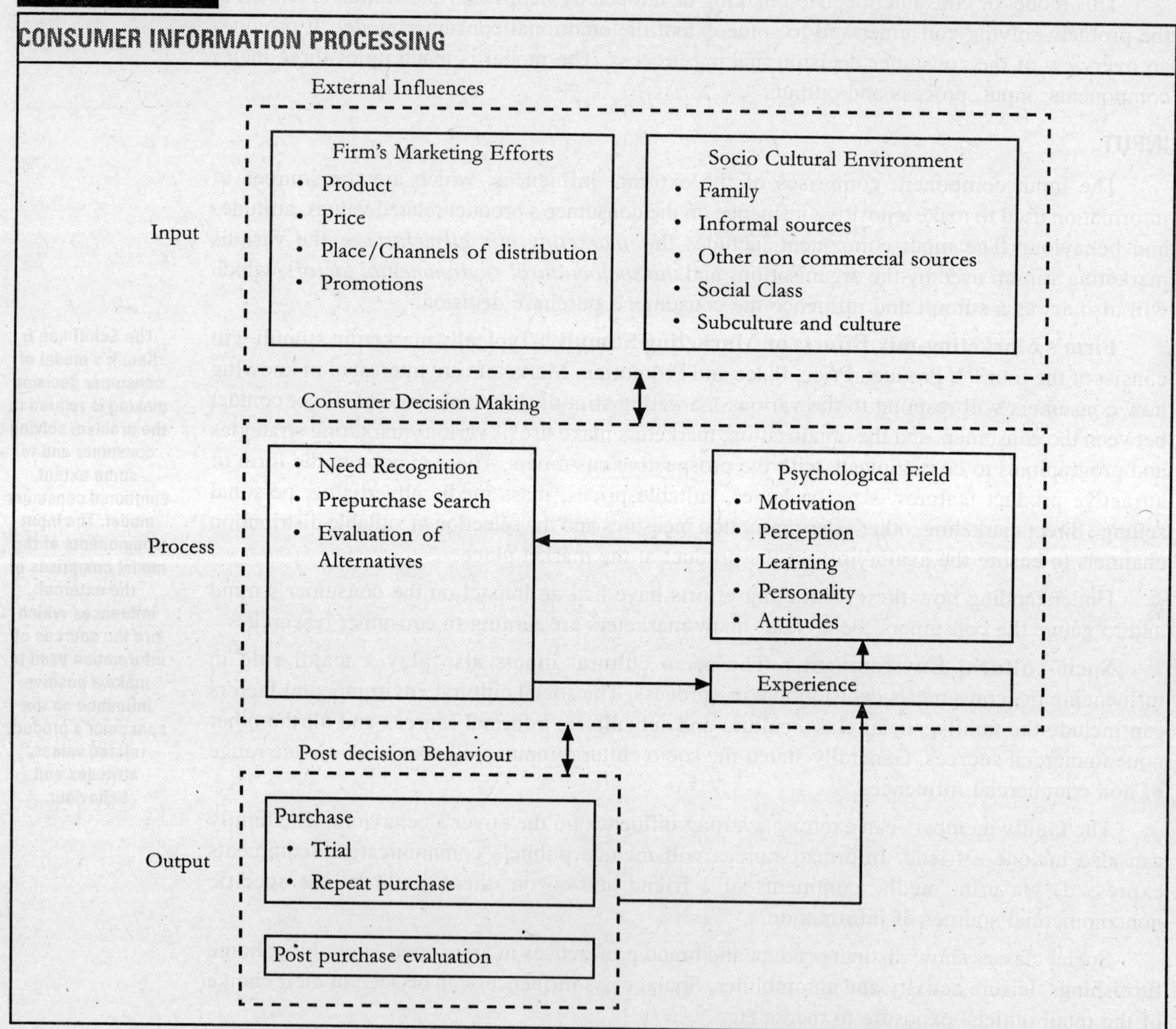

(*Source : Consumer Behavior*, L.G. Schiffman, L.L. Kanuk, 8th Edn., 2005, pp. 554)

Process : The process component of the model is indicative of the consumer decision making. This starts with the psychological field. *i.e.,* the psychological factors such as motivation, perception, learning, personality and attitudes which will determine the consumers' needs or wants, their knowledge about the various product choices, how they gather more information and then their evaluation of alternatives. From the figure 10.4, we can see that the consumer decision making process consists of three stages:

1. Need Recognition stage.
2. Pre-purchase search stage.
3. Evaluation of Alternatives stage.

Need Recognition : The consumer is likely to 'recognise a need" when he is faced with a 'problem'. The need or problem recognition, among consumers can be of varied types. Some consumers may experience the *'actual state type of problem'.* This may occur when they recognise a problem in the form of a product not performing satisfactorily. For instance, the housewife may realise that the mixie she was using doesn't grind properly. Another type of need or problem recognition could be the desired state consumer. Here the consumer may experience the desire for something new, which again may trigger the decision making process. For instance, a young executive may desire to possess a 'mid segment car'. The desired state will be the starting point for the consumer to become involved in the decision making process.

According to the Schiffman & Kanuk's model, the consumer decision making process consists of three stages: (a) Need Recognition stage (b) Prepurchase search stage and (c) Evaluation of Alternatives stages.

The need or problem recognition can be either simple or complex. Simple problem recognition refers to needs that occur frequently and can be dealt with almost automatically, such as feeling thirsty and not having a 'Pepsi". Complex problem recognition is characterised as a state, when a problem occurs over a period of time and the actual state and desired state gradually moves apart. *For example,* a man who has been driving a motor bike for many years may consider selling it and going for a brand new car (running on diesel) so as to reduce the heavy maintenance charges.

Pre-purchase Search : During this stage the consumer recognising a need that requires to be satisfied, now is engaged in an information seeking process. In case of having been satisfied with the product in the past, the consumer will make a choice without going for an extensive search for information. On the other hand, in case of no prior experience, the consumer will go on an elaborate information seeking process before arriving at a particular choice.

The consumer will be influenced by his or her internal psychological field before being engaged in an external search for information. Very often, the past experience plays a relevant role in deciding the extent of information that will be sought to by the consumer. If the past experience is good, less will be the external information sought by the consumer to reach a decision. Many consumer decisions will be based on a combination of past experience (internal sources) and marketing and non commercial information (external sources). Perceived risk could be another factor considered at this stage of decision process. If the perceived risk is high, the consumers are likely to be engaged in a complex information search and evaluation. Whereas, when the perceived risk is low, the consumers are likely to use very simple search and evaluation techniques.

The consumer is likely to 'recognise a need' when he is faced with a problem. During the Prepurchase stage, the consumer recognising a need that requires to be satisfied, now is engaged in an information seeking process. The amount of information he will gather depends on various situational factors: experience, social acceptability of the product and value related considerations.

As explained earlier, while discussing about the various types of decisions, consumers get engaged in an external search effort when they have the least amount of product category knowledge. This goes to show that when consumers have less information about the product category and it is very important to purchase the product also, they will get engaged in an extensive pre-purchase search activity.

The amount of information a consumer will gather also depends on various situational factors. The situational factors can be broadly classified into three:

1. Experience.
2. Social acceptability of the product.
3. Value related considerations.

Experience will be in relation to whether it is a new experience or whether the past experience with the product has been satisfactory or not. *Social acceptability* will consider whether the product is socially visible and acceptable to the society. In case of *value related considerations,* the consumer will evaluate and consider whether the purchase is discretionary rather than necessary, all the possible alternatives, family members' assessment of product requirements, reference group influences and all the possible sources of information.

While being involved in a pre-purchase search, the consumer will try to search and gather information from all the possible known sources.

Evaluation of Alternatives

The usual human tendency is to select a brand from a sample of all possible brands. The evaluation of alternatives is carried out by using two types of information:

(a) The Evoked set: A list of brands from which they plan to make their selection.

(b) The Criteria used to evaluate each brand.

The evoked set refers to the specific brands a consumer considers while making a purchase within a product category. Usually a consumer's evoked set will comprise of only a few brands. Since the evoked set will vary from consumer to consumer, the marketer must use promotional techniques designed to impart a very favourable and more relevant product image to the target consumer. At times this may also include a change in product features or attributes.

Compensatory and Non-compensatory Rules

The model speaks of certain decision rules which provide guidelines or routines to make the process less taxing. These decision rules can be broadly classified into two categories: compensatory and non compensatory decision rules. The output component of the consumer decision making is closely related to two kinds of past decision activities: Purchase behaviour and Post-purchase evaluation.

When firms know that consumers are evaluating alternatives, they make use of advertisements, through which they can suggest the criteria to be used by consumers in assessing the product or service options. This will enable the consumer to go through the experience of comparing or evaluating different brands or models of a product and finding the one that just feels, looks and or performs "right". In this connection, the model speaks of certain decision rules which provide guidelines or routines to make the process less taxing. These decision rules can be broadly classified into two categories: *Compensatory and non compensatory decision rules.*

According to the compensatory decision rule, the consumer evaluates brand options in terms of each relevant attribute and computes a weighted or summated score for each brand. The computed score will indicate the brand merit as a potential purchase choice. It is assumed that the consumer will select the brand that scores highest among the alternatives evaluated. Another unique feature related to the compensatory decision rule is that it allows a positive evaluation of a brand on one attribute to balance out a negative evaluation on some other attribute.

Whereas the non compensatory decision rules do not allow consumers to balance positive evaluations of a brand on one attribute against a negative evaluation on some other attribute.

At times, an individual's or family's decisions may be based on a particular lifestyle followed by them. A consumer's decision making process can also get influenced-when faced with incomplete information, no equally comparable alternatives or when the situation demands making a choice which involves multiple decisions.

Thus understanding the decision rules used by the consumers' in selecting a particular product or service will help the marketers to formulate a promotional programme.

OUTPUT

The output component of the consumer decision making is closely related to two kinds of past decision activities.

- Purchase behaviour
- Post-purchase evaluation.

Purchase Behaviour

The consumer may make three types of purchases, namely: *first time or trial purchases, repeat purchases* and *long term commitment purchases.* When the consumer is purchasing the product for the first time, he or she may buy lesser quantity than usual. This will be a trial purchase because the consumer would purchase the product to try it out on an experimental basis. The consumer would prefer to evaluate the product through direct use on a first time trial basis. This can happen especially when purchasing a new brand.

If the consumer finds the new brand, after the trial to be satisfactory, he/she is likely to repeat the purchase. When a consumer goes for repeat purchase, it is an indication that the product has met the consumer's approval and that he or she is willing to purchase it again for consumption purpose. Then the firm can look forward to a long term commitment from the purchaser. Of course, in case of certain type of durable goods like refrigerators, washing machines, ovens etc., a consumer will directly move to a long term commitment (through purchase) without being involved in a trial purchase.

Post Purchase Evaluation

There are three possible outcomes of the consumer's evaluation of the product's performance in the light of their own expectation. These could take the form of: a) actual performance matches expectations b) Performance of product surpasses or exceeds expectations or c) performance of the product falls below expectations.

There is a general tendency among consumers to judge their experience against their expectations when being involved in a post purchase evaluation process. There are three possible outcomes of the consumer's evaluation of the product's performance in the light of their own (consumers) expectations: These outcomes could take the form of:

1. Actual performance matches expectations, leads to a *neutral feeling.*
2. Performance of product surpasses or exceeds expectations, which results in *positive disconfirmation of expectations* and this leads to satisfaction.
3. Performance of the product falls below expectations, causing *negative disconfirmation of expectations* leading to dissatisfaction.

A very important component of post purchase evaluation is the reduction of uncertainty or doubt that the consumer might have regarding their selection. Generally consumers, as a part of their post purchase evaluation will try to reassure themselves that their decision was the right one. That is, they try to reduce their post cognitive dissonance by adopting one of the following strategies:

- They may rationalise that the decision is a wise one.
- They will look out for advertisements to support their choice and avoid those of competitive brands.

Children involvement in the decision making process

- ◆ They may attempt to persuade friends or neighbours to buy the same brand and thus confirm their own choice.
- ◆ They may turn to other satisfied owners for their reassurance.

The degree of post-purchase analysis that consumers undertake will depend on the importance of the product decision and the experience in using the product. The consumer's post purchase evaluation 'feedback' is an indication of the consumers, likely purchase behaviour in the future. If the product performs as per consumer expectation, it is likely that the consumer will buy it again. However, if the product's performance is disappointing or falls below expectations, they will look out for alternative products or brands in the future.

TYPES OF HOUSEHOLDS 

A **household** comprises of individuals living either singly or together with others in a residential unit. A family unit can compose of two or more people living together and who are related by blood or marriage.

A household comprises of individuals living either singly or together with others in a residential unit. Traditional households are represented by households having married couples with children (under or above 18 years). Where as, non-traditional households could be represented by married couples without children, single parent households, unmarried couples (or live-in couples) and individuals living with others.

Traditional and Non-traditional Households

Traditional households are represented by households having married couples with children (under or above 18 years). Whereas non traditional households could be represented by married couples without children, single parent households, unmarried couples (or live-in couples) and individuals living with others.

Traditional families can further be categorised into :

- **Nuclear family** – married couples with one or more children under 18 years.
- **Extended family** – nuclear families with at least one grandparent living at home.

In most of the cities and upcountry towns, with grown up children taking to work and moving out, the trend of nuclear family is very much visible, especially after these individuals get married. In such households there is sufficient purchasing power, especially if both the spouses are working. Marketers try to work out strategies which will communicate about products and services that can make their life more easy and comfortable. Today marketers have also identified a growing trend related to the purchase decisions influence of (children between the ages of 8-12 years) the tweens and teenagers in nuclear family households. The *tweens* who are almost entirely dependent on their parents and the *teenagers* who would like to believe that they are not dependent on anyone, have over the past few years become a direct market segment for products ranging from gaming consoles to books, apparel to cricket lessons and burgers to beyblades.

This market must have already been existing but it was with the arrival of the television channels such as Cartoon Network, Disney, POGO, Hunganna T.V and so on that advertisers realized the tweens' and teenagers power and involvement in the purchase decisions. In fact, this segment is the biggest influencer of decisions like – what to eat or which movie to see or which mall to visit. Sometimes the advertisements show tweens influencing purchase decisions in product categories not relevant to them. For instance, *Asian Paints* shows involvement of children in selecting colours or *Maruti Esteem's* advertisement shows a young child demanding to know whose big car her father is driving (he apparently cannot afford one).

In case of *Dabur's Real fruit juices*, the brand communication is two ways a) it is addressed (indirectly) to the mother conveying about the health benefits of the product. (b) it conveys the fun element to woo kids. In case of FMCG (Fast Moving Consumer Goods), the physical shape (or characteristic) of the product is particularly important. Marketers have been trying to attract the tweens and children by drawing their attention to the colour of the toothpaste, magic pops that crackle when popped into the mouth or the fruity smell of shampoos.

Today, the kids are known as the technology generation who get very excited by hi-tech products. These children play a far larger role in the purchase decision because their parents do not know as much as they do. This could probably be the reason why Microsoft India's Windows XP business unit had chosen to sponsor the 'Start Your Story' contest on *Disney channel* or run a promotional campaign at Delhi multiplex *PVR* for the company's PC games age of *Empires 3* and Fable : *The lost chapters* to coincide with the release of *'Harry Potter and The Goblet of Fire'*. The children of today are better exposed to the capabilities of a computer and this gets extended into the consumer durable space. *i.e.,* they offer suggestions on the brand of TV or home theatre or personal digit music player to buy. In the words of Ravinder Zutshi, Deputy Managing Director, Samsung India Electronics "Tweens are exerting increasing influence in the purchase of products across all categories and especially so when there is something new and cutting edge released in the market."

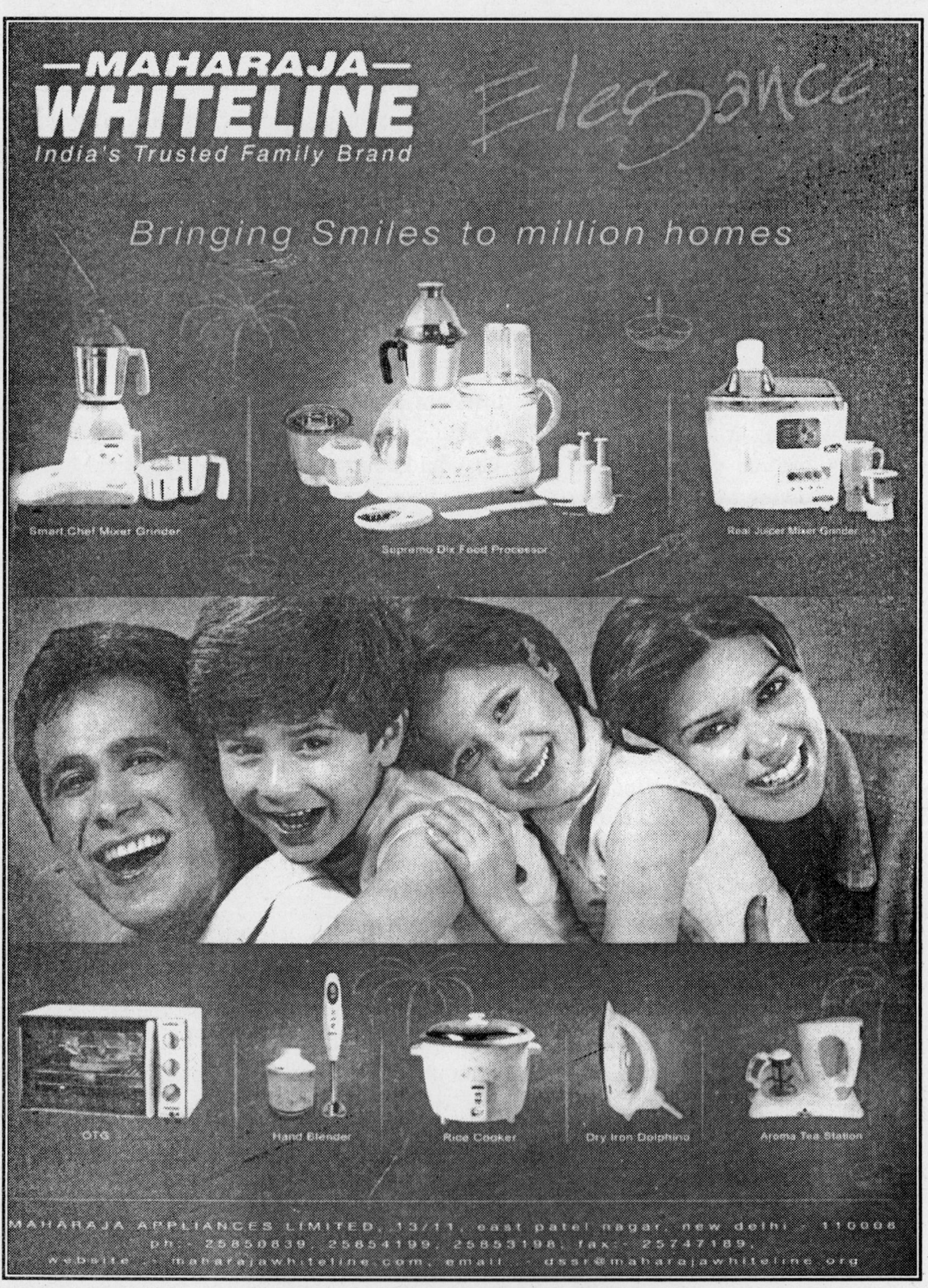

Ad will appeal to nuclear family households

Incidentally, the fact that children are the largest consumers of media and entertainment products have made them an attractive consumer segment. According to media analysts children are more involved viewers than adults who are mostly passive TV consumers. The latter not only remember ads but even the jingles that go with them. They spend time which is divided between watching kiddie channels (Table 10.1 gives information on viewership among 10-14 year olds, channel wise) watching Hindi movies and Hindi mass entertainment channels.

Today the kids are known as the technology generation who get very excited with hi-tech products. Incidentally, the fact that children are the largest consumers of media and entertainment have made them an attractive consumer segment.

The older tweens read newspapers and general interest magazines, tweens from higher income households surf the net and a significant proportion of them prefer to frequent multiplexes with their parents or friends. This type of behaviour indicates the making of a very media savvy consumer and decision makers for various products and services.

TABLE 10.1

CHANNELWISE VIEWERSHIP AMONG CHILDREN BETWEEN 10-14 YEARS.

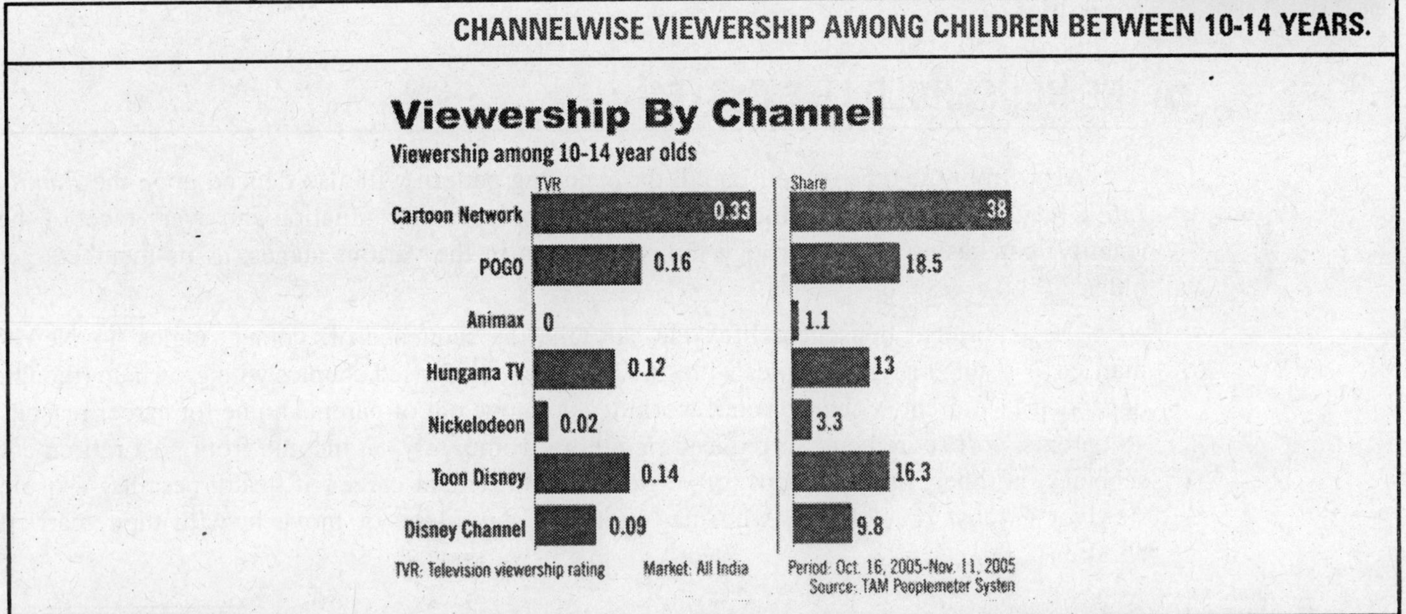

Today with mobility, geographic dispersion and changing patterns of migration it will not be uncommon to find the unmarried aunt or (at least) one grandparent living with the married children and family. This trend of *extended family* is visible in major cities and metro, where both the spouses are working and also having growing up children.

Non Traditional Households

There has also been an increase in the non traditional category of households. They are briefly described hereunder :

• **Married Couples without Children :** Another trend common today is keeping self and professional interests in mind, the young married couples postpone having children. At times being career oriented, the young may delay marriage then it is more likely that they will be childless for both biological and lifestyle reasons.

Such married couples without children have more discretionary income and are good targets for travel, entertainment and higher priced durables and hi-tech electronic items.

• **Single Parent Households :** At times the husband may be staying alone separated from his family due to professional postings away from the hometown. Or the marriage must have ended in divorce resulting in the emergence of single parent households.

The spending pattern will also depend upon the family life cycle *i.e.,* the changes which occurs in the income, family situation and every facet of the (family) purchasing power through the progression in the various stages as its members get older.

In such households apart from the financial burden, the single parent also faces time pressure, so they are wanting to spend more on their children partly out of guilt. The children in such households are likely to have more purchasing power and influence in the decision making of a wide number of purchases.

• **Unmarried (or live-in) Couples :** There is more acceptance of unmarried couples staying together especially in major cities. Such couples choose not to follow convention and though unmarried, live together. Such households have higher disposable income, with dual income – an affluent group and are a good target for luxury goods. Such households may be oriented towards spending discretionary income on travel, entertainment and high priced durable goods.

• **Individuals Living with Others :** There are some individuals who decide not to marry, so rather than living alone, they may live with another relative or sibling or friend or even with their parents. Such individuals may, to a certain extent, save money on housing and other necessities.

THE HOUSEHOLD LIFE CYCLE

Apart from the type of household, the spending pattern will also depend upon the *Family Life Cycle i.e.,* the changes which occur in the income, family situation and every facet of the (family) purchasing power through the progression in the various stages, as its members get older.

The traditional household lifecycle can take the sequence of: young singles → Newly married → young married couples with small children → married couples with grown up (though dependent) children → children start working and move out of parents home for career reasons → parents, post retirement, so reduced monthly income, rely on income from post retirement schemes (at times, they may opt for second post retirement career, if health permits) → sole survivor (widow or widower, who may prefer to stay alone or move in with their married children).

TABLE 10.2

NON-TRADITIONAL HOUSEHOLD LIFE CYCLES

SEQUENCE 1	
• Young married couple with children	• Young divorced parent
• Single parent with older children	• Older unmarried.
SEQUENCE 2	
• Young divorced couple without children.	• Middle aged married couple without children
• Older married couple without children.	
SEQUENCE 3	
• Young married couple with children	• Middle aged divorced parent.
• Middle aged married parent with children and step children.	
SEQUENCE 4	
• Young unmarried couple without children	• Middle aged married couple without children
• Older married couple without children	• Widow.

(*Source : Consumer Behavior*, Henry Assael, 6th Edn., 2001, pp. 571)

However, in the modern world with the break up of the joint family set up, migration of youth to bigger cities in search of better prospects, change in the lifestyles and various other demographics have resulted in the rise of the non traditional households.

Murphy and Staples had in the 70's suggested a new non-traditional household life cycle categories in the form of sequences 1 to 4. These are presented in Table 10.2.

In the above given examples, depending upon the category of the household, there will be income constraints and family responsibilities which in turn will affect many of the purchase decisions. With regards to the type of decisions and pattern of family influence, it will vary depending upon the type of household. *For example,* in case of married couple with children, a disproportionate income will be used for education, recreation activities, and other household expenses. While, for single parent with older children, given the paucity of time available to spend with children, there could be a reasonable amount of income spent on toys and day care centres. During the early stages of the family life cycle, the husband tends to be more influential. Over a period of time the wife will be assertive in decision making, especially if she is employed and enjoys financial freedom. Once children arrive, the nature of decisions may change especially with older children acting as influencers in a number of household decisions (purchase of consumer durables, selection of vacation holiday decision etc.).

Depending upon the category of the household, there will be income constraints and family responsibilities which in turn will affect many of the purchase decisions. Although there are variations in the way households make their purchase decisions, depending on their stages in the life cycle, there are certain consumer denominators in household decision making.

A MODEL OF HOUSEHOLD DECISION MAKING

Although there could be variations in the way households make their purchase decisions, depending on their stages in the life cycle, there are certain common denominators in household decision making. This aspect is discussed in the model of household decision making.

As seen in figure 10.5, there are three factors involved in the household decision making:

- The possibility (or likelihood) of joint decisions.
- Different role specifications for family members in the process of decision making.
- The need to resolve conflict among family members in the process of decision making.

We will consider a hypothetical example of household decision making involving a father (Ramesh), wife (Rita) and their two children Kirti (14 years) and Karan (12 years). Ramesh is planning to take his family on a week or 2 weeks summer vacation trip. In all likelihood, the decision would be a joint decision because : *(a)* the decision is *important* to all of them *(b)* the *perceived risks* of the decision (the expenses involved, the fact that they will be close together and also the importance of having a good time) are reasonably high and *(c)* the *absence of time pressure* as they are planning for May vacation in the month of January. Thus in the above example, a joint decision will be taken.

Prof. J.N. Sheth has suggested the following situations involving joint decision making :

1. Joint family decision are likely to occur when the *level of perceived risk* is high and a wrong decision could adversely affect the whole family. *For example* decision to purchase a new home will be a joint decision because of the involvement of financial risks, social risks (neighbourhood selection) and psychological risks. So a joint decision could help to reduce the risk and uncertainity.
2. When the *purchase decision is important* to the whole household. *For example*, purchase of a car or other major home appliances will involve discussions amongst all family members.

Once it is established that a joint decision is to be taken, there will be certain decision roles specified for individuals in the household.

FIGURE 10.5

A MODEL OF HOUSEHOLD DECISION MAKING

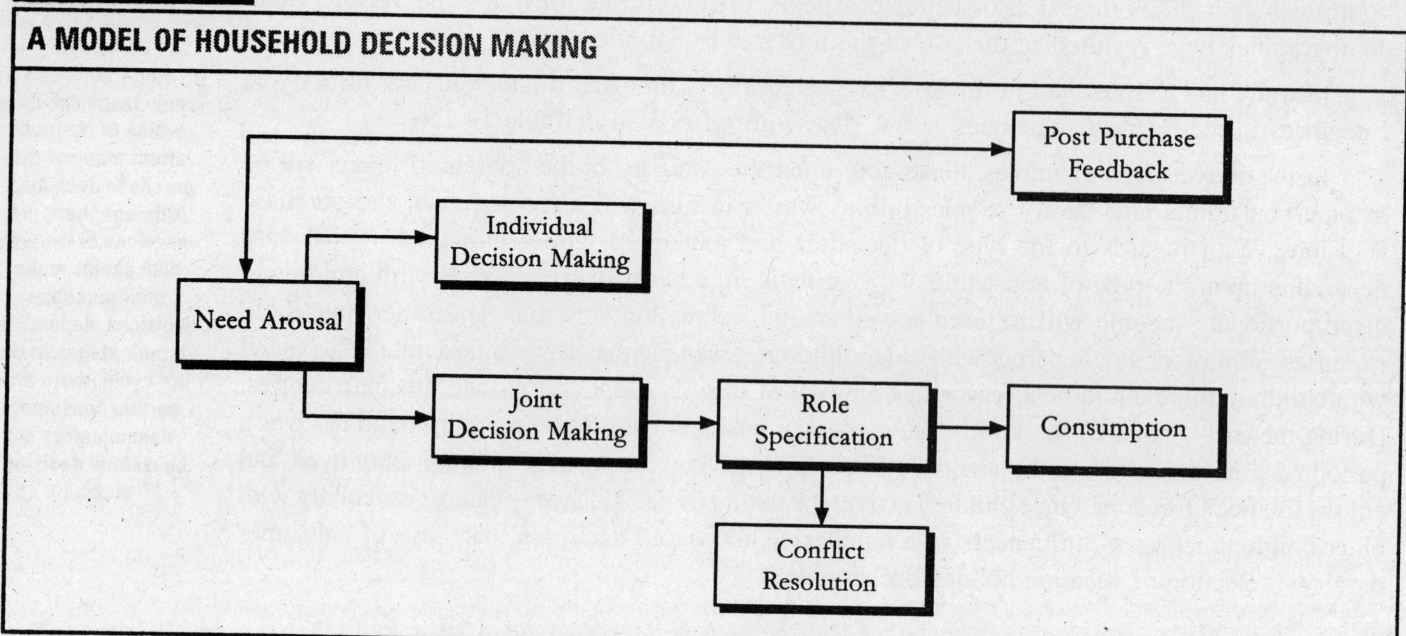

(*Source : Consumer Behavior*, Henry Assael, 6th Edn., 2001, pp. 573)

3. *Time pressures can result in joint family decisions*. With the rise in dual income households and along side the time pressures that go with it, there are situations when an individual may make the decision for many products that otherwise would have been purchased on a joint basis.
4. There are *certain demographic groups* which encourage joint decision making. In *middle income groups*, there is more likelihood of joint decisions taking place. Young *newly married families* show a higher frequency of joint decision making. Couples *before the arrival of children* opt for joint decision making. Joint decision is more likely if only one of the parents is working as time pressures are less.

Either the roles may be explicitly assigned to an individual in the household or it will be assumed that the individual in the household will perform the role.

Once it is established that a joint decision is to be taken, there will be certain decision roles specified for individuals in the household. Either the roles may be explicitly assigned to an individual in the household or it will be assumed that the individual in the household will perform the role. The household members may play one or more of the roles as shown in Figure 10.6.

- The *information gatherer* (or gate keeper) can influence the family's processing of information because of his or her ability to acquire and evaluate information.
- The *influencer* tries to establish the decision criteria by which brands are compared (looking to the cost, durability etc.) and influence the other family members' evaluation of alternative brands.
- The *decision maker* because of his or her financial power over the budget, would be the final decision maker on the particular brand to be purchased.
- The *purchasing agent* carries out the decision of purchasing the product for the family.
- The *consumer or user* will be the one who uses the product, evaluates it and provides feedback post usage on the satisfaction (or otherwise) and whether, it is worth while to purchase the product again.

Joint Decision

Conflict Management

Roles perfomed in the process of decision making

FIGURE 10.6

ROLES PLAYED BY HOUSEHOLD MEMBERS IN THE DECISION MAKING PROCESS

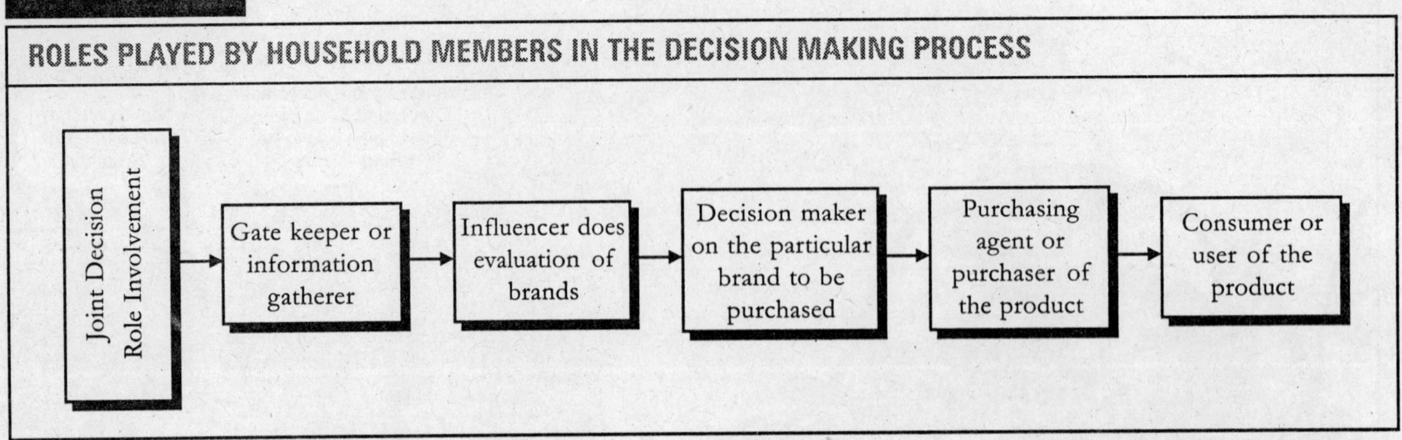

Going back to our example of Ramesh. When Ramesh told his kids about going for vacation, Kirti and Karan started collecting information on the various vacation trips offerings across India. They can be referred to as *information gatherers* and in the process of information search make their father aware of the many attractive options, a trip to Goa, a trip to Simla and surrounding places, attractive package for a trip to Kodia Kanal – Ooty or the attractive package of 'Taj Resorts'.

Here, the children are the prime *influencers* who specified the alternative vacations. Ramesh, being the father has budgetary power and control over the logistics, will be the *decision maker*. The wife Rita, is working in a travel agency and can easily make arrangements, so she will be the *purchasing agent.*

In the process of collecting information and evaluating alternative vacation spots, a *conflict* arises between the children – Kirti was keen to visit the beach resorts of Goa, while Karan was keen on the trip to the hill station-Simla. Ramesh settles the conflict by deciding that they will go to Goa this year and Simla next year. After the vacation, it is concluded that they thoroughly enjoyed the trip *(post purchase evaluation).* In fact they even discuss about going back to Goa during Christmas break and plan the trip to Simla during the next summer vacation.

An Example of 'Experimental Marketing' to Aid Decision Making

There could be a gap between when a consumer decides to buy something and when he or she actually buys it. This could be referred to as the phase when the buyer looks for more product information.

There could be a gap between when a consumer decides to buy something and he or she actually buys it. This could be referred to as the phase when the buyer looks for more product information. Realising this, a certain company tried to convert it into a business opportunity. Take for instance, *mEssence Consulting* which had opened a *'digital lounge'*, *"Xplore"* on Mumbai's Lamington Road, where the customer could try out products of various brands at leisure.

The 1,700 sq feet lounge had been set up·in partnership with IT distribution house Neoteric, which had over 6,000 channel partners in India. Xplore started with over 20 clients including *Kodak, Apple, IBM, Logitech, AMD* and *BenQ*. Unlike the typical electronics showroom, Xplore is an experience – oriented outlet, with a team to guide, explain how the gadgets work and provide information on features and prices. Visitors are not pressurised into buying something simply because they have tried it. In fact, when a visitor after trial wants to buy a product, Xplore calls the dealer in to make the sale or directs the customer to a retail outlet near his home.

You promised her the stars.
Now at least take her closer to them.

Delight her - with a New Home

Interest rates at a glance	
Upto 5 years –	9.25%
> 5 years & < 10 years –	9.75%
10 Years & above –	10.25%

There cannot be a better time to take a home loan. State Bank of India offers the lowest interest rates. With so many other additional benefits • **No processing fee • FREE SBI Classic International Credit Card • Flexible repayment option • Group Life Cover at concessional rates of premium • Interest calculated on daily reducing balance basis • Benefits for timely repayment of loans • Take over of housing loans from other banks/financial institutions • Free personal accident insurance cover to be offered shortly.** So visit your nearest branch. And move into your own home sooner than you expect.

SBI Housing Loans

State Bank of India
With you all the way
http://www.statebankofindia.com

Ad of "SBI Housing loans", provides information to help in decision making.

Thus companies are spending more money to build direct contact with the consumer, especially for electronic durables, where touch, feel and ease of use play a lot of importance in the process of decision making.

Conflict Resolution and Household Strategies

As in any group decision making, even in household decision making, conflicts are likely to arise related to purchasing objectives, attitudes toward alternative brands and choosing or selecting the most desirable alternative. Marketers must be aware of such conflicts and work out marketing strategies accordingly.

In households, strategies used to resolve conflicts can be related to

- Which option (choice of product or service) to select.
- The criteria used to evaluate alternative choices.

As in any group decision making, even in household decision making, conflicts are likely to arise related to purchasing objectives, attitudes towards alternative brands and choosing or selecting the most desirable alternative. Marketers must be aware of such conflicts and work out marketing strategies accordingly.

Whenever conflicts arise in homes over product alternatives, it gets resolved through *concensus*. It is through discussions and compromise that households arrive at a concensus (as seen our example of the vacation trip). Consensus could also result in the household deciding to go for individual decisions rather than a joint decision, in order to avoid a conflict. And in this way the responsibility for the decision can be delegated to any one member of the family. Usually, conflicts can arise in household over the selection of product alternatives. However, when conflicts arise over buying goals it could lead to politicking among family members.

One way of politicking is to form coalitions among family members. The children may support one parent over another in a conflict. Coalitions may be formed to bring those who dissent into line. *For example*, say everyone in the family want to buy a home theatre but the teenage son wants to buy an ipod. But with a majority of the family members favouring a home theatre, the teenage son may be forced to comply. In extreme cases, coercion may be adhered to. *For example*, the father may threaten the son that he may reduce his pocket allowance, if he spends most of it on purchasing and playing computer games.

'Recent studies have indicated that in the contemporary families, where both the spouses enjoy financial independence, they tend to use problem solving strategies in case of conflicts and then select the alternative of the spouse with the strongest preference.

There could be three situations when the family conflicts are most easily resolved. These situations are:

(a) when the family accepts one member as the legitimate authority. Then conflict can be resolved by delegating decision making to this person.

(b) when a single family member is more involved in the decision than others, then the family will accept the decision made by this member.

(c) when one family member may be more emphathetic to the other member's needs.

➲ SUMMARY

The process by which a person is required to make a choice from various alternative options is referred to as decision making. The various models of consumers decision making expressed in terms of an Economic view, the Passive view, a Çognitive view and an Impulsive or Emotional view of consumer were discussed.

A buying motive can be said to all the desires, considerations and impulses which induce a buyer to purchase a particular product. Product motives can be classified on the basis of the nature of satisfaction sought by the buyer, into: emotional product motives and rational product motives. Consumer decision making can be examined at two levels (a) by examining the extend of decision making (b) by understanding the consumer's degree of involvement in the purchase.

Consumer information processing can be understood by linking it with the nature of consumer involvement. This involves situations which can take the form of: low involvement purchase decisions, inertia, limited decision making and high involvement decision making. The model developed by Schiffman and Kanuk, which provides an overview of the consumer decision making process was discussed.

A household comprises of individuals living either singly or together with others in a residential unit. There can be traditional as well non traditional households and accordingly there may be differences in their spending pattern. Similarly the family life cycle *i.e.*, the changes which occur in the income family situation and every facet of the family purchasing power through the progression in the various stages as its members get older, can also affect the spending pattern of the family. Marketers must be aware of the likely conflicts to occur in household decision making and work out marketing strategies accordingly.

CHAPTER QUESTIONS FOR DISCUSSION

1. What do you understand by the term decision making? Why is this term of great interest to marketers? Explain giving a real example of any brand.
2. What steps of consumer decision making will work out in the following instances:
   - A house wife is thinking of purchasing a Dish TV Antenna.
   - A college student is planning to purchase a mobile phone.
   - A consumer is considering the purchase of a over the couter (OTC) medicine available for common cold.
3. Suppose a marketer is thinking of launching "instant ready mix and eat food items", in a market which already has other well known brands. What type households should be targeted and what marketing strategy should he work out?
4. Meet five different type of households in your locality and ask them about the decision making followed by them in the purchase of T.V, washing machine, furniture and vehicle (car or two wheeler) at their homes. What differences do you find in the nature of information search, evaluation of brands, conflicts (if any) and final selection of the brand, amongst these types of households?

SUGGESTED READINGS

1. Jim. Blythe, '*The Essence of Consumer Behavior,* Prentice Hall, Europe, Hertfordshire, 1997.
2. Leon. G. Schiffman, Leslie Lazar. Kanuk, *Consumer Behavior*, Prentice Hall of Indian Pvt. Ltd., New Delhi 2005.
3. C. Roy and N. Raghavendra, Riding the Tiger (Women take most buy Decisions), *The Economic Times,* Bangalore, 14 August 2005.
4. Samidha, Sharma., Female Power Stirs Marketing, *The Economic Times,* Bangalore, 17 February 2006.
5. Preethi, Chamikutty, Rules of Engagement', Brand Equity, *The Economic Times,* Bangalore, 5 July, 2006.

6. Priya, Srinivasan, Rahul Sachitanand and Archana Shukla, 'The Tween Economy, *Business Today*, January 1, 2006, pp. 53-56.
7. Henry, Assael., *Consumer Behavior and Marketing Action,* 6th Edition, Thomson learning, Singapore, 2001, pp. 565-601.
8. Namitha, Jagadeesh, Experience Sells, *Business World,* 3 April, 2006.

CASE

'GILI' – GILI INDIA LIMITED (GITANJALI GROUP)

Jewellery has always been a proud possession of Indian women. Before branded jewellery had caught the eye of the consumers, decisions related to the purchase of jewellery was preferred to be at the outlets owned by the traditional Indian family jeweller. Jewellery was treated as a proud possession only to be worn at specific occasions such as weddings, festivals etc.

However in 1994, Gili became the first branded jewellery of India, who successfully brought about a change in the paradigm "from occasionally... to the need of every occasion."

Branded jewellers had been an unknown concept then. So it was indeed an uphill task – creating a new brand for working women, changing the mind set of traditional Indians, inspiring trust among them and so on.

Working towards the changeover

The challenges before the company included certain facts :

- Traditionally in India, women did not wear diamond jewellery often, apart from special occasions such as marriages and festivals.
- Purchase of diamond jewellery was meant only for a privileged few who could afford it.
- Possession of diamonds was considered to be a real privilege.
- Indian consumers were aware of 22 karat jewellery in the market. The notion of 18 karat jewellery was completely unheard of.

So the challenge was to introduce a brand in diamond jewellery and offer consumers something unexpected, unbelievable and unheard of. Gili felt the need to bring about a change in the long-standing beliefs, practices and customary conventions.

Extensive research and study revealed that the market was ready to receive branded jewellery which was wearable, beautiful and affordable. At a time when diamond was the prided possession of the rich and there were very few diamond retailers, *Gili* was unwavering in its endeavour to present affordable and elegant ornaments to all.

Birth of the Brand Gili

The birth and growth of Gili has taken everyone by surprise because of its unique, inimitable and never seen before products. The beautiful designs which are a blend of Indian and Western nuances has made Gili jewellery a stupendous sensation. Gili, branded jewellery has successfully brought about a change in the Indians perception regarding wearing diamond jewellery for occasional wear to an everyday affair, when women consumers adorn themselves, since it is beautiful, contemporary and affordable too.

The New Consumer of Today

The consumer shopping for jewellery today has a vastly different profile from what she looked like a decade ago. Today's buyer of jewellery is one who is young, financially independent and fashion conscious. She is shopping for ornaments she can wear to work, at her business conferences, on her evenings out and so on. Being busy since she is working, she has to manage her precious time. Hence she is a shopper in a hurry – squeezing in the time to select clothes and accessories suitable to her lifestyle, in between her commitment at the office and her responsibilities at home.

The challenge before the jeweller is to influence such customer's decision making process through branded product offerings. The jeweller must have the ability to strike an instant connect with the buyer as soon as she sights their products, giving her a sense of confidence in the quality and value of the item.

Positioning through Specific Branding

The company realised that for products such as jewellery, value is most often judged by how it is perceived rather than the sum of its individual components. That is the reason why the Gitanjali group embraced the concept of **Purpose branding** or focus on different brands so that they cater to specific need based states of the consumer. *i.e.,* careful attention is paid to ensure that the specifics of individual brands have been more clearly identified and demarcated. *For example*:

- **Nakshatra** – This is a premium range brand primarily positioned as a lifestyle statement for women, which reflects the brilliance of the constellations and gives the person adorning it an incomparable celestial radiance.
- **Asmi** – **Asmi** is positioned as a symbol of woman's empowerment and a celebration of the various achievements in her life.
- **Sangini** – The **Sangini** brand is for couples where the jewellery is characterised by a bezel set centre stone slightly larger than the others used in the same piece as the perfect expression of wife's position in the husband's life.
- **Solitaire** – This one-in-a billion **Solitaire** is for the consumers seeking exclusivity.
- **Glitterate** – **Glitterate** is the star power meant for the Bollywood crazy consumer.

Competition : The last few years has seen a huge growth in jewellery brands such as **Tanishq, Sparkles, Kiah, Ishi, Swarnanjali** (from Adora).

The Future Challenge

Apart from diamond studded products, Gitanjali has also taken the concept of branding into the comparatively more tradition bound segment of plain Gold jewellery. The launch of **'Gold Expressions'**, a range of Italian designed and crafted jewellery has opened out a new avenue of choice for the Indian women.

Apart from positioning of the brand, the real challenge for the Gitanjali group will be in the **communication** *i.e.,* getting the concept and the message of the brand across to the consumer. The pace of change in the Indian retail scenario is gathering momentum, impacting the jewellery industry in a huge way and alongside is the competition from the other branded jewellers.

(*Source :* www.gili.com, Mehul, Choksi, 'Gilding the future, Branding : The Future', *A. Strategic Marketing Presentation*, 3 May, 2006.

QEUSTIONS FOR DISCUSSION

1. As demographic changes have occurred with younger individuals taking to work, do you feel the present positioning of the Gili jewels is sufficient to aid these consumers in their decision making process? Why?
2. Contemporary jewellers have to work towards "impacting the consumer's mind and winning her loyalty." In this context can you suggest a suitable communication strategy whereby message about the brand can be conveyed across to a wider segments of consumers?

UNIT IV : CONSUMER DECISION MAKING, AFTER SALES AND RELATED ISSUES

CHAPTER 11

DIFFUSION OF INNOVATIONS AND OPINION LEADERSHIP

- Case : **Crosswords** and **Strand Book Store**
- Meaning and Definition of Diffusion of Innovations
- The Diffusion Process
- Characteristics that encourage the adoption process
- The Adoption process
- Multiplicative Innovation Adoption (MIA) model
- Opinion Leadership and Personal Influence
- Methods to identify Opinion Leaders
- Opinion Leadership and Marketing Strategies
- Summary
- Chapter Questions for Discussion
- Suggested Readings
- Case : **Standard Chartered Bank's Mumbai Marathon**

CASE

CROSSWORDS AND STRAND BOOK STORE

In today's highly competitive scenario, companies are reading the consumer demographics and trying to understand their explicit and implicit needs and offer suitable products and services. After developing consumer insight, they have used the marketing strategy, with the right combination of the product mix and media mix which will motivate consumers to adopt their offerings in a big way. Today, with the influx of T.V and computer in most of the urban homes, individuals seem to have no time to experience the pleasure of book reading. However, we will gave a brief view of two book stores which have through constant innovations brought about an increase in the customer base.

- **CROSSWORDS**

Crosswords is a brand which has changed the perception of book retailing in India. Crosswords started in 1992, when its first store itself was positioned as a family store. The store has focused on having a right media, product and service mix, all backed up by a cost-benefit analysis. The children's section has been aggressively promoted through school programmes and reading hours which eventually transformed a non performing area into the highest individual gross earner for the company, contributing almost 25 percent to the total sales figure. It has used the well known retail approach of Wallet and Watch where the store competed for the customer's time and ultimately for money. Crosswords also ably supported events like Authors' meet, reading hours, loyalty programmes and other services such as dial-a-book, fax-a-book and email-a-book.

The marketing strategy followed by Crosswords has been in complementing more for same with great services, features and facilities rather than just offering more for less or same for less. This essentially involves attractive layouts, facilities, interiors, services and products and a convenience factor for browsing and reading books freely.

Crosswords retail strategy has evolved around the *pentagon* and the *triangle model*. Over and above the three internal elements of systems, logistics and supplier, place, product, people, communication and value were the five external areas which has been innovated and contributed to the healthy retail environment at Crosswords. The unique product mix includes CD ROMs, toys, music and stationery, a comfortable browsing place, great layouts, design and amenities, knowledgeable and helpful staff and innovative communication through events and public relation activities. They also have an internal book retailing training programme to develop the knowledge and skills of the staff.

Thus, it is following a *feature centric* strategy *i.e.,* laying more emphasis on integrating information, knowledge, entertainment and enlightenment in its product mix. These efforts have proved to be a big differentiator and the cutting edge built on the innovation has converted many non readers into long term consumers of 'Crosswords' today.

- **STRAND BOOKSTORE**

The *Strand Bookstore* was started by (late) T.N. Shanbhag in 1948 at Mumbai. The bookstore offers an illuminating range of rare to just-published bestsellers' book to the book loving customers. It was quoted that along with a branch opened in Bangalore, the turnover of the Strand bookstore was more than Rs. 20 crore (Retail Biz, May 2005)

Some of touches which have helped the store to earn a cutting edge are: offering extra ordinary discount delivery within the accepted fair trade norms, competitive price deals and the availability of wide range of rare and interesting books. Strand bookstore uses the following differentiating factors: (a) Personalised service by using a readers-to-reader approach where the sales person advises customers on the type of purchase which will help and be beneficial to them. (b) It also believes in bulk order with hefty discounts from publishers. The benefits from such discounts is passed on to the customers. This personalised service offerings is a unique factor which is a key feature behind the success story of the strand bookstore.

The above two examples of the Crosswords and Strand bookstore show that it is possible for business ventures to succeed by adopting innovative techniques. In this chapter we have tried to explore the diffusion of innovation process and the MIA model and present a profile of the consumer innovators and the other adaptor categories. The latter section in the chapter has been devoted to discussions on the role of opinion leader and the extent of their influence in their consumption behaviour as well as in the consumption behaviour of others.

MEANING AND DEFINITION OF DIFFUSION OF INNOVATIONS 

Diffusion of innovation is the process by which the adoption of an innovation spreads over a period of time to other consumers through communication.

Diffusion of innovation is the process by which the adoption of an innovation spreads over a period of time to other consumers through communication. Consumer researchers trying to explore the area of consumer acceptance of new products are primarily interested in understanding two closely related processes (a) The diffusion process (b) The adoption process.

Group communication are an important (or primary) source of information and can influence the consumer decision making. Group communication can occur within or across groups. Communication within groups refer to *word-of-mouth* influence which is considered to be highly credible since it comes through family, friends, peers and neighbours. Communication across groups takes place through the above mentioned process of *diffusion of innovation and influence.*

The process of diffusion will occur for new products as informational influence and is likely to affect the adoption of new products across groups. Consumer researchers trying to explore the area of consumer acceptance of new products are primarily interested in understanding two closely related processes

- The diffusion process.
- The adoption process.

The diffusion process is a *macro process* related to the spread of a new innovation from its source (or manufacturer) to the final consumers. Whereas, adoption is a *micro process* focusing on the stages through which an individual passes when deciding to accept or reject a new innovation. Over and above these two interrelated processes, marketers are also interested in identifying the *"Consumer innovators"*, those who are first to purchase a new product for it is felt that this group will play a major role in the success or failure of the innovation.

A consumer is likely to find a new idea, or product or even a new service attractive. But the organisation which is trying its hand at the new innovation is likely to be concerned about how fast the diffusion of the innovation is likely to take place. Even though, it is only after an intensive research that a new concept or product is launched, there is always an element of risk involved. Through research, answers to certain questions are sought.

- Does the innovation cater to the need of the target customer?
- Have the target consumer understood how the innovation is relevant to their need?
- Is the new product available and being demonstrated widely?
- Has the firm identified the opinion leaders? If yes, is the firm making efforts to convert opinion leaders into committed customers?
- Is the company providing suitable incentives to sceptics to get them converted to adopters?

These questions are pertaining to certain broad areas which can be of concern to marketers launching new products. One way of educating customers about new innovations will be by communicating the benefits the new innovations would provide. Thus diffusion of innovation is a challenge before the marketer to identify the 'value added benefits' which can be associated with the product and communicate it to the consumer.

Table 11.1 gives an overview of certain innovations which had gained acceptance among consumers because of the benefits communicated across.

TABLE 11.1

EXAMPLES OF POPULAR NEW PRODUCT INNOVATIONS

Product	Benefit Communication
• Cellular phones	Compact, wireless, telephone device.
• Credit card	Plastic card convenient to use facilitating cashless transactions.
• Laptop computer	Mobile computer which is compact, is portable, Wifi enabled with internet and other communication network facility.
• MP3 player	Compact, easy to use, alternative to Walkman.
• Ipod	Compact, stylish, portable device facilitating audio, video photo albums etc.

➲ THE DIFFUSION PROCESS

The diffusion process is concerned with the acceptance of an innovation (a new product or service or idea or practice) when spread by communication (mass media, sales personnel or informal communication) to members of a social system (the target market) over a period of time. The approaches used to define an innovation can be classified as firm oriented, product oriented, market oriented and consumer oriented.

The diffusion process is concerned with the acceptance of an innovation (a new-product or service or idea or practice), when spread by communication (mass media, sales personnel or informal communication) to members of a social system (the target market) over a period of time. Thus the diffusion process includes four basic elements:

- The innovation
- The channels of communication
- The social system
- Time.

THE INNOVATION

There are various approaches used to define an innovation. These can be classified as *firm oriented, product oriented, market oriented and consumer oriented* definitions of innovations.

Firm oriented approach will consider newness of a product or service from the perspective of the manufacturer or marketer. This definition ignores the newness of the product or service at the market place. For, as long as the innovation is 'new' to the company it is treated as new. However, if one is trying to understand the consumer acceptance of a new product, this definition may not hold good.

Product oriented approach focuses on the inherent features of the product and the effect they are likely to have on consumer's established buying patterns. As per this product oriented framework the innovations can take the form of:

- *A continuous innovation* involves introducing a modified product instead of a totally new product. *For example*, revised versions of *Zen (Zen Estilo), Lifebuoy soap,* latest version of *Microsoft windows* etc.
- *A dynamically continuous innovation* though more disruptive than a continuous innovation, will not result in changing an established behaviour. It could take the form

of creation of a new product or the modification of an existing product. *For example,* the 8 mm camcorder, C.D players (Compact Disk) etc.

- *A discontinuous innovation* will result in consumers adopting new behaviour patterns. For instance, Airplanes, radio, T.Vs, personal computers, internet etc.

Market oriented approach will look into the newness of the product in terms of how much exposure consumers have of the new product.

Market oriented approach will look into the newness of the product in terms of how much exposure consumers have of the new product. There are two market oriented definitions of product innovation which been used extensively in consumer studies.

Products such as mobile phone and laptop computers, are innovations that have gained acceptance among consumers

Some marketers have defined an innovation using a consumer oriented approach. As per this view, newness of the product will be based on the potential consumer's judgment on the 'newness' of the product and not necessarily on the physical features or the market realities.

(*a*) A product is considered to be new if it has been purchased by a relatively small though fixed percentage of the potential market.

(*b*) A product is treated as new if it has been available in the market for a relatively short period of time.

The above two market oriented definitions are basically subjective in nature, for, the researchers will be required to establish the degree of sales penetration with the market which will quantify the product as an "innovation" (say the first five percent of the new product users) or define the time period within which the product available in the market can be considered as 'new'.

Some marketers have defined an innovation using a *consumer oriented approach.* As per this view, newness of the product will be based on the potential consumer's judgment on the 'newness' of the product and not necessarily on the its physical features or the market realities.

'A continuous innovation'

'A dynamically continuous innovation'

THE CHANNELS OF COMMUNICATION

Communication also plays a big role in determining how quickly an innovation spreads through a market. This communication can be of two types: a) communication between marketers and consumers, b) Communication among consumers (word of mouth communication).

Consumer information sources fall into four categories:

- Personal sources — Family, friends neighbours, acquaintances.
- Commercial sources — Sales people, advertising, sales promotion techniques.
- Public Sources — Mass media, consumer rating organisations.
- Experimental sources — Demonstration, handling samples.

Apart from the above traditional communication media, today, marketers are looking out for an integrated marketing communication media. This includes off-line activities (like road shows, exhibitions, point of purchase danglers and posters). Direct marketing (direct mail), telemarketing etc., and Internet marketing (on-line direct marketing).

Depending upon the innovation (new product) and the prospective customers, firms try to adopt a cost effective way of communicating with them. The social system serves as the boundary within which the diffusion of the new product must exist.

Depending upon the innovation (new product) and the prospective customers, firms try to adopt a cost effective way of communicating with them.

Consumer's shopping behaviour cannot be understood or predicted outside the context as neither the consumer nor the product (or brand) exist in isolation. Consumers have the tendency to go through a process of 'see-touch-sense-select' while shopping. Here again the behaviour will vary depending upon the brand and product category.

In order to influence the purchasing power of customers, marketers make use of point-of-purchase systems and make them aware of new brands available in the market. For instance, *Johnson & Johnson* used environment friendly teddybear multiple options of displays made of paper board, with multicoloured printing to showcase the baby products in a cost effective manner. *Titan Slim* and *Titan Fast Track Watches* are displayed on cylindrical poles which are made of plywood and attached to the base or alternatively having digital display image made on one side. In this way various communication channels are used to attract consumer's attention.

THE SOCIAL SYSTEM

The diffusion of a new product and the consumer behaviour occurs in a social setting or social system. The *social system* is a *physical, social or cultural environment* to which people belong and within which they function.

The social system serves as the boundary within which the diffusion of the new product must exist. The orientation of our social system has its own special values or norms, which is likely to influence the acceptance or rejection of new products. With the changes occurring in the social system, a lot of changes are taking place in the outlook of the consumers.

In the past, consumers had to depend on neighbourhood Kirana shops for purchasing groceries or travel all the way to the centre of the city to purchase certain products. Now with a positive change in the mind set of the consumers, they are looking out for cost effectiveness, convenience and personalised services. This has resulted in easy acceptance of the concepts of 'Supermarket' and Mall shopping.

Today, more and more young girls are keen to participate in various fashion shows and contests. There is seen a growing awareness of the killer diseases 'AIDS' and Hepatitis-B'. Many public and other social organisations and NGO's are actively involved in organising programmes to increase the awareness of the problems associated with the above diseases. There are many consumer action groups to protect the consumer from any wrong practices adopted by the traders and business firms. The social system will act as a barrier and not allow them to adopt values and norms which go against the society at large. Organizations and marketers have to bear this in mind while launching new products or services. For, these aspects are likely to determine the acceptance or rejection of new products.

TIME

Time also plays a very important part in the diffusion process. This can be understood by determining (a) the purchase time, (b) determining the various adopter categories and (c) the rate of adoption.

Time also plays a very important part in the diffusion process. Knowing the purchase time will help the marketer to determine the average time a consumer is likely to take to adopt the new product. The rate of adoption will indicate how long it will take for a new product or service to be adopted by the members of a social system.

(a) Purchase time : There is usually a time gap between consumer's initial awareness of a new product or service and the time when he or she makes the purchase or rejection of it. Knowing the purchase time will help the marketer to determine the average time a consumer is likely to take to adopt the new product. This information in turn will be a predictor of the overall length of time taken by the product to achieve widespread adoption.

Firms are using innovative ways to inform the consumers about their new products or services and also going out of way to build relationship with them. For instance, when the new concept of *"Home land"* supermarket was introduced by Asha Chavan in (then the suburb) Pune, apart from offering a variety of quality products, they also gave an unconditional guarantee of replacement or refund, home delivery to all, even single item telephonic orders at no extra cost. And beyond business, Homeland also offered free services like phone, electricity, credit card and cell phone bill payments.

Consumers, with an increase in disposable income are increasingly looking towards shopping at malls offering products (and services) along with entertainment. Retail activity in malls primarily include branded apparel, discount and department stores. In order to woo customers, these retailers use creative promotions, charity fund raisers, VIP party events, drawings and fun contests. Take the example of *Fun Republic*, a chain promoting out-of-home entertainment concept. Fun Republic, the young-adult entertainment center, at Andheri, Mumbai had come out with a unique *'Rewards programme'* with its *Ginnie Combo offer*, wherein the customer who spends a minimum of Rs. 65 takes home a guaranteed prize. For instance, when a consumer watches a movie at Fun Republic, she gains access to the concession area of the theatre and there on the purchase of any combo (Pepsi + Popcorn), she gets a scratch card that entitles her to win gifts ranging from a *Kinetic Zing* to Air conditioners, Refrigerators, Colour Televisions, Walkmans or even Free Movie Tickets, Snack Coupons and so on. The unique aspect of the Ginnie offer is that scratch cards come with assured gifts which can be used at the purchase time.

(b) Rate of adoption : The rate of adoption determines how long it will take for a new product or service to be adopted by the members of a social system. The rate of adoption will indicate how quickly a new product or service will be accepted and then adopted by them. We can take the example of clothes. Firms are interested in knowing the rate of adoption for clothes. Apparel firms are looking to fashion and trends before launching brands. Take the example of corporate dressing. *Indigo Nation* has *Contra Formals* which is targeted at corporate executives who are interested in making a statement through their clothes. Surveys had indicated that these corporates did not want to wear outfits (or brands) catering to their 40 plus bosses. This led to the launch of *Contra Formals,* with distinct styling options in over 50 designs crafted from high quality 100 percent cotton and CVEs fabrics. Contra formals promises to be a pioneer in setting fashion trend for men in their late 20's or early 30's.

Depending upon the product category and target audience, marketers are using various marketing strategies to increase the speed of the rate of adoption. *For example, Ray Ban sunglasses* from *Bausch & Lomb* used premium pricing to convey that their product matched the lifestyle of the rich and famous (using Hollywood celebrities in its advertisements).

Two well known examples of the new products and services gaining fast acceptance from consumers can be narrated by explaining the marketing strategies used by *Akai* and *Narula's fast food chain.*

In the mid-nineties, Akai realised that there was a growing segment of consumers who had bought a colour T.V. set in the 80's and wanted to exchange it for a new T.V. set. These consumers also wanted some value for the old TV's they possessed while expecting a reasonably Good feature-Price performance ratio on the new TV they planned to purchase. That is when 'Akai" became the first firm to come up with a scheme of exchange offers. There was wide acceptance among the consumers and even the competitors in the colour Television market had to follow suit.

People vary remarkably in their readiness to try out new products or innovations, just as any product goes through a product life cycle, for each new product there are adopter categories too. This adoption process curve shape is almost similar to the PLC (product life cycle) of a product.

Another example can be of the Narula's *fast food chain of restaurants* in Delhi. *Narula's* creation for the customer a fast food chain based on Indian cuisine, had made it one of the pioneers to offer fast food in Indian delicacies. Of course, now the fast food market has many global restaurant chains like *Kentucky Fried Chicken, Pizza Hut* and so on.

In the above cited examples, the rate of adoption for the new product and services was very fast.

(c) ***Adopter categories :*** It must be remembered that people vary remarkably in their readiness to try out new products or an innovation. Everett M. Rogers *has defined a person's innovativeness as the degree to which an individual is relatively earlier in adopting new ideas than other members of his social system.* Just as any product goes through a product life cycle, for each new product there are adopter categories too. We can categorise adopters of the new products based on the relative time of consumers' adoption of the innovations.

This adoption process curve shape is almost similar to the PLC (Product Life Cycle) of a product.

FIGURE 11.1

TIME PERIOD OF ADOPTION OF NEW PRODUCTS

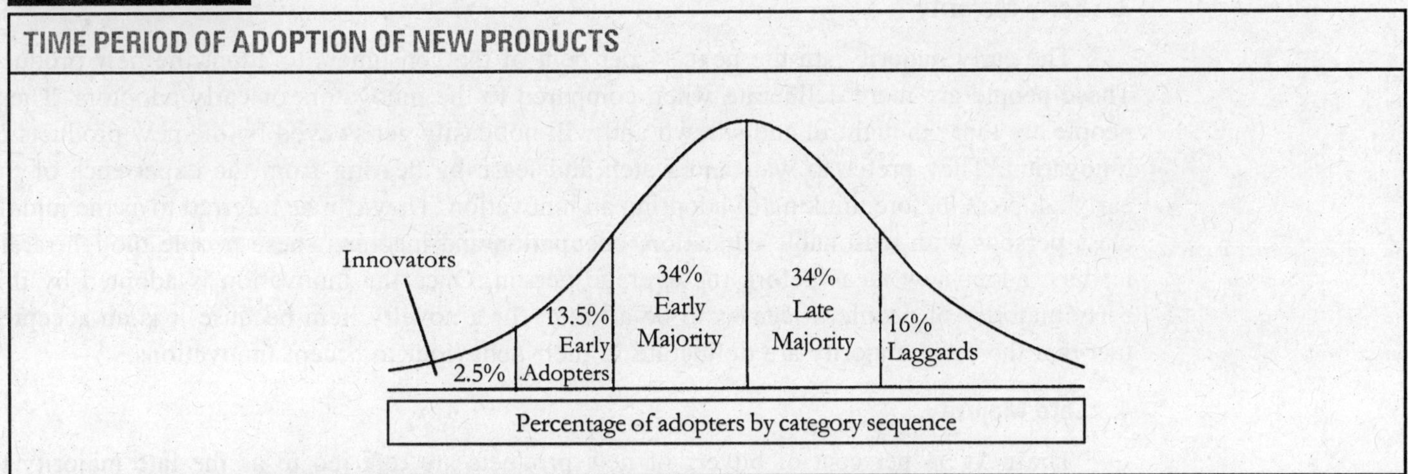

(*Source : Consumer Behavior,* L.G. Schiffman, L.L. Kanuk, PHI, 8th Edn., p. 528)

The diffusion process shown in Figure 11.1 takes the shape of a normal distribution (a bell shaped) curve, when considered over a period of time. The process starts with a slow beginning, then picks up momentum with more number of persons adopting the innovation, then after a certain number reaching the peak, there is a decline with less number of adopters remaining. A brief description of the category of adopters is given here under:

1. Innovators

After being aware of and seeking more information of new products, only 2.5 per cent of all the customers normally try out the new products. These people are referred to as the pioneers or innovators of the new product. Innovators are venturesome. They are easily acceptable to new ideas. They do not deliberate when new products are launched in the market. There is always a willingness on their part to try out new products even at the risk, that being the 'consumption pioneers', there is no feedback available on the use of the innovation from others. These people are usually found to be outgoing, gregarious, more educated and generally follow a lifestyle matching the high social class *'status'*. They consider it a chip to their shoulders when referred to as the innovators of the new product. Though, it may be remembered that this category of innovators of the new product is only a negligible 2.5 per cent of the entire target potential customers identified for the new product.

2. Early Adopters

The category of adopters in the diffusion process can be referred to as *innovators, Early Adopters, Early Majority, Late Majority and Laggards.*

The early adopters are the next 13.5 per cent of the buyers who adopt the new idea or new product. These people do not immediately plunge into buying as soon as a new product is available in the market. However, they also purchase the new product reasonably early though only after carefully verifying and gathering information about the new idea or new product from authentic sources. Companies have identified that the early adopters are usually recognised as opinion leaders in their social circles or community. These people are looked upon with respect, as they are social leaders of the community. Their views, opinions and facts expressed are heard with lot of respect and concentration by the community members. Their personality traits indicated that they are educated, of high social status with a favourable financial position, more successful than average and with a willingness to try new products or innovations, if convinced about the same. Due to these characteristics, early adopters are identified by companies and considerably exposed to information from all sources especially the mass communication media.

3. Early Majority

The early majority are the next 34 per cent of the consumers to adopt the new product. These people are more deliberate when compared to the innovators or early adoptors. These people are more thoughtful and shrewd and will not easily get swayed by the new products or innovation. They prefer to wait and watch and learn by hearing from the experience of the early adopters, before thinking of adopting an innovation. They can be referred to as the middle class persons with reasonable education, occupation and income. These people though rarely leaders, adopt new ideas before the average person. Once the innovation is adopted by this early majority of people, it ceases to be a luxury or a novelty item because it is an accepted fact that the early majority are deliberate in their behaviour to accept innovations.

4. Late Majority

The next 34 per cent of buyers of new products are referred to as the late majority to adopt the innovation. These people unlike the earlier mentioned categories of adopters are more conservative in their approach and do not immediately respond in favour of a change. Their acceptance of the new product will come into effect only after a public opinion is in favour of the new product or innovation. These late majority are people with limited education, an average social status, drawing limited salary and consequently having limited purchasing power. They are more skeptical and will adopt an innovation only after a majority of the people have tried it.

5. Laggards

This is the last category of buyers to adopt a new product, comprising of 16 percent of the total market. As the term *'laggards'* indicate, these are people who lag behind in their acceptance of an innovation. These people are very conservative, tradition bound and are vary or suspicious of changes. A lot of deliberation, caution and suspicion is exhibited in their buying behaviour for new products. They generally prefer to mingle with people who share a similar traditional outlook. They will adopt the innovation only because the innovation has taken a step in the direction of tradition in itself.

The above mentioned classification of adopters of a new product suggest that the firm introducing a new product should do research on the demographic, psychographic and media characteristics of innovators, and early adopters and specially work out communication programmes, directed at them. An understanding of how a consumer seeks and processes information about new products and the decision making process adopted by him can improve the adoption rate of new products. As seen above only 16 percent of all the customers, namely the innovators (2.5 per cent) and early adopters (13.5 per cent), normally try out new products soon after the launch. So firms can exploit the natural tendency of this section by meeting their needs, in particular, and accelerate the pace of acceptance. This is because, these segments endorsement of the product will have a positive impact in terms of appeal to the other categories of adopters comprising the 34 per cent of early majority, another 34 per cent of late majority and the remaining 16 per cent of the laggards.

An understanding of how a consumer seeks and processes information about new products and the decision making process adopted by him can improve the adoption rate of new products. Since each new product will be unique in its usage, the innovating firms have to work out innovative ways to tap the target market especially by concentrating on the top two segment categories of adopters.

This method was followed by *Dabur India,* in 1996, when it launched *'Real' a* natural fruit juice - a first of its kind in a market familiar with canned juices. The company had aimed at the early adopters, identified as the health conscious SEC Al, A2 housewife. The product *'Real'* was made available at 1400 select outlets out of the 20,000 outlets in the capital, concentrated in the affluent part of South Delhi. Added to this the company had also used attractive 'P.O.P' material all over the stores and even advertised on 'Star Plus' communicating that the product held out real value especially to early adopters of the product. The basic objective of the company was to ensure usage by these adopters rather than trying to broad base the appeal.

Since each new product will be unique in its usage, the innovating firms have to work out dynamic ways to tap the target market especially by concentrating on the top two segment categories of adopters.

Non Adopter Categories

There is another opinion to include the category of non adopters also, which will be in accordance to the market place reality, because not all potential consumers will necessarily adopt a product innovation. Suresh Subramanian and Robert A. Mittelstaedt (mentioned in *Consumer Behavior,* L.G. Schiffman, L.L. Kanuk, 6th edn, pp. 540) have given another classification of the different types of non adopters. These are:

1. *The unaware group* - Those consumers who are not aware of the new product
2. *Symbolic-rejectors* - Who, though aware of the product, have decided against buying it.
3. *Symbolic adoptors* - Who know the product will be useful for them but have not tried it.
4. *Trial adopters* - Who have tried the product but have not gone for a repurchase or actual purchase.
5. *Trial rejectors* - Who have tried the product and also rejected the same.

An attempt to induce non adopter's interest in Pears Soap

Role of Communication in the Diffusion Process

As seen in the definition of the diffusion, communication is a key element in the process. During the initial stages of a new product's launch, consumers tend to rely more on the mass media for information. Advertisements in mass media such as magazines, Newspapers, Radio FM and TV can be used to create an awareness as well as convey product information to the target consumers at large.

Once consumer awareness is created, early adoptors will look upon friends and close relatives to help in the evaluation of the new products. As seen in Figure 11.2, early adopters will rely more on mass media for information. Further, when they move across the various stages in the adoption process-from awareness to evaluation, trail and adoption, the word of mouth communication increases in importance. While for later adopters, the word of mouth communication is likely to be the dominant influence throughout the adoption process. Initially, these late adopters learn about the innovation from friends, relatives and neighbours rather than from the mass media. From this, it can be said that marketers must work at encouraging diffusion by using an informational campaign initially to create awareness among early adopters. Subsequently, they can then work towards stimulating favourable word-of-mouth communication among the late adopters.

Marketers must work at encouraging diffusion by using an informational campaign initially to create awareness among early adopters.

Spykar Lifestyles which markets *Spykar Jeans* had used the magic of films-the 70 mm screen to gain the mind share of the movie goers (prospects) by strategically weaving their products as the films are played on screen. In order to increase awareness and knowledge of their brand Spykar jeans, the company had done in-film advertising in more than seven Hindi movies such as Kya Cool Hain Hum, Namastey London etc., and established their presence in the North and West of India.

For entering the southern market, Spykar jeans planned to take the mass media route like advertising in Surya's (a leading Tamil Movie Star) movies apart from other southern films. To woo the late majority the company was to focus at below the line activities such as sponsoring college events and popularising the brand.

FIGURE 11.2

THE COMPARATIVE INFLUENCE OF 'WORD-OF-MOUTH' IN THE ADOPTION PROCESS

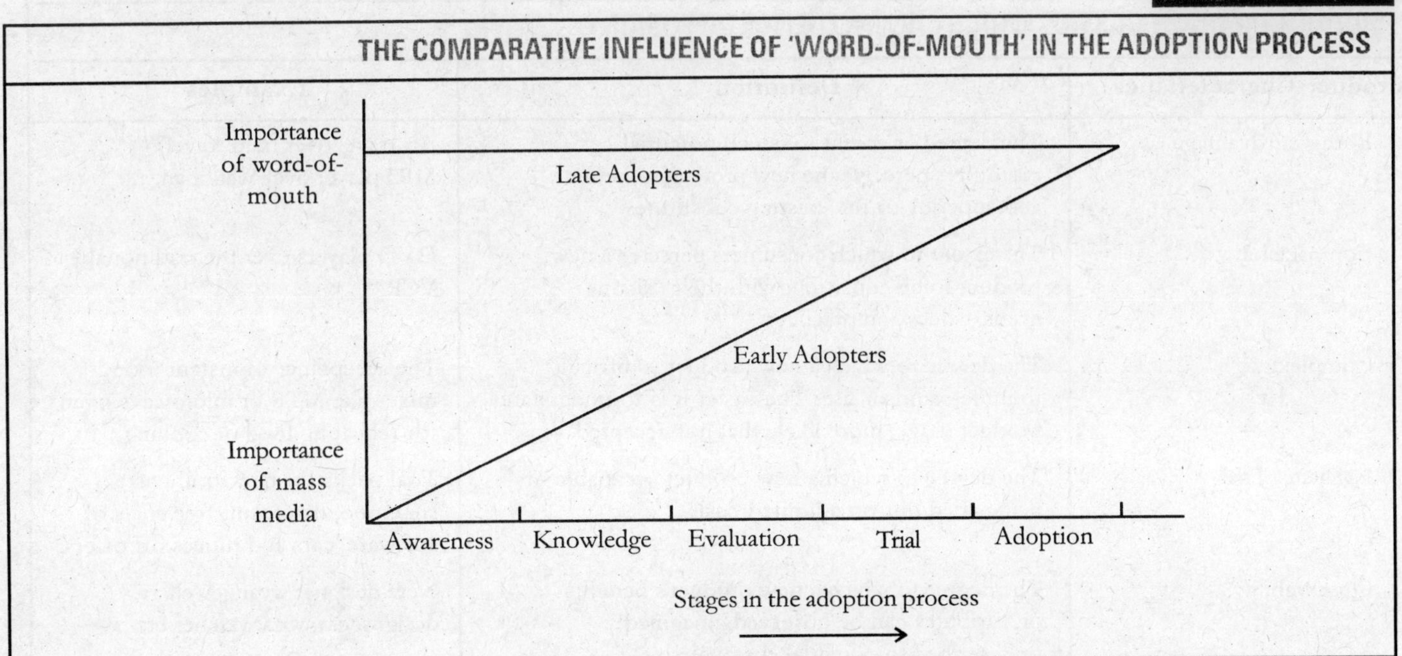

(*Source : Consumer Behavior*, Henry Assael, 6th edn., 2001, pp. 631)

Seiko Watch India before launching its products (watches) targeted at the premium watch segment, had a pre-launch campaign where it had advertised with a teaser campaign with 100 sports on TV (mass media). Post the launch, the company continued communication programme through print and other mass media and also had a tie up with *FI Sport.* It had assumed that post launch, the early adopters (the self assured individuals) will provide the necessary word of mouth to motivate the other adopter categories.

➲ CHARACTERISTICS THAT ENCOURAGE THE ADOPTION PROCESS

The uncertainties associated with product marketing can be greatly reduced if marketers could anticipate how consumers would react to new products and develop a promotional strategy accordingly.

All new products or innovations are not always easily accepted by consumers. Some products gain easy acceptance or are easily accepted by consumers. For instance, *Nirma detergent powder* (when *HLL*'s *Surf* was the market leader), *Maruti 800 c.c. car* etc. While there are other new products or ideas which took a long time to be accepted. *For example,* ownership of a personal credit card. There are still others which inspite of being available in the market since quite some time, (the new product) had never gained wide spread consumer acceptance as anticipated by the marketers, for example the *pagers.*

The uncertainities associated with product marketing can be greatly reduced if marketers could anticipate how consumers would react to new products and develop a promotional strategy accordingly. The characteristics of the new product or innovation also affects its rate of adoption or the adoption process. Five characteristics have been identified which play an important role in influencing the diffusion process.

1. *Relative advantage :* The first characteristic is the new product's relative advantage *i.e.,* the degree to which it appears to be better and superior than the existing products. If the consumer perceives, the new product to be relatively superior as compared to the existing products, more is the chance of the innovation being adopted. *For example, 'E-mail'* and *Fax* were considered to be better and superior to *Telex.*

TABLE 11.2

PRODUCT CHARACTERISTICS WHICH CAN INFLUENCE DIFFUSION

Product Characteristics	Definition	Examples
• Relative Advantage	The degree or extent to which potential customers perceive the new product as better and superior to the existing substitutes.	Air travel over train travel, MP3 player over Walkman.
• Compactability	The extent to which consumers perceive a new product to be consistent with their existing needs, values and practices.	DVD players over the traditional VCR.
• Complexity	The degree to which a new product is difficult to understand or use. The easier it is to understand product usage, more likely that it is accepted.	The acceptance of instant food mixes like MTR or microwave oven for reheating food or cooking.
• Facilitates Trial	The degree to which a new product is capable of being tried out on a limited basis.	Trial packs for new toothpaste, shampoo, detergent, free trials of software, cars and rupees off offers.
• Observability	The degree to which a new product's benefits or attributes can be observed, imagined or described to potential customers.	New-designer wear, jewellery designs, car, wristwatches etc.,

"Relative Advantage" and "Facilitating Trial" can influence diffusion.

Similarly, *cellular phones* over took *pagers*, because they were accepted to have better communicative features in comparison. This perception of greater relative advantage in using *'E-mail'* as well as *cellular phones* as communication network, resulted in sooner acceptance of this concept or new idea.

There are various characteristics which influence the diffusion (adoption) process. These are relative advantage of the innovation, compatibility (the degree to which potential consumers feel that the new product is consistent with their existing needs, values and practices), innovation's complexity and triability (the degree to which the new product may be tried on a limited basis).

2. *Compatibility :* The degree to which potential consumers feel that the new product is consistent with their existing needs, values and practices is a measure of its compatibility. Greater the degree of compatibility, sooner will the innovation be acceptable to the consumer. *For example, 'Laptop'* computers are highly compatible with the needs and lifestyle of senior executives of companies.
3. *Complexity :* The third characteristic is the innovation's complexity. This means the extent or degree to which the new product is relatively difficult to understand or use. Greater the degree of complexity, more time will be required for the product to be accepted. *For example, personal computers* are complex and therefore took a lot of

time to penetrate Indian homes. This issue of complexity is important when entering a market with hi-tech consumer products.

4. *Divisibility or Facilitates Trial :* The degree to which the new product may be tried on a limited basis. This means the extent to which the new product can be tried on a small scale basis before going for full fledged use of the same. If the consumers have got the option of trying out the product and then decide to buy if trial result found satisfactory, the innovation's rate of adoption increases. For instance, when *'Braun India'* pioneered the 'epilator' in a market, where its target consumers were using the traditional method of waxing, the company needed to convince women that using *'Silk Epil'* was more convenient, so it offered a six day money back trial offer to its consumers, reassuring that if she didn't feel comfortable with the product, she (the consumer) could always return it. At times marketers, when introducing products such as shampoo or detergent powder or tooth paste, use small trial packs (free samples) or rupees-off coupons to enable consumers have a first hand direct experience with the product. Even car manufacturers such as Maruti, Hyundai, Ford etc., offer 'test drive' for their new car models to provide customers a direct product experience.

5. *Communicability or Observability :* The fifth characteristic is the innovation's communicability. The degree to which the results are observable or can be described to others or the ease with which a new product's salient features are observed. A new product concept will work if the new technology or new product usage can be described and demonstrated. *For example, 'Eureka* Forbes' has been able to gain easy acceptance of its products such as the *'Aquaguard'* and *'Vacuum cleaner'* through adopting the method of observation through demonstration.

There could certain barriers which come in the way of adoption of an innovation. These are *value barrier* (i.e. a product's lack of relative advantage when compared to its substitutes), *usage barrier* (a product or service is not compatible with the consumer's exiting habits) R*isk barrier* (consumer's physical, economic performance or social risk in adopting an innovation).

The above are the typical product characteristics which can influence an innovation's diffusion process but, apart from the above, there are certain other characteristics which could influence the rate of adoption like initial costs, ongoing costs, risk and uncertainty, scientific credibility, selection of channel of communication and social system or social approval. These characteristics are also important determinants affecting the rate of adoption. So marketers involved in new products development have to undertake research and also consider the above factors. When *Air Deccan* had entered the market as a low cost air flier, it had used various mass media (T.V newspaper, magazines etc.,) to communicate about the various product services, offering benefits such as low costs, saving of time spent on travel and so on, in an attempt to woo potential customers. The key factor affecting the diffusion process may vary from product to product. So marketers have to pay maximum attention to the key ones while developing new products and then design a suitable marketing programme accordingly.

Characteristics of Barriers to an Adoption of an Innovation

Just as the characteristics encouraging adoptions, there could be certain barriers to adoption of an innovation, Ram and Sheth have put such barriers under three heads: value barrier, usage barrier and risk barrier. (*Consumer Behavior*, Henry Assael, 6th edn, pp. 624-626)

Value barrier: The value barrier can be said to be a product's lack of relative advantage when compared to its substitutes. When cellular phones were launched in India, being costly, it was considered to be the product of exclusive customers. It was also accepted in business markets as a good mobile communication device and hence worth the cost. Since landline phones were already available, most consumers felt that the cost of mobile phone was too high in relation to the value they could get from the landline phones.

Subsequently, the mobile phone market saw phenomenal changes with many manufacturers such as Bharti *(Airtel), Hutch, Reliance* etc., entering it and pushing down the price of the handset and offering various schemes that help in reducing the monthly charges. Simultaneously, the mobile phone companies are also using various media to convey information on their product-service offering's value to their target market.

Usage barrier : A usage barrier takes place when a product or service is not compatible with the consumer's existing habits. For instance, even though we are in the I.T (Information Technology) age with a reasonable percentage of the consumers being tech savvy, online shopping has not found wide acceptance. There is resistance from customers who prefer to visit shops, examine the merchandise, and have their queries attended to by the store personal. Moreover, they feel there is a fun element involved when shopping with friends and relatives. The usage barrier in online shopping occurs because they feel it is not compatible with their desire for visual treat and social interaction involved in shopping when compared to e-shopping.

To a certain extent, marketers are handling this barrier by having opinion leaders (persons who have personal experience with the benefits of e-shopping) communicate about the positive aspects of online shopping.

Risk barrier : A risk barrier refers to the consumer's physical, economic, performance or social risk in adopting an innovation. When cellular phones were introduced, consumers were worried about risks due to reports about physical risks of radiation from frequent and long usage of the mobile phones. But technological improvements and media communication to educate consumers, helped to reduce consumers perception of these risks. Initially, consumers had fears about personal computers (PC) price (economic) and performance (complicated software languages). This risk has been largely reduced by lowering the price of PCs as well as new, easily understandable software packages being made available in the market. Consumers' social risk of adopting designer wear clothes can be overcome through endorsements made of consumers' peer groups who have already used the same.

An effective way of reducing consumer risk is through offering free samples or trial or unique online strategies. Some marketers use their distribution network by offering off-line transaction services to customers.

An effective way of reducing consumer risk is through offering free samples or trail or unique online strategies. Free samples are given during the launch of continuous innovations for products such as tooth paste and detergent powders. Car manufacturers are offering free test drives when new models are launched *(Zen Estilo, Corolla, Logan)*. Auto companies are using a combination of online and off-line strategies to interact with prospective customers. For instance, Toyota has taken the online route to sell its limited edition model of *Toyota Corolla.* Internet research has become an important part during the purchasing process of cars. The company feels that using tools like microsites, direct mailers through the internet, SMS campaigns and having set up a back office operation which will provide the link to its dealers will help the customer in his internet research. Travel portals are now partnering retail chains to increase their volumes by having their presence at such high footfall areas. For instance, ***make my trip.com*** had set up a separate counter at Spencer's after receiving an encouraging response for a similar pilot study done at Subhiksha. So apart from flight/hotel bookings which can be done through internet interface, complete holiday packages can be offered through face-face interaction.

Some marketers use their distribution network by offering off-line transaction services to customers. *Yatra online* has tied up with *Hughes* a broadband satellite network provider to offer its travel related services to customers particularly in smaller cities. Through this tie-up, Yatra will use select Hughes Net Fushion centers across the country to create an off-line model of booking and payment. Thus customers who still have the fear of using their credit cards for e-commerce transactions and those who don't have credit cards will have comfort and feel secure about cash transactions.

Communication can be two types (a) between marketers and consumers, (b) among consumers (word of mouth communication).

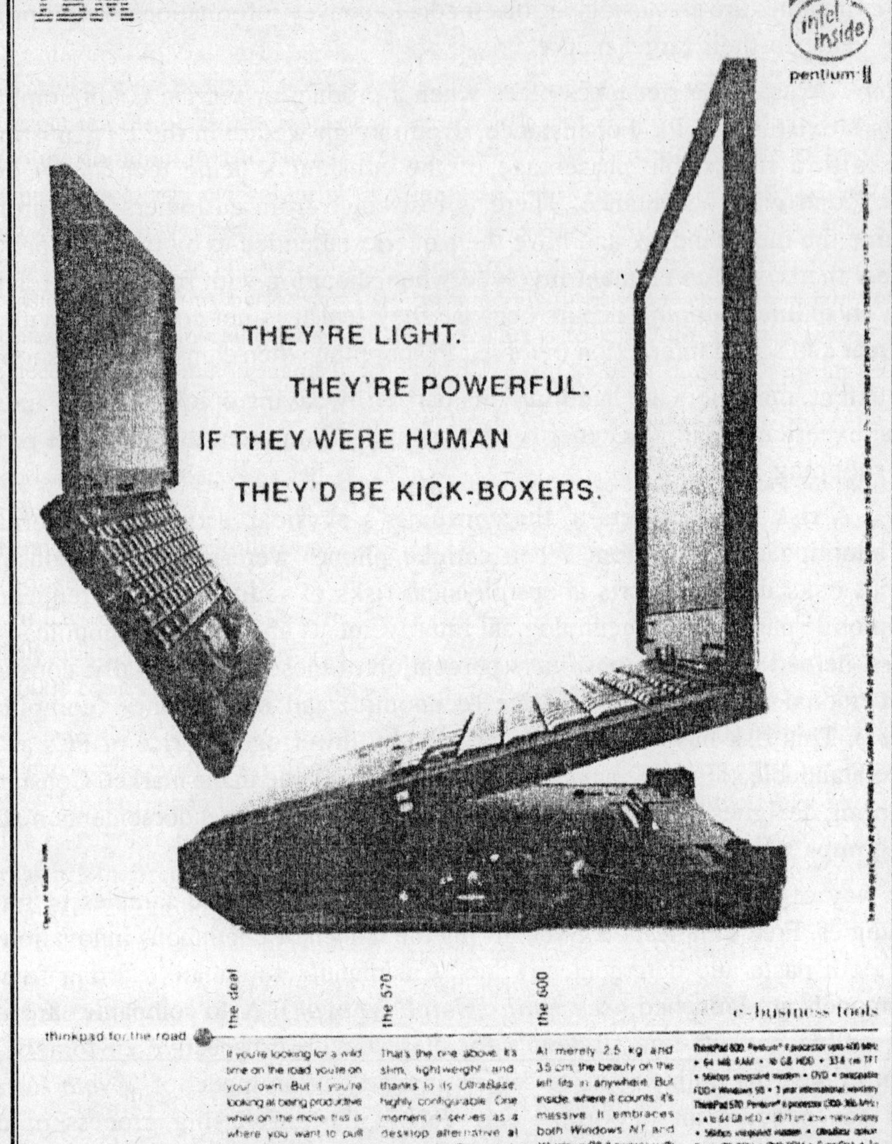

Ad communicates about the compatibility of the product 'Think pad'

➲ THE ADOPTION PROCESS

Marketers are interested in knowing how consumers learn about new products and the decision making process involved in adopting them. Adoption process may be defined as *the mental process through which an individual passes from first hearing about an innovation to final adoption.* (Philip Kotler, Principles of Marketing, 2nd ed^{n}, 1985, pp. 158) So adoption can be said to be the decision by an individual to become a regular user of the product.

When marketers introduce a new product or a new innovation to its target market, a lot of planning goes into managing the resistance to adopt the new innovation. This is because it involves bringing about a change in buyer's attitude and perception. Generally it is assumed that the consumer goes through five stages in the process of adopting new products. The five stages are represented in Figure 11.3.

Marketers are interested in knowing how consumers learn about new products and the decision making process involved in adopting them. When they introduce a new product or a new innovation to its target market, a lot of planning goes into managing the resistance to adopt the new innovation.

1. Awareness Stage

In this stage an individual comes to know about a new innovation or new idea or new product/ service. He becomes aware of the innovation from any source of information such as from friends, neighbour, co-workers, commercial sources etc. The individual only learns about the new innovation from either of the sources of information mentioned above. This means his knowledge about the new innovation is only limited to the extent of the information generated by the source of information from where he first learns about the new innovation.

FIGURE 11.3

STAGES OF ADOPTING NEW PRODUCTS

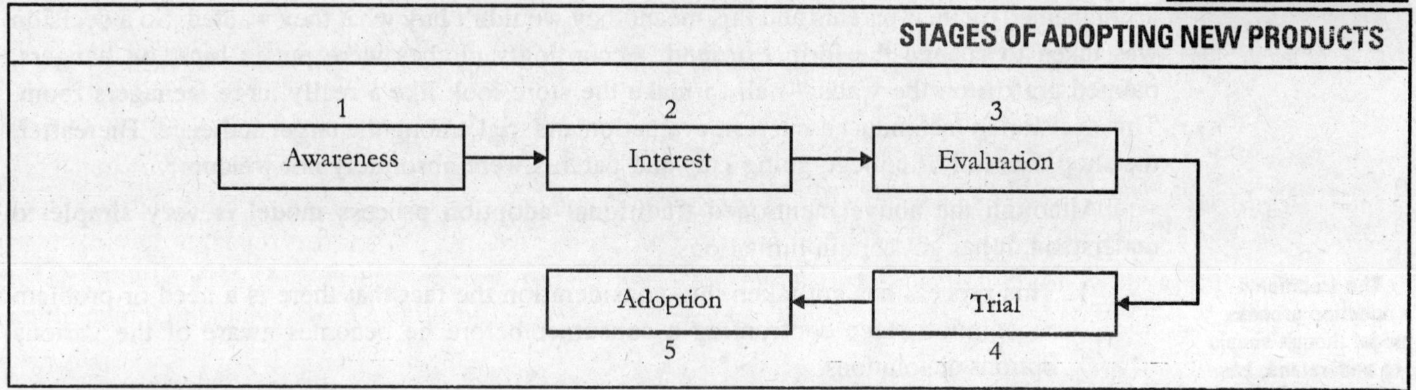

2. Interest Stage

After being aware of the new product or innovation, in this stage, the consumer gets stimulated and interested in the innovation. He goes about seeking more information about the new product. He is interested in gathering more detailed information related to the innovation in terms of its utility aspects, performance, durability and so on.

Generally, it is assumed that the consumer goes through five stages in the process of adopting new products. These five stages are the Awareness stage, Interest stage, Evaluation, Trial stage and the Adoption stage.

3. Evaluation Stage

The consumer 'interested' in the innovation will seek more information on it from all the sources he finds reliable. After collecting all the information on the innovation, the consumer will mentally try to evaluate the worthiness of the innovation. He will assign weights to the product attributes and work out to what extent the new product will be useful to him and then decide on whether or not to buy the new product.

4. Trial Stage

After evaluating the worthiness of the new product, the consumer may decide to try out the innovation on a small scale basis initially and make an actual assessment of the value of the new product. This stage also indicates that now the consumer is mentally prepared to try out the innovation, though initially on a small scale. He/she wants to experiment with the innovation and depending on how comfortable they are with the product, they will decide whether or not to go for large scale use. Since the consumer is not sure about the outcome of the use of the new product or innovation, it looks more logical and practical to go for a sample trial before opting for full time usage.

5. Adoption Stage

On being satisfied with the use of the new product, purchased by him on a trial basis, the consumer now decides to make full and regular use of the innovation. This is the last stage in the adoption process. The consumer takes the decision to go for a full fledged and continuous use of the new product or innovation.

The marketer must think of ways to help or facilitate easy movement of consumers through all these stages. Understanding how a consumer seeks and processes information about new products and the decision making process can help marketers to devise suitable ways which will help in the early adoption of the new products. When the Future group's Managing Director, Kishore Biyani started *Top 10*, a store that targets fashion for the college campus, tee-shirts, jeans, accessories and so on and also ranks the top 10 selling items in the store, the store was not able to attract consumers. A study carried out revealed that teenagers always came accompanied by their parents and this meant they wouldn't buy what they wanted. So a decision was taken to change the format around. Accordingly clothes were put in bins, on hangers, painted graffiti on the walls — all to make the store look like a really large teenagers room. This decision in fact induced interest, evaluation and trial among the target audience. Thereafter, the shop was full of college-going kids and parents were absolutely not welcome.

Although the above mentioned traditional adoption process model is very simple to understand, it has got certain limitations.

The traditional adoption process model though simple to understand, has certain limitations. It does not consider a need or problem recognition stage, does'nt mention the possibility of evaluation taking place throughout the decision making process, ignoring the fact that the consumer could reject the product after trail (or he may not use the product on a continuous basis) or include the post-purchase evaluation process.

1. This process has not taken into consideration the fact that there is a need or problem recognition stage confronting a consumer before he becomes aware of the various options or solutions.
2. The model does not consider that there is a possibility of the consumer rejecting the product after trial or that he may not use the product on a continuous basis.
3. Another fact which is not adequately recognised is that usually the evaluation takes place through out the decision making process and not necessarily at the evaluation stage only.
4. The model does not include the post purchase evaluation behaviour, which may either lead to a firm commitment or a decision to discontinue usage of the product.

In view of the above cited limitations, consumer researchers have suggested including two more stages between the trial and adoption stages, direct product experience (consequences) and product evaluation (confirmation) stages. The proposed modification to the adoption process is given here under.

From the above figure 11.3 it is seen that the adoption process starts with: Stage 1 → awareness, which leads to stage 2 → interest and then to stage 3 → evaluation. After this stage the product can either be rejected or tried out (stage 4) either before or after purchase. The trial stage may lead to stage 5 → direct product experience and the consequences of the experience stage 6 → product evaluation, this will ultimately result in either rejection or adoption (stage 7) of the product.

Examples of adopting innovations which were directly visible in the changes in behavioural pattern and lifestyle of consumers are automobiles, air conditioners, microwave oven and PC (Personal computer).

FIGURE 11.4

A PROPOSED MODIFICATION TO THE TRIAL ADOPTION PROCESS

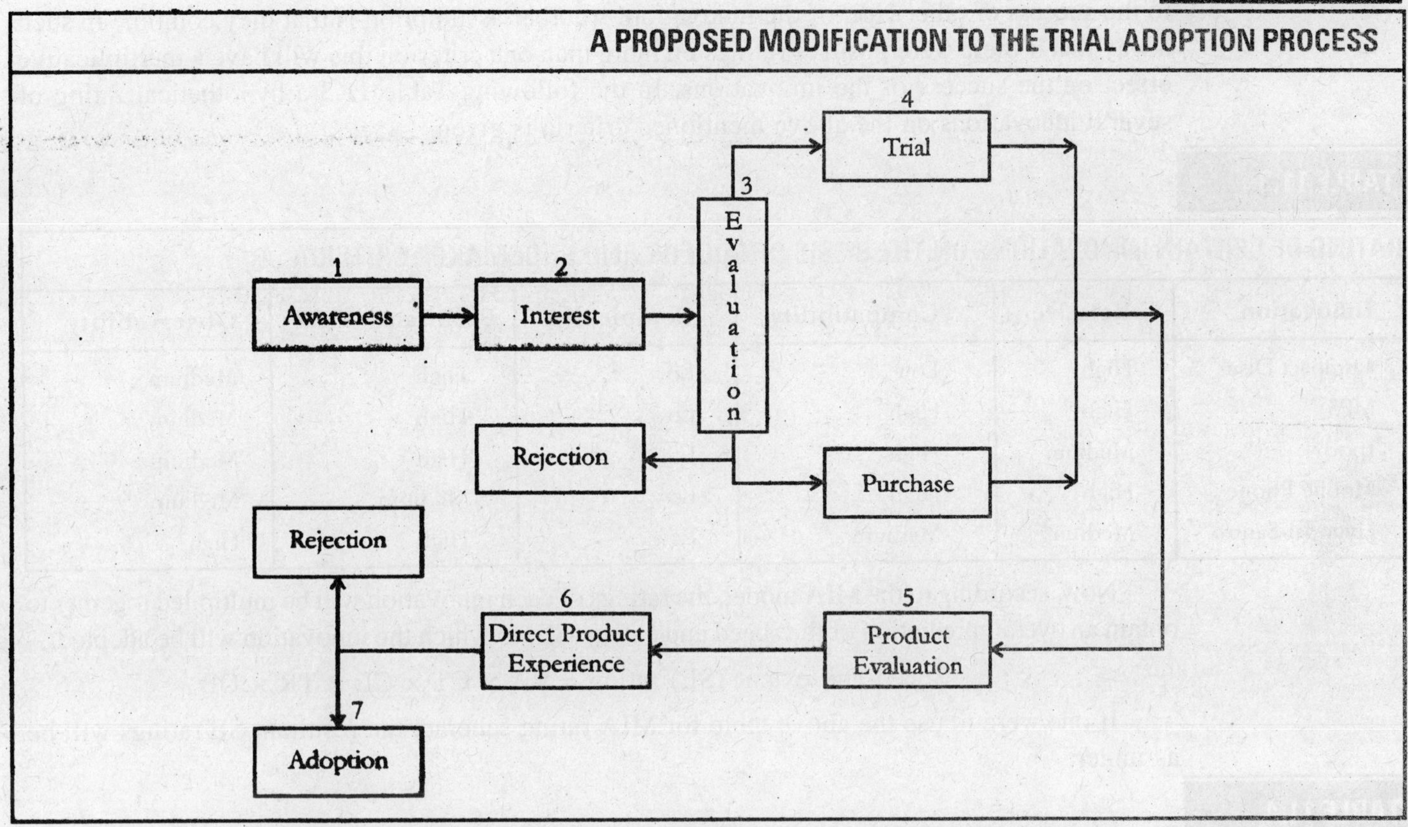

(*Source : Consumer Behavior,* L.G. Schiffman and L.L. Kanuk, 6th Edn., 1997)

MULTIPLICATIVE INNOVATION ADOPTION (MIA) MODEL

Rosemary Phipps and Craig Simmons had proposed a model of innovation adoption process, which is based on the Roger Shoemaker Criteria. Their idea was to understand what makes an innovative product, service or idea successful. (Understanding Customers 1996-97, Rosemary Phipps, Craig Simmons 1997).

Rosemary Phipps and Craig Simmons had proposed a Model of Multiplicative Innovation Adoption (MIA), which is based on the Roger Shoemaker Criteria. Under the MIA model, it is assumed that each of the criterion makes an equal contribution to the success or otherwise of the innovation.

To assess an innovation using the MIA model, it will be necessary to rate the innovation (product, service or idea) on the Rogers and Shoemaker criteria. This is done by using the following scheme:

- *Relative advantage :* The rating under this is referred to as RA. If the relative advantage is high, the innovation is rated 3, if it is medium, it is rated '2' and if it is low then '1'.
- *Compatibility :* This is referred to as 'CT' rating. If the compatibility is high, a rating of '3' is given, if it is medium, a rating of '2' is given and '1' if it is low.
- *Complex : This* is referred to as 'CL' rating. The rate of innovation is '3' if it is simple, '2' if it is medium (complexity) and ' 1' if it is judged to be highly complex.
- *Facilitates Trial :* This rating is referred to as TR. If the opportunity to offer trial is high the rate of innovation is '3', '2' if it is judged to be medium and ' 1' if it is low.
- *Observability :* This rating is called 'OB'. If the observability is high, the innovation is rated '3' if it is judged to be medium it is '2' and ' 1' if it is low.

Under the MIA model, it is assumed that each of the criterion makes an equal contribution to the success or otherwise, of the innovation. Another assumption is that they combine in such a way that if there were positive ratings on more than one criterion this will have a multiplicative effect on the success of the innovations. In the following Table 11.3 a hypothetical rating of several innovations on the above mentioned criteria is given.

TABLE 11.3

RATING OF CERTAIN INNOVATIONS ON THE BASIS OF ROGERS AND SHOEMAKER CRITERIA

Innovation	Relative	Compatibility	Complexity	Facilitates Trial	Observability
Compact Disc	High	Low	Low	High	Medium
MP3	High	High	Low	High	Medium
Ipod	Medium	High	Low	High	Medium
Mobile Phone	High	High	Low	Medium	Medium
Hyundai-Santro	Medium	Medium	Low	High	High

Now, according to the MIA model, the ratings of each innovation will be multiplied together to obtain an overall prediction of the speed and extent (SE) to which the innovation will be adopted:

$$\text{Speed and extent (SE) rating} = RA \times CT \times CL \times TR \times OB$$

If one were to use the above table for MIA rating scheme, the resultant SE ratings will be as under:

TABLE 11.4

SPEED AND EXTEND (SE) RATINGS USING THE MIA MODEL

Innovation	Speed/Extent (SE) Rating
Compact Disc (CD)	$3 \times 1 \times 3 \times 3 \times 2 = 54$
MP3	$3 \times 3 \times 3 \times 3 \times 2 = 162$
Ipod	$2 \times 3 \times 3 \times 3 \times 2 = 108$
Mobile Phone	$3 \times 3 \times 3 \times 2 \times 2 = 108$
Hyundai-Santro	$2 \times 2 \times 3 \times 3 \times 3 = 108$

The higher the SE rating, the higher or more the predicted success of the innovation.

Based on the above example of ratings provided it is predicted that the most successful innovation is likely to be MP3 while the least will be of CD (Compact disc).

Evaluation of the MIA Model

The researchers made the following observations while evaluating the MIA model.

1. The term success is a difficult term to define and is open to criticism on the basis that what they attempt to describe is itself vague. For the term 'success" will mean differently to various individuals - for one it may mean high sales figures, to another higher profit margins and so on. For instance, a manufacturer of premium jewellery may not sell in high volumes but may earn the reputation as an exclusive jewellery maker. There my be another jeweller who is well known for selling all types of jewellery purchased by many customers. In a sense then, both these jewellers are successful. Then we will have to redefine 'success' so it is best to accept a general definition based on cultural expectations.

2. The MIA model is purely theoretical. Tools do not yet exist to measure the five criteria and hence have to be constructed.
3. The criteria and model are based on perceived characteristics and hence are useful. This means different individuals could rate the same innovation in different ways. This would help in the application of this model for target marketing.

OPINION LEADERSHIP AND PERSONAL INFLUENCE

Word of mouth communication is the interpersonal communication which can take place between two or more individuals. For instance, between members of a reference group or a consumer and the sales personnel. All these persons can influence the purchase decisions of consumers. There is a well known adage "a satisfied customer is your best sales person", for they can through positive word-of-mouth influence, friends and relatives to buy certain goods or services. Whereas, dissatisfied customers through negative word-of-mouth may inhibit sales.

Opinion Leadership is the process by which one person (opinion leader) informally influences the actions or attitudes of others, who may be opinion seekers or merely recipients. This informal flow of consumption related influence between two or more people is referred to as word-of-mouth communication.

The word-of-mouth communication influence is closely linked to the concept of *opinion leadership.*

Opinion Leadership is the process by which one person (opinion leader) informally influences the actions or attitudes of others, who may be opinion seekers or merely opinion recipients. This definition of opinion leadership emphasises on informal influence. This informal flow of consumption related influence between two or more people is referred to as *word-of-mouth communication.*

Opinion Leader

These opinion leaders are very often a part of the social groups and also have social communication network. The biggest advantage of the informal word -of-mouth communication is that it is informal and interpersonal in nature and it takes place between people who are not directly associated with the commercial selling source or the firm. Very often, it is seen that the informal word-of-mouth communication is more influential than mass advertising in determining which product or brand is bought. The word-of-mouth communication can involve a face-to-face communication or over the telephone (conversation) or even surfing the internet while seeking information. Irrespective of the type of informal word-of-mouth communication, opinion leadership has been found to be more independent, effective and very often carry with it a pressure to conform.

Typically, persons most likely to influence others through word-of-mouth are opinion leaders while those most likely to be influenced are followers.

Opinion leaders are viewed as potential ambassadors of good-will by the consumers. Hence, their word-of-mouth communication will be the deciding factor in whether the consumer will go for a particular brand in the specific product category, based on the information or advice obtained from the opinion leader.

Characteristics of Opinion Leaders

Opinion leaders are found in various levels of social status. They are very good word-of-mouth communicators and can influence consumer's product related decisions.

1. **Opinion Leaders are Perceived to be Highly Credible Sources of Product Related Information :** Opinion leaders are persons who are considered to be knowledgeable. Opinion leaders often voice their opinion based on first hand information. Since they are informal sources of information, it is perceived that they have the best

interests of the opinion receivers. This first hand information from the opinion leaders helps in reducing the perceived risk or anxiety inherent in the purchase of new products.

Ads convey usage of brand ambassadors as opinion leaders in different product categories

Opinion leaders are perceived to be highly credible sources of product related information. They are also found in equal numbers in various levels of social groups.

2. **Opinion Leaders are Gregarious and are People with Experience :** Opinion leaders are found in equal numbers and in various levels of social groups. But what sets them apart from the other people is their experience (as a shopper and user) and their gregarious nature. Current experience count a lot when they are giving information or advice to the opinion receivers. Because of their outgoing and sociable nature, people enjoy interacting with them and since their opinion is based on first hand experience, opinion receivers have a lot of confidence in their advice .
3. **Opinion Leaders usually Provide Unbiased Information, that is they Provide both Favourable and Unfavourable Information to their Opinion Seekers :** It is presumed, marketers give only favourable information about the product. Whereas, a commendable aspect of the opinion leaders is that they provide both favourable and

Opinion Leader's view can influence purchase decision.

unfavourable information of the product. This quality of the opinion leader adds to their credibility. It is because of this characteristic of opinion leaders, that opinion seekers have faith in them and are confident that they are receiving the correct information which will help them in taking product related decisions.

Opinion leaders tend to provide both favourable and unfavourable information of the product and thus are not only a source of information but also advice opinion seekers on whether or not to purchase a specific product. They tend to be consumer innovators and have greater exposure to the media, especially in their area of leadership.

4. **Opinion Leaders are both Sources of Information and Advice :** Apart from communicating first hand information on their experience with the product, they would also voice their concern and advise others on whether to buy or not buy a specific product. Partly based on their experience and partly based on their information they will advise the opinion seekers on the various product or service oriented aspects. They generally pass an opinion on the performance of the various brands in a particular product category, which (brand) according to them is the best, where to shop, how best to use a specific product and so on.
5. **Opinion Leaders have got Greater Exposure to the Media, Especially in their Area of Leadership :** Opinion leaders are considered to be more knowledgeable than others because of their always being in the limelight, they are awarded a certain status and are persons who least deviate from the group norms. Because of the above mentioned qualities, these opinion leaders are always exposed to various media and also sought after by marketers.
6. **Opinion Leaders tend to be Consumer Innovators :** Opinion leaders have a tendency to seek more information or advice in the specific product or service category in which they are interested. Because of this interest to express their views based on first hand experience, they are likely to try new products in a particular product category as soon as it is introduced.

   Some studies, to understand the behaviour of consumer innovators have shown that for products like stereo, motor cycles, etc. the innovators function as opinion leaders and recommend specific products or services based on their own experiences.
7. **Opinion Leaders have got some Personal Product Specific Characteristics Like Personality Traits, Social Status and Demographic Features :** Opinion leaders are said to be having personality traits which include self confidence and gregariousness, are socially inclined, outspoken and possess a certain amount of knowledge, and interest in areas where they are looked upon as opinion leaders.

TABLE 11.5

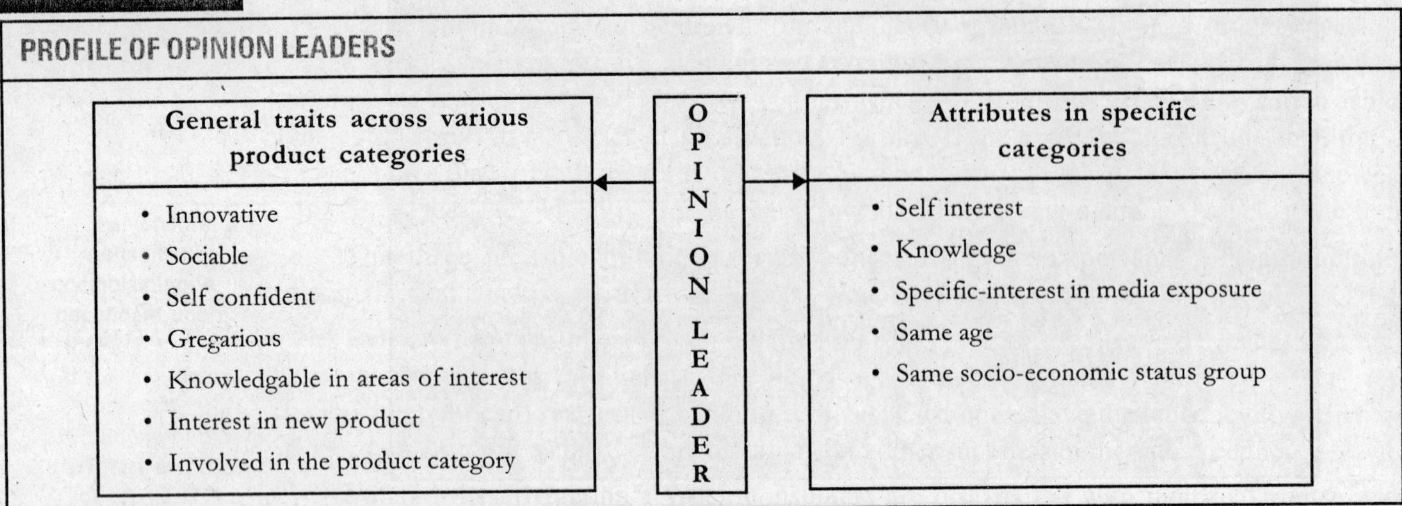

PROFILE OF OPINION LEADERS

General traits across various product categories	OPINION LEADER	Attributes in specific categories
• Innovative • Sociable • Self confident • Gregarious • Knowledgable in areas of interest • Interest in new product • Involved in the product category	⟷	• Self interest • Knowledge • Specific-interest in media exposure • Same age • Same socio-economic status group

(*Source : Consumer Behavior,* L.G. Schiffman, L.L. Kanuk, 6th edn., 1997, pp. 511)

Consumers who have been identified as market maven have a wide range of information right from the different types of products to all the other dimensions of markets. They like to shop and also share their shopping experiences with others.

Many marketing studies have shown that the opinion leaders and the people who seek their opinion are more or less alike and typically belong to the same socio economic group as them.

Marketers are interested in identifying opinion leaders and their demographic characteristics which will differentiate them from others, permitting the former to select the media likely to reach them. But studies have indicated that opinion leaders tend to communicate with consumers similar to themselves and that there is little difference between the demographic and lifestyle characteristics of opinion leaders and followers. So it will not be possible to identify a particular media to reach opinion leaders. Moreover, the profile of the opinion leaders is more likely to be product specific. For, instance the characteristics of the fashion opinion leader will be very much different from the food opinion leaders. Table 11.5 provides an over view of the general traits across various product categories and attributes in specific product categories.

Overlap of Opinion Leadership and the Market Maven

There is a persistent question concerning whether there can be a "generalised" opinion leader. In other words, can opinion leaders in one product category be opinion leaders in other product categories? In an attempt to answer this question, consumer researchers have agreed that opinion leadership tends to overlap across certain combinations of interest areas. For instance, in case of product categories with related interests like stylish clothes and cosmetics, soaps and personal care products etc., there is likely to be an overlap of opinion leadership.

Researchers Lawrence F. Frick and Linda L. Price have suggested the existence of a special category of opinion leader-*the market maven.* These consumers who are identified as market maven have a wide range of information right from the different types of products to all the other dimensions of markets. These market mavens like to shop and also share their shopping experiences with others. So their characteristics appear to fit the profile of opinion leaders. Unlike opinion leaders, they tend to help diffuse information on low involvement products such as razor blades and laundry detergent too.

➲ METHODS TO IDENTIFY OPINION LEADERS

Marketers and consumer researchers have been using four basic methods to identify opinion leaders: The socio metric method, the key informant method, the self designating techniques and the objective method.

• **Socio Metric Method :** In the socio metric method, specific individuals (group members) are asked to identify others with whom they communicate about a product or an idea. In this way, through interviews, efforts are made to trace the network of communication. Marketing studies require information beyond a single social group. So sociometric analysis will be useful in identifying the common characteristics of opinion leaders by studying many groups and constructing a number of sociograms. *For example,* more on a general level, any intact community (say an apartment housing 20 families) will provide an opportunity to measure and evaluate the flow of word-of-mouth communications in relation to a new product and its likely effect on the product trial.

• **Key Informant Method :** Key informants in a social group are asked to identify opinion leaders. These informants could be those who are engaged in frequent word-of-mouth communication within a group (say the college professor who could serve as a key informant for a college class), but not necessarily be an opinion leader. Through this technique, the key informant could be asked to identify the opinion leaders (from the class in the above example) and rate the prestige or leadership of members of that group. Although inexpensive (since it requires interviewing only one or few individuals). The practical difficulty is in identifying an individual who is capable of objectively identifying an opinion leader in a relevant consumer group.

Marketers and consumer researchers have been using four basic methods to identify opinion leaders, which are socio metric method, key informant method, self designating techniques and the objective method. Marketers try to influence consumer's decision making behaviour by stimulation of positive word of mouth communication that can induce product trial.

• **Self Designating Techniques :** These self designating techniques are used by marketers because they help to identify opinion leaders beyond a single social group. This technique involves asking consumers a series of questions to determine the degree to which they perceive themselves to be opinion leaders. The questions are restricted to a particular product category and consumers are asked to rate themselves on whether they are more or less likely to be asked an opinion (or advice) by others about the product in comparison to their friends. They are also asked whether friends and neighbours consider them to be a good source of information and seek their opinion on the product.

The self designating techniques are used more often than other methods by consumer researchers for measuring opinion leadership because it is easy to use. However, since a lot depends on the respondents it may be open to a biased view.

• **The Objective Method :** This method of determining opinion leadership is much like a *controlled experiment.* It involves imparting new product information with selective individuals and then tracing the resulting "web" of interpersonal communication. For instance, a new gym opened in the newly developed township may send out pamphlets informing the new residents of the township about the opening of the gym and inviting them to take advantage of the facilities offered at a special introductory discounted price. If the residents find the gym's health equipments to be the latest and of superior quality, the customers availing of the facilities are likely to provide the necessary positive word of mouth (or opinion) which will motivate many others to opt for a first hand experience with the gym.

OPINION LEADERSHIP AND MARKETING STRATEGIES

Marketers are trying to influence consumers decision making behaviour through various ways. It is keeping this in mind, that they are identifying ways to encourage word-of-mouth communications and other innovative ways to get the consumer interested in their product or service offerings. These could take the form of:

• **Stimulate Positive Word of Mouth Communication :** Marketers are trying to stimulate positive word of mouth from the consumers who have experience with the product. With the help of product design, marketers are trying to offer a new kind of consumer experience. For instance, *Mudra Marketing Services* helped *Asian Paints* and *Hyundai* standardize their stores across the country. It meant that the consumer would have the same shopping experience, irrespective of the size or location of the showroom. This marketing strategy was to let the customer know that they could take purchase decisions in a brand friendly ambience. The objective being to create a shopping environment which will prompt consumers to discuss the instore benefits and their experience to others.

In order to take advantage of the effectiveness of direct work-of mouth communication, marketers are moving away from the traditional marketing to experimental marketing *i.e.*, through direct selling, personal experience and advertising.

• **Stimulate Word-of-mouth to Induce Product Trial :** Marketers design innovative ways which can stimulate product discussions through informal communication and indirectly induce product trial. Marketers of Gurgaon based confectionery firm, Perfetti, realized that their product *Mentos* was not something that someone would leave the house to buy after watching a commercial. For chewing gum is purchased by customers who recall the brand while out shopping for other products. So Perfetti decided to create and get on to the website mentoshelpline.com, where a lot of young people surf. Using the website, Perfetti positioned Mentos as a fun product among youngsters. The initial feedback was overwhelming. The young surfers were having a good time having a hit at the website communicating with their contacts. Through prerecorded videos on the site, female executives gave cheeky answers to various questions. Thus the positive word-of-mouth helped in building up the brand recall for Mentos. It was because of Perfetti being able to associate Mentos with a feeling of camaraderie along with the usage of humour, which has made it popular among the youth.

• **Stimulate Word-of-mouth through Direct Selling :** In order to take advantage of the effectiveness of direct word-of-mouth communication, marketers are moving away from the traditional marketing to experimental marketing. For instance, in order to expand its user base beyond Mumbai, *Airtel* tied up with Nutan Mumbai Tiffan Box Suppliers Trust (The dabbawallahs) to sell new connections. The dabbawallahs who reached 2,00,000 households in Mumbai had long held the trust of their clients. While on their daily rounds, dabbawallahs hand out Airtel Registration forms to prospective customers in the morning and collect the filled forms in the evening. If the dabbawallah was able to get Airtel a new subscriber, he would earn Rs. 250 and a smaller commission on sale of prepaid vouchers. Even though they have not undergone formal training in sales management because of the trust they have built up, the dabbawallahs were able to provide the necessary word-of-mouth communication which people would easily accept. In this way Airtel was able to reach out to more customers.

Airtel used the dabbawallahs word-of-mouth network to expand its market

Stimulate Word-of-mouth through 'Experience' and Advertising

In order to stimulate word of mouth, marketers invite prospective customers (through advertising) to come forward and enjoy the 'experience' of the product or service offering. The Indian Hotels Company (IHC), the Tata Group's hospitality arm has redefined the budget category of *Ginger* chain of Hotels which offers modular rooms promising guests a consistently fresh experience at affordable rates. Ginger Hotels promises the customers a unique hospitality experience. For, right from checking in or out to even dining, one does not need the help of the hotel staff since everything is automated. These Wi-Fi enabled Ginger Hotels, with individually air conditioned rooms, come with ergonomically designed work areas, tea/coffee makers, a cyber cafe and even digital safe deposit boxes.

Because the emphasis is on the user experience the Ginger Hotels rely on positive word-of-mouth to sell the concept.

And so as to fetch potential customers, Ginger even built a replica hotel (complete with a model acting as a guest) in one of Mumbai's busiest areas Mahim Causeway. After this campaign, the Ginger Chain of Hotels saw a leap in bookings.

The Ginger Hotel looks for positive user's experience to stimulate and sell their concept

SUMMARY

Diffusion of innovation is the process by which the adoption of an innovation spreads over a period of time to other consumers through communication. Consumer researchers trying to explore the area of consumer acceptance of new products are primarily interested in understanding two closely related processes (a) The diffusion process and (b) The adoption process. The diffusion process is concerned with the acceptance of an innovation, when spread by communication to members of a social system over a period of time. Approaches to define an innovation can be classified as firm oriented, product oriented, market oriented and consumer oriented. The five characteristics which can influence the diffusion process include: relative advantage, compatibility, complexity, facilitates trial and communicability. Barriers to adoption of an innovation have been identified as value barrier, usage barrier and risk barrier. The channels of communication, the social system and time can also play an important part in the diffusion process.

How 'time' plays a very important part in the diffusion process by determining the purchase time, the various adopter categories and the rate of adoption were discussed. The adoption process has been defined as the mental process through which an individual passes from first hearing about an innovation till the final adoption. The stages involved in the adoption process include the Awareness stage, Interest stage, Evaluation stage, Trial stage and the Adoption stage. The Multiplicative Innovation Adoption (MIA) model, proposed by Rosemary Phipps and Craig Simmons based on the Roger Shoemaker Criteria was discussed to understand what makes an innovative product, service or idea successful.

Marketers are interested in identifying opinion leaders who can informally influence the consumption related decisions of consumers and thereby select the media likely to reach them. They use four basic methods to identify opinion leaders – the socio metric method, the key informant method, the self designating techniques and the objective method.

➲ CHAPTER QUESTIONS FOR DISCUSSION

1. What do you understand by the terms 'Diffusion process' and 'Adoption process'?
2. Why are marketers interested in the role of 'personal influence' and 'opinion leadership' in consumer decision process? Explain giving suitable examples.
3. Make a list giving of examples of new products which have been launched in the market in the past one year. Discuss about this with your classmates and determine the purchase time and rate of adoption for the same.
4. Write a brief note on the adopter categories by quoting a real example.
5. Describe about the importance of the adoption process and explain the stages involved in the adoption of new products

➲ SUGGESTED READINGS

1. www.strandbookstall.com
2. Jim Blythe, *'The Essence of Consumer Behavior'*, Prentice Hall, Europe HertfordShire, 1997.
3. The Learning Curve, *Retail Biz,* May 2005, pp. 30-31.
4. Leon G. Schiffman, Leslie Lazar Kanuk", *"Consumer Behavior"'*, Prentice Hall of India Private Limited, New Delhi, 2005 & 1997.
5. Henry.Assael., *Consumer Behavior and Marketing Action,* Thomson Learning, Singapore, 2001, pp. 603-641.
6. Gautam.K. Bhattacharya., Purchasing Power, *Retail-Biz,* February 2005, pp. 43-45.
7. S. Ram and Jagdish Sheth, Consumer Resistance to Innovations: The Marketing Problem and its solution *'Journal of Consumer Marketing'* 6, Spring 1989, pp. 5-14.
8. Urvashi. Jha., Travel portals reach retail chains to grow e-ticketing, *The Economic Times,* Bangalore 23 May, 2007.
9. Urvashi. Jha., Skykar Jeans bets on tinsel town, *The Economic Times,* Bangalore 26 May, 2006 pp. 4.
10. Sushmita. Mohapatra., On Time: Seiko Watch to make entry on June 7, *The Economic Times,* Bangalore, 26 May, 2006 pp 4.
11. Irshad. Daftari., 'Shopping with Kishore Biyani', *The Economic Times*, Bangalore, 19 May 2007.
12. Everett.M. Rogers, "*Diffusion of Innovations*", 4th Edition, Free Press, New York, 1995.
13. Virasat. Mirza., New Product Concepts, *Business Today*, Vol. 6, Number 1, January 7-21, 1997.
14. Rosemary Phipps and Craig Simmons, "*Understanding Customers*" 1996-97, Butterworth Heinemann, Oxford, 1996.
15. Janhavi. Abhyankar, Joshva. Newtonn., Direct-to-hearts, *Business World,* 30 April 2007, pp 64-65.

CASE

STANDARD CHARTERED BANK'S MUMBAI MARATHON

Standard Chartered Bank (SCB) in India is one of the country's largest international bank's with 80 branches in 31 cities and is one of the Group's key markets worldwide in terms of profitability and growth potential. The Bank has played a significant role in the history of the banking industry in India since the time it opened its first branch in Kolkata in 1858.

Competition

In the banking industry all the private and public sector banks were looking for image overhauls since there were very thin differences in their product service offerings. For this purpose local private banks like *ICICI and HDFC* were putting in lots of money in advertising besides literally purchasing market shares. Even the Public Sector Undertaking (PSU) banks were willing to spend liberally in the wake of economic reforms and liberalization.

Many of the banks have been trying to connect with the masses through association with a sports or by using a bollywood star. For example *ABN Amro Bank* had associated itself with the game of tennis.

Standard Chartered Bank's Strategic Approach to Build Brand Value

Standard Chartered Bank wanted to get customers relate to their brand in a different and unique way. Since many brands were associated with cricket, they wanted to do something different that genuinely lived up to the values of the Bank and also deliver the right stakeholder value. Standard Chartered Bank decided to re-inforce the focus on its five values (Responsive, Trustworthy, Creative, International and Courageous) in the minds of the stakeholders. So the challenge before the bank was to demonstrate the above values both internally and externally. Specifically put:

- Help people to relate to their brand, where in the bank will rise above their product promises and their role as a bank.
- To be a part of the community, in a never tried before way to help individuals and the community realize their potential and also make them proud.
- Research had indicated that since Standard Chartered Bank in India had previous sports association it would be good to stay in that arena. Globally it was seen that the brand benefits, community benefit and community ties were well visible and proven in countries where large marathons were organized. Standard Chartered Bank also felt 'Marathon' as an event would best fit to deliver their values and the desired marketing objectives.

The Difficulties

Marathon was not considered to be a popular sports or fitness activity in India. This difficulty had to be addressed and the challenge was to sell the marathon to the people as a marketing idea and solutions. SCB had to create brand awareness from community ties and showcase their values through the event. Although SCB had experience organizing Marathons in other markets, the health and awareness levels of the target groups there was more evolved compared to developing countries.

Moreover, in India, the learning and the target group fit was too radical and required a complete change of target group mindset for 'Marathon', to succeed here. Finally, running a Marathon would involve bringing a large part of the city to a complete halt on the day of the event. So this would require the support of the government and city administrative office, a good organizer to take care of the logistics, involvement of money and identifying the 'Right Partner' to help.

The Marketing Efforts and Communication

A multimedia approach was adopted for communication. The marketing and communication activities were broken into two phases. Pre and post registration. The pre registration phase was to create excitement and market the event and post registration would work to drive charity association, land mark announcements, participation, special efforts countdown etc. Marathon being a local and community event, a strong focus was to be on below-the-line (BTL) activities. BTL was to be concentrated at airports, railway stations, housing societies, jogging parks, shopping malls, schools, colleges, gyms and also take the form of special promotional activities.

The Event and Post Event Benefits

The communication *'Run Mumbai Run'* (in the first year) slogan invited the city to challenge themselves to do something new and different. Based on the very positive response, in the second year the communication was taken to the next level through *'Me Mumbaikar Me Marathoners''*. In the third year the "Me Mumbaikar Me Marathoner" was taken to one more level by Mumbaikar voicing their earlier experience conveying strong determination and pride (the very essence of Me Mumbaikar Me Marathoner).

SCB gained in many ways through its 'Standard Chartered Mumbai Marathon, which has been said to be a highly successful marketing initiative.

- Mumbai city saw its first ever international marathon of a massive scale never thought of before.

- A total number of around 23000 people participated as against the target of 15000, which included over 100 celebrities and 150 international participants.
- Standard Chartered Mumbai Marathon has been voted as the biggest marathon in Asia (both in terms of the largest participation and highest price money) and also to be amongst the top ten marathons of the world.
- Standard Chartered Bank's brand awareness rose to 74 per cent and advertising awareness to 69 percent.
- Over US $ 220,000 worth of free publicity was generated through media articles and events 'with India's premier daily newspaper even changing its masthead for the event.
- The TRP Ratings for the telecast of the event on the ESPN were the highest ever for a non-cricketing event, in a nationwide live telecast.

The success of the above marathon is reflected in the fact that other brands have organized marathon events in other Indian cities in an attempt to replicate SCB's success.

(*Source : Strategic Marketing,* Volume V, Issue IV, July-August, 2006. pp. 30-37)

QUESTIONS FOR DISCUSSION

1. Do you feel SCB could have used the internet to foster positive word-of-mouth among consumers regarding the marathon? Why?
2. Supposing a decision is taken to organize a Marathon run involving only management students in the city of Bangalore or Bengaluru:
   - Discuss how to go about developing a communication network.
   - Will it be possible to identify an opinion leader for the above event? If yes, how?

UNIT IV : CONSUMER DECISION MAKING, AFTER SALES AND RELATED ISSUES

CHAPTER 12

CONSUMER SATISFACTION

- Case: **Kalnirnay**
- Customerisation – Meaning and definition
- The relationship between consumer expectations and satisfaction.
- Implications for shaping expectations.
- Satisfaction - no satisfaction judgement.
- Measuring of consumer satisfaction.
- The concept of perceived value, customer satisfaction and loyalty.
- Customer satisfaction versus service, quality level and customer loyalty
- Few studies to measure customer satisfaction.
- Towards building customer loyalty
- Customer satisfaction in services market
- Tackling customer dissatisfaction
- Handling of customer complaints
- Summary
- Chapter questions for discussion
- Suggested readings
- Case: The leader in the small car segment, **"Maruti Suzuki"**.

CASE

KALNIRNAY

Long back in the 1970's Jayantrao Salgaonkar, a professional astrologer who used to write on astrology for a leading Calendar, Nirnayasagar felt the need to bring the 'Sanskrit panchang' closer to the common Indian. He felt that we live in a society which has a rich and colourful legacy. The common man did not have access to an authentic source to obtain basic information on dates for celebrating auspicious occasions, propitious periods to observe traditional ceremonies or plan important events. Understanding this unmet needs of the common man led to the birth of the calendar 'Kalnirnay', in 1973. With financial assistance from his friends the first edition of Kalnirnay which hit the stands in various towns and cities of Maharastra received an over whelming response from the day one itself. Apart from being economically priced at Rs. 1.25 (then), the housewives could easily get information about important days of the Hindu calendar, exotic recipes and other daily utility information also. In the first year itself around 10000 copies of Kalnirnay were sold.

Initially Kalnirnay (KNY) had a customer base, which comprised mostly of the elite Maharastraians in the cities. However, over the years the Salgaonkar family launched various versions of Kalnirnay in other regional languages such as Hindi, English, Gujarati, Tamil, Telugu and Kannada. In the mid 90's it became one of the first publication's to use the Internet to sell its product primarily to the expat Indians. Today, the publishers of Kalnirnay are happy to note that Gujaratis, Tamilians, North Indians and a huge number of expat Indians are their satisfied customers, who regularly follow the Hindu calender. The founder of Kalnirnay, Jayantrao Salganokar, takes immense pride in the fact that today almost half of the calendars sold are purchased by non-Maharastrian families. An interesting testament of Kalnirnay's success is that it is prominently displayed even in the nighbourhood butcher shop. This is to know the **titheas** (dates) for Sankashthi and Ekadashi as both these days mean lean business for them. Further, Kalnirnay gives dates on Muslim events like Bakri Id as well.

Although, initially, Kalnirnay was launched as a product for the decision making lady of the house, it has been able to build up a clientele of satisfied customers by adopting itself to their changing needs. Accordingly, over the years it has introduced speciality calendars too like Arogya KNY (health special) Saundarya KNY (beauty), Swadishta KNY (cuisine) and even a Braille special. Incidentally, since KNY has acquired a sizeable subscriber base it is in a position to charge a premium from companies and brands which have realized the benefits of advertising in Kalnirray which stems from value adds the calendar provides.

The above case of Kalnirnay shows that even for a product such as the calendar, customer satisfaction goes a long way and can be extended to built up a long term relationship with the clientele.

Existing customers are and will continue to be the best prospects for the organisation. *Henry Ford* has rightly said, "If there is any secret of success, it lies in the ability to get the other person's point of view and see things from his angle." This aspect was visible in the case of the calendar 'Kalnirnay', discussed above. Every marketer today is engaged in working towards satisfying every consumer for, they have realised that, while marketing is a core element of management philosophy, its success lies in focusing more on satisfying the needs of their customers.

Customerisation is a process where-in all the employees in the organisation are engaged in building up a platform of interactive communication techniques so as to add value and increase customer satisfaction.

The conventional argument put forth by organisations is that the purpose of production is consumption and this will be served provided (their) consumers' interest are attended to. This is because of the conventional response which evolves around what consumers think, i.e., satisfied customers are presumed to be loyal too. Moreover, in the long run, such loyal customers will help in bringing in repeat business, a higher share of their expenditure and referrals and word of mouth recommendations to other customers.

Nevertheless, ultimately only if the organisation is able to provide quality product or service which matches customer expectations that consumer satisfaction will be achieved.

In this chapter we have looked into the various aspects of customer satisfaction. We begin with defining customerisation and understanding the relationship between consumer expectation and satisfaction.

The satisfaction, no satisfaction judgement and the Oliver's expectancy disconfirmation model are then briefly touched upon. The concept of perceived value, quality level, satisfaction versus service and customer loyalty are also emphasised upon. And finally the issues related to customer satisfaction in services market, implication of customer dissatisfaction and how to handle complaints have also been discussed.

CUSTOMERISATION (MEANING AND DEFINITION)

Customerisation can be defined as the process wherein all the employees of the firm interact directly with the customer and end user. Such a process enables them to have access to every person and function within the organisation, be involved in designing and fine tuning key products and processes and turn every interaction with the customer into a platform of interactive communication so as to add value and increase customer satisfaction.

Today, with the availability of multiple product or service choices, consumers are seeking 'value' for the money spent. Marketers on the other hand, are trying to identify this value which can attract and appeal to the customers through unique delivery methods. For this purpose, they are evolved around the process of customerisation, wherein the entire organisation (including all the employees) are engaged in identifying customer aspirations and perceptions and match it with suitable product and service offerings. All these efforts at building up a platform of interactive communication techniques are to add value as well as to increase the consumer satisfaction leading to consumer delight.

Customerisation will help the organisation to :

- Focus on consumer needs and offer value added benefits to them.
- Identify new customers, new market segments and new applications for existing products and services.
- Provide quality service to match the customer aspiration and requirement.
- Help to enhance the organisation's operational efficiency through employees high

motivational level and involvement.

- Enables the organisation to work towards total customer satisfaction and maximum customer delight.

The term *satisfaction* has originated from Latin and literally means (when translated to English) 'to have enough'. A customer is satisfied when she feels "Yes, I have had enough." So the entire issue before the marketer is to know what happens in the consumer's mind which prompts or enables her to make a judgement about a product or service offering.

FIGURE 12.1

THE INTERACTIVE FUNCTIONAL ACTIVITIES TO ENHANCE CUSTOMER SATISFACTION

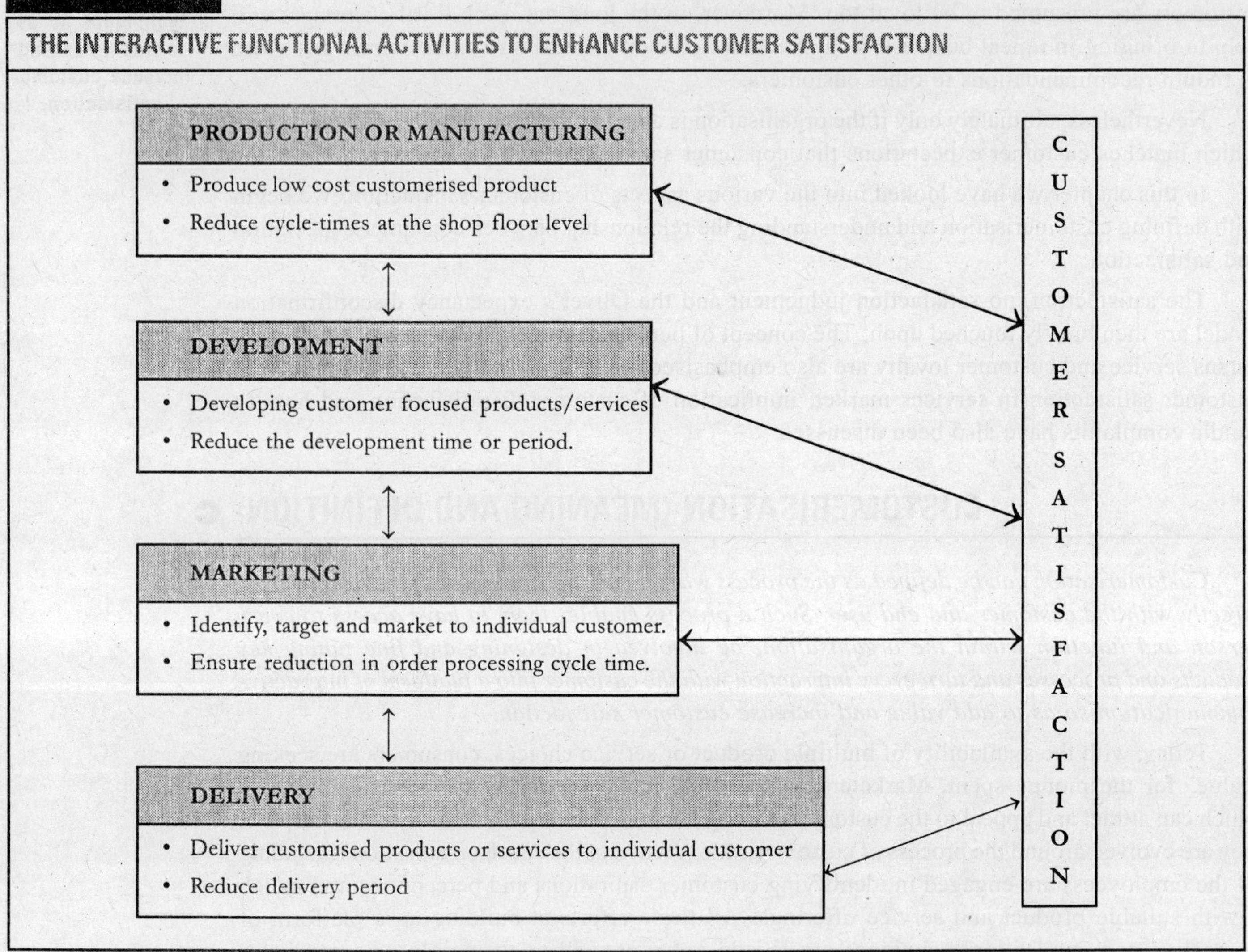

THE RELATIONSHIP BETWEEN CONSUMER EXPECTATIONS AND SATISFACTION

Consumer expectation can be said to be a belief or expectation or confidence of a certain outcome. Very often, consumer expectation is built up on a certain platform, which will accordingly affect the consumer satisfaction level.

In order to avoid consumer dissatisfaction, the marketer must adopt an approach wherein he can classify markets in relation to the degree of opportunity to deliver consumer satisfaction. The factors likely to influence consumer expectation and thereby their satisfaction level include:

Consumer expectation is the belief or expectation of a certain outcome from the purchase of a certain product or service.

- Market size
- Rate of growth of the market
- Stability of demand
- The 'price factor' influencing the purchase decision
- The consumer expectations of pre-and post-purchase service
- Consumer desire for product innovation.
- The level of competition (including both the existing as well as potential competitors)
- The organisation's competitive strength in terms of price and product performance.

Consumer Expectation Levels

Consumer expectation can exist at four levels :

***(a)* Expectation at the general level :** A general expectation of functional aspects like quality, durability reliability, style etc., of a high level of quality of product or service along with some negative external effects. For instance, when Vijay Mallya launched his *Kingfisher Airlines,* there was a lot of consumer expectations (excellent inflight services, hard drinks offerings etc.) build up. Consumers expected a high level of services from the UB group Chairman's airlines, provided the government gave the permission (probable external negative effect).

***(b)* Expectation at the category level :** At times, consumer's expectation is built upon a particular product category or class.

For instance, Park Avenue realised that premium customers were interested in exclusive men's wear in line with global lifestyle. Their answer was in the form of offering a complete range of fashionable men's wear made from the finest of fabrics and exceptional craftsmanship, in line with the global fashion under the brand name of *Park Avenue* in the premium category level.

***(c)* Expectation at the brand level :** At the brand level, the consumer's expectation is built up on the basis of his or her knowledge and information about the expertise and reputation of the organisation. The brand name *'Canon'* is immediately associated with camera. The company has been able build upon its customers expectation for making the best camera in the world in 1937 and even today it is known as a renowned brand in digital imaging. Other examples include brand names such as *Xerox* or *McDonald's* which have become identified with the product or service itself.

Consumer expectation can exist at four levels: Expectation at the general level, Expectation at the category level, Expectation at the brand level and Expectation at the transaction level.

***(d)* Expectation at the transaction level :** Such expectations are built up at the time of a transaction between the customer and the organisation. When Vijay Mallya was launching *Kingfisher Airlines,* he had made a bold mission statement "We are not in the transportation business we are in the aviation hospitality business." Given the Kingfisher brand, the consumer expectation was built up at the transaction level itself – they expected a lifestyle, quality, and services and Kingfisher Airlines, by positioning their service offerings was able to address those needs too.

Consumers have the tendency to compare their expectations with their post-purchase experience. If this experience falls short of expectations, it is referred to as negative discrepancy,

Park Avenue was launched to meet consumer expectations at the category level.

otherwise it is a positive discrepancy. Such discrepancies can induce customer satisfaction or dissatisfaction.

In a study titled 'Assessment of Quality of Banking Services in India' conducted by 'Consumer Voice' to analyse the perception of consumers and their satisfaction levels with their banks, certain interesting facts were revealed. Contrary to the popular belief, private sector banks did not score as well as other nationalised banks with the exception of Vysya Bank and Standard Chartered Bank. More details are provided in Box 12.1.

Marketers are engaged in trying to understand the consumer's product or service usage outcome. The outcome can be characterised as satisfaction or dissatisfaction.

To a great extent, consumer dissatisfaction can be reduced, if organisations are able to offer reliable, qualitative and customised product or service offerings.

Trying to understand the 'why' of customer satisfaction or dissatisfaction

Marketers are engaged in trying to understand the consumer's product or service usage outcome. This outcome can be characterised as satisfaction or dissatisfaction. It would be quite easy to measure overall satisfaction or dissatisfaction. This can be done by asking the consumers a question – "How satisfied or dissatisfied are you with our (mention the brand name) product or service offering?"

BOX 12.1

CITIBANK TOPS IN DISSATISFACTION LEVEL WITH 45% UNHAPPY - CUSTOMERS VOTE FOR PSBs

Time for banks to put in their ear to their ground. This is what their customers have to say. For customers who have been relying on advertised claims of banks, can now look to a survey conducted by "Consumer Voice" backed by the Union Ministry of Consumer Affairs, that reveals interesting findings including banks that are riding high on customer confidence and those that are over-charging their clients.

While Syndicate Bank, State Bank of Mysore, CentralBank, and Karnataka Bank scored the highest overall satisfaction score rated by customers, Citibank had the most number of dissatisfied customers with nearly 45% of them reporting a problem with the bank.

This study, named 'Assessment of Quality of Banking Services in India', analysed the perception of consumers and their satisfaction levels with their banks covering over 3,000 customers in eight cities. The methodology adopted for this bank was communicated to all banks in September 2005. The surprise winner was United Western Bank (UWB) with a loyal customer base in western India.

Contrary to popular perception, private sector banks did not score as well as their nationalised companies with the exception of Vysya Bank and Standard Chartered Bank. UTI Bank, Bank of Baroda, Canara Bank, HSBC were some of the banks where nearly 60% of their customers would recommend the banks to their friends. Customers of State Bank of Hyderabad, Citibank India and HDFC Bank, among others, would not recommend these banks to friends with nearly half of them deciding against it. Other banks where customers had a problem were Corporation Bank, UTI Bank and HDFC Bank.

While most banks wear credit card operations on their sleeve, the survey reports that the good old cheque deposit and draft facilities still drive the banking sector with 98% of the consumers endorsing the cheque facility.

Source : *The Economic Times*, 31 July, 2006 (Bangalore)

What is more relevant and challenging for the marketer is in trying to understand "why" customers feel the way they do. This aspect can be addressed by using two approaches. One approach could be to get the consumer rate a product or service on its various attributes. For instance, for a DVD player – its CD support format, PMPO mega bass effect, Random play feature, FM tuning, compatibility and pricing. The overall satisfaction or dissatisfaction with these product attributes can be looked into to explain the customer's overall satisfaction or dissatisfaction with the DVD player. But this approach does not explain what causes satisfaction or dissatisfaction.

The 'why' of consumer satisfaction or dissatisfaction will depend upon how the actual performance compares with the expected performance.

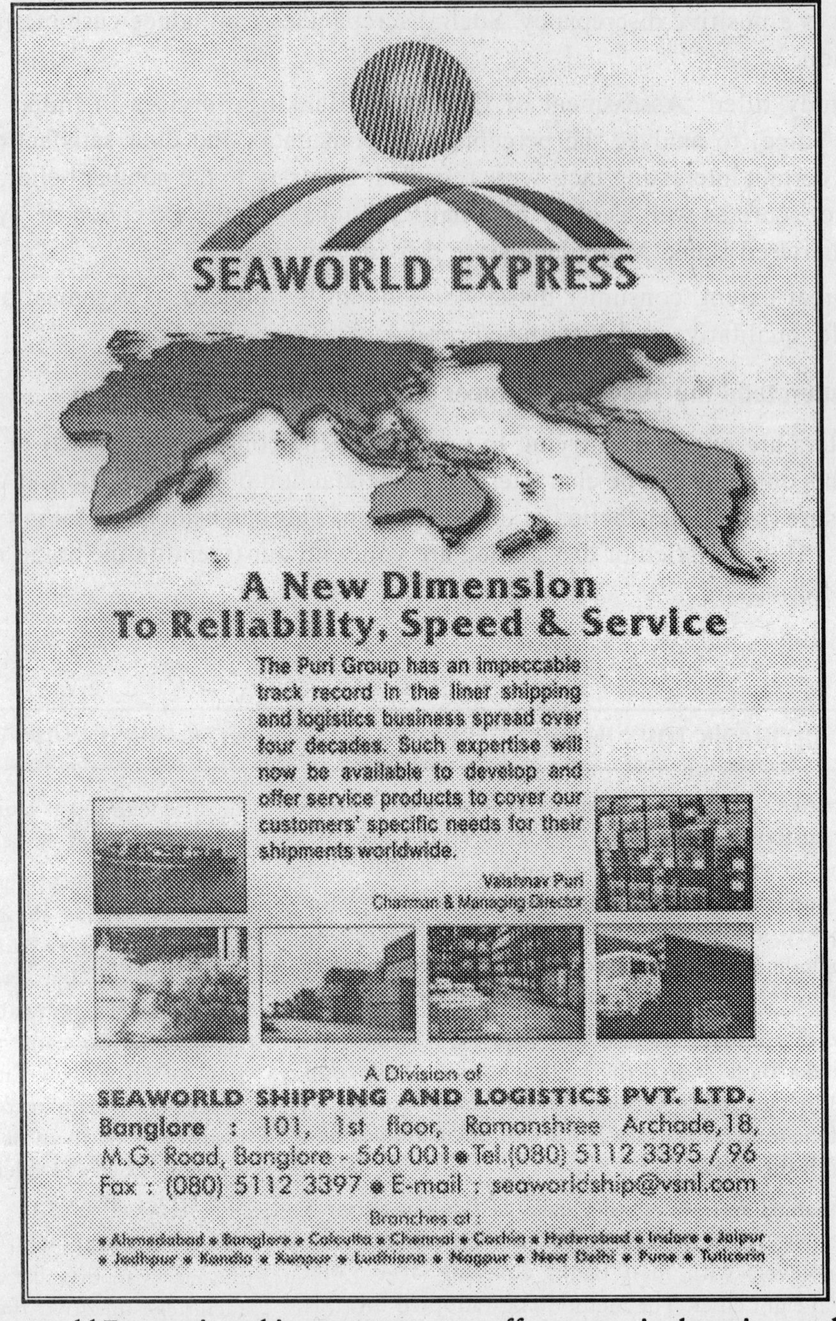

The Seaworld Express is making an attempt to offer customised service products to consumers and satisfy their shipment requirements

Three possible outcomes after experiencing satisfaction or dissatisfaction could be exit, voicing dissatisfaction or loyalty.

The second or theoretical approach helps to address this issue. Customer behaviour scholars have advocated that consumer satisfaction does not depend on the *absolute* levels of performance of the various attributes but more on a how the actual performance compares with the expected performance. Thus, if the product or service experience matches the pre-purchase expectations, it leads to customer satisfaction, and if it doesn't, dissatisfaction takes place. So, satisfaction or dissatisfaction will rise from the confirmation or disconfirmation of the consumer's expectation. This explaination is very relevant to how one makes intuitive sense of the everyday experience. *For example*, one may find the restaurant cleanliness unsatisfactory at the Coffee Cafe Day outlet but quite satisfactory in, say an ordinary restaurant. This is because one has a very high expectation from a Coffee Cafe Day outlet when compared to an ordinary restaurant.

"Price Factors" can influence purchase decision.

The satisfaction measures in terms of expectations from a hotel could be assumed to be as illustrated in Table 12.1.

TABLE 12.1

SATISFACTION MEASURES IN TERMS OF EXPECTATIONS

Attributes Measuring Satisfaction	Levels of Expectations		
	Fall below Expectations	Met Expectations	Exceeds Expectations
• Appearance of room	–	–	–
• Cleanliness of room	–	–	–
• Efficiency of front line staff	–	–	–
• Friendliness of in house staff	–	–	–
• Promptness of room service	–	–	–

* Few attributes have been assumed here, but it could vary on a customer to customer basis.

IMPLICATIONS FOR SHAPING EXPECTATIONS

Certain implications can be drawn from the theory of satisfaction for shaping expectations. If the various marketing mix elements (marketing communications, advertising, price etc.) promise too much, they could raise expectations which the product or service may fail to achieve, this could result in customer dissatisfaction. Further, if the expectations are too low, the sale may not take place. Thus, the right strategy would be to create realistic expectations, indicating a performance level which the target market would find attractive enough to select the brand.

The likelyhood of a consumer complaining is dependent upon three factors – dissatisfaction salience, attributions to the marketers and the consumer's personality traits.

The three possible outcomes or responses from the experience of satisfaction or dissatisfaction can take the form of – Exist, Voicing dissatisfaction or Loyalty.

Exit : When consumers are dissatisfied with the performance (or experience) of a brand, they may decide not to purchase that brand again. Such customer behaviour is very much visible in credit card services or banking services. Customers have the tendency to switch over from suppliers, with whom they are dissatisfied to other suppliers of the same product or services.

Voicing dissatisfaction : When consumers are dissatisfied with their experience with a particular brand, they may complain and then either decide to give the brand another chance or switch over to the competitor's brand *i.e.,* exit.

The likelihood of a consumer complaining is dependent upon three factors – dissatisfaction salience, attributions to the marketer and the consumer's personality traits.

Is this ad of IDFC trying to build up consumers expectations?

Dissatisfaction salience : Usually, the importance of the product or service and the degree of performance - expectations gap will determine dissatisfaction salience and this in turn will determine the likelihood of consumer complaints. For instance, consumers may ignore or let go small gaps between performance and expectations. Further, even substantial gaps are not likely to be noticed if the product (or service) is only of small value or importance. For example, if the vending machine of *Nescafe* is not functioning properly or the non-availability of the food items mentioned in the menu card of the restaurant can cause dissatisfaction but may not be enough for it to become salient.

Attributions to the marketer : Customers can make attributions about who is to be blamed for the product or service's poor performance. For example, if Air India flights are delayed, more often than not customers attribute the cause of the delay to the organisation or company, even though the actual delay may be related to weather problems. It is interesting to note that if customers blame themselves or circumstances, then they are not likely to complain. Similarly, if they thought that the failure was less likely to be repeated, they may be less motivated to complain. The consumer must be confident that the organisation is very likely to take the corrective action. If they believe that redressal from the marketer or organisation is unlikely, they make consider complaining a waste of effort.

Customers can make attribution about who is to be blamed for the product or service's poor performance. If they thought that the failure was less likely to be repeated, they may be less motivated to complain. But once the complaint redressal is successfully carried out, the customer may experience the feeling of perceived justice.

Consumers Personality Traits : Customers' personality traits can also play an important role in complaining. Personality traits such as the degree of self confidence and aggressiveness/submissiveness can drive a consumer to act. For instance, traits such as self confidence and aggressiveness can make consumers open up and complain rather than accept poor product or service performance.

Reactions after Complaining

Once the complaint redressal is successfully carried out, the customer may experience the feeling of *perceived justice.* Perceived justice refers to customer's perceptions that during the conflict resolution process they were treated with respect and the decision outcome was fair because unbiased policy and procedures were followed. Usually, once the customer gives a complaint, negative word of mouth is less likely. In fact, if the complaint has been successfully redressed, repatronage is more likely to occur.

Loyalty : The third outcome can take the form of loyalty. When consumers purchase the same brand again and again it is referred to as loyalty. However, this concept of brand loyalty has been debated upon because it can be defined in various ways. For instance, one can define brand loyalty as the consistent repurchase of the same brand. But this definition has two limitations. Firstly, in certain product or service (eating the same cereal or eating at the same food joint daily) categories, the consumer may purchase an assortment of brands to satisfy his need of variety sought in the consumption experience. Say, he may get bored or may not be satisfied eating the same food daily. In this case, the marketer could try to find if the particular brand is at least a part of the assortment of food consumed by them.

When consumers purchase the same brand again and again, it is referred to as loyalty. If one were to relate brand loyalty and customer satisfaction, it is often presumed that consumers would not switch brands if they are satisfied.

Secondly, it may be difficult to measure brand loyalty as a consistent repurchase. This is because the consumer may be buying the particular brand as it is a routine purchase decision and may not actually reflect a genuine preference for the brand.

If one were to relate brand loyalty and customer satisfaction, it is very often presumed that consumers would not switch brands if they are satisfied. However, studies have indicated that while consumers are less likely to switch brands when they are satisfied, than when they are not, being satisfied does not guarantee loyalty.

There could be several probable reasons for this.

- Although consumers' behaviour may indicate she is satisfied with a particular brand, she may also be satisfied with competitor's brand.
- Sometimes, regular or repeated usage of a brand could lead to a decline in its marginal utility value, with the need for 'variety' resulting in brand switching.

- At times, consumers may patronise or switch brands because they expect to receive more value and satisfaction from some other brand.

To take care of the above, the marketer could :

- try to measure consumer satisfaction with a brand in relation to competitor's brands.
- in order to reduce variety seeking in the focal category, try to provide variety in a different product category which is purchased simultaneously with the focal category.
- use promotion techniques highlighting the key features and value which consumers are likely to receive from using the particular brand.

ICICI Bank is trying to create a niche market of loyal customers for itself with a new concept. The bank had worked out a plan to offer reward points for its home loan/auto loan loyal customers by tying up with service providers like *Airtel, Hindustan Petroleum, Air India,* retailer *Lifestyle* and travel portal - *MakeMyTrip.com.* The loyalty programme card is called *Imint* and each point is equivalent to 50 paise and can be exchanged for over 300 products or services. More on this loyalty programme is given in Box 12.2.

Titan Industries Limited (formerly was known a as Titan Watches) was able to establish itself as the leader in the Indian quartz watch market during the 1990s. Titan was able to unseat HMT (Hindustan Machine Tools) the reigning market leader at that time, by adopting an aggressive marketing strategy and focusing on its *customer service objectives*. To quote Titan's corporate concern for its customers :

"It is our belief that when a customer walks into a shop to get a Titan watch serviced, there are three types of repairs which need to be effected : repairing the watch, repairing the feelings of the customer and repairing the damage done to the company's image. Attention, therefore has to be given to the physical environment in which the customer is received, the manner in which he or she is dealt with by the service personnel, the speed and quality of the actual repair jobs and the charges collected for the repair."

BOX 12.2

REWARDS GALORE WITH ICICI BANK HOME AND CAR LOANS

The next time you take a home loan or an auto loan from banking major ICICI Bank you would be in line for a reward. The bank is planning to offer reward points for its home loan/ auto loan customers and trying to create a niche market for itself with a concept which is traditionally associated with credit cards. ICICI Bank is spearheading one of the biggest loyalty and customer rewards programme in the country in association with service providers like Airtel, Hindustan Petroleum, the national airline carrier Air India, retailer Lifestyle and travel portal-MakeMyTrip.com.

"Our aim is to reach out to a large number of customers who could use either card or cash to transact. We aim to have as many as five million customers spread across over 20 cities and with over 20,000 merchant establishments," said Mr Vijay Bobba, CEO of Loyalty Solutions and Research Limited (LSRL), a company funded to the tune of Rs 18 crore by ICICI Venture Funds. The card for the loyalty programme is called 'Imint.'

Reward points accrue to a user on any of the above mentioned services/products.

Each point is equivalent of 50 paise and can be exchanged for over 300 products/services. According to Mr B Madhivanan, GM (retail asset products group) of ICICI Bank, the aim of providing reward points to home/auto loan customers was to expand the scope of offering. As current regulations forbid banks from rewarding customers on the capital, the reward points would be structured to cover the processing fee for these loans. Participants like Hindustan Petroleum intend to use this reward point system to tap those customers who transact in cash at the petrol stations. "currently on a pan-India basis we get as many as five million cards. Plastic only constitutes about 10% to 12% of our total sales realizations," said Mr S P Chaudhry, executive director – retail of HPCL.

(Source: *The Economic Times,* Bangalore, 9 August 2006)

The corporate concern shown by Titan for its customers and for the quality of services provided for was a very unusual feature in the Indian business scenario at that time. Due to its various efforts today, Titan has not only gained entry, with its various range of watch models but is also able to cater to the different segment of buyers – children's segment, the youth segment, the woman segment and more recently the rural market.

Organisations try to induce customer's interest in their product or service offerings and then gain their loyalty ultimately by adopting unique marketing programmes.

Organisations try to induce customer's interest in their product or service offerings and then gain their loyalty ultimately by adopting unique marketing programmes. Till *Titan* entered the watch market, HMT had positioned its watches as time keeping devices, positioning it as *'The time keepers of the nation'*. So watches were treated as a *utility thing*. Although customers gave due attention to their style of dress, ornaments and even foot wear, not much concern was

Ad suggests the core benefits of Ultra Dou to enhance consumer satisfaction

given to the wristwatch as it was merely treated as a time knowing device. But things changed with Titan's aggressive positioning strategy. Titan positioned its watches as a part of dress and ornamentation, such that customers now started viewing it as a product which displays the individual's taste and style. Subsequently, Titan popularised its watches by presenting them as ideal gifts for wedding (or other festival occasions) and as a corporate gift. Its corporate campaign read as "It is something your customers will be happy to receive." This campaign helped Titan to build up a loyal corporate customer base including the likes of *HLL, Brooke Bond, Eureka-Forbes, Lipton, Diners Club, Nestle* etc.

➲ 'SATISFACTION', 'NO SATISFACTION' JUDGEMENT

Satisfaction can be derived by comparing a chosen product with a rejected product.

Satisfaction is a relative term and involves making a comparison between a chosen product and a rejected product. The chosen product will be the one which has been selected or purchased by the consumer, while the rejected product is the one which was considered but not selected finally. If the chosen product is perceived to be superior to the rejected alternative, the consumer will experience satisfaction. But, if the chosen product seems to be inferior in comparison to the rejected one, the consumer will experience dissatisfaction. *For example,* a consumer, when required to select between *Pizza Hut's* offerings and *Pizza Corner's* offerings, may choose the latter. If he (the consumer) seems to treat *Pizza Corner's* offerings to be of a superior quality, he will be satisfied after the consumption of the same, otherwise he may experience dissatisfaction.

The term 'satisfaction' has implications for the marketer because it can influence repeat purchase behaviour among consumers. So, if a consumer is satisfied with a product, he or she will not only continue to patronise the same but also communicate a positive word of mouth. Similarly, dissatisfaction can influence complaining behaviour, reduce the likelihood of repeat purchase and at times even result in a negative word of mouth.

Satisfaction Judgement Versus Preference Judgement

As mentioned earlier since satisfaction involves comparison between a chosen product and a rejected (or not chosen) product, the direction of comparison can influence *satisfaction judgement* as well as *preference judgement.* That is, different judgements may be formed depending upon whether the consumer is comparing the chosen brand with a rejected brand or a rejected brand with the chosen brand.

A Study

In 1991, a study was carried out by Houghton, Sherman and Baker (*Consumer Behavior and Managerial Decision Making*, 2nd edn., Frank R. Kardes, 2002, Pp. 96) in order to test the prediction or hypothesis by presenting the descriptions of two products to consumers. The descriptions were in the form of either good unique attributes and bad shared attributes or bad unique attributes and good shared attributes. It was found that most of the consumers selected (or chose) the product described second (the focal product) when the unique attributes were good and most consumers chose the product described first (the non focal product) when the unique attributes were bad. Once the consumers indicated their choices, they were given a 15 minute distraction task. Thereafter, they were, once again given the description of the chosen or rejected product. Then, consumers were asked to indicate on a scale from 1 (very unhappy) to 12 (very happy), how satisfied they were with their prior choice. Consumers also indicated the extent to which they wanted to change or keep their choice on a scale 1 (strongly prefer to change the choice) to 12 (strongly prefer to keep the choice). It was seen that those who received the description of chosen product were more satisfied when the unique attributes were good. Conversely, those who received the description of the rejected product indicated that they experienced greater dis-satisfaction when the unique attributes were bad.

It may be noted that this asymmetry in judgement occurred even though pre-testing ensured that the two products were actually equally good or equally bad. The direction-of-comparison effect arises from the fact that more (or greater) attention is given to the unique attributes of the product described second as against the first.

OLIVER'S EXPECTANCY DISCONFIRMATION MODEL

Expectancy disconfirmation model indicates that consumers form expectations about product performance before purchasing the same.

R.L. Oliver gave the expectancy disconfirmation model which suggests that consumers form expectations about product performance before they purchase the same. After purchasing a product consumers compare the product's actual performance with the level of performance that was expected prior to the purchase. Consumers are satisfied if the actual performance is better than expected. But, if the actual performance is not as per the expectation or even worse than expected, then consumers are dissatisfied with the product. Further, consumer's *prior expectations are confirmed* if actual product performance is exactly as was expected. While, consumer's *prior expectations are disconfirmed* if the actual product performance is better or worse than expected.

Both expectations and disconfirmation influence satisfaction. In a general way, as expectancies increase, satisfaction decreases. This is because most products cannot meet consumer's highest expectations. When disconfirmation increases, satisfaction increases if the disconfirmation was positive *i.e.,* the product performed more or better than expected. Whereas, dissatisfaction increases if the disconfirmation was negative (the product performed worse or less than expected).

The expectancy disconfirmation model suggests that if consumers' expectations exceeded actual product performance, they will be dissatisfied even with excellent products. Conversely, if consumers' expectations fell below the actual level of performance they will be satisfied with poor products too. Thus, both, that which exists in the mind of the consumer (expectations) as well as that which exists in reality (actual product performance) are equally important. Hence it can be said that there are other factors other than comparison which can influence satisfaction judgements.

Another factor which has an important impact on satisfaction judgements is *consumers' attributions* or causal inferences concerning why a product performed worse than expected. (Oilver R.L., & DeSarbo, W.S-1988). There could be two reasons why a product performed worse than expected :

- The user may have used the product inappropriately (internal attribution since the fault lies within the user) Or
- The product was poorly designed (since the fault lies outside the customer, it is an external attribution).

Although, negative disconfirmation can lead to dissatisfaction, even more dissatisfaction will be experienced if the consumer forms an external attribution (as opposed to an internal attribution). In this way, one can try to search for explanations for product failure which can have a powerful influence on judgements of satisfaction or dissatisfaction.

MEASURING OF CONSUMER SATISFACTION

When we talk of measuring consumer satisfaction, there are two issues which need to be addressed :

(a) How does one measure customer satisfaction?

(b) How does one use the information received after measuring customer satisfaction?

Measuring consumer satisfaction will help organisations to understand what 'value' consumers are seeking from their product or service and whether they are satisfied after using the same.

It is possible to measure consumer satisfaction by going for *customisation*. Customisation refers to receiving the product or service in a personalised form or tailored to the individual's need and requirement. This can help consumers to experience a positive value during interactions with the organisation. A brand's success can no longer be evaluated on the basis of its market share but has to be measured by the share of the customers. Organisations which fail to do market research and try to understand the consumer's choices or wants and what is the value for money that buyers are looking out for, will ultimately have to be satisfied with the second best. With the constantly changing consumer choices, the organisation must understand the real customer satisfaction indicator – value. Value can be said to be what the buyer is willing to pay for the product or service. The concept of value though universal, its delivery has to be unique. In today's competitive scenario, with plenty of modern and economical alternatives available, the marketer should provide value and add to customer satisfaction. They can do this by offering superior value products at lesser price than their competitors or by providing benefits that more than offset a higher price.

Moves to Measure Customer Satisfaction

Organisations can adopt various ways to measure customer satisfaction, these measures can broadly be put as :

- Develop different concepts of customer satisfaction which can be evaluated.
- Design effective customer satisfaction data collection and report systems, which vary in sophistication.
- Use methods for institutionalising customer satisfaction measurement into organisational control systems.
- Develop systems for responding effectively to customer dissatisfaction and customer complaints.

Market research agencies use a full range of products to measure customer satisfaction. These include customer satisfaction survey methodologies, focus groups to study customer satisfaction issues, standardised packages for monitoring customer satisfaction and computer software package to analyse and report customer satisfaction data to management.

Factors Affecting Customer Satisfaction

The rise in consumer's buying power and their awareness of the existence of the new generation of customers are forcing organizations to identify ways of enhancing customer satisfaction. They have realised that they need to be vigilant about customer's perceptions of their products and services vis-à-vis that of the competitors. They also continuously seek ways to innovate their product offerings and differentiate themselves from competitors.

There are some factors which can affect the level of customer satisfaction. These are namely : the core product or service, value adding features, price vis-à-vis perceived benefits, external and contextual factors and personal factors.

◆ **The core product or service :** The core product or service indicates those product related functional attributes offered by organizations who are targeting the same or similar group of customers and adopting same or similar strategies. These functions and attributes will satisfy the basic or core requirements of the customers. Generally at the core product level, there are not many differences among the main players.

Organisations have realized that they need to be vigilant about customer's perception of their products and services vis-à-vis that of the competitors. Organisations which are able to differentiate themselves by not only understanding 'what' and 'why' of their customers wants but more so on what are those value added benefits being sought by them, will be able to enhance customer satisfaction.

◆ **Value adding features :** In order to differentiate themselves from competitors when offering core products or services, marketers must think of value additions in the form of tangible or intangible features which could offer additional benefits. The tangible additions could be in areas such as exclusive specification, range, cost, packaging, delivery and so on. However, organisation's must remember that such tangible features are quantifiable and measurable and thus could be imitated by competitors.

On the other hand, it will be difficult to imitate intangible features. The type and quality of intangibles offered by an organisation will depend upon the three 'R' (key) factors.

- Reliability
- Responsiveness
- Reputation

The organisation needs to develop a favourable perception in respect to these three 'key' factors in the consumers' mind, which is not an easy task. For this, they will have to develop the right business processes, proper employee attitude, work on creating a customer friendly culture and lastly, establish a network between the external (suppliers/venders and customers) and internal employees. If an organization succeeds in it's intangible features offerings, it can result in benefits such as :

- Reduce the customer's hidden costs
- Ensure customer satisfaction by clearly communicating about the way in which organisations transact business.
- Through two way communications bring satisfaction with their external stakeholders (suppliers).

FIGURE 12.2

FACTORS INFLUENCING CUSTOMER SATISFACTION

ORGANISATION'S CUSTOMER SATISFACTION INFLUENCES

- ***Core Product/Service :*** Those functional attributes which can meet the core requirements of consumers
- ***Value additions :*** This can be in the form of tangible and intangible features resulting in additional benefits to customers.
- ***Price versus perceived benefits :*** For a given level of perceived benefits the consumer should feel the benefit.
- ***External factors :*** Organisation must consider those external (or contextual) factors affecting consumer's decision making process, while determining their marketing mix policies.
- ***Personal factors :*** Organisations will need to additionally segment their customers into distinct categories of personal factors to enhance customer satisfaction.

Organisations which are able to offer distinct tangible and intangible benefits duly supported by superior product and service offerings will not only be able to meet the real and psychological needs of their customers, but also create a goodwill and strengthen the brand's equity in the minds of their customers.

Thus organisations which are able to differentiate themselves by not only understanding 'what' and 'why' of their customers want but more so on what are those *value added benefits* being sought by them, will be able to enhance customer satisfaction.

Customers prefer the price of the product or service being offered to be significantly lower than the perceived benefits both functional and emotional.

◆ **Price vis-a-vis perceived benefits :** Customers prefer the price of the product or service being offered to be significantly lower than the perceived benefits-both functional and emotional. It is necessary that organisations understand the customer's point of view of perceived benefits, for these could vary from what the former may consider it to be. If the marketer feels that its value or benefit offerings are substantially higher than those being offered by its competitors, they may prefer to price their product offerings on the higher side than the latter. Whereas, for the customer, generally, for a given level of perceived benefits, the benefit to price ratio should be higher. Further, dissatisfaction may be caused, if the ratio is lower than what is considered logical.

◆ **External and contextual factors :** Beyond the organisation's product and or service offerings, there could be certain external variables which could have a positive or negative influence on the consumer's satisfaction level on the basis of how favourable or unfavourable are the context in which the transaction between the marketer and customer takes place. Such external variables or factors could include the state of the physical infrastructure, the extent to which the logistics and transport system is reliable, the level of professionalism of the vendors (or dealers), after sales service network and performance etc. Organisations which want to achieve high customer satisfaction levels must take care while working out marketing mix policies. For instance, full time air carriers such as the *Air India, Jet Airways* etc. may not be able to solve all the customer complaints (or problems) related to issues concerning the late arrival the flight or say cancellation of the flight due to technical engine snags. However, looking to the context of the problem, the concerned airline can make up alternative arrangements such as accommodating the passengers (or those customers) on other flights or make arrangements to serve them with food and refreshments via coupons issued to the concerned passengers or if need be make arrangements for their stay at a hotel, at the carrier's expense. This aspect may not hold good for the frills free air carriers (like the SpiceJet), so it is likely that passengers opting for these type of airlines, when facing similar problems may experience customer dissatisfaction on a higher side.

There could be certain external variables which could have a positive or negative influence on the consumer's satisfaction level on the basis of how favourable or unfavourable are the context in which the transaction between the marketer or customer takes place.

◆ **Personal factors :** A customer's emotional and psychological state of mind *i.e.,* personal factors can also affect his level of satisfaction. For instance, the anxieties a customer experiences or how he or she feels (or thinks) can also affect his or her satisfaction level. To take care of or in order to enhance customer satisfaction, organisations can try to consider the personal factors and segment customers accordingly.

Life Insurance Corporation of India (LIC) has been able to earn the reputation as a brand trusted by its customers. This is because it has been able to build up their trust through its customised service offerings, provided by its dedicated employees.

'LIC' has repeatedly earned a reputation of immensely satisfying its customers

THE CONCEPT OF 'PERCEIVED' VALUE', CUSTOMER SATISFACTION AND LOYALTY

Perceived value is a blend of quality and price being sought to by customers in product and service offerings.

Satisfaction for the customer with regard to the product or services received will in reality be the difference between what is being delivered and what is expected by him or her. Consumers look for "Perceived Value" and not necessarily the price factor alone. This value will be a blend of both quality and price. There could be both tangible and intangible parts in the perceived value concept. A consumer could be willing to pay a particular price for a particular quality (expectation).

There could also be different categories of segments of consumers with different 'Perceived Value' points and not necessarily be only looking at the price of the product or service. This can be referred to as the *tangible part* of perceived value. The intangible part of perception could be a combination of the image and emotional value, which can also influence the consumer's purchase and consumption decisions.

Ultimately it will be a combination of both the tangible value and intangible perception of any brand which will be the *perceived value* imprinted in the minds and hearts of the consumers.

Today, when there is intense competition and the consumer can choose from a wide range of brands it will be perceived value loyalty which will ultimately decide where one brand stands when compared to another.

So, finally, it will be such perceived value points that the consumer is looking out for in products and services, leading to customer satisfaction (or dissatisfaction).

Korean major brands such as *LG Electronics, Samsung* etc. were able to get Indian consumers excited and interested in their television sets and other consumer electronic goods by offering innovative exchange schemes, unique tie-ups and liberal consumer financing.

The above when accompanied by sound positioning and excellent after sales services has enabled the brands to earn a high 'perceived value in the minds of the consumer.

In the area of entertainment also when the Indian consumer was already enjoying the various programmes aired by the *Starplus, Sony* etc, *Zoom* channel through its varied mixture of entertainment programmes had been able to lure many consumers from competitors'. Zoom channel with its better programmes was able to communicate a *higher perceived value* image to its viewers (or consumers).

Jagdeep Kapoor, Managing Director, *Samsika Marketing Consultancy* refers to the consumer behaviour of exploring various brands, momentarily and evaluating them according to the perceived value he or she is receiving, as 'imaginary remote control.' So if a brand continues to deliver perceived value over a period, it will attain sufficient brand loyalty.

Today, when there is intense competition and the consumer can choose from a wide range of brands it will be perceived value loyalty which will ultimately decide where one brand stands when compared to another.

This concept of perceived value is very important for the consumer, for he or she seeks brands and not a product which satisfies them, evaluates each brand and finally selects that which matches the perceived value.

'Elita Promenade' is trying to match it product offerings with consumer expectations.

CUSTOMER SATISFACTION AND MANAGING PERCEPTION

When the consumer receives a product or service, the satisfaction will work out to be the positive difference between what is being delivered and what is expected by him. It can be said that two types of perceptions (perceived value) can affect the ultimate levels of customer satisfaction.

Customer satisfaction with regard to a product or service will work out to be the positive difference between what is the perceived value and what is actually delivered.

- The customer's expectation of perceived value.
- What the consumer perceives he is actually receiving from the manufacturer (which may be different from what the supplier organization may think it is providing).

Thus, organisations will have to manage perceptions at two levels *i.e.,* (1) manage the consumer's own perception about his needs and (2) how the consumer perceives the offerings made by the service provider (or organisation) vis-à-vis his or her perception.

Organisations can work towards creating a positive customer satisfaction by:

- Either delivering a higher level of satisfaction than expected by the target customer

  Or

- Manage the expectation level such that their product or service offerings exceed such managed expectations.

FIGURE 12.3

MARKET RESEARCH TO ENHANCE CUSTOMER SATISFACTION

Organisation Undertakes

⇩

Market Research to :

- Identify the demographic and psychographic profile of consumers.
- Understand consumer's specific needs in terms of core product and value added benefits sought.
- Understand the functional and emotional aspects being sought in the product or service.
- Identify various ways to satisfy the consumer needs.
- Understand the customer's real costs of buying and using products and services.
- Identify the contextual factors which can influence the consumer's thought processes either favourably or unfavourably.
- Identify if there are any compromises which the consumer feels he is making while purchasing products or services, which could be viewed as opportunities for further value creation.

⇩

Customer Satisfaction

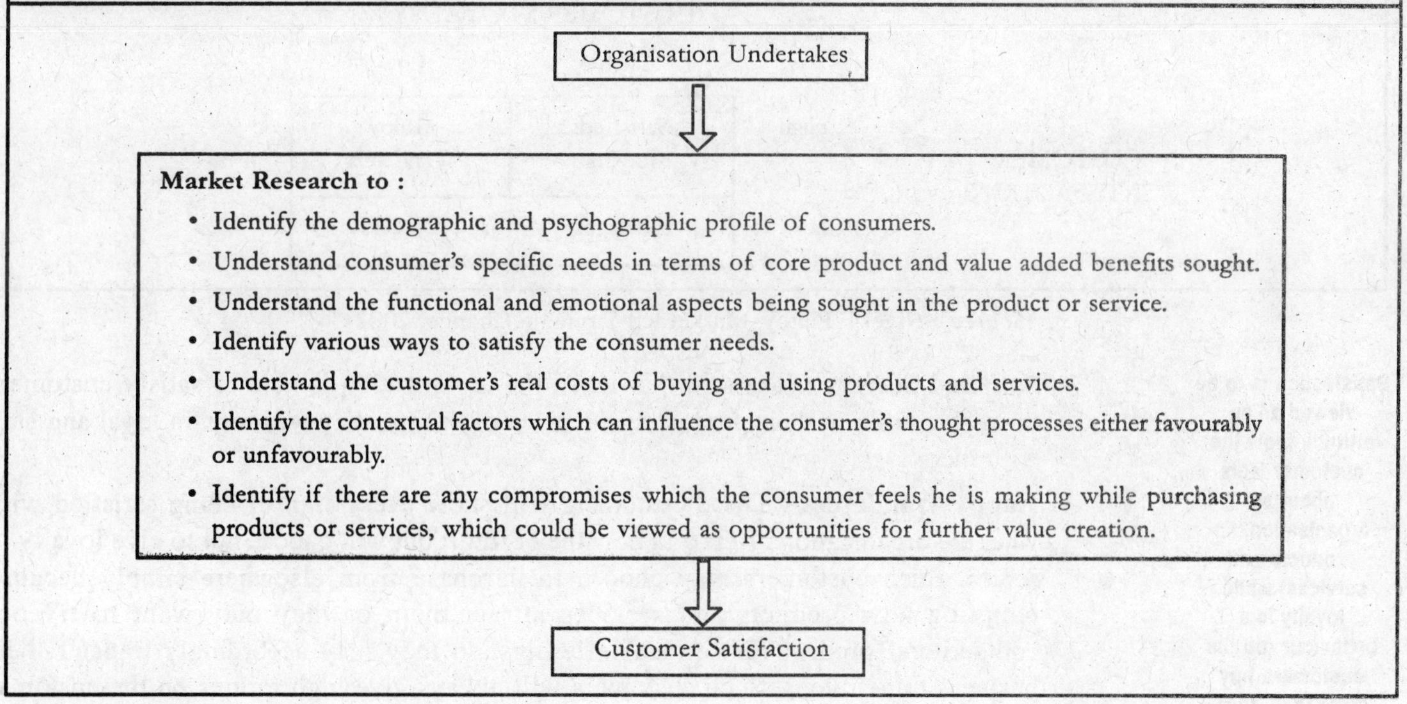

Tackling Perception through Market Research

We have already mentioned about the role of the two levels of perception and how it can affect the ultimate customer satisfaction levels. So it becomes obvious that organisations will need to undertake periodic market research and use the findings from such exercises to design and offer suitable product and service offerings. Simultaneously, they also need to develop a high quality communication with their customers. Through the formal research, organisations will be able to ask customers about their unmet needs, wants or requirements. Ideally, the

Periodic market research can help organisations to understand customer perceptions and offer product and services accordingly.

research should be both qualitative and quantitative in nature. The qualitative research will help to provide key insights, perspective and sensitivity with regard to customer satisfaction. While the quantitative studies will empirically establish important trends in relation the nature, attitude and behaviour of customers. Such researches with provide sufficient inputs on both the perception and expectations of consumers, which are the critical determinants of consumer satisfaction.

THE LINK BETWEEN CUSTOMER SATISFACTION AND CUSTOMER LOYALTY

Simply put, customer loyalty or customer retention is about how long the organization can keep a customer or how much share of their business is continuously obtained and retained by the company, whereas, customer satisfaction is expressed in terms of what the consumer thinks of the organization by virtue of their product quality, services provided, value and so on.

Nigel Piercy has made an attempt to work out the possible links between customer satisfaction and loyalty which is presented in the figure 12.4.

As shown in figure 12.4, Piercy suggests four possible links between customer satisfaction and loyalty.

FIGURE 12.4

CUSTOMER SATISFACTION VERSUS CUSTOMER LOYALTY

↑ CUSTOMER SATISFACTION	→ CUSTOMER'S LOYALTY	High	Low
	High	Satisfied Stayers	Happy Wanderers
	Low	Hostages	Dealers

(*Source :* Nigel F Piercy, Market led Strategic Change, 2002)

Satisfaction is to be viewed as an attitude (how the customer feels about an organisation, its products and services) while, loyalty is a behaviour (do the customers buy more than once from the organisation?)

- **Satisfied Stayers :** It is said that when the organization is able to satisfy customers through quality in their product and service offerings, they will remain loyal and stay with them.
- **Happy Wanderers :** These customers will show every sign of being satisfied with what the organization offers and how they offer it but will choose not to give loyalty in return. Such customers may choose to purchase from elsewhere simply because tempting new products and services attract them or they may want to try out competitors' product (or service) offerings, so they may accordingly transfer their business transactions. Such customers will always give high ratings on the customer satisfaction questionnaire but will not be loyal to the organisation always.
- **Hostages :** It is possible that some of the most loyal customers may be highly dissatisfied but may continue displaying loyalty due to reasons such as :
  - Product compatibility (only this brand works properly)
  - Get loyalty incentives (accumulate frequent flyer miles by the same airline to get the free ticket)
  - Avoid the costs of switching – economic (not worth switching bank accounts)

Such category of customers are not satisfied but can be retained for a particular time of period.

- **Dealers :** This category of customers are not satisfied and move brands and suppliers frequently.

From the above model it can be seen that **satisfaction** is to be viewed as an attitude (how the customer feels about an organisations its products and services) while, **loyalty** is a behaviour (do the customers buy more than once from the organisations?).

An example of customer satisfaction.

CUSTOMER SATISFACTION VERSUS SERVICE, QUALITY LEVEL AND CUSTOMER LOYALTY

Organisations need to offer services and quality to match consumer expectations which can result in consumer satisfaction leading to customer loyalty in the long run.

We have always referred to customer satisfaction in terms of expectation. The consumer will treat each product or service bought by him as a package with all the ingredients thrown in – basic utility, performance, after sales service, ease of purchase, delivery of promised promotional schemes and so on – every expectation associated with the offering that's on her (or his) mind. She will consider the package as a whole, compare it with her own expectations and if they exceed it, she will be delighted otherwise not. If consumer satisfaction is all about understanding expectations and fulfilling them, the issue ends here. But, in reality, it cannot be termed as unidimensional. To illustrate this we will take the example of a train journey undertaken, from Mysore to Bengaluru or Bangalore in the morning say. A senior citizen traveling by this train has expectations that she will have a comfortable journey even if the train arrives an hour late. On the other hand, a marketing officer, who has to attend a meeting with a prospective customer, desperately wants the train to arrive on time even if non-availability of a seat may force him to undergo the journey standing. Likewise, a small family with kids undertaking the journey may want comfortable seating with the availability of refreshments once in a while, to pacify the hungry children. The above example illustrates the fact that although the final destination (of reaching Bengaluru) is the same, for the same offering, the expectations of different customers will be diverse. So, marketers need to segment their target customers and offer products or services to cater to the expectations of the particular segment. Take for example, the *Nokia model 1100* was modified (in Copenhagen) to address a pertinent problem faced by Indian mobile users : dust was a major irritant. Accordingly the modified Nokia 1100 model was made dust resistant. The keypad was made a single unit with a miniflash-light attached.

Organisations need to focus on the quality and service provision issues, which can impact the customer satisfaction level. Nigel F. Piercy has illustrated a relationship between 'Service and Quality level' and Impact on customer satisfaction (Figure 12.5).

FIGURE 12.5

SERVICE AND QUALITY VERSUS CUSTOMER SATISFACTION

→ IMPACT ON CUSTOMER SATISFACTION

↑ SERVICE AND QUALITY LEVEL ↓		High	Low
	High	High Servicers	Over Servicers
	Low	Under Servicers and Dumb Servicers	Non Servicers

(Source : Nigel Piercy, Market led Strategic Change, 2002)

Customers may have the tendency to watch and compare the performance (in terms of service and quality) of one organisation over its competitors and draw their own conclusions.

Organisations need to work out appropriate **service** and **quality strategies** which match the important needs of their target market as well as their ability to deliver the same.

Customers may have the tendency to watch and compare the performance (in terms of service and quality) of one organisation over its competitors and draw their own conclusions.

As shown in figure 12.5, the conclusions, having an impact on customer satisfaction will indicate whether they are over or under servicing, or have got it about right, or non services.

➲ FEW STUDIES TO MEASURE CUSTOMER SATISFACTION

(A) JD Power Asia Pacific 2006 India Original Tyre Customer Satisfaction Index (TCSI) Study

The TCSI study analyses perceptions of new-vehicle buyers on five critical factors :

- Appearance of tyre
- Ride quality

- Traction
- Durability of Tyres
- Handling

The 2006 India Original Tyre Customer Satisfaction Index Study was based on response from more than 2600 new vehicle owners of 33 different vehicle models in India. The customers were surveyed between June and August 2005, to examine customer satisfaction with original tyres at 12 to 18 months of ownership. J D Power Asia Pacific associates have been keeping a track of the major tyre manufactures in India since the inception of the study.

The TCSI study indicated gain in terms of overall satisfaction by MRF and J K Tyres.

The 2006 Industry average score was worked out as 789 index points (on 91,000 points scale), with the top two positions being taken by MRF and J K Tyre respectively (refer to Table 12.2).

The study also indicated gain in terms of overall satisfaction by **MRF** and **JK Tyre**. Both these brands procured a larger share of the original tyre market in India, with each increasing their **share by 8 percent, when compared to 2005.**

TABLE 12.2

TYRE INDUSTRY CUSTOMER SATISFACTION RATING

Brand	Sastisfaction Rating on 1000-Point Scale
1. M R F Tyres	822
2. J K Tyre	803
3. Apollo	778
4. Bridgestone	771
5. GoodYear	758

(Source : J.D. Power Asia Pacific 2006 India Original *The Customer Satisfaction Index Study*)

(B) JD Power Asia Pacific 2005 India Customer Satisfaction Index (CSI) Study

This study examines the satisfaction of new vehicle buyers with the authorized service experience at 12 to 18 months of ownership. More than 4,200 buyers of 33 different vehicle models were surveyed in the 2005 study, during the period of June to August 2005.

This customer satisfaction with regards to the after sales service in the Indian automobile industry was assessed on 42 attributes grouped into seven pre-defined factors such as :

- Problems experienced
- Service quality
- User friendly service
- Service advisor
- Service initiation
- Service delivery
- In-service experience

The CSI study found that the operation costs for new vehicles rose from 11 to 15 percent for petrol and diesel vehicles respectively.

As per this study *Maruti Suzuki* continued to set the industry benchmark and was ranked the highest in India Customer Satisfaction study for a sixth consecutive year. *Mahindra* emerged as the most improved name plate with an increase in score of 30 index points from 2004. *Ford* and *Honda* also showed improved performance across all seven factors from the 2004 study.

The industry average also improved its overall performance by three index points. It was also found that the operation costs for new vehicles rose from 11 to 15 percent for petrol and diesel vehicles respectively.

While the *Tata Indica* and *Indigo* car models, showed strong performance in the diesel segment in terms of cost of operation, Maruti models performed better than their competitors in the petrol segment.

TABLE 12.3

CUSTOMER SATISFACTION CSI STUDY RATING FOR 2005

Company	Customer Satisfaction Index Rating On a 1000 Point Scale
Maruti Suzuki	823
Hyundai	739
Ford	735
Honda	723
Toyota	714
Chevrolet	712
Opel	709
Skoda	706
Mahindra	702
Tata	658
Fiat	654

(Source : J.D. Power Asia Pacific 2005 India *Consumer Satisfaction Index Study*)

(C) IDC India and Data Quest Survey (2004)

In the year 2004, *IDC India* in association with the Data Quest Magazine carried out a survey among 400 CIO's (Chief Information Officers) to understand different functional and service attributes which drive customer satisfaction and also develop a brand score of customer satisfaction for various product and service categories.

The survey covered large organizations across various verticals and was spread over six cities namely – Delhi, Mumbai, Bangalore (now Bengaluru), Chennai, Hyderabad and Kolkata. The products and services covered in the survey included desktops, laptops, servers and enterprises applications (SCM, CRM, ERP) and IT Services (Integrated and outsourced services).

In each category, a sample size for each brand was identified. In order to remove anomalies, IDC India weighed the results with the brand – share among the sample surveyed. Separate parameters were developed for each category. Based on the understanding of the market and the previous year's study report, some of the parameters and sub parameters were also modified accordingly.

The CIO's were asked to rate the level of satisfaction for each parameter and sub parameter on a five point scale, depending on the usage of the product. The scores of importance were derived from the satisfaction score, which was used as a weight for each of the sub parameters. In order to obtain the overall satisfaction scores, IDC India, measured satisfaction against each of these 'important' (or importance) parameters and then arrived at a weighted score of satisfaction on a possible maximum score of 100.

(D) TBR's Study

Technology Business Research's (TBR) Corporate IT service and support customer satisfaction study or TBR's study is carried out on a quarterly basis, when hundreds of corporate IT buyers are surveyed on eight aspects of service support. TBR considers various factors such as phone support, replacement, parts availability, warranty, upgrade price and overall satisfaction and then assigns each factor a weighted score for a total of 100 possible points.

The above studies will indicate that today, in a highly competitive market, the challenge before the marketer is to ensure customer retention especially in the face of the promiscuous behaviour displayed by the consumer. This is possible if they ensure continuous customer satisfaction which can lead to customer loyalty.

TOWARDS BUILDING CUSTOMER LOYALTY

Customer loyalty can be defined as a customer's commitment to a brand or a store or a supplier, based on a strong favourable attitude and is manifested in repeated patronage (Sheth and Mittal 2003). As per this definition, loyalty includes both behaviour and attitudes. These two components can result in four possible behaviour – attitude Loyalty situations as shown in Figure 12.6.

Sheth and Mittal have defined customer loyalty as a customer's commitment to a brand or a store or a supplier, based on a strong favourable attitude and is manifested in a repeated patronage.

When both attitude and behaviour are weak, *no loyalty* exists. Weak attitude means the customer does not like the brand while weak behaviour indicates the customer does not buy the same brand consistently. When both – attitude is favourbale and the same brand is purchased consistently, *strong loyalty* exists. The remaining two situations are interesting.

When behaviour is high but attitude is low, it can lead to *spurious loyalty*. *I.e.,* the customer purchases the same brand again and again at the same outlet regularly but does not have any preferential attitudes towards it. This could be probably because the customer perceives all brands to be more or less the same or probably the store is conveniently located. In such a situation, if competitors display more choice or attractive price deals the customer is likely to switch brands. Thus, in such situations, the marketer must work towards strengthening the customer's perception of the brand image.

In the quadrant with high attitude and low behaviour, the customer shows *lalent loyalty*. In this situation, the customer likes the brand but is unable to buy it probably because the price is too high or he (or she) does not have access to the brand or the store. Here, the marketer should try to tap this hidden potential market by lowering whatever barriers are there preventing the consumers from purchasing this brand.

FIGURE 12.6

HOW BEHAVIOUR AND ATTITUDE AFFECTS LOYALTY

		BEHAVIOUR →	
		Strong	Weak
ATTITUDE ↑	Strong	Satisfied Loyalty	Happy Latent loyalty
	Weak	Spurious loyalty	No loyalty

(Source : *Customer Behavior*, Sheth, J.N., Mittal. B, 2003, pp. 404)

Customer satisfaction can result in customer retention.

It can be said that although customer satisfaction will be a poor predictor of customer loyalty, customer dissatisfaction will be a good predictor of customer's defection.

Can Satisfaction Lead to Loyalty?

Using satisfaction (an attitude) to indicate loyalty (a behaviour) may not always work. *For example* 90 percent of customers purchasing Maruti 800 are very satisfied when they drive away from the showroom but less than half of them will buy the same car next time. So, one can think of distinguishing between behavioural loyalty (what the customer does) and attitudinal loyalty (how the customer feels about the organization and its products and services). For, only considering attitudinal loyalty (measuring satisfaction intention to re-purchase etc.) could lead to taking bad marketing decisions especially since only a small proportion of those who show behavioural loyalty in reality show attitudinal loyalty as well.

The many non-attitudinal factors which can affect behavioural loyalty to a great extent are :

- ***Committed loyalists*** – Such customers place high value on the company's offerings, are willing to pay a premium price and may not switch brands.
- ***Feature loyalists*** – These customers place a high value on certain one or two 'must have' features of the product or service.
- ***Convenience loyalists*** – Such customers may stick or be loyal to the existing option for an easy and convenient life. *For example,* a customer may not like his bank but may not find it worth undergoing hassles to shift his savings account to another bank.
- ***Channel loyalists'*** – Such customers place a high value on the channels of distribution. For instance, a customer, may think "I prefer *Pepsi* but if I eat at McDonalds daily, I will have to be loyal to *Cocacola* because this is what *McDonalds* sells.
- ***Lack of choice*** – When there are no other alternatives available, the customer may be forced to buy a particular brand. *For example,* the employee (customer) may have a preference for *Lenovo Thinkpad 261* laptop but is forced to use Dells laptop because that is what his employer buys for his employees.
- ***Price loyalists*** – Such customers are seeking the *best price* for the basic product performance.

Thus, it can be said that although customer satisfaction will be a poor predictor of customer loyalty, customer dissatisfaction will be a good predictor of customer's defection. A satisfied customer may or may not remain loyal but the dissatisfied customer will make all efforts to leave if he can. Hence, the bottom line is what marketers need to explore and understand why some customers defect to competitors while some remain with them and then make efforts at making proper investments in customer satisfaction, relationship marketing and loyalty programmes.

Fostering Successful Loyalty Programmes

Loyalty, as seen above is not just about attracting new customers, but more about retaining profitable customers. So, while working out loyalty programmes, the critical element would be in identifying the particular segment of the customer base being targeted and adopt features in the loyalty programme which will allign with the product and services being rendered. For instance, a super market chain like *Food World* may go for an in-store redemption offer but the same cannot be adopted by the *Metro Shoe Mart,* for here the next visit of the customer will not be immediate. A possible solution in this case could be – Metro shoes could go for a tie – up with another partner. Further, the loyalty programme should also be aligned with external market factors with the time period (or life cycle) of the loyalty programme clearly defined.

The critical element would be in identifying the particular segment of customer base being targeted and adopt features in the loyalty programme which will allign with the product and services being rendered.

Care need to be exercised such that customer attraction for the loyalty programme is sustained throughout the period it is being offered. Inspite of all the best efforts there could be 3 major distractions that any loyalty programme faces:

- Customers have the tendency to *compare loyalty programme benefits with* those being offered by *competitors* also.
- The loyalty programme should ensure that customers reap the benefits with a *tangible value.*
- *'Redeem and out' mindset* : Studies have revealed that 30 percent of the customers (loyalty) tends to switch over after their first redemption. The loyalty programme has

to be designed such that it constantly triggers customer preference. For, a dissatisfied customer can easily deter about 10 potential new customers.

Nevertheless, the benefits of a successful loyalty programme are many – higher customer retention rates, better referral rates and an increase in customer spending. All this will result in incremental revenue for the organisation.

➲ CUSTOMER SATISFACTION IN SERVICES MARKET

Today, a very powerful driver of any business is very similar to Murphy's first law of business. "Every consumer has a choice." In India also the range of choices has gone much beyond only competing players in the same service category to new competitive services from different categories so as to satisfy the same need. The Indian customer can no longer be taken for granted. He/she will no longer be contented with average service. He is aware that he is being charged for every little odd job and thus expects top quality treatment. Thus if he feels his wellbeing is not being taken care of, he may look out for other options.

Since the nature of customer needs is different, the service markets exhibit certain *unique characteristics.*

1. The nature of the product-service exhibits varying degrees of intangibility because unlike a product, services can be considered to be a deed, a performance or an effort.
2. The service may become perishable if remained unsold for a long time because unlike product it cannot be stored for later consumption.
3. Here the production and consumption go hand in hand and are often inseparable.
4. The firm or organistion which provides the services retains ownership and the consumer only has temporary access to it (for instance, taking credit from *Citibank* or say renting a car from a "Car Rental Agency".

Going by the conventional wisdom –in the face of changes in the technology and capital movement, increasing competition, every brand (except for the name and packaging) will represent a product or service. Thus the only way an organisation can differentiate its products or service is by offering added values of an emotional or symbolic nature.

Philip Kotler (Principles of Marketing, 1985, pp. 592) has given the definition of services "*As any activity or benefit that one party can offer to another that is essentially intangible and does not result in the ownership of any thing. Its production may or may not be tied to a physical product.*"

Types of Services Markets

The service industries are vast and varied. From the consumer's point of view, a service is also a bundle of benefits just as a physical product.

The service industries are also vast and varied. It includes : in the *government sector* – the courts, hospitals, banks, insurance companies, post offices, defence services, police and fire services, other regulatory agencies and schools. In the *business sector* – airlines, banks, computer services offering agencies, hotels, law firms, management consultancy firms, medical services, theatre, courier, plumbing repair companies and real estate firms. In the *private sector* – various NGO's (Non Government Organisation's), religious organisations, educational institutes and hospitals.

From the consumer's point of view, a service is also a bundle of benefits just as a physical product. And here again the consumer is paying his hard earned money in order to avail of services. Hence the fact that services are not something which is visible and can be held in hand is irrelevant.

For instance, if we are referring to a hotel, the consumer will purchase a complete bundle of services and facilities that are available for the price that he/she pays for the room. Research by Professor David Garvin (Harvard Business Review for Quality Management, 1983) in America has shown that the unique characteristics of service industries make customer use and consider a range of factors as parameters which influence purchase satisfaction for tangible goods or intangible services. These factors as identified by Prof. Garvin in the order of preference are given here under:

1. The communication ability of the staff especially in listening and in giving proper response to the customers.
2. The feeling of courtesy conveyed by the staff while dealing with all types of customers and their problems.
3. A genuine sense of caring for the customer.
4. The credibility of information communicated.
5. The information and knowledge exhibited by staff concerning all the aspects of the organisation, policies and service provision procedures.
6. A genuine feeling, concern and willingness of the staff to respond to customer needs.
7. Reliability with which the service is provided.
8. The tangible evidence of service seen in the physical appearance of facilities and staff.

From the above factors it is clear that the bundle of services must include certain vital aspects such as:

(a) *The formal product* – The image, quality, elegance etc., of the organisation set up.

(b) *The core products* – All the services which are bought by the consumer *i.e.*, in case of a hotel the accommodation, food and beverages.

(c) *The augmented product* – In total all the consumer benefits and experience of the service felt by them.

Though the tariff or (service) charges will be part of the deal entered into between the customer and organisation, this will probably represent a very small percentage of the total bill. The bulk of what the customer pays for availing of the services will be the *intangible* part of the deal. This will comprise of environment, atmosphere, the attitude – socialising and attention paid by the staff to their customer.

However, some people argue that service industry deals with intangibles while manufacturing industry or consumer products deal in tangibles which is a myth. They opine that every industry satisfies a customer's need and there is no dividing line in the customer's mind between tangible and intangible. The customer does not really care about the physical properties or the touch and feel of the stereo system, they are only looking out for the sound effect and to experience the overall unique and thrilling experience *i.e.*, the intangibles more than the tangible aspect. All these aspects are used by *Taj Hotels Resorts and Palaces.* To quote a few of them, they have won many Awards and Accolades which proves their ability to ensure customer satisfaction. They won the (Aug. 2006) – *Dun and Bradstreet American Express Corporate Award 2006,* for being the top company in the hospitality sector, *India's Most Trusted Hotel Brand* – Brand Equity Most Trusted Brand Survey 2005 (Feb. 2006), *Avaya Global Connect Customer Responsiveness Brands Survey* – 2005 (Dec.2005).

Organisations are working towards offering additional services value to persuade prospective customers because it is often observed that the customer does not mind paying more if he gets what he wants.

Few Examples of Efficient Customer Services

Organisations are working towards offering additional services value to persuade prospective customers because it is often observed that the customer doesn't mind paying more if he gets what he wants. All the services offerings are given in the name of customisation. To quote a few examples:

- ***ICICI Prudential*** was successfully able to change behaviour, inducing consumers to invest in retirement planning early-amongst those of the age group of 30-40 years. ICICI was able to bring about a change in their target market consumer attitudes and behaviour through its, creative advertising message "Retire from work – not life" along with a multi-dimensional communication usage campaign. The end result was that *ICICI Prudential* was able to outperform competitors as well create a new market leadership for retirement planning within the younger population.
- ***Master Card Users*** (Whether Platinum Card, Titanium Card or Gold Card) can enjoy exclusive access to premium airport lounges across India. Master Card Users can avail of the special Taipei, 'surprises which includes entertainment, dining, great shopping and ultimate relaxation. Master Card's advertisement says "there are some things money can't buy. For everything else there's *Master Card*".
- ***Housing Development Finance Corporation (HDFC)*** extends customer services which are appreciated by customers. A prospective customer wanting to avail of a housing loan, is able to complete all the formalities by interacting with a single company representative, who will conduct the whole process at the customer's pace and convenience handling queries and also clearly explaining everything at each step. Such gestures not only help the consumer in his decision making but also satisfies him (or her) immensely.

Efforts to maintain customer satisfaction.

ICICI Prudential **was able to change the behaviour of customers to invest, while young itself, for post retirement schemes**

As in case of products, in customer services industry also, customer satisfaction occurs when customer expectation matches the perception formed by them during all stages – selection, purchase and consumption of the desired service.

As in case of products, in customer services industry also, customer satisfaction occurs when customer expectation matches the perception formed by them during all stages-selection, purchase and consumption of the desired service.

From the Figure 12.7 it can be seen that the parameters that influence customer perceptions are the client interface and the service provision process. The interface components will include all the events which the customer had the opportunity of availing and interacting on a one to one basis with an employee of the service industry or organisation. The service provision process will include all occasions or events when the customer can observe (For example when customer is being attended to at the bank) or even if the service is being provided to at a place or location removed from the customer (For example Administration related to an insurance claim). In the latter case, in the absence of direct exposure to being served, the customer forms a perception about the efficiency of the provision process by considering the time factor and the accuracy of the response.

FIGURE 12.7

THE INTERACTION BETWEEN THE CUSTOMER & ORGANISATION DURING THE SERVICE PROVISION PROCESS

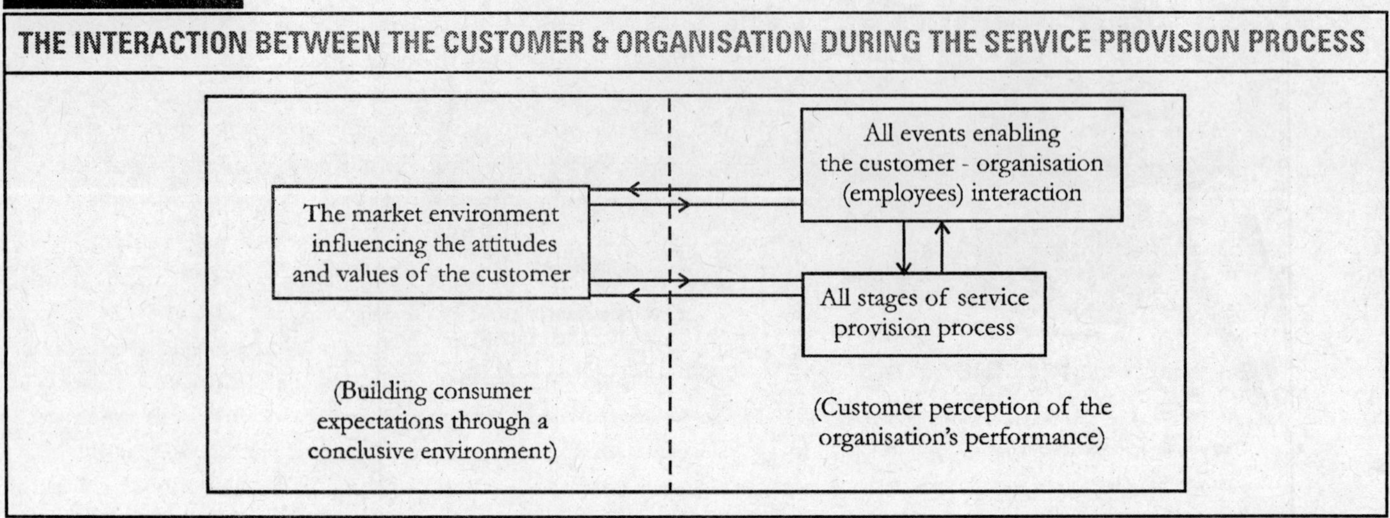

Today we have entered an era of true choices and real competition. Marketers have realised that the business will be driven by what consumers think. So the only way to beat competition is by concentrating on their customers' on a one-to-one basis.

➲ TACKLING CUSTOMER DISSATISFACTION

Customer dissatisfaction can set in due to ambigious or discrepant expectations, realisations or perceptions of quality associated with the product or services provided.

Customer dissatisfaction may occur due to ambiguous (or discrepant) expectations, realisations or perception of quality. *Ambiguous expectation situations* could take place when:

- The consumer or customer is not familiar with the purchase of a new product (ipod say).
- The product or service purchase could be a trend untried by the consumer (e-ticketing say)
- The service may not be physically present, when the purchase decision is being taken. (home – tele shopping say)
- The quality of service may not always be the same (the same tailor may not perform the same way at different times.)

At times, expectations are built up due to **making comparisons**, which in turn could lead to dissatisfaction. For instance, customer expectations get built up due to an attractive leaflet display, positive word of mouth from personal sources (friends or neighbours), personal use of the company's other product. (which gave satisfaction) etc.

Dissatisfaction can Occur due to the Customer's Perception of Quality

Quality is a term frequently used in relation to a product or service. Though every one has an idea of what quality is, it is very hard to define the same. According to D.A. Garvin. (Garvin D. A., *"Quality on the Line"*, Harvard Business Review 1983) The term 'quality' may be approached from various perspectives :

- ***Transcendental quality :*** This is a kind of innate excellence which is generally recognised. Skill and love for one's profession work as indicators for the quality of service provided.
- ***Production design quality :*** Here the product or service has to conform to its design specifications as an assurance of quality.
- ***Product character quality :*** This refers to an accurately measurable product characteristic. *For example* the proportion of fruit pulps and other ingredients in the *Kissan Jam*, the Cocoa content of chocolate etc.
- ***Value directed quality :*** This is defined in terms of price or cost. A product has a high quality if it functions well at a reasonable price. This is in relation to the equity of the price-value ratio of the product. For instance: *Hewlett Packard's* Laptop could outscore over its competitor *Lenova* based on the customer's perception of better quality and reasonable prices.
- ***Perceived quality :*** Perceived quality is associated with consumer's perception. Products and services have high quality if they meet the desires and expectations of consumers. For instance *British Airways* had made history when it came to be known as a '*World's Favourite*' *Airways* on account of its exclusive customised qualitative services.

People vary in their knowledge and expectations regarding products, this results in customer's perceiving different qualities in the same product or services category.

It can be seen that the definitions of perceived quality fits best with the consumer perspective. High perceived quality will include its utility or usefulness, durability, safety, comfort, reliability, low frequency of failure and good performance. *For example,* the quality of fruit juice will be judged on the basis of its freshness and fruit content. Whereas, the quality of a car will be determined by its failure frequency, its features and driving characteristics. If a product performs as expected, we consider it to have adequate quality. If the product performs beyond expectations we speak of high quality. Because consumer's associate to quality level, increasing quality levels can lead to demand for higher quality products. Moreover, people vary in their knowledge and expectations regarding products, this results in customers perceiving different qualities in the same products or services category. Similarly, in case of services also, measurable quality indicators will include warmth, care, time and accuracy and efficiency with which the service is offered.

Levels of Consumer Dissatisfaction

Discrepancies, consumer satisfaction and dissatisfaction can be measured at general, category and micro levels. Here we will discuss about four levels of dissatisfaction with increasing specificity.

- ***Dissatisfaction at the general level :*** This type of dissatisfaction can be associated with the consumption system itself. For instance: dissatisfaction may be with the demand and supply or use of goods and services (consumption system), or it may occur due to the non-availability of the goods and services at all places (shopping system) or say dissatisfaction with the choice possibilities (purchase system).
- ***Dissatisfaction may occur at the category levels :*** Here certain product classes itself may be the causes of dissatisfaction for the customer. For example, say washing machines, package tours etc.
- ***Dissatisfaction at the brand level :*** Here dissatisfaction can be directed towards certain specific brands, retailers or the organisation itself.
- ***Dissatisfaction may occur at the specific level :*** This is with reference to certain services and offers affecting the consumer's satisfaction level. For example, the repair of the scooter, faulty service performed on the refrigerator and so on.

Dimensions of Satisfaction and Dissatisfaction

Inhibiting and facilitating factors can influence consumer satisfaction. Inhibiting factors cause dissatisfaction and removal of these though may prevent dissatisfaction may not create satisfaction. Facilitating factors cause satisfaction provided inhibition is absent.

It is also important to make a note of the dimensions of satisfaction and dissatisfaction. Sometimes since satisfaction may have more than one dimension, a distinction between facilitations and inhibition is necessary. Too high a price may deter consumers (inhibition) whereas, a reasonable price may not stimulate them enough to purchase or accept the product. At times it may be an unfriendly salesman who may put off a prospective buyer, at the same time a friendly sales person may not act as a sufficient reason for buying. But manufacturers or producers have to remember to dispose off inhibition factors and create facilitating factors.

Likewise presence of inhibiting and facilitating factors can influence consumer satisfaction. Here also inhibiting factors cause dissatisfaction and removal of these though may prevent dissatisfaction but this may not create satisfaction. Facilitating factors cause satisfaction provided inhibition is absent.

In the words of Nelson Foote (The then manager of General Electric, 1961) *"In case of durable goods we observe more and more that consumers find certain product characteristic obvious especially for functional performance and values, such as safety. However, if it is lacking, it is an inhibiting factor, but if it is present, the producer is not given credit for it."*

FIGURE 12.8

ROLE OF INHIBITION AND FACILITATION

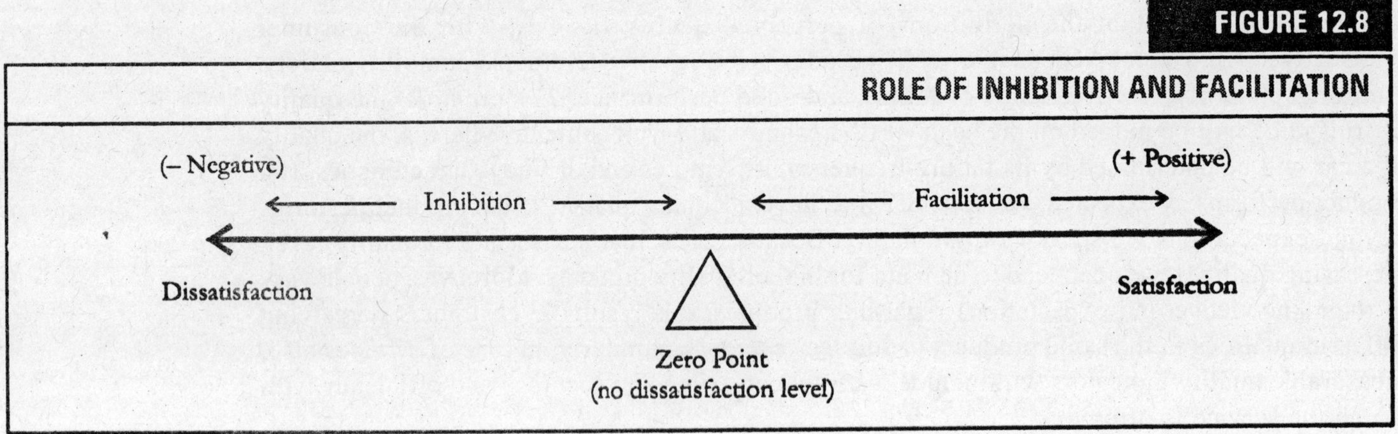

A good example of dissatisfaction caused by inhibition can be illustrated with the public transport system at Bengaluru. All the daily commuters or travelers are dissatisfied if the bus is late or if no seats are available, but this is taken for granted if the bus arrives on time (or schedule) and if they are able to procure seats. So the priority of a public transport management is to avoid or remove inhibition and not the creation of facilitation. Another example can be of the inconvenience caused to air travelers when the staff of Jet Airways resorted to flash strikes and all the pilots went on mass leave. These inhibition factors are causes of dissatisfaction for the customers. Here a facilitating factor such as providing snacks or lunch at the airport cannot compensate the inhibition caused by the delay in departure of the flights. So the management in the above instances should make all attempts to remove inhibiting factors, then only will facilitating factors have a positive effect.

Attribution and Dissatisfaction

Dissatisfaction with a product or service offered will occur if in reality there is a mismatch between the consumers expectations regarding the same and also on the basis of the availability of alternatives in the particular product/service category. Whenever dissatisfaction occurs, the consumers try to attribute the cause of dissatisfaction.

According to *V.S. Folkes* (Consumer Behavior, L.G. Schiffman, L.L. Kanuk, 1997), Attribution theory is concerned with the causes to which individuals attribute certain events. Consumers behave as lay-scientists and try to work out or detect the cause of events. During this process, three causal dimensions have been identified namely: Locos of control, stability and controllability.

Dissatisfaction with a product or service offered will occur if in reality there is a mismatch between the consumer's expectations regarding the same and also on the basis of the availability of alternatives in the particular product service category.

Locus of control will indicate which party is considered to be the cause of the event: the consumer or the supplier, that is indicating internal or external attribution, respectively. *For example,* the motor bike repair service may have not been up to the mark. The reason for this could be probably the motor bike rider had not communicated the 'exact problem' to the after sales service provider (internal attributions) or the latter may have knowingly not provided the desired service (external attribution). **Stability** refers to the duration of the cause. The motor bike repair had been carried out incorrectly because the mechanic had a bad day (temporary cause or phase) or the mechanic was not good at the job (permanent cause).

Controllability refers to the extent to which somebody has control over the cause. For instance, if the mechanic consciously and knowingly carries out a repair badly, hoping that the customer will not detect it, he is said to be the controller of the cause in a negative manner. Whereas, if the mechanic unknowingly uses the incorrectly adjusted measuring equipment, and as a result is responsible for the bad repair service provided, he does not control the cause. Here the mechanic will be less responsible for the result of his work.

FIGURE 12.9

ON ACCOUNT OF DISCREPANCY BETWEEN CUSTOMER EXPECTATIONS AND ACTUAL EXPERIENCE, THE SUBSEQUENT BEHAVIOUR

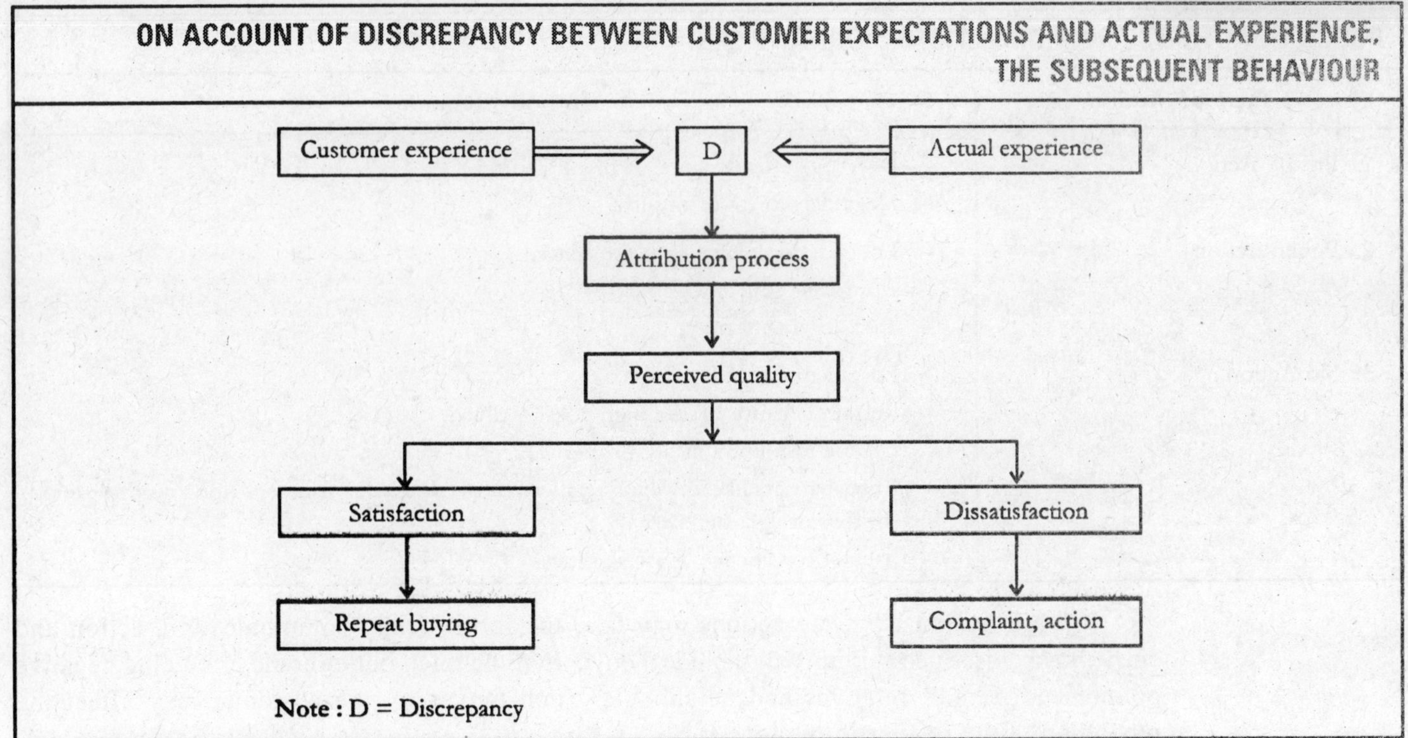

According to Folkes, the greatest dissatisfaction and most complaints occur in the case of *external attribution* and a stable controllable cause. When *dissatisfaction* is associated with an *external attribution* most consumers will demand a supplier's apology and compensation for the damage sustained.

If the cause of dissatisfaction is identified as stability, consumer will prefer repayment of the money as against a replacement of the product or another repair. This is because when

The consumer action is influenced by certain factors such as availability of time and other resources, experience with lodging complaints, expected benefits from complaining and the attitude towards complaining behaviours.

stability acts as the cause of dissatisfaction, the consumer will presume the other products or services of the supplier to be equally bad, probably the customer may never return to this supplier. Conversely, if the consumer becomes aware that the supplier has intentionally deceived him or her then they may become angry and may even take action against the supplier.

As shown in Figure 12.9, we can see that the result of the attribution process influences the perception of quality and the degree of satisfaction. When customers are satisfied they are likely to make more purchases and be loyal to the brand. While in case of dissatisfaction, it is more probable that they may make complaints or take action against the supplier. Sometimes the consumer may undergo stress–feel anger, tension and frustration, when he realises that the cause of dissatisfaction is attributed to the supplier and also is perceived to be under his or her control. In such cases, the tension will reduce only if he or she resorts to taking private or public actions.

Consumer Actions Post Dissatisfaction

Studies have revealed that dissatisfaction may activate consumers differently. They may either take no action or take private action, or take public action. Typically, the consumer action is influenced by certain factors such as availability of time and other resources, experience with lodging complaints, expected benefits from complaining and the attitude towards complaining behaviour.

TABLE 12.4

POSSIBLE ACTIONS FROM DISSATISFIED CONSUMERS

Type of Action	Method/Reason
1. Private Action	– Boycott of the retailer or manufacturer. – Negative word –of-mouth.
2. Public Action	– Lodge a complaint with the seller. – Approach consumer courts. – Take legal action.
3. No Action	– Forget about the problem. – Refrain because of the high cost involved. – Unable to communicate properly. – Entry barriers like unwilling retailers, or overloaded consumers' (long waiting period for redressal) forums etc. – Lack of confidence or assertiveness.

Private Action : Private actions may take the form of low communication, action and entry thresholds. Such actions will include a boycott of the retail outlet/brand or voicing negative opinions to friends, relatives and neighbours. Such moves by the customer may affect the reputation of the retailer in the long run.

Public Action : The dissatisfied customer is free to adopt a public action in the form of lodging a complaint with the seller or approach the Consumers Forum or file a legal suit against the seller.

No Action : There are many possible causes for consumers not taking any action over dissatisfied service provided. These may be :

- Consumers may forget or refrain from taking action because of lack of time and they do not foresee a balance between benefits and success especially if the problem is very small and the damage is minor in nature. Sometimes, disability to communicate properly may come in the way of consumer lodging the complaint. If consumers are not confident about themselves and not assertive enough they may not take any action. At times the consumer forum may be overloaded with complaints or there is a long procedure to seek redressal or even social and personal norms may stop a consumer from taking the trouble of complaining.

Another tactic used by the consumer is to caution the seller of the possible threat of going to the press (print media) to voice their complaint. Fearing bad publicity, the seller more often is likely to apologies and see how best he can reduce the customer dissatisfaction. The process of complaining may ultimately end with either satisfaction or with further dissatisfaction and then complaint, depending on how the complaint was handled. But unless the firm listens to their customers complaints and suggestions, it will lose its image in the market.

Book retailing is one area, where the book stores have to constantly try out innovative ways to retain and increase the customer base. Below is an example of how book retailing can be used to provide customer focused service.

Oxford Book Store is an independent store with its virtual retail site www. oxfordbookstore.com, with the largest data base of books in India with links from websites like www.penguin.com and www.bazee.com. The store is able to satisfy consumers by offering large discount for purchases made online with an easy to order and secure gateway that accepts different modes of payment.

The process of complaining may ultimately end with either satisfaction or with further dissatisfaction and then complaint, depending on how the complaint was handled.

The above example shows that an organisation which uses its ingenuity, resources and consumer insights to offer functional value and differentiate itself from its competitors will go a long way in ensuring customer satisfaction, and then earn loyalty in the long run.

In this age of e-technology, organisations are looking for a long term relationship with their customers. The length of the relationship between them will be determined on the basis of opportunities for mutual gain. So organisations need to, on an ongoing basis, carry out research programmes and process this information to build up a reputation as 'the service provider model, for the industry. For this, the organisation will have to make significant investments in database management, specifically with demographic data, segment-wise profiles, and needs, satisfaction survey details, forward positioning surveys etc.

Box 12.3 will throw light on how *i-flex* has earned the reputation of being the No.1 in the market for providing core banking solutions to satisfied consumers.

BOX 12.3

I-FLEX

It's the kind of story that would be a clinch for Harvard's sales textbooks. Eager to bag a prestigious banking account, the sales team at I-flex had prepared detailed spreadsheets and glossy presentations, and were ready to talk business. So when the officials of a large American bank walked into the conference room and brushed aside those presentations and the sales team, it naturally created a flutter. Apparently, they'd done the rounds of many Indian companies and were tired of all the sales talk thrown at them. So at I-flex, they wanted to meet just one person – the prospective project manger – and grill him not on technical skills, but his knowledge of the banking industry. The bank execs got a pleasant surprise: they clearly hadn't thought that the depth of understanding of the banking business shown by project manager designated by I-flex could exist in an essentially software company. Satisfied, they signed on the dotted line, I-flex has won yet another deal.

I-flex made a big splash when Bank of America signed up to install the company's core banking solution in its units across six Asian countries in late May, 2006.

(Source: Nandita Datta, *'I-Flex'*, *Outlook Business,* July, 2006, p. 52)

➲ HANDLING OF CUSTOMER COMPLAINTS

In order to do well in the market, organisations have to work towards developing a system of *Zero error delivery. For example,* organizations offering financial services are individualizing their service offerings to satisfy their customers. Like the *HDFC Asset Management Company Limited,* which has been assigned the highest *Crisil rating of Fund House, Level-1.* This is the highest Fund Governance and Process Quality rating (FGP) awarded and is clearly an indication of customer confidence and satisfaction In the area of mobile service operations, *Airtel* has been able to secure the second position (after BSNL) in the list of most trusted mobile service providers, in the *Brand – Equity's most trusted Brands* Survey of 2005. In the words of Hemant Sachdev, CMO, *Bharati Televentures* and Director – Mobility "we have played a relationship strategy rather than a price strategy, last year. Whether it was our customer in Trichy, in Mumbai or in the rural heartland, we have invested in building long term relationships with them".

Above were examples of how marketers are able to achieve customer satisfaction. But, at times, the marketer may not be able to understand the specific service requirements of an individual customer and offer a matching product. Or in case of providing services, which is intangible in nature, the marketer may find it difficult to ensure a few defect deliveries every time. Such situations can result in customer dissatisfaction and if not handled amicably the customer will adopt the complaining behaviour.

Organisations and marketers must remember that if they do not receive any customer complaints, it does not indicate that all is well. For, it is the human tendency to believe that being silent is an indication of satisfied customers. On the contrary, it could be that the customers think so poorly of the organisation and its offers that they do not even bother to give a feedback on how they think the offerings are. So it would be appropriate for organisations and marketers to treat customer complaints as 'eye openers', providing them opportunities to improve relationships with them.

It would be appropriate for marketers to treat customer complaints as 'eye openers', providing them opportunities to improve relationships with them.

N. Piercy has given some information on dissatisfied customers and their complaining behaviour.

- Most dissatisfied customers do not complain to the organization (around 4-5 percent bother). The silent majority may detect to a competitor or put up for a short time and then detect.
- Dissatisfied customers buy less and also do their best to get others to purchase less.
- Typically, the cost of complaint resolution will be very less compared to the cost of finding a new customer.
- There is some evidence which conveys that when complaints are resolved satisfactorily, these customers tend to be more loyal than those who have never experienced a problem before.

Research has shown that the chances of doing repeat purchase transaction with a complaining customer is more, if the organization just *listens* to the complaints. Further, this situation can turn for the better (or pales to insignificance) if the organisation not only listens but also *does* something about the complaint. So organisations, must on identifying *'unhappy customers'* make all efforts to convert them to one's most loyal customers all the time, by virtue of the way, they are treated.

Complaining customers can help the organisation to :

- Learn about the areas where business improvement methods need to be adopted.

- Satisfy these customers by replacing the product or service and get repeat business.
- Make efforts to potentially build real customer loyalty.

HDFC Mutual Fund is able to deliver customer satisfaction, as identified by the 'Crisil Fund House Level-1, given by CRISIL.

Proactive Model of Complaint Handling

The traditional view of the organisation had no place for complaints in the loop. However, now firms have realised that to keep pace with the changes taking place in the market place, listening to customers needs, views, suggestions, handling their complaints etc., will go a long way in communicating that they 'care' for their customers. This has given rise to the pro-active model where conscious effort is made to handle customer complaints at every stage.

The way in which the organisation handles complaints will reflect its commitment to the services it is offering. Problems identified by an analysis of complaints will prove to be a valuable element of market research and addressing such problems before they begin to have a measurable impact on the firm's market share, is a key goal of the development process. Moreover, analysis of complaints can also be viewed by the organisation as positive opportunities for service improvement.

FIGURE 12.10

THE ROLE OF COMPLAINT HANDLING IN A PROACTIVE ORGANISATION

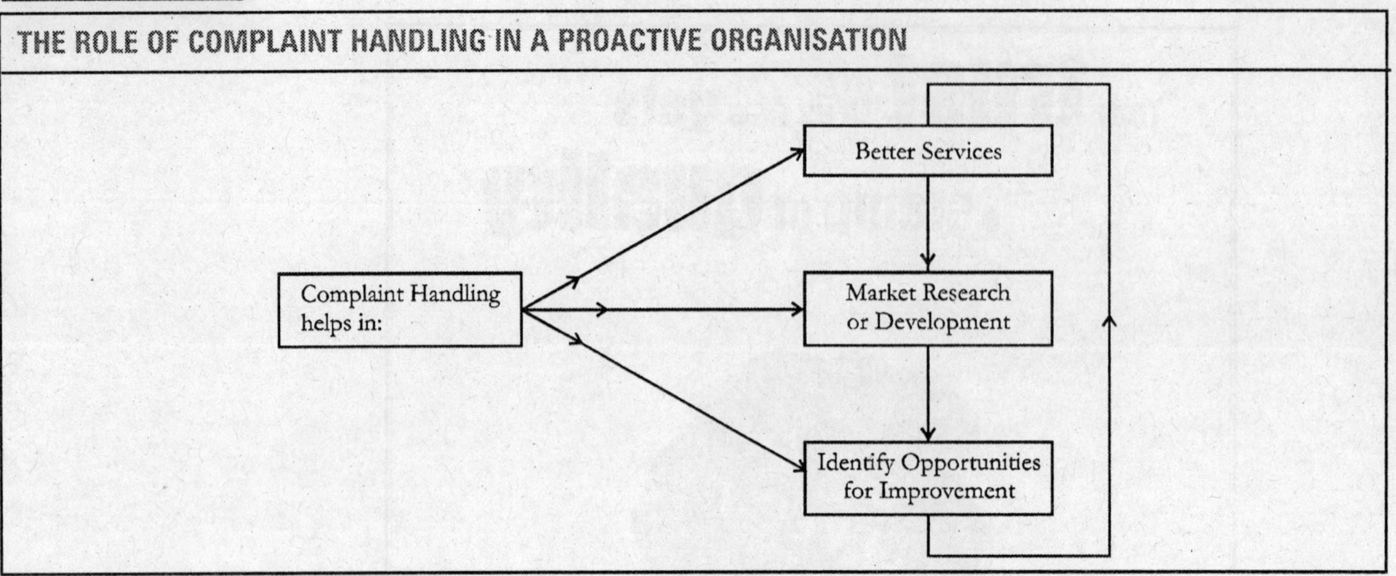

If the complaint handling function is to be a real influence at each stage, it is necessary that it is integrated into the decision making level at the board.

If the complaint handling function is to be a real influence at each stage, it is necessary that it is integrated into the decision making level at the board. This is because if a company wants to show genuine concern and respond effectively to grievances then it will be sometimes necessary to probe and take decisions to effect changes which may actually be the root causes of complaints. Thus involvement of the management at all the levels is necessary, so that the decisions pertaining to complaint handling redressals are amicably discussed and taken.

Today since the customer cannot be taken for granted, organisations with a genuine commitment to their customers, are involving their senior managers to directly deal with customer complaints.

1. The Indian subsidiary of the telecom equipment manufacturer '*Motorola*' has linked every manufacturing process by developing network of teams that assemble themselves as a cross functional team called The *Total Customer Satisfaction* teams (*TCS*). All the members of the team together interact and listen to customers. This team identifies the problem area for a particular process based on the feedback and prioritises its tasks.
2. *Bharti Televentures* (Airtel – brandname) as a mobile service operator has earned the reputation of occupying the second position in the list of the most trusted mobile service provider in 2005, Brand Equity Survey. Its quality statement is" We will deliver error-free service to our customers by doing our jobs right the first time, every time". The company has taken many initiatives such as Business Process Management based on voice of customers using six sigma methodology and knowledge management, etc. right from the grass root level enabling it to improve customer satisfaction level leading to customer delight.
3. In 2006, *ICICI Bank* had been awarded three awards for outstanding performance from *Asian Banker,* 'Best Retail Bank India', 'Excellence in Multichannel Distribution,' and Excellence in Automobile lending Award. Consumers also voted for, ICICI as 'Reader's Digest India – Most Trusted Brand Award for 2006.'

ICICI Bank has got a 24 hour customer care cell or Help Desk where the customer can register the complaint and a response from the organisation can be expected within 2 business days. ICICI's official statement says "When you make your complaint on the phone or by email, the action that will be taken to resolve your complaint and the time required to do so, will be explained to you. You will also receive a unique service request number of your complaint, which can be used for any future communication relating to that particular complaint.'

The image of the organisation will be reflected in the way customer complaints are handled and the necessary redressal is effected.

Similarly, '*Siemens*' communication systems division had also set up a customer information centre (CIC). This centre apart from serving as a showroom for its products, holding demonstrations for its hi – technology products and systems also had an operator sitting at the CIC to log into the machine installed at the client's site and carry out maintenance work and repairs. In short, the CIC could also attend to nearly 40% of its customers problems.

It will do to remember that even if a marketer fails on the first occasion to offer the required service, he has an opportunity to recover dramatically, the second time to control the damage. If he falters again then he is actually working away from providing a basis for a happy, long-term customer relationship.

The image of the organisation will be reflected in the way customer complaints are handled and the necessary redressal is effected. Sample of a complaint form which can be used for listening to customer grievance is given below.

COMPLAINT FORM

Name : ______________________

Address : ______________________

____

____

Contact Telephone Number Office : ______________________

Residence : ______________________

My Complaint is regarding

____

____

____

____

If you have already approached the firm to lodge a complaint, whom did you contact?

Name of the company person : ______________________

Designation : ______________________

On ______________________

Date : ______________ Signature : ______________

There are certain things which should be borne in mind and can help customers to communicate and register the complaint and also enable the organisation to set the scene for follow up action.

Always acknowledge receipt of the complaint. The organisation must communicate spelling out their understanding of the situation and what they intend to do about it.

- Customers (people) may be reluctant to complain. So the organisation needs to positively encourage them to do so.
- Ideally complaints, should be handled face to face by well trained staff who are empowered to deal with customer's problems.
- Complaints should be recorded with assurance of management backup to support staff dealing with difficult complaints.
- In case of handling telephone complaints, have an established telephone procedure to ensure all calls are dealt with properly.
- In case of written complaints, make the procedure easy for customers by keeping the form simple and also having staff to help in filling them up.
- Always acknowledge receipt of the complaint. The organisation must communicate spelling out their understanding of the situation and what they intend to do about it.
- Always have a positive, open and friendly environment so that most complainants will respond.

➲ SUMMARY

Customerisation is a process where-in all the employees of the firm directly interact with the end user, by building up a platform of interactive communication techniques so as to add value and increase customer satisfaction. In order to avoid customer dissatisfaction, the marketer must adopt an approach, where-in he can classify markets in relation to the degree of opportunity to deliver customer satisfaction. Consumers have the tendency to compare their expectation or dissatisfaction results from a positive or negative discrepancy with the outcome and expectations from a purchase. There can be three possible consumer responses from the experience of satisfaction or dissatisfaction: exit, voicing dissatisfaction or loyalty.

While measuring consumer satisfaction, there are two issues which need to the addressed: (a) how does one measure consumer satisfaction? (b) how does one use the information received after measuring consumer satisfaction? Perceived value is a blend of quality and price being sought to by customers in the product or service offering. Few studies in India (TCSI, CSI, IDC India and Data Quest Survey (2004) and TBR's study) were briefly touched upon. Organisations have to work towards building customer loyalty. A satisfied customer may or may not remain loyal but the dissatisfied customers will make all efforts to defect. Organisations offering services can add to customer satisfaction by offering 'it' with added values which are emotional or symbolic in nature.

Efforts must be made to take care of customer dissatisfaction which may occur due to ambiguous (or discrepant) expectations, realizations or perception of quality. Organisations need to develop a proactive model for handling customer complaints.

➲ CHAPTER QUESTIONS FOR DISCUSSION

1. Why should every marketer be concerned with the issue of "customer satisfaction"?
2. Discuss about the link between customer satisfaction and customer loyalty, with the help of an example.
3. 'Customer dissatisfaction can lead to reduction in purchase intention, brand defection, negative word-of-mouth and complaining behaviour'. Comment.
4. Carry out a survey in your college involving ten fellow students and another ten faculty members. Prepare a questionnaire to measure customer satisfaction/dissatisfaction, related to the purchase of:

(a) For students, consumer durable products such as mobile phone, motor bike or ipod (purchased within the last year).

(b) For faculty members, consumer durable products or service such as car, credit card or home theatre (purchased within the last year).

Try to find out their level of satisfaction post purchase. In case of dissatisfaction, how did the customer (particular respondent) react and what action was taken by the firm to resolve dissatisfaction?

SUGGESTED READINGS 

1. www.kalnirnay.com
2. Gaurav.Pai., The Date Keeper, Brand Equity, *The Economic Times*, Bangalore, March 18, 2009.
3. Nigel, F. Piercy, *Market-Led Strategic Change*, Butterworth – Heinemann, London, 2002 p. 51.
4. Khama Sundeep; G., Skaria., Pareena, Kawatra; "Customerising the Corporation", *Business Today*, January 7-21, 1997
5. Vijay Mallya; Innovation makes you sour, *Businessgyan*, BG 64, Vol.6 Issue 4, July 15-14th August, 2006, pp.16-20.
6. Jagdish, N. Sheth., Dr. Banwari, Mittal., *Customer Behavior : A Managerial Perspective*, Thomson South Western Learning, Singapore. 2003, pp.302-305.
7. C. Goodwin and I. Ross, 'Salient Dimensions of Perceived Fairness in Resolution of Service Complaints, *Journal of Satisfaction, Dissatisfaction and Complaining Behavior* 2, 1989, pp. 87-92.
8. V.S. Ramaswamy, S. Namakumari., *Marketing Management – Global perspective Indian Context*, Macmillan India Ltd, 2005, pp. 206-216.
9. A.D,. Houston., J.S. Sherman, & M.S. Baker., "Feature Matching Unique Features, and the dynamics of the choice process : predecision conflict and post decision satisfaction" *Journal of Experimental Social Psychology*, 27, pp.411-430.
10. R.L. Oliver., "A Cognitive Model of the antecedents and consequences of satisfaction decisions", *Journal of Marketing Research,* 17, 1980, pp.460-469.
11. Frank R. Kardes, '*Consumer Behavior and Managerial decision making*', Prentice Hall of India Pvt. Ltd, New Delhi, 2002., pp.94-97.
12. Dr. Ranjan. Das., Understanding Customer Satisfaction, *Strategic Marketing*, Vol 1, Issue 1. July-August 1999, pp.10-13.
13. Jagdeep. Kappor., A Switch in time, *Strategic Marketing*, Jan-Feb, 2005, pp.24-29.
14. Dr. Kaushik. Mukherjee, 'The Satisfied Customer', *Strategic Marketing* Vol. III, Issue V, Sept-October 2004, pp. 51-54.
15. www.jdpower.com
16. V. Ramkumar, Fostering Loyalty', *Strategic Marketing* Jan-Feb, 2005, p p. 12-14.
17. D.A. Garvin; Quality on the line, *Harward Business Review for Quality Management*, 1983.
18. *'Brand Equity' The Economic Times,* 15 February 2006.
19. Nandita. Datta., i-flex, *Out look Business* July 5, 2006, pp.52-57.
20. Bearden, W.O, and Teel, J.E, "Selected Determinants of Consumer Satisfaction and Complaint Reports", *Journal of Marketing Research*, 1983.
21. Kolodinsky J., "Usefulness of Economics in Explaining Consumer Complaints", *Journal of Consumer Affairs,* 29, 1995.
22. Williams Tom, "*Dealing with Customer Complaints*", Gower Publishing Ltd., England, 1996.

THE LEADER IN THE SMALL CAR SEGMENT, "MARUTI SUZUKI"

THE INDIAN CAR INDUSTRY

The Indian car industry has witnessed a seachange in the past few years. The historical sales figures indicate that there has been a rush among auto majors to become a part of (and gain a share) the fast emerging small car market. In the early 1980's, the annual sales volume of this market was around 30000 cars but in 2005-06, this figure grew to 1.1 million cars. Incidentlly, while the automobile industry grew by 20% in the first quarter of 2006-07, the passenger car segment grew by 24% during the same period. Added to this is the fact that the small cars (which includes the mini and compact or A1 and A2 car) segments account for nearly 76% of the passenger car market. During the first quarter of 2006-07, these segments grew by 27%. This can probably be because car manufacturers realized that sales volume and increase in market share came from investing in the mini car category. Ofcouse due to the recession, there is a slow down visible in the purchase of cars in 2008, unlike the earlier period.

MARUTI SUZUKI INDIAN LIMITED (MSIL) "THE BEGINNING"

Maruti Suzuki India Limited (MSIL) was established in February 1981, through an Act of Parliament in order to meet the growing demand of a personal mode of transport especially due to the lack of an efficient public transport system. In October 1982, a licence and a joint venture agreement was signed between the Government of India and the Suzuki Motor Company (now Suzuki Motor corporation of Japan) and thus began the long journey. Suzuki Motor Company was selected from seven prospective partners worldwide because of its envied 'undisputed 'leadership position' in small car segment. Suzuki Motor Corporation has been a global leader in mini and compact cars for three decaders. Its technical superiority lies in its ability to pack power and performance into a compact, light weight engine, which is clean and fuel efficient. Thus, Maruti Suzuki started as a government company, with Suzuki as a minor partner, to make a people's car for the middle class of India. It had brought to India, a very simple yet powerful Japanese philosophy "Smaller, fewer, lighter, shorter and neater".

MSIL's **core values are:**

- Customer obsession
- Fast, Flexible and Fast mover
- Innovation and Creativity
- Networking and Partnership
- Openness and Learned.

It's **vision** has been "To be the leader in the Indian Automobile Industry, Creating Customer Delight and Shareholder's wealth, A pride of India".

INDIA'S SMALL CAR MARKET SEGMENT

Since the past few years, there has been an increase in the purchase of small or compact cars by Indian consumers. The industry has attributed the reasons behind the sudden interest in the purchase of compact cars to:

(a) The boost the segment got from the 8% excise duty cut in the 2006 union budget.

(b) The reduction in the fuel price adhered to by the central government.

(c) The growing desire of most of the middle-class families to own at least one car.

The above were some of the indications that suggested that 'the small car' would be ruling the Indian automotive turf for quite some time. Based on the customer requirement, Maruti Suzuki gained popularity by offering different car models accordingly. Starting with the iconic Maruti Suzuki which offers 12 models with over 100 variants. The company has manufactured around seven and half million cars in India (till December 2008) and leads the automobile industry in India with a market share of over 54% among passenger cars.

Reasons behind Maruti Suzuki's popularity

(a) The quality advantage: Maruti has been ensuring that it's cars maintain a high level of quality. The J.D power Asia-Pacific study 2008, indicated that Maruti Suzuki owners_experienced fewer problems when compared to customers of other car manufacturers across 9 parameters. Another study, the J.D power Asia pacific 2008, India customer service Index (CSI) study, measuring ownership in terms of design, content, layout and performance of vehicles across 8 parameters had proclaimed that brands **Wagon** and **Swift** were rated as the best in the compact car segment and **SX4** and **Swift Dzire** as the No.1 in the mid size car segment.

(b) Providing efficient quality service through dealer network: Maruti Suzuki has a strong vendor base of around 225 Vendors. It has also over 600 sales outlets in 393 towns and cities along with 2628 workshops covering 1220 cities. Very good quality service is provided across all the service centres as proven by the J.D Power Asia Pacific 2008 CSI Study where Maruti Suzuki was rated as the best across all parameters. It is also the ninth consecutive year that Maruti Suzuki has been ranked the highest in customer satisfaction.

Maruti Suzuki achieved an overall CSI score of 820 on a 1000 point scale. Overall customer satisfaction with dealer service for the industry had moved up by 3 points when compared to the 2007, with six of the eleven ranked brands showing improvements and gains. Certain simple procedures were implemented:

- Greeting service customers quickly upon arrival and fully explaining charges and repairs.
- There was customer satisfaction with value of work performed and perceptions of the fairness and honesty of the dealer.
- The study found that the proportion of vehicles brought in and serviced within the same day, which was 49 percent in 2007 increased to 55 percent in 2008. Quick service provision is a key source of customer delight, especially for those who visit the dealer for regular maintenance.

The above mentioned practices by MSIL has helped to foster trust and delight among customers, which can result in building customer relationship through loyalty of future service and sales opportunities.

(c) Low maintenance cost and lowest cost of ownership: In the economy car segment, Maruti scores over its competitors in terms of affordability of spare parts and easy to maintain the vehicle. In this product category, the highest satisfaction ratings have been indicated for its top 6 models *Maruti 800, Alto, Omni, Zen Estilo, Wagon* R and *Swift Diesel.*

(d) One roof shop: All customer needs met under one roof at Maruti Suzuki. Whether it is easy finance, insurance, fleet management, services or exchange, the company has provided a single window solution for all the above related needs.

BRAND NAME	ENGINE CAPACITY	SPECIAL FEATURES OR BENEFITS HIGHLIGHTED	PRICE (APPROX)	MILEAGE IN TEST CONDITIONS
1. Chevrolet Spark	995c.c	Small turning radius of 4600 mm	Rs.3-Rs.4 lakhs	14-15 km/liter
2. Fiat Palio Stile	1105c.c	260 litres of boot space expandable upto 950 litres	Rs.3.5-Rs.4.25 lakhs	12-13 km/litre
3. Hyundai i10	1086c.c	New age 1.1 LIRDE engine with electric control unit	Rs.3.50-Rs.5.00 lakhs	–
4. Hyundai Santro Xing	1086c.c	Improved fuel efficiency, reduced emission, increased power	Rs.3.0-Rs.4.00 lakhs	12.13 km/litre
5. Maruti 800	796c.c	Low cost and highly fuel efficient	Rs.2.0-Rs.2.25 lakhs	13-14 km/litre
6. Maruti A-star	998c.c	Equipped with light weight KB series engine for refined performance	Rs.3.5-Rs.4.25 lakhs	18-19 km/litre
7. Maruti Alto	796c.c	Powered with 32-bit computer technology	Rs.2.50-Rs.3.0 lakhs	13-14 km/litre
8. Maruti Zen	993.c.c	Ergonomically crafted seats with rich upholstery	Rs.3.50-Rs.4.0 lakhs	11-12 km/litre
9. Maruti-Zen Estilo	1061.c.c	Sporty looks and roomy space	Rs.3-Rs.4 lakhs	12-13 km/litr
10. Maruti Wagon-R	1061c.c	Roomy interiors, 32 Bit Electronic Control Module (ECM)	Rs.3.50-Rs.4.50 lakhs	12-13 km/litre
11. Tata Indica	1405.c.c	Micro processor based Engine management system	Rs.3.50-Rs.4.50 lakhs	12-13 km/litre

Table 12.5 : A comparative picture of brands in the compact car market

COMPETITION

Till the end of 1998, Maruti had enjoyed a very high market share of 80%. As the car market grew and along with it the sales of each brand in obsolute terms, the market share of Maruti also came under pressure. In fact, within a year of the launch of Hyundai's **Santro,** Daewoo's **Matiz** and Tata Motor's **Indica** in 1998-99, Maruti's market share fell to be just a few notches above 50%. This competition is likely to intensity in the future. For, General Motors (GM) was thinking on rolling out a revamped version a of Matiz, which could give Maruti Alto a run for its money. Also there will be the formidable Hyundai Motor India, India's second largest passenger car manufacturer Maruti's nearest and most aggressive competitor and (holding 22% market share in the passenger car segment) to be wary of. Futher, the launch of Tata motor's **Nano** (the Rs.1 lakh people's car) in March 2009, is a tough competitor. Nano's launch in the recession period could lead to price wars and possibly the end of Maruti's reign at the top of the small cars market.

Measures to counter competion

- MSIL is focusing on getting its Rs.350crore plant at Manesar running and quickly roll out the diesel version of its **Swift model** to capture the booming diesel segment.
- Maruti is also beefing up its sales network and targeting tire 2 cities in a big way. It has launched several special car buying schemes across verticals to reach out to potential customers in these markets. Some of these schemes which have already hit the market include **Dil se** (for NRIs), **School Teachers Wheels of India** (for state and central government employees), Do Aor Char (it has changed the catch line from Do Ka Char to this one) (for two-wheeler owners) and Railways Scheme and Auto card (a part of its loyalty programme)
- As a part of its Market penetration Strategy, MSIL has increased its own marketing and sales team (from 45 in 2003 to 600 plus in 2008) and is building on its core strength of sales and service network. Of the 380 plus sales outlets in 230 cities, as many as 115 are in the country's tier 2 cities. And this number is only likely to go up in the future.
- The remarkable performance of MSIL's 'Swift' since its's launch in May has commited itself to launch five new models over as many years, starting 2006. It has launched a revamped Wagon R and also an LPG driven variant of Wagon R (called Wagon R Duo)
- Maruti is also planning to launch an export focused model in 2008-09 with a target of exporting, 100000 units per annum.

Commenting on future of compact cars in India, In the words of Mr Shinzo Nakanishi, Managing Director and CEO (Maruti Suzuki) " with growing incomes and aspirations, Indian consumers have exposure to global design. Most of them would want compact cars to be more stylish, loaded with features and superior engines and at least as reliable and efficient as their earlier cars. We would meet the needs of these customers" (The Hindu, Business line, September 2008)

QUESTIONS FOR DISCUSSION

1. **What measures should be adhered to by MSIL to offset the possible price war it may encounter from its competitors Hyndai Motors and Tata Motors?**
2. **Apart from the new roll-outs that Maruti is planning to fight back competitively in the small car segment, can you suggest the relative promotional programmes that can also help MSIL to induce a positive buying behaviour among consumers leading to a long term relationship?**
3. **'The entry of GM, Honda, Toyota and Volkswagen is likely to disturb the existing small car equilibrium' In the light of this statement, do you think that with its expertise in leading the small car segment, it can also try explore emerging markets like electric car or gearless car? Why?**

(Source : www.maruti_suzuki.com, "*Maruti'-Road Warrior, Outlook Business*, August 5, 2006, pp.48-52)

UNIT IV : CONSUMER DECISION MAKING, AFTER SALES AND RELATED ISSUES

CHAPTER 13

RELATIONSHIP MARKETING

- Case : **Anandabazar Patrika**
- Relationship Marketing – Meaning and importance
- Can organisations retain customers through loyalty programmes?
- Six model markets and relationship marketing
- The Relationship Management chain
- Positioning, segmenting and targeting
- Customer Retention improvement plan
- Understanding of brand equity and brand loyalty.
- Summary
- Chapter questions for discussion
- Suggested readings
- Catering through CRM, **'Mom's Kitchen'** and **'Calorie Care'**

CASE

ANANDABAZAR PATRIKA

In the present world of cut throat competition there are some Indian brands which have been able to strive a name for themselves in the mind of the consumers. This is because the organisation and the marketer have been able to understand the mindset of the target market and align the product-services offerings through relationship marketing. *Anandabazar Patrika*, a Bengali newspaper is a leading newspaper which has been able to understand the Bengali's mindset, touch their hearts and continuously connect to new consumers even though there is stiff competition from English newspapers.

Anandabazar began its journey as an evening newspaper about eighty six years ago and today it reaches more than thirteen lakh homes and seventy three lakh individuals in the state. Probably due to India's colonial past, even though we celebrated sixty years of independence, simultaneously our awe and respect for the English language has only increased in the last six decades. Every morning three out of every five newspaper readers in Bengal read the *Anandabazar Patrika*. This means that there are not enough gentlemen in Bengal. For, goes the gospel, 'Only English papers are for the gentry'. This indicates that an Indian language daily has to meet their standard to challenge it. Eighty-six year old 'Anandabazar' has been able to strive and create a name for itself in the mind of its consumers, amidst tough competition from the English daily. Research has revealed that Anandabazar reaches 42 percent of the identical deep pocket target group in Kolkatta. This is a clear indication that even the famous people in Kolkatta seem to read the Anandabazar (vernacular) by choice. It is not surprising that many describe this newspaper as the English newspaper printed in Bengali. It has achieved the success it enjoys by always walking that extra mile. By offering something different from the typical newspaper. It has fully made use of rich Bengali literature.

Over the eight (and more) decades of its existence, the Anandabazar has outgrown the role of a mere news provider. Eminent editors and erudite columnists, global correspondents and local reporters have helped to project Anandabazar as a *thought reader.*

It 'has truly remained a flag bearer in the cultural arena. Through its annual issue published during the Durga Puja, Anandabazar has harvested a literary crop. Anandabazar has played a role of a catalyst for many reputed authors who have written their first novel on these pages. Further, every year through an award *'Ananda Puroshkar'*, it recognises outstanding literary talent especially for those who have enriched the cerebral space of a Bengali. The standard of excellence that this award epitomises has earned it the soubriquet - Booker of Bengal. Perhaps it would not be easy to find a parallel where a single newspaper anywhere has taken such a huge responsibility of keeping a culture alive through its literature and relationship marketing.

By understanding the Bengali's mindset and love for their culturally rich literature, Anandabazar has tried innovative ways to be in touch with its consumers.

- Anandabazar has struck to provide food for thought through its editorial columns.
- Over the changing times spanning more that eight decades of a century, Anandabazar has touched the hearts and minds of Bengalis world over (both old and new) by ensuring that their culture is kept alive through its literature.

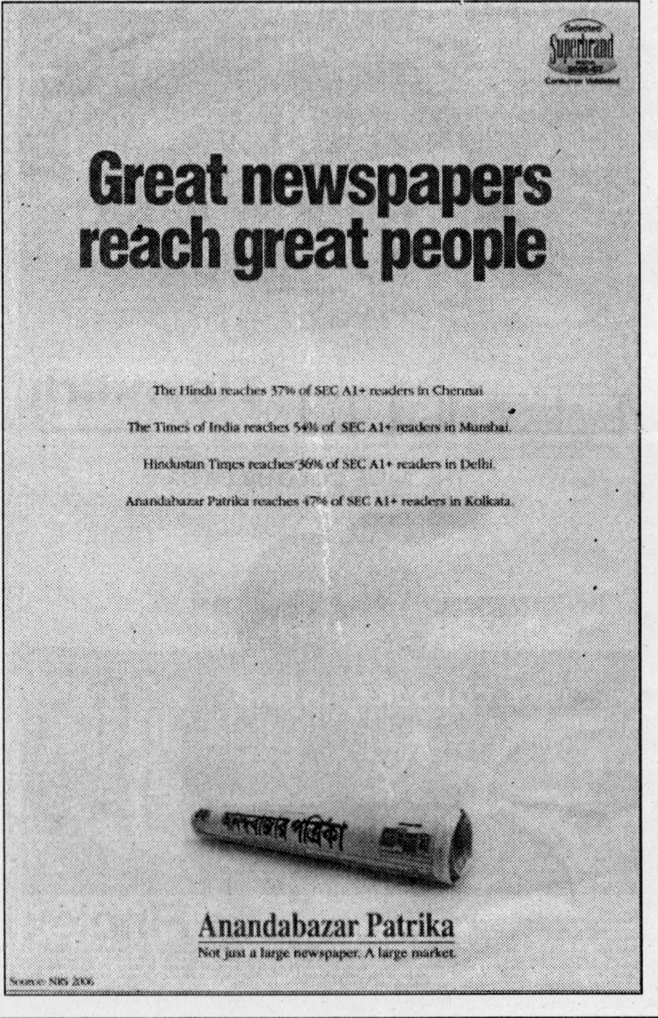

Post liberalisation has brought about dramatic shifts in the market place triggered by sharp changes in the demography, lifestyle pattern of the consumers, topography of the competition and the so called evolution in the communication technology. Marketers have realised that time tested concepts of brand loyalty, mass marketing cannot be taken as the only devices to gauge the behaviour of the new generation consumers.

This behaviour is characterised by the individualised customer expectations. Apart from insisting on consistent quality and improved price performance ratio, they are looking out for more customisation and availability of products 'anytime' and 'anywhere' and more information through advertisements rather than merely being a passive participant. Seeing the new emerging face of the customers, companies have realised that it is necessary to understood the changing demographic profile of the population in terms of education, income, size of family etc. What will be more substantive in days to come will be the psychographics of the customers *i.e.*, how they feel, think or behave. Further, the competition has become very intense at the market place and consumers have to choose from parity products. With this continuous entry of new competitors to explode the choice of consumers, marketers have realised the value of being customer focused and also are looking out for ways to retain existing customers and gain more revenue from them. This aspect was visible in the case of Anandabazar Patrika, discussed above. Thus has emerged the saga of Relationship Marketing.

Relationship marketing charts a new different path advocating high customer contact and service and customer relation in order to build long term relationship with them.

Relationship marketing charts a new different path — advocating a high customer contact and service and customer relation in order to build long term relationships with them. In this chapter we will discuss indepth the emerging marketing scenario of relationship marketing, with firms learning and relearning that consumers are looking for quality and value for money. So all their moves at segmenting, targeting and positioning is to constantly upgrade the consumer and the product by finding new dimensions and also about a paradigm shift on concepts such as 1:1 marketing. The key to brand loyalty is through ensuring customer satisfaction and working towards the beginning of a long term relationship.

RELATIONSHIP MARKETING - MEANING AND IMPORTANCE

According to Professor Philip Kotler, *"Relationship marketing is the process of building long term, trusting, win-win relationships with customers, distributors, dealers and suppliers. Over time, relationship marketing promises and delivers high quality, efficient service and fair prices to the other party. It is accomplished by strengthening economic, technical and social ties between members of the two organisations or between the marketer and the individual customer"*.

As per the above definition, organisations must strive for building long term relationships with their customers through creating trust and life time value for them. This can be done by assuring as well as delivering the promised high quality product and service offerings, efficient services and conveying the feeling of 'value for money'.

In today's competitive scenario, every organisation is working at increasing it's value. The value of an organisation is directly related to the value of customer which will be the outcome of the organic growth of the former. Such an organic growth will occur through a vibrant organisation which works at creativity and innovation resulting in increased customer value.

Traditional Marketing and CRM

The traditional transaction marketing was focussed only on one need — one product, marketed to as many customers as possible. In CRM (Customer relation management), the focus is on a customer and how the marketer tries to satisfy more and more of his (customer's) needs and create life time value, trust and relationship with them.

Marketers have understood that transaction marketing will not be fruitful in the long run and if the past and future are not linked, buyers and sellers will become adversaries. Only by understanding customer needs better, will the marketer be able earn his loyalty.

When transaction marketing was in vogue, the focus was on communicating about the product features and short term gains and achievement. Since the primary motive was to get adequate return on investments quickly, the quality aspect was limited to design and manufacturing. Moreover, customer contact and services were not emphasised and if existed, it was only a shallow attempt at achieving the organisation's short term goals and objectives.

Marketers have understood that transaction marketing will not be fruitful in the long-run and if the past and future are not linked, buyers and sellers will become adversaries. Only by understanding customer needs better, will the marketer be able earn his loyalty. Today marketers have understood that focusing on individual customer, treating him or her differently, building up their trust in them and then engaging themselves in customer specific actions will go a long way in building customer loyalty and CRM.

The emerging customer relationship marketing was initially advocated by L.L. Berry and then discussed by many others when describing a long term approach to marketing. C. Gronroos has given a relationship-focused definition of marketing which says *"The purpose of marketing is to establish, maintain, enhance and commercialise customer relationships (often, but not necessarily always, long term relationships) so that the objectives of the parties involved are met. This is done by the mutual exchanges and fulfillment of promises". (Payne Adrain, 1995)*

Few of the key elements which give a broader perspective of this new customer relationship marketing are:

- Interaction between suppliers and customers is moving from a transaction one to a relationship focused one.
- The relationship marketing emphasises on maximising the life time value of customer segments and on enhancing customer satisfaction.
- Relationship marketing is concerned with working, developing and enhancing relationships with *'internal'* markets within the organisation and building substantial *'external'* relationships with customers, suppliers, referral source, influence markets and recruitment markets.
- In the relationship marketing approach, the three closely related terms are — *Quality, Customer Service and Marketing.*

The relationship marketing concept suggests that as against the traditional, narrow, transactional, one-sale-at-a-time view of marketing, the new marketing concept focuses on relationships between the marketer and the customers more strongly.

Customers (Markets)

Customers will always remain the prime focus area for marketing. Under relationship marketing all the activities will be towards acquiring new customers but simultaneously, emphasis is more on building long term customer relationships.

A comparison on the specific characteristics included in the transaction marketing and relationship marketing are given here under:

DIFFERENCES BETWEEN TRANSACTION MARKETING AND RELATIONSHIP MARKETING	
Transaction Marketing	**Relationship Marketing**
• Focus on a single customer • Orientation on product features • Short -term sale • Less emphasis on customer service • Limited customer commitment • Moderate customer contact • Quality-Primarily a concern of production department	• Focus on customer retention • Orientation of customer values • Long term basis • High emphasis on customer service • Long term customer commitment • Regular customer contact • All are concerned with quality

The Liberalised Generation Consumer of Today

Consumer researchers have acknowledged that the Indian market has confounded their predictions about conventional wisdom and emerged with its own unique changes in the consumer buying behaviour. Some of the expected things did not occur, while many others not foretold are unfolding and visible today. Some of the important happenings are:

Consumer researchers have acknowledged that the Indian market has confounded their predictions about conventional wisdom and emerged with its own unique changes in the consumer buying behaviour.

- Unlike the assumption of *price-sensitive* consumers, Indians have emerged as *value sensitive* buyers *i.e.,* as long as a product or brand or service delivers value, they are willing to buy. *For example,* the increase in the number of Indian families travelling abroad on holiday.
- The fear that liberalisation would mean the arrival of *western cultural imperialism* was unfounded. Consumer trends 2006-07 study revealed that the Indian youth is strongly espousing on Indian values and attitudes. Even though there is a ready market for Valentine's Day cards and gifts, with even more guts and enthusiasm, is celebrated our traditional Indian festivals like Raksha Bandhan, Karva Chauth etc.
- In the past Indian consumers were very brand loyal and refused to change their brand. However, today no marketer can take brand loyalty for granted. The present generation is living in an atmosphere where the parental generation had designed the family unit in such a way that the former can live a better and more comfortable life than them. Moreover, this generation is willing to take risks and experiment with new ideas, products and new ways of doing things. Infact this type or these types of consumers are willing to go for *credit facilities* offered by various banks and other financial institutions. With the market being exploded by a number of brands in various product categories, there are many consumers willing to buy everything from a house and car to an appliance on credit.
- Post liberalisation has brought with it many socio-economic changes - more disposable income in the hands of consumers, increase in the number of educated and working women and rise in the number of nuclear families. This has affected the psyche of the consumer, who has become more indulgent with a greater focus on technology, willingness to go for credit purchases and aspiring for a global lifestyle. This has impacted their purchase decisions related to clothes, eating habits, travel and home appliances. In these categories, consumers are trying to optimise their spends between

the product categories and not necessarily between brands. All the consumers are interested in upgrading to the higher consumer class level. So a value seeker will try to upgrade to higher middle income class and higher middle income household will want to upgrade to and behave like rich consumers and trade up in some categories. For instance, *Fabindia and Hidesign* are two examples showing the emergence of mass-premium product offers.

➲ CAN ORGANISATIONS RETAIN CUSTOMERS THROUGH LOYALTY PROGRAMMES ?

In today's context, most of the loyalty programmes are offered in the form of points earned on each purchase, which can be redeemed later on against future purchases.

Organisations are spending a lot in trying to map how consumers go about deciding what to buy. As a part of this exercise, some have even launched loyalty programmes in an attempt to retain customers.

Loyalty programmes are essentially sophisticated marketing devices that seek to reward a *'loyal'* customer, *i.e.,* encouraging him or her, with incentives, to spend more on the same products in the future too. In today's context, most of the loyalty programmes are offered in the form of points earned for every purchase, which can be redeemed later on against future purchases. At times customers may be issued cards or granted membership to a lumpy club of players.

Various surveys have indicated loyalty programmes are not able to achieve what they set out to do *i.e.,* retain 'loyal' customers. This could probably be attributed to the fact most loyalty programmes attempt to accumulate buyer data for the organisation. The applicant, for membership to the programme, is required to furnish certain essential demographic data. By obtaining data on the customer's buying patterns, income levels and possessions, marketers hope to gain insights into what could be the likely needs required to be fulfilled in future. Or, at least get a rough outline of his mental mapping. Hence the studies concluded that loyalty programmes end up giving the consumer satisfaction, but are still far away from ensuring loyalty. Take for instance, *JetAirways* had communicated about its frequent flier programmes for its loyal *i.e.,* regular customers and expected an overwhelming response. But once the other low-cost carriers entered the market, many regular customers deserted the JetAirways preferring to fly the former. Another example would be related to credit card purchases. Most of the credit card holders are required to convert the points earned through purchases in order to avail the loyalty benefit and the annual walk would look like a stroll through the park.

The above tactics point to an insincerity on the part of the marketers. It looks as though the marketers are only keen to obtain data on consumers or ensuring immediate sales, even at the cost of sacrificing long term value. The customer may end with a feeling of not having gained anything. *For example,* cards issued by many retail outlets force customers to make purchases against their accumulated points within a stipulated time frame, making buyers feel that the retailers programme is only a subterfuge for short term expediency.

India has been acknowledged as an economy which is growing very fast. So in this developing scenario, when the market is flooded with domestic and global brands competing equally, marketers should go beyond loyalty programmes and work towards relationship marketing.

In a newly emerging economy like India, relationship marketing as a concept, is not new. The present scenario shows that growth rates in most of the product sectors are strongly positive, although there is still a lot of the population waiting to be tapped by aggressive marketers. Moreover, the penetration of goods and services on a per household basis or the per capita is slowly increasing. In spite of this, markets in India have remained fragmented and insular as is the case of rural markets, social, communal or ethnic and it is relationships which have helped in building up a customer base. Very often, when offerings from competing organisations are nearly at par in terms of quality and performance, it is the personal touch or an equation between a buyer and a seller which will tilt the scale in favour of the seller. This implies that in such a business scenario it is relationship marketing which can earn the goodwill of the consumers.

Working Towards Customer Retention

With stiff competition mounting up from domestic as well as global players, marketers are seeking newer and cost effective ways to retain their customer base. Tactical segmentation is one such technique adopted by marketers to identify customers who are likely to discontinue using or purchasing a company's products and services. Customer retention marketing is thus a tactically driven approach based on consumer behaviour and is a core activity carried out behind the scenes in relationship marketing.

The basic philosophy used by retention oriented marketer is that past and current behaviour is the best predictor of future customer behaviour.

The basic philosophy used by retention oriented marketer is that - past and current behaviour is the best predictor of future customer behaviour. Active customers are happy (retained) customers and they like to 'win'. They like to feel that they are in control and have made smart choices and feel good about their purchase behaviour. Marketers take advantage of this by using promotional offers (ranging from discounts and sweepstakes to loyalty programmes) and higher concept approaches such as thank you notes and birthday cards to make the consumer feel good.

FIGURE 13.1

THE PROCESS OF RETENTION MARKETING

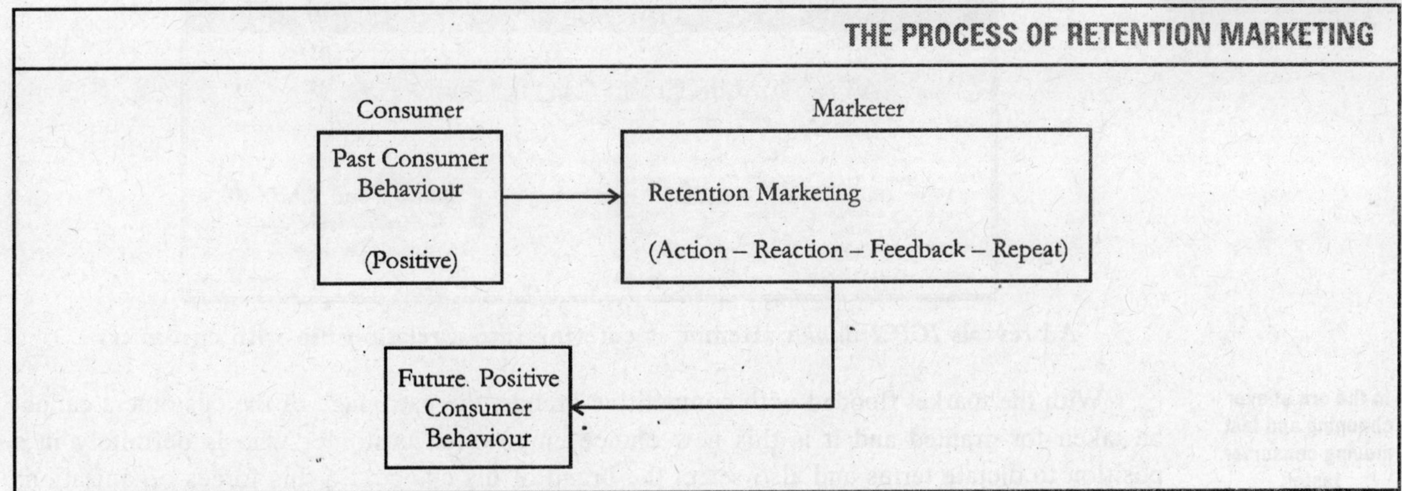

In retention marketing, the marketer is required to listen and *act* upon the customer data (which is often found to be highly evolved and a valuable conversation). It is very critical for the marketer to 'listen' to the customers opinions, reactions and feedback. It is the transaction data which will provide the correct feedback on the marketing actions. Based on this information, the marketer would go for a repeat of the marketing actions in order to generate better profits.

Thus retention marketing requires the marketer to develop a way to allocate resources to target and retain consumers in the most profitable way. This can be accomplished by using the data customers create through their interactions and transactions with the organisation, using simple models on analytics or rules which are easy to follow. Typically the organisation's listening system is data and the technique for informed decision making (Data Mining Analytics and Modelling).

Free for Life

ICICI Bank Credit Cards.
India's First Free for Life Credit Cards.
Because free is the way to be.

ICICI Bank
VISA

A Free for Life Credit Card for Every Indian.

ICICI Bank
Credit Cards

Ad reveals *ICICI Bank's* attempt at entering into a relationship with customers

In the era of ever changing and fast moving consumer tastes, organisations are developing flexible manufacturing and marketing systems in order to enable it to respond to the shifting requirements of the customers at the market place.

With the market flooded with competitive brands, the patronage of the customers cannot be taken for granted and it is this new choice empowered customer who is definitely in a position to dictate terms and also select the brand of his choice. So this forces organisations and marketers to respond and attend to the customers *i.e.,* talk to them, understand their overt needs, do psycho analysis to unveil their innermost desires and wants etc., and then use all the available resources to meet (or even surpass) them leading to customer retention.

In the era of ever changing and fast moving consumer tastes, organisations are developing flexible manufacturing and marketing systems in order to enable it to respond to shifting requirements of the customers at the market place. They are required to continuously update their understanding by anticipating and adjusting to the needs of the moving target. For instance, world automobile major such as *General Motors, Volkswagon* and *Honda*, had always focused on satisfying the needs of the top customer segments. However, realising the big market waiting to be tapped (small car segment) in an emerging market like India, have prompted them to work out marketing plans to serve this market's needs.

Even Toyota Kirloskar Motor (TKM) known for its successful *Innova* and *Qualis* (MUV) brands is of the opinion that the Indian market's character is that of a small car market. Says A. Toyoshima, CEO, Toyota Kirloskar Motors "In the Indian Market seven out of 1000 people drive a car today. Thus there is a huge potential to tap. Just having 1-2 years of difference in launching our small car doesn't matter. All that matters is that we offer an attractive product to the Indian consumers".

Re-engineering to Compete

In pursuit of its goal of *'customer focus'* organisations are trying to maintain a balance between quality (value) and cutting costs. They are going for process re-engineering by streamlining processes, and focusing on three vital elements — cost, quality and speed of implementation, to help it to add value to the customer.

Relationship marketing advocates very high customer contact and service and customer retention in order to build long term relations.

This is what *Timex India* had done so as to become the lowest cost operator among all other Timex operations worldwide. For instance. *Timex was* able to reduce the turnaround time for watch repairs to 96 hours from seven days to improve the dealers' perception of Timex quality.

During this process, the company discovered new ways of managing the processes that have boosted productivity. Simultaneously, *Timex* also resorted to random field-checks to gauge the consumers' perception of its performance. Then based on its feedback, Timex has built new competencies targeted at the customer by expanding its capabilities and getting into the commercial tool making and injection moulding business.

According to Ashoke Dutt, Ex-Director Consumer Banking, Citibank says "To *add value to the consumer, you have to offer him services on his term. Long ago, our research showed that people want to do banking at their convenience. That is why we created the 24 hour banking service"*.

Relationship marketing as we have discussed above advocates very high customer contact and service, and customer retention in order to build long term relations. When differentiation between brands ceases, there arises an increasing necessity for marketers to focus on intangibles over tangibles. Hence, the thrust or focus on quality and service related values is very necessary.

Interestingly, in the past, there was an assumption and perception that relationship marketing was best suited for the companies offering services. This was because only the service industry had felt it important to have long term relationship with their customers. But now even organisations selling products for mass consumption are feeling the pinch and the need to treat each customer as unique and also offer products which would suit his/her individual need. That is to say the concept of relationship marketing has come to stay in the Indian marketing environment.

Retaining Customers with the Help of 'Data Mining'

Data Mining is the art and science of extracting hidden patterns from accumulated data on consumers which helps in decision-making. Data Mining will provide insight into the consumer data which is collected. For the data mining initiative to be effective, there are three essential requisites

Date mining is the method of extracting hidden pattern from accumulated data on consumers which help in decision making.

- Domain expertise in the area of business
- Extensive knowledge of data mining tools, advanced statistics and modelling expertise.
- A data mining vision that includes willingness to commit time and other resources.

With passage of time the returns on investment in data mining should grow exponentially. For, insights obtained initially can be used to collect more relevant data, which in turn will provide more clarity. Data mining projects require putting in substantial initial effort in data preparation. Research has indicated that 75 percent of the total project time is spent in collecting the data. Thus organisations need to first develop a data mining vision and then develop a data warehousing solution in the context and background of the data mining vision. Some of the data mining techniques used by organisation's include:

Ultimately, the utility of the data mining techniques will be dependent on the ability of the decision makers to accurately interpret the information.

- ***Artificial neural networks*** - Non-linear predictive models which resemble biological neural networks in structure.
- ***Decision trees*** - Classification And Regression Trees (CART) and Chi Square Automatic Interaction Detection (CHAID).
- ***Genetic Algorithms*** - Optimisation techniques which use processes such as genetic combination, mutation and natural selection based on the concepts of evolution.
- ***Nearest neighbour method*** - A technique which classifies each record in a data set based on a combination of the classes of record(s). Most similar to it in a historical data set.
- ***Rule induction*** - Based on statistical significance, the 'useful-if-then' rules are extracted from the data.
- ***Analytics*** - Using analysis which will help the marketer to collect, condense and categorise information in a highly efficient manner.

Nevertheless, ultimately the utility of the above techniques will be dependent on the ability of the decision maker to accurately interpret the information.

The essence of CRM is that organisations are extending it to customer retention management wherein they build defences against competition and fluctuating customer loyalty. The CRM system begins with data collection - integrating and obtaining data from multiple sources (this is crucial to create one view of the customer) and do analysis of the data to segment customers and determine or predict important information such as:

- Who are the most valuable or potential customers?
- What is the current unmet need and what is the next most likely product to be bought by the potential customer?
- What is the optimal mix of offers the organisation should present to customers, keeping in mind the business constraints?

The CRM system must be able to present all the above information in a way that will enable the decision maker to make decisions quickly and easily.

Examples of the Practice of CRM

Ajay Aggarwal, CEO and MD Seacom solutions, Pune has given three perspectives on the practice of CRM.

(a) Managing or Controlling Out-of-stock Situations

Customer satisfaction surveys have indicated that many a time, customers complain about the non availability of merchandise of their expectations at the retail outlets. This could lead to losing customers to competitors. For instance, when *Subhiksha* outlets were opened in Mumbai, during the initial phase of the launch, many customers had to return without purchasing due to the non-availability of many products on the shelves. Subsequently, the situation was handled by re-engineering the end-to-end processes. In early 2009, due to severe finanical problems, Subhiksha had to close down most of its outlets in all the major cities.

Procter and Gamble (P&G), makers of brands such as Airtel, Pantene, Vicks etc., had successfully implemented the first phase of a solution which helped in reducing upto 50 percent of the inventory while delivering over 25 percent improvement in retail out-of-stock situations.

At the system level, the business process were reviewed to capture real time data at the point of sale. For this Microsoft Biz Talk Server 2000 adapters were connected to the various points of sale systems used by the stores. Biz Talk Server 2000 has the interpretability and integration required across a variety of retail platforms. Further, it can also manage the POS data feed as well as the customised retailer notification process. This programme has helped *P&G* strengthen systems to manage loyalty, shrinkage and loss prevention.

(b) Self-Service Kiosks

The new consumer trends indicate lack of time, desire for entertainment, purchase-choice linked with value and increased access to the e-technology via the internet and mobile phones. It also signifies that certain concepts such as self-service kiosks and self checkouts could prove to be beneficial to both-the customer as well as the marketer.

The new consumer trends indicate lack of time, desire for entertainment, purchase-choice linked with value and increased access to the e-technology via the internet and mobile phones.

For instance, in bookstore kiosks, customers are provided with an online catalogue service to identify titles and reviews before making a purchase decision. Established branded retailers (Reliance fresh, Foodworld, Indiatimes.com) have online kiosks for customers to place order for products which will be delivered at home or can be collected buy the customer later on. *Big-Bazaar* are using kiosks placed in other stores (tie-up) to take customer orders for their everybody shopping without entering their store.

(c) Loyalty Card Management

Organisations and marketers must try to make the best use of loyalty card management systems. Very often though they use this tool to create the desired loyalty, they are unable to deliver the value they promise through the card. They let go the opportunity to capture customer buying behaviour and use it to make their merchandise planning more customer oriented.

Seacom Solutions, Pune undertook an assignment for the Pantaloon group. In the first phase, it integrated and delivered a Dual Screen Module for its (Pantaloon's) POS tills. This module is able to :

- Give complete billing information to the customer, with itemwise details, loyalty points gained and so on.
- Indicate and display schemes and promotional events to the customer,
- Offers an additional source of revenue through display of vendor advertisements.
- Keep the customer entertained at the checkout counter.

In the *next phase*, Seacon reviewed Pantaloon's existing Green Card System and found that, it was not very customer friendly and there was no system to monitor customer loyalty across the group of chains. To handle this problem, the new server based system was provided to:

- facilitate online integration with the POS system, which gave an immediate credit of loyalty points to the customer.
- since all the stores in the country were connected online the customer could redeem loyalty points at any of their stores.
- stores could create their own schemes, events etc.; for loyalty card customers.
- instant upgradation of loyalty customers across all PRIL store formats.
- a facility to issue temporary cards to all walk-in customers and obtain their data.

In this way, when the system became fully operational and linked to the company's enterprise system, it was possible, to collect data (and information) on each buyer's buying habits.

The above examples indicate that while working out CRM strategies, the organisation much use the software, rich in customer related features including registering customer profits to handling loyalty cards.

Role of Customers in Relationship Marketing

Going by the above perspectives we can say that there has to be a new approach and way of looking at the customer while going for relationship marketing.

In the new scenario, unlike the conventional marketing which is based on one way communication method *i.e.*, segmentation and mass media tools, have to be supplemented by one-on-one communication methods.

1. Organisations instead of concentrating on keeping a track of the sales, would have to keep a check on customer desertion figures more minutely and also identify the causes for these desertions and then work out ways to prevent it from recurring.
2. A sale is never closed, rather the sale will become the starting point of a long term relationship. Unlike the transactional marketing, a customer is no longer considered to be a one time or even a multiple purchaser, he or she is referred to as someone who patronises the particular brand over an entire life time. This means that share of life time value and not market share will be the key performance indicator.
3. In the new sçenario, unlike the conventional marketing of one way communication method *i.e.,* segmentation and mass media tools have to be supplemented by one-on-one communication methods.

As shown in Figure 13.2, in relationship marketing the role of customers can take the shape of a pyramyd, moving from being a prospect to that of an ambassador.

FIGURE 13.2

ROLE OF CUSTOMERS IN RELATIONSHIP MARKETING

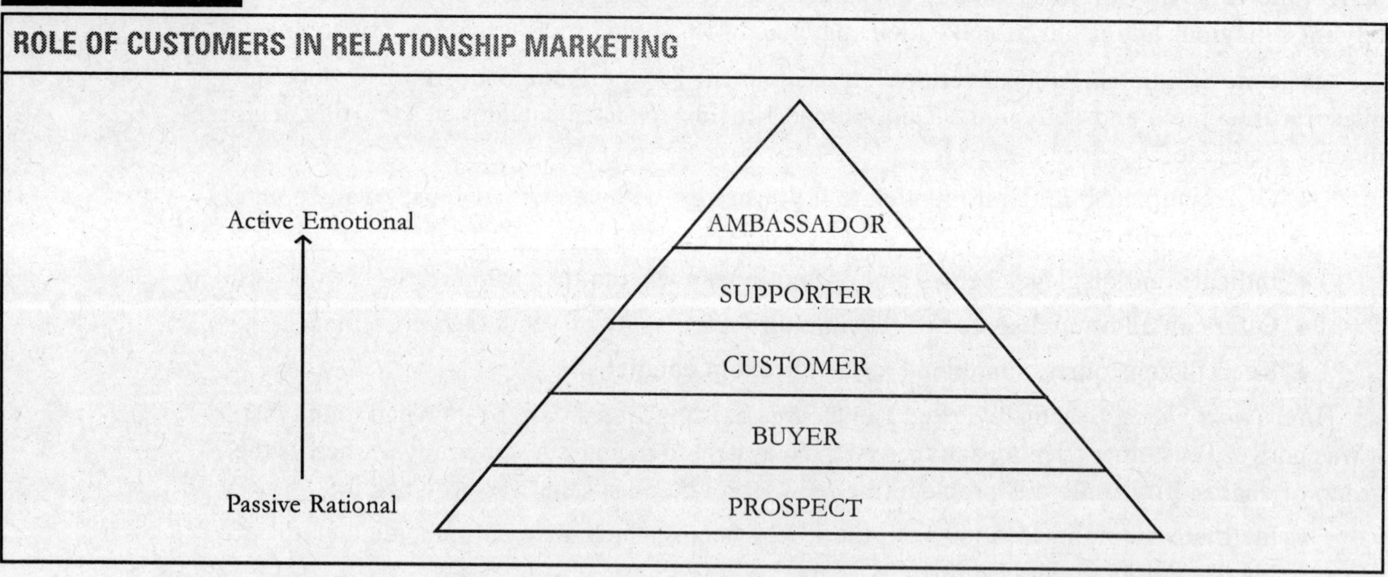

(Soure : *Advances in Relationship Marketing,* Adrain Payne, Kogan Page Ltd., London, 1995)

Various research studies have shown that companies lose roughly 15 per cent of their customers every year. This means that within three years, the company will be left with half the customers it started with. Of course, these customers will be replaced. But as competition increases it will become very expensive to do that. Studies indicate that in the US automobile industry, the penetration levels are substantial and the frequency of purchase is also on the higher side, yet it costs much more in getting a new customer than to motivate an existing customer to buy a new automobile. Likewise, other researches by US' Forum Corp. done across other industry categories show that there were chances that one in two of the existing customers would buy the product but in case of new customers, the possibility is that one out of sixteen prospective customers end up buying the product. This only reiterates the fact that relationship marketing is very much a part of the present market scenario.

In the present age of stiff competition, treating each customer as unique and offering products that would suit his or her needs will be the deciding factor for its success.

What exactly can relationship marketing do? *Relationship marketers leverage their data bases* to *convert potential buyers into customers and then build a long term alliance with them through a range of insightful, targeted programmes.* In the present age of stiff competition an organisation is known by its customers. So treating each customer as unique and offering products that would suit his or her needs will be the deciding factor for its success.

Ad of Bosch India claims to have loyal satisfied customers.

For instance, *Readers Digest* has for over the years been patronised by many customers. It has built up a reputation of a magazine which provides valuable information in a condensed and well presented manner to its delighted customers. Even today the magazine is primarily driven through subscription sale worldwide. It has already tested the market for 1:1 marketing. Now, it has moved up to market fiction and non fiction books, music albums on cassettes, CDs and CD ROMs. The magazine claims to have been successful in retaining two out of three subscribers every year.

Organisation tries to retain customer loyalty through promotional offerings.

Today when a reader has numerous options of having access to the kind of reading material that the Digest provides, its success cannot be attributed to the product quality alone. What has substantially contributed to its success is the intangible benefit of service quality. According to S. Sharad Sarin, Professor of Marketing, XLRI, Jamshedpur *"The ultimate test of relationship marketing is the ability of a marketer to retain a customer in a choice situation. It is here that the intangibles play a crucial role over the tangibles."*

Marico Ltd., had entered the health platform through its, *kaya* brand, with products ranging from sunscreens, cleaner, toner and so on. This kaya skin care products earned the company commercial success, it could breakeven in 2006 with an annual turnover of Rs. 75 crore. Riding high on the trust and success of the above products, Marico is further planning to extend its relationship with its consumers and expand into the health and wellness space with professional weight control centres under the kaya brand name. For this purpose, the Chairman and MD, Harsh Mariwala brought in retail lifestyle consultants from the UK to design a concept which looked at lifestyle counselling, weight loss, inch loss and body shaping, food planning and energising exercise, motivating and maintenance as a whole.

The design, right from colours to space was planned keeping in mind those customers who may not like exercising, diets etc. In the words of Mr. Mariwala "We have built a credible brand in *kaya skin care* and have learnt that beyond skin, people want to look good and be healthy. Lifestyles have changed a lot and a recent trend is obesity. About 40 percent of people in urban cities are obese and there is a great demand and potential for this business". These kaya life centres offer customised solutions for skin, hair and life and such offerings can help to tap more of the health conscious customers.

ICICI bank, has earned the reputation of a brand which is trusted worthy. The brand has been highly successful because of its USP statement "To provide customers the largest variety of products at affordable prices across a wide network of branches". Further, it also has better brand recall because of its USP, which is a culmination of multitude of information received and opinions formed by customers through exposure to advertising, competitors' claims and advertising, word-of-mouth, personal likes and dislikes etc. Thus ICICI's image of a technology savvy with wide spread network and reliable bank found it many loyal customers.

The above two examples of Kaya and ICICI Bank brands show that relationship marketing provides more scope of interaction between the marketer and the consumer by entering into a dialogue with them.

SIX MODEL MARKETS AND RELATIONSHIP MARKETING

Classical marketing has tended to focus on the means by which the individual or the organisation might be converted into a 'customer'. In the relationship marketing model the buyer may have bought the product for someone else but when he purchases the products and does business with the organisation once or occasionally he is referred to as a customer. Since he only does business occasionally, all efforts will be made to convert him to a 'supporter'. Once this is done, the strength of the relationship becomes apparent. These people now like to be associated with the organisation and can even be persuaded to become Ambassador's — in other words to actively recommend the firm and its products to others.

In the relationship marketing model, the buyer may have bought the product for someone else but when he purchases the products and does business with the organisation once or occasionally he is referred to as a customer.

Thus unlike transactional marketing, in relationship marketing, a wider view of the market is adopted. Rather than focusing only on the end user, concentration on a wider view of the markets would be more appropriate.

Adrian Payne in his "Advances in Relationship Marketing' has recommended a six markets model. The idea is that in order to build and sustain real customer value it is important to recognise that relationships must be built with a number of important constituencies. According to Adrian Payne and others the six markets model are :

- Internal markets.
- Referral markets.
- Influence markets.
- Employee markets.
- Supplier markets.
- Customer markets.

There has to be a direct relationship between well-designed service encounters, enhanced customer satisfaction and employee satisfaction.

Internal Markets : There are various definitions of internal marketing. However, the generally accepted view is that it is concerned with the creation of an internal culture and orientation which assists and supports the organisation in the achievement of its goals.

A very important and critical determinant of long-term success in relationship marketing is based on the development and sustenance of the customer-oriented culture within the organisation itself. An organisation's culture visible in its deep seated unwritten system of shared values and norms has a lot of effect on the employees, their behaviour and attitudes. According to *C. Webster "The culture of an organization in turn dictates its climate— the policies and practices which characterize the organization and reflect its cultural beliefs"*.

There has to be a direct relationship between well-designed service encounters, enhanced customer satisfaction and employee satisfaction. A satisfied employee is likely to be a retained employee. Organisations have realised that employees are not only a valuable and finite resource but can also be a potential source of competitive advantage. Employee retention is a very important aspect of the long term relationship with customers.

Very often customers are found to be more loyal to the employee who deals with them rather than to the wider organisation. It has been rightly said that despite having the best of the technology and the most carefully worked out procedures - the final test of relationship marketing will be dependent on the quality and willingness of the people who implement it.

Referral Markets : Such markets can be an effective source of new business. The best type of marketing referred markets is done for the firm by its own customers. This is the reason why the customer loyalty illustrated in figure 13.3 was suggested by Adrian Payne in his book 'Advances in Relationship marketing'.

FIGURE 13.3

THE RELATIONSHIP MARKETING LADDER OF CUSTOMER LOYALTY

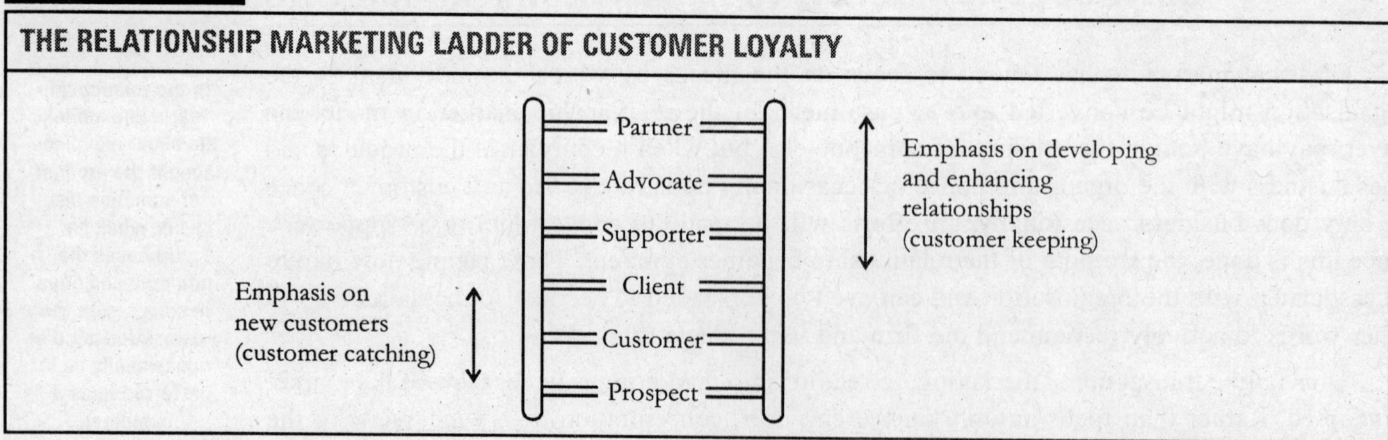

(*Source : Advances in Relationship Marketing,* Adrain Payne, Kogan Page Ltd., London, 1995)

From the customer loyalty ladder it can be seen that creation of advocates is very important for the organisation. It may be noted that existing customers are not the only sources of referral for there could be other groups who can refer business to organisations. Sometimes referral markets are also known by various names like intermediaries, connectors, multipliers, agencies and so on.

Referrals can also come from sources of professional advice such as doctors, lawyers, bank managers and accountants as well as the existing satisfied customers. Thus building relationships with these sources of word-of-mouth recommendation should be the integral part of the marketing strategy.

For instance we can illustrate this with an example of a bank. The referral sources for the bank will include insurance companies, real estate agents, accountancy and law firms as well as existing customers and internal referrals. The power of word-of mouth will be more prominently seen in this case. Satisfied customers can prove to be powerful advocates of a company's products or services. Since there may be many referral sources, it is possible to have a high leverage response in terms of new customers.

From the customer loyalty ladder it can be seen that creation of advocates is very important for the organisation. Successful organistions tend to have a good understanding and relationship with critical sources of influences relevant to their markets.

We can also take another example of McDonalds. Realising the rage for fast food which the present generation has and thus looking for convenience food, many fast food chains have set up outlets in India. These include *Nirula's Chain, McDonalds, Pizza Hut, Pizza Corner, Subway, KFC, Yol China* and *Bread & More*. Studies have indicated that this industry is growing at 40 percent annually and generating over a billion dollars in sales (till 2005). Each of the fast food chains have used innovative menus which convey a feeling of international and taste Indian to tickle Indian tastebuds. Says Vikram Bakshi, JV Partner of McDonald's India and MD of Connaught Plaza Restaurants "We have made our mistakes but we have constantly accepted and heeded-customer feedback. One such feedback we received was that the Indian consumer was looking for an international form with Indian taste". This led to the innovative offerings of Maharaja Mac., McAloo Tikka Burger, Veggie Taka Tak, Tandoori Paneer, Chutneywala Pizza and so forth.

But the challenge before these marketers is to maintain international quality standards. An incident highlighting how McDonald works hard to maintain its international image, was mentioned in 'The Gateway Magazine', March 2007. It was quoted that when a consumer found pieces of glass in an McAloo Tikka Burgur, McDonalds had a look at the entire supply chain to find its origin. It was soon discovered the glass piece had come from an employee's glass bangle which broke while working and happened to slip into the food. The bangles themselves had been hidden under the long sleeves of the employee's coat when she entered the plant. So McDonald's decided to ask their employees cut coat sleeves short in order to avoid a recurrence. In fact, the entire batch of food was stopped and flown back, resulting in incurring a loss of over Rs. 82 lakh for the company. Such gestures as above, have helped McDonalds to ensure customer satisfaction leading to brand loyalty in the long run. Further, these satisfied customers also provide the necessary referral and positive word-of-mouth.

Influence Markets : This market will comprise of entities, organisations and individuals who have the ability either positively or negatively to influence the marketing environment in which the company operates. The management of public relations —or public affairs has been viewed as a separate activity from the main stream of marketing. However, under the relationship marketing, parading the 'influence' or 'influence market' is seen as an integral component of the customer relationship building process. Successful organisations tend to have a good understanding and relationships with critical sources of influences relevant to their markets.

Influencers can come in many forms. The list of potential sources of influence could be - Government ministries or agencies, senior civil servants, the media, consultants and advisers, the stock markets etc. Organisations can either gain (benefit) or lose, from the influence that may be exerted from these sources. So as to manage public relations or public affairs effectively, many organisations have appointed' liaison officers.

Another way to influence markets is by providing a solution for consumer's concern even before the problem crops up.

Another way to influence markets is by providing a solution for consumer's concern even before the problem crops up. For instance, seeing the unprecedented growth in the number of mobile phone users, has enabled banks to transform mobile phones into an alternative channel for payments. Till recently, most transactions on the mobile would only give customers information on their bank accounts.

Some of the major banks are looking out for tie-ups with companies facilitating payments through the mobile phone. *SBI* and *ICICI Bank* have undertaken pilot projects to study mobile banking in association with *Airtel* and payments company *mChek*. *Standard Chartered Bank* and *HSBC bank* are also in the process of evaluating their mobile commerce options. *Citibank* has entered into a service partnership with Paymate, another mobile payments provider. To start with each bank will use its own payment-gateway. M-payments operate on a very simple mechanism globally. The details of the credit or debit card are stored in the user's phone, transactions are done via SMS.

So when a user wants to make payment using his mobile phone, he needs to share his mobile number with the merchant. Immediately he will receive an SMS (with the merchant's name and amount) asking him to authorise the payment. The customer can then confirm the alphanumeric code sent to him as well as the amount. Within a few seconds, the bank concerned will authenticate the details and debit the amount. Of course, the merchant will have to be a part of the system.

Realising that less than half of the mobile phone users have high-end handsets, organisations are trying to encrypt card details onto SIM cards, so as to target the users of entry level handsets. Those with sophisticated handsets can download a software to facilitate the process. One of the biggest benefits of using mobile phones apart from making small-value payments is that it reduces chances of credit card frauds as the card details are not shared with the merchants.

FIGURE 13.4

THE SIX MARKETS MODEL TO FACILITATE RELATIONSHIP MARKETING

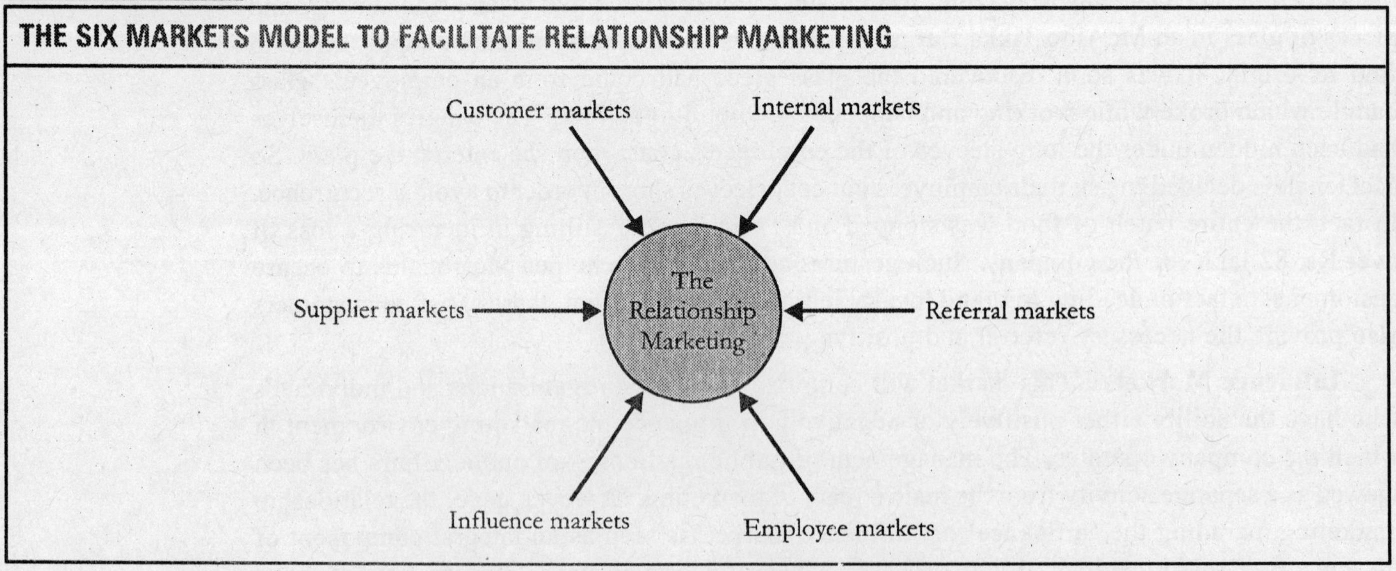

(*Source : Advances in Relationship Marketing,* Adrain Payne, Kogan Page Ltd., London, 1995)

Contactless Payment System : As with any technical devise usage, there is a fear of misuse or fraud. Contactless Payment System (CPS) is a fast emerging technology, which as the term itself indicates promises fast, easy and secure cashless transactions. CPS works on wireless automatic identification technology and comprises of a device with tiny chip antenna embedded in it, which communicates through radio frequency (RF). The device may encompass plastic cards, like credit cards, mobile phones, money clips, key fobs, watches etc. Radio Frequency Identification (RFID) enabled devices such as credit/debit card, key fob or cell phone or watch are activated and most commonly used for contactless transactions. Contactless card use the international standard ISO/IEC 14443 for contactless communications and are known to offer better security, which are relatively harder to duplicate in comparison to a magstripe payment card. Thus usage of CPS can help to improve customer experience and satisfaction.

In order to enhance competition, the company will need to service every link that constitutes each process into its value chain.

Employee Markets : Employee market is another focal point of relationship marketing. There is always an urgent need to recruit and retain employees who will further help in satisfying the aims of the company at the market place. This implies that the organisation should strive to create an attractive working environment so that each employee will be highly motivated and work towards customer satisfaction.

FIGURE 13.5

THE RELATIONSHIP MANAGEMENT CHAIN

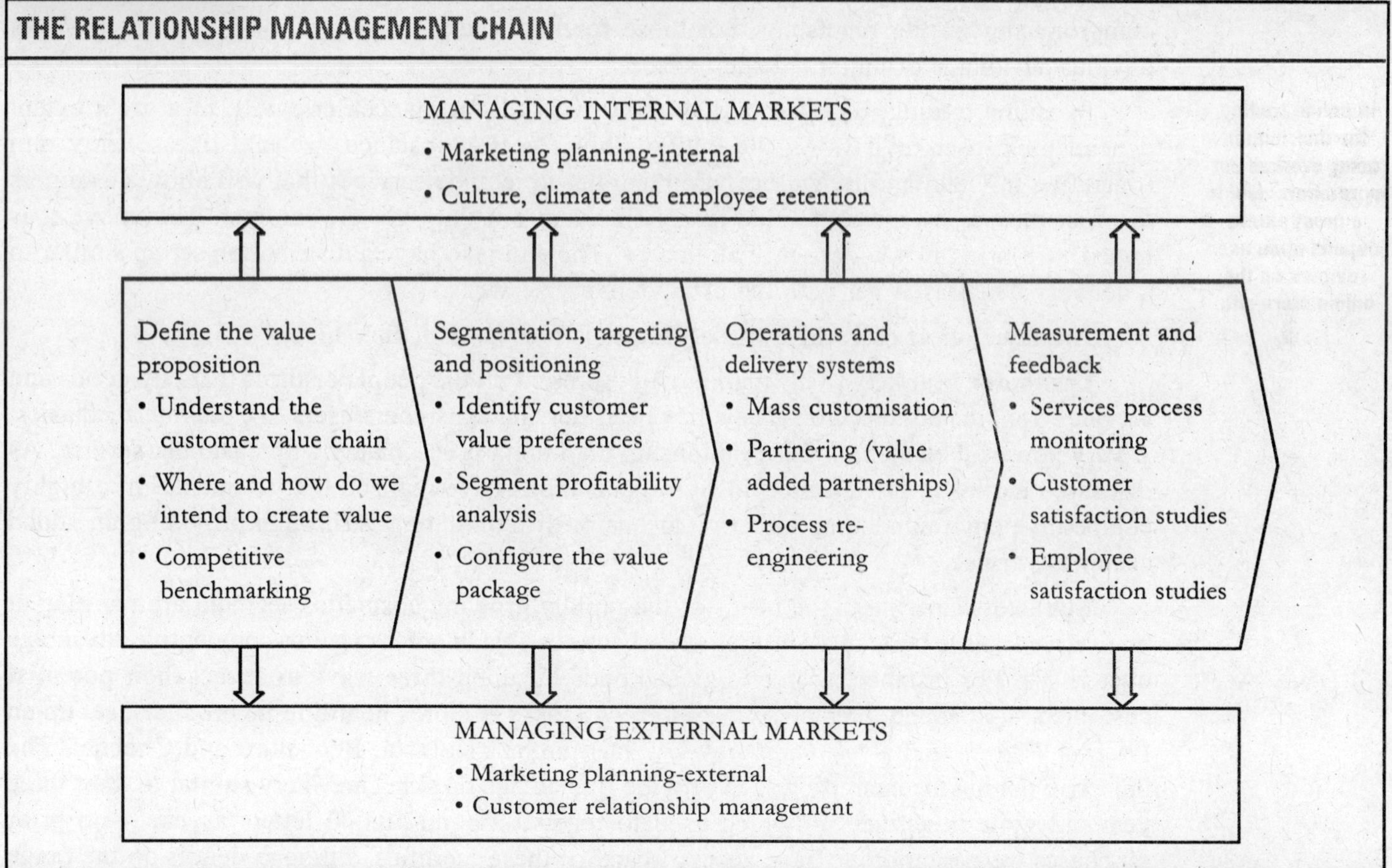

(*Source : Relationship Marketing for Competitive Advantage* - Adrain Payne, M. Christopher, M. Clark and H. Peck, Butterworth Heinemann, 1995)

In the words of Deepak Parikh (HDFC) *"Ultimately all the employees have to act as the trustees of our customers and depositors. To do that you need a level of motivation that comes from an empowered corporation"*.

In order to enhance competition, the company will need to service every link that constitutes each process into its value chain. This in turn will help it to create a strong internal customer value chain.

Supplier Markets : As the name suggests, this market refers to the network of suppliers, vendors or organisations which provide or supply the necessary materials, products or services to which the firm will add further customer value. It is necessary for companies to understand the importance of building closer, mutually beneficial relationships with their suppliers. Significant advantages can be gained by companies having close relationship with their suppliers—improved quality of materials/service, faster time-to-market, more innovative products and lower levels of inventory. This means when firms enter into a closer, mutually beneficial relationship with their suppliers, the result would be seen in the cost effective way of doing the business.

Renting movie DVDs or a cartoon series via the internet or mobile phone is gradually becoming popular trend today. Of the 42 million and more PC users in India, nearly 80 percent own an internet connection, indicating that there is a lucrative market for online video rental stores. Professionals, who are active members of online video rental stores feel that such services help them to spend weekends peacefully, away from the hustle bustle of the crowds without compromising on the fun factor. For those running music shops *i.e.*, online stores have an obvious advantage of unlimited shelf space.

In online trading, the distribution being worked out by retailers, will to a great extent depend upon user reviews on the online store site.

In online trading, the distribution being worked out by retailers, will, to a great extent depend upon user reviews on the online store site. For instance, website like seventy mm (operating in Delhi and Bengaluru) are planning to include services that will allow customers to order movies by messages through phones and not only via the internet. This move it is hoped, will bring in a wider set of audiences. The aim is to have a distribution set up similar to a delivery which is at par with the pizza delivery services.

A unique effort of CRM by Tata Motors is presented in Box 13.1.

Customer Markets : This market will represent all the people or firms that buy goods and services from the organisation. They may be either end consumers/users or even intermediaries. A very powerful element in this relationship marketing is associated with customer service. As discussed earlier in this chapter, today organisations have realised that to operate in a highly competitive environment, an effective means of differentiating is through providing an added customer service.

Marketers catering to the needs of the rapidly growing cosmetics segment are working at innovative ways to build relationships as early as possible in order to gain a competitive advantage over rivals. For instance, cosmetic giant Ponds hit upon three ways to attract their potential customers:— it added interactive *torch-screen* kiosks at stores hoarding its products, set up an *Internet Website* and a *telephone helpline* in Mumbai, Kolkata, Bengaluru and Chennai. The objective behind the exercise was to provide free advice on skin care. Very similar to their three year old write-in service — which used to receive around 50,000 letters a year —no prior purchases were required to have access to any of these facilities, although details on the range of Pond's products were available for those who were interested. Likewise, global hair colour manufacturer *L'Oreal* also set up a consumer advisory cell in Mumbai in April 1998, together with a write-in service and telephone helpline.

BOX 13.1

WORLD'S LARGEST CRM SYSTEM CONNECTS 1200 TATA DEALERS & 25K BUYERS

Networking helps Tata Motors improve efficiency, to woo buyers

When Tata Motors suffered a record loss of nearly Rs. 500 crore in 2000, it searched for ways to become *a* more efficient operation. An online customer relationship management system and a dealer management system were among the ideas that came up, and the first took off in 2003. Recently, Tata Motors connected the 1,000th dealer to its online integrated Customer Relationship Management-Dealer Management System (CRM-DMS). This milestone, coupled with the monitoring of the service to more than 25,000 customers, makes it the largest implementation of a CRM program in the automobile industry anywhere in the world, according to Siebel and Tata Motors.

Says Shyam Mani, Vice-President for sales and marketing at Tata Motors, "We were clear that we would drive CRM more as a tool, and the primary benefit had to come to customers." But that wasn't the way CRM was envisaged worldwide by the auto industry. When the CRM-DMS was first mooted in 2002, KR Sreenivasan, the project head, found virtually no global precedent. He says, "Globally, CRM was largely restricted to lead management,' or follow-ups to enquiries for purchasing a vehicle." Tata Motor show has nearly, 200 dealers connected online, and will scale this up to 1,600 in a few months. At the dealer level, Tata Motors monitors both finances and inventory, and at the customer level, it monitors services, spares, replacements etc.

Tata Motors has derived some clear benefits from this initiative. Mr Mani says customers like the online solutions to their needs and are quite happy with the service levels they receive at workshops. SM Bafna, Chairman of Bafna Motors, and the first dealer to hook up to Tata Motors' system, says: "We think that nearly 65-70% of our existing customers come back, either to replace their old vehicles or to buy new ones."

Since all dealers and factories are on the same platform, the inventory costs get reduced significantly, for both dealers and company. For both company and dealer, time lost due to such non-availability is a loss of revenue, albeit national. For Mr. Bafna, cutting down inventory means there is less money and resources tied down to it. Moreover, the turnaround time for trucks has reduced from 6 hours to just two, since monitoring has become better.

For Tata Motors, it also provides rich data by region and by brand instantly, rather than at the end of a month or a quarter. On-ground activation, coupled with analytics and information about the competition has worked out to be far cheaper than advertising - for a few thousand Rupees, Tata Motors could potentially reach target their customer, according to Mr. Mani.

(*Source : The Economic Times*, Bangalore, 1 September 2007)

Marketers are also trying to make their value chains competitive by creating distribution equity and then enhancing it. *Hindustan Lever Ltd.* has more than 300 differently packaged products each called a stock keeping unit (SKU). So as to keep track of the SKUs the company makes use of the infotech. And this facility is extended to its complete distribution network. Their distribution value chain comprising of — the carry and forward (C & F) agents, the redistribution stockists (RDSS) the stockists and the retailers—are electronically linked to the company's headquarters and to each other via V-SATS. Over and above, along with increasing its depots to ensure good distribution management, it has a fluid stocking system that is fleet footed enough to be responsive to the customer.

Along with increasing competition there has been an increase in consumer expectations for personalised service, making it imperative for organisations to focus on relationship management and customised solutions not only to sustain but also grow their customer base.

Along with increasing competition there has been an increase in consumer expectations for personalised service, making it imperative for organisations to focus on relationship management and customised solutions, not only to sustain but also grow their customer base.

THE RELATIONSHIP MANAGEMENT CHAIN

The term *relationship chain* is used to describe the basic proposition for all organisations — to create, and sustain mutually advantageous relationships *throughout the chain* , culminating in customer value enhancement.

The critical issues mentioned in the relationship management chain are:

Defining the Value Proposition : Simply stated, value can be said to represent the perceived benefits that customers believe they will receive from the consumption of a product or service. The customer value can be measured in terms of the impact of the supplier's offer on the customer's own value chain. In case the offer will result in enhanced performance, or increased perceived benefits or lower customer costs, then from the customer's perspective there is a clear value addition.

Identifying Appropriate Customer Value Segments : In order to meet the customer value requirements and different perceptions between customers the marketer will have to go for market segmentation. According to Christopher ("Relationship for Competitive Advantage"), "In depth customer research will help to reveal the silent dimensions of value and through the use of techniques such as *trade-off* analysis, it will be easy to identify groups of customers who share common value preferences". This means segmentation can be done on the basis of grouping of customers sharing common value preferences. It is likely that for segmenting one may have to cut across the more traditional basis for segmentation such as demographic or socioeconomic variables. Nevertheless, one cannot deny the fact that segmentation by such variables helps the organisation to work out marketing strategies based around enhancing relevant customer values which are more likely to succeed.

In order to take care of the differences in the profitability from different type of customers, organisations will have to go for successful value based marketing strategies.

Delivery system goes beyond the physical delivery of product or presentation of services. Employee satisfaction and customer satisfaction should form an integral part of the management of the service delivery process.

Designing Value Delivery Systems : The term *'value delivered"* to customers in itself conveys that it is going to contribute towards building relationships. Simply stated, delivery system goes beyond the physical delivery of products or presentation of services. It will include the marketing channels employed, the flexibility of response, the linking of buyer/supplier logistics and information systems and so on. The increasing fragmentation of the market place in many industries, has led to customers demanding a variety of goods and services and hence the need to engineer more flexibility into the delivery systems.

Now the primary focus of the organisations will be to deliver customer value. This has led them to recognise the need for re-engineering processes and other methods to be able to enhance the cost-effectiveness of the value delivery process.

Managing and Maintaining Delivered Satisfaction : Today it has come to be widely accepted that just as the quality of physical products is dependent on the control of the process that manufactures them, similarly the quality of customer service will be determined by the extent to which the delivery process is under control. There should be a continuous monitoring of the entire service process so as to identify and control the potential *'fail points'*. Such methodologies will make the difference between customer satisfaction and customer disappointment in the service process.

It must be noted that employee satisfaction and customer satisfaction should form an integral part of the management of the service delivery process. It is necessary to view the process of relationship building as a cross functional process and to bring together all the previously dispersed activities.

Another related and distinguishing feature is the management of internal and external markets parallel to the relationship management chain on an integrative basis. Internal markets will comprise of the people who work within the organisation and whose attitudes and motivation will have a direct or indirect impact upon customer relationships. External markets will include

Organisation's attempt at relationship marketing.

not only the final customers market but also the suppliers, referral sources, influencers and the recruitment market. So an integrated approach to marketing and human resources management is required because the final analysis of relationship marketing will be dependent on the quality and willingness of the people who implement it.

Creation of Customer Value

What does one understand by the term *'customer value'?* This term can be addressed from the customer's perspective as well as from the organisation's perspective. *From the customer's perspective*, 'value' can be understood as that what the consumer is willing to pay *i.e.,* the perceived value by the customer in an offer. In other words, it will be the value that the customer perceives as being relevant (or superior) and hence willing to pay for the purchase and consumption of the products/services.

From an organisation's perspective, customer value can be understood as the value of a single customer to the organisation's profit and market share *i.e.,* the customer's life time value. Research has shown that organisation's need to focus on enhancing the life of a customer as they (firms) gain more through their retained customers. This can be attributed to the 80 : 20 rule. This means that 20 percent customers generate 80 percent of profits. Generally, organisations will try to enhance the life of these 20 percent customers through different value maximisation strategies. Consumer researcher Morris Holbrook, has suggested a framework to understand two terms — 'value' and 'values'.

Value — value refers to preferential judgement.

Values — values refers to the decision criteria that shapes this preference.

For instance, when the housewife selects a brand of washing machine, she is communicating that this brand is more valuable than others. Marketers are interested in knowing what made her choose that brand. Research suggests the following factors which can influence a consumer's perception of 'values' and thereby his or her purchase decision.

- ***Personal :*** 'Personal' will be something specific to the individual which can trigger the 'want'. *For example,* the customer's demographics and lifestyle can play a significant role in determining customer values.
- ***Esteem Value :*** A significant factor which can influence customer's purchase decisions is its (product or service) esteem value. For instance, luxury products or premium priced products are often bought to enhance the esteem of the buyer. It may be noted that typically esteemed value is attached to all those products which are perceived as aspirational by the target market.
- ***Utility Value :*** The utility of a product will lie at the core of its purchase proposition. For instance, the young generation cannot do without a mobile phone with the latest fancy features. Whereas, for persons who are in the 45 plus age group, a mobile phone will serve a primary utility - a means of communication when there is a urgent need to do so.
- ***Social :*** Many a times, it is the customer's social needs which drives him or her to buy the product. During such instances, the primary value of the product will be social. Marketers of products which require social acknowledgment or admiration such as purchase of an apartment (with attractive neighbourhood) or jewellery involve affiliation, acceptance by peer (and neighbours), opinion leadership, friendship etc. These are some important social motives which direct a customer to a brand or service.

From an organisations's perspective, customer value can be understood as the value of a single customer to it's profit and market share i.e. the customer's life time value.

Customer's social needs may drive her to purchase jewellery

- ***Price :*** The price tag on the product is an indicator of its value. *For example, 'Big Bazaar or Food Bazaar'* attract customers who value low price and product quality, while those customers seeking exclusivity or designer wear will prefer to visit show rooms of *Allen Solley, Globus, Westside* etc.

  In case of price sensitive market segments researchers have established a relationship between price, perceived quality and perceived value. *i.e.,* the so called 'trade-off' concept used in marketing. It says that invariably, customers make a trade-off between price and quality and purchase the brand which maximises value at a given price level.

- ***Quality*** *:* Quality, just like price and utility is an important core value in the customers decision making process. It must be noted that for the customer it is his or her perception of quality which will influence the decision.

It is possible to understand customer value by examining a purchase situation as an experience.

It is possible to understand customer value by examining a purchase situation as an experience For this three key situations have to be examined:

(a) Value in Purchase : Value in purchase will be examined by having a look at the convenience in buying, experience in the store and with the sales personnel, payment options, delivery at the point at which it is desired by the customer and even the comfort with technology in today's market scenario. For instance, when making online purchases the customer is concerned about the security with the payment terms and disclosing information about his or her credit card or debit card.

(b) Value in Consumption : *Value in consumption* is a goal that is served directly through product consumption. It has got a functional outcome and value is measured in terms of the consumer's experience *post consumption*. In fact Joseph Pine II and James H. Gilmore (Harvard Business School Press) have in their work, *The Experience Economy*, concluded that companies need to focus on customer's experience with their products and services. They have opined that today competition is viewed on the basis of the consumption experience rather than the tangible product features or intangibles like services alone. More than acquisition of services, customers today pay for experience. For, the more encouraging (or positive) and rewarding an experience is, higher will be the price he or she is willing to pay. The popularity of the fast food chains such as *McDonalds, Cafe Coffee Day, Starbucks* etc., is a proof of how these outlets focus on maximising the target customer's total experience.

For the organisation, the value of a customer can be known by working out the cost of acquiring the customer. This can be done by analysing the buying patterns of both new as well as existing customers.

Marketer's aim is to create customer value through innovations, service, convenience in product acquisition and use, brand imagery and value for money propositions.

'Ad tries to build up customer value and relationship marketing'

Norman and Ramirez (Harvard Business Review) have proposed the concept of *Customer's Value Chain* - as a customer's activity cycle, relationship management chain and as a constellation of values which the customer buys. From this study they concluded that the focus has to be on a value creating system itself within which all economic factors (suppliers, business partners, allies and customers) jointly work to coproduce value.

Literature available on contemporary marketing has indicated that brands are a set of values for which the consumer is willing to pay.

So, the marketers aim is to create value through innovation, service, convenience in product acquisition and use, brand imagery and value for money propositions.

In this way, the value maximisation trial strategy can be worked out involving a value-based price, product quality and service quality as the three interdependent ends.

FIGURE 13.6

THE VALUE MAXIMISATION TRIAL

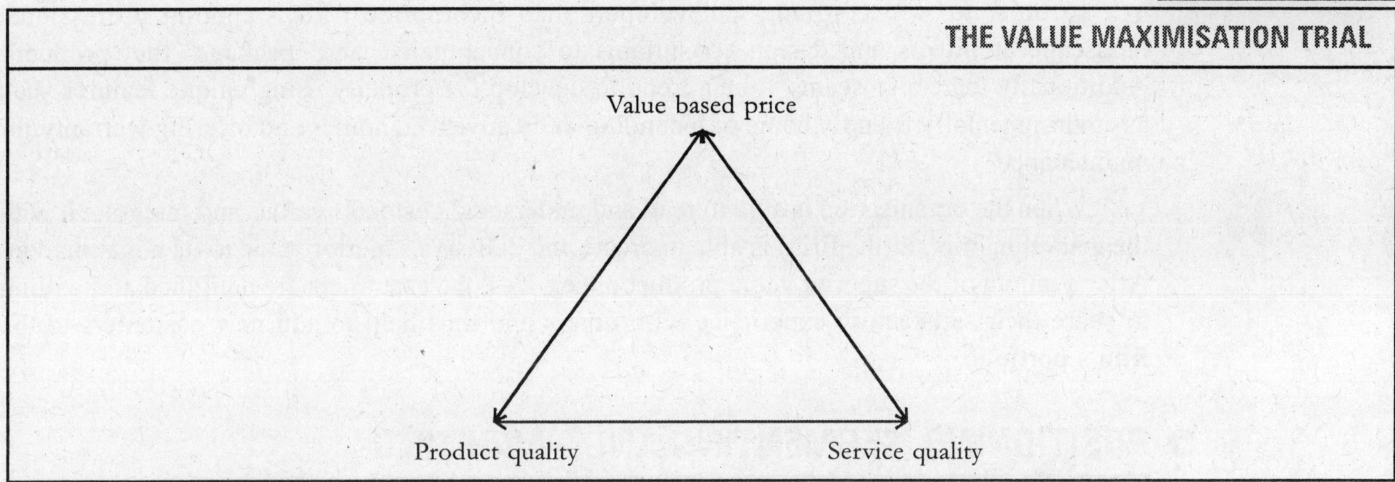

Every movement or development on the technology front or competition can affect the customer value paradigms. Therefore it is necessary for the organisation to monitor all the developments and innovate it's product and service offerings in order to retain the customer, on a continuous basis. Of course, in order to deliver this value and build relationships, all the key partners (mentioned earlier in the chapter) need to work jointly. These key partners who can work towards building relationships with customers are:

- Supplier markets
- Referrel markets
- Manpower suppliers
- Influencers such as financial and investor groups, regulatory bodies, media, interest groups
- Customer markets

Since each of the above markets are interrelated relationship with customers can be strengthened only if all of them work together.

The customer will display brand or product loyalty only if they believe the suppliers and perceive them to be fair, transparent, trust worthy and equitable in their relationship with them.

(c) Customer Value and Loyalty : Ultimately, every organisation is interested in creating a base of trustworthy, loyal customers. Customer relationship works on the premise of trust. The customer will display brand or product loyalty only if they believe the suppliers and perceive them to be fair, transparent, trustworthy and equitable in their relationship with them. In the long run it will be the loyal customers who will be the engine drivers of growth.

Today nuclear family set up has made customers bolder in their decision making and unlike the earlier generations, they are open to buying things on credit. Further, price is a low barrier and the consumers also have access to more options, even when it comes to finance. Says well known builder, Niranjan Hiranandani, MD, *Hiranandani Constructions*. "Earlier people's tendency was to save, but now its a credit card economy". Consumers have the option of home improvement loans, which can be taken to facilitate internal and external repairs, essentially anything considered a value addition. The average size of home improvement loans is Rs. 2 lakh which is quite sufficient to enable the customer to make purchases at a home speciality store.

In order to motivate and attract more customers, builders are offering something extra to their customers. They are offering some value additions as differentiators. These amenities include swimming pools, go-karting, schools, shopping malls, hospitals, etc., within the residential complex apart from marble flooring and modular kitchens.

In order to woo consumers, developers also incorporate frills - appoint professional landscape architects and design consultants to conceptualise and 'package' the 'product'. Additionally there also seems to be a trend to develop the property using unique features such as environmentally friendly home or technologically advanced homes and offering warranty for maintenance.

When the organisation is able to read and understand customer values and integrate it with the marketing mix, it (the firm) is able to create and deliver a superior value to its target market. After availing of the superior value product or services, the customers are delighted and willing to share their satisfactory experience with others and thus help to add new customers to the firm's portfolio.

➲ POSITIONING, SEGMENTING AND TARGETING

With intense competition taking place organisations are working out interactive marketing methods to woo the ultimate consumer. This is done in the form of three steps - segmentation, targeting and positioning.

With intense competition taking place organisations are working out interactive marketing methods to woo the ultimate consumer.

- ***Segmentation :*** Identify a set pattern of buying behaviour among the consumers and segment the market accordingly.
- ***Targeting :*** Use the database of the existing customers, whereby their profiles are analysed to correlate the demographic features along with their buying pattern - which can help to develop and target a customer value added focussed strategy.
- ***Positioning :*** This is concerned with differentiation (based on subjective criteria like image and communication or objective criteria (the marketing mix elements or in terms of nature, style and quality of relationship also) and use all this information to advantageously fit the organisation and its products and services to a market segment.

To quote a few examples where the firms tried to position their product and services differently when compared to other marketers.

- A well known Indian concern *Birla Super Shoppes* (sells cement) had differentiated itself from its competitors by offering free consultancy to various levels of cement buyers such as masons, civil engineers, contractors, architects, etc. At *each Super Shoppe* outlet a civil engineer and a task force to assist him are available. If the need arises, they may even visit the customer site to give a demonstration or solve a particular problem. Added to this, to 'cement' the relationship 'masons meets' were also organised, where users are invited and given further technical information, knowledge etc., The outcome — each Shopper started doing much more (almost double) business than before.

FIGURE 13.7

THE ROLE OF SEGMENTATION, TARGETING AND POSITIONING IN THE RELATIONSHIP MARKETING CHAIN

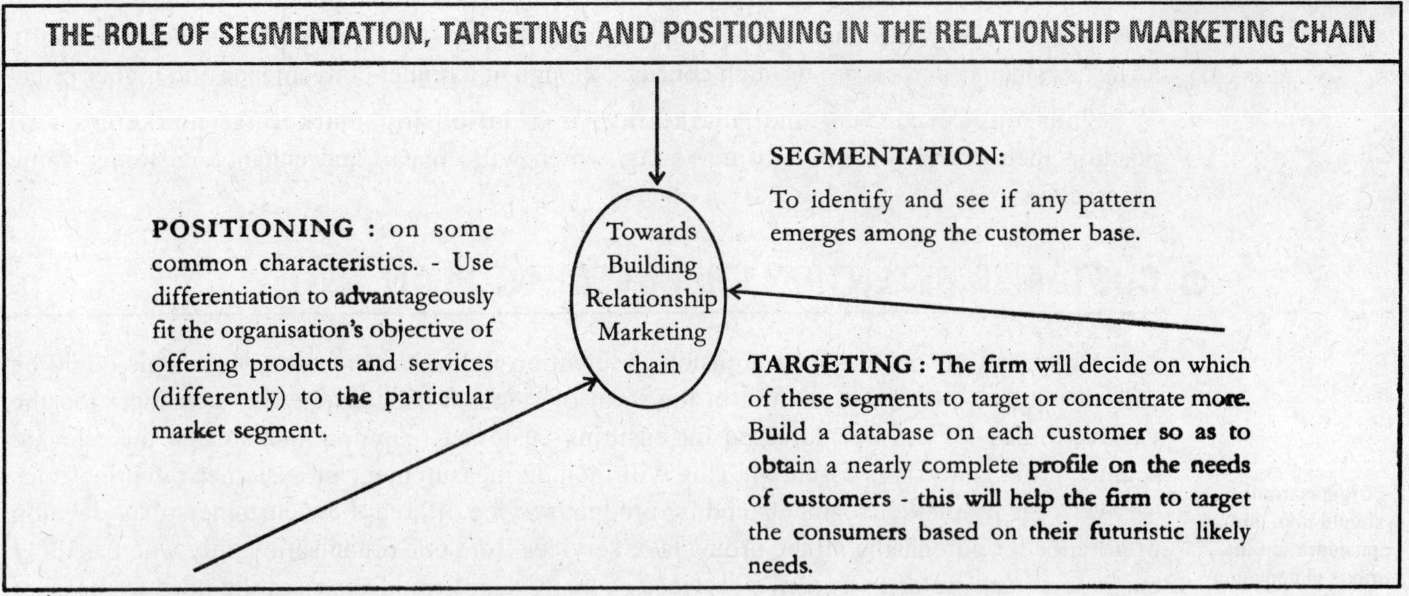

- Another organisation which many years ago made relationship marketing a smart marketing tool is *'Apollo Tyres'*. On the basis of a detailed research, Apollo discovered that the life time value of a truck owner in India (there were approximately 1,50,000 truck owners then, each owning seven trucks on an average) was Rs. 1.68 crore. Hence, it was felt that it is very important for the organisations to communicate with truck owners in a personal and intense way. So Apollo designed a programme on how to retain their customers with the help of HTA direct.

Apollo launched a privilege card for its customers through its 100 exclusive dealers. On the purchase of every tyre, a customer collects certain points on his card. These points can be redeemed for various rewards - ranging from a music system to a trip to New York. This programme runs in the same line like the frequent flier programmes of the various airlines. The objective of this scheme/programme was to buitlt long term relationship with the identified Apollo customer.

Unlike conventional marketing, in relationship marketing, marketers will position their brands on a totally new axis, which will appeal and enhance customer value satisfaction.

Having realised that it would need a separate cell to monitor and run its marketing relationship programme, Apollo created a separate 'Apollo Membership Centre (AMC), which was manned by a 23 - member full time team. In the words of the then Apollo Chief G. Udayan Dravid (Corporate Strategy Organisational Development), "With the help of such cells you can track your sales and even find out when the brand switch happens" For instance, if an average truck requires at least eight tyres in a year, and an AMC member does not return to buy new tyres in the given period of time, there is *a* possibility that he's bought another brand. If that happens, *Apollo* immediately gets in touch with the customer and tries to understand the reasons for his having switched brands.

Organisations also try to position their product or service such as to provide distinctive value to the customer. The courier company *DHL's* research team had identified a segment of customers who comprised of exporters, wanting to send samples of their products (usually very big and large) through courier quickly to their prospective customers in foreign markets. Here speed played a very crucial role for the customer. Especially in the world market, a delay in delivering the parcel could result in losing customers to competitors. Sensing this business opportunity, DHL decided to extend it's services to this new segment by charging extra for the bigger packages. They felt that customers wouldn't mind paying more for, the extra value would justify a premium price on the existing prices. The company then positioned its *brand Jumbo Box* —a services enabling packages of upto 25 Kg , which could be delivered virtually as fast as smaller parcels are through couriers, though at a higher convenience and higher price.

Thus unlike conventional marketing, in relationship marketing, marketers will position their brands on a totally new axis, which will appeal, and enhance customer value satisfaction.

➲ CUSTOMER RETENTION IMPROVEMENT PLAN

Organisations should take into consideration the various dimensions to be addressed for ensuring customer retention and for that the relevant segmentation analysis is essential.

Organisations could go for a customer retention improvement framework. This could be carried out as a particular process in the form of steps. It should take into consideration the various dimensions to be addressed for ensuring customer retention and for that the relevant segmentation analysis is essential. This will include measurement of customer retention rates — over time by market segments and by product/service offered. Few customers may develop preference for purchasing all the products or services from one organisation only whereas other customers may prefer to avail the services of many suppliers. Thus rises the need to measure and weigh customers by the amount they spend. Or else high customer retention rates can hide a serious problem. For instance, various banks may claim to have a high level of customer retention. But in reality, this may not be so. This is because customers may have defected to other banks but not closed their accounts with the previous bank. So this could amount to high level of account dormancy.

(a) Segment Profitability Analysis

The first step requires to undertake a segmentwise profitability analysis. This is because some customers may actually be too costly to serve whereas the returns may not be worthwhile and profitable. Thus investment in such customers may seem to be undesirable.

It is necessary on the part of the organisation to do a profitability analysis and identify and retain the customers from whom they are likely to earn most profitable returns. This method can also be used to identify the type and frequency of the marketing activity which have to be directed at the different market segments.

(b) Identify Causes of Defection and Key Service Issues

The second step involves identifying the underlying causes of customer defection. Four analytical approaches can be used for this purpose - root cause of defection analysis, trade off analysis, competitive bench marking and complaints analysis.

Identify Root Causes of Defection : Organisations can seek help of specially trained researchers who may be able to probe in detail and ascertain the reasons behind customers' deflection. The questionnaire should be framed such that it will help them identify the underlying causes for the customers switching their loyalty to another brand. For instance, a customer may say that she no longer patronises a particular retail outlet because of the high prices quoted there. However, the root cause may be unhelpful sales staff, products not displayed properly, non availability of all the products and so on.

Trade off Analysis : It is also important to undertake research to identify the key issues which have retained customers. This can be done through a trade-off analysis. Such an exercise enables the organisation to evaluate the implicit importance customers attach to the various and specific aspects of customer service. For instance, many of the financial institutions such as HDFC Bank, *HSBC bank* etc. have a large database and customer retention because of specific elements like helpful staff, convenience time facility and so on.

FIGURE 13.8

THE STEPS INVOLVED IN CUSTOMER RETENTION IMPROVEMENT

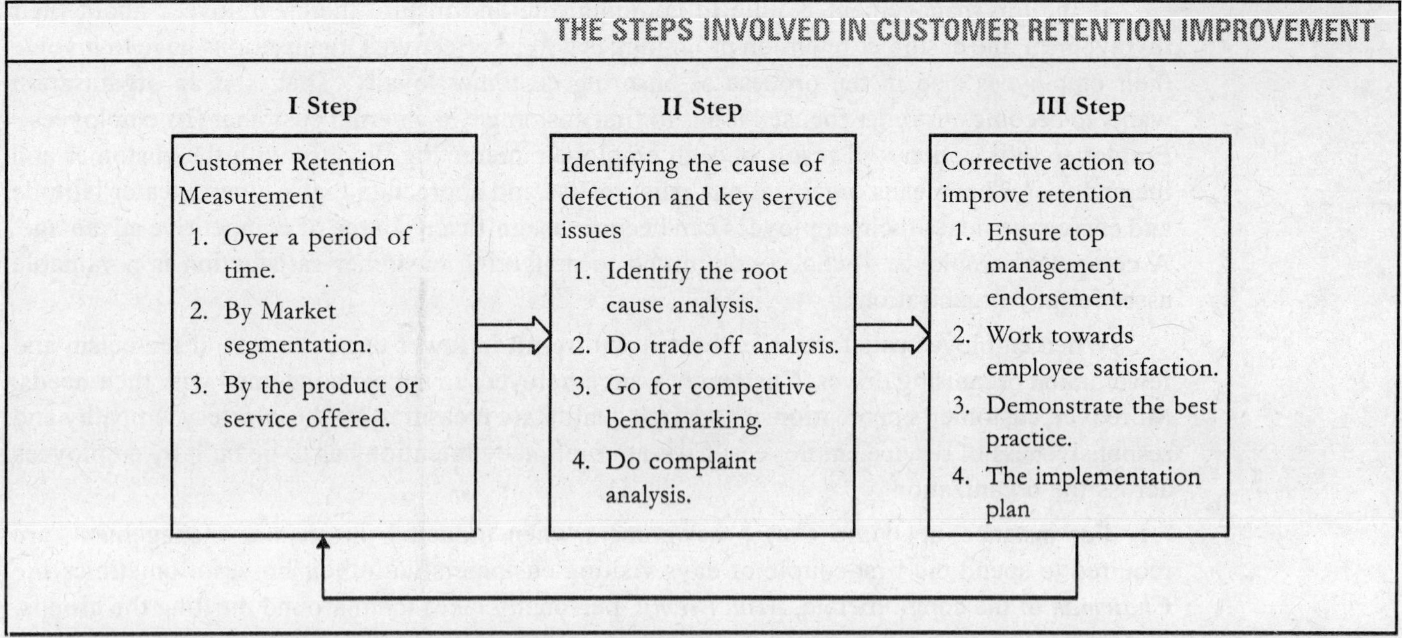

Competitive Benchmarking : Competitive benchmarking will help organisations to rate their performance with that of the competitors on certain vital elements of customer service and in the order of their perceived importance. Through this it would be possible to establish standards for the service to be offered to customers. Some of the aspects which need to be probed could be: Ideally for how long should the customer be left waiting in a queue? What is the level of product knowledge which employees are expected to have while serving customers? Are there any additional services being provided to customers and so on.

Competitive benchmarking will help organisations to rate their performance with that of the competitors on certain vital elements of customer service and in the order of their perceived importance.

Customer Complaint Analysis : Another very important aspect is to identify the key issues leading to customer complaints. This will not only help organisations to identify the causes of customer deflection but also act as an early warning system for the organisation and enable them to resolve a problem with the customer before it becomes too late. Simply said, such analysis will be beneficial to the organisation to identify the real causes of complaint and rectify it before they become too costly errors.

(c) Corrective Action to Improve Retention

The third and final step is concerned with taking the necessary corrective action so as to improve customer loyalty. The whole exercise involved in the customer retention programmes is evolved around the concerned organisation. The organisation can keep in touch with their regular customers. For this they will have to find answers to the following questions:

- Has the organisation made an attempt at identifying the most loyal amongst their customers?

- Has the organisation tried to provide additional services to their loyal customers?
- Is the organisation working at designing special recognition and reward schemes for them?
- How to make use of these schemes to establish long term relationships with their customers?

The answers to the above questions can be obtained if it is addressed to the top management and also involve them in generating employee satisfaction and commitment to build long term relationships, utilising best demonstrated practice techniques to improve performance and finally the development of an implementation plan.

If the top management is able to communicate and inspire their employees about their involvement, the customer retention programmes will be effective. Organisations have to involve their employees also in the process of ensuring customer loyalty. That is if an organisation wants to become customer focused it has to first customise its internal customer (its employees). Employee satisfaction will result in each employee interacting directly with the customer and the end user. This means organisations must realise and appreciate that—given greater latitude and encouragement - their employees can become a significant source of competitive advantage. A competent employee - who is committed to delivering customer satisfaction is a valuable asset for any organisation.

When employee satisfaction is there it will result in lower turnover, less absenteeism and fewer union organising drives. Customers want employees to appear concerned with their needs. Moreover, customer's perceptions of service quality are measured by the courtesy, empathy and responsiveness of service employees. Customer intimacy/retention has to be built by employees across the organization.

For instance, at *Wipro Corp.,* newcomers when inducted into senior management, are required to spend the first couple of days visiting customers with their bosses. Sometimes *the Chairman* of the conglomerate, *Azim Premji,* personally takes them around meeting the groups, customers, dealers and stockists. From the above example we can see that customer centric organisations involve employees across hierarchies and functions to talk to and listen to customers. Such employee customer interactions will not only increase the operational efficiency but also help in implementing a system where - in self managed and self directed employees are working towards ensuring customer satisfaction and delight.

➲ UNDERSTANDING OF BRAND EQUITY AND BRAND LOYALTY

Meaning of Brand

Brand name is the title given to a product by the manufacturer. It will convey a promise from the manufacturer to deliver a specific set of attributes like quality, value or services to the buyer.

Before going to brand equity, we start by defining a brand. According to the *American Marketing Association*. A brand is defined as *"A name, term sign, symbol or special design or some combination of these elements that is intended to identify the goods or services of one seller or a group of sellers. A brand differentiates these products from those of competitors".*

From the above definition it is seen that a brand name is the title given to a product by the manufacturer. It could take the form of symbol, logo, words, letters and or numbers that can be vocalised. The brand name will convey a promise from the manufacturer to deliver a specific set of attributes like quality, value or services to the buyer.

The brand clearly acts as a powerful differentiator in a highly competitive market. It gives the marketer enough power to deflect competitors moves. For instance, there is the *Most Trusted Brand Survey*, conducted by research agency A.C. Nielsen ORG-MARG. The survey is the largest of its kind in India, with a sample of over 7000, distributed across socio-economic class, age, income and geography. In the most trusted brand 2007 survey, *Colgate* continued to hold on to its No. 1 brand (top slot) for the fourth time in a row. Colgate has completed over 70 years of existence in India. The brand *Colgate* has been a very popular brand ruling over its competing brands such as *Pepsodent, Close-up* among others because of its total focus on oral care backed by a relentless focus on quality and innovation, a formidable distribution network and a commitment to continuously innovate. Colgate has set up a consumer innovation centre in Mumbai, which helps to develop ideas for new products that address diverse consumer needs in India and other emerging markets. Colgate's marketing and research teams spend time onsite with consumers in their homes, to try and translate observations and insights into new product ideas. *For example, Colgate's Active Salt Toothpaste* is promoted by communicating the importance they (consumers) associate with this toothpaste and, for its gum-care properties. Colgate India, since 1976, has been working with the Indian Dental Association to reach out to consumers through free dental check ups, special education programmes in schools and oral health month, a health awareness campaign.

All the efforts put in by the organisation have paid off and today as a strong brand, Colgate evokes feelings of trust, confidence, comfort and reliability in the consumers' mind.

Similarly, *British-Airways* is also knwon for putting in many efforts at ensuring customer satisfaction which has resulted in its loyal customers data base, who continue to patronise the brand.

British Airways is particular about customer satisfaction and building up "Brand Loyalty"

Brand Equity

David Aaker says Brand equity is a set of assets and liabilities linked to a brand, its name and symbol that add or subtract from the value provided by a product or service to a firm and or to that firm's competitors.

David Aaker has defined brand equity as the unique set of brand assets and liabilities that is linked with a brand. (*Marketing Research,* Aaker David A., Kumar V., Day George S., 6th Edn., John Willey & Sons, 2001) He says "Brand equity" refers to a *"set of assets and liabilities linked to a brand, its name and symbol that add to or subtract from the value provided by a product or service to a firm and or to that firm's competitors"*. He felt that brand equity is the outcome of all the investment and efforts put in by the marketer towards building the brand. How often the brand is used, consumer loyalty towards it, its perceived quality, positive symbols and favourable feedback about the brand..... a bundle of all these attributes together will create the brand equity. Only continuous efforts on the part of the marketer to focus and monitor all the above attributes will make a brand of the product. Thus, brand equity will add to (or subtract) value to an organisation, taking the form of price premium, trade leverage or competitive advantage.

FIGURE 13.9

CONSTRUCTS OF BRAND EQUITY

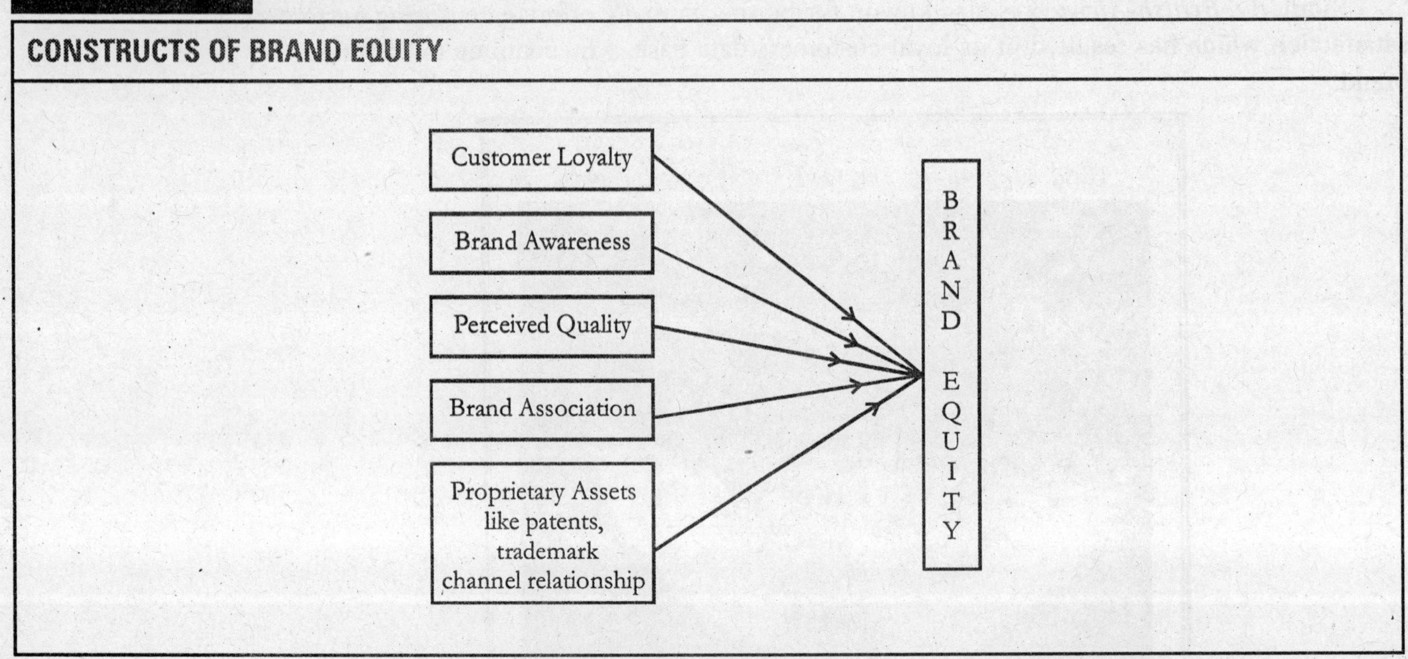

Simply put, brand equity is the value or the worth of the brand.

Having brand equity is beneficial to the firm in the long run. For instance when a brand has high brand equity, consumers are willing to pay a premium for the brand and its extensions. Typically, brand equity is measured using criteria such as market share, market ranking, brand stability and track record, stability of product category, global acceptability, market trends, advertising and promotional support and legal protection.

Figure 13.9 summarises what attributes can result in the brand equity. A brand with a strong brand not only enhances its value but can affect the share prices of its parent organisation. Valuation of a brand is also important as it shows how the organisation is using resources in creating and augmenting the brand equity. Today, when we are operating in a global market and dealing with global brands, a lot of importance is given to value the brand accurately. Thus a brand's value can be said to be the function of the consumer's perception, his or her attitude towards it, and the economic value or price that the customer attaches to the brand.

Brand Loyalty

All marketers aim at having as well as encourage brand loyalty among consumers. Brand loyal customers provide the impetus for a stable and growing market share of the company. The term brand loyalty is not a very simple concept. The dilemma is based on the issue that the concept is to be defined in terms of consumer behaviour. There is a concern among advertising professionals: whether customers view the brand as a person or is it merely the firm's fantasy?

Brand loyal customers provide the impetus for a stable and growing market share of the company.

This is because very often customers buy a brand not only for *it's functional value* but also for what it stands for— its *symbolic* or *psychological* value. Hence, the debate on whether to view brand loyalty in terms *of consumer behaviour* in general or whether it is to be associated with consumer *attitudes.* The argument put forth by the behaviour theorists is that behaviour of the consumer seen in the frequency of purchase or as a major proportion of the total purchases made cannot be indicative of the behaviour of an actual brand loyal consumer. The reasons behind the above consumer behaviour may be advocated to a spurious brand-loyal purchase, whose repetitive behaviour could probably be attributed to the fact that the particular brand was the only one available at the retail outlet.

Another view based on consumer attitudes is that a more favourable attitude towards a brand, service, and store when compared to the available competing brands along with repeat patronage can be said to be the requisite component of customer loyalty.

An integrated conceptional framework considers consumer loyalty as the relationship between an individual's relative attitude towards an entity - the brand, service, store or supplier -and patronage behaviour. The consumers' relative attitude will include:

- Strength of the attitude
- The extent of attitude differentiation found among competitive brands.

Thus the combination of the consumers *relative attitude* and *degree of repeat patronage* will reveal a consumer's loyalty. As seen from the figure 13.10, a consumer with a high relative attitude and high degree of repeat patronage can be said to be *loyal,* whereas, a consumer with a low relative attitude and high repeat patronage may be considered to be *spuriously loyal.*

FIGURE 13.10

BRAND LOYALTY MEASURED AS A FUNCTION OF RELATIVE ATTITUDE AND PATRONAGE BEHAVIOUR

Repeat patronage High Low

		High	Low	
Relative Attitude		Loyalty	Latent loyalty	High
		Spurious loyalty	No loyalty	Low

(*Source :* Consumer Behavior L.G.Schiffman, L.L.Kanuk, 6th edition)

Another view is that brand loyalty can be co-related with the consumer's degree of involvement; high involvement could result in an extensive information search finally culminating in brand loyalty. Conversely low involvement may lead to slight exposure, brand awareness and then to possible brand habits. Simply stated satisfied customers will show more loyalty in terms of strong commitment to a brand (product) or service or store and will not succumb to the persuasive attempts of competing firms.

The Brand Loyalty Pyramid

The brand manager will have to work towards creating a positive feeling which the consumer will nurture towards the brand.

The role of the brand manager is to create and strengthen the relationship between the customer and the brand. That is, he/she will have to work towards creating a positive feeling which the consumer will nurture towards the brand. In this connection David Aaker has suggested the development of *'a Pyramid of loyalty"*. According to him, loyalty stretches all the way from the switchers, the deal prone buyers, whose loyalty is at best fickle, right to the top of the pyramid, where consumers consider their brands as icons.

FIGURE 13.11

THE BRAND LOYALTY PYRAMID

THE BRAND LOYALTY PYRAMID
The Committed Buyer: Champion and spokesperson of the brand
Likes the brand considers it as a friend
Satisfied buyer: with switching costs
Satisfied buyer: No reason to break off relations
Switchers: No loyalty

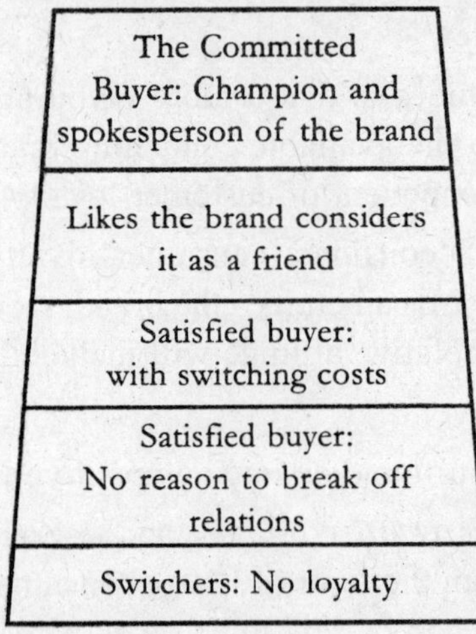

(*Source* : 'Brand Persona And Value' Subroto Sengupta, *Business Today*, January 7-21, 1997)

It is very difficult for the marketer to influence the deal prone switcher or switchers who do not show any feeling of loyalty. They are often referred to as deal prone (buy the brand on sale) or variety prone (want to buy something different each time) and are usually fickle minded buyers.

When the market has products in the particular segment which are on par in terms of performance, it will be tough for the customer to display loyalty for longer periods.

In the next level are the satisfied buyers. Here the role of the marketer is to work towards reinforcing the 'feeling good" image of the brand, so that the consumer continues to patronise the habitual purchase behaviour of its brand. Today with the market filled with many products (brands) which are similar in quality, performance etc., the marketer has to work even harder at promoting the brand and conveying the reasons for ensuring consumers on his brand's superior image over competitors. Such efforts will help in re-inforcing the brand's superior performance.

When the market has products in the particular segment which are on par in terms of performance, it will be very tough for the consumer to display loyalty for longer periods. For instance, in the mid size car segment, there are brands such as *Indigo, Accent, SX4* etc., which are well known. So each marketer will have to put in more efforts at building a brand personality which is likeable as well as ensure consumer loyalty for a long time.

At the next level is the satisfied buyer with switching costs. Such consumers play a greater role in maintaining loyalty. This type of behaviour is seen in businesses involving computer hardware and software, banking and insurance services, durables which offer long term service contracts, retail outlets, airlines with frequent flier schemes and so on. For instance retailers such as *Fabmall, Reliance Fresh, Vivek's, Nilgiris, Foodworld,* etc. are making shopping a sheer bliss for buyers by offering them a wide array of brand multifarious choices, superb pre and post-purchase services and excellent ambience. These branded retailers are positioning themselves to appeal to a loyal base of customers. The role of the brand personality will be to offer innovative schemes, services etc. so as to offset cognitive dissonance.

In the next level, the marketers have to adopt the relationship marketing strategy. Apart from adding to constant product or service improvements, the marketer have to continuously ungrade the product so that a picture of a familiar yet new, fresh and vivid brand gets associated with the brand personality. This can also result in strengthening the brand name and the consumer entering into a relationship with it since it is considered to be a friend. Organisations adopting this strategy are *Hindustan Unilever Ltd., Godrej, Procter & Gamble, Colgate etc.* Take *for example,* when the present Hindustan Uniliver had introduced *six hair specific variants of Sunsilk shampoo,* incorporating an upgraded mix in its elements *or Braun, a* division of Gillette Diversified operations, launched *Combimax, a* multiprocessing system which combines a super bowl with a food processor. Since Combimax was equipped with a 600- watt motor and special German stainless steel blades, it was able to simultaneously mix blend, knead, chop, whip, slice and shred ingredients. *Braun* had wanted to introduce 'Combimax' as a *kitchen mate* to its consumers.

Apart from adding to constant product or service improvements the marketer will have to continuously upgrade the product so that a picture of a familiar yet new, fresh and vivid brand gets associated with the brand personality.

Finally, right on top there are the icon brands where the consumers would rather fight than switch. Here the consumers are totally committed to the brand. There is no question of switching the brand. They will always act as spokespersons and consider their brands to be icons.

Nature of Brand Loyalty

Thus brand loyalty is a very challenging goal for every marketer to achieve. In a study to understand the repeat purchase behaviour for nine products on a *Chicago Tribune* purchase panel, the following brand loyalty pattern was observed:

- *Undivided loyalty* is displayed by families purchasing brand A in the sequence A A A A A A
- *Dividend loyalty* is displayed by the family purchasing brands A and B in the sequence A B A B A B
- *Unstable loyalty* is displayed by the family purchasing brands A and B in the sequence A A A B B B
- *No loyalty* is shown by families purchasing brands A B C D E F in the sequence A B C D E F.

On the basis of the products studied, a conclusion was drawn that most of the consumers tend to purchase a favourite brand or set of brands. Even though the degree of loyalty may vary product wise, the percentage of consumers displaying certain brand loyalty was rather high. It appeared that there existed a definite relationship between the strength of brands and the nature of the loyalty shown. Loyalty seemed to be high for well established products in which little or no changes have occurred and less where product entries were made frequently.

Other studies have used these and other measures of brand loyalty and drawn a general conclusion that brand loyalty exists and is a relatively widespread phenomenon.

Probable Reasons (or factors) Explaining Brand Loyalty

Although many studies attempting to explain brand loyalty have been largely inconclusive, the following results seem to have been observed :

- Some socio-economic, demographic and psychological variables are related to brand loyalty (when extended definitions were made use of) but these have a tendency to be product specific rather than general across all the products.
- It is the loyalty behaviour of an informal group leader which can influence the behaviour of other group members.
- There are a few consumer characteristics which are related to store loyalty and these in turn are related to brand loyalty.
- Brand loyalty is directly related to perceived risk and other market structure variables such as the extensiveness of distribution and market share of the dominant brand, but it is inversely related to the number of stores shopped.

Towards Measuring Brand Equity

Brands are valuable strategic assets and it is necessary to measure the value of a brand to assess its value. The value of a brand can be assessed from its underlying brand equity. Simply stated brand equity refers to the value inherent in a well known product brand.

Brand equity is associated with distinctiveness of a brand, its popularity, perceived quality, and above all enhanced value to the customers.

Certain terms which are associated with brand equity are brand awareness, brand loyalty, perceived quality and brand associations. For a customer brand equity refers to the added value bestowed on the product by the brand name. Brand equity is an asset and also a source of sustainable competitive advantage. Brand equity is associated with distinctiveness of a brand, its popularity, perceived quality and above all enhances value to the customer. Some measures of brand equity are:

- *Premium price* that the brand name supports. For instance *L.G.* is able to enjoy brand equity even with higher priced brands.
- *Customer preference* for a brand compared to the competitors brand. For instance customers preference for *'Lifebuoy* to *Nirma Bath.*
- The *replacement cost* especially when the new brand replaces an old one. For instance, IPCL's unsuccessful attempt at trying to replace its popular *'Cash Milon'* brand with *Indocrylon'.* Many factors like performance of the product, the communication and advertisements endorsements, consumer's satisfaction and experience on after sales support will all add to the brand equity. In order to overcome the threats of imitation and substitution, the managers can build up the brand equity by continuously adding value to it.

Marketers will have to look out for ways to enhance the brand value which in turn will play a big role in building equity among the customers.

Thus marketers have to look out for ways to enhance the brand value which in turn will play a big role in building equity among the customers. A well known success story of an Indian brand is given hereunder. Usha sewing machines was a very popular, household name and an essential component of the Indian brides wedding trousseau right from 1950's. Heading the company was a man with a vision Lala Sriram who was able to read the real need of the consumer. He created a category and a service extension to the main brand. He started a chain of *'UshaSilai Schools'* for teaching girls how to stitch and sew using a machine. The schools charged a fee and was highly popular. They provided service, enhanced brand value and earned a brand equity in the process.

Marketers have to identify the core values of a brand, plan for its improvement or amendment so as to get a better focus on the consumer's perception of the real brand personality. Amendments help in building brand intangibles and thus increase the brand equity.

Given below Table 13.2 provides a view of the "Fifty Best Brands in 1998", based on survey done by A & M-ORG-MARG.

TABLE 13.2

FIFTY BEST BRANDS IN 1998

Brand Name	Score	Brand Name	Score
1. Colgate	48.23	26. VIP Luggage	25.02
2. Iodex	38.35	27. Close-Up	24.96
3. Ponds	38.29	28. Dalda	24.59
4. Britannia	38.19	29. Titan	24.49
5. Bata	37.40	30. Hawkins	24.34
6. Lifebuoy	36.81	31. Johnson & Johnson	23.65
7. H.M.T.	36.77	32. Vim	23.42
8. Vicks	36.75	33. Bajaj	22.81
9. Doordarshan	35.10	34. Clinic	22.54
10. Dettol	35.04	35. State Bank of India	22.37
11. Tata	34.23	36. Bombay Dyeing	22.33
12. Philips	31.49	37. Burnol	22.32
13. Godrej	31.44	38. ZeeT.V.	21.17
14. Lux	29.35	39. Crocin	19.83
15. Parachute	28.80	40. BPL	19.78
16. Usha	28.10	41. Topaz	19.76
17. EverReady	27.88	42. Cadbury's	19.73
18. Nirma	27.86	43. Cinthol	19.14
19. Ariel	27.82	44. Coca-cola	18.76
20. Horlicks	27.80	45. Band Aid	18.31
21. Surf	26.76	46. Hero	17.99
22. Parle	26.52	47. Prestige	17.15
23. Rin	26.11	48. Bournvita	16.71
24. Amul	25.89	49. Wheel	16.65
25. Anacin	25.10	50. Complan	16.57

Scores are on a scale of 100.

(*Source :* A&M-ORG-MARG, 1998, Survey of Top Brands in India, October 31, 1998)

SUMMARY 

Relationship Marketing is the process of building long-term trusting, win-win relationships with customers, distributors, dealers and suppliers. In today's competitive scenario, every organisation is working at increasing their long term relationship with their customers. Unlike the transactional marketing which focused only on the product features, today's marketers are concentrating on each individual customer, to earn their trust and build up a long term relationship with them and enjoy their loyalty. With stiff competition from domestic as well as global players, marketers are seeking newer and cost effective ways to retain their customer base. Some of the tactical moves to add value to the customer include process re-engineering, retaining customers with the help of data mining, self service kiosks, and through loyalty card management.

The six markets model suggested by Adrain Payne to build up long term relationship with customers were discussed. The critical issues used to build up the relationship management chain, which will ideally culminate in customer value enhancement were examined. Organisations could go for customer retention improvement plan, which involves: segment profitability analysis, identify causes of defection and key service issues and corrective action to improve retention.

All marketers aim at having loyal customers and to encourage brand loyalty among them. Brand equity is the outcome of all the investment and efforts put in by the marketer towards building the brand.

➲ CHAPTER QUESTIONS FOR DISCUSSION

1. Compare and contrast the transaction marketing with relationship marketing.
2. The recession in the economy has generally slowed down the buying behaviour of individuals especially in the purchase of homes. So what steps should be used by a real estate agent if he has been asked by the company to work out relationship marketing programmes?
3. Interact with a local retailer in your area and determine the demographic and socioeconomic characteristics of the customers who seem to be loyal to the shop? Try to find out on what common basis has the retailer identified the customer's loyalty criteria?
4. Suppose you are the manager of an economy hotel at Bengaluru, what type of retention plan frame work has to be worked out to ensure brand loyalty?
5. Select a product category and search for three advertisements (in that category) which communicates of brand loyalty. What differences or similarly do you find in the potrayal of brand loyalty in each of the ads?

➲ SUGGESTED READINGS

1. Super Brands, *The Economic Times*, Bangalore, Wednesday, March 14, 2007.
2. Payne Adrian, Christopher Martin, Clark Moira Peck Helan, *"Relationship Marketing for Competitive Advantage"*, Butterworth - Heinemann Ltd., Oxford, 1995.
3. Payne Adrian, *"Relationship Marketing: Towards a New Paradigm"*, Kogan Page Ltd., London, 1995.
4. Meenakshi, Verma, *Times Auto*, Bangalore, March 8, 2007.
5. Don. Peppers, Seminar on Customer Relation Management, *Retail Biz*, Sept. 2004, pp. 47-49.
6. Rajrishi. Singhal., Customer loyalty a myth *The Economic Times,* Bangalore, June 4, 2007.
7. Harnessing information, *Retail Biz*, November 2004, pp. 47-49.
8. Ajay. Aggarwal., Customer capture, *Retail Biz*, April 2004, pp. 27-29.
9. Nandini Raghavendra, Marico plans weight control centres under kaya brand, *The Economic Times,* Bangalore, June 9, 2007.
10. Radhika, Pandeya., Fast Food First, Routes : *The Gateway Magazine,* March 2007, Vol VII, issues 5, pp. 40-43.
11. Aniruddha. Ghosh, Cards are Passe, mobile payments are the in thing, *The Economic Times*, Bangalore, 4 June 2007, pp. 5.
12. Priyanka. Joshi, Now, rent a movie on the net, *Routes : The Gateway Magazine*, March 2007, pp. 67-69.
13. Pine, II, B. Joseph and James H. Gilmore, *The Experience Economy*, Mass : Harvard Business School Press, Boston, 2004.
14. Norman R. and R. Ramirez., 'From Value Chain to Value Constellation', *Harvard Business Review*, July-August, 1993.
15. Preethi. Chamikutty, Full house, Brand Equity, *The Economic Times,* Bangaluru, 1 August, 2007.
16. Preethi Chamikutty, The Most Trusted Brand Survey 2007, White is Right, *The Economic Times*, Bangalore, 30 May, 2007, pp. 3.
17. Aaker. David.A., *Managing Brand Equity-Capitalising on the value of a Brand Name*, The Free Press, 1991, p. 15.
18. Aaker.A.David, *"Building Strong Brands"*, The Free Press, New York, 1996.
19. George H. Brown, "Brand Loyalty - Fact or Fiction?" *Advertising Age*, 1953, January 26, p. 75.
20. David L. Loudon, Albert J. Della Bitta, *Consumer Behavior*, 4th edn., Tata McGraw Hill Publishing Company Ltd., New Delhi, 2006, pp. 564-565.

CASE

CATERING THROUGH CRM, 'MOM'S KITCHEN' AND 'CALORIE CARE'

[A] MOM'S KITCHEN

Mom's Kitchen was started by Techies Vinamra Pandiya and Ashwin Rathod in September 2006 in the city of Pune, with an initial capital of Rs. 1 lakh each. When it began Mom's Kitchen had just 11 customers which has grown to 550 customers with another 3,000 on the wait list. Mom's Kitchen's USP is to deliver good quality food at reasonable rates to the more price conscious customers. They follow a simple, no frills food service which follows the pattern of *'no repeats for 30 days'*. They cater to a clearly defined market segment: the value conscious bachelors, students and the elderly. Regular meals are priced at Rs. 30/ each along with a Rs. 25/ budget option.

The 'Idea', Beginning and Growth

Pandiya and Rathod had spent two months seriously thinking over their idea - picking a brand name and building a website (www.momskitchen.in). For the food recipes, not much research was undertaken apart from taking tips from home. This is because the aim was to provide good quality food service to those who are deprived of home-cooked food, at a reasonable rate. Mom's Kitchen started operating from a rented apartment, which doubled up as sleeping quarters for the cooks at night.

On the first three days, the entrepreneurs (Pandiya and Rathod) had personally delivered the food (or dabbas). Later on, when the business started growing, Mom's Kitchen invested in seven motor-bikes, driven by delivery boys who have been trained to customise delivery of dabbas up to 36 at a time.

Unlike the neighbourhood *dabba service* Mom's Kitchen used a software programme which keeps a track of the meals availed of by the customer. This ensures there are no billing problems. So, in case a customer wants to cancel an order for the evening, he (or she) merely has to call or email the service and it is taken care of in the bill.

Mom's Kitchen uses CRM initiatives *i.e.,* they take care of their internal customers (employees), who will take care of the external customers.

Being a labour intensive business, a lot of effort is put into searching, identifying, training and motivating their cooks and helpers. The entrepreneurs, instead of being addressed as *'Sir'* or *'Maabit'* are addressed to as *bhaiya*. All (employers and employees) share meals and watch motivational films together. Even the suggestions and problems of the staff are listed and addressed to by the bosses. All these initiatives have led to a feeling (or sense) of loyalty among the employees! The cooks had even worked without salary for four months, toiling hard without ever grumbling. Though today the cooks who started a year ago on Rs. 1800, are earning a decent Rs. 6000.

The customer service put in by Mom's Kitchen has been able to generate a lot of goodwill and positive customer feedback. With a waiting list of 3500 customers (as in August 2007).

The Future Plans

Mom's Kitchen had plans to open 10,000 dabbas in Pune by 2008, apart from planning to start similar outlets in Chennai also. They also are thinking of opening a *theme restaurant* where customers will feel everything is *just like home.*

[B] CALORIE CARE

Calorie Care is said to be India's first customised, calorie counted meal service, in Mumbai started by a former investment banker, Cyrus Driver in 2004. Calorie Care offers customised menus, high grade ingredients with focus on health food dressed up in a range of designer recipes, from various cuisines - all at Rs. 150 a meal.

Cyrus had taken a whole year to create 150 calorie counted receipes, with the help of dietician Lisa John. Calorie Care's USP is offering menus which addresses, the problem of weight management either for the health-conscious customers (about 20-25 percent of the customer base) and those with medical conditions like diabetes, who require special meals (about 5 percent fall in this category). However, a majority of customers are well paid professionals, hard pressed for time and willing to pay for health and convenience.

Calorie Care's chef is Kamlesh, whose prior experience with *Ambassador Skychef*, a airline catering service has proved invaluable for the business. It is located on the ground floor of a centrally located building in Mumbai. The kitchen has interiors along the lines of Skychef, with gleaming steel counter tops, a giant walk-in freezer and an air-conditioned packing and salad zone. The company also owns a fleet of seven vans which delivers food to customers.

Use of I.T and Future Plans

Calorie Care makes use of I.T for its operation. The first step involves consultation with the dietician in person or over the phone. In the next step, the customer has to indicate his or her preference in detail. *For example,* "I like Indian and Chinese food but not continental. Allergic to brinjal and hate carrot. No salad with yoghurt dressing. Delivery at office Monday to Friday, Saturday at home please".

There is a specially developed software which will convey about the daily aggregate orders as well as how much food needs to be packed for each individual tiffin box or dabba. Further, depending upon the dietary goal and body type there will be variations in the serving sizes.

Calorie Care already operates cafes in select gyms. It was to enter Baroda in August 2007 on a profit share basis at a health mall. It had also planned to set up services in Delhi and Bengaluru in 2008, following a seed fund investment by American private equity firm Culbro LLC. In order to expand their customer base the company also plans to start a "no frills" dabba service at half of the regular prices. Says Driver, "the challenge is maintaining quality and adding variety".

(*Source :* Rashmi .Bansal, Catering : The New Age Dabbawala, *Business World*, 6 August 2007, pp. 76-78)

QUESTIONS FOR DISCUSSION

1. Over and above whatever is mentioned in the cases, can you suggest more initiatives to increase the amount of 'trust' and 'commitment' of the 'internal customer' and 'the organisations'?
2. If 'Mom's Kitchen' and 'Calorie Care' want to build up a chain of their services across the metros, what measures should be adopted to ensure increased buying of their services, favourable word-of-mouth and enjoy customer equity?

UNIT V : ETHICS AND APPLICATION

CHAPTER 14

CONSUMERISM

- Introduction to Consumerism
- Consumerism in India
- The Indian Consumer
- Reasons behind rise of consumerism
- Benefits of consumerism
- Government Measures
- The Consumer Protection Act No. 68 of 1986
- Monopolies and Restrictive Trade Practices Act, 1969
- ICRPC
- Summary
- Chapter Questions for Discussion
- Suggested Readings

INTRODUCTION TO CONSUMERISM

The marketing concept is a philosophy of providing services to mutual gain. If this concept is followed, it can help the economy to satisfy the diverse and continuous needs of its ever-growing number of consumers. However, not all marketing practices follow this theory.

Very often, firms are seen engaging themselves in questionable marketing practices and transactions, which though may seem innocent in themselves, have profound implications on the society at large. For instance, if one were to consider the sale of cigarettes as a transaction between the marketer and the smoker, the transaction involves public interest also. This is because the smoker may be shortening his life by smoking. This will cause harm and places a burden on the smoker's family and the society at large. Lastly, other people in the presence of the smoker may have to inhale the smoke, feel uncomfortable and can also be prone to cancer through passive smoking. Hence the government's decision to ban such transactions especially at public places. This only goes to show that private transactions may invite profound questions about public policy and intervention.

In order to advocate its role as a public decision maker the government uses intervention in the form of regulation measures and consumer education programmes to communicate and encourage desired behaviour.

Public policy does affect the field of consumer behaviour when the public policy-makers are confident that Government intervention in the marketing transactions is necessary, so as to ensure that such transactions are beneficial to the society as a whole. With the changes occurring in the socio-economic environment, very often market place abuses are brought to the notice of the policy decision-makers, either through the media, consumer awareness groups, consumers themselves or through the public recognition of the need for the economic or social-welfare programmes.

In order to advocate its role as a public decision-maker, the Government uses intervention in the form of regulation measures, and consumer education programmes to communicate and encourage desired behaviours. The regulation measures include prohibiting certain types of marketing practices (selling of unsafe goods), make certain practices mandatory (provide information on the food label), and restrict against indulging in certain practices like misleading and deceptive advertising. Consumer education can be done by using various media to communicate, inform and educate them about the importance of eating healthy food, the importance of pre-natal care, to live in harmony with nature, i.e., environmental conservation, importance of education, the reasons behind drug abuse, etc. The people at large believe that it is the Government's responsibility to promote and protect the public interest and also to contribute for the general welfare.

Social critics have accused the marketers of hurting and harming the consumers by engaging themselves in practices such as: high prices, deceptive practices, high pressure selling, shoddy or unsafe products, planned obsolescence and poor services. Thus, firms are confronted with important changes in the socio-political environment, which has led to the growth of consumerism and legislative measures to protect the consumers. Originally, the consumer movement had its conspicuous beginning and had picked up momentum in the United States. Slowly this awareness spread to the other countries, resulting in the growth of consumerism and the growing awakening and the demand for consumer protection.

This consumer awareness and the impact, though still in the infancy stage, has started growing in India. Here, there is felt a growing consumer awareness and feeling of being exploited. Several organisations are active in conducting researches and exposing substandard quality of products and other activities like indulging in adulteration practices, etc. These consumer organisations are also involved in responding to public outcries against dishonest or unethical business practices. They also play an active role in redressing consumer grievances.

In this chapter, we will discuss about the growing importance of consumer rights and the spread of consumerism in India. We will also examine the consumer-oriented legislative measures enacted to protect the consumers.

CONSUMERISM IN INDIA

In the words of *Peter F. Drucker,* the father of management science *"Consumerism is the shame of the total marketing concept".* Every organisation should take marketing decisions keeping in mind the company's requirements, the consumers' long-term interests and lastly the society's long-run interests. Neglecting the consumers and the society's long-term interests will not only prove to be a disservice, but also give cause to raise the wrath of the consumerists. So, it would be preferable if companies recognise societal problems as presenting opportunities. As stated by *Peter Drucker, "Consumerism actually should be, must be and hope will be the opportunity of marketing. This is what we in marketing have been waiting for.* "

In India, as a developing economy, it is felt that the plight of the consumers are not different from that of their counterparts in the rest of the world. Inspite of the fact that not all Indian consumers are well-educated and hence, unable to comprehend and understand the complex methods of marketing, they are also exploited and very often become victims of false claims for products, misled by deceptive advertisements, deceitful packaging, poor after-sales service and so on. Because of the above felt abuses, there is observed and seen a growing consumer awareness leading to the growth of consumerism and an increasing demand for consumer protection in India.

Consumer movement is slowly gathering momentum. It is a social force used to protect the consumers against the unfair marketing practices occurring in the transactions between the sellers and the buyers.

Consumerism can be said to be still in its infancy stage. But the consumer movement is slowly gathering momentum. It is a social force used to protect the consumers against the unfair marketing practices occurring in the transactions between the sellers and the buyers. At times, there is a deliberate attempt on the part of the marketer to adopt misleading, false or deceptive advertisements, where only half-truths are offered to the consumers, so as to give a different impression and create a different image as compared to the actual fact. It has been observed that the Indian consumers are cheated to the tune of Rs. 2000 crores annually through various devises invented by the clever businessmen and traders, unsafe products, adulteration, misleading advertisements, black-marketing, false warranties, etc. In 1990s also, after the liberalisation of the economy, the market was again flooded with varieties of goods and services. The difference in the scene now is the continuous entry of new competitors, willing to make enormous investments for long-term market shares, fast falling margins cutting into the profitability of many marketers, rapid rise in the consumer earnings, fall in the savings rate resulting in generating increasing amounts of disposable income to be spent on consumer products and services. The advent of the information age has brought with it real time images of the global lifestyle; and thus making high spenders and budget shoppers spend lavishly on products and services.

Under the above circumstances, "Survival of the fittest" was the motto. This resulted in marketers using wrong means to increase their market share rather than facing the situation of being wiped out from the market place. The following situational factors also aided the marketers:

- The vastness of a country like India, along with an imbalance in the distribution of income and wealth and backwardness of the people came in the way of organising consumer awareness and movements
- The high rate of illiteracy and ignorance among the majority of the population

- Onslaught from the unscrupulous businessmen due to the traditional outlook of the people to suffer in silence, lack of education and information
- Unable to understand the technical complexity of the goods and thus, accepting the information given by the manufacturers or sales persons on face value
- Indian consumers getting carried away by the clever advertising and promotional tactics used by the marketers

It must be remembered that while on one hand the manufacturer has got the right to design manufacture, distribute, advertise and price the product, the consumer has got the right to decide whether or not to purchase the product. However, the consumer is not in a position to exercise this power, while purchasing a product or service. This is because of either the lack of information or excess of indigestible information or conflicting information received from one or more competing firms. This has resulted in the rise in consumerism. To quote Mr. T. Thomas (Ex - Chairman, HLL). *"It is worthwhile to note that consumerism, like several other social movements, e.g. Independence Movement, Civil Rights Movement, etc. has been the result of a social conflict and cannot therefore, be wished away. It will be till the conflict facing the consumer is resolved".*

THE INDIAN CONSUMER

Consumerism today, as a collective action of the consumers to protect their own interests indicates failure on the part of the business system, which includes public-policy makers and the government to guarantee and ensure the legitimate rights of the consumers.

Philip Kotler had long back emphasised that the original marketing concept has to be broadened to include the societal marketing concept. According to him, alongwith the inclusion of the long-run consumer welfare concept, the businessmen must also consider including social and ecological considerations in their product and market planning. By doing this, they are not only meeting their social responsibilities but also taking care so as to avoid hurting their long-term interests as producers. Only if such a concept is practiced will an enlightened marketer be able to prevent the rise of consumerism.

But consumerism today, as a collective action of the consumers to protect their own interests indicates failure on the part of the business system, which includes the public policy-makers and the Government to guarantee and ensure the legitimate rights of the consumers. And this is also the reason behind consumer seeking protection. To ensure consumer protection, the onus of responsibility lies on the shoulders of three groups of people namely: the business, the Government and the consumers themselves.

There are several problems faced by the Indian consumers, thus making it necessary to have an effective and more involvement from the Government and consumer movements to safeguard the consumers rights. The factors responsible for the sad plight of Indian consumers are given hereunder:

(a) Very often, India faces a severe imbalance in the demand and supply of essential commodities. This has produced evils in the form of hoarding and black-marketing profiteering, corruption, nepotism, red tapism, irresponsibility and arrogance while dealing with the consumers.

(b) With low literacy levels and incorrect and unsatisfactory information generated, many of the Indian consumers are not consciously aware of their rights. This further encourages businessmen to develop indifferent attitudes and behaviour towards their consumers.

(c) Though the market is flooded with many goods and services, there is seen an imperfect and ineffective competition. For, in a perfect (competition) market, the buyer may be

Government tries to educate consumers on the harmful effects of consuming "Tobacco".

in a position to substitute one product for another with visible differences in the quality, service and price of the products. But in the existing scenario, apart from the lack of general essential information, there are very few sellers available in the market, who can keep the competition alive and also work to avoid the threat of potential competition by offering equally good alternative products and services to the consumers. Thus, the Indian consumer becomes a victim of ineffective competition and is forced to make a choice from the available few alternative goods and services. This holds true, more often for consumables purchased in the medium price ranges.

(d) In the absence of proper information and unfamiliarity with some of the new product features, consumers, at times, become easy victims and accept substandard, inferior or even defective products.

(e) Consumerism is still in its infancy stage and hence, not well-organised and developed as in the developed countries.

(f) The legal framework and system in India is a time-consuming and tiresome process. Thus, consumers are hesitant to seek redressal of their grievances by taking the help of the judiciary.

(g) The Government had started the public sector undertakings (PSUs) to serve the public interest by providing effective competition to the private sector, increase production, etc. However, these units are yet to produce benefits that will be commensurate with the investments. The basic objective behind investing and encouraging the growth of public sector was to encourage the concept of consumer welfare. But as far as performance is concerned, many of the public sector monopolies are making the life of consumers miserable. To quote a few examples, the services provided by some of the State-owned electricity boards is very poor. Very often, consumers are compelled to make hard payments for the services hardly received by them. The state of the public roads in the various cities and towns are always uneven with many potholes, thus causing more inconvenience and harm to the people and all the vehicle users, who make use of the roads.

(h) The existing laws which have been framed to protect and safeguard the interests of the consumers at large, are not being effectively implemented and enforced to achieve the said objectives.

The Government can come to the help of the consumers and prevent them from being exploited by passing certain legislations to protect the consumer and also by having certain statutory bodies to prevent firms from exploiting the consumers.

From the above discussions, we can see that many of the above pitfalls can be removed if active participation is there from the business, Government and the consumers.

- The business, comprising of all the manufacturers and intermediaries must take up the responsibility to ensure efficiency in production and quality of the output. They must also abstain from resorting to unhealthy practices like charging exorbitant prices, or hoarding and black marketing. Thus, voluntarily the businessmen themselves should take up the responsibility to ensure that qualitative goods and services reach the ultimate consumer in time and at reasonable prices.
- The Government can come to the help of the consumers and prevent them from being exploited, by passing certain legislations to protect the consumer and also by having certain statutory bodies to prevent firms from exploiting the consumers. The Government has also included consumer protection as an item of the 20-point programme. A Consumer Advisory Council has been set up by the agencies, including the State Governments, the Textile Committee and the Department of Science and Technology. Added to this, the Government is seeking to increase the awareness of the consumers'

rights through various media. Doordarshan has been organising programmes like Lok Samasyani, Jansad, Janavani, etc.

- And lastly, consumers themselves should assert their rights and protect themselves from business malpractices. They should accept consumerism and work towards making the businesses and Government more responsive to the rights of the Consumers. Various consumer movements have also been organised in many parts of the country and there are as many as 237 or so consumer organisations working towards consumer protection.

REASONS BEHIND RISE OF CONSUMERISM

Consumerism as a social force can help to:

(a) Make the business community more honest, efficient, responsive and responsible. The manufacturers and sellers will be compelled to adopt fair trade practices, when consumers learn to exercise their rights and are not taken for granted.

(b) Consumerism can also be viewed as an opportunity for businessmen to serve the consumers in a better and more efficient manner. It will prove to be a weapon for marketers to effectively implement the societal concept of marketing.

(c) In case of imperfections in the demand and supply situation in the market, concerned marketers can help the consumers to get rid of the traders who resort to practices such as hoarding, black-marketing, etc.

(d) Consumerism will also ensure that the Government takes the necessary measures to protect consumer interests by guaranteeing their legitimate rights.

Advertising is a vehicle through which the marketer seeks to communicate, inform, appeal and guide consumers in their decision making process. But at times, the advertiser will mislead the viewer by imparting incorrect information.

Deceptive Advertising

Advertising is a vehicle through which the marketer seeks to communicate, inform, appeal and guide consumers in their decision-making process. But at times, the advertiser will mislead the viewer *by* imparting incorrect information. An *unfair ad* is one in which the advertiser withholds information, which may result in causing harm to the consumer. *A deceptive ad contains explicit or implied claims or omissions which are likely to mislead a consumer acting reasonably under the circumstances.*

For instance, the claim made sometime back by *Colgate* toothpaste to be 102% better as compared to the competitors or the claim of HLL that in *Wheel detergent powder,* lemon is an inbuilt ingredient which helps in removing the dirt. The above mentioned instances are just two of the many advertisements which were used by businesses to take their consumers for a ride.

Unfortunately, till recently there was no proper legislation to put a check on the misuse of advertisements by the marketers. Now the *MRTP Act* empowers the MRTP Commission to deal with such false claims or in the event of misuse of advertisements by advertisers.

Over and above this, the advertising professionals have also adopted a self- regulation mechanism by observing a code of conduct which is to be followed for advertising products. The Advertising Club of India (ACB) in 1982, formulated a regulatory code of conduct for the profession and was to be applicable to all those concerned with advertising — advertisers, the ad agencies and the media. The advertising code is as follows:

- The concerned people (in the advertising) have to make 'honest' claims and should not mislead the consumer.
- The portrayal of the advertisements should be within the accepted standards of public decency.

Consumers raising voices against illegal hoarding of foodstock by a trader.

- Ensure and safeguard against the excessive promotion of products, which are considered to be dangerous or hazardous to the society or individual.

The advertising code seeks to : ensure the consumers protection against spurious advertising and works as a guarantor that a self regulation measure is adhered to and guarantee that the set standards of morality are upheld.

There have been instances when companies had to seek the help of the MRTP Commission when competitors made false or misleading claims about them in the advertising campaigns made by the latter, observe fairness in competition between different brands of the same product or a product and its substitute. Box 14.1 is one such illustration.

As seen above, the advertising code will seek to meet two purposes:

(a) Ensure consumers protection against spurious advertising

(b) Works as a guarantor that a self-regulation measure is adhered to and guarantee that the set standards of morality are upheld.

Those connected with the advertising profession have also established a public body (a public limited company, *The Advertising Standards Council of India* (ASC)), whose job is to ensure the implementation of the advertising norms and standards. This is a non-profit organisation set up by 43 members who are connected to advertising in one way or the other. By formulating a regulating code, it has got the necessary authority to adjudicate on whether an advertising is offensive in nature. The final decision taken by the ASCI will be binding on its members. It also poses to deal with the Government, in case of any disputes.

The above mentioned code of conduct was worked out, inspired by a similar code of the *Advertising Standards Authority (ASA), U.K.* The ultimate aim being to ensure the adoption of fair advertising practices in the best interest of the ultimate consumers.

BOX 14.1

MRTPC BLOCKS BPL CLAIMS IN EXCELL AD CAMPAIGN

The Monopolies and Restrictive Trade Practices Commission (MRTPC), has directed BPL Ltd, the consumer electronics and alkaline battery manufacturer, to drop claims in its advertising campaign that its 'Excell' brand of batteries are 'the longest lasting in the world'.

The Commission has ordered BPL to stop advertising this claim in any manner and in any form and through media, whether print or visual or through any packaging material'.

This order has come on an application made by Duracell India Pvt. Ltd. before the MRTP Commission whereby, the former had questioned the objectionable and Superlative claim of BPL, in respect of its Alkaline batteries.

During the course of the proceedings, the Commission had directed BPL to submit its batteries for a joint evaluation along with Duracell to an international acclaimed laboratory at Sweden, having facilities for testing in accordance with IEC and JIS parameters.

After due consideration of the report, the MRTPC had stated that it was prima facie of the view that the test report of the Swedish laboratory shows that the aforesaid claim made by and on behalf of the respondent (BPL Ltd), with respect to its alkaline batteries, to the effect that it is the longest lasting battery in the world, is not genuine, and as such is not justifiable.

The Commission has said that, on the contrary, if we go by the Swedish laboratory test report, in certain respects, we might have to consider that alkaline battery manufactured and marketed by and on behalf of the applicant/complainant (Duracell India) to be longer lasting than that manufactured and marketed by the respondent.

The MRTPC has also ruled that 'no person has any right to mislead public by misinterpretation as to the quality of the products manufactured and /or marketed by such persons. Because of such claims in the advertisement campaign, the choice of people in need of alkaline batteries is likely to be deflected'.

Earlier in the year, on March 6, 1998, the Commission had issued a notice of enquiry against BPL for adoption of unfair and restrictive trade practices, under section 10 (A) (I) and sub-section B as well as Section 2(0) of the MRTP Act 1969, in relation to their claim.

The MRTPC had also directed BPL to discontinue its television commercial wherein batteries manufactured by its competitors were shown in a disparaging, manner.

(*Source : The Hindu, Business Line,* Wednesday, December 30th, 1998)

Apart from the above, there are three professional bodies concerned with the three types of people connected with the advertising world in India - the advertiser, the advertising agency and media of advertising. The ISA — The Indian Society of Advertisers, is the only representative body of advertisers. The AAAI, the Advertising Agencies Association of India are the agencies who undertake advertising on behalf of the advertisers. And the INS - the Indian and Eastern Newspapers Society which refers to the media or the organisations of newspapers, magazines and other publications.

All the problems start only if advertising is misused or deliberately gives wrong information to the consumer.

Advertising, if used properly can contribute to consumer welfare, because in a persuasive language it can inform the consumers and tell them what to buy, how to buy, where to buy and why to buy along with the price to be paid for the products or services. But all the problems start only if advertising is misused or deliberately gives wrong information to the consumer. Box 14.1 had thrown light on how the MRTPC cautioned *BPL* against giving false claim in its ad. In the words of Rothenberg *"Advertising does not work by entertaining or assaulting the intellect of its audience... Nor does it work through subliminal manipulation. Instead,* as *the great ad man, Bruce Barton had acknowledged decades before, was "Something big, something splendid, something which goes deep down into an institution and gets hold of the soul of it* (*Source :* S. A. Chunawalla, K.C. Sethia, *"Foundations of Advertising Theory & Practice"*, Himalaya Publishing House, Mumbai, 1997).

Truth about Labelling and Product Performance

There also arises questions related to the truth in labelling and packaging. Good packaging will communicate about the quality of the product and helps in creating a value for the product. The packaging is used as a vehicle which carries details related to the manufacturer's name, brand name, trademark, all other information about the ingredients and also gives directions on its usage.

Given below are complaints received against Ads by ASCI and MRTPC in Table 14.1 and Table 14.2.

TABLE 14.1

THE COMPLAINTS LIST

Advertiser	Product or brand	Nature of Complaint
The ASCI complaints:		
Reckitt & Coleman of India	Martein mosquito repellent	Claims that Mortein is "more smart, more safe" is dangerous
Weekender Kids	Clothes range	Ad implies superiority of rich children over poor, and promotes violence
Kinetic Engineering	Kinetic Safari V2	Ad shows riders on KS driving dangerously through traffic.
Videocon International	Bazooka 21 TV	"The greatest offer of century – own a Bazooka 21 Free" is misleading
Paras Pharmaceuticals	Moov	The ads claim that Moov is better than Iodex, is unsubstantiated

Kenstar Kitchen Appliances	Kenstar Ultra care water purifier	Ad makes unsubstantiated claims of destroying harmful micro-organisms.
Nivaran Herbal	Memory Plus	Claims that the product gets rid of wrinkles, due to age are untrue.
Johnson & Johnson	Stayfree silky dry napkin	Claims of a survey in Mumbai proving product is better are unsubstantiated.
RCI	Lizol Disinfectant	Ad claiming Lizol is true germ-cleaner is unsubstantiated.
Pidilite Industries	Fevikwick	Ad showing the secretary sticking the the boss's fingers show unsafe practices.
Daewoo Anchor Electronics	Daewoo Refrigerator	Claims of the refrigerator cooling 3 times faster is not true.
Hindustan Lever Ltd.	Clinic All Clear Dandruff shampoo	Claims that an ingredient ZPTO, moisturizes hair is unsubstiated.

TABLE 14.2

THE MRTPC COMPLAINTS

Advertiser	Product or brand	Nature of Complaint
Colgate Palmolive	Colgate Dental Cream	Claims of Colgate Dental Creams being 2.5 times superior over any toothpaste
Castrol	Castrol base oil	Ad make disparaging reference to Bharat Shell.
Perfetti	Big Babool	Ad shows rival Candicos product Freedom being disfigured and thrown out
ICI	Supercote Acrylic Paint Chewing gum	Ad discredits Snowcem by showing a bag of cement paint being thrown out.
BPL	Excell alkaline Battery	Claims of the "longest lasting alkaline batter in the world" in untrue..
Voltas	Master Laundrete Washing Machine	Ad claims that it is the country's largest twin-tub machine, which has been disputed
Marico	Parachute hair oil	Ad hinted that HLL's Clinic Plus Oil was'nt pure cocount oil

(*Source :* 'Campaigning against Ads,' Nanda Majumdar, *Business Today*, January 22, 1999)

Thus, labelling is a part of the package giving additional information to the consumer about the product. Just as ads, even labels could be misused. To put a check-on such misuse, the Government has passed the Central Packaged Commodities (Regulation) Order, 1975. This act makes it mandatory on the part of the manufacturer to ensure the following information is disclosed on the label of the product:

- Name of the manufacturer, Date of manufacture
- Date of expiry
- Net weight of the product
- Maximum Retail Price (MRP)

Good packaging and labelling will communicate to consumers about the quality and also create value for the product.

In the marketing environment today, when more and more complex and varied products are available, it is the moral responsibility of the manufacturer to provide the necessary instructions manual to the consumer along with the product.

Consumers also have the right to expect the products they purchase to perform as stated and claimed by the manufacturer. Further, it is also the moral responsibility of the producer to ensure that the products are safe. In the marketing environment today, when more and more complex and varied products are available it is the moral responsibility of the manufacturer, to provide the necessary instructions manual to the consumer along with the product. It is also necessary to get the product tested before getting it affixed with the necessary quality standards approval.

It has been assumed that consumers can purchase products which have got the above mentioned marks which will ensure quality and safety for the consumer. Inspite of all these measures, it is said that Indian consumers are cheated to the tune of Rs.2000 crores annually through various devises created and used by clever businessmen and traders. Eighteen out of twenty-two pressure stoves tested at the instance of CGSI failed to clear the Important Safety Tests and all thermometers tested failed to register temperature accurately. Similarly, there are also many products which have been tested by various consumer organisations and found not to be as accurate in performance as it should have been.These organisations are demanding governmental action against the manufacturers to ensure that the quality standards are met with. This calls for effective State intervention and Consumerism is necessary to ensure and protect the right of the consumers.

Ad advises consumers to ensure the 'Handloom Mark' is affixed on the product, as an assurance of genuine quality.

Typical Malpractices and Unfair Trade Practices

The business malpractices could include improper: quality of the product, pricing of the product, non availability of products (improper distribution), misleading advertisement of the product, tax evasion, violating laws such as FEMA, etc. Some of the typical malpractices affecting consumers are :

- **Absence of Quality Control and Safety Measures :** Indian manufacturers in the past have shown indifference towards maintaining the quality of the product. As a result of this, the product finally reaching the lands of the consumers may not be of the desired quality. As we are competing with global competitors today, Indian manufacturers need to view the 'quality' aspect of the product very seriously so that it is built into the product right from the idea inception stage.
- **Improper Weights and Measures :** Most of the commodities in retail outlets are sold in terms of weight of a particular quantity, for which the customer is paying the price. However, often customers have found that there are variations in the quantity mentioned and received by them. Probably due to faulty weighing equipment used by the retailer. Inspite of the government's efforts at informing and educating consumers about such practices, the existing legal formalities is grossly inadequate to deal with such malpractices.
- **Adulteration :** Adulteration is mostly found to be related to the sale of food products. This practice can be found to the food products sold in loose by some of the Kirana shops; where the food products could be mixed with cheaper or inferior substances. Outlets indulging in such practices often take the consumers for a ride. Inspite of the Food Adulteration Prevention Act since its implementation is very slack and due to many loopholes in our legal system, such traders are able to go scot free.
- **Black Marketing and Profiteering :** Sometimes traders adhere to black marketing, especially when there is a big gap between the supply and demand owing to shortages of certain commodities in the making. Under such circumstances, some traders resort to selling those products at exorbitant prices, which is a type of profiteering. Such actions on the part of traders not only causes consumer exploitation but can also put genuine customers at a disadvantage.

Apart from the above there are other types of trading activities such as selling imitation products in the guise of real goods, smuggling, gambling etc. These are practices which can affect the customer satisfaction and their loyalty in the long run.

➲ BENEFITS OF CONSUMERISM

It is very necessary to have a well developed consumerism in India, for the benefit of and to protect the consumer rights.

It is very necessary to have, a well-developed consumerism in India, for the benefit of and to protect the consumer rights. But, inspite of the best efforts put forward by the various consumer organisations few names were given in (the list mentioned earlier in the chapter), not much consumerism with practical utility has taken place in the country. This is partly because of the lack of consumer education among the public and partly, because very often the mass consumer protests demonstrated against market imperfections, (shortages or price rise, etc.) has the involvement of the vested interests of the political parties. Further, the little organised consumer movements has generally been confined to the major urban cities and towns, whereas there is a huge majority of consumers in the rural areas, who have not been involved in such movements.

If organised well, with involvement of many more consumers, consumerism will gain momentum and benefit the consumers in many ways, such as:

(I) Consumer Education : Over and above protective legislation and regulation, consumers need to be informed and educated to enable them to make wise purchase decisions. It is observed that even the presence of Government regulations and consumer action groups cannot always protect the consumers against all the marketing abuses. So the best weapon in the hands of the consumers will be to-have more information and knowledge about the product, company, etc. This is possible only if the consumers are educated in the real sense. Even the marketing firms could help by providing the necessary education material to consumers. Another proposal is for the firms to make provisions through the development of computerized data banks containing product information (prices, availability, etc.) and general educational information to their potential customers. By sharing such information, the firms cannot only develop relationship marketing with their customers but also make them educated customers. As the saying goes *"Educated consumers make better customers."*

(ii) Liaison with Government and the Producer : Consumer advocates who are organising the various consumer movements should realise that in a developing economy like India, where consumerism is still in its infancy stage. Government efforts can go a long way in meeting consumer needs. Thus, they can play the key role by maintaining liaison with the Government on one hand, and the manufacturers on the other.

(iii) Product Research and Inform the Consumers : Product research is a part of the broader term *consumer research,* which is a part of the marketing research. Product research will help in the generation of more product knowledge, in terms of its various attributes, information related to prices, ingredients, competing brands, utility value and so on.

There are various research organisations such as MARG, ORG, etc which conduct researches on an ongoing basis. At times, such findings get published in various leading magazines also. Similarly, product ratings will enable the consumers in making a choice of products. The consumers can use such information to ascertain the merits of the product in terms of its convenience, portability, style, comfort, durability, etc. So when consumers make a purchase decision after the receipt of such information, it is less likely that they are misled or taken for a ride by the marketers.

Consumer researches and market segmentation will ensure a better *'match'* between the products and consumers and also enable the marketers to communicate more efficiently with their target markets.

GOVERNMENT MEASURES

In India, the Government has taken a number of measures to protect the consumer interest. These measures can be classified into two categories:

(a) Statutory regulations of private business.

(b) Development and expansion of the public sector.

The statutory regulation empowers the Government of India to control the product, supply, distribution, price and the quality of a large number of goods and services.

Statutory Regulations

These statutory regulations empowers the Government of India to control the product, supply, distribution, price and the quality of a large number of goods and services. Our Government can exercise control over the terms and conditions of sale, the nature of trade and commerce and so on. According to an ex-chairman, Hindustan Lever Ltd., "Unlike in the West, the Government in Indian has a large number of controls on industry and is therefore, in a position to respond more swiftly and effectively than Western Governments. In some ways, our bureaucracy has perfected the art of assuming the guardianship of all interests of the consumers and the vulnerable sections".

Government cautioning customers to be aware of retailers who are illegally hoarding food stock.

The many important legislations enforced by the Government to protect the consumer interests are as follows :

- The Monopolies and Restrictive Trade Practices (MRTP) Act, 1969.
- Industries Development and Regulation Act, 1951
- Essential Commodities Act, 1955.
- Prevention of Food Adulteration Act, 1954
- Prevention of Black-Marketing and Maintenance of Supplies of Essential Commodities Act
- The Indian Sale of Goods Act, 1930
- ISI Certification Mark Act, 1952, AGMARK
- Trade Marks and Merchandise Marks Act, 1958
- Agricultural Products Grading and Marketing Act, 1937
- Drugs Control Act, 1950
- Indian Standard Institute's Certification Act, 1952
- Standard of Weights and Measures (Packaged Commodities Rules, 1977)
- Consumer Protection Act. 1986
- Imports and Exports Control Act, 1947
- Packaged Commodities (Regulation) Order, 1975
- The Drugs and Cosmetics Act, 1940
- Foreign Trade (Development and Regulation Act), 1992

The Monopolies and Restrictive Trade Practices Act, 1969 and the Consumer Protection Act, 1986 are of great relevance to consumerism and in the consumer's interest. A very significant aspect of the MRTP (Amendment) Act of 1984 is the provisions to control unfair trade practices.

Growth and Expansion of the Public Sector

Our economy is characterised by the co-existence of the public, private, joint and co-operative sectors. There is a lot of significance in the growth and expansion of the public sector in India. The most important objectives of the public sector undertakings is the enhancement of consumer welfare by increasing production, improving efficiency in production and supply, to ensure the availability of goods and services at fair prices, to reduce market imperfections and curb private monopolies, improve the distribution system, etc.

According to the Bureau of Public Enterprises, "The public enterprises is born as the outcome of the conscious policy of the Government to speed up the industrialisation of the country, with a view to give added impetus to economic growth as well as to achieve certain socio-economic goals as enunciated in the Industrial Policy resolutions of the Government. These enterprises today cover a wide spectrum of activities in basic and strategic industries like steel, coal, minerals and metals, petroleum, heavy engineering, chemicals, fertilizers and pharmaceuticals, etc. on the one hand, and consumer goods, trading and marketing activities, transportation services, contracts and consultancy services, tourist services, financial services, development of small industries, etc. on the other. While some of these enterprises operate under monopoly or near monopoly conditions, there are others working under competitive conditions. There is yet another segment of the public enterprises, *viz.,* sick enterprises taken over from the private sector to protect employment. Thus, public enterprises comprise units

The public sector has a very important role to play in the development of this vast and populous developing economy characterised by the dearth of capital, entrepreneurship and technology.

engaged in different spheres of industrial and commercial activities, some capital-intensive - long gestation-low profitability enterprises; some sick and hence, requiring special treatment, while some others are low-sick high profitability enterprises. Added to this basic diversity in the composition of the units is the multi-dimensional objectives of public enterprises in general, which is another significant factor to be considered while making any realistic analysis of their performance."

Thus, the public sector has a very important role to play in the development of this vast and populous developing economy characterised by the dearth of capital, entrepreneurship and technology. But in India it has been observed that the public sector is lagging very much behind in the objectives set at the time of its formation. Most of the public sector undertakings are enjoying either monopolies or near monopolies in their areas of operation, but their performance is far from satisfactory. Examples of such units which are operating with accumulated losses are some of the SOEs like the State Electricity Boards, State Transports, etc. These SOEs and PSEs (Public Sector Enterprises), enjoying monopoly are not only making huge losses but are also, causing severe resource constraints in the face of the large revenue, budgetary and fiscal deficits which the nation has been enduring. To make up for the deficits, the Government is compelled to put the burden on the public by increasing taxation. Why should the Government impose financial burden on the citizens by running inefficient enterprises? Why should the public bear the brunt for the loss making State-owned luxury rioter and buses, making soaps and detergents, cosmetics, bread and a variety of other products? Indeed, we as consumers do have a right to choose. One of the objectives of the *Consumer Protection Act,* 1986, is *"the right to be assured, whereever possible, access to a variety of goods at competitive prices ".*

One of the objectives of the Consumer Protection Act, 1986 is the right to be assured, whereever possible, access to a variety of goods at competitive prices.

Further, certain laws like the MRTP Act are not binding on the public sector. It has been rightly observed by the Sanchar Committee. There is no justification for exempting Government and Government-controlled/owned undertakings from the provisions relating to control and prohibition of monopolistic and restrictive trade practices and the provisions related to unfair trade practices The beneficiary of monopoly legislation is the consumer and it is only fair and reasonable that undertakings owned or controlled by the Government should be subjected to the same type of rigour and discipline as the private sector undertakings, where the interests of the consumers are involved.

Due to the operational inefficiency of the public sector undertakings, the Government had announced in the Industrial Policy, 1991, that it was thinking of opening up to the private sector many of the industries reserved for the public sector, except the fields on strategic or military considerations.

CONCLUSIONS

The combined efforts of the consumers, business and government will be required to give consumerism the desired upliftment and make the government more responsive and effective and the business more responsible and obliging.

With post-liberalisation many dynamic enterprises having made their presence felt, the industry itself could consider consumerism as a unique opportunity and respond by involving itself in a more positive manner. Today, most of the industries have realised the value of adopting relationship marketing with their customers. In a broader prospective, this can be extended to become its social responsibility. This means the firms must adopt a sound and proper marketing system. It must ensure that all the products offered by it have been tested and proven to be within the safety norms. In case of consumer complaints, the same has to be handled properly and also a quick and smooth method of redressal is to be adopted by the firms. They should also use advertising as a method of communication only to convey the correct information. So as to be able to contribute to consumerism, the firms also should extend a helping hand and give information and educate the consumers, apart from investing in Research and Development to come out with products and services to match the rising needs and expectations of the consumers.

Thus, combined efforts of the consumers, businesses and the Government will be required to give consumerism the desired upliftment and make the Government more responsive and effective and the business more responsible and obliging.

THE CONSUMER PROTECTION ACT No.68 OF 1986

The Consumer Protection Act, 1986 is a very important legislation passed by the Government of India, to ensure a proper system is established for the protection of the consumer rights and the redressal of consumer disputes. This act also includes the amendments made vide the Consumer Protection (Amendment) Act, 2002 and was brought into force w.e.f. 15.3.2003.

This Act applies to the whole of India, except the State of Jammu and Kashmir and as otherwise expressly provided by the Central Government by notification, it applies to all goods and services.

The objectives of the act are:

1. To provide for the better protection of the interests of the consumers.
2. To fulfill the above objectives, make provisions for the establishment of Consumer Councils and other authorities for the settlement of consumers' disputes and for matters connected therewith.

Meaning of Complainant and Service

As per the act 'complainant' means a consumer, or any voluntary consumer association registered under the Companies Act 1956, or under any other law for the time being in force or the Central Government or any state government, one or more consumers where there are numerous consumers having the same interest or in case of the death of a consumer, his legal heir or representative who or which makes a complaint.

According to the Act, services of any description made available to potential users can be termed as *service.* Services can include all "facilities made available for the purpose of banking, finance, insurance, transportation, processing, supply of electrical or other energy, boarding and lodging, entertainment, amusement or the purvey of news or other information, but does not include the rendering of any service free of charge or under a contract of personal service.

According to the Act, services of any description made available to potential users can be termed as service.

Explanation

As per the act

1. *'commercial purpose'* does not include goods bought and used by a consumer for the purpose of earning his livelihood, by means of self employment.
2. *'consumer dispute'* means a dispute, where a person against whom a complaint has been made denies or disputes the allegations mentionsed in the complaint.
3. *'defect'*, refers to any fault, imperfection or shortcoming in the quality, quantity, potency, purity or standard which is required to be maintained or claimed by the trader under any contract or as under any law for the time specified or in any manner whatsoever, in relation to any goods.

4. *'deficiency'* refers to any fault, imperfection, shortcoming or inadequacy in the quality, nature and manner of performance as is required to be maintained under any law for the specified time period or is required to be performed by a person in pursuance of a contract or otherwise in relation to any service.
5. *'goods'*, refers to goods as defined in the Sale of Goods Act, 1930 (3 of 1930).

Consumer Protection Councils

Under the Act, provision is made for the establishment of the Central Consumer Protection Council by the Central Government and a State-level Consumer protection council in each State, by the respective State Governments.

The Central Council will consist of the Chairman, the respective Minister in charge of the consumer affairs at the Central government- level and such number of other official or non-official members/representing such interests as may be prescribed. The Council of members may meet as and when necessary. However, at least one meeting of the council shall be held each year.

The State Council shall consist of the Minister in charge of Consumer Affairs at the state level as its Chairman and such number of official or non official members (not more than ten) representing such interests as prescribed by the state government. Here also the council may meet as and when necessary though not less than two meetings shall be held every year.

The objectives of the Councils both the Central and State Councils are to promote and protect the rights of the consumers. However the State Council's objectives will be restricted to within the concerned State only as per clauses (a) to(f) of section 6 of the act.

More specifically, the objective of both the Councils are to protect the right of the consumers such as:

The objectives of both the central and state councils are to promote and protect the rights of the consumers.

(a) The right to be given protection against marketing of goods which are hazardous, dangerous to life and property.
(b) The right to get correct information on the quality, quantity, potency, purity, standard and price of various goods. That is to protect the consumer from unfair trade practices.
(c) The right to be able to make a choice from a variety of products, at competitive prices.
(d) The right to be heard and assured that consumers' interests will receive the due consideration at appropriate forums.
(e) The right to seek redressal against unfair trade practices or unscrupulous exploitation, and
(f) The right to consumer education.

Process of Consumer Disputes Redressal

Under the Consumer Protection Act, there is a provision for a three-tier consumer disputes redressal system at the District, State and National levels. Thus, the Act provides for the establishment of the following consumer disputes redressal agencies:

- A District-level forum, in each district of every State.
- A State-level Commission in each State, and
- A National-level Commission.

The National Commission was established by the Central Government in August, 1988, whereas the responsibility for the establishment of the State Commission and District Forum lies with the respective State Governments, after a prior approval is obtained from the Central Government.

Under the Consumer Protection Act, there is a provision for a three tier consumer disputes redressel system at the District, State and National levels.

The District Forum will include:

(a) A person who is, had been or is qualified to be a District Judge nominated by the State Government. This person will also be its President.

(b) Two other members, one of whom is a women and possesses the following qualifications namely (i) Should not be less than thirty five years of age (ii) possess a bachelor's degree from a recognized university (iii) be persons of ability, integrity and standing and have sufficient knowledge and at least 10years of experience in dealing with problems related to economics, law, commerce, accountancy, industry, public affairs or administration.

In the case of State Commission will include:

- A person who is or has been a Judge of a High Court and is appointed by the State. This person will also be the President of the Commission.
- Not less than two and not more than such number of members, as may be prescribed and one of whom shall be a woman having the following qualifications i.e. be not less than thirty five years of age, possess a bachelor's degree from a university.

Action taken by the consumer court against a complaint received.

- Members who shall be persons of ability, integrity and standing with adequate knowledge or experience or have shown capacity in dealing with problems relating to Economics, Commerce, Law, Accountancy, Industry, Administration or Public Affairs. (One of the members shall be a woman)

A complaint may be filed with a District Forum or State Commission, related to any goods sold or delivered or any service provided, as the case may be. The complaint may be filed by:

The District Forum is empowered to deal with complaints where the value of the goods or services and compensation if any, does not exceed five lakhs of rupees.

- A consumer to whom such goods are sold or delivered or such service is received;
- Any recognised consumer association, irrespective of whether the aggrieved consumer is a member of such association or not; or
- One or more consumers where there are numerous consumers with the same interest with the permission of the district forum on behalf of all consumers so interested.
- The State or Central Government.

The National Commission will comprise

- A person who has been a Judge of the Supreme Court and is appointed by the Central Government. This person will also be the President of the Commission.
- Two other members who are persons with ability, integrity and standing and with the adequate knowledge and experience or has shown capacity to deal with problems related to Economics, Commerce, Law, Accountancy, Industry, Pubic affairs or Administration.

The District Forum is empowered to deal with complaints where the value of the goods or services and compensation if any, does not exceed five lakhs of rupees. In case the value exceeds five lakhs, but does not exceed twenty lakhs of rupees, the State-level Commission is empowered to deal with the complaint, whereas complaints where the value is more than twenty lakhs of rupees, are to be dealt by the National Commission.

The State is empowered to deal with appeals against the orders of any District Forum within the State. It can also call for all the records and pass appropriate orders in any consumer dispute which is pending or a decision taken by any District Forum within the State, where it may appear to the State Commission that the concerned District Forum has exercised a jurisdiction not vested in it by law or it has failed to exercise a jurisdiction vested in it by law or may have exercised its jurisdiction in an illegal manner or not made use of proper regular material.

Appeals against the orders of the State Commission can be made to the National Commission. The National Commission is also empowered with similar jurisdiction (as mentioned in the above paragraph) over the State Commissions. It may also be noted that appeals against the orders passed by the National Commission can be made to the Supreme Court.

Regulations

In case any of the consumer disputes redressal agencies feel that any of the allegations filed by the aggrieved person or persons is true, it will issue an order to the effect that, the opposite party may have to do one or more of the following:

(a) To remove the defect from the goods in question, as pointed out by the laboratory.

(b) To replace the defective goods with new goods (which are free from all defects) of similar description.

(c) To return to the complainant the charges or price paid by them.

(d) To pay an amount as the case may be, as a compensation for any loss or injury suffered by the consumer, due to the negligence of the opposite party.

In case of any trader or person against whom a complaint is made, fails or omits to comply with the order passed by the redressal agency, he will be punished with imprisonment for a period not exceeding three years or with a fine not exceeding ten thousand rupees or with both.

Any person, aggrieved by the order of the particular consumer protection council has to appeal to the council at the higher level within a period of thirty days from the data of the order.

Every order of a District-forum, the State Commission or the National commission shall, if no appeal is made against such order under the provisions of this Act, will be final.

MRTP ACT

The Monopolies and Restrictive Trade Practices Act, 1969, aims to prevent concentration of economic power to the common detriment, provide for control of monopolies and probation of monopolistic, restrictive and unfair trade practice and protect consumer interest. As per the act, the practices which can be categorised into monopolistic, Unfair and Restrictive trade are given below:

(a) **Monopolistic Trade Practice :** Monopolistic trade practice is that which represents abuse of market power in the production and marketing of goods and services by eliminating potential competitors from market and taking advantage of the control over the market by charging unreasonably high prices, preventing or reducing competition, limiting technical development, deteriorating product quality or by adopting unfair or deceptive trade practices.

(b) **Unfair Trade Practice :**

- Misleading advertisement and False Representation
- Falsely representing that goods and services are of a particular standard, quality, grade, composition or style.
- Falsely representing any second hand renovated or old goods as new.
- Representing that goods or services, seller or supplier have a sponsorship, approval or affiliation which they do not have.
- Making a false or misleading representation concerning need for or usefulness of goods or services.
- Giving to public any warranty, guarantee of performance that is not based on an adequate test or making to public a representation which purports to be such a guarantee or warranty.
- False and misleading claims with respect to the price of goods or services.
- Giving false or misleading facts disparaging the goods, services or trade of another person or concern.

(c) **Restrictive Trade Practice :** To maximise profits and market power, traders often attempt to indulge in certain trade practices which tend to obstruct the flow of capital into the stream of production. It may also bring manipulation of prices or conditions of delivery or affect the flow of supplies in the market so as to impose unjustified costs.

Procedure

All consumer Complaints regarding monopolistic trade practice, unfair trade practice and restrictive trade practice can be made to the MRTP commission. All the complaints will have to be addressed to the 'Director General' (Investigation and Registration), MRTP Commission. The following procedure is followed by the MRTPC on complaint.

- Inquiry may be initiated through a complaint by an individual or registered consumer organisation.
- Fact finding investigation is carried on by the Director General.
- If no prima facie case is made, the complaint is dismissed, else an order is passed to that effect.
- The commission may restrain the party concentrated from carrying on the impugned trade practices by granting temporary injunction.
- Final order is passed. Compensation may be granted to the complainant.

➲ ICRPC

International Consumer Rights Protection Council (ICRPC)

ICRPC is a registered non profit, non political, Non Government Organisation (NGO) which works for the benefit and welfare of consumers who have grievances. The aims of the International Consumer Rights Protection Council, based at Thane (Mumbai) are :

- To work for a corruption free society.
- To educate the public on consumer issues and bring consumer awareness among masses.
- To help consumers fight against the powerful and corrupt officials and organisation.
- To guide and counsel consumers for filling their consumer complaints with the consumer count.
- To provide with the latest information on consumer laws through the website (www.icrpc.org).
- To take action against corrupt government officials and report the same to the concerned authorities.
- The enlighten and encourage the citizens of India to become aware of their rights as a consumer.
- To unite the public by offering them a platform to voice their grievances against defaulting companies and corrupt officials.
- Facilitate redressal of consumer grievance through out of court settlement and thereby reduce the load on the consumer courts.

Given below are examples of a few consumer complaints which were resolved due to ICRPC's intervention:

(a) Godrej Refrigerator : Replacement of Defective Unit : Mrs. C. Almeida of Thane (West) received a new Godrej refrigerator from the company within a month through ICRPC's action. She had approached them after she got fed up when nothing happened even after following-up the matter with the company for three years.

(b) APTEC Computer Institute : Refund of Fee : Full course fee refunded to Parminder from APTECH against consumer complaint for their low grade educational services. The case was filed at Sonipath (Haryana) but was withdrawn due to out of court settlement through ICRPC's notice.

(c) Chemist Shop : Refund against Defective Item : Miss Delia Antao of Nirmala Niketan received full refund against ICRPC's notice for a defective item sold by New Bombay Chemists, Mumbai. The item did not have manufacturer's name and address printed on the packing.

(d) LPG - Hindustan Petroleum : Connection Sold Fraudulently : LPG gas consumer receives a new gas connection from the Chairman, Hindustan Petroleum Ltd., Mumbai as a result of action taken against the dealer of HP who mischievously sold the complainant's consumer number to someone else.

SUMMARY

Consumerism is an organised movement of citizens and government to enhance the rights and powers of buyers in relation to sellers.

Since the 1980's even though changes have been occurring in the socio-economic environment like the rise in consumers earnings, growth of the media with a growing consciousness to adopt lifestyles more in line to global lifestyles, growing aspirations, etc. marketers in their quest to beat competition are also adopting unethical marketing practices. All these has led to the rise of consumerism in India.

To protect consumers against unethical marketing practices, the industry have put certain self-regulatory codes of conduct for the particular profession (for example, the Advertising Standards Council of India (ASCI). The Government has also brought in certain regulations like — Central Packaged Commodities (Regulation) Order, 1975, the Monopolies and Restrictive Trade Practices (MRTP) Act, 1969, Industries Development and Regulation Act, 1951, The Consumer Protection Act, 1986 etc.

QUESTIONS FOR DISCUSSION

1. Define consumerism.
2. Late Peter F. Drucker had said, "Consumerism is the shame of the total marketing concept." Comment giving your views on the rise of consumerism in India.
3. Explain how consumerism can benefit consumers.
4. Briefly explain the Consumer Protection Act, 1986.
5. How does the MRTP ACT describe unfair practices and restrictive trade practices?

SUGGESTED READINGS

1. Cherunilam Francis, *'Business Environment and Policy'*, Himalaya Publishing House, Mumbai, 1997.
2. Kotler Philip, *'Principles of Marketing'*, Prentice Hall of India Pvt. Ltd., New Delhi, 1985.
3. Schiffman. Leon. G, Kanuk Leslie. L, *'Consumer Behavior'*, Prentice Hall of India Pvt. Ltd., New Delhi, 1997.

4. *Consumer Protection Act*, 1986.
5. *Consumer Protection Regulation*, 2005.
6. www.monopoliesandrestrictivetradepracticesact.com
7. Chunawalla.S.A., *Commentary on Consumer Behaviour*, Himalaya Publishing House, Mumbai, 2001.

CHAPTER 15

MARKET SEGMENTATION

- Case : **Lifebuoy, Radio Mirchi**
- Concept of Market and Segment
- Benefits of Market Segmentation
- Criteria for selecting a market segment
- Bases for segmenting Consumer markets
- Bases for segmenting Industrial markets
- Strategic implications of market segmentation
- Summary
- Chapter Questions for discussion
- Suggested Readings
- Case : **Khadim Foot-wear**

CASE:

LIFEBUOY, RADIO MIRCHI

Lifebuoy from Hindustan Unilever Ltd. is one of the oldest soap brands in the world and has been available in India since 1895. Right from the beginning *Lifebuoy* has been segmented so as to meet the macho Indian males' need of a soap which takes care of their health and hygiene.

Even though India got Independence in 1947, it was only in the mid-fifties that the advertising industry came of age. The popular jingle, *'Tandarusti ki raksha karta hai Lifebuoy'* was as coined in the 50's. The jingle had struck a chord with the mothers then, who had made it mandatory for their children to wash themselves with lifebuoy when they got home in the evening after playing. In fact the above mentioned popular jingle had takers even in the rural market, where Lifebuoy was positioned as a soap for hand wash.

In 1964, Lifebuoy are relaunched with a slight modification in its shape and in the wrapper design. Although the health benefit' continued to be highlighted, the brand now started associating itself with sports events, portraying it as a champion's soap. This positioning reinforced the 'health and body fitness' dimension of the soap.

During the 1970's, with the advent of more competition, Hindustan Unilever Ltd., attempted to expand the scope of the lifebuoy brand through product line extensions.

- *Lifebuoy personal*
- *Lifebuoy plus* (targeted at the new, urban consumers, the old Lifebuoy with a new perfume)
- *Lifebuoy Gold* (targeted at the urban consumer, in a pure white colour with a different fragrance and also priced slightly higher)
- *Liquid Lifebuoy* a modern soap to strengthen the brand's presence in the urban market.
- *Lifebuoy Active* to counter the challenge posed by competitors selling non-carbolic soaps.

Lifebuoy, right from the time of its launch days until early 2000, has been consistently positioned as a soap which takes care of health and hygiene. Thereafter the brand Lifebuoy was repositioned as a soap which takes care of hygiene along with skincare. Its look was made more sleek and contemporary with an attractive, TV Campaign, which shows a group of kids trying to help clear rain water from a cricket stadium (because of which the match has been delayed), after taking a shower with Lifebuoy soap. The campaign claims that since the kids have the Lifebuoy protection, they are untouched by germs and diseases.

Right from the beginning, Lifebuoy has served the market segment which targets the Indian woman, who is interested in using a soap which would help her family fight germs and keep illnesses at bay. This consistency in its core positioning has helped the brand to retain its glory and even earned it the status of a heritage brand.

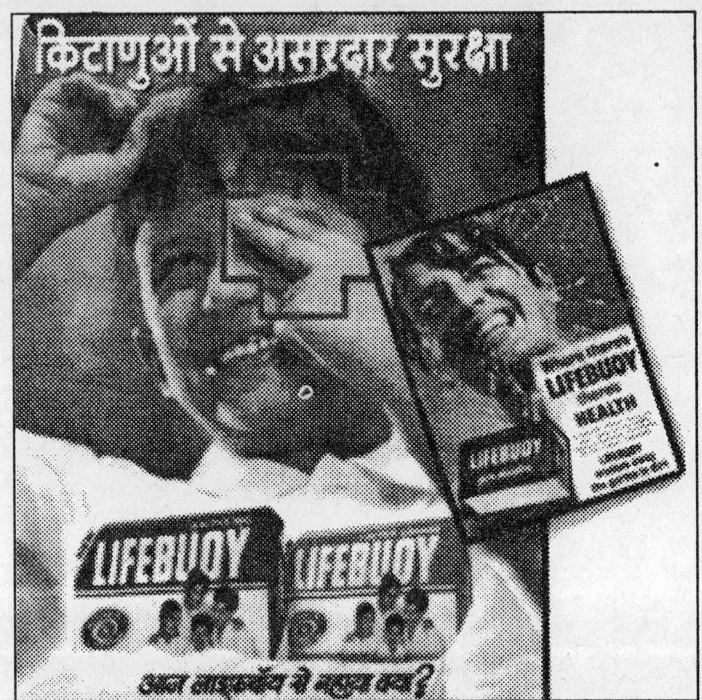

'*Lifebuoy's* positioning is changed from a macho male soap to a soap meant for the family

Positioning through *Communication* is another vital and powerful instrument with which the marketer tries to create a positive impact on the minds of the people. This can be illustrated with an example.

Radio Mirchi has always positioned itself as a mass premium brand of radio. Mirchi has woven itself in the minds of the people and gone beyond being just a 'Radio brand.' Mirchi is perceived as a state of mind and is often used in films to indicate youthful fun. It is ubiquitous with Bollywood, and with music. The campaign used for Radio Mirchi has brought out the essence of what the brand stands for, without featuring the product up front.

Information on Radio Mirchi has been conveyed in a very creative manner. Live sound is recorded, (in the commercial) during the shoot to add a touch of reality - in place of the usual practice of using dubbed dialogues and background music. Radio Mirchi had come out with a new commercial, using the television as a medium of communication.

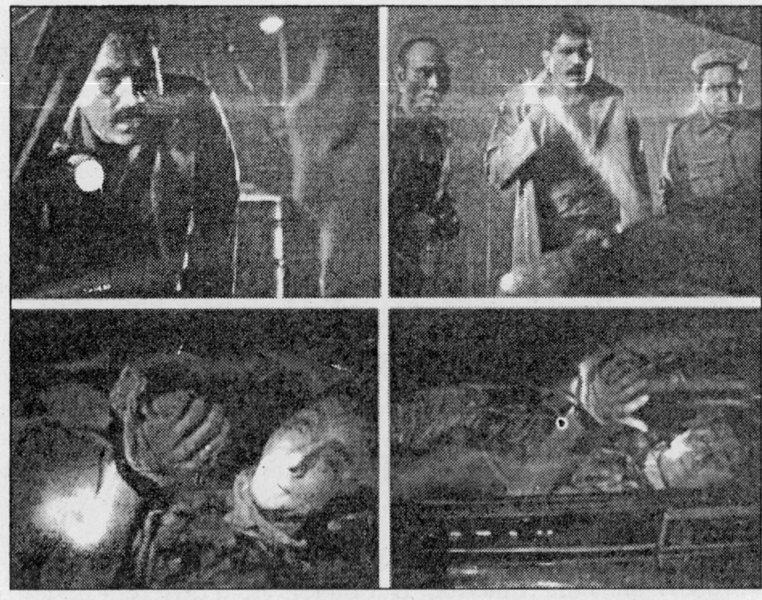

'Radio Mirchi' uses humour to communicate its unique positioning - "Mirchi sunnewale always khush"

This commercial had on television worked on a simple concept. A person has been kidnapped and locked up in the boot of the car. Yet, when he gets a chance to escape, he is not interested and bothered, for he is in a trance, obviously because he has been listening to Radio Mirchi.

In the earlier Mirchi's 'manhole' commercial, also the positioning of 'those listening to Radio Mirchi are always happy' was used. Continuing from where they left off, the new TVC had build on Mirchi's long standing positioning of *"Mirchi Sunnewale Always Khush."* Further, as the brand's commercial goes beyond just being a radio brand, indicating youthful fun, the TVC has also been put on YouTube. This move is to interact with the tech savvy generation who are actively engaged in undertaking interactive web experiences. This medium of communication (YouTube placement) has elicited some very good feedback on the station's website and email boxes.

The above two examples have illustrated that segmenting the market properly and using of suitable positioning will help to increase the brand awareness and create a positive image in the minds of the consumers.

Market for a given product will comprise of several consumer (market) segments. But these consumers are rarely homogeneous. They typically vary in terms of various characteristics and buying behaviour variables. So it is necessary for the marketer to divide the heterogeneous market for his brand into various segments based on certain common homogeneous consumer characteristics.

Consumers of a market segment are rarely homogeneous. They vary in terms of various characteristics and buying behaviour variables.

Alongside, the marketer will also have to use attractive, persuasive communication so as to transfer - the set of meanings, feelings and tones about their brand such that the prospective customer's perception of the product brand will match the same set.

In this chapter the focus is on market segmentation, targeting and the role of communication in planning, the marketing strategy. We start with defining the term market segmentation, discuss about its benefits and criticism and learn about the criteria for selecting a market segment. In India, we have a conglomeration of several markets and consumers displaying a varied consumption behaviour pattern within each market. Hence, we have had a detailed discussion of the various bases for segmenting consumer markets. This is followed by an examination of the strategic implications of market segmentation, the role of product positioning and a brief view on the technique of perceptual mapping.

Marketers are looking out for markets that exploit the firm's distinctive capabilities within the firm's markets and also for those market segments wherein it will have an edge over competition. But for this the firm will have to know the exact market to which it has to cater and then develop a suitable marketing strategy accordingly.

➲ CONCEPT OF MARKET AND SEGMENT

The term market has several meanings. It can be used in the sense of the network of institutions like wholesalers, dealers etc. dealing in the product. It can also be used to refer to the nature of demand for the product, as when we speak of the market for toothpaste. However, it must be remembered that the above two meanings of market are related yet distinct, so a change in one does not necessitate a change in the other.

For the term 'market', it can be inferred that buyers in the same market seek products for broadly the same function. Market segmentation is the process of dividing a heterogeneous market into homogenous sub-units.

Usually market is used to identify competition and to break down the market into segments. If viewed this way, the *'market for' will be referred to in relation to the function (s) served by the product.* Products having the same utility and performing the same function will be competiting with each other and hence in the same market. A firm's business is defined in terms of technology, customer group and function(s) served. So it would be more appropriate to refer to (or define) market in terms of its function (or purpose) served, which in turn will coincide with the customer group it is to serve.

Going by the above discussion on the term 'market' it can be inferred that buyers in the same market seek products for broadly the same function. But buyers hold different beliefs on what their interpretation is about that product which performs the functions efficiently. As a result, they are aware of the various brand options and will be attracted to different offerings based on how the brand will cater more closely to their wants.

DEFINITION OF MARKET SEGMENTATION

Market segmentation is the process of dividing a heterogeneous market into homogeneous sub units. Usually, marketers divide the heterogeneous market for any product into segments on the basis of some homogeneous characteristics. Market segmentation works on the premise that:

- Any market will be made up of several sub-markets or sub-groups of consumers, who can be distinguished from one another by their varying needs and buying behaviour, and
- It is also possible to disaggregate consumers into segments such that across or among segments the consumers may vary significantly in terms of needs, characteristics and buying behaviour but there will be homogeneity within each segment.

The Indian Consumer

In order to gain an understanding of the Indian market, let us have a brief look on the profile of the Indian consumer. According to the census 2001, as of May 2001, the population of India stood at 1,027 million, of which 742 million people (73 percent) lived in the rural areas and 285 million (27 percent) people in the urban areas. India is a vast country with people scattered over a wide territory.

Even India is diversely distributed in terms of climate, religion, language, literacy level, customs, economic status and lifestyles etc. This heterogeneity affects the consumption pattern and buying behaviour of the people.

The diversity in religion and language affects the social customs, tradition and cultural practices followed by the customers belonging to his or her religion. Although Hindi is recognised as the official national language, sixteen languages have been specified in the constitution of India. Over and above there are hundreds of dialects. This will be considered as a challenge for the marketer who is targeting the entire nation (India) as a market. While recognising the linguistic diversity, the marketer will have to work out a suitable media of communication for the consumers. Almost every religious community and every state follows its own traditional style of dressing and eating habits. As mentioned earlier, there is a great divide among people living in the urban India and rural India. This divide affects the consumption pattern of the people as well as the availability of infrastructure and mobility, level of health care and education.

India is diversely distributed in terms of climate, religion, language, literacy level, customs, economic status and lifestyles etc. This heterogeneity affects the consumption pattern and behaviour of the people.

Studies carried out by the Centre for Monitoring Indian Economy (CMIE) has indicated that there have been structural shifts in the consumption pattern of the Indian consumers which has especially gained momentum in the post-liberalisation period. Studies by NCAER also reveal that economic liberalisation has had a positive impact on Indian households, pushing up their incomes and expenditures.

The average Indian is a new phenomenon, spending more freely than before. NCAER's survey suggests that there have been changes in the conventional notion of what is a luxury product and what is to be treated as an essential commodity. This change can be attributed to the influence of the media, especially television. The television has worked as an eye opener, whereby the viewer gets exposed to the lifestyles of the well-to-do, international lifestyle and the sophisticated or modern products that are displayed on the screen. As a result, there have been significant changes visible in the lifestyles and buying pattern (or habits) of the Indian consumer. There is more acceptance of convenience foods and ready-to-eat foods, modern gadgets such as microwave ovens, vacuum cleaners, water purifiers and so on.

In the new nuclear family set up, there has also been a change in women's attitude towards cooking and eating habits.

Categorising Indian Consumers on the Basis of Economic Status

The above discussion reveals that India has got a huge and varied market. Thus, it is all the more necessary that marketers divide the market into various segments considering the more homogeneous characteristics, in order to tap it. A better understanding of the Indian consumers can be gained by classifying them looking into their economic status. As per this classification, a fourfold classification emerges:

◆ **The Affluent Group :** In terms of percentage this group may be small (about 40 million people as per Morgan Stanley Study). This market segment is suitable for luxury products. NCAER has estimated the affluent population in India to be those households whose income per annum will be above Rs. 10 lakhs. This segment is looking out for buying something new and upgrading to the styles set by those affluent in the west. They like to be conscious and display a willingness to spend on products and brands which will get them noticed by others.

◆ **The Middle Class :** The socio-economic developments that have taken place over the past many years has led to the emergence of the middle class. This class is referred to as the *'consumption community'* of the country. It is estimated, that the size of the middle class will be around 300 million.

The members of this class are equipped with better education, good jobs and income and with more exposure to global lifestyle, their aspiration levels are also constantly growing. There are other socio-cultural and lifestyle factors which have brought about a rapid shift in the consumption pattern of the middle class. These include – growth of urbanisation, breaking down of the joint family set up and women taking to work (resulting in more dependance on domestic help or modern gadgets). With many nuclear families becoming double income households, it has resulted in increased affordability and consumption of modern time saving gadgets. In such situations there is more acceptance to purchase products or services on credit. In such households, generally the wife also joins her husband while taking consumption related decisions. By virtue of her being educated and employed, the woman has become an active partner in the family decision making. She is well informed, not averse to change, though cautious and yet quality as well as cost conscious.

With the India middle class's upward economic mobility through increase in income and purchasing power, marketers need to study and understand this class more indepth and develop marketing strategies to target and segment this market.

A survey carried out by Pulse (Mc Cam Erickson Study) provided consumer insight on the new age urban Indian woman. The study used focus groups from the socio-economic classification groups (SECs) A & B and woman professionals from SEC A_1 in the age group 25-35 – across the cities of Delhi, Mumbai, Kolkata and Chennai. The study indicated a changed power equation in the way she sees herself today. She displays an enhancement of self esteem and confidence. She is comfortable donning both her traditional as well as modern outlook life roles. She is exercising greater control over her life and open to expressing her yearning for - recognition, personal grooming and pleasure and for emotional support.

The profile of the Indian middle class reveals that they form a huge demand base for various consumer durables. With their upward economic mobility through increase in income and purchasing power, marketers need to study and understand this class more in depth and develop marketing strategies to target and segment this market.

◆ **The Relatively Poorer Section :** Although the purchasing power of the consumers falling in this category is not much, they account for a reasonably good sized demand base for certain type of products. A study by NCAER revealed that over 75 percent of the purchase of products in categories such as cooking oil, tea, detergent cake, bath soap, tooth powder, transistor radios, and certain kinds of footwear was from consumers whose income level was below Rs 25,000 per annum. Although this group is economically backward presently they are beneficiaries of many social, educational and economic programmes. This has created a yearning amongst them – they aspire to join the middle class segment. So it is only a question of time, when this segment will become economically forward.

◆ **The Below the Poverty Line or BPL Segment :** As the term itself indicates, those falling in this segment are very poor and cannot be considered for the demand base for most consumer products.

➲ BENEFITS OF MARKET SEGMENTATION

There are many advantages or benefits of market segmentation:

◆ **Helps in Distinguishing one Customer Group from another, Selecting (or choosing)** the market and tapping it effectively. Through market segmentation, the marketer will be able to distinguish the customer group within a given market. This will also enable him to decide and select the segment which will form his target market.

◆ **Helps to Adapt the Offerings to Suit the Target Market's Needs and Tap it Effectively:** Through segmentation the marketer is able to identify and crystallise the needs of the target market. This will facilitate them to make an accurate prediction of the likely responses

Outlets catering to different category of customers based on their economic status.

from the various segments of the target market. Such exercises are also likely to obtain consumer responses which are homogeneous in nature. This will further help the marketer develop programmes and make offers suitable to each market segment. By understanding the consumers and adapting the product-service offerings, the marketer will be able to tap the market.

◆ **Enables Dividing the Markets and Conquering them :** Through market segmentation the marketer will be able to identify the differences among the customer groups and work out the suitable marketing strategy for each group. For instance, prior to liberalisation, there existed a *'mindset of scarcity'* and consciousness of *'value'* consumers, probably due to the socialistic learning that India as a nation had. However, post liberalisation, there has been a slow yet steady redefinition of the term value. Earlier, anything that was material had value, be it containers or durables, they were never disposed of with. But now a choice paradigm has set in. Earlier, every time one paid money, one got smaller; whereas, now there is an increasing tendency to use one's ability to buy things as a measure of 'success'.

Earlier, everytime one paid money, one got smaller, whereas, now there is an increasing tendency to use one's ability to buy things as a measure of success.

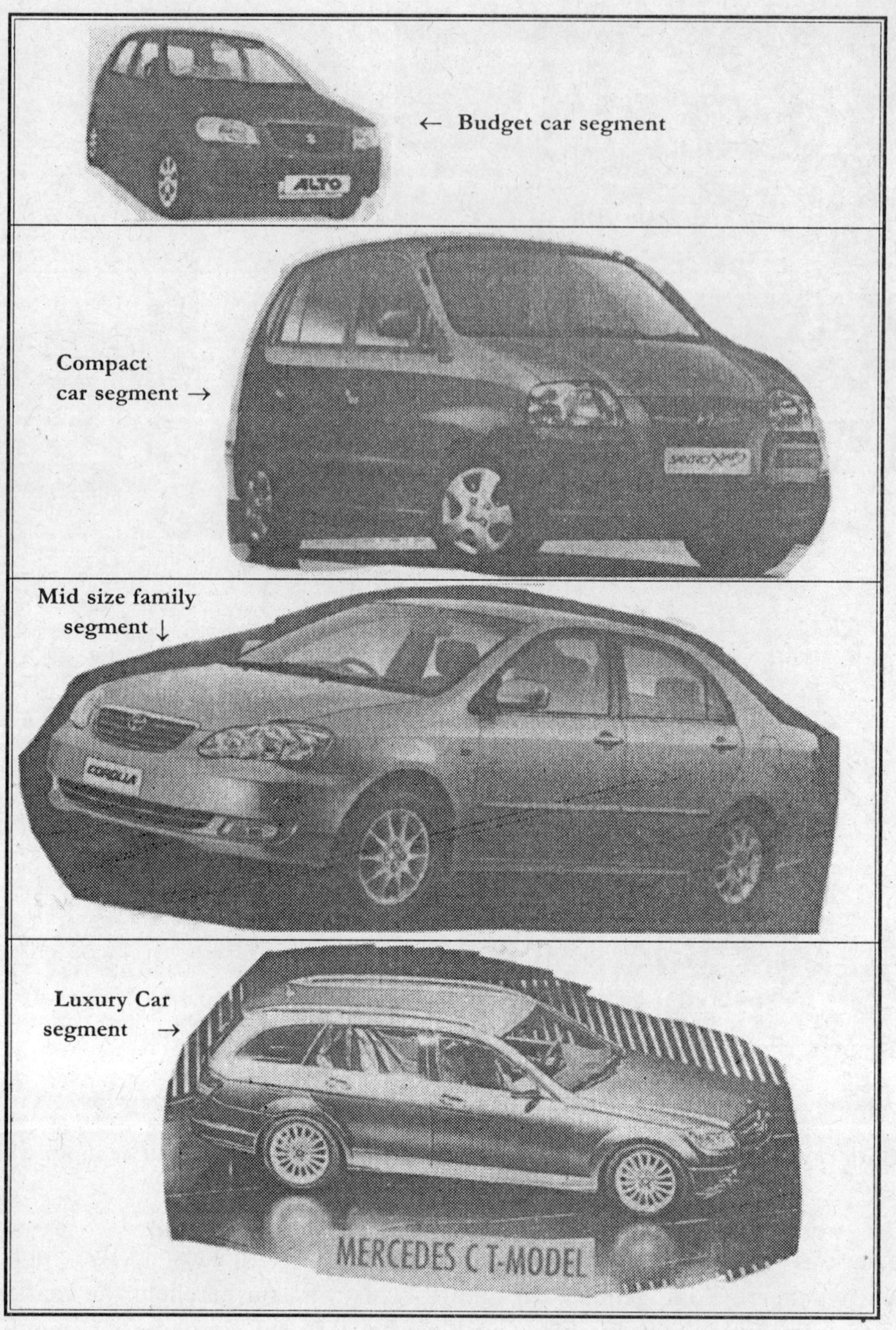

Examples of market segmentation for cars

Understanding the change in consumer behaviour and positioning the product to suit the particular market segment is what marketers of today strive to achieve. We can take the example of *Bajaj scooter.*

Till the mid 1990's *Bajaj Scooters* had been associated with the phrase *'value for money, for years'.* The owner of Bajaj scooter was not willing to part with it even after 15 years. Now, there is a growing sense within the middle class, that it can afford to spend today as more will come tomorrow. In fact, consumers are up-trading their cars at the first given opportunity. Realising this Bajaj Auto has dropped their *'value for money, for years'* and came out with a more contemporary phrase *'Inspiring, confidence'* and conquered the market.

◆ **Market Segmentation Helps to make the Marketing Effort more Efficient and Economical :** Through market segmentation, the marketer will be able to ensure their efforts are more efficient and economical. It will ensure that the marketing efforts are concentrated on well defined and carefully chosen segments. This will not only help in tapping the market but also ensure that resources are utilised properly by concentrating on segments that are most productive and profitable ones.

Market segmentation helps to make the marketing effort more efficient and economical and also helps to concentrate on less satisfied segments.

◆ **Helps to Identify and Concentrate on Less Satisfied Segments :** *Market segmentation helps the marketer to identify customers who belong to the less satisfied segments.* Based on the needs of the different customer segments marketers will make different product service offerings. They can also assess the customer satisfaction levels when compared to competitors offerings and identify the relatively less satisfied segment and make efforts to rectify the same.

◆ **Market Segmentation Helps Customers Too :** Market segmentation will benefit customers also for marketers will recognise their needs and customise products and offerings suitable to the particular segment. Take the example of the marketing war between the undisputed leader (till then) HLL and a new, emerging small firm *Nirma Chemicals*.

FIGURE 15.1

BENEFITS OF MARKET SEGMENTATION

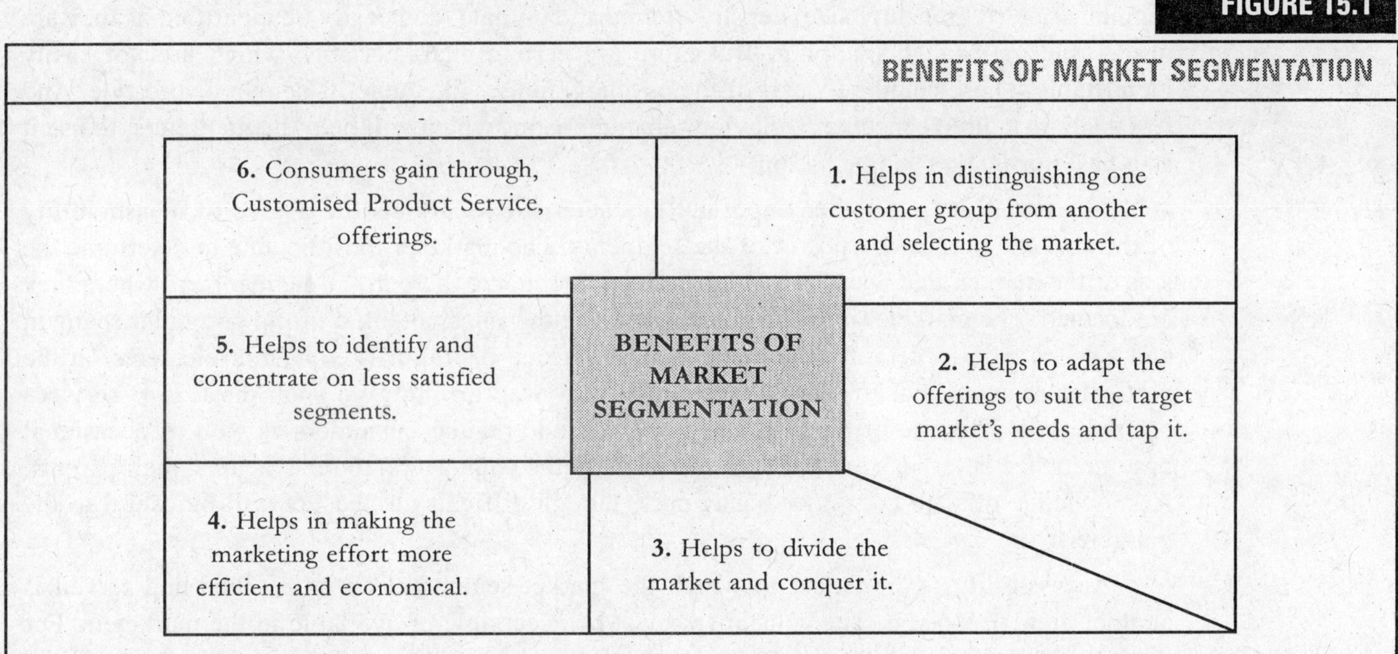

The launch of *Nirma* washing powder had shaken *Surf's* market No. 1 positioning, which Hindustan Unilever Limited (earlier known as Hindustan Lever Ltd.) could not recapture inspite of having many sales promotion campaigns. It was around that time (early 1980s) a fresh research was carried out across the country by HLL. This study revealed that consumers belonging to different income groups had varying expectations from washing powders and detergents. *For example,* middle and lower middle income group preferred purchasing yellow coloured washing or detergent powder. Middle class consumers washed expensive clothes with *Rinbar* or the white *Lux* flakes. In fact blue or white coloured detergent powders were associated with washing clothes clean and purchased by middle to higher income group of customers. Even housewives were said to be adding 'blue' to get the extra whiteness from their laundry of white clothes. Surprisingly, even the colour green was perceived by the target customers, to clean very dirty clothes. The study findings led to HLL launching the brand. *Sunlight* (yellow colour), *Rin* (blue colour), *Wheel* (green colour) and the *Surf Ultra* (White colour) detergent powders to cater to the customer requirements of the various market segments.

Thus, marketing segmentation will not only help to increase the firm's productivity but can also be used to add customer value.

CRITERIA FOR SELECTING A MARKET SEGMENT

Marketers will have to select one or more segments to target with an appropriate marketing mix.

Another aspect is the criteria for effective targeting of market segments. The marketers will have to select one or more segments to target with an appropriate marketing mix. For a segment to be viable, it must have the following characteristics:

Identification : To facilitate division of the market in various segments based on certain common characteristics relevant to a particular product or service, the marketers must be in a position to identify these characteristics. It is easy to identify certain segmentation variables because they are easily visible or observable. These *are demographics* such as age, sex, marital status, education and occupation. This information about demographic variables can be obtained either through observation or through research (by using questionnaires). Similarly, geographic segmentation (region, city size, density of area and climate) can easily be identified as they are observable or through mapping. But there are certain characteristics which are not easily identifiable. These could be a part of the psychographics, like benefits sought or lifestyle. And it is such intangible consumer behaviour characteristics which will help the marketers, to use it as a base for market segmentation.

Measurability : Another important characteristic ascertains the degree of measurability of the size and purchasing power of the segments. The marketer must be able to determine the size of the market, that is to find out how many people are there in the segment and where they are located. The marketer must be able to measure the sales potential of the particular segment and also be able to determine the extent of influence of the marketing mix elements on the particular segment. For instance, a restaurant may want to improve upon the F & B services offered by it. The size of the customers will include regular customers as well as occasional customers, the latter may eat and drink (especially the youngsters) to rebel against their parents. A knowledge of such consumer behaviours, though difficult to measure will be useful to the marketer.

Accessibility : The extent to which the market segments can be reached and served is another area of concern. The consumers must be accessible or available to the marketers. For instance, a company which sells *'skin care products'*, may find that heavy users of its brand are teenagers and young women, who are frequent visitors at fastfood centres and beauty parlours. But unless the firm is able to get more information on places or store preferences and exposure to various media's it will be difficult to reach this consumer segment. Because once the firm has found a medium that reaches their consumers, it can communicate with it's target segment effectively. Marketers try to reach their consumers through *"differentiated marketing for differentiated consumer profiles"*.

Substantiality : Another matter of concern for the marketer is the extent to which the segments are large enough and worthy of investment. For a market segment to be worthwhile, it must have a large number of people with specific needs and interests. The size of the large segment must be big enough to be economically viable. The size of the market is not the only indicator of the economic worthiness of the segment. It is also necessary to undertake consumer research methodology to determine whether the consumers are dissatisfied or only partly satisfied with the existing products and whether they are willing to pay for the firm's product. The target segment should be a large homogeneous group worth focusing with a tailored marketing programme. For instance, a company may observe that *'retired persons'* prefer to have a rocking chair. But going by the problem faced of space availability in houses, the size of the market is shrinking in nature. In this case the particular segment will not be substantial to make it a market.

Prestige Group's Forum mall has used suitable criteria while segmenting the market.

A matter of concern for the marketer is the extent to which the segments are large enough and worthy of investment?

Stability : Marketers would like to target consumers whose behaviours can be predicted. The marketers want to be sure of the stability of the consumers in terms of their demographic and psychological characteristics and wants and needs which are likely to grow faster over a period of time. Marketers would like to avoid 'fads' which may disappear one day because it is unpredictable in terms of durability.

A few years ago the travel industry noticed that when the 'airfares' were reduced (especially with the entry of the low cost airlines) many middle class customers were exposed to a taste of international travel for leisure. Today, when economic recession could have a negative impact on the travel plans of most persons, the industry is attempting at segmenting the market by offering special product service offerings to niche market segments. This is aimed at out bound tourists who are moving beyond the popular all family group tours.

Travel companies are now offering segmented (customised) holiday offerings for men and women separately. For instance, ***Kesari Travels*** (Mumbai) has 'My Fair Lady' offering trips for the woman who would like to let her hair down in the company of other women. They have built up a community around its 'My Fair Lady' travellers. The woman customers are offered a Club Card, with discounts from Card associate companies such as Tanishq, VLCC. They also keep the link alive through get-togethers organised periodically. The offerings include trips to a variety of domestic and international destinations.

FIGURE 15.2

CHOOSING A SEGMENT

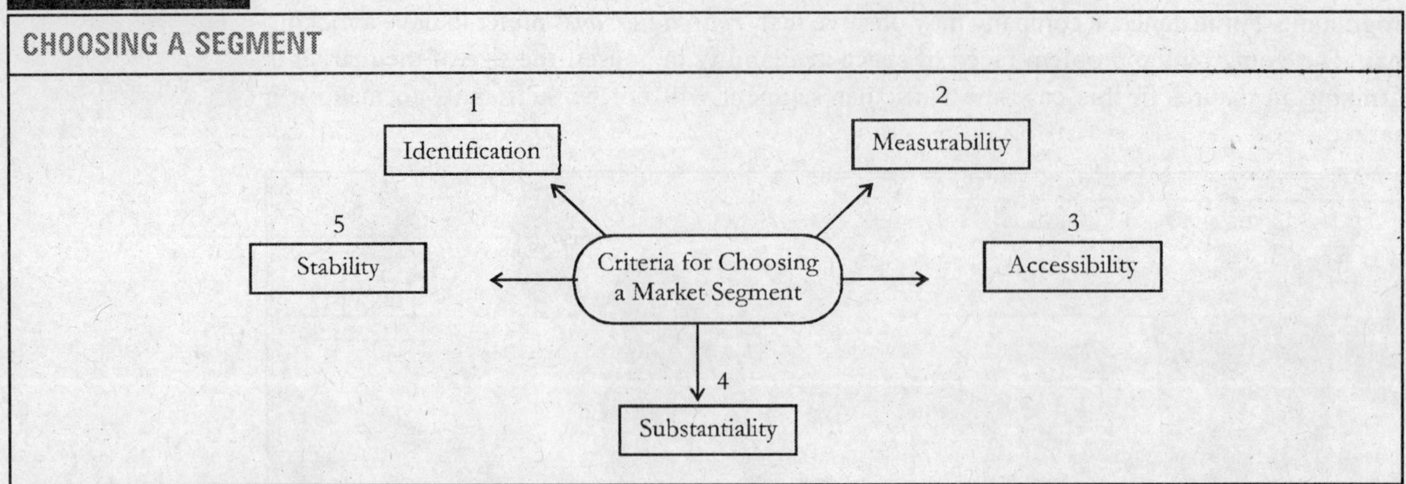

BASES FOR SEGMENTING CONSUMER MARKETS

In order to avoid the situation where the consumer may reject the firm's offering, marketers are looking beyond the conventional demographics to map the market.

The present day market scenario reveals the existence of a complex Indian market. There is no indicator to identify the motivators and demotivating factors affecting consumer behaviour. Marketers are trying to understand what motivates the consumer. In order to avoid the situation where the consumer may reject the firm's offering, marketers are looking beyond the conventional demographics to map the market. They have realised that consumer's purchase decision is strongly influenced by the interplay of various environmental factors like personal influences, family, situations, social class culture; individual differences in education, knowledge, interest, attitudes, personality, values, availability of resources and involvement level. Another related factor to consumer behaviour today is their willingness to try more products and the awareness of brand as compared to the consumer of yesteryears. All these indicate that there is a need for doing market segmentation to discover the needs and wants of the specific groups of consumers, uncover the factors which act as motivators for purchase and identify the segment where the product adds most value.

Markets consist of many buyers who vary in many respects as mentioned above. So there is no single way to segment a market. Hence marketers use different variables either singly or in combination, so as to get an insightful view of the target market. Here we have used the major geographic/demographic, psychographic and behaviouristic variables as bases for segmentation.

GEOGRAPHIC SEGMENTATION

Under geographic segmentation the market is divided according to the place or location. By and large, the rural consumers market is diverse in terms of religious, social, cultural factors, languages spoken and understood.

Under geographic segmentation the market is divided according to the place or location. The rationale behind this type of segmentation is that people located in the same area will share similar needs and wants which will be different from the needs and wants of people living in other areas.

Consumption behaviour will vary according to the climate of the particular region. In the North East region where it rains very heavily almost throughout the year there is a better market for umbrellas and raincoats, whereas in the West where there is extreme climate there will be better opportunities for selling cotton clothes and air conditioners in summer and woollen clothes during the winter.

The marketer may operate in one or more geographical areas or they may operate in all areas but pay more attention to variations in geographical needs and preferences. For instance, 'Bru *Coffee*' is sold nationally but is more preferred in South India. Similarly *'Red Label tea'* has got nationwide market but is more popular in the North India as compared to South. There are also other products brands like *Dabur, Amul, Glucon-D and Fevicol* which enjoy a premium position in the Eastern India, though they are national brands.

Rural Consumers

The rural market in India is not only widely geographically scattered but there are also visible differences in the rate of development (availability of infrastructure facilities, literacy rate etc.), from state to state. By and large, the rural consumers market is diverse in terms of religious, social, cultural factors, languages spoken and understood. Till some time back, the rural consumers were viewed as a conservative and tradition bound segment. However, since the past few years, there have been certain factors which have brought about lifestyle changes among them. These factors are:

- Growth in income and a change in the income distribution among the rural customers.
- The literacy rate among the rural people is slowly rising.
- Enlarged mass media-reach especially through the television.
- Many corporates are using developmental marketing programmes and trying to reach out to rural consumers and develop a market for their products. With lifestyle changes, studies (by NCAER, CMIE) have indicated that rural consumers consume a broad range of products from packaged tea, washing products, to personal care products, through to scootors and motor cycles. An interesting fact was revealed by NCAER survey, which showed that the rural market is growing faster than the urban market for certain product like packaged tea, analgesics, detergent (cake and powder) and washing soap. Rural demand is more seasonal, where income from agriculture plays a predominant role. Usually, marriages and festivals coincide with the harvest and influence the buying pattern and behaviour of the rural consumers.

Thus, firms interested in tapping the rural market will have to analyse these consumers in depth, and select relevant market segments through market segmentation.

Various researches by NCAER have indicated that of the total 1.1 billion Indian population, around 8-10 million comprise India's rich *i.e.,* households whose yearly income works out to be in excess of Rs. 45,00,000. Then there is an exclusive set of around 50-60 million consumers (mainly living in the metros) whose average annual household income hovers between Rs. 3 lakh and Rs. 10 lakh. This group is followed by some 250 million consumers with an annual household income of around Rs. 45000-2 lakh, they are referred to as India's real consuming class, mostly living in the country's top 27 cities.

According to the National Council of Applied Economic Research (NCAER), India's middle class had constituted less than 10 percent of its population in mid 80's. But post liberalisation with increased level of industrialisation and the subsequent rise of the services sector resulted in growing employment opportunities and the income levels also went up. All this has led to the growth of the middle class and today it comprises over 30 percent of the total population. With better education, good jobs, high disposable income, the middle class has been exposed to the best global consumption culture and are willing to indulge in the same. Table 15.1 gives an overview on what Indian consumers spend on.

With better education, good jobs, high disposable income, the middle class has been exposed to the best global consumption culture and are willing to indulge in the same.

The Indian economy has been growing with a GDP of over 6 percent (on average) in the past one decade. Strategic Consultant Gurcharan Das, the author of *India Unbound,* has opined that if the economy grows over 7 percent annually in the foreseeable future and the population increases by 1.5 percent and literacy rate keeps rising, then half of India will comprise of the middle class between 2020 and 2040.

Tables 15.2 and 15.3 indicates NCAER estimates on how the number of households are likely to move up in terms of income levels and rise in households to a higher class.

TABLE 15.1

SPENDING PATTERN OF INDIAN CONSUMERS

Category	Percentage (%)
Food and Beverages	42
Transport and Communication	15
Rent, Fuel and Power	12
Health care	8
Clothing and Footwear	5
Furniture and Fixtures	4
Recreation and Education	3
Miscellaneous	11

TABLE 15.2

ESTIMATION OF THE MILLIONS OF HOUSEHOLD LIKELY TO JOIN THE MIDDLE CLASS BY 2013

Rich Households	3 million	11 million	(Per annum income which is more than Rs. 2,10,375)
Aspirers	46 million	124 million	(Per Annum between Rs 43, 875-210,375)
Strivers	131 million	96 million	Per Annum income less than Rs. 43, 875.
Household Category	2003	2013	

DEMOGRAPHIC SEGMENTATION

Demographic variables are the most popular bases for distinguishing consumer groups. Marketers can easily get access to demographic variables and it is also easily verifiable and measurable.

The most frequently used bases for market segmentation are the demographic characteristics like age, sex, marital status, income, occupation education, religion and caste. Demographic variables are the most popular bases for distinguishing consumer groups, marketers can easily get access to demographic variables and it is also easily verifiable and measurable. Consumer needs and wants, preferences, and usage rate are also closely related to demographic variables. If information of psychographic or sociocultural variables are available, they have to be linked back to the demographic variables in order to get a better interpretation of the findings. This will help to work out the size of the market and also on how to reach it efficiently.

Age : Marketers have often found age to be a very useful factor indicating a change in the consumer interests and product needs which vary with consumer's age. Even babies who are six months old differ from babies who are one year old in their interest and consumption potential. *'Leo Toys'* & *'Funskool'* are two names associated with makers of children's toys. These two companies have designed different toys to be used by children of all ages, starting sequentially from babyhood, to pre-scholar, to school-goers and so on.

TABLE 15.3

THE ESTIMATED INCREASE IN INCOME IN INDIAN HOUSEHOLDS BY 2010

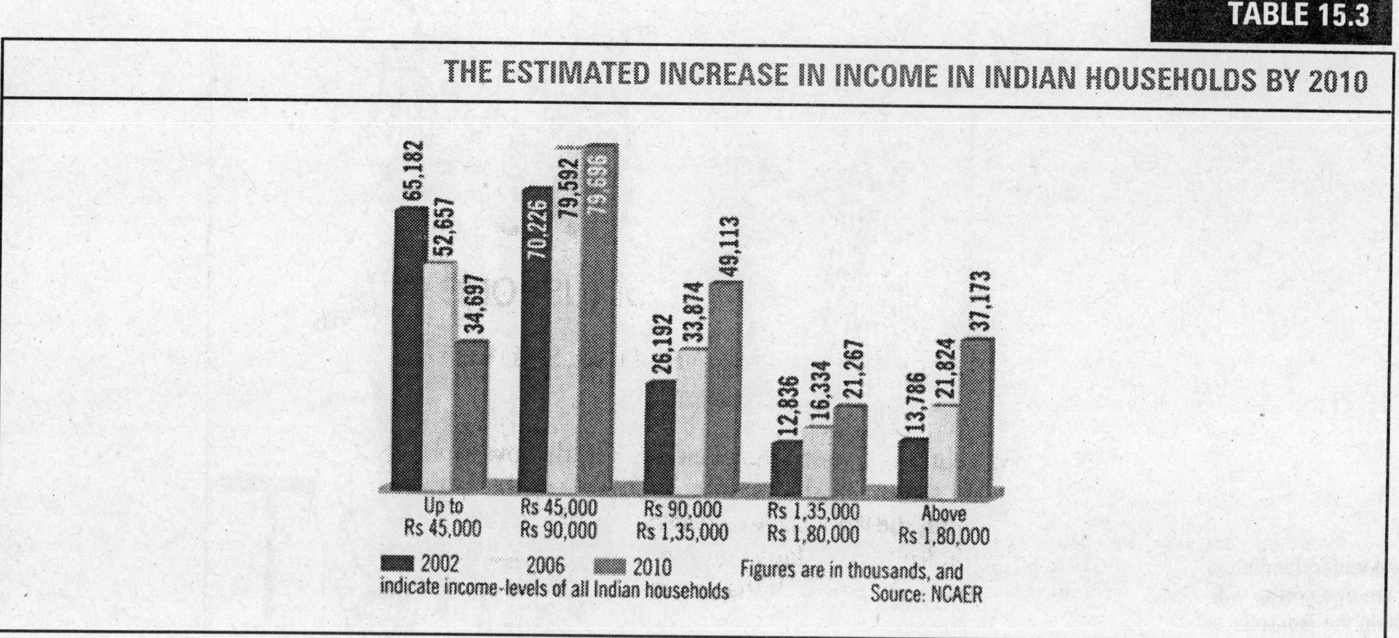

(Business Today, January 14, 2007)

Based on the assumption that all those belonging to the same age group are likely to behave or display an identical buying behaviour, marketers typically follow the agewise division as:

- Infants market (newly born - 1 year)
- Toddler market (from 1 - 2 years)
- Child market (2 - 12 years)
- Pre-teens market (11 - 13 years)
- Teens market (13 - 19 years)
- Adolescent market (16 - 19 years)
- Youth (young) market (20 - 35 years)
- Middle age market (36 - 50 years)
- Retirement age approaching (51 - 60)
- Senior citizens (Above 60 years)

An understanding of the age profile will help the marketer to design the marketing strategy to suit the particular age segment. Children are said to be a key influencer in the family purchase decision. Take for instance, the tween market. It is estimated that there are about 120.47 million tweens (as in January 2006) and over the next 10 years. *i.e.,* by 2016, it is believed that this number will rise to 116.19 million. The market can said to be children who are between the ages of eight and twelve. They lie between the younger children (infants, toddlers, pre-schoolers and early schoolers) who are almost dependent on their parents and teenagers (who would like to believe that they are not dependent on anyone). It has been observed that children start defining themselves around the age of eight. This is done in terms of their parents, friends (peer pressure plays a big part in their consumption habits) school, activities and so on.

Market segmentation based on 'Age' and taste in dressing

An understanding of the age profile will help the marketer to design the marketing strategy to suit the particular age segment.

Marketers have identified several facets of tweens that make them ideal targets for marketing programmes. Tweens are aware of brands. In urban areas, a substantial number of them come from double-income homes and thus are empowered early to make purchase decisions and spend money. There is also *pester power,* which drives tweens purchase decisions even in categories such as TV and Cars. Says R. Suresh, Deputy Managing Director, *TNS India "Children in the age group are seen as tomorrow's consumers and the segment is important to companies from the point of view of entry and brand awareness"*.

Another important segment is the youth market in India. As compared to the previous generation, the contemporary Indian youth are experimentative, daring, financially more secure and more educated, with a modern outlook. Parents of today's youth have developed more acceptance of the aspirations, changing tastes and eccentricities of their children. This is reflected in the ads of *Fair & Lovely, HDFC Standard Insurance, Franklins Institute of Airhostess training, Idea cellular* (women card). The youth believe in style and substance and are more aware of the consequences of relationships, Sex, AIDS, politics and career. Titan had introduced *Fastrack,* watches with a positioning statement *Fastrack - Cool watches by Titan.* This lifestyle positioning was to match the *young, vibrant and cool* youth market. Even television channels such as *MTV, V* and Music Stores such as *Planet M* cater to the tastes and preferences of today's youth.

As compared to the previous generation, the contemporary Indian youth are experimentative, daring, financially more secure and more educated with a modern outlook.

Ads of *TVS Apache, Bajaj, Hutch* typically use commercials which reflect the tastes of the young of today.

Ad tries to reach out to the youth who listen to FM Radio.

Gender : Gender is also a very important and a distinguishing segmentation variable for marketers. This is prominently visible in the clothing, hair dressing and magazines read by both the sexes. Traditionally women have been users of hair products and cosmetics whereas men were identified to be users of tools and shaving products. However, today one cannot clearly distinguish consumers in some product categories merely based on gender. For instance, women are actively involved in buying household appliances and vehicles whereas men have become significant users of skin care and hair products. Very often we get to see magazines and T.V. commercials depicting men and women in very different roles as compared to their traditional roles. For instance, the ad *of Nivea for men', "who says care is not for men"* reflects the child-nurturing role undertaken by young fathers in today's society.

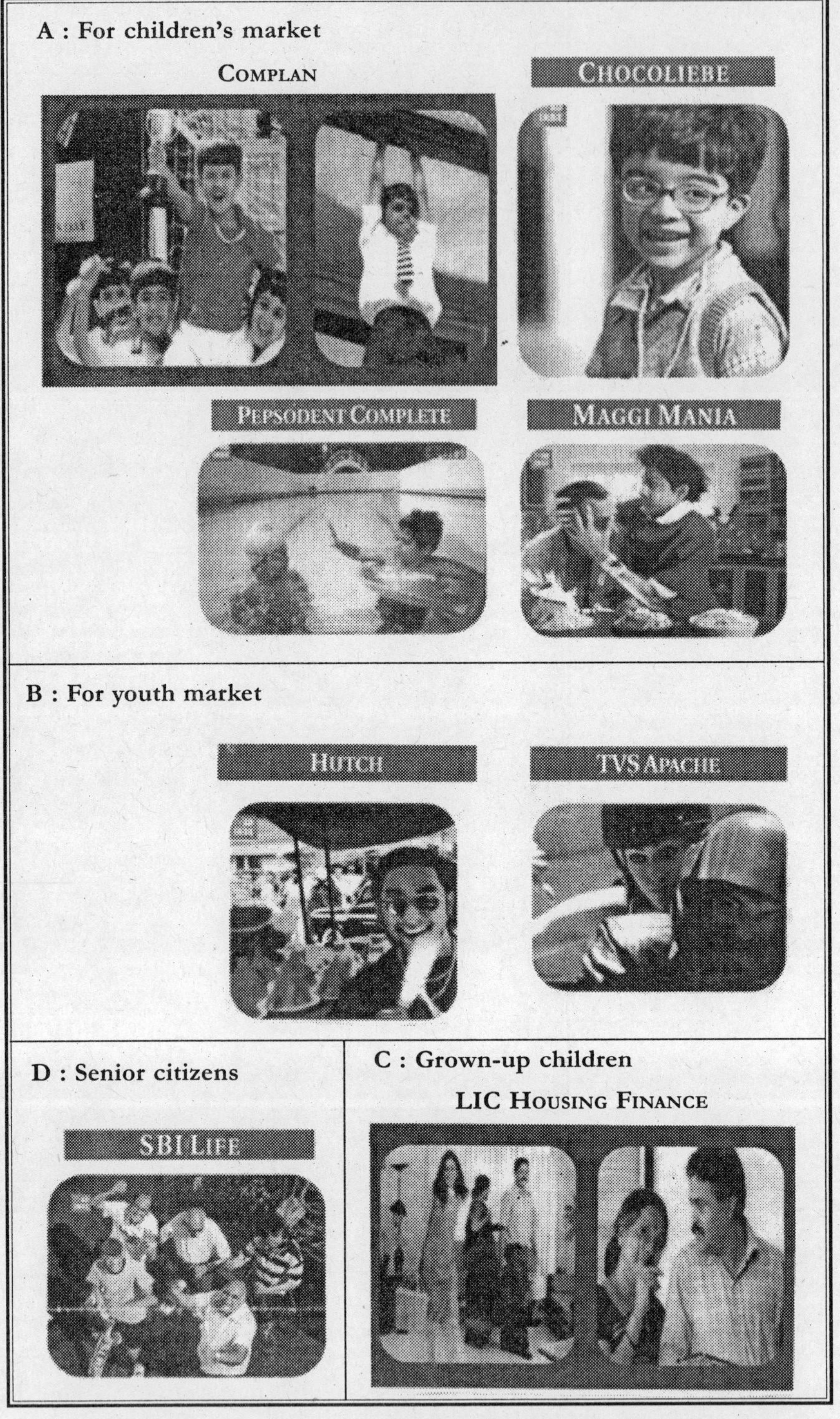

Ads reflecting the tastes of different age group of consumers

Gender is a very important and a distinguishing segmentation variable for marketers. While formulating marketing strategies, marketers, have to take into consideration the gender factor keeping in mind the change in the roles of both the male as well as female consumers of today.

The change in the sex roles can be attributed mainly to the change in role of a housewife of yesterday as against the role of the working women-cum-housewife of today. This has given rise to dual income households especially in urban India. Being hard pressed for time, as their role involves making an ideal combination of a working woman or professional-cum-housewife-cum mother, most of the women today do not have much leisure time to watch T.V. or listen to radio etc. Realising this, advertisers are using various media like Direct mailers, or Catalogue, Tele marketing etc. to communicate and help the working women in shopping for personal clothing, personal care products, household and family need products. *For example, 'HDFC bank'* uses tele marketing for inducing customers to open account with them and avail of all the financial benefits offered by it by enabling operating the account from home. Tele marketing today in India, is a growing activity from financial services to times shares, corporate gifts to at times even golf club memberships.

Ad is targeted at the "New Age Man" of today.

For the New Age man of today, looking good is important. A survey done by a marketing information organisation in India, revealed that more than 60 percent Indian men are grooming themselves, with the male grooming market in India having touched Rs 650 crore and is growing at the rate of 11 percent. Grooming and beauty consciousness have penetrated the male psyche like never before. Women of today are independent, confident, educated, well groomed and ready to match shoulder-to-shoulder with her male counterpart. In order to match steps, the Indian males are also grooming themselves to get the perfect looks and personality.

Liberalization, education, awareness of international styles (and trends), employment and a more tolerant and supportive family have helped the Indian women to develop a broad attitude in her purchase decisions. Although for products like apparel and clothing, gender is used for segmenting the market, it may vary for personal care and self grooming products.

Thus, while formulating marketing strategies, marketers, have to take into consideration the gender factor keeping in mind the change in the roles of both the male as well as the female consumers of today.

Marital Status and Family Life Cycle

The family has been very relevant for most of the marketing efforts. Further, for most of the products and services, the household continues to be a very important consuming unit. Marketers are also interested-in knowing the roles of the various family members especially the persons involved in the actual selection of the product. Marketers are basically keen and interested in knowing the number and the kind of household of their target market, the details of the demographic variables and the media profiles of the various households.

Marketers are also targeting consumers keeping in mind their marital status and family life cycle. For example: *'Gili' jewels* conveys the message by showing the love a husband has for his wife (couple having a grown up child) by gifting her a diamond ring: *'Acquaguard'* is targeted at young mothers with young children, (she is anxious about the health of her children). The various 'real estate' advertisements are meant for different categories of consumers - like bachelors (professionals and career oriented) young, married couple with children (reasonably priced, may be a 2 bedroom flat) and so on. Similarly, the various college education loan schemes offered by financial institutions such as *The State Bank of India, Canara Bank* are targeted at youngsters aspiring to study further. Most of the home appliances such as microwave oven, home theatre, etc., available in the market are meant for household consumption.

Marketers segment the market on the basis of income for it is assumed that there exists a relationship between a person's income and his or her consumption behaviour.

Income, Education and Occupation : Income is a very important and distinguishing demographic variable because it indicates the capacity or ability of the consumers to purchase the product. Marketers segment the market on the basis of income for it is assumed that there exists a relationship between a person's income and his or her consumption behaviour. Research has indicated that when consumer income increases, from the total expenditure, the percentage of expenditure on food and other basic amenities declines. For instance, this behaviour is visible (among) the young professionals of today. These young people are able to procure exciting jobs with an attractive salary, at a young age (usually in their early 20s). Such persons with higher income start buying branded products and become consumers of the so-called luxuries such as domestic or global tourism, air travel, automobiles, perfumes, microwave ovens, cooking ranges, washing machines, mobile phones with camera and other latest technically advanced gadgets. Usually, marketers segment markets on the basis of income for they feel that this parameter will help them to analyse the ability (or inability) of the consumers to pay for a particular brand of product or service. However, to get a more accurate consumption behaviour picture of the target market, an ideal combination will be income-cum-education cum occupation. These three variables are very often closely related. Usually, the Indian market has been stratified from the rich to the poor by considering the annual family income and their consumption of goods and services. As per the NCAER research findings (India's Market Demographics Report, 2002), income-wise basis of consumer segmentation can be:

'The ad is directed at the women of today'

- *The Affluent* (Households owing personal car/jeep with other products)
- *The Well off* (Households owing many durables but no car/jeep)
- *The Climbers* (Households with any/all - moped, VCR/VCD B/W TV etc. But not those under the above categories)
- *The Aspirants* - Households owning any/all of - bicycle, electronic fans, electric iron with other durables but not households mentioned under the first three categories.
- *The Destitute* Households other than those classified under categories 1 to 4 above.

The behaviour pattern of each of these household categories is different. So the marketer is required to customise products and prices to match the particular segment. For instance, the affluent consumers may own multiple houses, cars, jewellery etc. These consumers try to seek social exclusivity, social esteem and power. While, for those belonging to the lower end of the market, the marketer needs to use imaginative and innovative approaches. This is because they have brand awareness but are price sensitive.

'The product service is unisexual and directed at both (women and men) segments'.

The inter relationship between education, occupation and income also indicates a closeness to the social class of the consumers. This, in turn, will reflect values, tastes, attitudes and lifestyle of the individual consumer.

The above three variables of education, occupation and income will also throw light and help the marketer gain insight on the media preferences of the target group. This information can be used by the marketer to plan a communication mix of the various media. *Mudra Communications,* 'prepared a traffic update programme on *FM Radio* for mobile phone makers, *Hutchison Max cellphone service',* to drive home the message about the benefits of mobile phone service, fully knowing the comments, annoyance about stalled traffic.

It may be noted that the inter relationship between education, occupation and income also indicate a closeness to the social class of the consumer. This, in turn, will reflect values, tastes, attitudes and lifestyle of the individual consumer.

Religion : Indian consumers can also be differentiated on the basis of the religion or caste to which they belong. Religion as a basis of segmentation categorises consumers as Hindus, Muslims, Parsis, Sikhs, Christians, Jain and Buddhists. To a certain extent the effect of religion is seen in the food consumption behaviour and clothing habits of the consumers.

Reading habits will vary among consumers depending upon their lifestyle and education.

PSYCHOGRAPHIC SEGMENTATION

Here the marketer will divide the consumers into various groups on the basis of their social class, lifestyle and or personality characteristics. Even within the same demographic group, consumers can reveal very different psychographic profiles.

Social class : This is a very important variable clearly seen in the consumer's buying behaviour. Social class has always been a potential market segmentation variable for the marketer. The concept of social class indicates a hierarchy in which people in the same class generally have the same degree of status whereas members of other classes occupy either a higher or lower status (This concept of social class has been elaborately discussed in a separate chapter in the book). Studies have revealed that social class plays a role in consumers buying habit, product preferences, attitudes and values.

Studies have revealed that social class plays a role in consumer's buying habit, product preferences, attitudes and values.

FIGURE 15.3

AN ESTIMATE OF THE LIKELY HOUSEHOLDS, THE VARIOUS SOCIAL CLASSES IN 2013 AND ACTUAL FIGURES IN 2003

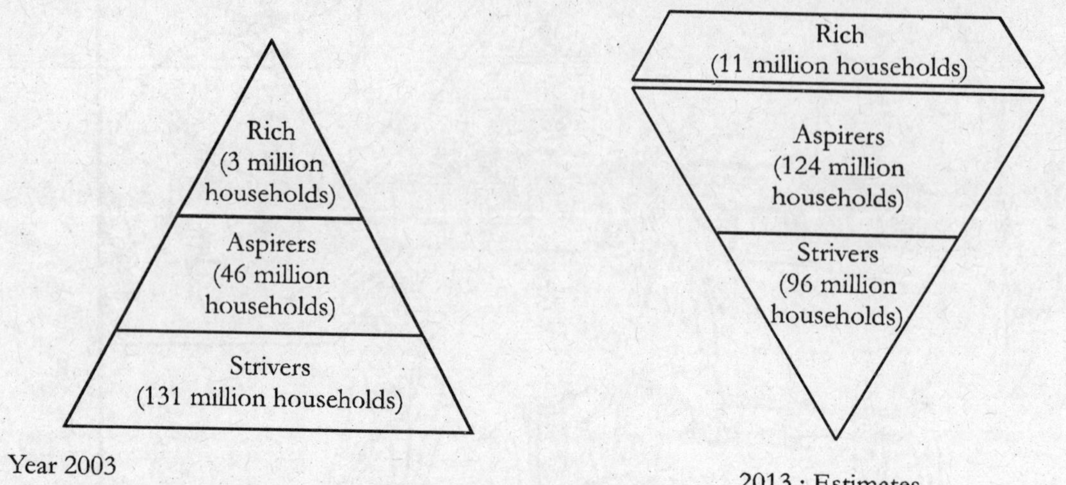

Note : (a) Rich households with per annum income more than Rs. 2,10,375
(b) Aspirers with per annum income between Rs. 43,875 to Rs. 2,10,375
(c) Strivers with per annum income below Rs. 43,875

(Sources : NCAER Study, *Business Today*, Jan 14, 2007)

A study conducted by NCAER to identify the real figures and facts about the 'rich' - has resulted in a redefinition of the rich.

A broad classification of the social classes can be put as :

- The Rich Class,
- The Aspirers,
- The Strivers.

Studies carried out by Technopak indicate that today there are about 1.6 million households earning over $ 100,000. These households belong to the rich and above social class who spend nearly $ 9000 per annum on luxury goods and are estimated to be growing at the rate of 14 percent per year.

For the middle class or aspirers, gone are the days of scrimp and save or struggle for survival. These households have moved on in life from mere availability of products and goods to demanding better quality and experiences.

For the middle class or aspirers, gone are the days of scrimp and save or struggle for survival. These households have moved on in life from mere availability of products and goods to demanding better quality and experiences. Apart from the market being filled with many products, the easy credit offerings from banks have helped these households to demand and experience better shopping facilities. With better per capita and disposable income these consumers are becoming open to indulging themselves and adopting a better lifestyle.

Liberalisation has changed the landscape of the Indian market. The increased level of industrialisation and consequently the growth of the services sector led to a growth in the employment opportunities and rise in the income levels.

According to the NCAER, India's middle class had constituted less than 10 percent of its population in mid 80's but now it comprises over 30 percent of the total population. Another reason for the growth in the size of the middle class can be attributed to the various transformations occurring at the social level. This includes a younger population which is financially independent at a much earlier age, the rise in the number of nuclear households and an increased media exposure giving rise to a new consumption culture in the country. NCAER has identified the number of households with per annum income ranging between Rs. 43, 875 - Rs. 2,10, 375 or the Aspirers in 2003 was 46 million and this segment is estimated to increase to 124 million households by the year 2013.

Ad will appeal to the affluent social class segment.

Marketers will have to work out more self sustaining scalable models which will not only make consumers out of the poor but also provide them opportunities to raise their income levels and motivate them to purchase products and services with their disposable income.

C.K. Prahalad has suggested that marketers can also make profit by focusing on the consumption needs of those belonging to the bottom of the pyramid. According to C.K. Prahalad's theory of "the market at the bottom of the pyramid" *What is needed is a better approach to help the poor, an approach that involves partnering with them to innovate and achieve sustainable win-win scenarios where the poor are actively engaged and, at the same time, the companies providing products and services to them are profitable"*. This segment is price sensitive though brand conscious and value conscious with increasing awareness of the benefits of communication network. With ownership of cellular phones and T.V. this segment of the consumers have unprecedented access to information as well as opportunities to enter into a dialogue with the larger community. However, since these consumers are price sensitive, marketers need to carry out a careful analysis of price-performance relationship and then provide innovative solutions (suitable products and services). Some of the companies have started working on this. For instance, *Microsoft India* have chalked out programmes such as Project Shiksha - for accelerating IT literacy, Project Bhasha - to promote local language computing and Project Jyoti - for empowering women and rural communities. *HLL* (Now Hindustan Unilever Ltd) has a Project Shakti, which looks out for self help group (SHG) and invites rural women to become direct - to - consumer distributors. For this *HLL* has several products in its portfolio that are affordable to the poor - Shampoo Sachets at 50 paise, Soaps and detergents at Rs. 5 and toothpastes at Rs. 10. Apart from helping to penetrate the market, even the distributor gets a chance to earn a decent income of up to Rs. 10,000 per month. As a part of this project are the Shaktivanis, who are trained to communicate the brand's attributes alongwith the virtues of health and hygiene and basic healthcare. So the benefits are manifold: the women (Some 30,000 of them at least) get to earn a living, their fellow dwellers are educated about health and hygiene and an intangible benefit is of women empowerment. *HLL* through its Project Shakti has been able to increase the consumption of its core products, among the destitutes which account for 15 percent of rural sales (as in January 2007). *Dish* TV from the Essel Group has been able to increase its subscription to 1.7 million subscribers across the country through its DTH (Direct- To - Home) satellite TV which can penetrate into the remote areas of the country. *Bharti Airtel* has tied up with low cost hand set manufacturers in order to provide cellular services in the rural markets. For this segment of customers it had also introduced the Rs. 200/- recharge coupons and the Rs. 999 lifetime prepaid card. Thus marketers will have to work out more such self sustaining, scalable models which will not only make consumers out of the poor but also provide them opportunities to raise their income levels and motivate them to purchase products and services with disposable income.

Income Levels and Consumer Classification

NCAER research studies have indicated that there is an increase in income among the various income groups. When compared to the high (or top) level income group, the growth rate in the middle and higher middle income groups is faster. Further the households classified as destitutes and aspirants have showed a negative trend. The study had taken the following annual income ranges, at 1994-95 prices as the basis for each of the categories (Table 15.4).

TABLE 15.4

CLASS CATEGORY ANNUAL INCOMEWISE

Class Category	Annual Income Range
Very Rich	Over Rs. 2,15,000
Consuming Class	Between Rs. 45,001 and Rs. 2,15,000
Climbers	Between Rs. 22,001 and Rs. 45,000
Aspirants	Between Rs. 16,001 and Rs. 22,000
Destitutes	Below Rs. 16,000

This NCAER study findings indicated that the growth in affluency among Indian households can be attributed to :

- Existance of many double income families with one or no children.
- Re-emergence of joint families and parents taking care of the house.
- Emergence of a new breed of entrepreneurs.
- Higher incomes in the corporate sector.

The behaviour pattern of the various household categories will vary and so also their value systems.

NCAER's India's Market Demographics Report, 2002 had given the following basis of consumer classification :

1. *The Affluent/Very Rich :* Households owning personal Car / Jeep with other products.
2. *The Well-off / Consuming Class :* Households owning any / all of these - air - conditioners, motor cycle, scooter, washing machine, refrigerator, colour television with other durable products but no Car / Jeep.
3. *The Climbers :* Households owning any / all of these - moped, VCR/VCP, mixer grinder sewing machine, audio equipment (two-in-ones, etc.) black & white T.V, geyser with other durable products but not those mentioned under the first two categories.
4. *The Aspirants :* Households owning any / all of these - bicycle, electric fans, electric iron with other durables but not households mentioned under the first three categories.
5. *The Destitute :* Households other than those classified under the above 1 to 4 categories (owning any / all / none of these – wrist watches, pressure cooker, mono cassette recorder, transistor / radio).

The behaviour pattern of the various household categories will vary and so also the value systems. For instance, the middle class consumers will desire to dissociate themselves from their roots and display buying behaviour so as to move up to the ranks of the affluent or rich class. On the other hand, the affluent are always looking out for exclusivity, so their aspirations and buying behaviour will revolve around social exclusivity and power.

Another related aspect is the change in the value systems over time. However, there are certain terminal or acquired values which continue to be held even with passage of time - for instance, in India, strong family bondage and love for the family have always been a core value and a major driving force. Marketers have used product or service campaigns linking core values of family care into their product - service features.

For example, product / service brands such as *LIC, ICICI, Tanishq* diamonds are highlighting the strong family bondage and love for family in their advertising campaigns.

'G.K. Vale' uses family to highlight its product offerings.

Marketers have used product or service campaigns linking core values of family care into their product-service features. New values have been acquired by Indian consumers, due to exposure to international media channels and global lifestyles, with global travel.

Similarly, new values have been acquired by Indian consumers, due to exposure to international media channels and global lifestyles, with global travel. This has led to more willingness to spend more time and money on personnel grooming, leisure and leisure goods. The result is a boom period for the travel and tourism industry, consumer white goods and automobile industry. Unlike the earlier generation, today's consumers do not consider purchasing on 'credit' as a taboo. Thus, housing companies, leasing companies, financial institutions and credit card companies are growing steadily.

Even the communication media has influenced the development of new value systems. Apart from the television and telephone (land lines as well as cellular phones) the wide spread usage of the computer and the internet has led to the development of new value systems. Some of the current strong values with which Indians have come to be associated are acquiring competencies, striving hard to succeed, enjoying acquisition of products and acceptance of being rich.

The marketer, thus, needs to understand the impact of sociological changes on the behaviour pattern of consumers and devise strategies accordingly.

The Marketing Research Society of India (MRSI) has provided an important basis for understanding the Indian consumer behaviour through determining his or her social and economic class. (Marketing Management, Rajan Saxena, 3rd Edn.). This is illustrated in Figure 15.4.

According to the research, the consumption behaviour of a consumer is determined by his or her social and economic class. This social class is determined on the basis of the occupation of the earning member(s) of the family.

FIGURE 15.4

THE EIGHT SOCIO-ECONOMIC GROUPS OF CUSTOMERS IN THE INDIAN MARKET

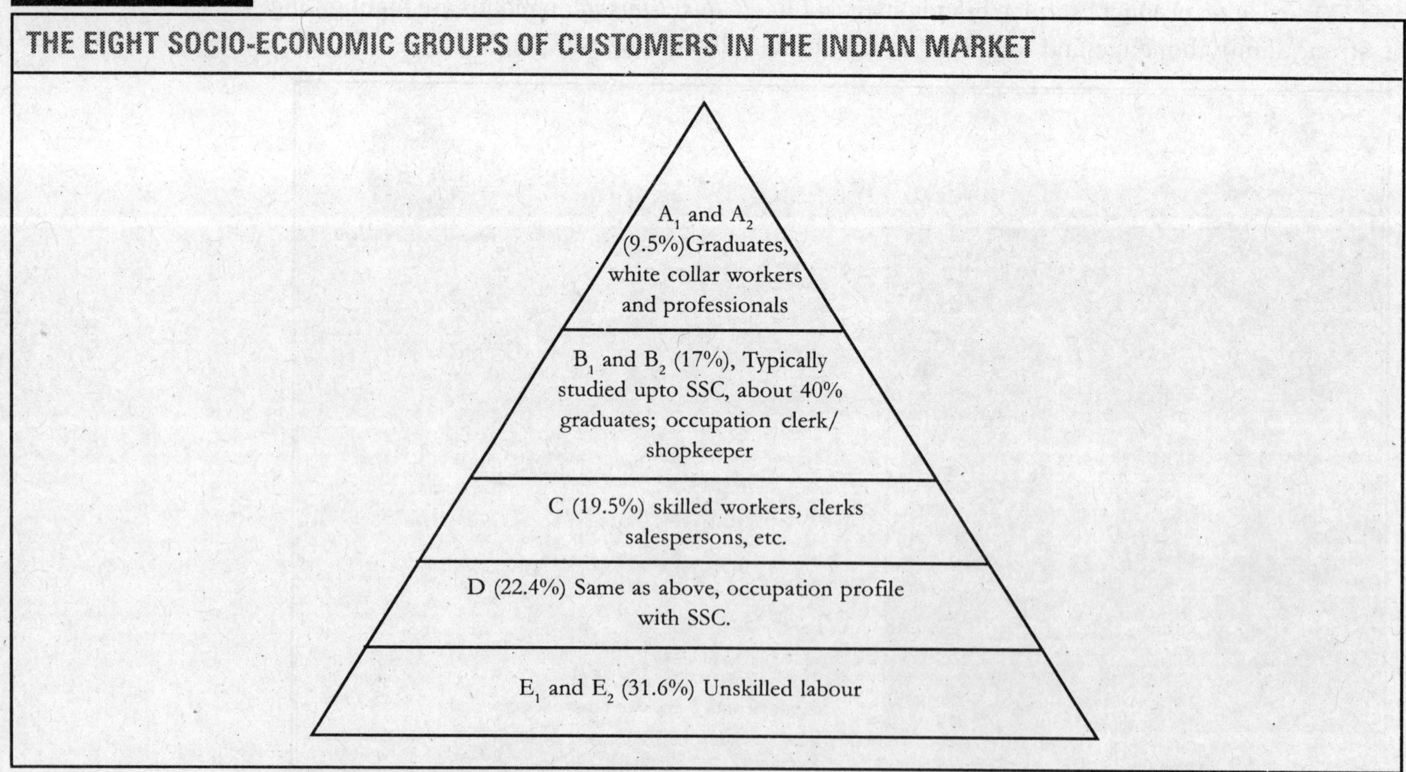

(*Source* : Rajan Saxena, *Marketing Management*, 3rd Edn., Tata McGraw-Hill, New Delhi, 2006. P. 210)

LifeStyle (Marketing through - VALS)

Lifestyle can be said to be the beliefs, interests and opinions each person has about himself. Lifestyle can be referred to as an individual's way of living in the world, which will be reflected in his attitudes, interests and opinions about other persons or towards things. Marketers have realised that each individual customer's buying behaviour will be dependent upon his perception of whether the brand (or product) will match his lifestyle. If he perceives the brand to be suiting his lifestyle he is likely to purchase the same, otherwise not.

Lifestyle can be referred to as an individual's way of living in the world, which will be reflected in his attitudes, interests and opinions about other persons or towards things.

SRI Values and lifestyle programme, popularly known as 'VALS' was first developed by Arnold Mitchell. It is a research oriented service undertaken to understand the relevant shifts in the benefits, values and lifestyles of the psychographic segments of the population. The original VALS programme (1970) was designed to understand the dynamics of societal change. In 1989, VALS 2 programme was developed to use it as a marketing tool to better explain the consumer purchase behaviour. The VALS programmes are closely connected to Maslow's need hierarchy.

The 'VALS 2' has referred to eight different segments of consumers having distinct attitudes, lifestyles and decision making styles. The demographic/ socio- economic factors relevant are sex, age, income, education, occupation, health, marital status and self confidence. The Figure 15.5 given below conveys a brief profile of eight segments of consumers in the 'VALS 2' model.

FIGURE 15.5

VALS 2 SEGMENT'S PROFILE

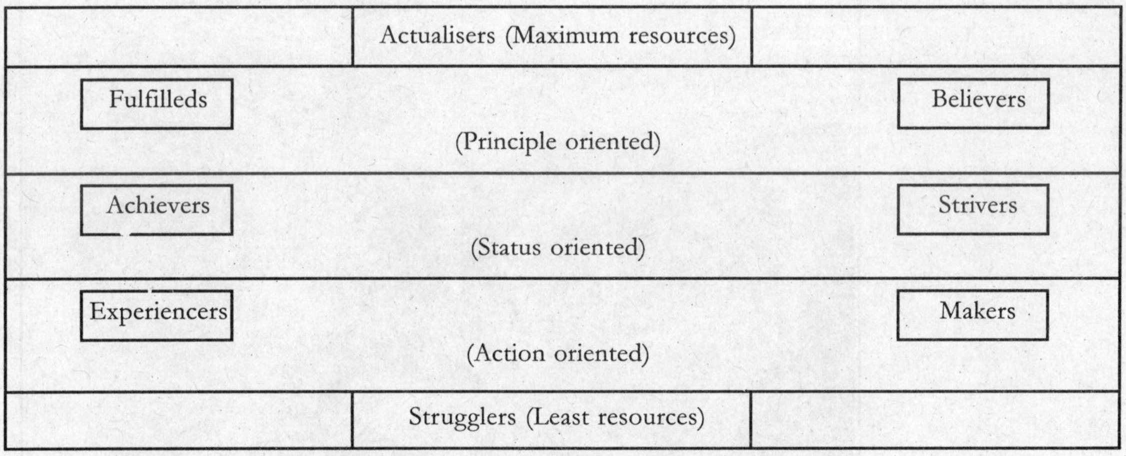

	Actualisers (Maximum resources)	
Fulfilleds	(Principle oriented)	Believers
Achievers	(Status oriented)	Strivers
Experiencers	(Action oriented)	Makers
	Strugglers (Least resources)	

(*Source : Consumer Behavior*, Leon C. Schiffman, Leslie Lazar Kanuk, 6th Edn.)

Actualisers	:	are receptive to new ideas or products, skeptical about advertising, readers of variety of publication works.
Fulfilled & Believers	:	are principle oriented consumers, whose choices are inspired and motivated by their beliefs rather than by desire for approval.
Achievers & Strivers	:	are status oriented consumers whose choice are dependent on the actions, approval and opinion of others.

Experiencers & Makers	:	are action oriented consumers motivated by a desire for a richer lifestyle, with variety and risk taking.
Strugglers	:	are price conscious, loyal though not very knowledgeable shoppers.

Lifestyle analysis will help the marketer to have a sharper focus on the demographic profile of the consumers.

Thus VALS can help to understand the demographic profile, attitudes, consumption pattern, brand preferences and the most preferred media of the various customers. Then on knowing the lifestyle of consumers, the marketer can devise suitable positioning and promotional strategies accordingly.

Lifestyle analysis will help the marketer to have a sharper focus on the demographic profile of the consumers. The behavioural pattern of consumers is more visible or observed in the lifestyle patterns adopted by the consumers. Of course, changes in the lifestyle pattern of individuals may be on account of the changes taking place in his or her social environment and other environmental factors.

Blue Sky Sunglasses and watches will appeal to specific lifestyles.

As already discussed, the average Indian is now spending money more than the earlier generations. One can also see visible changes in the lifestyles and spending habits. With the nuclear family set up gaining acceptance especially in the cities and towns, there has been a shift in the women's attitude to cooking and the type of meals served at home. Elaborately made home food has given way to convenience foods and ready to eat foods, and modern gadgets such as vaccum cleaners, microwave oven, and modern cooking ranges have become very popular among both housewives and working women.

The changes among Indians could have been stimulated to an extent by exposure via media (T.V) to the lifestyle of the well-to-do and global homes and the modern products used by them.

These lifestyle changes have made the lives of women more comfortable. What was considered to be luxury products yesterday have become todays necessities. This fact is reiterated in the data obtained from the NCAER's National Survey of household expenditure on consumer durables, which suggests that conventional notions on what is a luxury good and what is an essential commodity (or necessity) are fast changing.

Clarion Hotels invities customers to 'Live it up in style'.

This change, as already explained earlier in the chapter, could have been stimulated to an extent by exposure via media (Television) to the lifestyle of well-to-do and global homes and the modern products used by them.

In an article titled 'Seductive South', Mukerjea, Meenu, Shekar et.al have spoken about high literacy rates, knowledge and media boom which has made consumers down South adopt a different lifestyle, when compared to the earlier times. The writers on a visit to "Red E Food Court", a hip restaurant in Chennai were surprised to observe that there was an equal number of jeans clad consumers and middle aged consumers dressed in 'veshtis' happily enjoying the food junction's vegetarian fare at a little before midnight. This was unlike the traditional Chennaites lifestyle, according to which they were well in bed by that time.

The figure 15.6 refers to the nine different lifestyles, developed by Stanford Research Institute (now SRI International), found among U.S.A. consumers.

The knowledge of lifestyle pattern and attitudes is used to try and predict consumer behaviour.

The lifestyles of consumers, who are referred to as survivors, sustainers and belongers are essentially controlled by their basic needs (Similar to Maslow's, basic survival, security and belonging needs). After these basic needs have been met, some consumers become outer directed *i.e.,* they value or are concerned and have respect for other people's opinion. While other consumers become inner directed i.e. are more concerned with their own internal drives. Mitchell also refers to the ultimate integrated position adopted by consumers, where concern about others opinion is combined with a knowledge of their own inner drives.

FIGURE 15.6

VALUES AND LIFESTYLES

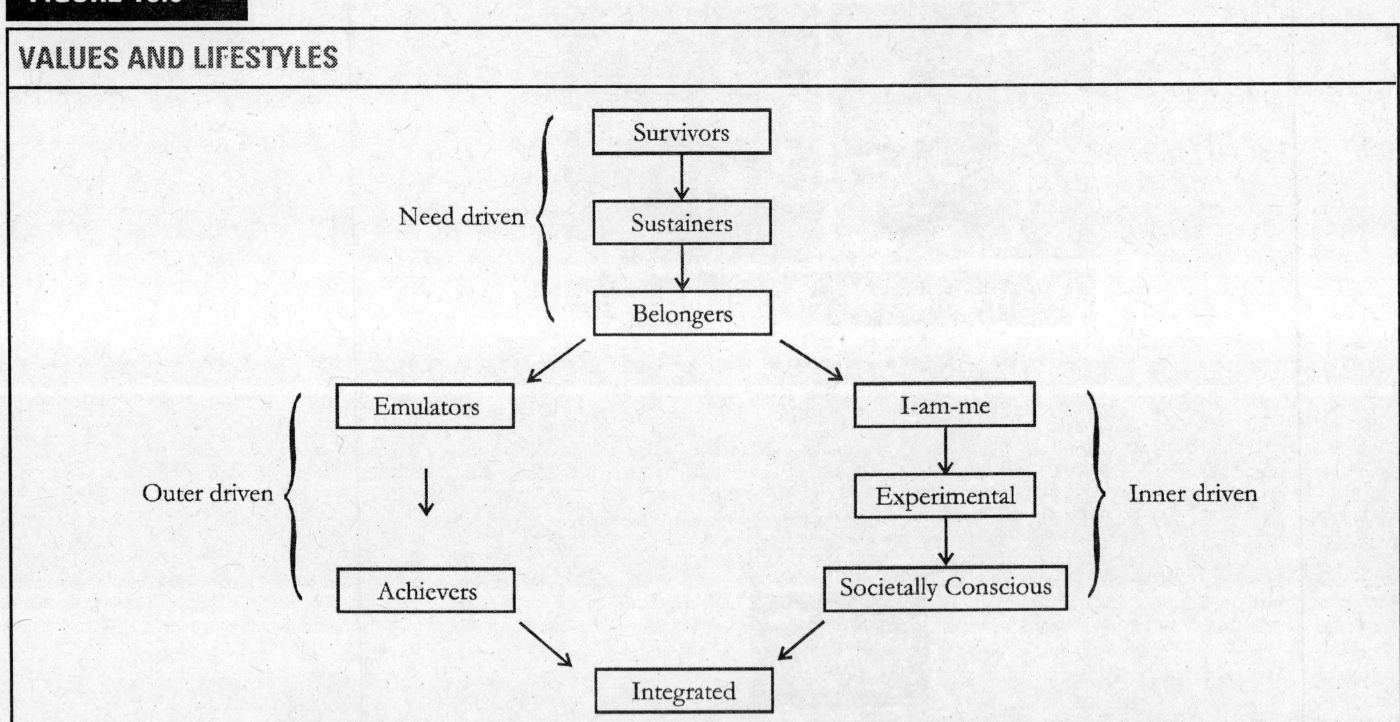

[(*Source :* Adapted from Arnold Mitchell, *The Nine American Lifestyles*, New York; Macmillian 1983)]

U.K's LifeStyle

The same basic lifestyle patterns were identified among the U.K. consumers and an equivalent to VALS was developed by Taylor Nelson as shown in the Table 15.5.

The knowledge of lifestyle pattern and attitudes is used to try and predict consumer behaviour. Though very informative, the drawback of this approach is that the research is wide and time consuming. Further, the end result greatly depends upon the ability of the researcher to decide on which factors will be appropriate to a particular lifestyle. But since most purchases have relevance to the particular lifestyle chosen by an individual, this approach can be used to decide on the type of products, positioning and promotional strategies to be considered by the marketer.

Personality : Marketers have also been using personality variables to segment the market. It has been observed by marketers that consumers are influenced not only by the functional aspects, utility and performance of the brand but it is the sum of a look, an attitude, its character *i.e.,* the psychological and symbolic values attached to it. Marketers try to co-relate the brand personality that corresponds to consumer personalities.

Consumers have personalities which will be inclusive of physical attributes, mental abilities and attitudes, beliefs and values.

In other words, the marketers role is to create and strengthen the relationship between the brand and consumer.

TABLE 15.5

U.K. LIFESTYLES

	Lifestyle Group	Characteristics	Percentage of Population
Sustenance driven groups, motivated by the need for security	Belonger	People who believe in traditional family values, patriotic and averse to change	19
	Survivor	People who are fighting a holding action, accept authority, hard working, quiet, traditional, strong class consciousness.	16
	Aimless	1. The young unemployed whose main aim is short term kicks. 2. The very old whose aim is simply day-to-day existence.	5
Outer directed	Conspicuous Consumer	Materialistic, values opinion of reference groups, friends, family, followers of fashion.	18
Inner directed groups, motivated by self actualization	Social resister	Caring group, goes by the principle of fairness and a good quality of life at the societal level. Altruistic, concerned with issues related to preservation of ecology, and nuclear disarmament.	11
	Experimentalists	Materialistic and pro-technology, individuals are interested in novelty	14
	Self-explorers	Self expression and self realization act as motivators, tolerant, think big not only in thoughts but also solutions.	16

(*Source :* W. Kirk Mc Nulty, *'UK Social change through a wide-angle lens', Futures*, August 1985)

Consumers have personalities which will be inclusive of physical attributes (looks, structure etc.) mental abilities (knowledge, skill to perform etc.) and attitudes, beliefs and value. Similarly, a brand also distinguishes itself on account of its personality which will be a blend of all the above features. Very often brand personality is seen as a vehicle to express the personality of the user. Brand personality should inspire feelings of confidence because of its functional performance. *'Dove'* (soap with 1/4th moisturiser) inspires confidence that it will improve the

Marketers work and develop successful market segmentation strategies based on personality traits which can be co-related to specific product (brand) personality.

complexion of women. Consumers view *'Titan Watches'* as a brand personality surrounded with style, design and accuracy. Another aspect of a successful brand personality will be if it has originality, attractiveness and is distinctive - *'Polo'* - the mint with the hole, is a popular brand personality because of the dry humour involved. Similarly, *'Amul'* with its 'Taste of India' positioning. (utterly Butterly delicious) is another well known brand personality. *Tide detergent* has developed its own personality by retaining its "stripe of surprise" positioning. So also is *'Horlicks'* which has kept its brand personality image of the "The Great Family Nourisher" intact over the years.

Marketers work and develop successful market segmentation strategies based on personality traits which can be co-related to specific product (brand) personality.

TABLE 15.6

MARKET SEGMENTATION WITH SELECTIVE VARIABLES

Segmentation Base	Selective Segmentation Variables
1. Geographic Segmentation	
• Region	East, West, North, South
• Density	Urban, Rural
• Climate	Hot, Extreme, Humid, Cold
2. Demographic Segmentation	
• Age	Below 6, 6-11, 12-19, 20-34, 35-49, 50-64, 65+
• Sex	Male, Female
• Marital Status	Single, Married, Divorced, Widowed, Live-in couples,
• Religion	Hindu, Muslim, Christian, Parsi, Jain.
• Income Level	The affluent class, the middle class, the relatively poorer section, the BPL section
• Education	Illiterate, school, secondary school, diploma, graduate, post graduate, professional graduate.
• Occupation	Unemployed, housewife, student, agricultural, skilled/semiskilled/ unskilled workers, clerk, sales persons, officers/executives, managers, proprietors, teachers, professional & technical.
3. Psychographic Segmentation	
• Social Class	Lower class, Middle class, Upper Class
• Lifestyle	Economy minded, well-off and couch potatoes, status conscious, extrovert-enthusiasts,
• Personality	Gregarious, ambitious etc.
4. Use-related Segmentation	
• Usage Rate	Light user, Medium user, Heavy user.
• User Status	Non user, ex-user, potential user, first time user, regular user.
• Brand Loyalty	Absolute, Strong, Medium, None.
• Occasion or Usage situation	Regular, Special Occasion.
5. Benefit Segmentation	
• Benefit Sought	Quality, Price/Economy, service etc.
6. Behaviouristic Segmentation	
Buyer readiness stage	Unaware, aware, informed, interested, desirous, positive intention to buy.

BEHAVIOURISTIC SEGMENTATION

Consumers are divided into groups based on their knowledge, attitudes, use or response to a product.

Use-related Segmentation

A very popular and effective way of segmentation involves dividing or categorising consumers in terms of product, service or brand usage characteristics. In other words consumers can be categorised in terms of rate of usage, awareness, status and degree of brand loyalty.

A very popular and effective way of segmentation involves dividing or categorising consumer's in terms of product, service or brand usage characteristics.

Usage Rate : Segmentation differentiates the consumers as heavy users, medium users, light users and non-users of a specific product, service or brand. Marketers very often have found heavy users though a small percentage account for a high percentage of the total consumption. In a research study conducted by A. Ghosh, A Mukherjee and V V P Badrinath (doctoral students at IIM Ahmedabad) to understand the demographic characteristics of the smoker in Ahmedabad city, it was found that: more youngsters smoke, with smoking habits being maximum between the ages of 19-30 years, varying between three and ten cigarettes a day. To mention a few of the above study findings:

1. Women who smoke though constitute a small proportion, amongst those who do, more than three out of four smoke between three to ten cigarettes a day.
2. Men, on the other hand, have a much higher proportion of light smokers by comparison.
3. A higher proportion of individuals in all the educated groups were found to be light smokers and very few were very heavy smokers.
4. The proportion of businessmen who smoke though less as compared to people in service, tend to be heavy smokers rather than light smokers.
5. The trend of fewer people smoking, but heavy smokers was found to be more pronounced among professionals.

Usage rate study will indicate the consumer profiles, in terms of demographic, psychographic and media habits, this information can help the marketers to develop the marketing mix programmes.

(*Source:* "Zero in on the Indian Consumer", Anirban Ghosh, Avinandan Mukherjee, Badrinath V.V.P., Strategic Marketing, March 1997)

The above study had included four variables namely income, age, education and occupation for understanding the consumer profile of smokers.

Similarly, for other products also such as beverages, liquors, credit card, mobile phone etc., marketers prefer to segment the consumers into heavy users, medium users and light users. Usage rate study will indicate the consumer profiles, in terms of demographic, psychographic and media habits; this information can help the marketers to develop the marketing mix programmes.

We will have a look at how usage of the Internet has brought about a change in consumer behaviour. Especially with the growth of the private ISP market, Internet has become a very important medium for information, entertainment, communications and commercial activities (electronic commerce).

Studies by NASSCOM have indicated around ninety percent of the times the Internet is used for sending emails. This could be because now, even in far away places, the private ISP has facilitated cyber usage at competitive prices. Around 93 percent use the Internet for web-browsing, 59 percent use it for online chat, 53 percent for information and data transfer and 6.5 percent for e-commerce.

Research has shown that more than one family member in the Indian household uses the Internet for various needs. Further, it was also revealed that in a family, the Internet is most used by an adult son/daughter or male head of the family. Thus when added up, it works out to be 42 percent of the Net users in the age groups of 15-24 years, 31 percent in the 25-34 years of age group and the rest are above 35 years.

The Internet has created awareness among an average Indian consumer about international quality and performance and obtaining the same at an affordable price. Today's generation (a major internet user) is very comfortable purchasing products (books, home appliances etc.) and services (holiday packages etc.) through the net. The younger generation of consumers are less brand loyal and since they are shopping for value, the net has come as a big boon for them. Further, the Internet has made it possible for all market segments to have access to the same information and also provide equal opportunity to buy products and services.

User Status : The markets can also be segmented on the basis of regular users, first time users, potential users, ex-users and non users. This segmentation is based on the exposure of the consumer to the product. Of particular interest to marketers are potential users and non-users. Marketers adopt different marketing approaches to attract potential and non users.

In the competitive environment of today, there are no dearth of competitors trying to innovate ways to induce potential and non-users to try their product offering. Marketers have realised that the key to success lies in creating customer expectations and inducing trial among them. This is exactly what *Procter & Gamble (P & G)* did for its shampoo *'Pantene'* and *Colgate-Palmolive* did for its shampoo *'Optima'*.

In order to launch the product by trial in the market place, P & G distributed free samples of *Pantene* among upmarket salons in Mumbai and actually invited 350 hair stylists at the launch party in November 1995, in Mumbai, who endorsed the brand after having used it themselves. They also explained to the invitees scientifically how the shampoo could help them to mend split hair ends and stall the loss of hair. The same strategy was followed in the other metros also.

Similarly, when *Colgate Palmolive* wanted to launch its *Optima* shampoo for women, it announced a *free Optima Hair wash week.* During this period customers were asked to walk into salons across the country and ask for a free Optima wash. Both products, Pantene and Optima drew a good response from the customers.

High market share companies are particularly interested in attracting potential users to their brand, while smaller firms try to attract regular users to their brand.

Marketers try to make use of the characteristics observed in their brand loyal consumer and work out promotional programmes to be directed at potential customers showing similar characteristics in the larger population.

Brand Loyalty is also used as one of the bases for segmentation. Marketers try to make use of the characteristics observed in their brand loyal consumer and work out promotional programmes to be directed at potential customers showing similar characteristics in the larger population. Marketers are also trying to target consumers who are not brand loyal or brand switchers in the belief that if a USP (Unique Selling Proposition) is present, they may switch over to their brand. *Videocon International* (Videocon) has used a Unique Value Proposition while marketing its low priced TV sets, it created a variable based on price without allowing it to be viewed that way. The name *'Budgetline'* had a soothing effect differentiating from the 'Junta' type of products conveying the message "At this price we give you the best value".

Another method followed by marketers today is to stimulate and reward brand loyalty by offering various special schemes or benefits to consistent or frequent buyers or users of the product or service. The *'Frequent flier schemes'* of the Air India is one such example. Companies are also trying to attract and retain old customers through offering value added services. For instance, long ago *British Airways used to offer special Lounges - with showers attached at 199 airports* for its frequent passengers. The rationale behind this gesture from the company was that the most frequent passengers were from the business community and these travellers would like to freshen-up in between flights or before attending business meetings. So *the added benefit is on shorter business halts,* this will help the consumer to save on hotel fares.

Occasion or Usage Situation: Consumers or buyers can be distinguished according to the occasions when they may feel the need to purchase a product. Marketers have realised this and have often used usage situation as a segmentation variable. Depending on the situation, circumstances and occasion, consumers vary on their choices of various products.

Occasion segmentation help marketers to convey product usage benefits to consumers. The greeting card industry *(Archies, Cry, Hallmark* etc.) have *special cards* for a variety of occasions like Valentine's day, Mother's day, Wedding Cards, Birthday Cards and so on. *Titan Watches* suggest a dual set of a male and women's models of wrist watches as *a perfect wedding gift. Godrej* promotes *'Godrej Storwel'* as on ideal gift for the expectant mother.

Usage of brand loyalty as a base for segmentation

BENEFIT SEGMENTATION

A very practical and powerful form of market segmentation is to classify buyers according to the different benefits they look out for in the product. The benefit that is sought by consumers will vary according to the product. For doing benefit segmentation, the marketer will have to determine the major benefits that consumer seek in the product class, the kinds of people who are seeking the benefit and the other major brands which can deliver each benefit.

Related to benefit segmentation is the contribution of Russell I Haley "Benefit Segmentation: a decision oriented research tool". Haley had identified three variables geographics, behaviourist and psychographic, though none of the three by themselves were sufficiently selective. Since these factors rely more on descriptive factors, they cannot be considered as efficient factors for prediction of future buying behaviour.

Marketers and advertisers are constantly trying to communicate the benefit of their brand with the target groups. Examples of benefits communicated with the use of the particular brand are financial security *(LIC, HDFC Life Insurance ICICI prudential),* near instant fairness and great completion *(Fair & Lovely* active fairness moisturiser) reduces calories and controls cholesterol *(Saffola),* even toothpaste advertising often focuses on highlighting the associated benefit, *for*

Marketers and advertisers are constantly trying to communicate the benefit of their brand with the target groups.

example, Close up (sex appeal or attraction because of white teeth and fresh breath) *Pepsodent* (tooth decay prevention).

The ad of *SBI Life Insurance* is apt for 'Benefit Segmentation'.

The changes in the socio cultural environment resulting in changing lifestyles have prompted marketers to position their brand highlighting its benefits to consumers.

The changes in the socio cultural environment resulting in changing lifestyles have prompted marketers to position their brand highlighting its benefits to consumers. Washing Machine and Vacuum Cleaner was the ideal solution for the needs of working couples because both the husband and wife do not get sufficient time to dance to the tune of domestic help. There are also instant, ready to mix and make food products from *MTR*, *Everest* etc. Such products offer a lot of benefits to busy families who have less time at disposal to be involved and use elaborate methods for cooking food.

Benefit segmentation can also be extended to position various brands in the same product category. This is visible in the Shampoo Market and Toothpaste Market. Examples of a few brands of Toothpaste with benefits associated are :

HelpAge India cards are used for usage - situation segmentation.

Benefit segmentation can also be extended to position various brands in the same product category.

Benefit	*Brand*
Economical	Babool
Mouthwash	Close-up Gel
Freshness	Close Up
Prevents tooth Decay	Pepsodent, Colgate
Brightness of Teeth	Close-up, Colgate

In the 'Shampoo' market also marketers are communicating about various benefits associated with the different brands. To quote a few examples :

Brand Name	*Benefit Communicated*
1. Dabur Vatika	Root Strengthening with deep conditioner
2. Pantene	Pro-vitamin B (rich in proteins)
3. Heads and Shoulders	Anti dandruff with extra conditioning
4. Himalaya Herbals	Anti dandruff
5. Sunsilk	Nutra Care (Vitamin & Proteins)
6. Nyle	Herbal
7. Chik	Extra rich with milk proteins.
8. Clinic Plus	Rich in proteins
9. Medicare	Anti lice

Buyer's Readiness Stage : At times marketers have observed that people are in different stages of readiness to buy a product. Some people may not be aware of the product, few may be aware, others may be interested, while some others may desire for the product and some others may intend to purchase the product. Depending upon the number of people who are in the various buyer readiness stage, marketers have to design a suitable marketing communications programme.

At times marketers have observed that people are in different stages of readiness to buy a product.

For instance, when the U.S. Telecommunications giant *'Motorola'* was introducing its *pagers* in India during February 1995, realising that Paging as a service was not available in the country until then, the task before it was to introduce the targeted customers to the values of paging. For meeting this objective, Motorola used an integrated Marketing Communications programme.

Market Place Promotions: Motorola used road shows, mobile vans and home visits to educate and make the customer aware of the experience of using paging service.

Through Direct Marketing: Identifying three main target segments: The local shopkeeper, the executive and the businessman, the company addressed them direct mailers and one-on-one contacts.

Through the Trade: Motorola tied up with paging services operators to set up outlets where the customer could obtain information on the various types of pagers, accessories and also avail of free demonstration.

Through Public Relations: Motorola first educated the media and then used them as a channel to target a wide range of customers.

➲ BASES FOR SEGMENTING INDUSTRIAL MARKETS

There are many variables which can be considered for segmenting the industrial market. R.N. Cardozo has identified four dimensions, which can be used either separately or in combination for various organisational buying situations.

(a) *Familiarity with the buying task:* This dimension is based on the suggestions of 'P. Robinson, C. Paris and Y. Wind in Industrial buying and Creative Marketing' wherein they have identified three types of buying situations - straight rebuy, modified rebuy and new task. Depending on the particular buying situation, a relevant approach is used for segmentation.

(b) *Product Type:* Here the segmentation can be done based on the product use in terms of components, material and equipment required which, in turn, may be dependent upon the degree of standardisation.

Customer based - a unique design based on the customer requirement. Modular - a unique combination comprising of standard components or materials. Standard - This will be consisting of the combination of the ingredients offered previously.

(c) *Significance or importance of the industrial purchase to the buying organisation.*

(d) The *uncertainty* involved in the buying situation.

The above mentioned dimensions to be used for segmenting the industrial market reflects clearly the fact that industrial buyers also segment the set of potential suppliers. They also develop various criteria which are used to assess them and set up formal vendor rating schemes. H.G. Johnson and A. Flodhammer have opined in 'Industrial Customer Segmentation' that understanding buyer needs is as important in industrial buying as in consumer markets. This is because unless there is knowledge of the industrial users' needs, the manufactured product will be using the lowest common denominator - price. Quality and service will be unknown aspects.

TYPICALLY USED BASES FOR SEGMENTING INDUSTRIAL PRODUCT

Some of the typically used bases for segmenting industrial product markets include:

(a) *Size and purchase of the customer :* There could be various customer groups based on their size and purchase. For instance, large, category buyers, medium sized (category) buyers and small buyers. Depending upon the size of the customer, the organisation will be able to get an idea of its sales potential as well as it's competitive position in that customer group.

(b) *Geographical Location :* It is also possible to know the geographical location of the industrial customer and use it as a base to segment the market.

(c) *Differentiating the end users of the product :* Differentiating the end users of the industrial product is another way of segmenting the market. For instance, the plastic manufacturer may have end user segments comprising of cables, automobiles, office furniture, electrical, electronics and so on. Each segment has unique characteristics and thus a different marketing approach will be required to be adopted.

(d) *Purchase criteria :* Within a specific end use segment, it is again possible to further segment the market based on the purchase criteria. Say, by considering the 'price sensitivity' of the customers, they can be categorized as highly sensitive, slightly sensitive, sensitive or not sensitive.

(e) *Combination of size and geographical criteria :* Organisations tend to combine size, buying criteria and geographic location while carrying out industrial marketing. Another important consideration is segmenting the market on the bases of 'buying motives' as well as buyer characteristics.

Typically some of the bases used for segmenting industrial products are : size and purchase of the customer, geographic location, differentiating the end users of the product, purchase criteria and combination of size and geographical criteria.

STRATEGIC IMPLICATIONS OF MARKET SEGMENTATION

In order to remain competitive, marketers always try to add value and create a base of satisfied customers. This value addition strategy is also referred to as 'Value Added Marketing Strategy' (VAMS) (Harvard-Business Review, Nov-Dec. 1988). All moves towards value addition are evolved around the most important source - "Customer needs'. Thus organisations need to understand customers' inherent needs, their problems and then decide on the product category and product which will take care of the same. VAMS is based on market segmentation analysis and using this information for product design and market segmentation can help organisations to utilise resources in a well defined manner.

Once, the market is segmented, the organisation will have to work on the suitable marketing strategies. Generally, there are three marketing strategies to select from: Standardisation, Differentiation and Focused.

Standardisation

Under this strategy, the firm will offer the same product to different market segments.

The same communication, pricing and distribution strategies are used for various market segments. For instance, Cocacola and Pepsico have maintained the same distinctive taste, communication (or advertising) campaign and packaging across segments in different geographical areas for their *Coke* and *Pepsi* brands, respectively. The biggest advantage of this strategy is the economies of scale which the firm can gain through mass production and marketing. The reason behind standardisation could be : the firm realises that although consumers may be different, they may be sufficiently alike to be addressed as a homogeneous group for the product under consideration.

Differentiation

This strategy is just the opposite of the standardisation strategy. Under differentiation strategy the firm will offer different products to suit the various segments and expectations. If one were to consider the travel industry. Say, the train offers its services into three classes 1st A.C. class, 2nd A.C. Class, and the 2nd (or economy class). Each of these classes is targeted at a particular segment whose needs may vary from that of the other classes.

Focused

Market segmentation and product positioning are closely linked. A product's position is the place occupied by it in a given competitive market as perceived by the concerned target market segment.

Focus is a combination of standardisation and differentiation. The core strategy, here, remains the same although differentiation is made taking into consideration the specific customer group's requirements. For instance, the *Indica* or *Indigo* from Tata Motors have some basic features and offers certain specific benefits to its buyers. However, a customer who is seeking more features such as power steering and music systems can obtain the same by paying an additional amount. In this way Tata Motors is in a position to focus its strategy on both the economy and premium customer segments. Further, this strategy enables the firm to take the benefits of the economies of scale as well as bigger market penetration and thereby a higher market share.

In this way, the marketer has to choose the suitable strategy to address the particular market segment's needs.

PRODUCT POSITIONING

Segmentation involves taking care of different consumer groupings' or segments' wants through a suitable marketing strategy. Knowing that different consumers will respond differently to products (or services), promotions, prices and channels, marketers need to consider the overall market (or people's) action to the product (or service) as well as the reactions among the different market segments. Thus, market segmentation and product positioning are closely linked. A product's position is the place occupied by it in a given competitive market as perceived by the concerned target market segment. Positioning is carried out by the marketer and it involves determining how consumers *perceive* the marketer's product and also developing and implementing marketing strategies to achieve the desired position at the market place. Marketers try to make use of suitable price, promotional and distribution tools for positioning their product or service offering. So, market segmentation and positioning go hand in hand. Through positioning marketers try to gain competitive advantage through differentiation.

Typically, marketers use differentiation along the following lines to gain competitive advantage : Product, Service, Channel, Price, People and Image. Yet, the most basic and commonly used approach to positioning is through differentiation on account of *'product'* by modifying the features, form or benefits.

Typically, marketers use differentiation along the following lines to gain competitive advantage: Product, service, channel, price, people and image.

For instance, *HDFC Bank,* based on research learnt that women have over 30 percent higher usage of debit cards when compared to men. Further, debit cards are mostly used by them for purchasing low ticket and utility items, whereas, credit cards are used for lifestyle products. Realising that women play a significant role in household, decision making, HDFC Bank launched the Woman's Advantage Debit Card and Woman's Gold Plus Credit Card with special features like cash back on purchases in order to tap this emerging market segment.

Nevertheless, when the global market is characterised by standardised technologies and products, products based on differentiation may not last long. So some firms have attempted on ***(a) positioning on benefits*** - *Clinic All Clear* Shampoo (removes dandruff), *Pantene Pro V* (conditions the hair) shampoo, *Dabur Vatika* (natural ingredients, strengthens hair) *Shampoo* and *Chik Shampoo* (economical) in sachet form ***(b) positioning on Usage*** **:** This technique is related to benefit positioning in that, marketers will seek to associate their brand with a particular usage or situation. For instance, *Kellogs* advertises positioning its products to be used at breakfast time. *Vicks* is positioned as a mild Vaporub which can be used even by children to get relief from cough and cold ***(c) positioning on user:*** This approach associates the product with the user or a class of users who act as spokespersons. For instance, Celebrites portray a certain lifestyle in the ads for *Recova cream, Asmi diamonds, Whirlpool washing machine, Omega watch, Tajmahal Tea* etc. Successful models or celebrities are used as spokesperson or opinion leaders in positioning the brand after using it. ***(d) Lifestyle positioning*** **:** Lifestyle segmentation research measures-

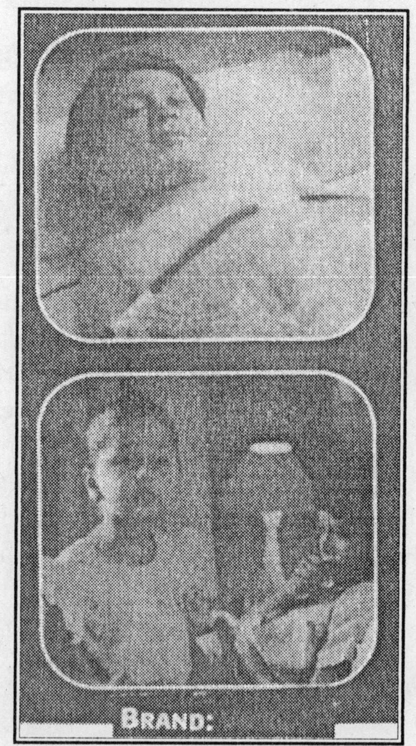

Vicks is positioned on usage situation.

- how people spend their time engaged in various activities
- what interests them the most in their immediate surroundings
- their opinions and views about themselves and the environment (world) around them. All these three areas together are generally referred to as activities, interests and opinions (AIOs).

For instance, Reliance Retail opened its first books and music store *'Reliance Time out'* in Bangalore. This speciality lifestyle store has an extensive range of merchandise in stationery, toys and gifts. *Time out* has differentiated from its competitors by its USP lifestyle positioning such as a *Karaoke Studio* (where customers can sing and record their voice in a professional quality recording studio), reading bar and a kids wall. The store has a wide range of vernacular and academic books and for those loving music, Time out offers sound domes which provide hygienic sampling of music and a cafe where, one can relax and consume tea.

Selection of the Product Positioning

There are various platforms which can be used to position the firm's brand. Nevertheless, each brand must try to be different from the competing brands on the following aspects:

- *Better (or superior)* – the difference must be noticeable when compared to the available methods of need satisfaction.
- *Conveyed (or communicable)* – the difference can be conveyed across in a clear and distinctive manner.
- Be able to *forestall competition.*
- *Be economical* – target must be able to purchase it since it is economical and affordable.
- *Earn profit* for the company.

There are various platforms which can be used to position the firm's brand. Marketers can also use lifestyle information and a technique called perceptual mapping for taking positioning decisions.

Once the above aspects are taken into consideration the firm can make a selection from the following positioning platforms.

- Position the brand using the *"Premium"* status. For instance, *Kingfisher Airlines* is positioned as an airline offering premium services when compared to competitors.
- Use the *'Value for money'* positioning. For instance, Alto, in the compact car segment is positioned as value for money.
- Offer products / services on par with competing brands.

Of course, ultimately, the firm needs to identify a suitable media for communicating about the brand's benefits, features etc. by selecting a suitable positioning strategy. Keeping in mind the change in the mind set of today's consumers who are leading busy lives with packaged schedules, some marketers have started positioning their brand using time as a selling proposition. For instance *DHL Express* has a campaign on air which promises, customers that DHL will answer all calls to its call centres in three rings - working on the logic that business can't be kept waiting on hold. The *Parachute hair oil* communicates the ease of an oil massage on a simple premise "One hour champi kiya?" General *Motors* offers a service called the "Free after three" running in certain select North Indian Cities, wherein it assures GM car owners service in three hours flat - anything longer means the service comes free. Thus for an effective market segmentation the firm will have to become more customer focused.

Perceptual Mapping

Marketers can also use lifestyle information and a technique called perceptual mapping for taking positioning decisions. We have already discussed about the consumers' perception of products or services, which is developed in a complex manner and not easily determined by the marketer. However, a process called perceptual mapping can be used to learn more about consumers' perception on products or services. Generally consumers perceive products on many dimensions such as quality, price and strength. This perceptual mapping technique is multidimensional in nature and so is able to measure the influence of more than one stimulus characteristics on product perceptions. Consumers will indicate their perceptions of the various characteristics and similarities of the competitors brands. Then computer analysis is done to identify those product characteristics or combination of characteristics which are important to the consumers and how they differ from competing brands. The result can then be plotted in the form of perceptual "maps", which display how consumers perceive the brands and their differences on a coordinate system.

➲ SUMMARY

Market segmentation is the process of dividing a heterogeneous market into homogeneous subunits. Market segmentation can help the marketer to become customer focussed. India is diversely distributed in terms of climate, language, literacy level, customs, status and lifestyles etc. This heterogeneity affects the consumption pattern and behaviour of the people. There are many benefits of market segmentation which will not only help to increase the firm's productivity but can also add to customer value. The criteria for choosing a market segment is generally based on identification, measurability, accessibility, substantiality and stability.

Some of the bases used for segmenting consumer markets were discussed. These included geographic segmentation, rural consumers, demographic segmentation, gender, marital status & family life cycle, income, education and occupation, religion, psychographic segmentation (Social class, lifestyles), behaviouristic segmentation (user related, usage rate, brand loyalty), and benefit segmentation. Once the market is segmented, the organisation will have to work on the suitable marketing strategies i.e. select from Standardization, Differentiation and Focused. Market segmentation can also help the organisation to work out product positioning decisions.

CHAPTER QUESTIONS FOR DISCUSSION

1. Define market segmentation. Indian consumers vary significantly in terms of needs, characteristics and buying or consumption behaviour. So through market segmentation it will be possible for the marketer to identify homogeneity in such a heterogeneous market. Discuss with taking the example of any consumer market.
2. Briefly explain the benefits of market segmentation, if one were to segment the market for FM Radio, MP3, Entry level car and Sports shoes.
3. Discuss generally what criteria is used for effective targeting of market segments?
4. Discuss the various bases of market segmentation to be considered in case of the rural consumers for:
   (a) Mobile phone
   (b) Branded men/women's wear
   (c) Multi Utility Vehicle
   (d) Branded Jewellery.
   Justify your selection of the particular base for market segmentation.
5. Do you think it is necessary for the airlines to consider behaviouristic segmentation while working out a suitable marketing strategy? Why?
6. Bring out the usefulness of lifestyle segmentation for markets, while working out media and promotion programmes.

SUGGESTED READINGS

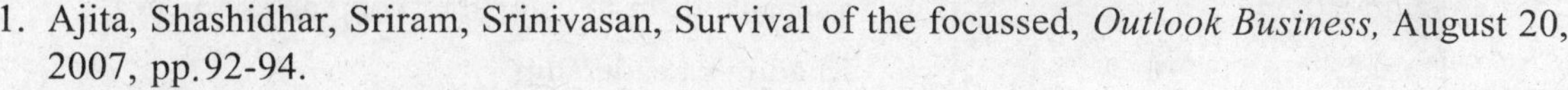

1. Ajita, Shashidhar, Sriram, Srinivasan, Survival of the focussed, *Outlook Business,* August 20, 2007, pp.92-94.
2. *The Economic Times,* (Brand Equity) Bangalore June 27, 2007.
3. V.S. Ramaswamy, S. Namakumari, *Marketing Management – Planning, Implementation & Control,* 3rd Edn., Macmillan India Ltd., 2005, pp. 234-261.
4. *Business Today,* January 14, 2007, pp. 145-152.
5. Priya. Srinivasan, E. Kumar Sharma & Achna. Shukla 'Tween Power', *Business Today,* January 1, 2006 pp. 48-56.
6. L.G. Schiffman and L.L. Kanuk, *'Consumer Behavior'* Prentice Hall of India Private Limited, New Delhi, 2005.
7. Dr. Rajan Saxena; *Marketing Management,* 3rd Edn., Tata McGraw-Hill Publishing Company Limited, New Delhi, 2006. pp. 47-67.
8. David. L. Loudon, Albert J. Della Bitta, *'Consumer Behavior'* (4th Edn.), Tata McGraw-Hill, New Delhi, 2002. pp. 73-76.
9. Henry. Assael, *Consumer Behavior and Marketing Action,* 6th Edn., Thomson Learning, Singapore, 2001. pp. 439-442.
10. Philip Kotler, *"Principles of Marketing"*, Second Edition, Prentice Hall of India Private Limited, New Delhi, 2005. pp. 53-68
11. John O' Shaughnessy, *"Competitive Marketing - A Strategy Approach"*, 2nd Ed. Unwin Hyman Ltd., London, 1988.
12. *The Economic Times,* Bangalore, 11 December 2007, p. 6.
13. N. Shatrujeet. 'In the thick of time, *The Economic Times,* (Brand Equity), 18 April, 2007. pp.1.

CASE

KHADIM FOOT-WEAR

The Journey From A Modest Beginning

Khadim's early beginning was as a modest footwear wholesaler in Kolkata in the 1950's. Gradually they diversified into manufacturing and exporting of leather products, real estate development, media, communication and chain-store retailing with a noticeable presence in almost all parts of the country. Khadim has today emerged as the market leader in the relevant sectors. However, it is its foray into footwear retailing in 1993, which can be said to be one of the biggest success stories in the footwear industry. Khadim had initially been a well known name in leather goods in the eastern part of India. But with it entering into the export and superstore divisions apart from footwear, today the Khadim group of companies commands respect not only from the east of the country but from all over India.

The Facets Behind Khadim's Success

For *Khadim,* their success can be directly related to the values cherished and abided by the company. Khadim can be said to have become such a potent player in the industry because of having a keen foresight, sharp business acumen, strong concern for its people along with a deep understanding of the market needs. By keeping a steady finger on the consumer's pulse, Khadim has been able to produce value-for-money products which cater to the needs of all strata of people across the society and satisfy their tastes. The company feels that the success of the brand Khadim can be attributed to:

- Excellent quality
- Cost effective practices
- Centralised control
- Extensive Information Technology Network
- Regulating Overheads
- Innovative Strategies
- Keen insight for consumer trends
- Catering to regional and cultural needs

Right from the time it entered footwear retailing, Khadim has become synonymous with quality products available at affordable prices. It is the state of the art production methods adopted by the company which ensure economies of scale, which they pass on to their customers. Consequently, customers are able to get the best of the leather products and footwear not only in terms of style and quality but also in terms of price.

In fact, in footwear alone, Khadim is able to stand out amongst the best in the industry. Khadim is among the top three national players in terms of organised footwear retailing. It has more than 250 exclusive retail outlets across the country.

'Egaro Chain of Departmental Stores'

Khadim launched a chain of departmental stores called EGARO on June 1st 2007. *Egaro*, the chain of departmental stores promises to be a different kind of shopping experience for the family. This chain offers solutions across multiple segments including apparels, footwear, cosmetics, gold ornaments, fashion jewelleries, home needs and grocery which is a one stop shopping hunt for shoppers. All these have been made keeping in mind the fashion and aspiration needs of the consumers which will make them feel free as well as enable them to enjoy the shopping experience.

Khadim's Leadership

In order to be in competition as a leader in the market various efforts have been made by Khadim. Their manufacturing facility is an ISO 9001 company and has been in operation since June 2001. Strigent quality control, round-the-clock production and usage of the latest technology has increased the company's competitive edge.

However, despite financial success, the company is yet to enjoy a Pan-India presence. So protracted efforts must be put in order to plan a Pan-India and a global presence in the future.

(*Source :* www.khadim.com, Debasish. Roy., 'Khadim's Leathership, *Financial Times,* Bangalore, December 23, 2007.)

QUESTIONS FOR DISCUSSION

1. With many global brands of footwear being available in the Indian markets, what type of bases and strategies can be used by Khadim, for catering to the relevant market segment needs?
2. Can you suggest a suitable communication programme which can help Khadim to obtain a pan-India like presence or positioning?

CHAPTER 16

ORGANISATIONAL BUYING BEHAVIOUR

- Case : **Castrol**
- Who is an organisational customer?
- Differences between Organisational buyer and Final customer.
- Participants in Organisational buying.
- Characteristics of industrial markets.
- Buying decisions involved in buying process.
- Factors influencing Industrial buying behaviour.
- Organisational customer's buying process.
- Reseller market.
- The Government market.
- Summary
- Chapter questions for discussion
- Suggested readings
- Case : **Crompton Greaves Limited.**

CASE

CASTROL

Charles Cheers Wakefield on 19th March 1899, had set up an oil company in England and ten years later, produced a new lubricant that revolutionised the transport industry. The history of **Castrol** in India can be traced to 1910 when certain automotive lubricants from C.C. Wakefield and Company entered the Indian market.

In 1919 C.C. Wakefield and Company set up its first overseas branch office in India and commenced operations as a trading unit. Today Castrol India Limited is the second largest player in the Indian Lubricant industry and the market leader in the retail Automotive lubricant segment. Castrol India is a part of the BP group worldwide.

Products

The company manufactures and markets a range of automotive and industrial lubricants under two brands, **Castrol** and **BP**. It has around 70,000 company services retail outlets in India. Castrol has a dominant suppliers position in the OEM (Original Equipment Manufacturers) workshop segment which is fast emerging as an important channel of distribution for lubricant sales. In the industrial business segment, Castrol has leading brands that cater to specific materials, applications, processes and speeds and feeds to achieve greater performance like finish, consistency, tool life and wheel life. Castrol metal working products are used in various segments of the manufacturing industry and comply fully with the stringent requirements of user companies. Over 5000 castrol formulations meet the requirements of different sectors of industry and transportation.

As per the AC Nieloon-Lubricants Retail Audit, Castrol was identified as the unchallenged market leader in the Indian retail automotive segment (*Source :* www.superbrandsindia.com). Castrol is India's second largest lubricant company with around 21 percent market share. The company has a number of firsts to its credit, including the launch of multigrade diesel engine oils, dedicated two stroke engine oils and new generation truck engine oils.

Castrol is also an established player in the B2B segment offering value-added products and services acknowledged to be the best in class. The company works closely with its customers to develope products specific to their unique needs and delivers tailor made solutions for each partner.

Castrol has been a preferred partner of Original Equipment Manufacturers (OEM) over the years with **Tata, Maruti Suzuki, Ford BMW, Volvo, Volkswagen and Hudi**, in the tractor segment with **Mahindra and Mahindra** and **John Deere** and in the off highway category, Castrol has tie-ups with **JCB, L &T, Komatsu Telcon** and **Case**.

In the industrial business, Castrol offers comprehensive lubricant solutions to clients. Further, through efficient chemical management and services it is able to present client's with complete management of onsite fluid consumables with guaranteed cost and process saving.

The company **Castrol** with its line **'It's more than just oil. It's Liquid Engineering'** conveys a lot about the company's confidence and unswerving belief in its products and brand superiority along with the strong relationship it has forged with its customers - OEMs, the trade, influencers service providers and end consumers.

Castrol's decision making process involves total commitment of working together with its customers for mutual benefits.

The above case of Castrol gives an overview of the working of the company which sells products to its industrial customers. The market place consists of both individual customers and organisational buyers. This chapter focuses on industrial or organisational buying. We begin with trying to understand who is an organisational customer. Then an attempt is made to understand to differences between the organisational buyer and the final buyer, participants in organisational buying, characteristics of industrial markets, buying decisions involved in industrial buying process, factors influencing industrial buying behaviour, organisational customers buying process, the reseller market and government market.

WHO IS AN ORGANISATIONAL CUSTOMER?

In some ways organisational buying can be said to be similar to consumer buying for it is not *organisations* but the *people* within it who are making the buying decisions. So, who can be referred to as an organisational customer? Apart from the business organisations, the government, educational institutions (universities, colleges), retail institutions, consulting firms, financial institutions (banks) and nongovernment organisations can be addressed to as organisational customers. Since it is a varied market, it will be a challenge for marketers to deal with their customised needs and wants.

Simply stated *a market is said to be composed of buyers and sellers involved in a exchange process of goods and services and money*. However, when we think of companies selling to other organisations, we can consider a market in terms of the channels through which buyers and sellers contact each other and which gets extended into a personal relationship rather than ending as a faceless transaction. A industrial marketing system, therefore comprises of participants, distribution channels and relationships.

The consumer marketing involves analysing the decision making process of an individual consumer, whereas, industrial marketing involves firms trying their best to understand the organisational buyer's needs, resources, policies and buying procedures.

The purpose of organisational buying is to reduce costs, make profit, serve internal clientele's requirements and sometimes for meeting social and legal obligations. Since the buying is done by the organisation, the participants involved in the decision making process, are people with different organisational responsibilities and hence use different criteria in the purchase decision. The organisational buyers have to operate within the frame work of the policies, rules and regulations established by the organisation. The buying instruments included in organisational buying are request for tender quotations, purchase contracts and proposals.

The above mentioned aspects, help in drawing the differences between organisational buying and consumer buying processes. The consumer marketing involves analysing the decision making process of an individual customer, whereas organisational or industrial marketing involves firms trying their best to understand the organisational buyer's needs, resources, policies and buying procedures.

Organisations provide a big and vast market for raw materials, semi processed goods, manufactured goods, accessories, supplies and business services.

DIFFERENCES BETWEEN ORGANISATIONAL BUYER AND FINAL CONSUMER

Generally speaking, the differences between a business or organisational buyer and the final buyer can be spoken to in terms of the buying motives. Typically, the organisational buyer purchases products (or services) so as to improve the operational efficiency in the work environment in the most economical manner. Whereas, the buying motives of the final household customers are primarily psychological in nature, unlike the organisational buyer whose motives are more rational in nature. There could also be differences in terms of the size of the purchases (in terms of sales volume), involvement of risk, concentration of buyers and type of decision making etc.

The major differences amongst both the type of buyers are discussed hereunder:

Purpose or Motive of Organisational Buying

Both organisational buyers and final consumers make purchase decisions so as to satisfy their goals, although there is a difference in these goals. The final (household) buyer will make purchase decisions for his or her own consumption. Whereas, the organisational customer will buy to add value to the product which is then sold to another customer.

An organisational consumer's buying motives are more rational whereas, the household consumers buying motives are more psychological in nature.

In a way the organisational buying can be said to be a derived demand. *i.e.,* their demand for a product or service is in turn based on the end customer's demand. For instance, consider the demand for tyres in the automobile industry. For the tyre manufacturers, the demand for tyres will be according to the automobile firm's production plans, which in turn will be dependent upon the final customer's demand for automobiles and the external environmental factors (technology, government policies etc.). The tyre manufacturers demand for rubber in turn will depend on his production plans. Of course, the organisation also becomes a buyer of certain products like computers, fax machines, franking machines etc., which are purchased for it's own use. These products are purchased to improve their own efficiency, work environment and in the long run it becomes an economical consumption.

So, it will be more apt to say that an organisational consumer's buying motives are more rational whereas, the household consumers buying motives are more psychological in nature. Nevertheless, in organisational buying there could be psychological motives also. For instance, a very important factor which can influence the buyer's decision can be : the previous experience he has with the supplier (or vendor) and the extent to which the latter has taken care of the former's esteem. This holds true today especially when most of the vendors supply product's which are on par as for as product specifications, technology and the type of after sales service are concerned. Under such circumstances, each supplier will try to build up the cutting edge by understanding the buyer better and satisfy the organisational buyer's needs better than others.

Size of the Market

Organisational buyers buy in bulk, though they may seem fewer in number when compared to household buyers. But in reality, the final (household) buyer is relatively smaller although they all go for retail buying too. For, even in the case of small organisational buying, the annual purchase budget can run into a few lakhs atleast, however, even in large households the retail buying usually will be restricted to only a few thousand rupees.

Market Structure and Demand

There are several factors related to market structure and demand which are associated with organisational buying. These factors can be broadly classified as geographical concentration, fewer though larger buyers, vertical or horizontal market and derived/inelastic/fluctuating demand.

Buyers are *more concentrated* based on where the *specific industries are located.* For example textile (silk especially) industries are predominantly clustered in Southern India, information technology in Bangalore, Hyderabad, Noida, rubber production in Kerala and Oil and related products in Western India.

Organisational buyers look out for a few good customers. *i.e.,* they are concentrated by the *size of the market*. For instance about one-half of the value added by manufacturing occurs among a few of the largest firms in this sector. For example *Tata Motors* may have only a comparative handful of original equipment tyre users such as truck, autorickshaw, mini truck and tractor makers. But in the consumer market there will be lakhs of vehicles needing tyre replacements, which is handled by their wholesalers and retailers who are a part of their distribution network.

Organisational buyer markets may be either *vertical or horizontal*. In a *vertical market* the product or service would be sold to most of the organisations in perhaps one or two industries. *For example,* drilling equipments are primarily used only by the oil exploration industry like the *ONGC, RIL* etc. Horizontal markets are those which are very broad and the product or service is sold to a wide spectrum of industries. Say, office stationary is used by many industries.

In organisational buying, demand for industrial goods is relatively not affected by changes in price in the short run, whereas in the consumer market, the demand is greatly influenced by price changes.

As mentioned earlier organisational demand is *derived from consumer demand*. For instance, the booming real estate industry has resulted in an increase in consumer demand for apartments and independent houses. So sanitary ware industry saw a big demand for the related products which is derived from consumer demand.

In organisational buying, demand for industrial goods is relatively not affected by changes in price in the short run, whereas in the consumer market, the demand is greatly influenced by *price changes*. If the rubber producers were to raise the rubber prices say by Rs. 3 to automobile manufacturers, it would have little effect on demand. For, the automobile manufacturers would continue to place orders for roughly the same amount as before, since rubber price will be a small contribution in the overall cost of the final output *i.e.,* the finished automobile. Thus a Rs. 15 increase in the final price will have very little impact on the total automobile demand. This situation may be prevalent for the industry demand but an individual firm's demand can get strongly affected by a price change. *For example,* if a single car manufacturer was to raise the prices of its particular car model, it could lead to a significant fall in demand for that car model with customer preferring to purchase competitor's car priced lesser in the same segment.

Another feature of the organisational market is that organisational demand shows more fluctuation when compared to the consumer market. Usually, organisational buying is greatly influenced by the economic cycle. When there is an increase in demand for consumer products, the industrial demand for products also goes up and organisational buyers will invest and buildup large inventories of raw materials, various component parts, other office equipments and other items. However, when the economy is going through the slow down phase, the organisational buyers (manufacturers, wholesalers and retailers) may prefer using up the existing inventories and postpone the purchase of the supplies, equipments and related items.

Differences in the Marketing Strategy

Organisational buyers are usually concentrated in the same geographical area. Going back to the tyre manufacturers example, say *Goodyear* will have all its business or organisational customers located in one geographical area. However, in the consumer market buyers of cars, two wheelers, trucks and tractors will be spread across India. So for its organisational buyers, Good year will have a more focussed marketing strategy with more emphasis on personal selling. Whereas, for the consumer market, Goodyear will use mass communication (advertising in T.V. periodicals etc.) and a dealer network (or trade channels) as its marketing strategy.

FIGURE 16.1

FACTORS RELATED TO MARKET STRUCTURE AFFECTING ORGANISATIONAL BUYING

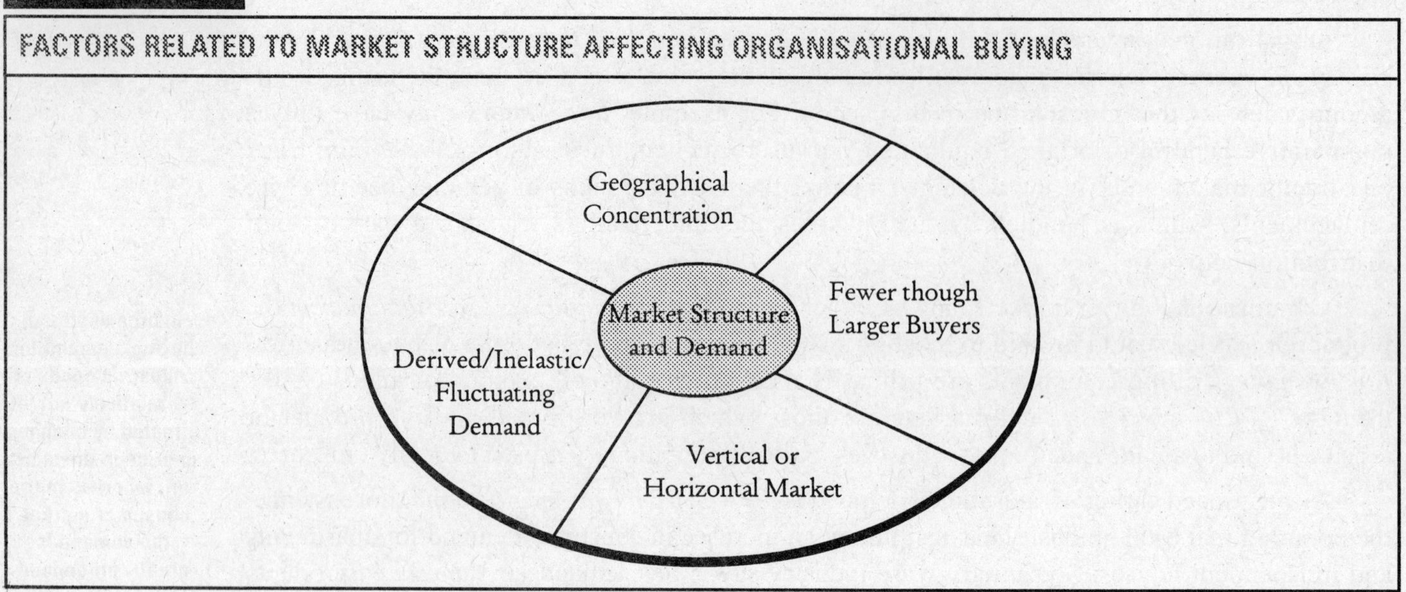

Buyer Characteristics

There are certain buyer characteristics which reveal differences between the business buyer and final consumer. Since purchase of products, by organisational buyers, are more complex and costly, *a group decision making* is involved in the decision making process. In case of final consumers, since the product is likely to be used by the consumer or a close friend (or relative), the consumer himself or herself takes the final decision on the purchase.

The nature of purchases in organisational buying requires the services of technology competent professionals within the organisation. The final consumer, generally purchases products for direct consumption. Under these circumstances there is no requirement for technical knowledge.

There is a difference in the economical rational considerations involved in organisational and final consumers purchase decisions.

There is a difference in the economical rational considerations involved in organisational and final consumers purchase decisions. In organisational buying, the rational considerations could include product quality specifications, consistency, prompt delivery assurance, price quoted, credit terms, warranty and service of the vendors etc. In final consumers purchase decisions, the rational considerations could be weighed in terms of rupees (cost) and the likely benefits from the purchases.

The organisational buyers purchase in bulk and even in case of small buyer, the budget will run into lakhs of rupees. So the risks in such purchases are very high. The organisational buyer will try to reduce risks by looking into certain factors such as : the previous experience with the supplier, vendor image and the supplier's standing within the industry among others. As the final consumer's purchase annual budget may run into few thousands only, the risks involved may not be very much, since most of available brands are more as less on par as far as quality and price are concerned.

➲ PARTICIPANTS IN ORGANISATIONAL BUYING

Webster and Wind in "Organizational Buying Behaviour", have called the decision making unit of a buying organization the buying center. The buying center can be defined as *"all those individuals and groups who participate in the purchasing decision-making process, who share some common goals and the risks arising from the decisions".* They have further, also stated that the buying center includes all members of the organisation who play any of the following five roles in the purchase decision process.

1. *Users :* These are members of the organisation who will use the product or service. Very often it is the user who initiates the buying proposal and also defines the product specifications.
2. *Influencers :* These are persons who are able to influence the buying decision. Very often such persons may be technical personnel who are often involved in defining specifications and also in providing information for evaluating alternatives.
3. *Buyers :* These are persons who are formally authorised to select the supplier and also work out the contract of agreement. Such persons may help in working out product specification and also play a major role in selecting vendors and negotiating the terms.
4. *Deciders :* These are persons who are formally or informally given power in the selection or approval of the final supplier.
5. *Gate keepers :* These are persons who control the flow of information to others. *For example,* the agent from the organization will use his authority and prevent salespersons from seeing users or deciders.

Within any organisation, the size and the composition of the buying centre will vary for the different classes of products.

However, it may be noted that within any organization, the size and the composition of the buying center will vary for the different classes of products. And on the other side, the industrial marketer has to work-out as to who are the major decision participants? Which are the decisions they will be able to influence? What is their degree of influence? What is the evaluation criteria used by each decision participant?

An easy way to identify the participants of industrial marketing system is to divide the economy into three broad divisions comprising of extractive industries, manufacturing industries and the consuming or user industries.

FIGURE 16.2

PARTICIPANTS IN INDUSTRIAL MARKETING

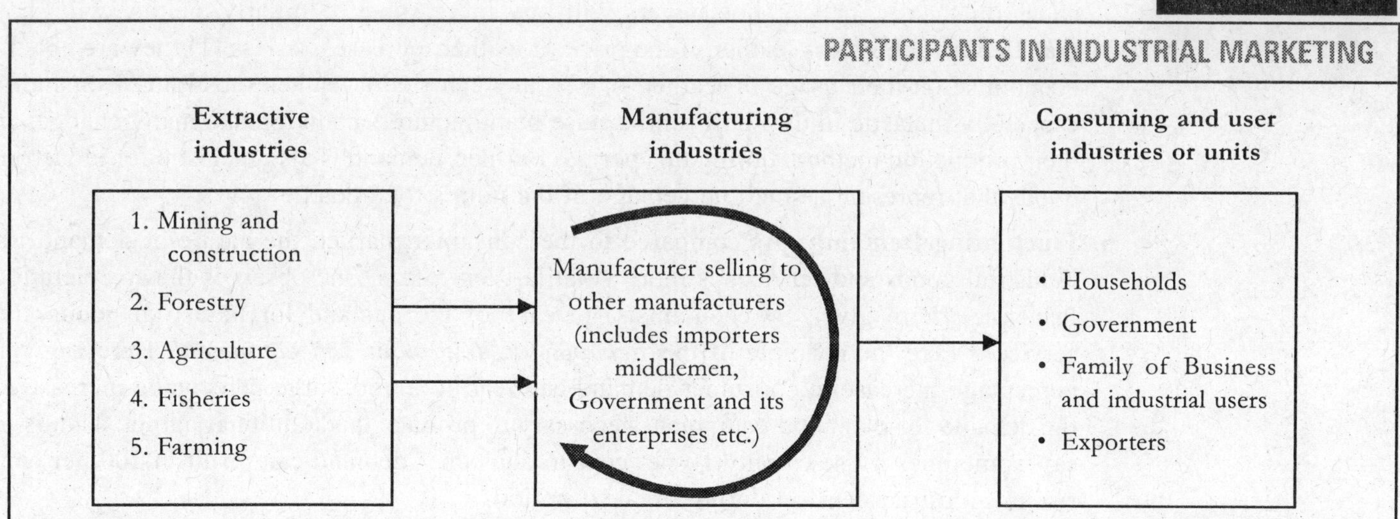

The above illustration shows a complex way in which product flows:

On one hand, the manufacturing industries procure raw and semi finished materials from the extractive industries and supply them with equipment and supplies. And on the other side, these manufacturing firms are selling capital goods, supplies and consumer goods to households, government, business firms/institutional users and exporters.

➲ CHARACTERISTICS OF INDUSTRIAL MARKETS

Characteristics of industrial markets include: fewer buyers, larger buyers, geographically concentrated buyers, derived demand, inelastic demand, fluctuating demand and professional purchasing.

1. **Fewer Buyers :** As compared to the consumer market, there are fewer/less number of buyers in the industrial market. Generally, bulk orders are placed by buying organizations with the selling firm. *For example,* the fate of *"MRF tyre"* company will depend on getting orders from the automakers or heavy good vehicle makers. But if *MRF* sells replacement tyres to consumers, the potential market will consist of the automobiles/or heavy good vehicles currently in use.
2. **Larger Buyers :** In the industrial market, there are a few large buyers who account for most of purchases. *For example,* in the industrial market for telephone and telegraph, it is only the top most four or so manufacturers who account for over 70 per cent of total production.
3. **Geographically Concentrated Buyers :** In industrial market most of the buyers show geographical concentration. *For example,* most agricultural output come from few states in India like, Punjab, Maharastra, Gujarat, South Indian states etc. Similarly, industries such as petroleum, rubber and steel also show geographical concentration. Such geographical concentration of manufacturers will help in reducing the cost of selling.
4. **Derived Demand :** This means that the demand for industrial goods will ultimately be derived from the demand for consumer goods. Today, world over due to recession, there has been a negative demand for automobile products. Since there is a fall in demand for these consumer goods, automatically there will be a decrease in demand for all the industrial goods entering into their production.
4. **Inelastic Demand :** If the total demand for the industrial product remains unaffected by price changes, the demand is said to be inelastic. *For example,* the foot wear manufacturers are not going to buy more leather if the price of leather falls unless (i) leather is a major cost in shoe manufacture or (2) the manufacturer will reduce the prices of the leather shoes drastically, or (3) shoe buyers will buy more shoes. Similarly, neither will shoe manufacturers buy less leather, if the price of leather increases, unless (1) they are able to economise on their usage of leather, or (2) they can find a leather substitute. Demand is especially inelastic in the short run because manufacturers cannot make many changes in their production method, during this period. Further, demand is also inelastic for industrial goods that represent a small percentage of the item's total cost.
6. **Fluctuating Demand :** As compared to the consumer market, the nature of demand for industrial goods and services is more volatile. Very often, one observes the Acceleration Principle, (term given by economists) in case of the demand for industrial goods and services. Take the example of the *demand for new plant and equipment.* Here a given percentage increase in consumer demand can lead to a very large percentage increase in the demand for plant and equipment necessary to produce the additional output. That is to say, sometimes a rise of only 10 per cent in consumer demand can result in 200 per cent rise in industrial demand during the next period.
7. **Professional Purchasing :** Since industrial buying is a complex purchase decision, more specialised personnel with the necessary technical expertise are involved in the purchase of such industrial goods and services. Generally purchasing firms have buying committees made up of technical experts and top management who purchase the industrial goods and services.

Taking an organisational buying decision.

8. **Other additional characteristics** of industrial buying are given below in brief:

(a) *Direct purchasing :* In case of technically complex or expensive items, industrial buyers often buy directly from producers rather than through middlemen.

(b) *Reciprocal buying :* Industrial buyers often select suppliers who also buy from them. *For example,* A paper manufacturer will buy the necessary chemicals from a chemical company that is buying a considerable amount of its paper.

The number of decisions involved in the purchase of an industrial product will vary and depend on the type of buying situation.

(c) *Leasing :* Industrial buyers sometimes prefer to go for equipment leasing instead of outright purchase. In this case the lessee stands to gain due to the availability of more capital, facilitates use of seller's latest products, provision for better servicing and he can gain some tax advantage. This is more visible in industries related to computers, packaging equipment, delivery trucks and so on.

FIGURE 16.3

CHARACTERISTICS OF INDUSTRIAL MARKETS

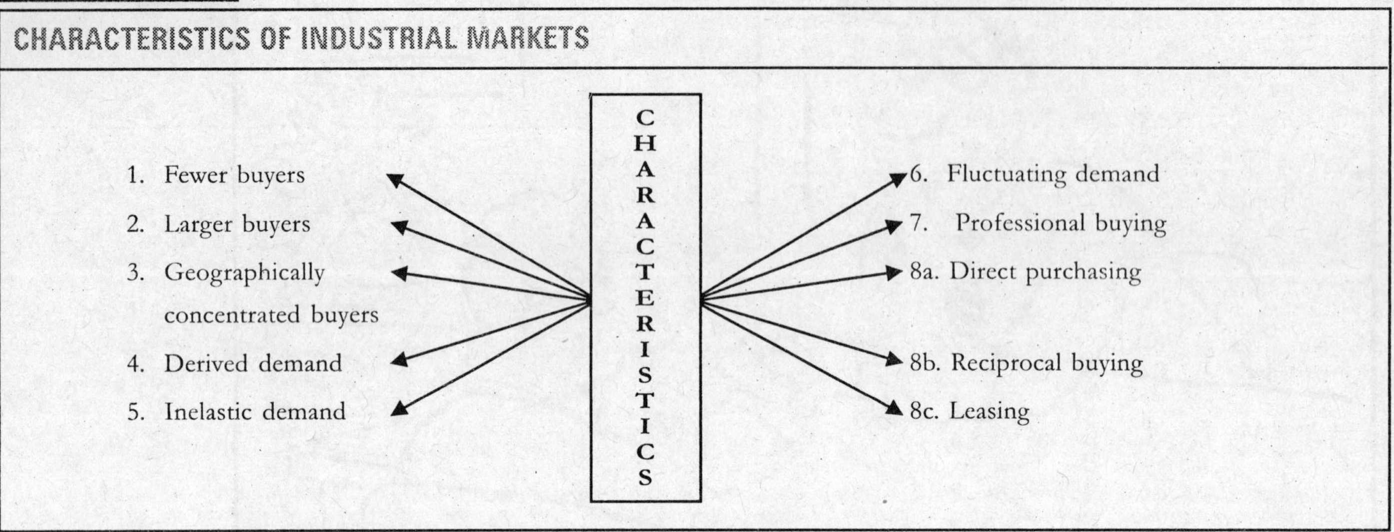

BUYING DECISIONS INVOLVED IN INDUSTRIAL BUYING PROCESS

The industrial buyer has to take a lot of decisions while being involved in the purchase of an industrial product. Of course, the number of decisions will vary depending on the type of buying situation. There are generally three types of buying situations.

FIGURE 16.4

TYPES OF BUYING SITUATIONS

Straight/routine rebuy	*Modified rebuy*	*Completely New task with negotiation*
1. Electricity, water, gas	1. New cars/trucks	1. Complex buildings bridges, dams
2. Office supplies	2. Electrical components	2. Installations (machinery etc.)
3. Gum, cigarettes	3. Computer terminal	3. Custom built office or house
4. Bulk chemicals	4. Consultancy services	

1. **Straight/routine Rebuy :** This straight or routine rebuy is concerning a buying situation where the purchaser will reorder the product without any modification. This is handled on a routine basis by the purchasing department. The buyer will select the supplier from the 'suppliers list' available with them, based on the past experience and satisfaction with the various suppliers.

   The 'in' suppliers will try to live up to their past image of providing product and service quality. They may also suggest automatic reordering systems so as to save on reordering time. The 'out/new' suppliers will attempt at offering something new so as to get a footing within the organisation. They may try for a small order to begin with.

2. **Modified Rebuy :** Here the term 'modified' indicates situations where the buyer/purchaser wants to modify product specifications, prices, other terms or specifications. Such situations may result in an increase in the number of participants. On the one hand the 'in' suppliers will try their best to procure or protect the account, whereas, the 'out' suppliers will see this as a business opportunity and make a 'better offer' to gain some new business.
3. **Completely New Task :** This means a company is buying a product or service for the first time. Higher the cost or risk involved, more will be the number of participants involved in decision making and more information will be sought by them. Under this situation the marketer will try to reach out to as many key buying influences as possible and also provide the necessary information and assistance. Under 'new task' buying situation because of the complicated buying situations, the companies or organisation will prefer to use the best of their sales persons.
4. **Other Related Decisions Involved in the Buying Decision :** From the above mentioned three buying situations, the new task situation involves the maximum number of decisions taken. Here the buyer will be interested in knowing and deciding on :
   1. *Product specification.*
   2. *Price limits.*
   3. *Delivery terms and conditions and time of delivery.*
   4. *Service terms.*
   5. *Payment terms and conditions.*
   6. *Order quantities.*
   7. *Reliable and acceptable suppliers.*
   8. *The supplier who has been approved of.*

   Of course the sequence of the above decisions will vary depending on the buying situation and the participants in the decision process.

For an industrial product there are three types of buying situations, routine rebuy, modified rebuy and new task.

Turn-key Operation or Systems Buying and Selling

Very often it is observed that organisational buyers, (especially when the government is a buyer) would invite bids from prime contractors who would assemble the package or system. The contractor who finally is accepted as the prime contractor would be responsible for bidding and assembling all the sub components. So the prime contractor will provide the turnkey operation *i.e.,* the buyer simply has to turn the key to get everything necessary.

The contractor who finally is accepted as the prime contractor would be responsible for bidding and assembling all the sub components.

The supplier will sell a group of inter connected components. *For example,* the supplier sells not only glue but glue applicators and dryers as well. Moreover, the supplier sells a system of production, inventory control, distribution and other services to meet the buyer's need for a smooth running operation. This is why this method is called *systems buying* and is an important marketing tool in industrial buying.

FACTORS INFLUENCING INDUSTRIAL BUYING BEHAVIOUR

Generally stated there are two sets of factors that shape the behaviour or demand of industrial goods. One is the direct factors namely, the variation in the nature and uses of products themselves *i.e.,* whether they are items of major equipment, component parts, process materials, operating supplies or raw materials. The other set of factors indirectly affects industrial buying. These are

Factors influencing industrial buying behaviour can be categorised into: environmental, organisational, interpersonal and individual.

business conditions, the nature of the ultimate buyer and financial conditions. Together these factors influence the industrial buyer behaviour.

However in a simplified way we can classify the various influences on industrial buyers into four categories : environmental factors, organisational factors, interpersonal factors and individual factors.

FIGURE 16.5

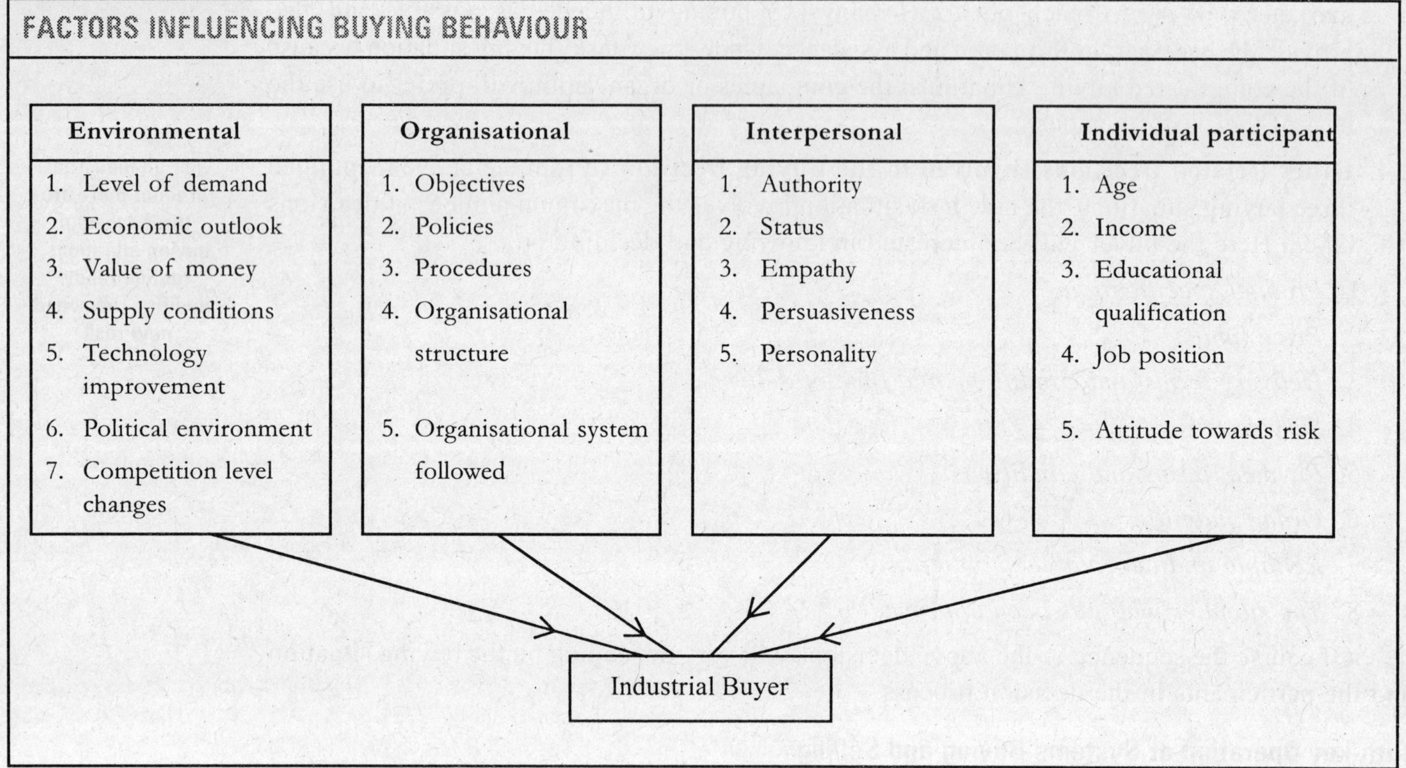

Environmental Factors

Industrial buyers are greatly influenced by the existing and expected environmental factors namely the level of primary demand, the economic outlook and cost of money (money value). If there is increased economic uncertainty, the industrial buyers would prefer to reduce their inventories and will not invest in new plants and equipment.

Another important environmental factor is the availability of key materials. Companies are willing to buy and hold larger inventories of scarce materials rather than facing a situation of shortages in key material.

Other environmental factors affecting the industrial buying behaviour are rate of technological changes taking place, political stability and regulatory developments and competitive developments in the environment. The industrial marketer has to monitor these factors, determine how they will affect the buyer, identify the problems if any and in turn work to convert these problems into opportunities.

Organisational Factors

. Since each buying organisation has its own objectives, procedures, organisational structure and systems, the industrial marketer will be interested in getting to know the answer to questions like:

1. How many people are involved in the buying decision?
2. Who are these people?
3. What is their criteria for evaluation?
4. What are the company's policies and constraints on the buyers?

The purchasing system generally followed by the organisations could take the form of :

(a) *Purchasing departments* : This department will be responsible for managing the company's cost related to purchasing, inventory control and production schedule. Sometimes these departments are also referred to as materials management department. The inside people handling these may be highly technically qualified persons or M.B.A's. So industrial marketers have to correspondingly ensure their sales persons also match the calibre of the industrial buyers.

(b) *Centralised purchasing* : The head office will identify the materials required by the various divisions and then consider buying them centrally. This method gives the company more purchasing clout and also produces substantial saving for the company. Here again the industrial marketers must have a sophisticated sales force and meticulous marketing planning effort.

(c) *Long term contracts* : Industrial buyers are seeking long term contracts with suppliers. These contracts call for skillful negotiation from industrial buyers as well as from the industrial marketer's sides.

(d) *Purchasing performance evaluation* : Sometimes organisation's have in place incentive systems to reward purchasing managers especially for good purchasing performance. This in turn will prompt managers to increase pressure on sellers for the best terms.

Interpersonal Factors

This refers to the various participants involved in the decision making process and their status and authority, and their empathy and persuasiveness qualities. Though the industrial marketer is not likely to know the kind of group dynamics which will take place during the buying process, whatever information they can uncover about the personalities and interpersonal factors will help them to be prepared while interacting with the participants of the industrial buying process.

The industrial marketer must know their customers and adapt their tactics to the specific environmental, organisational, interpersonal and individual factors which will influence the particular buying situation.

Individual Factors

Each participant in the buying decision process has got his/her own personal motivation's perception and preferences. These to a great extent are influenced by the participant's age, income, education, profession, personality, belief and value and attitude. Each participant also exhibits a unique buying style very often influenced by his lifecycle stage.

So the industrial marketer must know their customers and adapt their tactics to the specific environmental, organisational, interpersonal and individual factors which will influence the particular buying situation.

ORGANISATIONAL CUSTOMER'S BUYING PROCESS

FIGURE 16.6

ORGANISATIONAL CUSTOMER'S BUYING PROCESS

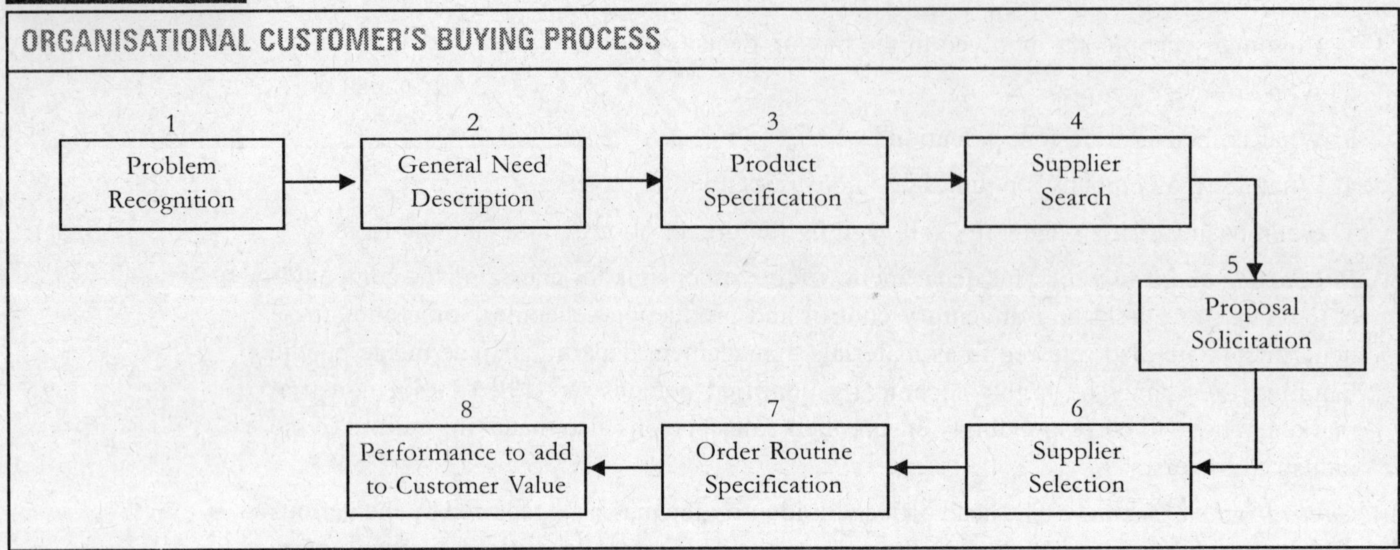

1. Problem Recognition

The buying process starts when someone in the organisation/company recognises a problem or need which can be met by purchasing a good or service. The problem can arise as a result of internal or external stimuli. Internal stimuli, which can trigger off a problem recognition situation are:

Unlike the ultimate customer, the industrial buyer will be motivated by budgetary considerations such as profit goals, expense quotas and cost benefit analysis.

- The company decides to launch a new product and requires new equipment and materials for manufacturing the new product.
- The breakdown of a machine which requires replacement or new parts immediately.
- The material purchased from a vendor proves to be unsatisfactory and the company is urgently looking out for another vendor.
- The purchase department head notices an opportunity to obtain better prices or quality materials.

The various factors which can act as external stimuli are :

- The buyer comes to know or gets new ideas at a exhibition or trade show or by seeing an advertisement in a technical magazine or from a sales representative who offers a better product at a lower price etc., the buyer becomes aware of the availability of a better product at a reasonable price.

So the industrial marketer has to act as the stimulant for problem recognition by developing informative and attractive advertisements, mail literature to industrial buyers about the availability of technical products, direct their sales personnel to call upon the buyers/prospects and so on.

2. General Need Description

Having recognised the problem, and realising the need for fulfilling the need, the buyer will now be involved in identifying the characteristic features and the quantity of the product which is required. Unlike the ultimate consumer, the industrial buyer will be motivated by

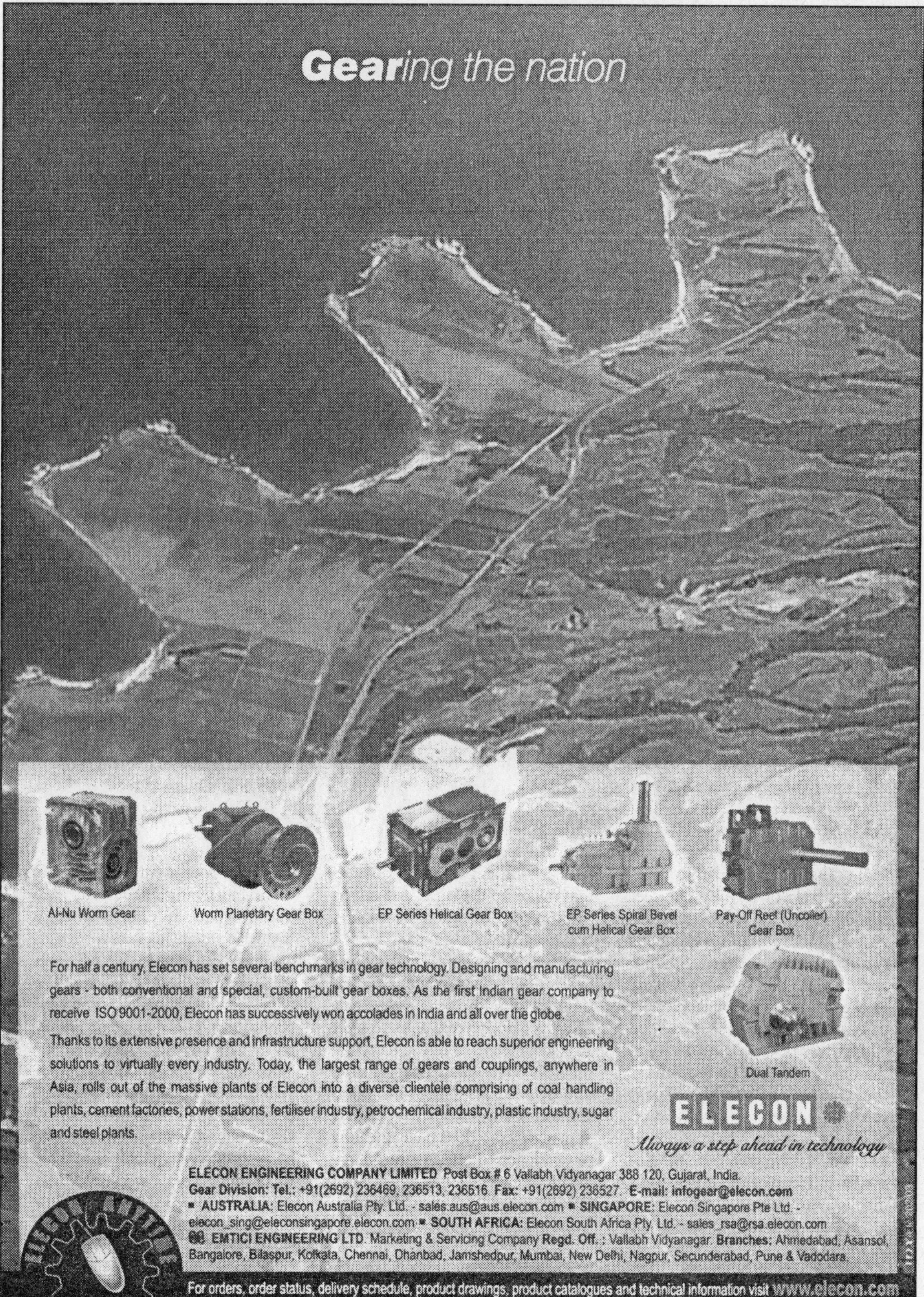

Elecon Engineering communicates about its ability to meet the Gear market's requirement through its specific products.

budgetary considerations, such as profit goals, expense quotas and cost benefit analysis. He is conscious of justifying the purchase based on some measurable parameter. Very often, hence, the buyer will select the vendor/supplier based on the sellers/marketer's quality, service and price generally in this order.

During this stage, the industrial buyer tends to define *product quality* as that combination of properties which fits the product for its use in the future. Related to this is the supplier's capability to deliver materials, components and supplies consistently in the required standard of quality. Then he should be convinced that the supplier will *provide a variety of services* in the form of technical, replacement parts, delivery, information and sales. And lastly, the industrial buyer will *work out the evaluated price,* on the basis of the amount of scrap or waste resulting from the use of material, the cost of processing the material, the work required to be done by the machine, the power it consumes, the damage or loss liability, and many other factors which should help in minimizing costs.

Typically, these parameters are verified after which the buyer will rank the attributes in a sequence or order of importance like reliability, durability, price etc., required in the item to be purchased.

Ideally, the marketer must take care of the product characteristics desired by the buyer and then interact with the industrial buyer and communicate about the availability of the same with them.

Ideally, the marketer must take care of the product characteristics desired by the buyer and then interact with the industrial buyer and communicate about the availability of the same with him.

3. Product Specification

The buying organisation will now proceed to the item's technical specifications. For this the buyer will do value analysis to appraise a supplier's effectiveness. *Value analysis* involves the review of product specifications in relation to requirements, the identification of unnecessary cost elements and suggestions for their elimination. This method requires participation by several groups of functional area specialists, such as engineering, manufacturing and production and accounting. These groups will be required to look for optional product characteristics and specify them accordingly. Moreover the buyer has also got the choice of refusing merchandise that fails to meet the intended standards.

In turn, value analysis can be used by the marketer as a tool for opening a new account with an industrial buyer.

4. Supplier Search

The buyer now tries to identify the most appropriate vendor. The buyer has to be certain that their suppliers meet the standard of performance and quality for which they have worked out their operational plans. They will find out ways to accurately assess vendor capabilities, mainly in the areas of technology, production, financial strength and management. So, at times the vendors will be dropped from the list of considerations because they may not be able to supply the needed quantity or because of a bad reputation in the market. And ultimately the buyer will be left to choose the supplier from the 'finally approved list' of qualified suppliers.

5. Proposal Solicitation

The next stage requires qualified suppliers to submit proposals. Generally, the supplier will furnish information in the form of a catalogue or send their sales representative to the buyer with the necessary information. In case of more complex or expensive item, the buyer will prefer to have a detailed written proposal from the supplier.

The proposals must include both the technical as well as the marketing documents. In case of oral presentations, the supplier must be able to generate confidence of the buyer in his company's capabilities and abilities to be able to stand out in the midst of competition.

6. Supplier Selection

Now the stage is set whereby the members of the buying center will review the proposals and take a decision for the final selection of the supplier. This buying center will generally draw up a list of the desired supplier attributes and their relative importance. A few of the attributes looked out for in a prospective supplier are :

1. *Technical support services*
2. *Prompt delivery*
3. *Quick response to customer needs*
4. *Product quality*
5. *Supplier reputation in the market*
6. *Product price*
7. *Extension of credit, and so on.*

In this stage the buyer will do *vendor analysis* so as to ascertain not only the technical competence of the various suppliers but also their ability to deliver in time and provide the necessary services. The buyer will rate the supplier's against the desired attributes and then identify the most attractive supplier. The buyer will negotiate with the preferred suppliers for better prices and terms before making the final selection. Usually, buyers opt for multiple sources of suppliers and prefer not to be totally dependent on one supplier in case of anything going wrong. Further, they will also be in a position to compare the prices and performance of various suppliers.

Under the 'blanket contract', the supplier will agree to re-supply the buyer as and when required on certain price terms over a specified period of time.

7. Order Routine Specification

This requires the buyer to specify and write out the final order in terms of technical specifications, quantity to be ordered, expected time of delivery, terms on goods returned, warranties and so on. Moreover, placing a new order each time the stock is required is a costly affair. Similarly neither would the buyer want to stock extra materials or items because it indicates carrying more inventory, which is also not a healthy sign. To avoid the above problems, the buyer very often goes for 'blanket contract' with the supplier. Under this contract, the supplier will agree to resupply the buyer as and when required on certain price terms over a specified period of time.

8. Performance to Add to Customer 'Value'

In this stage, the buyer will review the performance of the supplier. Today all industrial marketers suffer from the problem of product parity. So they are trying to build relationship with the buyers by adding value to the transaction. Suppliers are *customising* by knowing not only their own customers but also their *customer's customer*. For instance, *Asian Paints* had customised its paints portfolio to add real value to the buyer. *'Asian Paints'* tries to work out the autobuyers preferences, and tailor make its shades accordingly based on the findings of qualitative and quantitative research on preferred colours of automaker's interests. In this way, *Asian Paints* had customised its paints portfolio and used this flexibility to add real value to the industrial buyer.

Participants in organisational buying decision.

In another instance, *'Standard Batteries Ltd.' (SBL)* realising that *'Exide Industries'* was a big competitor to take on in the replacement market, put its focus on *Maruti Udyog Ltd. (MUL)*. It offered a two year warranty period - higher than the industry average of one year-as an assurance of indicating that it wanted a long term relationship and not short term profits. Based on this technique and also by proving its performance SBL was able to bag orders from new automakers like *Mahindra Ford, General Motors India and Mercedez Benz.*

During this stage the buyer reviews the performance of the particular supplier(s). Based on the performance review, the buyer will decide whether to continue, modify or drop the seller.

The reseller market consists of individuals and organisations who acquire and resell goods produced by others.

The above eight stages in the buy phase model represent the major steps in the industrial buying process. However, in a real situation, the industrial marketer will need to act according to the situational requirement.

From the above discussions it can be seen that industrial marketing is a challenging area, with the marketer required to identify the organisational buyer's needs and buying procedures before designing an effective plan to sell his products or services.

➲ RESELLER MARKET

Related to organizational markets is the reseller markets. The reseller market consists of individuals and organizations who acquire and resell goods produced by others. For instance *Geeta Electronics*, is a Bangalore based company which purchases in bulk the various components related to the 'computer' at wholesale rates and then resells the same to individuals and to other organizations like *'TVS Electronics'*, etc.

Resellers have to work out on their assortment, suppliers, prices and terms. The resellers generally face three types of buying situations (1) new items, (2) new vendors and (3) new terms. In case of small wholesalers and small retail organizations buying may be carried out by one or few individuals; in large organizations, this is carried out by the purchase department. Today we see that there is acceptance of the 'Supermarket' by the consumers. So in case of a supermarket chain, there will be a chain of participants - headquarters buyers, store-wide buying committees and the individual store manager, generally. In case of purchasing new items, the buyers will go through a buying process similar to the one adopted by the industrial buyer. And in case of purchasing standard items, the buying process consists of routines for reordering and renegotiating contracts.

THE GOVERNMENT MARKET

The government market consists of governmental units - Central, State and Local - who purchase or rent goods for carrying out the main functions of the government.

Government buying is based on acquiring goods and services to carry out public utilities and services like education, defence, public welfare programmes, health and hospitals, highways, roads and other infrastructure facilities, natural resources, postal service etc. Each good that the government buys requires further decisions on how to buy, where to buy, how much to buy and to other services required. Usually the concerned government will favour the lowest cost bidders, who are able to meet the required specification.

Government buying procedures are of two types (1) the open bid and (2) the negotiated contract.

The government buying procedures are of two types (a) the open bid and (b) the negotiated contract.

Open bid buying means the government office will invite from qualified suppliers for carefully described items and award the contract to the lowest bidder. The supplier must consider whether it can meet the specifications and accept the terms. At times, preference may be given to a supplier because of his superior product or reputation for completing contracts.

In *negotiated contract* buying, the agency works with one or more companies and directly negotiates a contract with one of them covering the project and terms. This usually takes place in case of complex projects often involving lot of research and development cost and risk and/ or where there is little effective competition. Such contracts may involve cost-plus pricing, fixed pricing or price-and-incentive methods of pricing.

Government contracts won by large companies give rise to substantial subcontracting opportunities for small companies also. However, government spending is determined by elected officials rather than by marketing efforts to develop this market. Nevertheless because the government is a vast one, many companies are now establishing separate marketing departments to guide government - directed marketing effort.

SUMMARY

Apart from the business organisations, the government educational institutions, retail institutions, consulting firms, financial institutions (banks) and non-government organisations can be addressed to as organisational customers. The differences between organisational buyers and final consumers can be in relation to : purpose or motive of buying, size of the market, market structure and demand, differences in the marketing strategy and the buyer characteristics.

It is possible to identify the participants of marketing system by dividing the economy into three broad divisions comprising of extractive industries, manufacturing industries and the consuming or user industries. The characteristics of industrial markets include fewer buyers, larger buyers, geographically concentrated buyers, derived demand, inelastic demand, professionals purchasing and the type of buying.

Typically, the buying decisions involved in industrial buying process are dependent upon the buying situations which could be related to straight/routine rebuy, modified rebuy or completely new task with negotiation. Generally, there are two sets of factors that shape the behaviour of demand for industrial goods. (a) the direct factors, (b) indirect factors. The organizational customer's buying process involves eight stages starting from the problem recognition stage till the performance to add to customer value.

The reseller market consists of individuals and organisations who acquire and resell goods produced by others. The government market consists of government units (central, state and local) who purchase or rent goods for carrying out the main functions of the government.

➲ CHAPTER QUESTIONS FOR DISCUSSION

1. Who can be categorised as an organisational customer?
2. What are the major differences between the organisational buyers and the final customer?
3. Briefly describe the characteristics of industrial markets as well as the three types of buying situations.
4. Explain the major factors influencing industrial buying behaviour.
5. Describe the various steps involved in the organisational customer's buying process.
6. Visit your college canteen interact with the person-in-charge of the canteen and find out which factors are involved in the buying behaviour for the purchase of raw materials (ingredients for cooking food) and other environmental factors involved in their buying behaviour. Prepare a brief report on your findings.

➲ SUGGESTED READINGS

1. www.superbrandsindia.com
2. www.castrol.co.in
3. Philip Kotler, *Principle of Marketing* (2nd edn.) Prentice Hall of India. Private Ltd., New Delhi, 1985.
4. Philip Kotler, *Marketing Management Analysis, Implementation and Control* (8th Edn.), Prentice Hall of India Private Ltd., New Delhi, 1994.
5. Fredrick E. Webster Jr. and Yoram Wind, *Organizational Buying Behavior* (Engle Wood Cliffs, N.J.: Prentice Hall, 1972)
6. Roopa Pai, Industrial Marketing, *Business Today* Volume 6 Number 1, January 7-21, 1997, Living Media India Ltd.
7. Rosemary Phipps, Craig Simmons, *Understanding Customers*, 1996-97, Butterworth-Heinemann, Oxford, 1996.
8. David L. Loudon, Albert J. Della Bitta, *Consumer Behavior*, 4th edition, Tata Mc.Graw Hill, New Delhi, 2006 (reprint), pp. 657-685.

CASE

CROMPTON GREAVES LIMITED

The Beginning

Crompton Greaves Limited was established in India in 1937 and is a part of the Avantha Group a conglomerate with an impressive global footprint. The early beginning of Crompton Greaves can be traced to 1878 when Col. R.E.B. Crompton founded R.E.B. Crompton and Company. The company merged with F.A. Parkinson to form Crompton Parkinson Ltd. (CPL) in the year 1927. Greaves Cotton and Co. (CGC) was appointed as their concessionaire in India. In the year 1937, CPL established its wholly owned Indian subsidiary viz. Crompton Parkinson Works Ltd. in Mumbai (then Bombay), along with a sales organisation, Greaves Cotton and Crompton Parkinson Ltd., in collaboration with GCC. In the year 1947, an eminent Indian Industrialist Lala Karamchand Thapar took over the company. Today, Crompton Greaves is India's largest private sector enterprise with headquarters at Worli, Mumbai.

Products

Crompton Greaves has diversified extensively and is engaged in designing, manufacturing and marketing technologically advanced electrical products and services related to power generation, transmission and distribution besides executing turnkey projects. It is also the single largest source for a wide variety of electrical equipments and products.

The company is organised into four business groups *viz.,* power systems, industrial systems, consumer products and telecom products. Crompton Greaves (CG) offers a wide range of products such as power and industrial transformers, HT circuit breakers, LT&HT motors, DC motors, traction motors, alternators/generators, railway signaling equipments, lighting products, fans, pumps and public switching, transmission and access products. Apart from offering a broad range of products mentioned above, the company also undertakes turnkey projects from concept to commissioning. CG exports its products to more than 60 countries worldwide, including the emerging markets of South-East Asia and Latin America. In short, CG offers products and services to all the segments of the power industry from complex industrial solutions to basic household requirements.

Customers

Crompton Greaves motors are used in a variety of industries including the railways, cement, fertilisers, textiles, paper and agriculture. CG's motors are designed to stand up to the rigorous of the most severe conditions. For instance in case the application calls for maximum power at the highest efficiency or resistance to harsh environmental conditions or extreme temperatures, Crompton Greaves motors are able to meet the requirements.

Crompton Greaves has a large customer base, consisting of State Electricity Boards, utility companies, railways, government and local bodies and large companies in public as well as private sectors. In other words, it addresses customer needs of many segments ranging from households to complex industrial sectors through its comprehensive range of products and services. CG's customers include:

- State Electricity Boards
- Power Grid Corporation of India
- Andhrapradesh Transmission Corporation
- Infosys Technologies
- Kirloskar Brothers
- Diesel Locomotive Works
- Reliance Energy
- Larsen & Toubro
- Whirlpool (India)
- ABB Ltd.
- Mather and Platt India
- Bharat Petroleum Corporation
- Indian Space Research Organisation

Competition

CG has different competitor(s) depending upon its particular product division. The names of a few: for instance include *Bajaj Electricals* is a competitor for Crompton Greaves in the area of Power Transmission, Power Distribution, Telecom Towers, Mobile Telecom Towers and Wind Energy Towers. *Bharat Bijlee* is another competitor involved in the manufacture of electric motors and transformers. Bharat Bijlee also has a project division which undertakes turnkey projects in the areas of outdoor EHV and HV Switchyards, Industrial Electrification, indoor substations, overhead and underground distribution system, power system study etc. *L&T (Larsen and Toubro Ltd.)*, which has an Engineering Design and Research Centre (EDRC) involved in providing comprehensive design, detailed engineering and constancy services for EHV sub-station and switchyards, distribution substations, GIS substations, total electrical solutions for industrial projects, electrical and automation for intelligent buildings and infrastructure projects, transmission line towers, telecommunication towers and railway electrification structures, is another competitor of Crompton and Greaves.

Future

As one of the country's leading engineering companies, Crompton Greaves has helped its customers use electric power efficiently as well as increase industrial productivity in a sustainable way. It has shown the market of its capability as an Indian company, with the products and technology to successfully compete in the global market too.

Its entry into the latest generation value added products has ensured that the company can capitalise on the growing demand for transmission and distribution (T&D) infrastructure equipment. With the government having ambitious plans to upgrade and modernise its sub-stations, it is expected that the market for this service will grow manifold in the coming years. In such a Scenario, Crompton Greaves (CG) will have a futuristic role to play.

(*Source :* www.cromptongreaves.com
www.cglonline.com)

QUESTIONS FOR DISCUSSION

1. What are the environmental factors which have helped Crompton Greaves to establish its brandname in the market?
2. Rural India is facing a lot of power shortage and the government is planning to upgrade and modernise its substations. Looking to its present market performance, what organisational and external factors have to be considered by Crompton Greaves, if it is planning to tap this market?
3. Meet any distributor of Crompton Greaves products and find out the decision making process followed by the company for selecting distributors or vendors.

CHAPTER 17

ONLINE CONSUMER BEHAVIOUR

- Case : **HDFC Bank Limited** and **www.shopping indiatimes.com**
- Brief History of the Internet and E-commerce
- The internet in India
- Online decision making process
- Developments and concerns in Indian net connections
- Summary
- Chapter questions for discussion
- Suggested Readings
- Case : **Games on Demand** – **India Games** and **Zapak.com**

CASE

HDFC BANK LIMITED AND WWW.SHOPPING INDIATIMES.COM

HDFC Bank Limited was incorporated in August 1994 with the Single minded focus on product quality and service excellence. As on December 31, 2006, the bank had a India network of 583 branches in 263 cities and over 1471 ATM'S.

For internet savvy customers, **HDFC Bank** has got the internet banking service **'Net Banking'**, which provides up-to-the-second account information and let one manage the account from anywhere, anytime, at one's own convenience. Customers can also view their Demat account through Net Banking. The bank also noted that customers found it convenient to use plastic cards as a preferred mode of payment. However, the HDFC Bank noticed that their customers were very much concerned with using their cards online. In order to address this issue HDFC Bank launched the **Net Safe,** offering a virtual card facility. It offers customers the flexibility and security for online shopping. This can be created online by the customer by using their credit card or debit card to fund it for the first time the card number, to shop, thereby eliminating the risk of their entire credit limits or account balances getting exposed.

In order to shop online, customers can **create a virtual card** on their existing debit or credit card with a pre-defined limit that is valid for a short time only, after which the card ceases to exist. *For example,* if customers wish to buy something from a particular site worth Rs. 1000, they can create their own Net Safe card where in they get a one-time use card with a limit of Rs. 1000 which is taken from the credit card/debit card. Further, in case the customer doesn't use Net Safe within 24 hours of creating the card, the card simply disappears and the credit limit or amount in the account gets reverted back to the customers credit/debit card.

Another innovative offering from HDFC Bank is the launch of **Mobile POS terminals** and **tying up with Reliance Infocomm** to enable merchants to deliver goods to customers', house, and offering them the option to make payments through their credit cards or debit cards. This service offers a lot of convenience and business opportunities for various categories of business customers-merchants, restaurants, supermarkets and grocery stores.

The **Times group** has created a website www.shopping.indiatimes.com to enable customers have an enjoyable online shopping experience. It helps customers to-

- **Click & shop**- after providing all the relevant customer personal information, the customer can click, place order for a wide range of products such as cell phones, digital cameras. jewellery, toys, car accessories, access to India's entertainment arenas, news, multimedia, movie games etc.
- **India.com feedback-** this facility is to take care of any technical query or related services.
- **DNV-India Times.com-** this effort is made to build consumer confidence in its online shopping mall with the help of DNV and its EB trust mark.

Ad invites customers to enjoy online book shopping

- Through **meracd.indiatimes.com** customers are provided India times store help in payment options. Say, Usage of credit card.
- **www.mumbaimirror.com** is a service offered to those using indiatimes.com shopping service of Times Internet Limited (TLL), who are communicated about the terms and conditions of using the India Times Shopping service.

The above two examples of **HDFC Net Banking** and **www.shopping indiatimes.com** represent the face of e-commerce today. The potential of the usage of internet is the youth population (it is said that more than 70 percent of Indians are below the age of 35 years) who not only enjoy increased purchasing power compared to the earlier generation but are also tech savvy and prefer taking advantage of the speedy online transactions. With many more corporates opting for online ventures and by bringing the best of the internet to customers, they have been awarded with a large customer base and loyalty.

www.shopping.indiatimes.com provides information of on the availability of products at very low prices.

Internet has brought about major changes in the way corporate do business. Manufacturers are able to produce customized products and services more quickly and efficiently. This is because of interactive shopping environments which are enabling manufacturers and retailers to learn on how to satisfy consumers' individual tastes and preferences more effectively. Internet has benefited consumers because they can obtain customer made products and services at reasonable price and also make better decisions along with more satisfying choices. Internet has provided interactivity and a easy way to perform comparison shopping by consumers.

Internet has provided interactivity and a easy way to perform comparison shopping by consumers.

In this chapter we have addressed different issues related to online consumer behaviour. The chapter begins with a brief *(a)* history of the internet and e-commerce and *(b)* internet in India. Then we discuss on the activities in the three main stages of online consumers decision making behaviour and development and concerns of Indian net connections. The chapter concludes with an over view on the trends in online consumer behaviour.

BRIEF HISTORY OF THE INTERNET AND E-COMMERCE 

Internet can be defined as a large system of interconnected networks. The origin of the internet can be traced to the 1960s when the U.S Department of Defense while preparing for the possible effects of a nuclear attack, had commissioned the development of network which could operate independently without central control. The network was used to connect four computers in 1969, one each at:

- The University of California at Los Angeles.
- SRI International
- The University of California at Santa Barbara
- The University of Utah.

This first network was called the ARPANET. Over the years, several computers were connected to this network and several applications such as e-mail, FTP (file transfer protocol) and Telnet were developed to send and receive messages and files across computers on the network. Subsequently, other networks, such as the BITNET, CSNET and USENET came into existence. In the early 1980s there was an explosion in personal computer use when powerful and affordable computers became available in the market. Soon, it was felt that there is a need for a public network across which businesses could interact with each other for commercial transactions. In 1986, the NSFNET, which functions, even in the current age as the backbone communication service for the internet was developed with funds from the NSF (National Science Foundation). By 1995, the internet was substantially available for private use and the operation of main Internet connections was taken over by a group of private companies. Since then, the usage of internet has grown with it being used for business activities and transactions.

According to **Tim Bernes-Lee,** the person who invented the hypertext system, the World Wide Web is an "abstract space of communication," which came into existence because of the programmes that communicate between computers on the internet. The web has helped in using the internet for commercial purpose by making it simple to organize and retrieve information.

E-commerce has come to stay. Researches have indicated that U.S.A Business-to-Consumer (B2C) revenues are rising and alongside there is an increase in the number of people (aged 14 and above years) who have purchased something online. The e-marketers feel that the **online customer conversion ratio** (proportion of web site visitors who end up making a purchase) which in 1999 was about 1.9 percent (in the U.S) would have definitely more than doubled by, now. This is because e-tailers attract and win new customers with more targeted customized programmes.

Corporates have realized the importance of the internet as a channel of communication and are working on it as an **'essential to be on'** for long term survival. In fact it is estimated that companies are spending roughly around 10-20 percent of the IT budgets on e-business initiatives.

It can be said that the launch of the Netscape Browser in 1994 started the e-commerce revolution. With this, the technology barriers were broken and anybody could have access to the internet and use it for commerce without being a technology buff.

Characteristics of the Internet

R.A. Peterson, S. Balasubramanian and B.J. Bronnenberg (Customer Behavior 2nd edn, J.N. Sheth, B. Mittal) have worked out a list of the special characteristics of the internet:

Unlike traditional retailing, the internet as a marketing channel has reasonably reduced the place and time constraints.

- It has the ability to inexpensively store vast amounts of information at different virtual locations.
- It provides a powerful and inexpensive means of searching, organizing and disseminating such information.
- It facilitates interactivity and also has the ability to provide information on demand.
- It has the ability to provide perceptual experiences to the user, which is better than the printed catalogue, though this may not be as rich as a personal experience.
- It can be used to serve as a transaction medium.
- It is able to serve as a physical distribution medium for certain type of goods such as software.
- For retailers, it involves relatively low entry and establishment costs.

Benefits of the Internet

From the characteristics of the Internet, it can be seen that as a marketing channel it has changed the way customers shop for products and services. Unlike the traditional retailing, the internet as a marketing channel have reasonably reduced the place and time constraints. Usage of the internet has brought about a change in the way consumers shop and buy products and services online. Moreover, via the internet, the customer can have access to vast (availability of) information, which can be easily searched and compared with the other available aids *i.e.,* evaluate the information-all leading to a well informed customer. When he is armed with so much information, the customer is able to display a lot of online purchasing power in the decision making process.

Using of the internet is beneficial to both (the marketer as well as the customer) :

- For the **marketer**, it result in **increasing revenues** by allowing them to personalize their products or services.
- And, for the **customer,** it acts as a **medium of marketing communications.**
- Internet can also **cut down the costs** for marketers through the use of web self service channels at the consumer end and through e-procurement and market research at the supplier's end. To quote an example of a service which has been made possible on the web at nominal cost includes - as a communication bandwidth, there has been an increase of broadband connections. This has resulted in the customer terminals (or internet access devices) becoming more powerful, easy to use, affordable and portable and making it possible to exchange a range of services on the web at nominal costs too.

- A relatively **high level of interactivity** occurs on many web sites. Both the retailer and the manufacturer (or retailer) communicate back and forth until an agreement is made or the customer leaves or moves away from the site. Moreover, the retailer will keep an electronic record of the customer's purchase history and preferences, which can be utilized by them for all future transactions.
- Shopping becomes **quick and easy** on the net. With the click of a button customers can tell the manufacturers to ship the requested items to a particular address, and bill it to their credit card. The transaction takes place very quickly. Customer's can shop for products offered by retailers in their home town, other cities or even in other countries from the comfort of their home. All the hassles related to shopping-traveling long distances, waiting in lines, searching for parking slots for the vehicle etc. can be avoided by shopping on the net.

Although the number of choice options available aids in the decision making process, too much information can be confusing and overwhelming to consumers.

Problems Associated with Web Usage

Consumers have learned that by using the web, they can obtain, information on custom made products and services *i.e.,* various alternatives at an increasing pace. Although the number of choice options available aids in the decision making process, too much information can be confusing and over-whelming to consumers. Similarly, manufacturers and retailers, though appreciate the benefits of interactivity, they also feel the problem of cost transparency. The web helps consumers to compare prices and determine if a given price is fair or unfair. This, feel manufacturers and retailers, will make consumers more price sensitive and could also erode profits dramatically. Moreover, most firms are not keen to have a price war on the web.

At times customers are not very comfortable in furnishing all their personal details for the fear of it being misused.

TABLE 17.1

BENEFITS AND PROBLEMS ASSOCIATED WITH ONLINE SHOPPING

BENEFITS	PROBLEMS
• Though interactive shopping environments, manufacturers and marketers are able to learn more about on how to satisfy consumers' individual tastes and preferences more effectively. • The customer is able to obtain custom made products and services at a reasonable price. • Using of the internet for purchasing products and services will result in a high level of interactivity between the prospective buyer and seller. • Internet can cut down the costs for the marketer through the use of web self service channels at the consumer's end and e-procurement and market research at the supplier's end. • For the customer, it becomes quick and easy to shop. All the transactions takes place quickly-with the click of a button from the comfort of their homes. • Unlike the traditional mass media, advertising, a relatively high level of interactivity takes place between the marketer and customer until an agreement is reached or the customer leaves the website.	• Although customers can obtain more information about various products and service alternatives, at times too much information can prove to be confusing and over whelming. • Since the customer is able to compare prices of various alternatives and determine if the given price is fair or unfair; manufacturer's fear that customers can become price sensitive and this could even erode profits. • Customers are hesitant to provide all their personal details for the fear of it being misused.

(*Source : Outlook Business*, January 5, 2007, p. 74.)

THE INTERNET IN INDIA

In the year 2000, NASSCOM (National Association of Software and Service Companies) had estimated that the Internet user base in India would be around 7.5 million, compared to an urban population of 250 million or a population of 30 to 40 million in the upper and upper middle-income segments, by March 2001. Further it was felt at that time that looking to the number of C&S (cable and satellite) television households, it will not be far when the compounded growth rate of Internet usage will be in excess of 100 percent per year.

Internet usage is seeing the emergence of communication where like minded people share ideas, information, photos, music etc., – all this will drive up the demand for personalised content.

As in early 2007, it was reported (Business Today, January 14, 2007) that India has around 110 million TV homes, of which 68 million are cable and satellite (C&S) homes, while the remaining 42 million homes are with access to cable or satellite TV. It is difficult to lay cables in the remote corners of the country (rural), that is why C&S TV is largely an urban and town phenomena. This problem has been reasonably solved with the entry of the DTH (Direct-to home) satellite TV. DTH has brought about a paradigm shift in TV viewing as it can penetrate even the remotest corners of the country without any difficulty.

Doordarshan TV had been the first mover in this business and take infortainment to the hinterlands in India. *Dish TV* had primarily focused on cable dry areas till 2006, had taken a lead in this segment and build up 1.7 million subscribers across the country to which it had planned to add on 2.5 million by the end of 2006.

The DTH is popular because on its platform, it promises an immense degree of personalization of content with features like active news service, which will help the viewer to watch news the way she wants. *Tata Sky* had introduced the personal video records service which would enable viewers to record programmes in their absence. Thus, in making efforts to reach out to one's target audience, marketers are working at offering niche or special content for the DTH platform.

Internet and Mobile Phones have helped individual consumers to move towards personal and informal media. The user of both the internet and mobile phones are predominantly young (between 20-40 years of age). They have a higher SEC and income profile when compared to nonusers (TNS-mode, a market research agency). Studies have also indicated that Internet users are online at home during TV prime time too. So, marketers are using Internet in conjunction with other media to target the young affluent consumer. For instance, when Maruti had launched its new model *Alto*, it had not only aggressively used mass media campaign, but also the Net for a creative and well executed teaser campaign which generated a lot of curiosity and inquiry. The theme "hottest little thing" was driven home by the combination of all media channels, Similarly there are other marketers of various products who have been using the Net for their products including - *Ericsson, Samsung, HLL, Intel, ICICI, Citibank and Parle.*

Internet usage is seeing the emergence of communication where like minded people share ideas, information, photos, music etc.-all this will drive up the demand for personalized content. Further, with the Indian online population likely to increase to 42 million by March 2007, (as per IMRB-IMAI study), it was estimated that this demand would to go up even further.

Marketers feel that the mobile subscribe base which had crossed the 100 million mark in April 2006, was expected to outpace internet penetration. This will result in a market for personalised content or value added services such as ring tones to wallpapers to games to the unknown, which can easily be expected to grow by 60 percent in the year 2007, making it a Rs. 2,750 crores market. According to Subho Ray, President, Internet and Mobile Association (IMAI), much of this demand will be from small towns. He says, "A person living in a small town will be more inclined to access movie clips or ring tones of a new block-buster as it would take some time for the film to be released in his town".

Most of the young consumers are living in an age of **'me (or personalized) media'** with access to the internet and smart phones, so they prefer media content to be consumed as and when one feels one wants to. It was assumed that by the end of this decade mass media would metamorphose into some sort of a heavily interactive personalized media and yet making room for some informal competition in the form of internet communities (My space, Orkut, Digg), blogs (have you got one yet?) and photo and video sharing sites (Flickr, Youtube). Today, media companies are already trying to reach out to their audience through multiple touch points such as mobile alerts, wallpapers and ring tones. For instance the reality shows (Sa Re Ga Ma Pa challenge or Indian Idol) have been using SMS-driven interactivity and news channels (NDTV) (Headlines Today etc.) are encouraging viewers to participate in news gathering. These are two such examples. So, although a lot of importance is given to the content, the loyalty to the channel would not be worked out by looking at how much time viewers spend on the channel but on how much they interact with the content.

Impact of Internet on Communications

The impact and coming together of the internet and wireless communications can truly be called an information-led convergence. Internet has helped in connecting people to people. It has created a sort of network of identities and relationship that transcend corporate or national affiliations.

Internet has helped in connecting people to people by creating a sort of network of identities and relationship that transcend corporate or national affiliations.

Ad appeals to online customers interested in sending Rakhi to their brothers on the occasion of Rakshabandhan.

Social networking software helps in organising social interactions, which can take the form of shared purchases and unified articulation of issues.

At one level, the creation of new communities is coming about by associations of common (or shared) interests and goals, brought together in the virtual world. At another level, there are new social networking software (shaadi.com. social network etc.) which are mining web traffic and looking for new relationships to acquire customers. They try to analyse the patterns of behaviour among existing customers and help them to improve the value of relationships by ways which will increase sales. For instance, www.shopping india-times.com can help customers to customize and send gifts to their dear ones on special occasions such as Valentine's day, Diwali, New year, Christmas, Rakshabandhan and many other festivals. Similarly social networking software helps in organizing social interactions, which can take the form of shared purchases and unified articulation of issues.

Internet as a Media

India is one of the few global markets where the media, including the internet is booming. According to TRAI's (Telecom Regulatory Authority of India) figures on connections, the internet reaches about 50 million people, making it one of the largest in the world.

TABLE 17.2(A)

THE COST INVOLVED FOR INDIA'S LEADING PORTALS (Average CPM on campaigns)

Portals	Pageviews (Per Month)	Ad Rates (2005)	Ad Rates (2007)
REDIFF	700,000,000	75	125
YAHOO!	600,000,000	150	200
INDIATIMES	400,000,000	75	125
MSN INDIA	300,000,000	75	100
SIFY	150,000,000	75	100
SULEKHA	100,000,000	50	100
WEBDUNIYA	60,000,000	100	125
INDIAINFO	30,000,000	50	100
INDYA	20,000,000	150	150
NDTV	80,000,000	150	125
HINDUSTAN TIMES	40,000,000	75	100
CRICINFO	90,000,000	100	150
MONEYCONTROL	50,000,000	75	125

(Note : Ad rates refers to Rupee cost per thousand impressions (CPM) *Source :* Starcom Media Vest Group)

TABLE 17.2(B)

CATEGORY DISPLAY AND ADVERTISING SPENDS

Category	Spends (Rs. Crore)	Category	Spends (Rs. Crore)
E-COMMERCE	45	FMCG	34
ONLINE SERVICES	23	BANKING PRODUCTS	23
INVESTMENT PRODUCTS	23	TECHNOLOGY/IT	23
AUTOMOBILE	11	TRAVEL/TOURISM	11
MEDIA/ENTERTAINMENT	11	OTHERS	23

Note : This does not include classified (Rs. 500 crore) and search advertising (Rs. 230 crore) revenues

(Adapted from *'Business world'*, 16 April 2007, pp. 30-34)

However, only about one fifth of the users can be reached by broadband, so the quality of accessibility has still a long way to go. Yet, the internet reaches about the same number of people as the largest read newspaper or about 10 percent of those who watch the most popular TV channel (IRS quoted figures).

Only about one fifth of the users can be reached by broadband, so the quality of accessibility, has still a long way to go.

There are three broad reasons why Indian media brands are trying to view the internet seriously.

- Inspite of its smaller base, online spends are growing roughly at twice the rate of off-line spends.
- Most of the prime users of the internet are young (more than two-thirds are youngsters from SEC A), who could be the prime audience for, big advertising spenders such as FMCG or telecom companies.
- Advertisers have developed positive attitude towards spends on the internet (for jobs monster.com/naukri.com).

Some of the established old media companies have started investing in websites because they feel that the net is eating revenues or the investor offers a better valuation for an internet brand. To quote a few examples:

Ad will appeal to those wanting to enter into wedlock and seeking to find one's spouse via the shaadi.com

- In early 2007, Bangalore based Yahoo! India tied up with jagran Prakashan of Kanpur, publisher of the Hindi Daily, **'Dainik Jagran'** in order to launch a co-branded Hindi Portal by mid 2007.
- The Mumbai based **Benett Coleman & Co.** earns a lot of revenue from its various portals- indiatimes.com, timesjobs.com among others.
- Mumbai based news broadcaster Television Eighteen (TV18) had initially in about two years, built, acquired or allied with partners to create a family of 10 websites such as poweryourtrade.com and yatra.com.
- India's leading news broadcaster, New Delhi Television (NDTV) has the ndtv.com, which **is said has 200 million page views a month and is among India's top five web sites.**

➲ ON-LINE DECISION MAKING PROCESS

The online consumer is also involved in a decision making similar to that of an off-line consumer. The internet affects consumer decision-making behaviour in all the three stages: pre-purchase stage, purchase stage and post-purchase-stage.

PRE-PURCHASE STAGE

In the pre-purchase stage, the marketers are interested in knowing how customers search for information, the sources they use and the mental processes they undergo while taking purchase decisions.

In the pre purchase stage, marketers are interested in knowing how customers search for information, the sources they use and the mental processes they undergo while taking purchase decisions. They are also keen to understand how customers evaluate the information collected, while arriving at a purchase decision, from competing alternatives. For an online shopper, the task of deciding from a range of alternatives is complicated by the options that are available. Let us have a look at activities involved in the pre-purchase stage:

Problem Recognition

Customer problem recognition can get triggered by internal or external stimuli. **Internal stimuli** are perceived to be states causing discomfort and can be physical or psychological (for example hunger or boredom). Here the problem stimulus can lie within the customer (say hunger pangs), and the customer on recognizing the problem will seek a potential solution. While using the internet, broadband providers (cable or *BSNL say*) will display advertising messages indicating 'your Internet connection is very slow,' which may act as an internal stimuli prompting the customers to lookout for faster alternatives to their existing dial-up ISP.

The occurrence of problem recognition due to **external stimuli** may be different. For instance, seeing a friend playing games on the internet, can act as a stimulus to go online and browse the Internet for similar activities. A customer may also be motivated to go online through off-line (say Television) advertising, *for example,* tele brands (*www.telemartime.com, homeshop18.com*) advertise about online product or service offerings. The customer may not have recognized a need in the past, but when exposed to the solution-product it would make him realize a latent deprivation. For instance, a health conscious consumer, when engaged in exploratory browsing on the internet, happens to come across information on the availability of various fitness equipments, this could act as a problem recognition stimulus.

The internet can generate both primary and secondary demand. When the consumer gets educated about what the new product or service can do and how it can solve a problem, this can lead to the generation of secondary demand. For instance, the banner advertisement could

Family involved in online decision making.

motivate the customer to click on and search for information on how to lose weight and manage a diet. Being interested, the customer may click on the banner, when he or she will be taken to a generic web site, where marketers will display pop-up-advertising on various exercising equipments, dietary control food and nutritional supplements. Similarly by comparing sites, the customer not only gains increased confidence about the risk of purchasing from unknown web sites but also provides him the opportunity to switch brands.

Today's technology savvy customer is always on the move, very mobile, prefers using the computer and mobile phone and owing to paucity of time prefers to shop online.

Information Search

Once the need (or problem) has been recognized, customers will be engaged in an information search about the alterative ways to solve the problem. Today's, technology savvy customer is always-on-the –move, very mobile, prefers using the computer and mobile phone and owing to paucity of time prefers to shop online. Such customers prefer using the internet which searching for information on various product categories.

According to well known market research firm T.D Power & Associates, more than half of all new-car buyers and a third of used car buyers search on the internet for reviews, feature lists and price details before making a purchase decision. Even for information on real estate or home loans, the prospective customer prefers to use the internet and search for the available information on the various home loan offers from various banks such as the HDFC Bank State Bank of India, Bank of Baroda, ICICI Bank, Corporation Bank etc. By seeking information on the net, the consumer not only saves time and effort but is also able to make comparisons

Ad conveys the many ways of using 'www.sbionline.com'

between the competing offers. Nevertheless, for the final decision transaction, customers are still not comfortable about making complex decisions such as the purchasing of a car or taking house loans on the internet.

Marketers need to encourage customers to search on the internet specially by conveying and creating an image of enjoying a risk free online shopping experience.

Studies have indicated that tourism and health are areas which are widely researched on the internet. This could probably be the reason behind so many foreigners seeking treatment for health related problems in India or foreign tourists visiting India, after making bookings and reservations online.

Research has indicated that one of the biggest benefit's of searching for information on the internet is the involvement of low costs. But of course only those customers who have a positive attitude towards online shopping are likely to search for information (and) with purchase intention. However, perceived behaviour control in terms of access to the internet, ability to navigate the internet with interest and time to do the same will be related to the intention to search on the internet. So marketers need to encourage customers to search on the internet specially by conveying and creating an image of enjoying a risk free online shopping experience.

Evaluation of Alternatives

It is observed that those consumers using the internet are very much informed about the relevant websites to visit for the particular product or service. Simultaneously, when a lot of information is available to the customers, they may find it different to make purchase decisions. Researches have indicated that although price does affect the purchase decision, there are other factors such as the retailer brand name which is considered as an important dimension in the decision making process. This is because customers use the brand name to make judgments on the product quality and the firm's ability to deliver it on time. Thus firm's should make efforts to build up the customers confidence in retail experience by providing an ease of use, prompt delivery services, and clear cut privacy and return policies.

With the internet growing into a medium used for commerce, marketers find that information given to consumers online, builds up their loyalty and interest, encouraging them to revisit the website and purchase products and services online. Finally even the marketer can use the information collected at the website on each customer as this will enable the former to personalize his marketing offerings and promotions.

PURCHASE STAGE

Typically, once customers evaluate the alternatives available for purchase, they have two options before them, using the information obtained from the internet:

- They may visit a retail outlet to buy the product or
- They could purchase the product online *i.e.,* via the internet itself.

In order to woo the customer towards online buying, the online marketer could make efforts at customizing and making the purchase experience more attractive through personalization.

Most of the internet users can be reached by broadband. We will take the example of Rajshri productions of Mumbai, who have been in the business of producing and distributing films for over 60 years, have been able to sell their film to online users. Initially, the Rajshri media launched *Rajshri.com* as a little more than a digital brochure. In April 2006, during a trip to Finland, Rajjat A. Barjatya, Managing Director, Rajshri media, discovered that there were 15,000 Indians there who knew all about every Indian film released and had seen them all on pirated DVDS. When asked by Rajjat if they would see the film **Vivaah** if it were released on

Online marketers must try to make the purchase process more attractive to customers through personalization.

broadband, brought out a positive response. So in November 2006, Rajshri.com was relaunched as a broadband portal. About 6,000 people, mostly from the US and Europe, purchased (down loaded) the movie at Rs.440 ($9.99). The bulk of Rajshri.com's half million page views a day come from the free downloads of films, TV or other content. From April 2007 onwards, Rajshri began shooting a 90 webisode sitcom (3-5 minutes long) for the portal.

Of course, for Rajshri, most of the buyers are overseas Indians (about 90 percent come from outside and half of it is from the US). In India, there are about 10 million online users who have broadband which allows full movie downloads.

Thus online marketers must try to make the purchase process more attractive to customers through personalization. But online consumers generally have certain concerns about online purchases, these are namely related to giving out personal information to retailers and the fear of breach of security of credit-card transactions on the Net.

Man Customization of Products or Personalization

Customers are unsure if the products such as clothes which fit them properly are available on the Internet. To tackle this problem, taking the help of the computer and flexible manufacturing technology, manufacturers can go for **'mass customization of products.**

Apart from this, in the online market, the marketer can go for personalization starting with addressing the customer by his or her name, when they visit the website. Thereafter on the basis of the preferences quoted by the customer, develop and maintain a personalized page for the customer.

Online customers are concerned about the amount of personal information that websites collect from them and how it is likely to be used.

Inform and apprise customers about promotional offers and deals pertaining to products of their choice and interest using data from their previous purchases and their preferences stated therein. Today, many online marketers such as **Amazon.com** or the famous **Dell computers** make efforts to 'identify' their customers, differentiate between their needs and value to the firm, 'interact' with them and then 'customize' the company's product offering based on his or her needs.

Researchers Eric Brynjolfsson and Micheal D. Smith in their study noted that, over a period of time, customers tend to prefer to stay with sites with which they are already familiar in terms of navigation and purchase expectations. They feel it is a waste of time to go through the whole procedure of visiting another site and searching just when the question is only of a difference of few rupees. Box 1 gives information on how ads are working towards personalization.

Tackle fear of misuse of personal information provided for online purchases

Online customers are concerned about the amount of personal information that websites collect from them and how it is likely to be used.

Various studies have indicated that customers are wary about furnishing websites with their personally identifiable information, fearing that it could land up in wrong hands and be misused.

The methods adopted by online marketers to collect data on customers could include:

- Through forms which are required to be filled by the customer at the website.
- Planting electronic 'cookies' onto the customer's computer which will enable them to get different kinds of data about the customer.

FIGURE 17.1

STAGES IN ONLINE DECISION MAKING

PRE-PURCHASE STAGE		PURCHASE STAGE		POST-PURCHASE STAGE
• Problem Recognition • Information search • Evaluation of alternatives.	→	• Mass customization or personalization • Fear of misuse of personal information providing online credit card details *i.e.,* security concerns • Building trustworthiness of the website • Turning Browsers into buyers.	→	• Working towards customer satisfaction and loyalty • Tackling Returns.

BOX 17.1

ADVERTISEMENTS ATTEMPTS AT PERSONISATION OF COMMUNICATION

Just For You – *It's time ads are tailor-made for various platforms and audience*

This is not good advertisement for the traditional ad industry. Jump Games, a Mumbai-based mobile and web game content creator, is giving advertisers a run for their money. It recently donned an advertiser's cap to design an online game for *Coca-Cola India* to promote its brand *ThumpsUp*. Says Salil Bhargava, CEO, *Jump Games*: "Since the positioning of the brand was about energy and challenge, we created a game which challenged the user to climb the Everest. On the corner of the screen was a ThumpsUp bottle, which indicated the energy level of the users." And, according to Bhargava, it has done well for the brand.

The good news for the ad industry is that these gaming and web content providers are not here to fight with the admen. Instead, they are providing new platforms-and therefore new challenges-to the ad world to reach out to their audience on a one-to-one basis. "The gaming platform enables an advertiser to interact with the consumer for six-seven minutes at a stretch," says Bhargava.

Not that advertisers are unaware of it. With users changing their preferences, the ad industry too has embraced non-traditional media. If mobile marketing and internet advertisement are already established, 2007 could see advertisers carrying the idea of creating tailor-made ads for various platforms further ahead.

That means, in the days to come, the commercial for a car brand on a youth channel would be different from the commercial of the same brand on a general entertainment channel. And your personal blog may well become an enterprise if you have a lot of online visitors.

Says Manish Porwal, Executive Director, Starcom: "The new media platforms would definitely give scope for micro-segmentation of communication." Starcom is already making specialised communications at a macro-level, says Porwal. "We have specialised *region-specific communications for brands like Western Union Money* and *World Gold Council* in Kerala and Punjab." Bhargava of Jump Games feels that the future would see a fair degree of cross-platform integration that would allow advertisers to seamlessly interact with their target audience both on the Net and mobile. "You could play a game online and also play components of it on your mobile."

The ad world is gung-ho about the advent of new media platforms and the tremendous scope for a high degree of personalisation of communication. But Pratap Bose, CEO, Ogilvy & Mather, doesn't want to jump the gun. "Technologies like 3G would open up new opportunities, but how personal can one get would depend on the degree of acceptability these platforms would receive. It is still early days." Early days, yes, but no doubting that the personalisation of communication is here to stay.

by Ajita Shashidhar

(*Source : Outlook Business,* January 5, 2007, p. 74.)

For instance, the World Wide Web Consortium had developed a standard called the 'platform for privacy preferences project' (P3P) and Microsoft's new version of Internet Explorer browser 6.0, comes equipped with the P_2P_3. This standard enables the customer to find out which website is sending 'cookies', the kind of information the cookie gathers and who is going to use the information. The P3P is equipped with an automatic blocking device with which the customer can put on hold 'cookies' from residing on the hard drives of their computers. Further, the P3P also helps the customer to decide on which cookies to put a block and those on which to allow access to. In this way, the customer can select the cookies that help sites recognize the customer, remember the passwords and also store information on the other preferences about the site. Simultaneously, the customer can put a block on the cookies that collect personal information to transmit to their concerned website.

The customer can select the cookies that help sites recognise the customer, remember the passwords and also store information on the other preferences about the site.

Website ezeego1.com enables customers interested in travelling to avail of the various facilities offered by the site.

Organizations on their part, are using authentication technology, fitters, audit controls, custom-tailored software, professional consulting services and permission based content technology-all to ensure privacy of customer data. They also install spaces which will provide a security check on unsolicited mails Nevertheless, when customers privacy concerns increase, they are more likely to:

- Provide incomplete information to websites
- Notify ISPs (example **VSNL or Sify etc.**) about unsolicited mail
- Request for removal from mailing lists.
- Cut off from online entities sending unsolicited mails.

Fear of credit and misuse

Another security concern which customers have in online purchases is related to the credit card payment. In a study to learn about 'online fraud' covering 16 different countries, involving 8,500 adults (aged 18 years and above), research firm Ipsos-Reid (2001) had found that potential online credit card fraud was quoted as a 'major concern' by 46 percent of the respondents (adults) and as a 'moderate concern' by another 26 percent. This concern for security was found to be varying from country to country.

- In **France,** 63 percent of respondents quoted security a major concern.
- In **China** about 15 percent of respondents cited it as a major concern.
- In the **U.S.** about 47 percent of people considered online credit fraud as a major concern.

It is seen that there are also gender based differences in the perceptions of risk associated with credit card misuse, fraudulent sites and the fear of losing one's privacy associated with online purchasing. Research has indicated that women perceive a higher level of risk in online purchasing when compared to men. Yet they are more than willing to purchase online when a site is recommended by a friend in comparison to men.

To tackle security issues, websites force customers to log in with a username and password. Companies also rely on encryption of data, such as credit-card information to ensure transaction security. Further, companies can also use the two protocols-Secure Sockets Layer (SSL) and Secure Hyper Text Transfer Protocol (S-HTTP) in order to provide secure information transfer through the internet.

Building Trustworthiness of the Website

Websites should make efforts at building trustworthiness of their brand through accumulative process which establishes customers:

- trust in the internet and the specific website.
- trust the information displayed on the website.
- start believing or have trust in the website's delivery schedule and service fulfillment.

A big way of tackling the security and privacy concerns of the online customers is by building trust in their brands.

A big way of tackling the security and privacy concerns of the online customers is by building trust in their brands. In a study involving 299 consumers across 12 countries in the North America, Western Europe and Latin and South America regions, it was found that there are three important factors affecting customers' online purchase decisions and loyalty:

- website quality
- affect
- trustworthiness of the website.

If the website has a positive impact in terms of trustworthiness, it can have a positive impact on purchase intentions and loyalty. So websites must make efforts at building trust by providing-service guarantees, privacy policies, third party credentials of credibility and customer or user testimonials.

Researchers G.L. Urban, F. Sultan and W.J. Quallis (Sloan Management Review, 2000) have suggested that websites could use software-enabled **virtual advisors** in the form of personal shopping consultants. Such virtual advisors could interact with customers, understand their needs and provide them with suggestions to fulfill those needs.

Online retailers need to keep a track of customer response to various tactics and make efforts to convert browsers to actual purchasers.

Online shoppers feel that in the area of delivery fulfillment, the shipping or delivery charges also come in the way of abandoning a virtual shopping cart. To handle this problem, the retailers can provide information related to shipping charges on the site, much before the online customer reaches the last stage in the purchase process.

Convert Browsers into Buyers

The challenge before the online retailer is to convert internet browsers into buyers. Researchers Wendy W. Moe and Peter S. Feder have worked out an online buyer conversion model which can help to determine when browsers will turn into buyers. (Customer Behavior 2nd ed^{n}, J.N. Sheth and L.B. Mittal, 2003, pp. 441) They have suggested a classification of the customer visits to the website, before they decide to purchase from the site. The visit can be classified as follows:

- Directed Purchase Visits: Customers visits the site to purchase a product or service.
- Search and Deliberation Visits: The customer visits the website seeking information, weighs the various options and intentions on future net purchases.
- Hedonic browsing Visits: The customer browses the net for pleasure and recreation.
- Knowledge building Visits: The customer goes for online scanning of the market and any information gathered in the process can affect future purchases.

Moe and Fader's model helps to analyze visits and the purchase data about a customer and predict the exact visit which can lead to a purchase. Web marketers could use this model to provide customers with the right cues to induce purchase. *For example,* when the website knows that a particular customer is going to purchase on his third visit to the site, the customer can be put on to a faster server on that visit, so that he can have a quick and convenient purchase option. If it is felt that the customer needs an incentive to purchase, he or she can be targeted with promotional offers. In this way online retailers need to keep a track of customer responses to various tactics and make efforts to convert browsers to actual purchasers.

POST PURCHASE STAGE

In the post purchase stage, the online marketer has to work towards providing online satisfaction, building loyalty and address the issue of returns.

Web marketing is beneficial to both the marketer as well as the customer. For the marketer, the major benefits include accessibility to widest markets and customers across the world, reduces costs (related to business, marketing, communication etc.), can personalize and build relationships with customers and so on. For the online customers the benefits include convenience to shop from home, scope to search for information and competitive buying, saves time and energy (otherwise be spent on travelling, vehicle fuel, parking the vehicle etc.), bargain and select the product or service and so on.

From the Table 17.3, it is seen that the medium of the internet, benefits both the marketers and customers too.

Some companies *(Baze Flash Couriers, Blue Dart etc.)* in order to provide satisfaction to customers have the web based-self service facility. By availing of this facility, the customers

TABLE 17.3

BENEFITS OF ONLINE BUYING TO MARKETERS AND CUSTOMERS

Benefits to the Marketer	Benefits to the Customer
• Accessibility to various markets across geographical boundaries. • Can provide enhanced customer value through product and service offerings from a single stop and in an individualized manner. • Can work towards building 'customer relationships' by personalizing product and service offerings. • Helps to reduce-business, marketing, channel, communication and promotion costs. • Provides flexibility to adopt to individual customer needs. • Flexibility in planning, marketing and communication *i.e.,* can adopt a mass medium as well as personalized medium.	• Provides convenience to shop at one's own time and pace from home. • Scope for informed and competitive buying. • Saves time on travelling and searching for suitable retail outlets. • Due to the interactive nature of the web, consumers can actually bargain and get the best price and terms. • Online buyers become aware of all competitive product and service offerings, due to the high degrees of transparency. • Access to accurate information related to promotional schemes discounts, guarantees, etc. making online buying attractive.

are able to take care of minor issues such as change of address, tracking the whereabouts of the package, or the status of a submitted application directly without having to call the company. It is felt that such initiatives helps to keep the customer satisfied as he feels that he has control over the whole process.

The web self service has been broadly divided into two:

(a) Content Based Services : These are related to customer queries which are general in nature and require static information. Such queries are put in the form of FAQ (Frequently Asked Questions) on the website.

(b) Transaction Based Services : These services are in dynamic form. *i.e.,* customers want to place orders, fill out application, make payment, know the whereabout of their purchased item etc. Such queries (transactions) require individualized information which is to be retrieved from back-end databases and then supplied to the customer whenever requested.

Research has shown that a website can break-even only after atleast four repeat visits from a customer, in a period of twelve months.

Sometimes the 'co-production' method is adhered to as in the case of purchasing railway tickets or airline tickets via the internet. Under this model the customers will state their preferences (data of travel, type (or class) of travel etc.) and the company (Railways or Airlines) will ask the customer to select from a set of alternatives which closely matches the customers consideration set. In this way, the company is able to provide the customer with the right choice.

The key driver of the online business's profitability can be measured from the customer loyalty. Loyalty by customers can be clearly seen in two ways-

- Repeat purchases at a site.
- Referring customers to the site.

Research has shown that a website can breakeven only after at least four repeat visits from a customer in a period of twelve months. Further, referrals will be the best way of acquiring new customers, for, without spending any money to get them to the site they will provide revenues and also refer the website to more customers, if they have a satisfying experience. Thus the key to succeed in online retailing is by fostering loyalty amongst one's customers.

Tackling Returns

A very annoying problem associated with online buying is to handle returns. Although there is a lot of convenience in purchasing online, customers find it annoying to return the purchased products to the manufacturer if it is not found to be satisfactory. So companies have to adopt suitable ways by which customers will find it hassle free to return products which are not found to be satisfactory.

➲ DEVELOPMENTS AND CONCERNS IN INDIAN NET CONNECTIONS

Domain names in Indian Languages

While there are websites with Indian language content, there were no web addresses in Hindi or Tamil or any other Indian languages.

In an attempt at Indianising the web, the Department of Information Technology (DIT) in association with the Center for Development of Advanced Computing (C-DAC) is working on preparing a variant table for characters of various Indian languages. This means that efforts are being made so that the 'Dot in' domain names which links the online user to the vernacular website will also be available in the Indian languages. Because as of now, the 'dot in' registry offers only English domain names.

While there are websites with Indian language content, there were no web addresses available in Hindi or Tamil or any other Indian language. The Information technology ministry through the National Internet exchange of India (NIXI) offers 'dot in' domain names to the public. So that the vernacular domain is available with NIXI, the web portal has to be positioned for local language characters. The ministry had proposed to carry out, a pilot project to enable this mechanism, in the year 2007.

The IT ministry is also working at preparing a web based software which will act as a search engine seamlessly running across all prominent Indian language scripts. For instance, a Gujarati seeking information which is available only on Tamil script, can use the software to search the web and obtain the necessary information back in Gujarati, translated from the Tamil version.

Local Websites of MNCs

It has been found that when it comes to online user interface for Indian consumers, or local websites of MNCs there is a lot of lacking in terms of user friendliness, interactivity and content. When compared to their global (or Western) counterparts or MNCs, Indian websites are way back in terms of content, look, levels of interactivity and user friendliness. To quote some such examples:

- **Motorola India :** If one is trying to locate the nearest Motorola dealer, click the 'local dealers' on the Motorola India's website and the message comes "Motorola's products are distributed through the main channels and shops for (mobile) communication. We advise you to contact your local communication specialist with regards to availability and prices of Motorola products". However, the Motorola's U.S website offers a drop-down menu for a user to find the nearest dealer.
- **LG Electronics :** L.G has two major websites lgindia.com (which appears first if you google LG India) and lgezbuy. An internet user visiting lgindia to locate the nearest LG dealer would not find the option. Well, first go to products, select a product and

then one will find the option to locate an LG dealer-click and then one is taken to the lgezbuy dealer locate page. However, it will be much easier finding LG service centers and the online shopping options on the global website.

- **Unilever Vs Hindustan Unilever :** The 'look and feel' factor can be seen in the case of Hindustan Unilever. The Unilever's website is colourful, vibrant and consumer oriented where as, Hindustan Unilever website leans more towards a corporate user. So, while the Unilever homepage has tips on staying fit, healthy and beautiful, on the Indian site quarterly results and other corporate information share prominence with information on Hindustan Uniliver brands.
- **Procter & Gamble :** The global website of Proctor & Gamble (P&G) offers tips on issues ranging from nutrition to stress busting and from beauty to baby care. While the Indian website goes just beyond the basic brand information to offer 'consumer care' tips on how to deal with cough, cold and flu.

Problem with local website when it comes to online user interface.

- **Mc Donald's :** McDonald's has always shown increased focus on projecting itself as a responsible brand. So while the Indian website has a restaurant locator, nutrition info and some fitness tips, the American site offers suggestions on topics ranging from nutrition tips while dining at McDonald's to 'food allergins' and 'sensitivity info'. It also has sections where a doctor and a personal trainer offer advice.
- **Levi's (denim major) :** If one wanted to seek the Levi's Indian website, one would go to Levis main website and point towards the Asia-pacific link. Although India is listed there, clicking on it would lead to the Asia pacific website of Levi's. Countries listed on the Asia Pacific website include Australia, Indonesia, Korea, Malaysia, Philippines, Hong Kong, Japan, New Zealand, Singapore, South Africa, Taiwan and Pakistan, but there is no mention of India.
- **Nike :** If one want's to check out Nike India, it doesn't exist. Nike's global website may lead one to the other regional websites, but doesn't have India or Asia at all on its list.

Experts feel that low Internet penetration in India could be one of the reasons for the Indian websites lagging behind their counter parts in the developed markets.

Experts such as Harish Bijoor (Marketing Consultant) feels that low Internet penetration in India could be one of the reasons for the Indian websites lagging behind their counter parts in the developed markets. Marketing professors of ISB (Indian School of Business) feel that the lack of consumer sophistication in India could be why brands think they can get away without paying so much attention to their websites and hence the low levels of interactivity and user friendliness.

Probably with more internet penetration among Indians to even rural areas could result in websites being designed to convey 'more information, be user friendly and connect well' with the user. Read Box 17.2 on how the common man's mode of long distance travel 'Indian Railways' has used its online booking site to reap profits.

Likely Trends in Online Usage

The developments being made in the field of technology offer ample opportunities for the internet customer. These are:

Mobile e-commerce Market : People are able to use their mobile phones to purchase goods, purchase cinema and train tickets and shop on the internet. Mobile phones penetration is very high and consumers are able to use their phones to connect to the internet more than personal computers. Wireless Internet services can be made more personalized for customers when compared to the other means of communication. This is mainly due to the following reasons:

- The customers possessing mobile phones, usually switch on the cellular phones which are with them.
- Wireless network operators using a GSM (Global System for Mobile Communication) standard are in a position to identify a user uniquely and send him or her personalized communication.
- The Wireless Network operator being able to exactly identify the user's location, can present him or her with an array of applications to select from.

Retailer **Reliance Retail** is working on strengthening its online presence seeing the growth in broadband penetration in the country. It is believed that in the next 2-3 years time, a significant 5-6 percent of Reliance Retail's overall revenues is expected to be generated through the e-commerce network. Efforts are being made to have an online retail channel alongside its physical stores. Such depots will be set up at various locations which will serve as a delivery point once the orders are placed through the internet. "Having physical delivery stores always adds to the convenience and success of the online business model for retailers." Says Arvind Singhal, Chairman, Technopak Advisors. Reliance Retail, in order to strengthen its e-commerce venture is thinking of having co-branded credit cards (it has already contacted the head of the credit card at American Express) and consumer financing schemes.

BOX 17.2

TRAIL OF FORTUNE

MUCH before (the ex) union railway minister Lalu Prasad Yadav achieved a turnaround for loss making public transport Indian Railways which is now raking in all the accolades, one division within the railways has chugged away to profitability —right from day one. And today, it is the biggest e-commerce site in India and is the fastest growing in Asia with a growth rate of 400% in just four years of operation. The numbers garnered by the Indian Railway Catering and Tourism Corporation's (IRCTC) online ticketing site with a daily turnover of Rs. 1.5 crore a day will make any other e-commerce venture stop and think.

From 112 tickets a day, when it launched in August 2002, the online site today averages around 13,000 tickets daily and is dispatched to over 200 cities in India. "When we thought of adopting an online model, we were warned that Indians are not very open to making payments online," says Amitabh Pandey, former COM, IT services, IRCTC, who was instrumental in implementing the idea. Despite the misgivings, Pandey presented the proposal and fortunately, both the department heads, who were involved were computer-savvy to give him the green signal. Accenture was appointed as a consultant on the project, and with Broadvision as the developer, the virtual ticket window took shape.

Initially the site only offered online booking, with tickets being couriered to consumers' homes. Recently, since February '06, the site started offering e-tickets, which has evoked a good response from the consumers. Sanjay Aggarwal, additional GM, IRCTC, says, "The introduction of e-tickets have given a boost to our sales and today out of 100 tickets about 55 tickets booked are e-tickets."

An interesting side effect of IRCTC's success has been the boost it's given to internet banking in India. Today IRCTC has tie-ups with 18 national and private banks for online booking. So consumers have the option of making payments using his credit or debit card as well as direct debit from bank accounts. While cash-on-delivery option was never considered viable, IRCTC now allows the option of making payments using 'Itz Cash' card— a pre-paid card available from denominations of Rs 100 to Rs 10,000. The card is available at a number of general stores and caters to consumers, who are sceptical of sharing their details online. Says Aggarwal, (Additional GM, IRCTC) "The reason IRCTC is popular is because of the level of security we offer our consumers. We do not store any card details with us; there are no files or databases."

One of the cornerstones of the site is the emphasis on technology, where the backend which supports seamless customer experience is mesh of systems at work. "The website is connected to the Passenger Reservation System (PRS), which enables updation of seats available on a train in real-time. In case any extra bogies are attached, then the PRS is updated and more tickets can be booked on the same train," reveals P K Goel, MD, IRCTC. PRS is the backbone which enables smooth conduct of day-to-day affairs of IRCTC. The bookings can be done within dedicated time frame, with the remainder time utilised for cancellation.

With revenues for the year 2005-2006 at Rs 330 crore, the profitable venture reflects the potential of e-commerce in India. And for players like Visa, tying up with IRCTC makes sound business sense; given the fact that regular internet users in India has increased from 40% to 51% over the last two years driven mainly by factors like saving time and the convenience of shopping anytime.

Going forward IRCTC is looking at other avenues to strengthen the online booking initiative. A step in this direction is the tie-up with Rail Travel Service Agents (RTSA), accredited IATA agents and members of Travel Agents Association of India (TAAJ). Mumbai Suburban Season Tickets (MSST) for first and second class can also be booked online now. Having begun when the internet penetration was still considered' nascent, IRCTC will be looking to ride the wave as more and more people log on to the net.

(*Source : The Economic Times*, Bangalore, August 30, 2006)

Interacting With Consumers Through Blogs

Corporates should think of creating blogs to give brands the much needed human face through networking and communicating about their quality products and services.

Blogs function as online diaries or a platform to provide commentary or news on a particular subject such as health, politics, local news or brands. *For example,* one has to just search on Goggle for "effect of blogs on brands" and the results page will speak for itself. For the online customer, blogs can influence their decisions. Infact blogs are being used by consumers as a forum to air their views, be heard and most importantly influence a brand choice. For instance, in the Jessica Lal's case, Jessica became a brand created by the media and public at large (long after her death) owing to the 'sms'es and blogs that hit cyber world. Similarly, though products are manufactured in factories, brands are created (or destroyed) in the minds of consumers. So corporates should think of creating blogs to give brands the much needed human face through networking and communicating about their quality products and services.

Telemarketing

Telemarketing is a form of direct marketing, facilitating personalized contact (though not face-to-face interactions) with the target customers. Telemarketing is usually done through specific campaigns run for a few days and contacts are established with many prospects. Tele-callers are hired for the tele-call operations and building up the rapport with the prospects.

Tele shopping or home shopping works when the marketer communicates about his products or services on the Television (*Tele Shopping Network, Asian Sky Shop, United Tele Shopping* etc.) or via the consumer's mobile network and the interested consumer will give a positive response to the marketers' offer.

Marketers should go for 'Ubiquitous Internet' which can be applied to any place where the consumer is physically present *i.e.,* Shopping centers, malls, railway stations, bus terminals, airport lounges etc., At such strategic locations, marketers can provide customers with mobile devices, which will provide them information relevant to their needs and in turn also obtain information for the marketers.

Internet Protocol Television (IPTV) Services

IPTV is a comparatively new concept, which uses the internet communication protocol to transfer content (data) from the broadcaster to the end user (online customer). It works as a two way communication wherein the online consumer can seek a host of value added services such as internet browsing, VOIP (Voice-Over-Internet Protocol), Video Conferencing and Personalized advertising. Hyderabad based *Goldstone Technologies* has signed an agreement with *BSNL* for providing IPTV services to its broadband customers in India. Goldstone has signed agreements with several Indian and European channels for worldwide distribution. They plan to provide features such as 'on demand' movies, game shows, serials and educational content and online gaming. The company is considering at getting licenses for using a huge library of movies on demand content.

A market research firm 'E MARKETER'S prediction on the future market for mobile video clips is given in *Box 17.3*.

BOX 17.3

GEARING UP FOR MOB-TV

EMARKETER, a market research firm, predicts that by 2011 there will be 120 million 3G subscribers who will, among other things, pay a premium for mobile video clips or streams. Of the 120 million 3G subscribers worldwide, 80 million are expected to watch TV on mobile phones by 2011. eMarketer believes that mobile TV subscribers will be among the top quartile of mobile customers in terms of income and revenue potential. These early-adopting mobile TV users will be courted by service providers and handset makers to buy the most cutting-edge mobile phones. Perhaps the ones on which you can watch TV without straining your eyes too much on a small screen!

	2007	2008
Total paid mobile video users	14.9	37.9
Total mobile TV paid subscribers	1.3	5.2
Mobile video revenues	31.4	1349.3
Mobile TV revenues	232.2	743

Revenues are in million dollars and subscribers are in millions.

(*Source* : *The Economic Times*, Bangalore, 17 April, 2007)

SUMMARY

Internet has brought about major changes in the way corporates do business. Manufacturer's are able to produce customised products and services more quickly and efficiently. For the consumers, internet has provided interactivity and an easy way to perform comparison shopping. Corporates have realized the importance of the internet as a channel of communication and are working on it as an 'essential to be on' for long term survival. With the launch of Netscape Browser in 1994 started the e-commerce revolution enabling anyone to have access to the internet and use it for commercial purpose. With the increase in online mobile population, in India, the internet and mobile phones have helped individual consumers to move towards personal and informal media. According to TRAI's (Telecom Regulatory Authority of India) figures on connections, the internet reaches about 50 million people.

The online consumer is engaged in a decision making process similar to that of the off-line consumer. The internet affects the consumer's decision making behaviour in all the three stages: pre-purchase stage, purchase stage and post-purchase stage. Some of the concerns in Indian net connections included: domain names in Indian languages and Local websites of MNC's. The likely trends in online usage could be related to: mobile e-commerce in market, consumer interactions through blogs, Telemarketing and IPTV (Internet Protocol Television services.)

CHAPTER QUESTIONS FOR DISCUSSION

1. Bring out the relevance of understanding online consumer behaviour by marketers, if they need to compete in the e-age of today.
2. Meet and interview three customers who have recently made purchase of products online and find out what all were involved in the stages when they were going through the online decision making process. Write a small report on your findings.

3. India is widely acknowledged as an emerging economy. Describe what are the visible concerns and developments in relation to Indian net connections.

➲ SUGGESTED READINGS

1. www.hdfcbank.com
2. www.shopping.indiatimes.com
3. Aspy.Engineer., Fast Forward, *Retail Biz,* September 2005, pp. 17-20
4. Jagdish.N.Sheth., Banwari. Mittal, *Customer Behavior,* Thomson South Western Learning, Singapore, 2003. pp. 425-452.
5. 'A Brief History of the Internet and Related Networks,'http: //www.isoc.org/internet/history/cerf.html
6. Robert A. Peterson, Sridhar Balasubramanian and Bart J. Bronnenberg, "Exploring the Implications of the Internet for Consumer Marketing" in Sheth, Eshghi and Krishran *Internet Marketing,* Orlando, 2001, pp. 120-147.
7. Frank R.Kardes '*Consumer Behavior and Managerial Decision Making,* 2nd edition, Prentice Hall of India Pvt. Ltd, New Delhi, 2002, pp. 226-280.
8. Ajita.Shashidhar; I, Me Media, *Outlook Business,* January 5, 2007, pp. 72-74.
9. Mukesh.Ambani., 'The New Convergence, *Business Today,* January 16, 2005, pp. 42-46
10. Vanita-Kohli - Khandeker, Big Media goes online, *Business World,* April 16, 2007, pp.30-34.
11. Neha Kohli., Domain names to go desi, *The Economic Times,* Bangalore, 16 April 2007. pp. 9.
12. Deepshikha.Monga., Not Connecting to Indian Consumers, *The Economic Times,* Bangalore 15 April 2007. pp. 1
13. Samidha. Sharma., and Mayer. Shekhar.Jha., Reliance Retail readies for click, *The Economic Times,* Bangalore, 19 April, 2007
14. 'Goldstone to launch IPTV service,' *The Economic Times*, Bangalore, 17 April 2007, p.6

CASE

GOD (GAMES ON DEMAND)-INDIA GAMES AND ZAPAK.COM

GOD - The Concept

The concept of GoD is popular in UK, Europe, U.S, Japan and Korea. Games on Demand (GoD) will enable all those games freaks (or users) to download the legal version of all the brand new blockbuster mega budget games at a nominal cost-almost the same as that is charged by the local CD library.

In India, companies like *India Games* and *Zapak.com* offer their own models. India Games has tied up with *BSNL, MTNL, Airtel, Tata Indicom* and *You Telecom*.

Online customers having a broadband connection of any of the above telecom companies can have access to the service.

Zapak Digital Entertainment, the ADAG group company which floated **Zapak.com** has tied up with the gaming companies to offer these games at a fraction of the cost to its online subscribers. Whereas, Indiatimes.com is offering free-to-play online games to those who visit their website. Although they too are planning to introduce the paid model of GoD very soon.

Working and Cost Involvement

Let us have a view of how this works. The online customer once connected to the net through broadband will be required to fill up a small registration form on the respective telecom service provider's website.

For India Games the customer will be taken to the 'India Games website dedicated for the telecom operator, and then he or she will have to download a software which will further enable them to download games.

INDIA GAMES and the telecom operator have made it clear that 'data downloaded for installing the games offered on to the online customer's is **free of cost.** India Games is offering the service on a 15 day trial basis to those who want to test it out. The company has tied up with the gaming company to offer the latest-in action, quick games, rote playing games, racing, sports and multiplayer games.

India Games offers gaming packages for two category of customers.

- For the **serious gamer** (customer), the gaming package comes at a cost of Rs 200 per month.
- For the **casual gamer,** (customer), the gaming package comes at a cost of Rs 100 per month.

For the Rs 200 per month package, the customer gets to play all the latest and favorite games (there are no other costs involved). The Rs 100 version package offers customers smaller yet popular games though with a limited choice of games.

In the words of Vishal Gondal, founder and CEO India Games.

"Each of these latest action games costs upwards of Rs.1500 per game. While one can play legal versions of as many games as possible at a little of Rs 200 per month. GoD will do the same to gaming in India, what cable TV has done to viewing TV channels."

However, there is a limitation, since it is a subscription based service, the user has to remain connected to the internet to play any of the games. Further, if the customers' subscription expires, he or she will not be able to play games (even those which are downloaded on their PC). The rule is simple play as long as you are subscribed. India Games has got about 1 lakh subscribers.

ZAPAK.COM

Zapak.com follows the 'pay-as-you-download' model. There is no monthly subscription fee. The customer gets to download the games at a fraction of the cost at which they are available on CDs. The members pay as they download each game through a payment gateway, which is configured. This will enable members to pay through credit cards. Initially all the games on the site were being offered free. By the end of April 2007, the company had planned to launch the service commercially. Till March 2007, Zapak.com had about 10 lakh registered users. The proposal for pay and use works as follows. If a game costs $ 20 in the overseas market, Zapat.com will change about $ 2 in India. Moreover, the user gets to play off line and can keep playing even when he or she ceases to be a member of Zapak.com

Expected Trends

Marketers associated with the entertainment industry feel that India has a gaming mindset waiting to explode. Further, 54 percent of the Indian population falls in the below 25 years of age group, making it not only the world's largest population but also an attractive market. There has been an upward swing in the internet usage, especially those in the younger age group. Moreover, entertainment features as a predominant spending area amongst the Indian consumers. This trend is expected to continue in the future also. It is estimated that by 2010 there will be 20 million broadband subscribers (up from 1 million in 2007) and 200 million internet users (up from 50 million today). The gaming market in India is expected to grow to 424 million by 2010.

(*Source:* www.indiagames.com, www.zapak.com
Debjoy Sengupta and Sreeradha D. Basu, 'It's Nirvara: On-demand goodies from the GOD of legal gaming,' *The Economic Times,* Bangalore, 17 April, 2007.)

QUESTIONS FOR DISCUSSION

1. In view of the expected growth of the gaming market in India, can you suggest ways to increase the interconnectivity between the online customers and marketers?
2. Discuss ways in which India Games and Zapak.com can increase trustworthiness of their sites.
3. What promotional activities could be worked out by gaming marketers to induce customers to visit their site?